Adversarial Learning and Secure AI

Providing a logical framework for student learning, this is the first textbook on adversarial learning. It introduces students to attacks and vulnerabilities of deep learning, and to methods for defending against attacks and making AI generally more robust.

It is the ideal resource for upper undergraduate and first-year graduate courses on AI security and adversarial learning. Students and instructors will benefit from these features

- application examples, case studies, and real-world student projects in each chapter, connecting theory with practice
- a project-driven approach that strengthens critical thinking when evaluating attacks and defenses
- a variety of application areas covered by the examples and projects, for example, image classification, text classification, point cloud classification, and a regression example from finance.

David J. Miller is professor of Electrical Engineering at the Pennsylvania State University.

Zhen Xiang is a post-doctoral research associate of Computer Science at the University of Illinois, Urbana-Champaign.

George Kesidis is a professor of Computer Science and Engineering, and of Electrical Engineering, at the Pennsylvania State University.

"This textbook is one of the first major efforts to systematically examine adversarial machine learning. It clearly outlines the most common types of attacks on machine learning/AI, and defenses, with rigorous yet practical discussions. I would highly recommend it to any instructor or machine learning student who seeks to understand how to make machine learning more robust and secure."
Carlee Joe-Wong, Carnegie Mellon University

"This is a clear and timely introduction to the vital topic of adversarial learning. As leading international experts, the authors provide an accessible explanation of the foundational principles and then deliver a nuanced and extensive survey of recent attack and defense strategies. Multiple suggested projects allow the book to serve as the core of a graduate course."
Mark Coates, McGill University

"Remarkably comprehensive, this book explores the realm of adversarial learning, revealing the vulnerabilities and defenses associated with deep learning. With a mix of theoretical insights and practical projects, the book challenges the misconceptions about the robustness of Deep Neural Networks, offering strategies to fortify them.
It is well suited for students and professionals with basic calculus, linear algebra, and probability knowledge, and provides foundational background on deep learning and statistical modeling. A must-read for practitioners in the machine learning field, this book is a good guide to understanding adversarial learning, the evolving landscape of defenses, and attacks."
Ferdinando Fioretto, Syracuse University

"In a field that is moving at break-neck speed, this book provides a strong foundation for anyone interested in joining the fray."
Amir Rahmati, Stony Brook

Adversarial Learning and Secure AI

DAVID J. MILLER

Pennsylvania State University

ZHEN XIANG

University of Illinois, Urbana-Champaign

GEORGE KESIDIS

Pennsylvania State University

CAMBRIDGE
UNIVERSITY PRESS

Shaftesbury Road, Cambridge CB2 8EA, United Kingdom

One Liberty Plaza, 20th Floor, New York, NY 10006, USA

477 Williamstown Road, Port Melbourne, VIC 3207, Australia

314–321, 3rd Floor, Plot 3, Splendor Forum, Jasola District Centre, New Delhi – 110025, India

103 Penang Road, #05–06/07, Visioncrest Commercial, Singapore 238467

Cambridge University Press is part of Cambridge University Press & Assessment,
a department of the University of Cambridge.

We share the University's mission to contribute to society through the pursuit of
education, learning and research at the highest international levels of excellence.

www.cambridge.org
Information on this title: www.cambridge.org/highereducation/isbn/9781009315678

DOI: 10.1017/9781009315647

© David J. Miller, Zhen Xiang, and George Kesidis 2024

First published 2024

Printed in the United Kingdom by CPI Group Ltd, Croydon, CR0 4YY, 2024

A catalogue record for this publication is available from the British Library

A Cataloging-in-Publication data record for this book is available from the Library of Congress

ISBN 978-1-009-31567-8 Hardback

Additional resources for this publication at www.cambridge.org/millersecureAI.

DJM dedicates this book to his children Joshua and Madeline

ZX dedicates this book to his son Ian

GK dedicates this book to Fozzie, Gonzo and Therese

The authors also share a dedication of this book to their collaborators Xi Li and Hang Wang

Contents

Preface

Why We Wrote This Book

In the past ten years, deep learning has been applied to many market and government sectors (e.g., health, finance, military, intelligence, manufacturing, sales), including in their critical infrastructure and supply chains (MLOps/AIOps). Application domains include those where operational conditions may change over time (model drift), where safety and security are of great concern, and where significant financial stakes are involved. As such, the deep learning process and the trained Deep Neural Networks (DNNs or "AIs") themselves have become targets of attack. More generally, basic questions about the robustness and explainability of DNN solutions have also been raised even in the absence of attacks, for example, [132]. A research sub-field assessing and addressing the risks associated with using AIs (and other machine learning models) is known as *adversarial learning*. This area essentially represents a merger between the fields of computer security and machine learning.

An important aspect of software security is to consider how the software will behave for *all possible* valid inputs. The reason for this is that an adversary may exploit a vulnerability that pertains to a range of inputs for which the software's behavior was not carefully considered by its developers. This is a daunting security task for a DNN, whose behavior depends on an enormous set of parameters (even billions) which are heuristically learned, and whose input space may be very high-dimensional. What this means is that DNNs have a substantial attack "surface," which makes them vulnerable to a variety of attacks/exploits. While some basic adversarial learning research dates back more than 20 years, this field really took off with the observation in 2014 that *adversarial inputs* may be easily constructed for DNNs – these are small changes to an input pattern, *imperceptible* to a human being, and yet which greatly alter the DNN's output (e.g., changing its class decision). Aside from being a security threat, adversarial inputs demonstrate that it is a fallacy – held by many researchers, educators, industrialists, and journalists – that DNNs are generally robust, reliable decision-makers, and are close to fulfilling the promise of artificial intelligence. In the year 2020 alone, more than 1100 papers on adversarial learning were submitted to arXiv.org. While there are a number of review papers, to date there are no books on this subject which are suitable for a course offering.

The Emphasis of the Book is Unsupervised Defenses

Generally, defenses and attacks continuously evolve. New vulnerabilities are discovered by attackers (either in the system being protected or in its defenses) and exploited. Defenses may evolve to address newly identified vulnerabilities (including those recently revealed by new exploits). It may be unrealistic to suppose that the defender has detailed knowledge of an attack that may be mounted. This is why we focus on unsupervised defenses that aim to protect against a whole family of attacks (rather than relying on somehow obtained knowledge of a specific *known* attack [269, 270])[1]. On the other hand, in the quest for the glory (and concomitant research funding) associated with finding a new vulnerability and devising an exploit for it, some researchers ignore existing or obvious defenses which would be effective against their attacks, or get carried away and unrealistically assume an omniscient or omnipotent attacker (e.g., one who completely controls the training dataset and training process, or controls how new samples are labeled in an active learning context). Given an omnipotent adversary, a defense may be able to do little more than increase the attacker's work factor. That said, though "security through obscurity" is commonly practiced and may be effective in some cases, assuming some attacker knowledge of a defense is not unreasonable. This is especially true considering spectacular leaks by insiders and breaches in privacy protections in the recent past.[2]

Purpose, Target Audience and Prerequisites

The targeted audience for this book is senior undergraduates and graduate students in all branches of science and engineering. The purpose of this book is to introduce students to existing attacks and vulnerabilities of deep learning (and machine learning in general) and to methods for defending against these attacks, as well as for making AI generally more robust (even in the absence of attack). Along the way, students will also enhance their appreciation for what deep neural networks are in fact learning (and what they are not learning). For example, students will learn that training dataset augmentation (i) may improve generalization performance, (ii) instead, may cause degradation in DNN accuracy (e.g., by overfitting through adversarially robust learning), (iii) or may result in the planting of a backdoor in the DNN. As another example, students will better understand the circumstances in which DNNs learn patterns that are spatially invariant (occurring anywhere in an image), or only patterns that are spatially fixed. The book covers many attack-defense scenarios and involves many case studies and real-world problems addressed by the state-of-the-art in recent research publications.

---

[1] Note that an antivirus system or firewall typically functions in response to known attacks, that is, they are supervised defenses. Hence periodic updates (with patching of exposed vulnerabilities) are needed, typically *after* a new exploit has been detected and carefully studied to identify its signature.

[2] Which can go both ways, that is, new attacks can also be leaked before they are launched; but, to reiterate, we focus on unsupervised defenses herein.

Prerequisites for this book include a basic introduction to calculus, linear algebra, and probability. Though the second and third chapters provide the necessary background material on deep learning, detection, and statistical modeling, a student would benefit from a more broadly scoped course on pattern recognition and machine learning based on, for example, [63, 190], and from an introduction to numerical analysis, for example, [8].

Projects

There are course projects at the ends of the chapters that give hands-on experience to students in devising and evaluating both attacks and defenses against machine learning systems. These projects are intended as the primary homework exercises for a course on robust and adversarial learning. They also serve the dual purpose of helping students to obtain familiarity and facility in machine learning design within the Python programming environment (in particular, the use of PyTorch for deep learning). Moreover, these projects provide a window for students into how much research work is being conducted in AI/machine learning – with promising new ideas postulated and then experimentally assessed, both to validate (or reject) them and to obtain greater insight into the problem at hand. Given some Python experience, students can learn PyTorch [209] while studying the first few chapters of this book. Also, a tutorial on the Pillow fork of the Python Image Processing Library (PIL) will be useful, for example, [88]. PyTorch code for projects given at the end of Chapters 4, 5, 6 and 13 is available at: www.cambridge.org/millersecureAI.

Quite a bit of code is provided for the first few preliminary PyTorch projects (the provided code should be carefully studied by the student), while little to no code is provided for subsequent projects. The idea is that the students can "fill in the blanks" for the first PyTorch projects that are assigned but have to produce all of the code for subsequent ones.

Chapter Roadmap

The first three chapters respectively provide background on attack types and attack nomenclature, on deep learning, and on detection and estimation. If students have taken a prior course on pattern recognition or machine learning, they may be able to skip Chapters 2 and 3. Note that subsequent chapters frequently refer back to material in Chapters 2 and 3.

Chapter 4 addresses defenses against adversarial inputs at test-time, also known as test-time evasion (TTE) attacks.

Chapter 13 addresses defense against general data poisoning attacks against classifiers.

Chapter 14 addresses defense against reverse-engineering (probing) attacks.

A road map for the remaining chapters on backdoor defense is as follows.

- Chapter 5 addresses backdoor defense implemented by the training authority, who has access to the (possibly poisoned) training set and who controls the training process.
- The next four chapters address *post-training* backdoor defense, where the defender does *not* in fact have access to the training set, but only to the trained classifier and to a (relatively) very small set of clean (unpoisoned) labeled samples.
- Chapter 6 addresses defense against imperceptible backdoor attacks. One approach reverse-engineers putative backdoor patterns that are additively incorporated either to the input (raw features) or to an internal layer of the neural network (embedded features). The reverse-engineered backdoor pattern has utility beyond post-training detection (it can also be used for test-time detection of backdoor triggers and for mitigating the effect of backdoors). Moreover, it is an important element of explainable AI (XAI), indicating patterns in the presence of which a DNN's decision-making is fragile.
- Chapter 7 addresses post-training defense against backdoors that are embedded by replacing a "patch" of input features by the backdoor pattern. These backdoor attacks can be implemented either digitally or *physically* (e.g., by placing an object – the backdoor pattern – in a given scene). One reverse-engineering defense exploits the fact that the attack should be "scene-plausible" in order to be evasive.
- The defenses in Chapters 6 and 7 are not very suitable when the number of classes in the problem is small (e.g., the two-class case), since in this case there are insufficient detection statistics available for estimating the parameters that specify a detection rule. The post-training defenses in Chapter 8 address this problem. The main defense developed there was found to be effective with a *constant* detection threshold ($\frac{1}{2}$), *irrespective* of the DNN architecture and classification domain.
- Chapter 9 considers defenses that aim to be *universal*, that is, without any explicit or implicit assumptions about the backdoor pattern or how it was embedded.
- Chapter 10 considers "in-flight" detection, that is, detection of backdoor triggers in input patterns at test time. Such detection may give the potential to catch culprits in the act of exploiting the backdoor mapping. One such described defense leverages a reverse-engineered backdoor pattern.
- Chapter 11 considers backdoor detection for non-image point cloud data classifiers.
- Chapter 12 considers backdoors for regression rather than classification and also discusses active learning.

The authors acknowledge the support of students and colleagues. In particular, we thank Yujia Wang (Chapters 4 and 14), Xi Li (Chapters 10, 12 and 13), and Hang Wang (Chapters 4 and 9), as well as Zhicong Qiu and Xinyi Hu. We also thank Vladimir Lucic for consultations regarding Chapter 12.

The authors acknowledge the sources of our research support through the Pennsylvania State University: an AFOSR DDDAS grant (2017–2021), an ONR NROTC education grant (2021–2022), an NRC Research Associate Fellowship with AFRL (2021–2022), and two Cisco Systems gifts (2019, 2022). Through Anomalee Inc., we also acknowledge the research support of an NSF SBIR Phase-One grant (2022–2023).

Notation

Typically,

- random objects are denoted by capital (upper-case) letters
- non-vector matrices are denoted by bold capital letters, for example,

$$\mathbf{V} = [v_{i,j}]_{i=1,\ldots,n,\ j=1,\ldots,m}$$

  denotes an $n \times m$ matrix with entry $v_{i,j}$ in the ith row and jth column, and both $m > 1$ and $n > 1$
- column vectors are denoted by underlined lower-case letters
- datasets are typically denoted by calligraphic capital letters
- some variables not defined below, such as $x, y, z, n, m, i, j, k, \alpha, \beta, \kappa, \theta$, are often re-purposed in various chapters
- some symbols, such as f, g, are typically used for functions and are also often repurposed

More specifically, we define the following mathematical symbols and operators

- $\mathbb{R}$ is the set of real numbers
- $\mathbb{Z}$ is the set of integers
- $\mathbb{Z}^+$ is the set of positive integers (natural numbers)
- N is the dimension of the input sample space (space of input patterns) of a feed-forward neural network, that is, the space of N-dimensional, real-valued column vectors, $\mathbb{R}^N$
- $\underline{z}'$ is the transpose of column vector $\underline{z}$, that is, $\underline{z}'$ is a row vector
- $\langle \underline{z}, \underline{y} \rangle = \underline{z}'\underline{y} = \sum_{j=1}^{N} z_j y_j$ is the inner (dot) product of (column) vectors $\underline{z}, \underline{y} \in \mathbb{R}^N$
- $\|\underline{x}\|_q = (\sum_{i=1}^{N} x_i^q)^{1/q}$ is the l_q-norm (or q norm) of vector $\underline{x} \in \mathbb{R}^N$
- $\|\underline{x} - \underline{y}\|_q$ is the l_q distance between $\underline{x}$ and $\underline{y}$ of the same dimension
- $\|\underline{x}\| = \|\underline{x}\|_2 = \sqrt{\underline{x}'\underline{x}} = \sqrt{\langle \underline{x}, \underline{x} \rangle}$ is the Euclidean (l_2) norm of $\underline{x}$
- $\underline{x} \odot \underline{m}$ is element-wise multiplication of the vectors (or matrices) $\underline{x}, \underline{m}$ resulting in another vector (or matrix), that is the ith element of $\underline{x} \odot \underline{m}$, $(\underline{x} \odot \underline{m})_i = x_i m_i$
- $\mathcal{X}$ is the set of data samples that are used for training a neural network (deep learning), where $\mathcal{X} \subset \mathbb{R}^N$
- $T = |\mathcal{X}| < \infty$ is the number of samples in the dataset $\mathcal{X}$
- K is the (finite) number of classes in $\mathcal{X}$ for classification problems (but K has different meaning in the context of K-means clustering or KNN classification)

- $\mathcal{Y}$ is the set of classes in $\mathcal{X}$, that is, $K = |\mathcal{Y}|$, for example, $\mathcal{Y} = \{1, 2, \ldots, K\}$
- $c(\underline{x}) \in \mathcal{Y}$ is the true class label of $\underline{x} \in \mathbb{R}^N$
- $\hat{c}(\underline{x})$ is the inferred class of input sample $\underline{x}$ by a classifier
- $\mathrm{E}X = \mathrm{E}(X) = \mathrm{E}[X]$ is the expectation of random variable X
- $\mathrm{P}(A) = \mathrm{P}[A]$ is the probability of event A
- $\{x_1, x_2, \ldots, x_n\}$ is a set with n elements
- $\{x_a \mid a \in A\} = \{x_a : a \in A\}$ is the set of elements x_a *such that* (: or $\mid$) parameter or index a belongs to the set A (here $x(a)$ or $x^{(a)}$ may be used instead of x_a to indicate the dependence of x on a)
- $A \cup B$ and $A \cap B$ respectively are the union and intersection of the sets A and B
- $A \backslash B$ is the set of elements in the set A that are not in the set B
- $\emptyset$ is the empty set
- $[a, b) = \{r \in \mathbb{R} : a \le r < b\}$, with $b > a$, is a contiguous interval of real numbers including a but not b
- $\mathbf{1}\{\xi\} = \mathbf{1}(\xi)$ is an indicator function, equal to one if the statement ξ is true and zero if ξ is false
- $\mathbf{I}$ is a square identity matrix, with 1s on the diagonal and 0s off diagonal
- $a := b$ or $a \triangleq b$ means a equals b by definition
- $\underline{0}$ is a vector all of whose entries are zero
- $\underline{1}$ is a vector all of whose entries are one
- $\underline{X} \sim F$ means random vector $\underline{X}$ has (multivariate) distribution F
- $\det(\mathbf{A}) = |\mathbf{A}|$ is the determinant of square matrix $\mathbf{A}$
- Δx is a change in the quantity x

List of Acronyms

- 3D: three-dimensional
- ACC: Accuracy (on a clean test/evaluation set)
- AD: Anomaly Detection (short name for I-PT-RED in Chapter 6)
- AI: Artificial Intelligence (often synonymous with a DNN)
- AL: Active Learning
- a.s.: almost surely (with probability one)
- ASR: Attack Success Rate
- AUC: Area Under the (ROC) Curve
- BA: Backdoor Attack (Trojan)
- BIC: Bayesian Information Criterion
- BP: Backdoor Pattern
- CDF or cdf: Cumulative Distribution Function
- CNN: Convolutional Neural Network
- CS: Cosine Similarity
- DNN: Deep Neural Network
- DP: Data Poisoning (attack)
- ET: Expected Transferability

- FPR: False Positive Rate (fraction or percentage)
- GAN: Generative Adversarial Network
- GMM: Gaussian Mixture Model
- HC: High Confidence
- i.i.d.: independent and identically distributed
- JSD: Jensen–Shannon Divergence
- KL: Kullback–Leibler divergence
- KNN: K Nearest Neighbors
- LC: Low Confidence
- LEM: Local Error Maximizer
- LeNet-n: Learnable Neural Network architecture with n layers [140]
- LR: Logistic Regression
- LSTM: Long Short-Term Memory (a recurrent NN)
- MAD: Median Absolute Deviation
- MAE: Mean Absolute Error
- MAP: Maximum a posteriori
- ML: Machine Learning
- MLE: Maximum Likelihood Estimation
- MM: Mixture Model (or Maximum Margin in Chapter 9)
- MSE: Mean-Squared Error
- NB: Naive Bayes
- NN: Neural Network
- OOD: Out-Of-Distribution
- OODD: Out-Of-Distribution Detection
- pAUC: partial (ROC) Area Under the Curve
- PCA: Principal Component Analysis
- pdf: probability density function
- pmf: probability mass function
- PMM: Parsimonious Mixture Modeling [86]
- PT: Post-Training
- RE: Reverse-Engineering
- RE-AP: Reverse-Engineering Additive Perturbation
- RE-PR: Reverse-Engineering Patch Replacement
- REA: Reverse-Engineering Attack
- RED: Reverse-Engineering Defense
- ResNet-n: Residual Neural Network architecture with n layers [97]
- RL: Reinforcement Learning
- ROC: Receiver Operating Characteristic
- SGD: Stochastic Gradient Descent
- SIA: Source-class Inference Accuracy
- SVD: Singular Value Decomposition
- SVM: Support Vector Machine
- TPR: True Positive Rate (fraction or percentage)
- TSC: Training Set Cleansing

- TTE: Test-Time Evasion (attack), that is, adversarial input
- WB: White Box
- XAI: eXplainable AI

The following list contains the "proper names" of some attacks and defenses used in this book, with bibliographic citations

- AC-GAN: Auxiliary-Classifier GAN based TTE detection [284, 285]
- ADA: Anomaly Detection of TTE Attacks [179]
- B3D: Black Box Backdoor trigger Detection [61]
- BIC-MM-TSC: BIC-MM based TSC against error generic DP [148]
- CI: Cluster Impurity defense [308]
- CIFAR-n: Canadian Institute for Advanced Research color image dataset with n object classes [129]
- CW: Carlini–Wagner TTE attack [33]
- FGSM: Fast Gradient Sign Method for TTE attacks [83]
- FP: Fine Pruning backdoor defense [156]
- i-FGSM or BIM: iterative-FGSM or Basic Iterative Method for TTE attacks [133]
- I-PT-RED: Imperceptible–backdoor PT-RED [303, 307]
- IF-RED: In-Flight backdoor trigger RED [149]
- JSMA: Jacobian based Saliency Map Approach for TTE attacks [203]
- KD: Kernel Density based defense [68]
- L-PT-RED: Lagrangian PT-RED [305]
- MD: Mahalanobis Distance based defense [142]
- MNIST: Modified National Institute of Standards and Technology dataset of hand-written digits [141]
- NC: Neural Cleanse backdoor detection [282]
- NC-M: NC based backdoor Mitigation [282]
- P-PT-RED: Perceptible backdoor PT-RED [304]
- PC-PT-RED: Point Cloud PT-RED against backdoors [306, 309]
- PGD: Projected Gradient Descent for TTE attacks [271]
- STRIP: STRong Intentional Perturbation backdoor trigger detection [73]
- T-PT-RED: Transferable PT-RED against backdoor DP [302]
- TSC-RED: Training dataset Cleansing RED against backdoor DP [301]
- UnivBD: "Universal" Backdoor Detection approach [286]
- UnivBM: "Universal" Backdoor Mitigation approach [286]
- ZOO: Zeroth Order Optimization based TTE attacks [41]

1   Overview of Adversarial Learning

In this chapter, we introduce attacks/threats against machine learning systems. Attacks that will be covered in much greater detail in subsequent chapters are discussed briefly, and attacks which will not be explored beyond this chapter are covered in greater detail. In much of the rest of this book we will focus on defenses against the attacks surveyed in this chapter.

A primary aim of an attack on machine learning, particularly deep learning, is to cause the neural network to make errors. Examples with severe implications include: fooling a biometric authentication system so that it grants access to sensitive material or building access to an unauthorized individual; fooling an automated breast cancer pre-screening system so that images with tumors are not forwarded to a radiologist; fooling an autonomous vehicle's recognition system so that it mistakes a stop sign for a speed limit sign. An attack may target the training dataset (its integrity or privacy, the former by data poisoning), the training process (deep learning), or the parameters of the deep neural network (DNN) once trained. Alternatively, or in addition, an attack may target vulnerabilities in the trained network by discovering test samples that produce erroneous output – such samples are called *adversarial inputs* or *test-time evasion attacks (TTEs)*. They have also been referred to as adversarial samples, adversarial examples, or (redundantly) adversarial attacks. All of these terms are ambiguous in light of backdoor triggers (Chapter 10) and querying/probing for purposes of reverse engineering (Chapter 14), which are also adversarial. Indeed, both TTEs (Chapter 4) and backdoor triggers produce incorrect outputs.

Defenses typically attempt to detect attacks and/or to proactively improve the robustness of machine learning in the face of them. They may also help to interpret the decision-making of a machine-learned system and to make it generally more robust even in the absence of an attack.

In this book, previously published attacks and defenses under various scenarios will be critically surveyed. The main focus is on unsupervised defenses with reasonable work factors against *strong* contemporary attacks on supervised machine-learned systems. Primarily, the examples are DNN classifiers applied to images, but there are some exceptions: Chapter 11 on 3D point cloud classifiers, Chapter 12 on non-image regression applications, and Chapter 13 on document classifiers.

In this chapter, after reviewing some jargon, an overview is first given of the three main types of attacks on machine learning that will be investigated in subsequent chapters.

1.1   Machine Learning and Its Attack Vectors

Machine learning involves learning predictive models (for tasks such as classification, regression, and time series prediction) from a finite training set of "examples." (Machine learning may also involve learning data "transformations," where one seeks the most informative/salient feature representation starting from high-dimensional feature vector examples that may involve many noisy/uninformative features.) Moreover, "deep learning" is simply machine learning applied to deep neural network (DNN) models – these involve numerous (in general nonlinear) layers of data processing applied to input patterns, culminating in the output of the DNN, which produces a classifier decision or a regression model prediction. Accordingly, attacks on machine learning/deep learning may target different stages of the machine learning model-building and use process: (i) corruption of the training data; (ii) malicious alteration of the learning process itself, or of the resulting model parameters; or (iii) disruption of the test-time use of machine learning models, so that they produce incorrect decisions/inferences. Attacks may also seek to reveal sensitive information, such as information about individual training examples (e.g., which patients participated in a large-scale medical study) or about a company's proprietary decision-making rule (e.g., for an investment bank, revealing how it makes its trading decisions).

The main attacks on machine learning that are comprehensively addressed in this book include: data poisoning attacks, backdoor attacks, test-time evasion attacks, membership-inference attacks, and reverse-engineering attacks. Data poisoning and backdoor attacks both involve corruption of the training set (and/or alteration of the learning process). However, backdoor attacks *also*, along with test-time evasion attacks, involve attacker exploits at test-time, that is, altering input patterns so as to produce erroneous model outputs. Membership-inference attacks seek to reveal sensitive information about training data, while reverse-engineering attacks aim to reveal a classifier's decision-making rule/a regression model's predictive rule, and the features on which it is based. All of these attacks (and defenses against them) will be studied in detail in this book.

1.2   Attacker/Defender Goals and Assumptions

Attack/defense scenarios typically begin by describing the attacker's specific goals and the knowledge and capabilities that the attacker and defender are assumed to possess. Also, attack/defense scenarios typically specify at what point the attacker/adversary and defender will act: before training, while the training dataset is being formed; during training; post-training but before operational deployment; at test/operational time; or during retraining or fine-tuning (including by "active" learning using judiciously chosen new supervised training data samples, or by "reinforcement" learning using recently observed test samples).

We now discuss the following post-training scenarios particularly germane to TTE attacks. In attack scenarios sometimes referred to as *black box*, the attacker does not possess detailed knowledge of the trained DNN, but is assumed to be able to freely query the DNN, so as to learn its decision-making rule. Alternatively, in what is sometimes referred to as a *grey box* scenario, the adversary has access either to the DNN's parameters or to a training dataset (presumed i.i.d. with the training data used to build the targeted DNN) that allows it to build a good proxy of the DNN. In the following, "black box" will typically be used to describe *both* of those foregoing attack scenarios, since in both cases the attacker possesses (or creates) knowledge of the classifier, but not of any supplementary defense that may be mounted against the attack. In *white box* attack scenarios [32], the adversary has knowledge of the DNN parameters and is also assumed to have detailed knowledge of any mounted supplementary defense.[1] The latter could be obtained by an *insider* (inside attacker). Alternatively, if attack detection results in the classifier making a "rejection" or "undecided" decision, then the attacker may be able to learn the mechanism of the supplementary (anomaly detection) defense by observing this output (rejection decisions). [21] makes a case for white box attacks, ostensibly because "security through obscurity" may fail: the DNN parameters (as well as the inner details of a supplementary defense) may have been leaked to the attacker. It will be argued, however, that the privacy of a supplementary defense may be protected in some cases.

Let us next consider pre-training attack scenarios, germane to data poisoning attacks. If an attack targets the training set of a classifier, then one can imagine reasonable scenarios where the adversary can manipulate only a small fraction of the training samples (for example, to avoid detection). The adversary may either be unaware (black box) or aware (white box) of the remaining training samples.

It is important to assess the relative *work factors* of the attacker and defender, especially in the white box case. Work factors particularly include the computational effort and memory storage needed to mount a given attack or defense.

Extreme case scenarios, where either the attacker or defender is *omniscient* (knows everything) and/or *omnipotent* (can do anything) will not be considered here. For example, it may be theoretically impossible to defend against an adversary who is aware of and can easily manipulate all of the training dataset X and all aspects of the training process, that is, an omniscient and omnipotent insider. See, for example, Appendix R.4 of [286].

Note that calling a defense unsupervised (i.e., without any knowledge about a specific attack that may be mounted) is analogous to calling an attack black box (i.e., where the attacker has no knowledge of any supplementary defense). Similarly, calling a defense supervised is analogous to calling an attack white box. White box attacks and supervised defenses require information that generally may not be available in practice – they are arguably less realistic than black box attacks and unsupervised defenses.

Genuinely unsupervised defenses are also obviously preferable as they afford some protection against *zero day threats*, never before seen attacks, which are also sometimes

---

[1] This terminology is not standard. In some articles, knowledge of the model (its parameters and architecture) is dubbed "white box" or "grey box," and "black box" means that the adversary can only query the model. In the following, we will clarify these definitions when describing attack/defense scenarios.

called unknown unknowns. Supervised defenses, on the other hand, may only be effective against threats that are already known. Many proposed defenses appear to be unsupervised but either make unrealistic assumptions regarding limitations of the attack or involve hyperparameters which are difficult to set in an unsupervised, anomaly-detection setting.

Some attacks are *targeted*. For example, a targeted attack may focus on ensuring a DNN classifier assigns either a particular subset of data samples, for example, from a particular class (even a single sample), or a particular region of feature space, to the attacker's chosen (target) class [14]. Other attacks are *indiscriminate* (untargeted, or *error generic* [21]). An indiscriminate TTE or data poisoning attack on a classifier seeks to induce decision change *without* the requirement to misclassify to a particular class chosen by the attacker.[2]

Attacks may be referred to as *strong* when they both (i) succeed in their objective of inducing misclassifications and (ii) are not easily detectable by man or machine. For example, strong TTE attacks on a classifier craft examples that induce misclassifications to a target class but which to a human inspector still appear to be natural (artifact-free) examples from some other class. In fact, in general, a TTE attack is *only* deemed to be truly successful if it induces misclassifications while *not* introducing artifacts that make the attack either easily perceivable by a human being or easily detected by a trivial anomaly detector; that is, only strong attacks are truly successful ones.

1.3   Test-Time Evasion Attacks (TTEs) or Adversarial Inputs

As aforementioned, TTEs [19, 260] involve the alteration of test-time input patterns, resulting in erroneous decision-making/test-time inferences. TTEs are most commonly launched against statistical classifiers. However, they can also target other systems that involve discrete decision-making such as those that involve object detection and image segmentation [313]. From this standpoint, they can also in fact target unsupervised data clustering, where a learned clustering solution/model may be applied to identify to which cluster a new (test-time) data object should be assigned. TTEs are typically constructed with knowledge of the model/classifier, but without relying on knowledge of the specific training samples used for deep learning. Again, if the attacker has full knowledge of both the classifier and any deployed defense (and seeks to defeat both), it is referred to as a white box attack. How plausible the white box assumption is will be explored in Chapter 4.

Given a trained DNN, a TTE typically modifies a "clean" input sample in a way that may not be noticeable to a human inspector (in which case we refer to the modification as "imperceptible") but which induces a significant change in the DNN's output (decision).[3] We refer to the attacker's change to the input pattern as an adversarial

---

[2] Some authors use "universal" instead of "untargeted" and use "label-specific" instead of "targeted," in either a data poisoning or TTE context.

[3] In contrast, some "spoofing" attacks are not innocuous and the resulting change in the DNN's decision is not necessarily incorrect (not a misclassification).

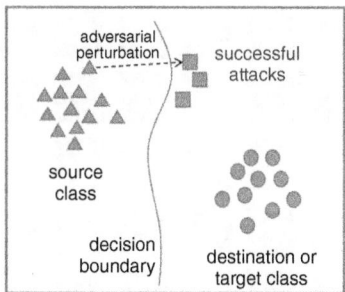

Figure 1.1 Illustration of a test-time evasion attack. Correctly classified source-class samples (triangles) are adversarially perturbed so that they are pushed across the decision boundary (represented by squares) and incorrectly classified to the destination/target class (the circle class). Reprinted from [179, 180] with permission.

perturbation of the input pattern. A strong, untargeted TTE modifies a clean, correctly classified sample x from class s, $\hat{c}(x) = c(x) = s$, so that the modified sample $\tilde{x}$ is not classified to s, that is, so that $\hat{c}(\tilde{x}) \neq s$ but while still appearing to be a *natural* (undoctored) class-s sample to a human inspector; see Figure 1.1. The imperceptibility objective is typically achieved by making the adversarial perturbation from x to $\tilde{x}$ as small as possible according to some measure. Likewise, a targeted TTE attack seeks to induce decision change to a *target* class chosen by the attacker.

Clearly, in non-image domains that are high-dimensional (for which human beings either cannot intelligibly perceive class-discriminating patterns, or would require huge time and resources, perhaps involving data visualization tools, to make such inferences), it is much less of an imperative that the attack example be "imperceptible" to a human. However, for such domains, the attack should still aim to be evasive to simple, automated anomaly detection systems.

Note that TTE attacks in general assume the attacker knows the true class of the sample to be altered – otherwise, the attacker would only know he/she succeeded in inducing a decision change (to the actual classifier, or to the attacker's proxy) – *not* whether the change actually results in a misclassification (the decision change could otherwise in fact "correct" a misclassification). The practical implications of this assumption will be further explored in Chapter 4.

TTE attacks often employ techniques of neural network inversion (see Section 2.10) applied to an objective function whose maximization is consistent with a change in the classifier's decision (see Section 4.1). Some proposed TTE attacks compute the gradient of this objective but take a single, large step rather than taking an incremental descent approach involving smaller step sizes and (potentially numerous) small descent steps. As a result, to succeed in inducing misclassifications, the former approaches may require larger adversarial perturbations than the latter ones. However, some TTE attacks of the latter variety, with relatively small perturbations, can still be quite weak/ineffective.

As an example of the latter, let us consider a DNN classifier of handwritten digits trained on the MNIST dataset [141] with $K = 10$ classes, $\mathcal{Y} = \{0, 1, 2, \ldots, 9\}$.

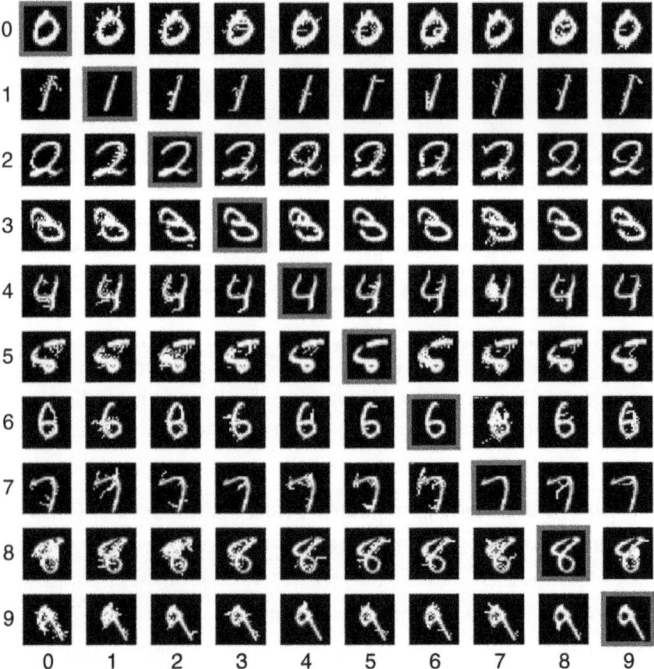

Figure 1.2 Images on the diagonal are examples of unmodified (clean) samples that are correctly classified by a DNN trained on MNIST [141]. Off-diagonal images are the result of the JSMA [203] attack applied to the diagonal image in the same row, which are classified by the DNN to the class corresponding to the column index. Adversarial examples are clearly doctored with significant salt and pepper noise. Reprinted from [179, 180] with permission.

Example JSMA TTE attacks (see Section 4.1), wherein individual pixels are modified sequentially until the desired misclassification is achieved, are depicted in Figure 1.2. Note the significant salt-and-pepper noise and extra white pixels introduced by the attack. A simple detection method based on the number of contiguous white regions in the image achieved 0.97 ROC AUC; see Table 6 of [179] and Section 4.10.2. Moreover, the attacked images should appear highly suspicious to a human observer. Thus, JSMA applied to MNIST is a weak TTE attack. Moreover, in some of the attack instances in Figure 1.2 even a human being cannot unambiguously assert the true class of origin for the image – note in particular many of the attacked '5's, some of the '3's, the attacked '6' classified as a '7', and the attacked '9' classified as a '0'. In this sense, the attack does not "fool" the classifier since even a human being cannot ambiguously determine the class of origin. Other TTE attacks such as FGSM [83] and CW [33] do exhibit grey ghosting artifacts on MNIST (see Figure 1.3) but these are less noticeable than JSMA artifacts. Moreover, all of these attacks exhibit much less noticeable artifacts for more complex image domains (involving textures and non-constant image background) such as CIFAR [129] and ImageNet [57].

A TTE attack may be on physical objects in the real world (e.g., altering a road sign or "camouflaging" a vehicle). However, in some cases it may be difficult to implement

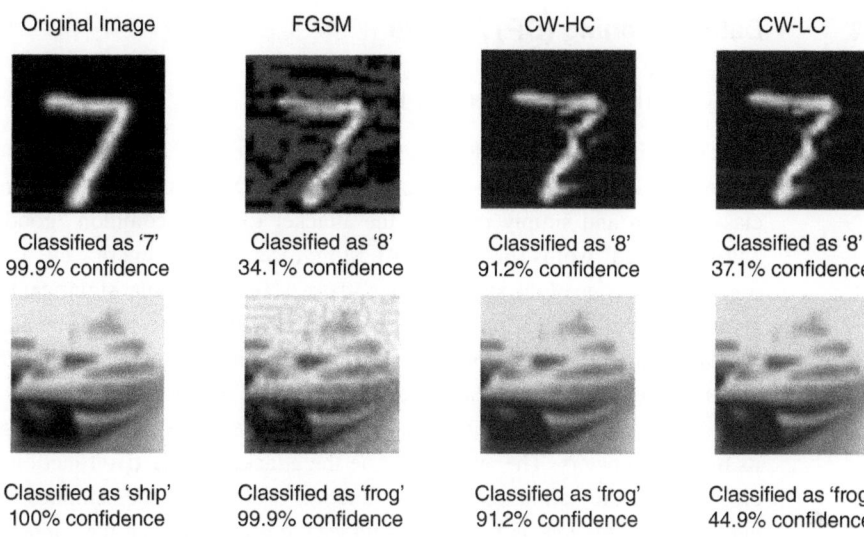

Original Image	FGSM	CW-HC	CW-LC
Classified as '7' 99.9% confidence	Classified as '8' 34.1% confidence	Classified as '8' 91.2% confidence	Classified as '8' 37.1% confidence
Classified as 'ship' 100% confidence	Classified as 'frog' 99.9% confidence	Classified as 'frog' 91.2% confidence	Classified as 'frog' 44.9% confidence

Figure 1.3 Examples of clean images, FGSM attack images [83], CW high confidence (CW-HC) images and CW low confidence (CW-LC) images [33], from MNIST [141] (first row) and CIFAR-10 [129] (second row) datasets. HC TTEs typically have much larger adversarial perturbations compared to LC TTEs. Reprinted from [284] with permission.

strong physical attacks. Alternatively, a TTE attack may alter data objects that have either already been digitally captured (e.g., digital images, voice files) or those which are *natively* digital (e.g., emails, documents, or computer programs). Such *digital* TTE attacks are invoked prior to the data object being input to the DNN.

While some attacks necessitate sophisticated defenses that may require significant innovations, other attacks may be defeated simply by invocation of standard techniques. For example, the use of encryption can defeat a man-in-the-middle TTE attack [135], that is, one wherein the data object is intercepted by the attacker, and modified, before being input to the classifier. As another example, the attack on voice systems in [31] could potentially be defeated by Apple Siri's existing built-in speaker-recognition system. Even if the speaker-recognition system can be overcome by existing voice cloning technology (especially under a white box scenario where the attacker has samples of the authorized party's voice), standard techniques of limited privilege can be applied. For example, Siri cannot enter data into the Safari web browser, and even if it could, there is standard multi-factor authentication to prevent unauthorized access to a private website even if the password were compromised.

Aside from use of standard security techniques, there are basically two different approaches to TTE defense. The first is robust classifier training, which seeks to be robust to (i.e., to correctly classify) adversarial inputs. The second, and more promising approach, is anomaly detection (AD) at test/operational time, which, unlike robust classification, makes explicit attack detection inferences. These two approaches are discussed in detail in Chapter 4.

1.4   Data Poisoning (DP) Attacks

1.4.1   Early Work on Error Generic DP attacks

Most early DP attacks simply seek to degrade the learned classifier's accuracy, see for example, [106, 176, 311]. For example, an early DP attack targeted spam/ham email classification and simply required the attacker to know common "good" words (in ham) and "bad" words (in spam) [14]. More recent "error generic" DP attacks require greater knowledge of the system under attack. [20] showed that significant degradation in the accuracy of a Support Vector Machine (SVM, see the Appendix) could be achieved with the addition of just one poisoned training sample – on MNIST the error rate increased from the 2–5% range to the 15–20% range. To achieve this, the attacker exploits knowledge of the training set, a validation set, the SVM learning algorithm, and its hyperparameters. The authors define the attacker's objective function as classifier error rate on the validation set as a function of the poisoned sample's location (and class label). This loss is maximized under the constraint that the support vector and non-support vector subsets of the training dataset are not altered by addition of the poisoned sample. Thus, [20] adds a single, new (adversarially labeled) support vector to the SVM solution. The constraint is met by performing gradient descent carefully, with a small step size. One would expect that even more classifier degradation could be achieved if the support vectors were allowed to *change* through the addition of the poisoned sample.[4] However, this would also entail a more complex optimization procedure. An illustrative example of such a DP attack on SVMs is shown in Figure 1.4.

While [20] required the attacker to possess substantial knowledge of the classifier, other works make even greater assumptions about an attacker's capabilities. In particular, in [176] it was noted that, in the data poisoning attack on active learning of an SVM in [175], the authors assumed that the *oracle* (typically a human expert) deliberately mislabels samples. Thus, the attack in [175] relies on even the human labeler being compromised.

While SVMs (which rely on a support vector subset of the training set to define the linear discriminant function) can unsurprisingly be fragile in the presence of DP attacks, there is little prior work investigating such attacks against DNNs. One reason may be computational complexity – one could in some way alternate gradient descent optimization in weight space (minimizing the loss function, i.e., the defender/learner's problem) and gradient *ascent* in pattern space (maximizing the loss function, i.e., the attacker's problem), to find a set of poisoned input patterns that maximally degrade the learned DNN's accuracy. However, such a procedure would be complicated and quite computationally heavy. Moreover, this assumes both that the attacker has access to the training set *and* that the attacker is the training authority.

DNNs should be less fragile in the presence of data poisoning than SVMs. To degrade a DNN's accuracy sufficiently, a larger fraction of poisoned samples may be

---

[4] On the other hand, if the attacker does *not* know the value of the margin slackness hyperparameter, he/she cannot ensure the poisoned sample will be a support vector; in such case, many more poisoned samples may be needed in order to significantly degrade SVM accuracy.

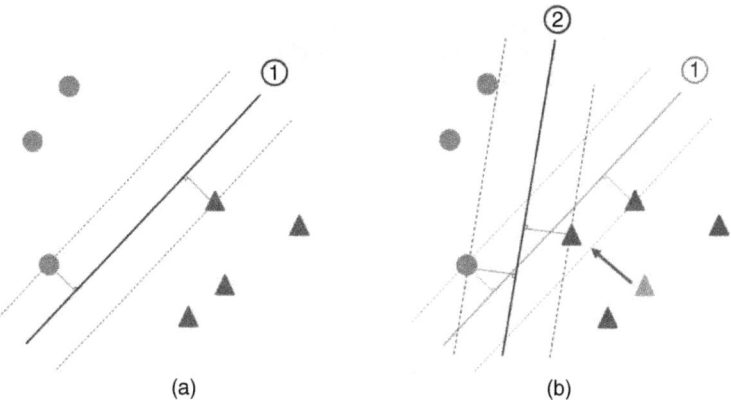

Figure 1.4 Linear SVM classifier decision boundary for a two-class dataset with support vectors and classification margins indicated (a). The decision boundary is significantly impacted in this example if just one training sample is changed, even when that sample's class label does not change (b). Here, the changed sample becomes a support vector. Reprinted from [180] with permission.

needed. For "big data" domains with, for example, one million training samples, even 2% data poisoning (with judicious selection of the poisoned samples by the attacker) means optimizing 20,000 poisoned sample locations and labels.

1.4.2   Backdoor DP Attacks on DNNs

On the other hand, DNNs appear to be quite vulnerable to *backdoor* DP attacks, as demonstrated in a number of works [44, 89, 150, 158, 268, 303, 304, 308]. Planted backdoors are also known as *Trojans*. To the training dataset, the attacker adds samples drawn from a source class with a backdoor pattern incorporated, and with the resulting poisoned samples labeled as belonging to a different (target) class. Thus, the classifier learns to classify to the attacker's target class whenever the attacker's *backdoor pattern* is embedded in a source-class test example to be classified, that is, when the test example is a backdoor trigger; see Figure 1.5. Successful backdoor poisoning does not significantly impact classification accuracy on clean (backdoor-free) test samples.

Triggering a backdoor of a (poisoned) DNN at test-time is typically much easier (and requires much less computation) compared to launching a TTE on a clean (unpoisoned) DNN with the same associated source and target classes.

The backdoor pattern could be an **imperceptible** (e.g., random-looking) local or global watermark-like pattern. Alternatively, it could be **perceptible but scene-plausible** – for example, the presence of glasses on a face [44], a plausible object in the background of an image scene (such as a tree or a bird in the sky, or a ball on a lawn), or a noise-like audio background pattern in the case of speech classification. Scene-plausible attacks on images may be implemented either by a physically "choreographed" scene or by photo-shopping a digital image to include the plausible object.

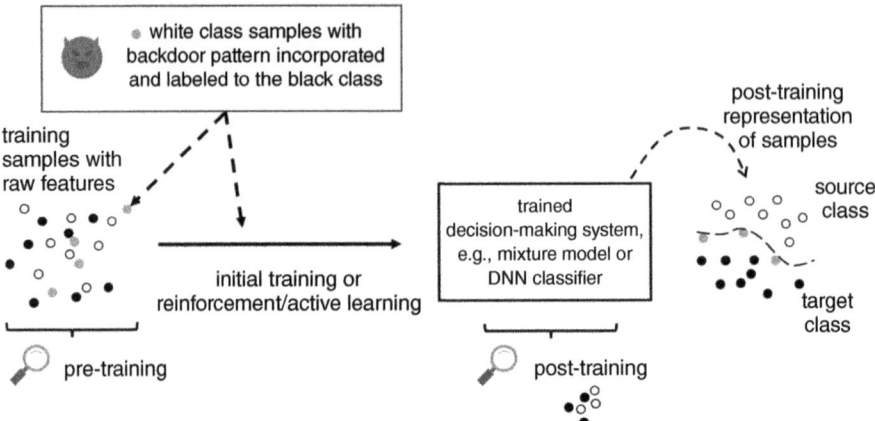

Figure 1.5 Illustration of a backdoor attack and the before/during and post-training defense scenarios. Also see Figure 6.1. The "in-flight" defense scenario, where backdoor triggers at test time are detected, is not depicted; see Chapter 10.

In Chapter 7, it will be argued that scene-plausibility implies that the backdoor pattern will be learned in a spatially invariant fashion by a DNN.

Various digital mechanisms can be applied to introduce a backdoor pattern into an image. These include replacing a local patch of pixels (consistent with the afore-mentioned perceptible, scene-plausible backdoors), applying an additive perturbation to the image, or applying a multiplicative perturbation. Noisy patch backdoor pat-terns are described in [144, 197]. [44, 316] employ a noisy patch u that is "blended" into a clean image x using an image-wide binary mask m (all elements are Boolean, $m_i \in \{0, 1\}$ for all pixels i) and a real-valued blending factor $\alpha \in (0, 1)$ to produce $\tilde{x} = (1 - \alpha m) \odot x + \alpha m \odot u$. Here, $\odot$ is a pixel-wise product (e.g., a 3×3-pixel square mask in the same location for each poisoned image $\tilde{x}$).

One very attractive aspect of backdoor attacks is that they may require *no* knowledge of the classifier – the attacker simply needs: (i) legitimate examples from the domain, into which it embeds the backdoor pattern; (ii) the ability to poison the training dataset with these samples labeled to the target (backdoor) class; and (iii) perhaps knowledge of the training set size, to know how many poisoned samples may be needed. On the other hand, if the attacker does possess knowledge of the classifier, its training set, and its learning algorithm, he/she can optimize the backdoor pattern to ensure: (i) the backdoor is well-learned; (ii) clean classifier accuracy is not compromised; and (iii) that (i) and (ii) are accomplished with the least amount of "attack strength," that is, with the fewest poisoned examples and/or using least noticeable backdoor patterns (so that the attack is not easily detected). An attempt at such an approach is given in [150].

Figure 1.6 is a low resolution picture of a car with a single pixel modification. A group of images with such changes could be used to poison a training set and thus plant a backdoor in the classifier. Note that, even at this level of resolution, it would be

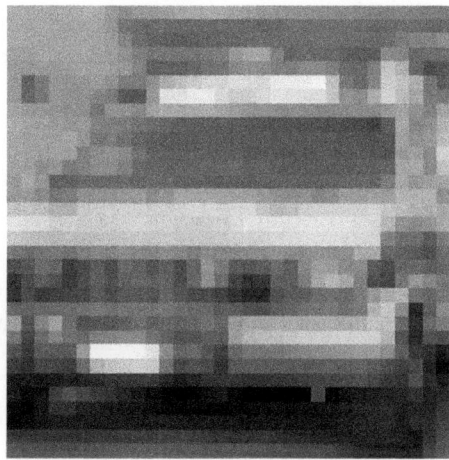

Figure 1.6 Modified low resolution CIFAR-10 [129] image of a car with a single pixel changed to trigger (or train) a backdoor.

difficult for a human inspector to detect the poisoned samples in the training set or the samples triggering the backdoor operationally (at test time).

In some defenses, it is assumed that initially there is a clean (free of poisoned samples) training set, but that subsequently it is altered by additional (potentially unreliable) data collection, by online learning, or by the actions of an adversarial insider – under this scenario, the learner knows a subset of the available training set that is guaranteed to be *clean* (attack-free). In this case, for DP attacks, one can detect poisoned samples by discerning that their use in learning degrades classification accuracy (on a clean, held-out validation data subset) relative to just use of the clean subset of data [193].

A more challenging DP scenario for attack detection is the *embedded* scenario [301, 308], where one cannot assume the training dataset is "initially" clean and where there is no available means (using time stamps, data provenance, etc.) for identifying a subset of samples guaranteed to be free of poisoning.

Defenses against backdoor attacks under different scenarios are discussed in Chapters 5–10 for image classification, Chapter 11 for 3D point cloud classification, and Chapter 12 for regression.

Clean Label Backdoor Attacks

In [275], a *clean label* backdoor attack was proposed. These attacks have two key aspects. First, they intend to induce classification to the target class whenever the backdoor pattern is present, *irrespective* of the class of origin of the data object. Second, and most importantly, these attacks do not require any mislabeling of training examples. As motivation for the latter, suppose that the training set is initially *unlabeled* and that an honest human expert is responsible for labeling all the training samples.

In this situation, the mislabeling required for conventional backdoor attacks cannot be achieved. So, the attacker applies the backdoor pattern to samples that originate from the *target* class of the attack, not from a source class. Moreover, the poisoned samples may be further altered, for example, by:

- adding noise in order to weaken, within these samples, the features that can normally be relied upon to correctly classify them (but somehow in a way that is not noticed by the honest human expert labeling the samples); or
- adding a sample-specific adversarial perturbation, causing an unpoisoned classifier (trained on clean data and assumed available to the adversary) to change its class decision from the target class.

However, even when such sample alterations are applied, clean label backdoor attacks appear to require much greater attack strength than regular backdoor attacks in order to be successful. One reason is that some normal target-class features need to persist in the poisoned sample in order to convince the honest human labeler that the sample belongs to the target class. Alternatively, if (sample specific) adversarial perturbations are used, there is no reason why those perturbations will be learned instead of the target-class discriminating features when the victim classifier is trained. So, clean label backdoor attacks either require poisoning a much greater fraction of the training set than regular backdoor attacks or they require much more overt (and hence less evasive) backdoor patterns in order to overcome the target-class discriminating features in the poisoned samples. The former may not be possible in practice (as the attacker may have access to, or contribute to, only a portion of the training set). The latter will make the attack more easily detected (by either an automated detector or a human inspector). Consequently, clean label backdoor attacks do not appear to be a significant practical threat. See the results given in Figure 1.7 which involved an additively incorporated chessboard-watermark backdoor pattern, shown in Figure 6.4b, without any other alterations. Here, ten ResNet-18 (see Figure 2.6) classifiers were conventionally trained, each on a different CIFAR-10 subdomain of five randomly selected classes among which the poisoned target class was also randomly chosen. Note that the attack success rate is high only when the number of poisoned samples is large or when the perturbation size is quite large.

There are other types of backdoor attacks, e.g., label smoothed and sample specific.

1.4.3   Post-Training Model-Adjustment Attacks

Post-training, deployment-stage backdoor attacks have also been proposed, see for example, [12]. These could occur if the *model* is intercepted by an adversary (if it is transmitted from a remote site), that is, by a man-in-the-middle, or if the model is compromised by resident malware. These attacks are not discussed in detail here, but it is expected that they can be detected by the post-training backdoor defenses discussed in this book. Note also that a simple hash against the trained model parameters can be used to check if the model has been altered, post-training.

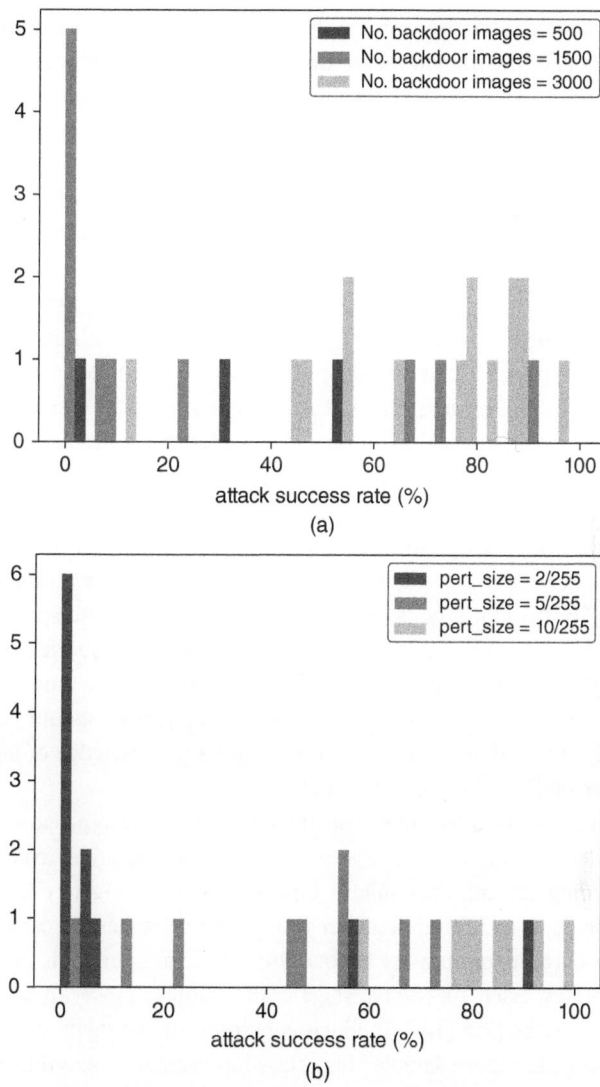

Figure 1.7 Histograms of attack success rate for clean label backdoor attacks, for the CIFAR-10 domain, with (a) different numbers of images for training set poisoning, and (b) different perturbation sizes for the backdoor pattern. To achieve a high attack success rate, either the poisoning rate must be very high, or the backdoor pattern size must be large (making the backdoor trigger potentially visually discernible).

1.5   Reverse-Engineering Attacks (REAs) Targeting the Deep Neural Network (DNN)

Let us now consider **privacy issues** related to reverse-engineering attacks (REAs) targeting the training set, the training process (algorithmic privacy), and/or the model parameters and architecture. The identification of some training samples or of some aspects of the trained model by an adversary is sometimes called "data leakage."

REAs may involve querying (probing) a DNN numerous times, either to learn its decision rule or to learn something about the dataset on which it was trained (an attack on data privacy). Repeated querying can be used to create a training set for the attacker (with the classifier's decision on each example used as the supervising label), allowing him/her to learn a surrogate of the true classifier. Several motivations have been given for reverse engineering a classifier's decision rule.

In [267], the authors consider black box machine learning (ML) services, offered by a company, where, for a given domain, a user (with limited resources for learning a model) pays for class decisions on individual samples (queries) submitted to the ML service. [267] demonstrates that, with a significant number of queries (e.g., tens of thousands, even for low-dimensional classification domains), one can learn a classifier that closely mimics black box ML service decisions. Once the black box has been reverse engineered, the attacker need no longer subscribe to the ML service. Perhaps more importantly, such reverse engineering enables TTE attacks by providing the attacker with knowledge of the classifier when it is not initially known. One weakness of [267] is that it considers neither very large (feature space) domains nor very large neural networks – for orders of magnitude more queries may be needed to reverse engineer a DNN on a large-scale domain. However, a more critical weakness of [267], discussed further in Chapter 14, is that its queries should be easily detected because they are *random*, that is, they do not use any knowledge of the nominal (training) data distribution for the given domain.

REAs based on more realistic queries have been proposed. In [202], the adversary collects a small set of representative labeled samples from the domain as an initial training set and uses this to train an initial surrogate classifier. Then, there is data collection and retraining over a sequence of stages. In each, the adversary augments the current training set by querying the classifier with the stage's newly generated samples. Each successive stage crafts samples closer to the classifier's true decision boundaries (see (14.1)), which is helpful for surrogate classifier learning (but which also makes these samples less class representative and thus more detectable). Once a sufficiently accurate surrogate classifier is learned, a TTE attack can be launched using it. Defenses against REAs are discussed in Chapter 14.

1.6   Attacks on Privacy of Training Data

Another emergent attack, referred to as a membership-inference attack, seeks not to alter classifier decision-making but rather to glean, from the classifier, (assumed sensitive) information about the training set on which it was learned. Relevant applications here include: discerning whether a particular person participated in a patient study that produced a disease classifier (or a diagnostic or prognostic decision-making aid) – one may then infer he/she is likely to possess the disease; or discerning whether a particular individual's data was used in training a system that grants secure access (to a building, data, financial records) only to company employees or vetted individuals. In the latter case, one might alternatively seek to infer what such individuals *look like* (estimate an image of an employee's face [71]). There are various scenarios we can consider for this type of problem.

An important scenario is one wherein the attacker only has black box (query) access to the classifier. A representative approach that investigates data privacy attacks on classifiers under this scenario is [244]. This work makes some strong assumptions, but shows that when these assumptions hold one can make quite accurate inferences of whether or not an individual's sample was used in training (a membership-inference attack), for example, accuracies as surprisingly high as 80–90% in inferring training-set membership on two classification domains. The authors pose the attacker's problem as learning a posterior model whose input is a data record (feature vector) and whose output is the probability that the data record was used in training the classifier under attack. There are three pivotal assumptions made.

- The attacker has query access to the victim classifier and, when queried, the classifier does not merely produce decisions – it gives decision "confidence" that could consist of the vector of posterior probabilities over all classes, just the "top" probabilities, or quantized values for these probabilities. The attacker does not query the victim classifier repeatedly to reverse engineer its function – this could be detected using the methods of Chapter 14. It simply queries using the data sample on which it is seeking to violate privacy, and elicits the victim classifier's decision and confidence on this sample.
- It is assumed that the attacker has access to a (surrogate) dataset that is statistically similar to the training set used in building the victim classifier [244]. This assumption is plausible only in some applications. In the patient study scenario, the attacker could have access to data records from hospital B, while the study yielding the victim classifier was produced by hospital A – hospital B's population could be very similar to that of A. However, it is less plausible that the attacker would have a training set statistically similar to a particular company's dataset, used to build its secure authentication classifier – unless, for example, members of this company also belong, in large numbers, to the same country club.
- Even though the victim classifier *is* assumed to be a black box with respect to the attacker, it is assumed that the victim classifier was trained using a particular online tool or "ML pay-for-service" system (e.g., provided by Google), that the attacker knows which tool/service was used, and he/she also has access to this tool. In this way, even without knowing what the classifier type is (e.g., SVM or a particular DNN architecture), the attacker can assume that, *given a similar dataset, with the same feature vector format, from the same classification domain*, the tool/service is likely to produce a new classifier (a shadow classifier) that "behaves in a similar way" as the classifier under attack. In particular, it should exhibit similar decision confidence patterns for samples used for training (high decision confidence) compared to samples not used for training.

Based on its surrogate training (and test) datasets, the attacker uses the tool/service to build an array of such shadow models. For each such model, he/she produces class decisions and the confidence scores on the surrogate training samples, and separately on the test samples. Each such triple class decision, confidence vector, training set example (Yes/No) is treated as a supervised instance of a *new* training set, used to learn a binary posterior model that infers whether a given sample was part of a shadow model's training set. After the attacker's binary classifier is trained, it can be applied to the output of the classifier under attack, when queried by a given data sample, and yield the probability that the query sample was part of the attacked classifier's training set.

It was noted there are strong assumptions in this work, whose violation could substantially minimize the amount of membership "leakage" obtained. First, if the victim classifier does not produce decision confidence, but merely a decision, this would defeat this attack. Producing confidence on decisions is important in order for classifier decisions to be trusted, but one could, for example, grossly coarsen the victim classifier's output confidence to "highly confident," "confident," "weakly confident," "uncertain" – such quantization could potentially defeat the membership-inference attack of [244] .

Second, as the authors note, this attack is successful because trained classifiers tend to overfit to training examples, producing patterns of "high confidence" on samples used for training, and patterns of lower confidence for non-training samples. The authors investigate defense strategies that seek to reduce classifier overfitting, or at least its signature in the victim classifier's posterior. These mitigations include use of regularization and altering the victim classifier's posterior to increase its decision entropy. While strong regularization can degrade the accuracy of the attacker's binary (training set example: Yes/No) classifier, it may also compromise accuracy of the victim classifier.

One can also likely defeat or weaken this attack by *not* using an accessible (and inferrable) service for training the victim classifier. This attack may not transfer well if the victim and shadow classifier decision rules are quite different.

One can also simply suppose that after training the targeted classifier, the training set that was used is (securely) retained by the platform/system that operates the classifier [180]. Now, when the classifier is queried by a sample, the system can first check whether the sample is part of the training dataset. If the sample is not part of the training set, the classifier can output its decision and confidence, as usual. However, if the query sample is in the training set (or is even essentially indistinguishable from a training pattern, i.e., if the attacker added a small amount of noise to the query sample in order to be evasive), the system can infer that this is very likely a data privacy attack query. In this case, the classifier should still output the correct decision, as well as confidence values that are at least maximum a posteriori (MAP) consistent with that decision. However, the system should randomize the confidence values to destroy any privacy revelation, and thus confound the attacker. This simple defense should be highly effective at defeating [244]. The attacker could add noise to his/her query so that it will not be recognized as a possible training instance. However, there is a fundamental tradeoff between successful evasion of this defense and the attacker's success rate in revealing training set memberships. If insufficient noise is added, the query may be detected as a training instance. On the other hand, if large enough noise is added to avoid such detection, the query sample may no longer elicit a high confidence "signature" from the classifier.

It is also noted that the system can ignore differences from training samples in features that anyway are not crucial for class discrimination, as the attacker might obfuscate such irrelevant features in order to be evasive to detection while at the same time not altering the confidence pattern produced by the classifier – in matching a query pattern against the training set, the detector should focus on the key, discriminating subset of the features. (See the discussions in Sections 2.12 and 2.13.)

Privacy of training data is not discussed further in this book.

1.7   Chapter Summary

In this chapter we introduced various kinds of attacks against machine learning systems, including test-time evasion, data poisoning, backdoor data poisoning, reverse engineering, and membership-inference attacks. We introduced jargon to describe an attacker's knowledge (black, grey, or white box), as well as the attacker's objective (targeted versus untargeted attacks). We indicated the importance of characterizing the work factor (computation and memory requirements) for implementing an attack, as well as a defense – for example, white box attacks, with full knowledge of the machine learning system as well as the defense, may *always* be able to defeat the ML system-plus-defense if given *limitless* computational resources. However, it may take substantial computational resources, for example, to construct a TTE attack example that defeats both the classifier and a detector-based defense. We indicated some attacks are digital (e.g., modifying the pixel values in a digital image) while others are physical (e.g., altering the scene which will be captured by a digital image). Membership-inference attacks were discussed in some detail, as they are not covered in the remainder of the book.

Some questions to test the reader's understanding of the chapter include the following.

- Why is it arguable that the attack examples in Figure 1.2 are not successful attacks?
- Why are TTEs demonstrative that AI still has a long way to go?
- Why is it important that a backdoor pattern be either imperceptible or scene-plausible?
- What are the three possible defense scenarios for backdoors?
- What are some possible ways of embedding a backdoor pattern in a digital image?

- What is the potential advantage of a clean label backdoor attack?
- Explain the simple strategy (described in this chapter) for defeating a membership-inference attack?

1.8   References for Further Reading

General introductions to computer and network security include [23, 249]. The following books focus on adversarial learning [112, 281].

2 Deep Learning Background

Artificial Neural Networks (NNs) have had an interesting boom-or-bust history, beginning promisingly with the McCulloch–Pitts proposal of an artificial neuron and Rosenblatt's Perceptron algorithm for learning a linear decision boundary separating data from a pair of classes [63]. Optimism for NN capabilities dimmed with Minsky and Papert's 1969 demonstration of the limitations of perceptrons. Optimism then waxed in the 1980s with the rediscovery of the back propagation algorithm applied to multilayer perceptrons and with the development of convolutional neural networks, inspired by classical paradigms from signal processing. (An interesting history of neural networks is found in [233, 234].) However, alternative machine learning solutions came to the fore in the 1990s and early 2000s, including semi-supervised learning, boosted classifier ensembles, and Bayesian learning frameworks. Finally NNs, in particular large deep neural networks (DNNs) with many hidden layers, became resurgent around 2010 with the greater availability of much faster computing and larger storage platforms for learning/training DNNs (particularly through the public cloud), and with demonstrated advances over state-of-the-art methods for problems in various domains [45, 261, 264]. For some application domains there could be at least tens of millions (in some cases billions) of DNN parameters to be learned using a labeled training dataset which, in some applications, may be commensurately huge and yet, in others is quite limited.

In this chapter we provide an introduction to "deep learning." This includes introducing pattern recognition concepts, neural network architectures, basic optimization techniques (as used by gradient-based deep learning algorithms), and various deep learning methods, for example, for coping with limited available labeled training data. Some topics, such as neural network inversion and robust classifier training strategies, will be revisited frequently in subsequent chapters, as they form the basis both for attacks against deep learning and for defenses against such attacks.

For a given supervised learning task involving a potentially huge training dataset, DNN architectures are heuristically formulated. Moreover, DNNs are trained through a "deep learning" process which is a combination of classical optimization techniques. The performance of these optimization techniques can be theoretically studied only in very special cases which do not apply to practical DNNs, for example, [259]. Deep learning has been greatly facilitated by software platforms such as PyTorch and TensorFlow which accommodate a wide variety of DNN architectures and optimization techniques.

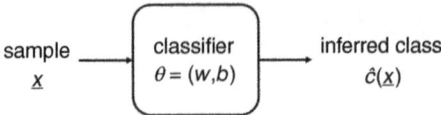

Figure 2.1 A classifier with input sample (input pattern) $\underline{x}$, output $\hat{c}(\underline{x})$ being the inferred class of $\underline{x}$, and learned parameters θ.

As discussed in Chapter 1 (and Chapter 4), adversarial inputs are easily constructed for DNNs. This demonstrates that it is a fallacy that DNNs are *generally* robust and reliable decision-makers. Another fallacy is that DNNs have "democratized" science and engineering, so that little technical domain specific expertise is required for their application – practical (supervised) deep learning typically requires the creation and curation of a vast training set of carefully labeled samples. This is a very time-consuming process requiring domain expertise. (Quality and integrity issues of the training dataset are also known as the "garbage-in/garbage-out" problem of deep learning.) DNN architecture design and feature preprocessing may also need to be customized for specific domains in order to achieve state-of-the-art performance. Such customization may also require insightful domain knowledge. Moreover, DNNs and deep learning respectively have inherent problems of explainability (e.g., [91]), and reproducibility (e.g., [100]). (Other choices of machine learning platform besides DNNs, e.g., [63], are better suited for certain learning tasks, but they may also have vulnerabilities and robustness issues.)

Having given this bit of *caveat emptor*, the remainder of this chapter provides a technical overview of deep learning.

2.1   Deep Learning for Classification, Regression, or Prediction

Suppose we have a large training set of labeled data samples X from a particular data domain, to be used for supervised design of a classifier. The dimensionality N of the data samples is often large, in many applications of interest. Deep learning, the process through which a DNN is trained on X, can be applied to a wide variety of applications. The samples may be based on, for example, images, segments of speech or video, documents, or may represent the current state of an online game. The trained classifier assigns any sample from the input data domain to one of a finite number of categories. The DNN classifier could thus be used to infer, for example,

- the type of animal in an image,
- the word that is being spoken in a segment of speech,
- the sentiment or topic of some text, or
- the action that is to be taken by a particular player at a particular stage in a game.

Suppose a sample $\underline{x}$ is an input pattern to a classifier; see Figure 2.1. The output $\hat{c}(\underline{x})$ is the inferred class label (decision) for the sample $\underline{x}$. The classifier parameters θ should be learned, using the training set, so that the inferred class decisions on *test* samples (unseen during training) are as accurate as possible. This is often referred to as the generalization capability of the classifier.

2.1.1 Types of Data

The samples themselves may consist of a collection of scalar features that are of different types, for example, categorical, ordinal, and continuous numerical. There are various ways to transform data from all other types into continuous numerical – the standard representation for inputs to a deep neural network. As one example, for documents, there are methods such as Word2vec [174] that map words (which are discrete-valued features) to continuous-valued feature vectors. How this is done may significantly affect classification performance. Such preprocessing is part of a potentially complex, initial data preparation phase of deep learning [189, 255]. In the following, we assume all input samples $\underline{x} \in \mathbb{R}^N$ for simplicity.

2.1.2 Training and Test Datasets

Suppose we have a finite training dataset $X \subset \mathbb{R}^N$ with **ground truth** class labels $c(\underline{x})$ for all $\underline{x} \in X$. X contains representative samples from all (K) classes. Using X and the supervising label for each training sample, one goal may be to create a classifier

$$\hat{c} : \mathbb{R}^N \rightarrow \{1, 2, \ldots, K\} =: \mathcal{Y}$$

that

- accurately classifies on X, that is, for most $\underline{x} \in X$, $\hat{c}(\underline{x}) = c(\underline{x})$, and
- generalizes well to a different production/test set $\mathcal{I} \subset \mathbb{R}^N$, which is assumed to follow the same distribution as X. Good generalization means that for most $\underline{x} \in \mathcal{I}$, $\hat{c}(\underline{x}) = c(\underline{x})$.

A held-out subset of the training set called the validation set, $\mathcal{H}$, containing samples from all classes, can be employed to choose hyperparameters associated with training (such as the stopping condition for learning, the DNN architecture, or its size). In particular, the *accuracy* of a classifier $\hat{c}$ on $\mathcal{H}$ is measured as

$$\frac{\sum_{\underline{x} \in \mathcal{H}} \mathbf{1}\{\hat{c}(\underline{x}) = c(\underline{x})\}}{|\mathcal{H}|} \times 100\%.$$

This accuracy can be maximized with respect to a discrete set of hyperparameter choices, under the premise that performance on the validation set is a good surrogate for performance on the test set. See Section 2.8.3.

2.1.3 Optimal Bayes Error Rate

For each input sample $\underline{x}$, there is a *true* posterior distribution on the classes κ, $\{p(\kappa|\underline{x})\}_{\kappa=1}^K$, where $p(\kappa|\underline{x}) \geq 0$ and $\sum_{\kappa=1}^K p(\kappa|\underline{x}) = 1$, that is, $p(\cdot|\underline{x})$ is a probability mass function (pmf) on the set of classes $\mathcal{Y} = \{1, 2, \ldots, K\}$ conditioned on the sample x. Employing a maximum a posteriori decision rule based on the true posterior gives the minimum possible misclassification rate on the given domain, known as the Bayes error rate. That is,

$$B := \int_{\mathbb{R}^N} (1 - p(c(\underline{x})|\underline{x}))\psi(\underline{x})d\underline{x},$$

where ψ is the (true) probability density function (pdf, or just "density") on the input sample space $\mathbb{R}^N$.

Note that ambiguity regarding the class of a sample $\underline{x}$ will be reflected in multiple classes possessing large posterior probabilities conditioned on $\underline{x}$.

A given classifier $\hat{c}$ trained on a finite training dataset X (hopefully sampled according to ψ) may have normalized outputs for each class, $\hat{p}(\kappa|\underline{x}) \geq 0$ (see Section 2.5.2), where

$$\hat{c}(\underline{x}) = \arg\max_{\kappa \in \mathcal{Y}} \hat{p}(\kappa|\underline{x}).$$

If these outputs also sum to 1, then $\hat{p}(\cdot|\underline{x})$ is a valid class posterior distribution on $\mathcal{Y}$ which, through deep learning, approximates $p(\cdot|\underline{x})$. The classifier will have error rate [63]

$$\int_{\mathbb{R}^N} \mathbf{1}\{\hat{c}(\underline{x}) \neq c(\underline{x})\}\psi(\underline{x})d\underline{x} \geq B.$$

Note also that in practice it may be difficult to evaluate the classifier's error rate as defined above, since the true density ψ is often unknown (and the integral may also be high-dimensional and potentially intractable to evaluate precisely). This is why, in practice, the generalization performance of a classifier is typically evaluated on a test/production set I which is *not* used for training the classifier. That is, the test error rate is defined as:

$$\frac{\sum_{\underline{x} \in I} \mathbf{1}\{\hat{c}(\underline{x}) \neq c(\underline{x})\}}{|I|} \times 100\%.$$

2.1.4   Regression or Sequential Prediction

DNNs can also be applied to many problems that intrinsically involve regression, rather than classification, for example, the problem of filtering noisy signals. As another example, DNNs can replace numerical solvers for differential equations that may be based on (deterministic) finite-difference algorithms or Monte Carlo methods. Deep learning in this case seeks to fit the DNN's output to the solutions of the differential equations for various initial conditions and/or driving input-signals. The motivation here is that DNN inference is much faster than explicit numerical solution of the differential equations; see Chapter 12.

DNNs are also often used to solve inference tasks involving time series and documents, where the latter is also essentially a "time" series as there is an ordered sequence of discrete features (words). Prediction problems can often be cast as regression problems. Both feed-forward networks (using a sliding window of time to select the

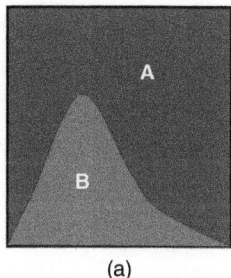 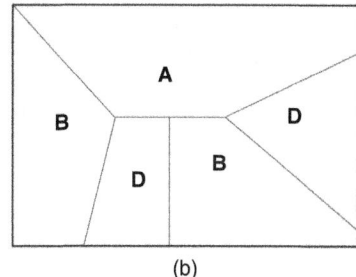

(a)   (b)

Figure 2.2 Illustrating class non-convexity in $\mathbb{R}^2$. (a) Two classes, A and B, with non-convex decision regions. (b) Three classes, A, B, and D, with class A having a convex decision region, while B and D have non-convex regions that are each the union of two convex component regions.

current inputs to the DNN) and recurrent networks have been used for these prediction tasks.

2.2 Motivating Deep Neural Network (DNN) Classifiers

There are many different classification frameworks besides DNNs, including decision trees, naive Bayes classifiers, support vector machines (SVMs), mixture model based classifiers, and ensemble classification systems. In many cases, the optimal class decision boundaries may be non-convex, for example, each class may consist of multiple disjoint regions ("components") in the feature space $\mathbb{R}^N$. Note that $A \subset \mathbb{R}^N$ is a convex set if and only if $\forall \underline{x}, y \in A$ and $\forall r \in [0, 1]$, $r\underline{x} + (1 - r)\underline{y} \in A$. See Figure 2.2. While other classification frameworks can represent non-convex decision surfaces, a highly parameterized classifier like a DNN has great capacity to represent a complicated decision boundary. Some commercial DNNs have on the order of a billion (or more) parameters.

2.3 Linearly Separable Data

If the dimensionality of the input feature vector, N, is much larger than the number of samples, that is, $N \gg T = |\mathcal{X}|$ (as in, e.g., some genomic and document datasets), then the classes of data in $\mathcal{X}$ will likely already be linearly separable, in other words, perfect accuracy on the training set can be achieved by a *linear* decision function. The following theorem of T. Cover [51] can be applied when the input data $(\mathcal{X} \subset \mathbb{R}^N)$ is not linearly separable, particularly when $N \ll T$.

Theorem 1 *For simplicity, let us consider a two-class problem. If the classes represented in $\mathcal{X}$ are not linearly separable, then there is a continuous mapping ζ such that $\zeta(\mathcal{X}) = \{\zeta(\underline{x}) \mid \underline{x} \in \mathcal{X}\}$ is linearly separable.*

Proof Choose an enumeration of $\mathcal{X} = \{\underline{x}_1, \underline{x}_2, \dots, \underline{x}_T\}$ as follows. Continuously map each sample $\underline{x}$ to a different unit vector $\in \mathbb{R}^T$; that is, $\forall k$, $\zeta(\underline{x}_k) = \underline{e}_k$, where $e_{k,k} = 1$

and $e_{k,j} = 0 \ \forall j \neq k$. For example, use the Lagrange interpolating polynomial, whose kth element is

$$\zeta_k(\underline{x}) = \prod_{j=1,\ j\neq k}^{T} \frac{\|\underline{x} - \underline{x}_j\|^2}{\|\underline{x}_k - \underline{x}_j\|^2}, \quad \underline{x} \in \mathbb{R}^N, \tag{2.1}$$

where $\underline{\zeta} = [\zeta_1, \dots, \zeta_T]' : \mathbb{R}^N \rightarrow \mathbb{R}^T$ and $\| \cdot \|$ is the l_2 norm.

Every partition of the samples $\zeta(\mathcal{X}) = \{\underline{e}_k\}_{k=1}^{T}$ into two different sets (classes), indexed κ_1 and κ_2, is separable by the hyperplane $\underline{w}'\underline{x} = 0$ with parameters

$$\underline{w} = \sum_{k \in \kappa_1} \underline{e}_k - \sum_{k \in \kappa_2} \underline{e}_k.$$

For this choice, $\underline{w} \in \mathbb{R}^T$ has entries that are ± 1. Thus, $\forall k \in \kappa_1, \ \underline{w}'\underline{e}_k = 1 > 0$, and $\forall k \in \kappa_2, \ \underline{w}'\underline{e}_k = -1 < 0$.   □

Thus, Cover's theorem motivates DNN classifiers that map the input features to a large number of *embedded* features (activations of an internal layer of the DNN). In this embedded feature space, the classes are likely to be linearly separable. See Section A.2.

2.4   From Binary to K-ary Classification

We can build a classifier for $K > 2$ classes from multiple binary classifiers in different ways. "One versus rest" classification works as follows.

- Consider the class partition $\mathcal{X}_1, \mathcal{X}_2, \dots, \mathcal{X}_K$ of the training dataset $\mathcal{X}$.
- The ith binary classifier separates $\mathcal{X}_i$ from $\mathcal{X}_{-i} := \cup_{j\neq i}\mathcal{X}_j$, that is, "one versus rest" discrimination.
- If just one of these classifiers i assigns input sample $\underline{x}$ to class i (i.e., classifier j assigns $\underline{x}$ to class "$-j$" $\forall j \neq i$) then decide $\hat{c}(\underline{x}) = i$.

Another approach, dubbed "all pairs" classification, involves $K(K-1)/2$ binary classifiers, separating all class pairs, with the class that "wins" the most such binary "competitions" the decided class.

Both of the above approaches, in general, may have *indeterminate* input regions, within which *no* class achieves a plurality of votes. A tie-breaker rule is needed in order to make decisions in these regions. See Section A.4.5. An alternative multiclass linear discriminant, known as a *linear machine* [63], is guaranteed to have no indeterminate regions. However, it is not guaranteed to always achieve perfect separability of the training set, even if the training set is in fact multi-class linearly separable.

2.5   Deep Neural Network (DNN) Architectures

In this section, we discuss several types of neurons/units (activation functions), network layers, and whole DNN architectures. A simple, illustrative feed-forward neural

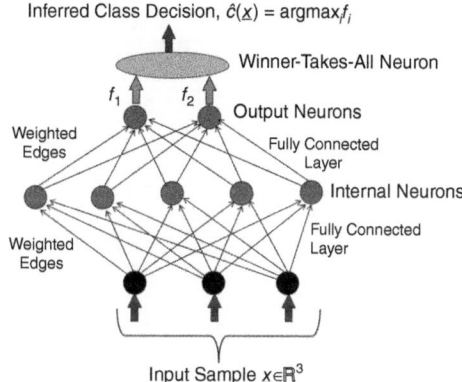

Figure 2.3 A small feed-forward neural network classifier, deciding between two classes.

network classifier, with two fully connected layers, for the case of two classes, is shown in Figure 2.3.

Let us consider a neuron/unit n in layer $\ell(n)$, that is $n \in \ell(n)$, with input edge-weights $w_{i,n}$, where neuron i is in the layer immediately preceding that of n, $i \in \ell_-(n)$. (In some feed-forward architectures, weights are conducted to a layer not only from the immediately preceding layer, but also from earlier layers in the network (i.e., via "skip connections"), see Figure 2.6.) The activation of neuron n is (for the example of a fully connected layer)

$$ v_n = f\left(\sum_{i \in \ell_-(n)} v_i w_{i,n} , b_n \right), $$

where b_n are additional parameters specifying the activation function.

2.5.1   Types of Neural Activations

If a neuron n is of the linear type, then it has an activation function of the form

$$ f(z, b_n) = z + b_n, $$

with bias b_n.

Example (nonlinear) sigmoid activation functions, as depicted in Figure 2.4, include

$$ f(z, b_n) = \tanh(z + b_n) \in (-1, 1), $$

$$ f(z, b_n) = \frac{1}{1 + \exp(-z - b_n)} \in (0, 1). $$

Rectified linear units (ReLUs) have activations of the form:

$$ f(z, b_n) = (z + b_n)^+ := \max\{z + b_n, 0\}. $$

Though ReLUs are not continuously differentiable at $z = -b_n$, they have a much simpler derivative than sigmoids. Also, both linear and ReLU activations are unbounded, whereas sigmoids are bounded. In practice, b_n is often not learned – instead it is just

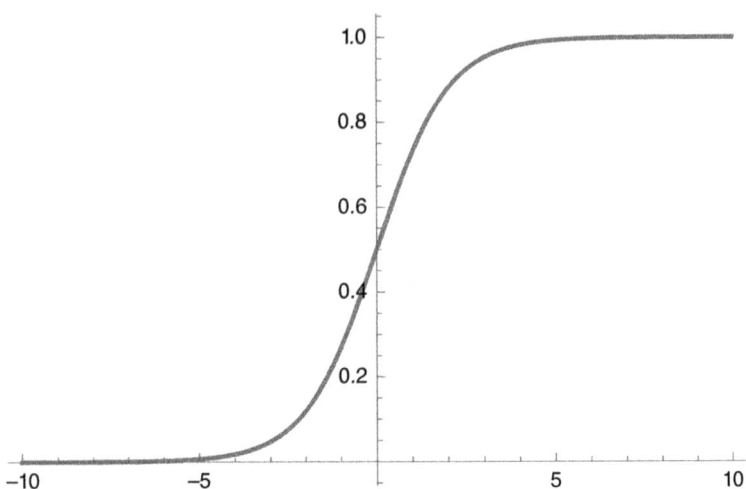

Figure 2.4 A sigmoid activation

taken to be 0, so that the operation is equivalent to simply zeroing out negative values, and preserving positive values,

$$f(z) = \max\{z, 0\} =: z^+.$$

"Hard threshold" neural activations, involving unit-step functions $u(z) = \mathbf{1}\{z \geq 0\}$, for example, $f(z, b_n) = u(z - b_n) \geq 0$, are obviously not differentiable at b_n, and have zero derivative everywhere else.

For the purposes of processing sequential data, *gated* neurons with inter-sample memory can be used to form a kind of *recurrent* neural network such as an LSTM (long short-term memory neural network) [101]. A simple gated neuron is one whose current activation v (i.e., for the current sample) depends on its activation v_- for the *previous* sample. Then, by extending the foregoing notation:

$$v = f(v_-, z, b).$$

2.5.2   Some Types of Layers

Now let us consider a layer of neurons ℓ and a previous layer (or layers) of neurons ℓ_-.

Fully Connected Layer
If $w_{i,n} \neq 0$ for all $i \in \ell_-, n \in \ell$, then layer ℓ is said to be fully connected.

Convolutional Layer
Suppose neurons in consecutive layers ℓ_- and ℓ are somehow ordered and indexed, for example, with activations $\{v_{\ell,1}, \ldots, v_{\ell,|\ell|}\}$ for ℓ. Layer ℓ is said to be **convolutional** if, for example, each neuron $n \in \ell$ has activation of the form:

$$v_{\ell,n} = \sum_{i=1}^{s} w_{s-i+1} v_{\ell_-,n+i-1}, \tag{2.2}$$

where the vector $\underline{w} \in \mathbb{R}^s$ is a *learned* (one-dimensional) *convolution kernel* or *convolution filter*; typically the kernel size $s \ll |\ell_-|$, and the layer-ℓ activation index n takes values in the range

$$1 \le n \le |\ell_-| - s + 1. \tag{2.3}$$

Note that each activation in layer ℓ, $v_{\ell,n}$, depends on a different *local region* of activations in ℓ_- according to how the neurons are indexed in ℓ_-. So, different neural activations in layer ℓ are dot products between the kernel $\underline{w}$ and different overlapping windows of size s of the activations of layer ℓ_-. That is, the s-window slides across the neurons of ℓ_-. A kernel $\underline{w}$ can be trained to detect localized, class-discriminatory patterns positioned somewhere in the activations of ℓ_-.

A single convolutional layer typically uses $r > 1$ different kernels $\underline{w}_k$, $k \in \{1, 2, \ldots, r\}$ of the same size s. Also, there may be an integer stride parameter m so that layer ℓ only has activations indexed n in range (2.3) such that n (or $n - 1$) is divisible by m. The quantities m, r, s are considered hyperparameters of a convolutional layer which, unlike the kernel parameters w, are not learned by back propagation, see Section 2.7.2.

For image based datasets, higher dimensional kernels are typically used. For example, 2D kernels can be used for greyscale images, 3D kernels when the image has multiple color channels per pixel, and 4D kernels for color video. Here, the kernel activations in ℓ correspond to spatially local (and also temporally local in the case of video) activations in ℓ_-.

Compared to fully connected layers with at most $|\ell_-| \cdot |\ell|$ non-zero parameters, convolutional layers have significantly fewer non-zero parameters, with this number given by:

$$\sum_{k=1}^{r} \|\underline{w}_k\|_0.$$

Convolutions are characteristic of linear, time-invariant filters, which have been used for decades in signal processing, long before their incorporation into neural networks (as a special case of a fully connected layer).

Pooling Layer

Pooling layers are intended to down-sample from a large layer ℓ_- to a much smaller one ℓ, that is, $|\ell_-| \gg |\ell|$ with $|\ell|$ a factor of $|\ell_-|$. Different pools (sets) of $|\ell_-|/|\ell|$ activations from layer ℓ_- are mapped to a single activation in layer ℓ. When this mapping is the maximum of the activations in the pool, this is called a max-pooling layer. Alternatively, when the mapping is an average, it is an average-pooling layer. Pooling layers operate similarly to convolutional layers, but they only involve hyperparameters such as the stride parameter (which is the down-sampling factor) and decisions such as whether to use maximum or average pooling.

Figure 2.5 (right) illustrates the max-pooling operation. Here $|\ell_-| = 16$ (left), $|\ell| = 4$, and the window of size 2×2 slides across the larger representation (ℓ_- at left) according to the horizontal and vertical stride parameter 2. Thus, $|\ell| = 4$ different

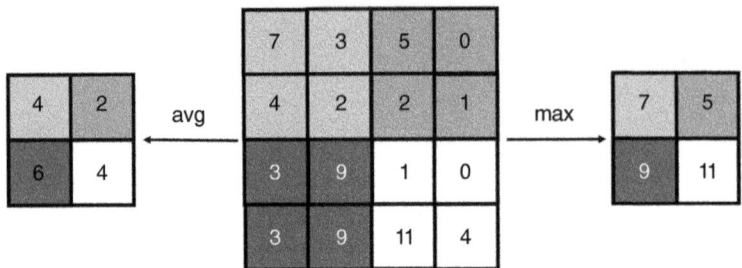

Figure 2.5 Example action of a max (right) or average (left) pooling layer with 2×2 filters and (horizontal and vertical) stride 2.

maximum readings are taken, forming the down-sampled layer ℓ. Down-sampling instead by average pooling (a linear operation) is also illustrated in the figure (left).

A pooling layer is often inserted following a convolutional layer. When there are $r > 1$ equal sized kernels associated with layer ℓ_-, pools may consist of local activations of one kernel or of activations with the same index across different kernels.

Nearest-Prototype Layer

Let us assume a penultimate layer with activations $\underline{z} \in \mathbb{R}^M$ for input sample $\underline{x} \in \mathbb{R}^N$. The idea here is to learn a prototype $\underline{b}_\kappa \in \mathbb{R}^M$ for each class $\kappa \in \mathcal{Y} = \{1, 2, \ldots, K\}$. The final-layer activations are, for example,

$$f_\kappa(\underline{z}) = \|\underline{z} - \underline{b}_\kappa\|^2$$

which is equivalent, in representation power, to a K-component Gaussian mixture model (GMM) with identity covariances for each component (see Chapter 3). For a final, *nearest-prototype* layer, for distance based activations as given above, the class decision corresponds to the *minimum* of the penultimate layer activations,

$$\hat{c} = \arg \min_{\kappa \in \mathcal{Y}} f_\kappa.$$

The final layer of the LeNet-5 architecture is a Euclidean nearest-prototype layer (see the explanation near Eq. (8) of [139]).

Softmax Output Layer

Again, suppose the DNN has a logit output (penultimate layer activation) f_κ for each class $\kappa \in \mathcal{Y}$. If $f_\kappa(\underline{x}) \geq 0$ for all DNN inputs $\underline{x}$, then one may define, for example,

$$\hat{p}(\kappa | \underline{x}) = f_\kappa(\underline{x}) \left/ \sum_{j=1}^{K} f_j(\underline{x}), \right. \tag{2.4}$$

else one may define, for example,

$$\hat{p}(\kappa | \underline{x}) = \exp(b f_\kappa(\underline{x})) \left/ \sum_{j=1}^{K} \exp(b f_j(\underline{x})), \right. \tag{2.5}$$

where the parameter $b > 0$. Note that $\hat{p}(\kappa|\underline{x})$ is a probability mass function on $\mathcal{Y}$ conditioned on $\underline{x}$. These probabilities approximate the true posterior (a posteriori) class probabilities and form the outputs of a *softmax* layer.

For each input $\underline{x}$, a *winner takes all* output layer gives the class decision:

$$\hat{c}(\underline{x}) = \arg\max_{\kappa} \hat{p}(\kappa|\underline{x}) = \arg\max_{\kappa} f_\kappa(\underline{x}).$$

Classification "confidence" can be defined as

$$\frac{\hat{p}(\hat{c}(\underline{x})|\underline{x}) - \max_{i \neq \hat{c}(\underline{x})} \hat{p}(i|\underline{x})}{\hat{p}(\hat{c}(\underline{x})|\underline{x})} \in [0, 1]. \tag{2.6}$$

The class decision for $\underline{x}$ may *not be accepted* unless it has some "margin" $\mu_\kappa > 0$, that is, unless

$$\frac{\hat{p}(\hat{c}(\underline{x})|\underline{x}) - \max_{i \neq \hat{c}(\underline{x})} \hat{p}(i|\underline{x})}{\hat{p}(\hat{c}(\underline{x})|\underline{x})} > \mu_{\hat{c}(\underline{x})}.$$

If this condition is not achieved, the decision for this sample may be chosen as "don't know," which is otherwise referred to as sample *rejection*. The parameters μ_κ can be set using a labeled validation set $\mathcal{H}$ held out from training. See, for example, [120].

Batch Normalization Layers

Batch normalization layers are used in ResNet architectures, see Figure 2.6. They may be needed because ReLU neurons have (positively) *unbounded* output signals. For example, the output activation v_n of the nth neuron of a batch normalization layer whose input is z is given by [16]

$$v_n = \frac{(z - \mu_n)}{\sigma_n}$$

with $\sigma_n > 0$. For each neuron n, using the current training data batch, see (2.11), estimates of the mean μ_n and variance σ_n^2 of its activation are dynamically updated by a simple first-order autoregressive mechanism with decay rate (forgetting factor) set as, for example, 0.9; see Section 2.7.6.

Self-Attention Layers

Different types of *attention* mechanisms essentially provide a gating function to all the signals in a given internal layer of the network based on the strength of their correlations with other signals in the layer. If correlations are measured between all signals in the layer, it is referred to as *global* attention. Alternatively, correlations may only be measured between "neighboring" signals in a layer, which is referred to as *local* attention. Global attention gives an alternative (and potentially more effective) way to capture long-term/range correlations than some other methods (such as by solely using gated recurrent networks) for applications that involve time series (including natural language processing tasks such as translation [114]). They can also be applied to image generation or image segmentation [205] and to object tracking in video. Local attention is most suitable, for example, when trying to capture local features (e.g., between words in the same sentence, or between pixels in the same region of an image). Attention mechanisms can also achieve a more sophisticated feature down-sampling/pooling, one which captures interactions among subsets of embedded features.

A *self-attention* layer [280] is designed to capture the connections between elements in a *sequence* of n vectors $\{\underline{x}_1, \ldots, \underline{x}_n\}$, where $\underline{x}_i \in \mathbb{R}^d$ may represent, for example, the feature-embedding of the ith input word. A self-attention layer is associated with three matrices, $\mathbf{W}_q, \mathbf{W}_\kappa, \mathbf{W}_v \in \mathbb{R}^{m \times d}$, where each element in these matrices is a learned parameter. First, for each vector $\underline{x}_i$ in the input sequence, one obtains:

$$\underline{q}_i = \mathbf{W}_q \underline{x}_i, \quad \underline{\kappa}_i = \mathbf{W}_\kappa \underline{x}_i, \quad \underline{v}_i = \mathbf{W}_v \underline{x}_i.$$

Then for each $\underline{x}_i$, the associated output of the self-attention layer is:

$$\underline{y}_i = \text{softmax}\left(V \left(\frac{\underline{q}_i' \underline{\kappa}_1}{\sqrt{d}}, \ldots, \frac{\underline{q}_i' \underline{\kappa}_n}{\sqrt{d}}\right)'\right) \in \mathbb{R}^m.$$

Here the matrix $V = [\underline{v}_1, \ldots, \underline{v}_n] \in \mathbb{R}^{m \times n}$ and the "softmax" operator on a vector exponentiates its elements and then normalizes them so that the elements form a pmf. In addition to an output sequence of vectors, a self-attention layer also outputs an *attention matrix* representing the connection (or "correlation") between element pairs, with the ith row being

$$\text{softmax}(\frac{\underline{q}_i' \underline{\kappa}_1}{\sqrt{d}}, \ldots, \frac{\underline{q}_i' \underline{\kappa}_n}{\sqrt{d}}).$$

Self-attention is usually implemented with multiple *heads*, that is, *multi-head attention*. For example, for a self-attention layer with h heads, there are h groups of matrices

$$(\mathbf{W}_q^{(1)}, \mathbf{W}_\kappa^{(1)}, \mathbf{W}_v^{(1)}), \ldots, (\mathbf{W}_q^{(h)}, \mathbf{W}_\kappa^{(h)}, \mathbf{W}_v^{(h)}).$$

These h heads are processed in parallel (as above for a single-head self-attention layer), with the outputs of all the heads concatenated for each input vector $\underline{x}_i$. Such multi-head attention can capture different types of connections between input vectors (which is the counterpart to multiple feature maps, each produced by a different kernel of a convolutional layer). Moreover, practical self-attention layers may be associated with *masking* to exclude the input of selected vector positions from being fed into the softmax.

2.5.3   Example Feed-forward DNN Architectures

Typically, the front-end of the DNN performs abstract feature extraction to produce a feature embedding (or feature map) of the input sample by, for example, using convolutional layers. The front-end may also involve downsampling using, for example, pooling layers. The back-end makes decisions based on combinations of embedded features using, for example, fully connected, pooling, or attention layers.

For a classifier, the penultimate layer of $K = |\mathcal{Y}|$ logits of the back-end feeds a softmax layer that allows for possible assessment of class decision confidence (recall (2.6) and see Section 2.9). Even if the class decision rule based on the embedded features is quite simple (e.g., linear), the induced decision boundary in the (raw) input feature space may be quite complicated, that is, the decision boundaries may be nonlinear and a single class may consist of unions of disconnected input regions (recall Figure 2.2).

In the ResNet-18 [97, 155] architectures depicted in Figure 2.6, activations in some layers are fed forward (via skip connections) and used to create a *residual* signal, see Section 5.5.3. Forming such residuals is commonly done in signal processing and control, for example, in linear prediction and various Wiener filtering realizations. Feed-forward branching also helps address the "vanishing gradient" problem, see Section 2.7.3.

Some example feature embeddings activated by a given image sample that is input to a trained, feed-forward Convolutional DNN (CNN) for the MNIST digit classification domain [141] are shown in Figure 2.7. Here, the different feature maps correspond to different kernels in the final convolutional layer.

2.5.4   Transformer Architectures

Transformers process temporally and/or spatially sequential data. Transformer layers may involve feature correlations by considering products of (i.e., nonlinear operations on) neural activation pairs. Unlike recurrent neural networks, transformers operate on an entire input sequence.

The idea of a vision transformer (ViT) was inspired by the success of self-attention based models in the field of natural language processing [58]. Initial ViTs divide an image into equal-sized patches. Then each image patch is treated as a vector, such that an input image can be represented by a sequence of input vectors, which can be directly processed by a self-attention layer. However, the length of the input sequence grows with the image size, which substantially increases the training time. As one example, self-attention is computed in a *local* window of, e.g., 4 × 4-pixel patches. However, *different* window selections are adopted in two consecutive layers to reduce redundancy and hence to enhance the information exchange between different image patches, in the signals propagated forward through the network [160].

2.6   Background on Gradient-Based Optimization

In this section, we first define directional derivatives and descent directions, define first- and second-order optimality conditions, and discuss gradient methods for achieving locally optimal solutions [208].

Suppose we have a continuously differentiable function $L : \mathbb{R}^n \rightarrow \mathbb{R}$ for (integer) $n \geq 1$. The objective is to find a local minimum $\hat{x} \in \mathbb{R}^n$ of L. The gradient of L is

$$\nabla L(\underline{x}) = \begin{bmatrix} \frac{\partial L}{\partial x_1}(\underline{x}) \\ \frac{\partial L}{\partial x_2}(\underline{x}) \\ \vdots \\ \frac{\partial L}{\partial x_n}(\underline{x}) \end{bmatrix}.$$

Note that $\nabla L : \mathbb{R}^n \rightarrow \mathbb{R}^n$.

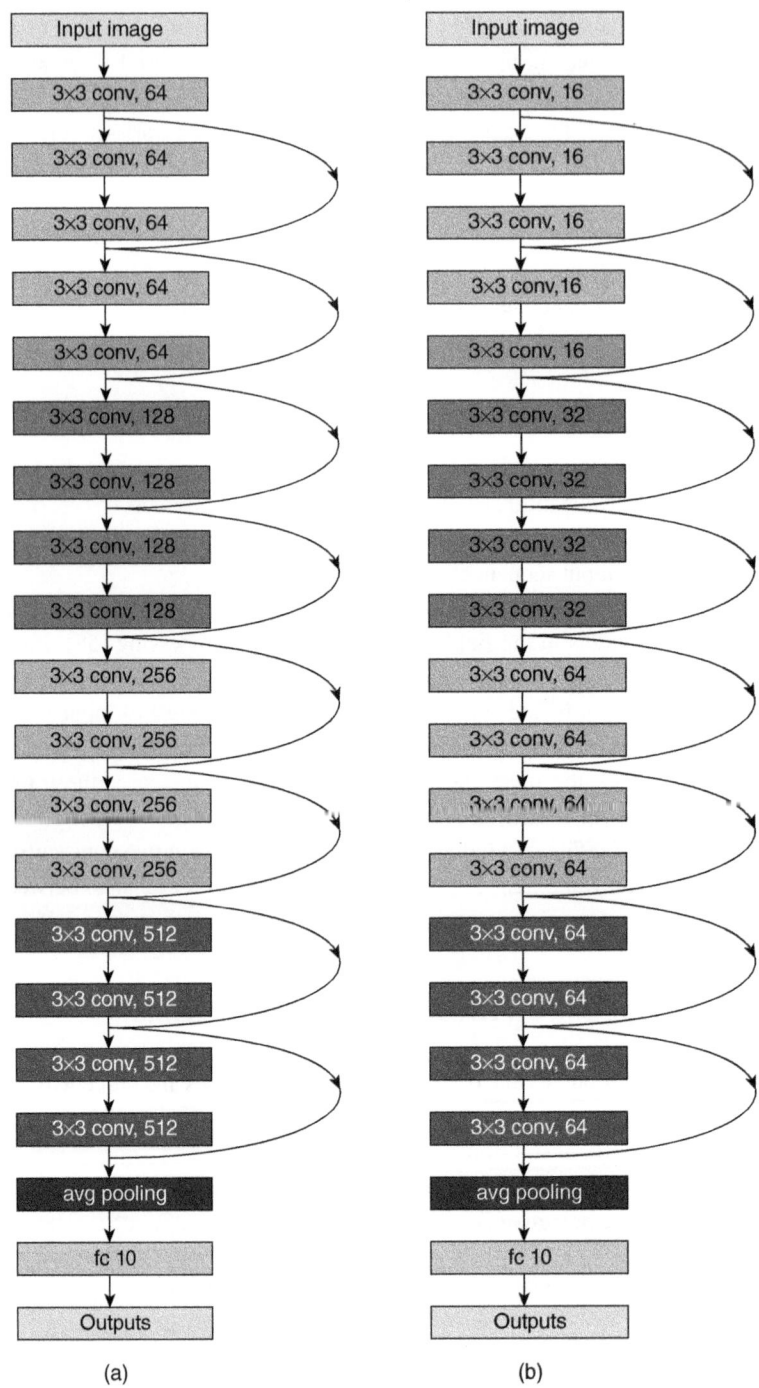

(a)   (b)

Figure 2.6 The wide (a) and compact (b) ResNet-18 architectures designed to classify CIFAR-10 images [129]. The points where branches meet are summers, that is, producing a "residual" signal. The final fully connected layer has ten outputs, as there are ten different image classes, for example, a class posterior probability for each class, given the input image. See [97, 210]. Reprinted from [304] with permission.

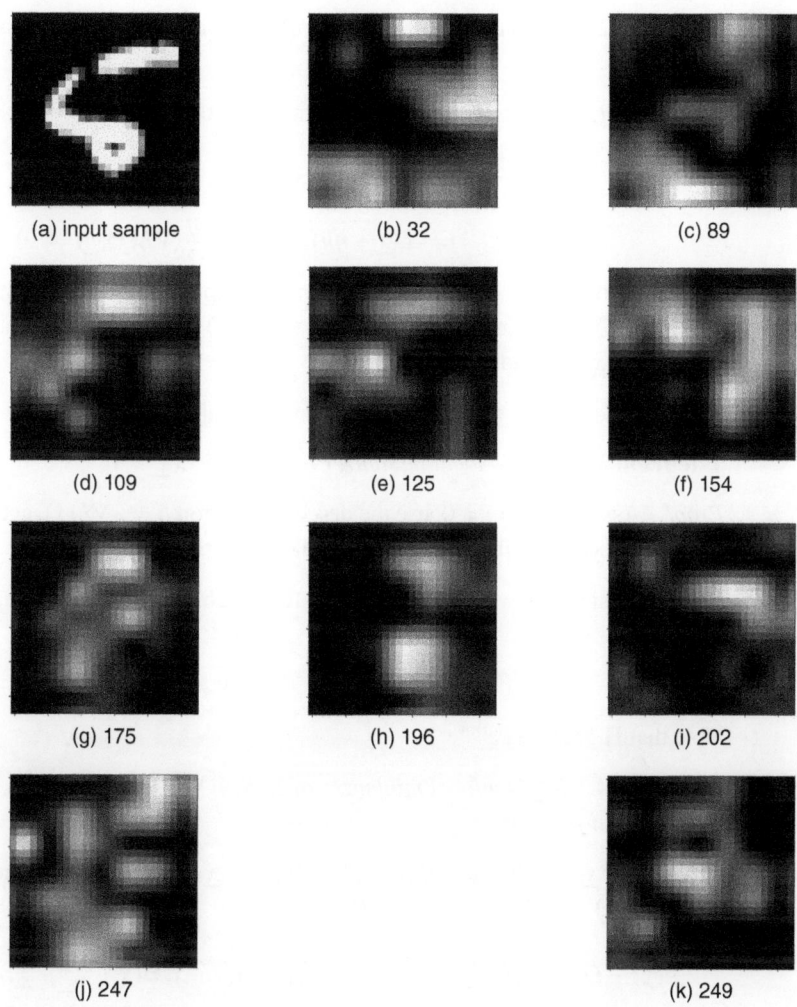

(a) input sample | (b) 32 | (c) 89

(d) 109 | (e) 125 | (f) 154

(g) 175 | (h) 196 | (i) 202

(j) 247 | (k) 249

Figure 2.7 A select subset of feature maps for an input image representing the digit '5'. The CNN was trained to classify 28×28-pixel greyscale images of hand-written digits taken from the MNIST dataset [141]. The feature maps are produced by a (final) convolutional layer with $256 \ 3 \times 3$ kernels. The number for each figure is the feature map index in $\{1, \ldots, 256\}$. For visualization, each feature map is rescaled to the size of the input image.

The derivative of L at $\underline{x}$ in the direction $\underline{h}$ (a vector with unit length) is the inner product

$$\langle \nabla L(\underline{x}), \underline{h} \rangle = \lim_{\eta \downarrow 0} \frac{L(\underline{x} + \eta \underline{h}) - L(\underline{x})}{\eta}, \tag{2.7}$$

where $\eta \in \mathbb{R}$ and $\underline{x}, \underline{h} \in \mathbb{R}^n$. Note that $\partial L / \partial x_k$ is the derivative of L in the direction of the unit vector $\mathbf{e}_k$.

$\underline{h}$ is a descent direction at $\underline{x}$ if $\langle \nabla L(\underline{x}), \underline{h} \rangle < 0$. Obviously, $-\nabla L(\underline{x})$ is a descent direction at $\underline{x}$ unless $\nabla L(\underline{x}) = \underline{0}$.

Theorem 2 *If $\underline{h}$ is a descent direction of L, then there is an $\eta > 0$ such that $L(\underline{x} + \eta \underline{h}) < L(\underline{x})$.*

Proof By (2.7), there is a sufficiently small $\eta > 0$ such that

$$\frac{L(\underline{x} + \eta \underline{h}) - L(\underline{x})}{\eta} - \langle \nabla L(\underline{x}), \underline{h} \rangle \le -\frac{1}{2} \langle \nabla L(\underline{x}), \underline{h} \rangle$$

$$\Rightarrow L(\underline{x} + \eta \underline{h}) - L(\underline{x}) \le \frac{\eta}{2} \langle \nabla L(\underline{x}), \underline{h} \rangle < 0. \qquad \square$$

The following gives necessary conditions for optimality. We say that $\hat{\underline{x}}$ is a local minimum of L if there is an $r > 0$ such that $L(\hat{\underline{x}}) \le L(\underline{x})$ for all $\underline{x}$ in an open l_2 ball centered at $\hat{\underline{x}}$ with radius r, that is,

$$\forall \underline{x} \in B_2(\hat{\underline{x}}, r) := \{ \underline{y} \in \mathbb{R}^n \ : \ \|\underline{y} - \hat{\underline{x}}\|_2 < r \}.$$

Theorem 3 *If $\hat{\underline{x}}$ is a local minimizer of L then $\nabla L(\hat{\underline{x}}) = \underline{0}$.*

Proof Assume $\nabla L(\hat{\underline{x}}) \ne \underline{0}$, use the descent direction $\underline{h} = -\nabla L(\hat{\underline{x}})$, and argue as in the previous theorem (with $\eta < r$) to contradict local minimality of $\hat{\underline{x}}$. $\square$

The Hessian of (twice continuously differentiable) L is the $n \times n$ matrix

$$\mathbf{H} = \frac{\partial^2 L}{\partial \underline{x}^2} = \left[\frac{\partial^2 L}{\partial x_i \partial x_j} \right]_{i,j=1}^n.$$

Note that $\mathbf{H} : \mathbb{R}^n \to \mathbb{R}^{n \times n}$.

Theorem 4 *If $\hat{\underline{x}}$ is a local minimizer of L, then $\forall \underline{h}$, $\langle \underline{h}, \mathbf{H}(\hat{\underline{x}}) \underline{h} \rangle \ge 0$, that is, $\mathbf{H}(\hat{\underline{x}})$ is positive semi-definite.*

Proof For $\underline{x}, \underline{y} \in \mathbb{R}^n$ and $s \in [0, 1]$, let $g(s) = L(\underline{x} + s(\underline{y} - \underline{x}))$. Integrating the identity $(g'(s)(1 - s) + g(s))' = g''(s)(1 - s)$ gives

$$L(\underline{y}) - L(\underline{x}) = \langle \nabla L(\underline{x}), \underline{y} - \underline{x} \rangle + \int_0^1 (1 - s) \langle \underline{y} - \underline{x}, \mathbf{H}(\underline{x} + s(\underline{y} - \underline{x}))(\underline{y} - \underline{x}) \rangle ds.$$

Substitute $\underline{y} = \hat{\underline{x}} + \eta \underline{h}$, $\underline{x} = \hat{\underline{x}}$, and $\nabla L(\hat{\underline{x}}) = \underline{0}$. Finally, let positive $\eta \to 0$. $\square$

The following gives sufficient conditions for optimality.

Theorem 5 *If $\nabla L(\hat{\underline{x}}) = \underline{0}$ and $\langle \underline{h}, \mathbf{H}(\hat{\underline{x}}) \underline{h} \rangle > 0$ for all $\underline{h}$, then $\hat{\underline{x}}$ is a local minimizer.*

Proof To prove this, assume $\hat{\underline{x}}$ is not a local miminizer. Then there is a sequence $\underline{x}_i \to \hat{\underline{x}}$ such that $L(\underline{x}_i) < L(\hat{\underline{x}})$ for all $i \in \{1, 2, 3, \ldots\}$. Then argue as in the previous theorems to show a contradiction follows from this assumption. $\square$

For $n = 1$, recall that if $L'(\hat{x}) = 0$ and $L''(\hat{x}) > 0$ then $\hat{x}$ is a local minimum of L.

Figure 2.8 shows local minima, local maxima and (when dimension $n > 1$) saddle points, where

- at a local minimum, $\nabla L = \underline{0}$ and $\mathbf{H}$ is positive definite,
- at a local maximum, $\nabla L = \underline{0}$ and $\mathbf{H}$ is negative definite, and
- at a saddle, $\nabla L = \underline{0}$ and $\mathbf{H}$ is indefinite (dimension $n > 1$).

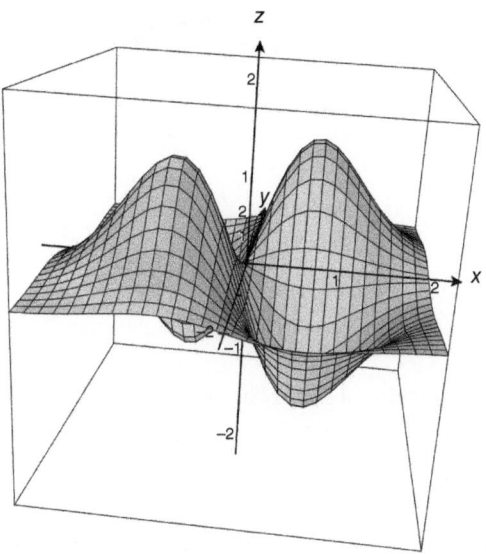

Figure 2.8 The example $L(\underline{x}) = 7x_1 x_2 \exp(-x_1^2 - x_2^2)$ has two local minima, two local maxima, and one saddle point at the origin. Plotted using [27].

2.6.1   Gradient Methods for Local Optimization

To find a local minimizer of L, one could try to solve $\nabla L(\underline{x}) = \underline{0}$ by the Newton–Raphson algorithm (which exploits both the gradient and the Hessian) and then assess whether the solution is a local minimum, maximum or saddle by considering the Hessian **H** of L there. If it is not a local minimum or if Newton–Raphson does not converge, one could restart Newton–Raphson at another initial point (perhaps chosen at random).

An advantage of gradient-based methods is that they do not require higher order derivatives (**H**), or estimates of them (BFGS or DFP quasi-Newton methods [8, 199]). Disadvantages of gradient-based methods are that they tend to converge slowly compared to Newton–Raphson and may converge to saddle points.

The steepest descent algorithm is a gradient-based method that works as follows:

1. choose the initial values $\underline{x}^{(0)} \in \mathbb{R}^n$, iteration index $k = 0$, small $\varepsilon > 0$
2. if $\|\nabla L(\underline{x}^{(k)})\| < \varepsilon$ then stop
3. search (descent) direction $\underline{h}^{(k)} = -\nabla L(\underline{x}^{(k)})$
4. line search to find step size

$$\eta_*^{(k)} = \arg\min_{\eta > 0} L(\underline{x}^{(k)} + \eta \underline{h}^{(k)})$$

5. update $\underline{x}^{(k+1)} = \underline{x}^{(k)} + \eta_*^{(k)} \underline{h}^{(k)}$
6. k++ and go to step 2.

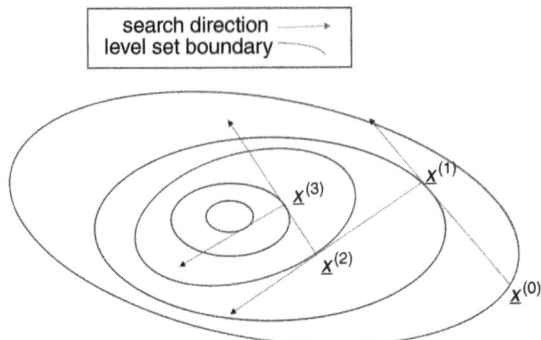

Figure 2.9 Illustration of steepest descent and the level sets of optimization objective L.

Note that determining $\eta_*^{(k)}$ is a one-dimensional optimization problem. Each update results in a point that is tangent to a level-set of L; see Figure 2.9.

One can show by contradiction that any accumulation point $\hat{\underline{x}}$ (limit of a convergent subsequence) of the sequence $\underline{x}^{(k)}$ must satisfy $\nabla L(\hat{\underline{x}}) = \underline{0}$. Thus, if the Hessian $H(\hat{\underline{x}})$ is positive definite (so $\hat{\underline{x}}$ is not a saddle), then $\hat{\underline{x}}$ is a local minimum. An additional Wolfe condition on curvature of L guarantees convergence of gradient descent to a local minimum: $\exists c > 0$ such that $\forall k$,

$$|\langle \underline{h}^{(k)}, \nabla L(\underline{x}^{(k)} + \eta_*^{(k)} \underline{h}^{(k)}) \rangle| \leq c |\langle \underline{h}^{(k)}, \nabla L(\underline{x}^{(k)}) \rangle|.$$

2.6.2   Optimization/Training Heuristics for DNNs

Approaches that leverage second-order derivatives (Newton–Raphson) or their approximations are too computationally complex for deep learning because the Hessian grows quadratically with the number of parameters to optimize (which may be in the millions or billions). There are simpler approaches to line search (e.g., by discretizing the search space as in Armijo), which may still be too complex for the DNN setting. In the following, we describe some heuristics that are used for deep learning; see [224].

2.7   Heuristic Optimization Methods for Deep Learning

In this section, we will discuss types of training/learning objectives, stochastic gradient descent (SGD) with momentum, background on first-order autoregressive (AR-1) estimators, overfitting and regularization, training dataset augmentation, and a held-out validation set to determine hyperparameters.

2.7.1   Training Objectives

The objective of learning is to choose classifier parameters θ, that is, to *train* the DNN, to **minimize** the following "loss" expressions over the DNN parameters on which final-layer activations (logits) $f_\kappa(\underline{x})$, inferred class decisions $\hat{c} = \arg\max_{\kappa \in \mathcal{Y}} f_\kappa(\underline{x})$, and inferred class posteriors $\hat{p}(\kappa|\underline{x})$ implicitly depend.

First note that the training set misclassification rate objective,

$$L(\theta) = \frac{1}{|\mathcal{X}|} \sum_{\underline{x} \in \mathcal{X}} \mathbf{1}\{\hat{c}(\underline{x}) \neq c(\underline{x})\},$$

has zero gradient almost everywhere, and so does not lend itself to training by gradient-based methods.

A cross-entropy loss objective can be expressed as:

$$L(\theta) = -\frac{1}{|\mathcal{X}|} \sum_{\underline{x} \in \mathcal{X}} \log \hat{p}(c(\underline{x})|\underline{x}), \tag{2.8}$$

based on the DNN's estimated class posteriors obtained as, for example,

$$\hat{p}(\kappa|\underline{x}) = \frac{f_\kappa(\underline{x})}{\sum_{j \in \mathcal{Y}} f_j(\underline{x})}$$

where the class-wise activations (the logits) $f_j \geq 0$ are differentiable with respect to the DNN parameters θ. Cross-entropy loss is commonly used for designing classifiers and is commonly optimized using gradient-based methods. To simplify the derivatives of L, the estimated class posterior $\hat{p}(k|\underline{x})$ may be replaced by the logit $f_k(\underline{x})$.

When the training dataset has high class imbalance (more training examples from some classes than others), one can instead use a weighted cross-entropy loss, for example,

$$L(\theta) = -\sum_{\kappa \in \mathcal{Y}} \frac{1}{|\mathcal{X}_\kappa|} \sum_{\underline{x} \in \mathcal{X}_\kappa} \log \hat{p}(\kappa|\underline{x}), \tag{2.9}$$

where $\mathcal{X}_\kappa$ is the set of class-κ training samples.

A mean-square error (MSE) loss objective is commonly used for purposes of time series prediction or regression (see Section 3.5 and Chapter 12). Here, the DNN $\hat{c} : \mathbb{R}^N \to \mathbb{R}^M$ is not treated as a classifier and the MSE loss objective is

$$L(\theta) = \frac{1}{|\mathcal{X}|} \sum_{\underline{x} \in \mathcal{X}} \|\hat{c}(\underline{x}) - c(\underline{x})\|^2, \tag{2.10}$$

where $\hat{c}(\underline{x}), c(\underline{x}) \in \mathbb{R}^M$, $c(\underline{x})$ is the correct output for training sample $\underline{x}$, and the DNN mapping $\hat{c}$ is differentiable with respect to the parameters θ. Issues of balance are also important in regression in that the generalization performance of $\hat{c}$ will depend on the distribution of the training set X in $\mathbb{R}^N$. The regressor roughly will tend to be more accurate in regions of high training set density, that is, interpolation error tends to be smaller than extrapolation error.

While not common for this purpose, MSE is also sometimes used as the training objective for a classifier. It has been shown in [63] that designing a classifier to minimizing MSE to the target distribution $(0, 0, \ldots, 1, 0, \ldots, 0)$ (with a '1' in the position of the true class) minimizes the MSE to the Bayes optimal discriminant function. In this sense, there is some theoretical justification for use of MSE as a classifier training objective.

Also, sometimes (e.g., in the context of anomaly detection) the training set consists of just one class, that is, $K = |\mathcal{Y}| = 1$. Here one can use different one-class training loss objectives, for example, see Section A.4.6.

Promoting Sparsity in DNN Parameters

Initially, a DNN may have excess parameters for the particular training task under consideration. Using excess parameters may result in overfitting to the training set (and also may require more computation and memory during both the classifier's training and its operation than are necessary for the given task). Note that the number of non-zero elements of θ can be expressed as

$$\sum_i \mathbf{1}\{\theta_i \neq 0\} = \lim_{q \downarrow 0} \sum_i |\theta_i|^q.$$

So, one way to promote sparsity among excess parameters (i.e., zeroing them out) is to suitably penalize the optimization objective with an approximate 0-norm (as in LASSO) penalty term,

$$L(\theta) + \lambda \sum_i |\theta_i|^q, \quad \text{where } 0 < q \ll 1.$$

Here, reducing $q > 0$ and increasing the penalty parameter $\lambda > 0$ promotes more sparsity in the DNN parameters θ. The number of non-zero elements itself is not very useful as it is not differentiable, and so would not lend itself to training by gradient-based methods.

DNN "regularization" [110] aims to improve generalization performance by preventing overfitting, including through the promotion of parameter sparsity, see Section 2.8.

2.7.2   Back Propagation

Back propagation is just the chain rule for differentiation applied to compute the gradient of composed functions. Given a function of two real variables $g(\underline{z}) = g(z_1, z_2)$, define the functions

$$\partial_1 g = \frac{\partial g}{\partial z_1} \quad \text{and} \quad \partial_2 g = \frac{\partial g}{\partial z_2}.$$

So, $\partial_k g$ is just the partial derivative of g with respect to its kth argument, as defined from left to right. Now consider the following composed function of four variables

$$L(\theta_1, \theta_2, \theta_3, x) = L(\underline{\theta}, x) = g_3(\theta_3, g_2(\theta_2, g_1(\theta_1, x))).$$

Here, L represents a loss function for a single, scalar input x of a simple, feed-forward neural network consisting of just three consecutive neurons (one per layer) having differentiable activations g. Also, θ_k is the parameter associated with layer k, g_k is the output of layer k, the DNN output layer is layer 3, and layers 1, 2 are *further back* (towards the input x).

If there is a single parameter per layer, then simply by the chain rule, the gradient of L with respect to the θ variables (in reverse order) is

$$\nabla L(\underline{\theta}, x) := \begin{bmatrix} \frac{\partial L}{\partial \theta_3}(\underline{\theta}, x) \\ \frac{\partial L}{\partial \theta_2}(\underline{\theta}, x) \\ \frac{\partial L}{\partial \theta_1}(\underline{\theta}, x) \end{bmatrix}$$

$$= \begin{bmatrix} (\partial_1 g_3)(\theta_3, g_2(\theta_2, g_1(\theta_1, x))) \\ (\partial_2 g_3)(\theta_3, g_2(\theta_2, g_1(\theta_1, x))) \cdot (\partial_1 g_2)(\theta_2, g_1(\theta_1, x)) \\ (\partial_2 g_3)(\theta_3, g_2(\theta_2, g_1(\theta_1, x))) \cdot (\partial_2 g_2)(\theta_2, g_1(\theta_1, x)) \cdot (\partial_1 g_1)(\theta_1, x) \end{bmatrix}.$$

Note that to compute $\partial L / \partial \theta_k$ for $k = 1, 2$, one needs to compute $\partial_2 g_3$, that is, the partial derivative of g_3 with respect to its second argument evaluated at $(\theta_3, g_2(\theta_2, g_1(\theta_1, x)))$. So, this quantity needs to be propagated **backward** from layer 3 to compute $\partial L / \partial \theta_k$ for $k = 1, 2$. Also note that the quantity $g_2(\theta_2, g_1(\theta_1, x))$ is propagated **forward** from the input.

In a similar way, for a more complex feed-forward neural network, to compute the partial derivative of a loss function with respect to parameters in layer ℓ of a DNN, the partial derivatives with respect to parameters from layers closer to the output need to be **propagated back** to layer ℓ. Moreover, for recurrent neural networks, one can employ back propagation *through time* [295] to account for memory state.

2.7.3 Vanishing Gradient Problem

In some neural network designs, the gradients computed using back propagation may become very small in magnitude as the number of layers increases. ResNet's use of "forward branching" mitigates this vanishing gradient effect. Recurrent neural networks which use inter-sample neural memory [101], as in simple gated units, also may avoid vanishing gradient problems.

2.7.4 Constant Learning Rate

Rather than attempting to compute an optimal step size per iteration of gradient descent, one can simply take a constant step size, $\eta > 0$, so that gradient descent proceeds as:

$$\theta^{(k+1)} = \theta^{(k)} + \eta \underline{h}^{(k)}.$$

Here, $\eta > 0$ is also called the *learning rate*, for example, $\eta = 0.1$. That said, η may be changed dynamically, for example, η may be made smaller as the iteration index k increases for greater "depth" of search (as well as to ensure that the parameter updates continue to be descent steps). For example, η may be reduced by a factor of 10 every 10 iterations.

2.7.5 Stochastic Gradient Descent (SGD)

Suppose an additive loss objective to be minimized

$$L(\theta) = \frac{1}{T} \sum_{\underline{x} \in \mathcal{X}} g(\underline{x}; \theta).$$

When $T = |X|$ is large, computing $\nabla L(\theta)$ over the entire training dataset X can be very costly. Alternatively, one can compute the average gradient over a small batch $B_k \subset X$ ($|B_k| \ll T$) at iteration k:

$$-\frac{1}{|B_k|} \sum_{\underline{x} \in B_k} \nabla g(\underline{x}; \theta). \tag{2.11}$$

Note that (2.11) might not be a descent direction for L. A training epoch may consist of a sequence of iterations using such search directions corresponding to a group of equal sized batches B_k whose union is X.

2.7.6   Background on First-Order Autoregressive Estimators

Suppose one wishes to iteratively estimate the mean of a sequence of random vectors $\underline{X}_n$, for $n \in \{0, 1, 2, \ldots\}$, which could either be non-stationary or with an unknown (stationary) limiting distribution. Since the distribution of the random vector $\underline{X}_n$ may change with n, one may wish to more significantly weight the recent samples $\underline{X}_k$ (i.e., $k \leq n$ and $k \approx n$) in computing the estimated mean $\underline{\hat{X}}_n$.

An autoregressive estimator of order 1 (AR-1) is

$$\underline{\hat{X}}_n = \alpha \underline{\hat{X}}_{n-1} + (1 - \alpha)\underline{X}_n$$

where $0 < \alpha < 1$ is the forgetting/fading factor and $\underline{\hat{X}}_0 = \underline{X}_0$. Note that all past values contribute to the current value of this AR-1 process, with weights that exponentially diminish over time:

$$\underline{\hat{X}}_n = \alpha^n \underline{X}_0 + (1 - \alpha)(\alpha^{n-1}\underline{X}_1 + \alpha^{n-2}\underline{X}_2 + \ldots + \alpha\underline{X}_{n-1} + \underline{X}_n).$$

Note that smaller α means $\underline{\hat{X}}_n$ is more responsive to the recent samples $\underline{X}_k$ ($k < n, k \approx n$), that is, lower tracking error, but may exhibit larger oscillations in the AR-1 process $\underline{\hat{X}}$, that is, higher steady-state error.

See Figure 2.10 for the scalar case. Suppose the initial marginal distribution of X_n is uniform on the interval $[0, 1]$ (i.e., $EX = 0.5$), but for $n \geq 20$ the distribution is uniform on the interval $[3, 4]$ (i.e., EX changes to 3.5). When $\alpha = 0.25$, a sample path of the first-order AR-1 process $\hat{X}$ responds much more quickly to the change in mean (at $n = 20$), but is more oscillatory, than when $\alpha = 0.75$.

2.7.7   Momentum

Momentum [224, 259] incorporates information into the search direction $\underline{\tilde{h}}^{(k)}$ from **prior** computed gradients $\underline{h}^{(j)}$ for $j < k$. For example, using simple first-order auto-regression with forgetting/fading factor $\alpha \in (0, 1)$, one can take the search direction

$$\underline{\tilde{h}}^{(k)} = \alpha\underline{\tilde{h}}^{(k-1)} + (1 - \alpha)\underline{h}^{(k)},$$

that is, $\theta^{(k)} = \theta^{(k-1)} + \eta\underline{\tilde{h}}^{(k-1)}$. Alternatively, one can update the parameters as:

$$\theta^{(k)} = \theta^{(k-1)} + \underline{\tilde{h}}^{(k-1)} \quad \text{with} \quad \underline{\tilde{h}}^{(k)} = \alpha\underline{\tilde{h}}^{(k-1)} + \eta\underline{h}^{(k)}.$$

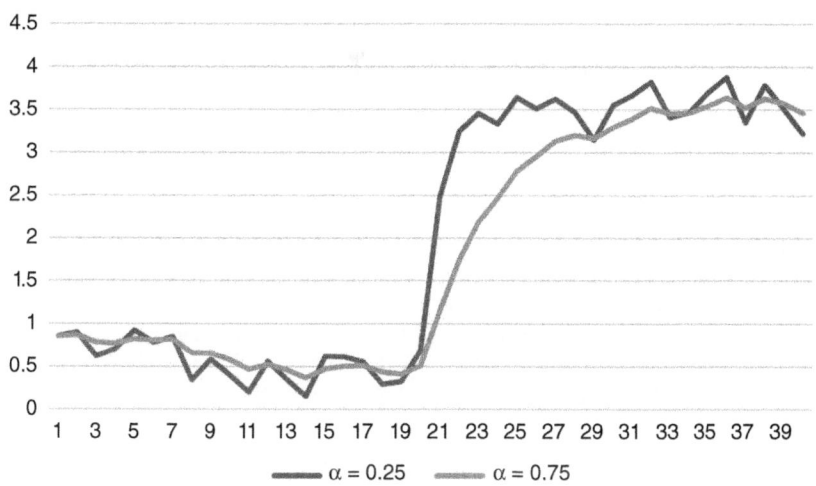

Figure 2.10 Two sample paths of an AR-1 estimator, $\hat{X}_n$ versus n, with a change in distribution at time $n = 20$, for two different parameters α.

Using SGD and momentum may avoid being trapped in shallow local minima of L and also may avoid zigzagging through "ravines" associated with them as may be indicated by a persistently negative sign for $\langle h^{(k-1)}, h^{(k)} \rangle$. Typically, α is chosen in $[0.1, 0.9]$. The commonly used "Adam" optimizer [123] and root mean square (RMS) techniques normalize an autoregressive estimate of the gradient by an autoregressive estimate of its (uncentered) second moment.

2.7.8 Dropout

Under "dropout" [248], only a randomly selected subset of DNN parameters are updated at each iteration of gradient-based deep learning. So at each iteration of gradient-based deep learning using dropout in combination with SGD, only a subset of training samples are used to update only a subset of the network parameters θ. Presuming that the network is over-parameterized, this has the "regularizing" effect of "spreading" the learning throughout the network so that overfitting is potentially avoided. The dropout action may be applied only to designated dropout *layers*.

2.8 Overfitting and DNN Regularization

Aristotle wrote in *Posterior Analytics*, "We may assume the superiority, other things being equal, of the demonstration which derives from fewer postulates or hypotheses." Also called *Occam's Razor*, this principle suggests that good generalization performance is achieved if a minimum number of parameters are used to explain the training data, in other words to avoid overfitting to the training set $\mathcal{X}$. Note that, a priori, one has no idea how many parameters are most suitable for very large and complex training datasets (with high feature dimensions).

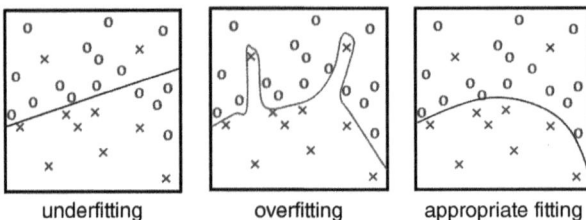

underfitting   overfitting   appropriate fitting

Figure 2.11 "Appropriate" fitting optimizes the so-called *bias-variance tradeoff* to give better generalization performance on the test set by not overfitting to the two "×" class outliers. Here these two class outliers do not justify the complex class boundary required to correctly classify them – this boundary will likely misclassify many "o" test samples. An evaluation set $\mathcal{H}$ held out from training could be used to navigate between underfitting and overfitting.

A DNN may be over-parameterized or under-parameterized. Low accuracy on the training set may indicate too few parameters (insufficient DNN capacity to learn, leading to, e.g., model bias). On the other hand, low accuracy on the held-out validation set (poor generalization performance) with high accuracy on the training set may indicate too many parameters (overfitting to the training set); see Figure 2.11. This so-called *bias-variance tradeoff* can be addressed by, for example, model order control using criteria such as BIC/MDL [238] (which will be seen in the context of mixture models in Chapter 3), or by the following heuristic means in the context of deep learning.

Assuming the DNN is over-parameterized, one can heuristically reduce the number of parameters, for example, by removing those which are close to zero during or following training, while checking performance on a validation set. Recall the discussion on promoting neuron/edge sparsity in Section 2.7.1.

Alternatively, one can simply apply dropout, possibly in combination with early stopping of training, see Section 2.8.3.

2.8.1   Training Dataset Augmentation

Let us now consider the training dataset of an image classifier, including images that belong to, for example, the *cat* class. To improve generalization performance on the test/production set, the training set can be augmented with a version of each cat image that is rotated, cropped, tint/color adjusted, contrast adjusted, has noise added, etc. But in some cases, augmenting with samples that are close to training samples (e.g., augmenting with "adversarial" samples in an attempt to be robust to test-time evasion attacks), may overly bias learning to the training samples and degrade generalization performance, see Sections 2.9 and 4.2.5. Such data augmentation may also bias the classifier and degrade its accuracy if the augmented samples are not truly representative of the classes to which they are labeled.

These considerations motivate use of early stopping in the deep learning process to avoid overfitting to a training dataset (which possibly contains some noisy and/or class-atypical examples).

For some applications of deep learning, new training samples can be automatically generated (but at some computational cost), particularly in regions where *improved* accuracy is required. In other applications, new training samples may require substantial human expertise (with concomitant financial expense and/or time demands) to label them. DNN *re*-training or fine-tuning can be performed based on these new samples, starting from the parameters learned from prior training (see Chapter 12).

2.8.2 Distributed Deep Learning

In *distributed* deep learning (DDL), for very large and high-dimensional training datasets and commensurately large DNNs, multiple graphics processing units (GPUs) may be used. In classical "data-parallel" configurations, the training dataset is partitioned into $J > 1$ equal sized subsets, with each subset assigned to a different GPU. Data-parallel configurations exploit how the deep learning objective is additive over the training dataset.

Operating synchronously, the J GPUs maintain a *common* DNN model, and based on it and on their subset of the training dataset, back propagation is used by each GPU to compute a set of gradients. In one configuration, layer-by-layer during back propagation, the GPUs communicate these gradients among themselves. The gradients are then aggregated and then used to update the DNN model parameters by each GPU.

Let us consider a loss function involving three single-parameter layers and two training samples $\mathcal{X} = \{x_1, x_2\}$,

$$L(\underline{\theta}, \mathcal{X}) = \sum_{i=1}^{2} g_3(\theta_3, g_2(\theta_2, g_1(\theta_1, x_i))),$$

with two GPUs used for training (the following is easily extended to encompass an arbitrary number of GPUs). Recalling Section 2.7.2, for all i, GPU i (using x_i) computes

$$(\partial_1 g_3)(\theta_3, g_2(\theta_2, g_1(\theta_1, x_i)))$$

and then shares this with the others, that is, with GPU $3 - i$. Then each GPU j sums the terms of the previous display for all $i \in \{1, 2\}$, while computing the next layer's derivative,

$$(\partial_2 g_3)(\theta_3, g_2(\theta_2, g_1(\theta_1, x_j))) \cdot (\partial_1 g_2)(\theta_2, g_1(\theta_1, x_j)).$$

This process repeats down the layers toward the input until a complete and common set of gradients is computed by all GPUs. Then all GPUs update the DNN's parameters $\underline{\theta}$. One such iteration of DDL, over which the commonly held DNN model parameters are adjusted, is called an epoch.

In an alternative configuration, a single (reducer) processor receives component gradients from the J GPUs and sends back the aggregated gradients (and optionally computes and sends back the updated θ parameters as well) layer by layer.

2.8.3   Held-out Set for Hyperparameter Setting

The validation set $\mathcal{H}$ is sampled uniformly at random (and removed) from the training set so that it is unbiased. $\mathcal{H}$ is not the production/test set $\mathcal{I}$. While only the remaining training set X is used to learn the classifier parameters θ, $\mathcal{H}$ can be used to:

- determine hyperparameters, for example, initial weights, learning rate, forgetting factors, and aspects of the neural network architecture and size;
- set parameters for representing and preprocessing data (before training); or
- early-stop training, when the accuracy on $\mathcal{H}$ starts to degrade (to prevent overfitting).

Also, in settings where the amount of data is limited, rather than using a fixed held-out validation set, a *cross validation* strategy may be taken. Under cross validation, the labeled dataset is partitioned into $J > 1$ equal-sized "folds." It is important that all classes be proportionally represented in each fold for classification problems. Training takes place J times, where, for the jth training, the jth fold plays the role of the (held-out) validation set, with the remaining folds used to learn the model parameters θ. Cross validation can be used to set hyperparameters, typically choosing the value for a hyperparameter that minimizes the average held-out fold error rate. It can also be used to estimate the held-out (test set) error rate, when there is insufficient data to create a held-out test set. The use of cross validation, rather than a single validation set, in a deep learning context will require a substantially larger amount of computation.

2.9   "Certified" Training and Classification Confidence

Robust training is surveyed in [290] and discussed in Section 4.2. One family of approaches to robust deep learning concerns the Lipschitz (uniform) continuity parameter of the DNN. Estimation and engineering of the Lipschitz parameter for a DNN is discussed in, for example, [15, 46, 67, 84, 260, 272, 294]. How to engineer class purity (class decision consistency) in an open ball of a certain radius about every training sample is addressed in, for example, [127, 272]. Maximum classification margin training is also discussed in some of these references, see Section 4.2.3.

2.9.1   Lipschitz Confidence

In the following, a local class purity result is derived *given* a Lipschitz continuity parameter for the DNN. Let us consider rectified (non-negative) logits $f : \mathbb{R}^N \rightarrow (\mathbb{R}^+)^K$ that are input to the softmax layer of the DNN; recall Section 2.5.2. Another definition of the classification **margin** for an individual input sample $\underline{x}$ is

$$\mu_f(\underline{x}) := f_{\hat{c}(\underline{x})}(\underline{x}) - \max_{i \neq \hat{c}(\underline{x})} f_i(\underline{x}) \geq 0. \tag{2.12}$$

Suppose there is an l_∞ / l_2 Lipschitz continuity parameter for f defined as

$$\Lambda_{\infty,2} = \sup_{\underline{x} \neq \underline{y}} \frac{\|f(\underline{x}) - f(\underline{y})\|_\infty}{\|\underline{x} - \underline{y}\|_2}, \tag{2.13}$$

which is somehow estimated. Now consider samples in an open l_2 ball centered at $\underline{x}$ with radius $\varepsilon > 0$, $B_2(\underline{x}, \varepsilon)$. The following locally consistent (robust) classification result is an example of *Lipschitz margin* [120]; also see Proposition 4.1 of [272] and Section 4.3 of [260].

Theorem 6 *If f is l_∞/l_2 Lipschitz continuous with parameter $\Lambda_{\infty,2} > 0$ and $\mu_f(\underline{x}) > 0$ then*

$$B_2\left(\underline{x}, \frac{\mu_f(\underline{x})}{2\Lambda_{\infty,2}}\right)$$

is class pure.

Proof For any $\underline{y} \in B_2(\underline{x}, \frac{1}{2}\mu_f(\underline{x})/\Lambda_{\infty,2})$, we have

$$\frac{1}{2}\mu_f(\underline{x}) > \Lambda_{\infty,2}\|\underline{x} - \underline{y}\|_2$$
$$\geq \|f(\underline{x}) - f(\underline{y})\|_\infty$$
$$:= \max_i |f_i(\underline{x}) - f_i(\underline{y})|$$
$$\geq \max_i |f_i(\underline{x})| - |f_i(\underline{y})| \quad \text{(triangle inequality)}$$
$$= \max_i f_i(\underline{x}) - f_i(\underline{y}) \quad \text{(since } f_i \geq 0\text{)}$$
$$\geq f_{\hat{c}(\underline{x})}(\underline{x}) - f_{\hat{c}(\underline{x})}(\underline{y}).$$

So,

$$f_{\hat{c}(\underline{x})}(\underline{y}) > f_{\hat{c}(\underline{x})}(\underline{x}) - \frac{1}{2}\mu_f(\underline{x}). \qquad (2.14)$$

If one instead writes $|f_i(\underline{y})| - |f_i(\underline{x})|$ in the triangle inequality above and then replaces $\hat{c}(\underline{x})$ by any $i \neq \hat{c}(\underline{x})$, one gets that

$$\forall i \neq \hat{c}(\underline{x}), \quad f_i(\underline{y}) < f_i(\underline{x}) + \frac{1}{2}\mu_f(\underline{x}). \qquad (2.15)$$

So, by (2.14) and (2.15),

$$\forall i \neq \hat{c}(\underline{x}), \quad f_i(\underline{y}) < f_i(\underline{x}) + \frac{1}{2}\mu_f(\underline{x})$$
$$\leq f_{\hat{c}(\underline{x})}(\underline{x}) - \frac{1}{2}\mu_f(\underline{x}) \quad \text{(by (2.12))}$$
$$< f_{\hat{c}(\underline{x})}(\underline{y}). \qquad \square$$

2.9.2 Maximum Margin Training

Since it is difficult to achieve a *prescribed* Lipschitz parameter (and since the value of the Lipschitz parameter for a DNN is anyway unknown in practice), we now consider maximum margin training based on (2.12). [272] suggests to add the margin "to all elements in logits except for the index corresponding to" $c(\underline{x})$. Alternatively, one can perform (dual) optimization of the weighted margin constraints, for example,

$$\min_\theta \sum_{\underline{x} \in X} \lambda_{\underline{x}} \left(\max_{i \neq c(\underline{x})} f_i(\underline{x}) + \mu - f_{c(\underline{x})}(\underline{x}) \right), \qquad (2.16)$$

where the DNN mappings f_i obviously depend on the DNN parameters θ, and the weights $\lambda_{\underline{x}} \geq 0 \; \forall \underline{x} \in \mathcal{X}$. For hyperparameter $\delta > 1$, training can proceed simply as follows (see Section A.1.5).

0. Select initially equal $\lambda_{\underline{x}} > 0$, say $\lambda_{\underline{x}} = 1$ for all $\underline{x} \in \mathcal{X}$.
1. Optimize over θ (train the DNN).
2. If all margin constraints are satisfied then stop.
3. For all $\underline{x} \in \mathcal{X}$, if margin constraint $\underline{x}$ is not satisfied then $\lambda_{\underline{x}} \to \delta\lambda_{\underline{x}}$.
4. Go to step 1.

Again, the parameters of the previous DNN could initialize the training of the next, and an initial DNN can be trained instead by using a cross-entropy loss objective. There are many other variations, including also decreasing $\lambda_{\underline{x}}$ when the $\underline{x}$-constraint is satisfied. Or additively (rather than exponentially) increasing $\lambda_{\underline{x}}$ when it is not, and changing $\lambda_{\underline{x}}$ in a way that depends on the degree of the corresponding margin violation.

Given a thus margin-trained classifier, one could undertake the difficult task (for a DNN) of estimating its Lipschitz continuity parameter, for example [67, 84, 294], and apply Theorem 6 or Proposition 4.1 of [272] to determine a region of class purity around each training sample.

When training with objective (2.16), increased margin $\mu > 0$ could result in reduced accuracy due to overfitting [120], see Section 4.2.5.

2.10   Neural Network Inversion

Given a neural network classifier, neural network inversion [54, 104] is the process through which one discovers an input sample $\underline{z}$ that achieves specified DNN outputs. In particular, neural network inversion can be used to discover input patterns that are very close to (or which cross over) the classifier's decision boundary. Given an initial sample $\underline{x}$ known to belong to class k and correctly classified by the DNN, that is, $\hat{c}(\underline{x}) = c(\underline{x}) = k$, in order to find a sample $\underline{z}$ near the decision boundary between classes k and $j \neq k$, beginning at $\underline{x}^{(0)} = \underline{x}$, employ gradient descent on, for example, the naturally *discriminative* objective [113]

$$\hat{p}(k|\underline{y}) - \hat{p}(j|\underline{y}), \tag{2.17}$$

and stop when $\hat{c}(\underline{x}^{(t)}) = j$. Alternatively, starting from $\underline{x}$ such that $\hat{c}(\underline{x}) = k$, one can use a one-class (or "untargeted") objective,

$$\hat{p}(k|\underline{y}) - \max_{j \neq k} \hat{p}(j|\underline{y}), \tag{2.18}$$

to find a sample $\underline{z}$ that is close to the decision boundary of class k with *any* other class. (Alternatively, just use the logits $f_k(\underline{y})$ instead of the estimated class posteriors $\hat{p}(k|\underline{y})$.) Here, computing the objective's gradient will involve back propagation with respect to the DNN's *inputs* (rather than the DNN's parameters, as during its training).

2.11   Identification and Visualization of Salient Features

Given a trained DNN, we may wish to investigate whether it is working properly on a validation set or to understand how it made a particular decision for a given test sample. That is, we would like to identify the primary features of an input sample that are used by a trained DNN to determine its class. To this end, again recall an input sample $z \in \mathbb{R}^N$ is inferred to be in class

$$\hat{c}(z) = \arg \max_{y \in \mathcal{Y}} f_y(z),$$

where f_y is the class-y logit (just prior to the softmax layer) of the trained DNN. Now consider an internal layer which produces (embedded) abstracted features of an input sample z, for example, the final layer ℓ of a bank of convolutional layers. Each kernel of a convolutional layer produces a (typically scaled down) representation of z. Suppose layer ℓ uses κ $m \times m$ convolutional kernels. Let $v_{k,i,j}$ be an activation of the kth kernel for $k \in \{1, 2, \ldots, \kappa\}$.

Using back propagation, one can compute the sensitivity of f_y to each $v_{k,i,j}$:

$$\frac{\partial f_y}{\partial v_{k,i,j}}(z) \quad k \in \{1, 2, \ldots, \kappa\}, \ i, j \in \{1, 2, \ldots, m\}.$$

In the gradient class activation map (Grad-CAM) approach [239], the average sensitivity per kernel is first computed for the decided upon class $y = \hat{c}(z)$,

$$\alpha_k(z) = \frac{1}{m^2} \sum_{i=1}^{m} \sum_{j=1}^{m} \frac{\partial f_{\hat{c}(z)}}{\partial v_{k,i,j}}(z).$$

This average intensity is used to weight the activations at (i, j) across layer ℓ's kernels,

$$\sigma_{i,j}(z) = \sum_{k=1}^{\kappa} \alpha_k(z) v_{k,i,j}(z).$$

$\sigma(z)$ can then be rectified and rescaled to the dimensions of the input z, and visualized (as essentially a heat map) to compare the "raw" features of z to the most significant features of $\sigma(z)$; for image domains, this approach helps a user to identify the spatial region(s) of the image that contribute most to the DNN's decision-making (i.e., classifying z to $\hat{c}(z)$), see Figure 6.17. This technique has been expanded upon to better *interpret* how a trained DNN functions, including identifying which internal neurons are important when making specific class decisions, for example, [230, 239]. Note that the feature maps k of Figure 2.7 are those with the largest α_k.

2.12   Handling Label-Deficient Data: Transfer and Contrastive Learning

There are a variety of approaches for seeking to learn an accurate classifier even when the available training set is limited in size or deficient in some way (besides the domain/application specific dataset augmentation discussed in Section 2.8.1, which may not adequately address this deficiency).

2.12.1   Semi-supervised Learning

Semi-supervised learning supposes that, while it may be difficult to obtain a large number of *labeled* examples from the given classification domain, it may be far easier to obtain a large set of *unlabeled* samples. These can be used to augment a relatively small labeled training set. One can then exploit both the labeled examples and unlabeled examples for learning the classifier's parameters. For generative classifiers, [178] proposed to learn the classifier model parameters to maximize the "total" log-likelihood, that is, the log-likelihood of the labeled samples plus the log-likelihood of the unlabeled samples. Use of unlabeled data in this way was found to yield more accurate classifiers than those obtained solely by making use of the (limited) labeled data. For discriminative classifiers, one can, for example, invoke a *regularizer* based on the unlabeled samples, for example, by imposing a constraint on the entropy of the DNN's class posterior, evaluated on the unlabeled samples [214]. Maintaining a certain level of entropy (decision uncertainty) may keep the DNN from overfitting.

2.12.2   Transfer Learning and Data Preprocessing

The key idea here is that even if two classification domains (A and B) are quite different, there may be key class discriminating features that are essentially common across them. For example, detected edges at certain orientations may be useful for discriminating between digits, but also possibly for discriminating between cats and dogs. Likewise, certain texture features may be important across multiple classification domains. Thus, one can leverage a classifier trained on domain A (not the task of interest) to extract a feature vector for each training example from the domain of interest (B). These feature vectors, combined with the class labels, form a new training set that is then used in the conventional way, to learn a discriminative classifier for the target domain (B). As a particular illustration, suppose that domain A is ImageNet (with more than 1000 categories) [57], with an existing, publicly available classifier, and domain B is CIFAR-10 [129]. One then feeds (upsampled) CIFAR-10 training images into the ImageNet DNN classifier and, for each, extracts an embedded feature vector from some internal layer of the Imagenet DNN. One possible choice is to extract the embedded feature vector of the layer directly preceding the logit layer of the ImageNet DNN as activated by CIFAR-10 images. These feature vectors are the input to a DNN that is then trained in the conventional way for CIFAR-10. Use of the ImageNet classifier for feature extraction may greatly reduce the number of needed free parameters and layers in the CIFAR-10 classifier. Moreover, it may reduce the training set requirements to achieve an accurate CIFAR-10 classifier.

Another way to generate highly salient features for purposes of deep learning is to leverage prior work from signal processing, for example, frequency-domain coefficients for audio (e.g., cepstral coefficients) and images (e.g., discrete cosine transform or wavelet coefficients).

2.12.3   Contrastive Learning

Recall that the back-end of some DNN classifiers consists of fully connected layers producing logit activations per class followed by a softmax layer to produce class posteriors. As for purposes of transfer learning, one can interpret the input to the logit layer (i.e., output of the front-end of the DNN) as producing salient embedded features needed for accurate classification that are produced implicitly by deep learning minimizing the cross-entropy objective. Contrastive learning instead explicitly controls these embedded features.

Let us consider a classification problem with a training dataset which is either only partially labeled or completely unlabeled. In the unlabeled case, one assumption is that individual samples can be *augmented* for purposes of training; for example, it is possible that an unlabeled image can be rotated, shifted, cropped, flipped or color/intensity adjusted without changing the class label. A second assumption in the unlabeled case is that for every training sample x used for learning, there are examples known to belong to a different category than x (or, even if from the same class, these examples are quite different from x, e.g., possibly originating from a different *sub-category* than the sub-category for x). It is possible these examples are just randomly chosen from the training set. Alternatively, these examples may be given, along with "cannot-link" supervision information, specifying example pairs that cannot belong to the same class/group.

In summary, there are *anchor* training samples $x \in \mathcal{X}' \subset \mathcal{X} \subset \mathbb{R}^N$ for which there is a known subset $\mathcal{P}(x)$ of the possibly augmented training dataset all of whose elements are very similar to x (positive samples of the anchor), and another subset $\mathcal{N}(x)$ all of whose elements are dissimilar to x (negative samples of the anchor). Here, similarity pertains to class-discriminative features, where again it is possible that somewhat dissimilar samples are from the same class. For example, a long snout may very well discriminate between the 'dog' and 'cat' classes for a poodle but not for a pug. The tail to body length may very well discriminate between 'dog' and 'cat' for a pug but not so for a poodle. The ear shape may pretty well discriminate from the 'cat' class for both poodle and pug but not for French bulldog (i.e., there are different sub-classes within the 'dog' class).

One can now formulate a simple *contrastive loss* learning objective to train a DNN

$$f : \mathbb{R}^N \to \mathbb{R}^M$$

which outputs features $\in \mathbb{R}^M$ to facilitate classification or other subsequent data processing.

To this end, using the inner product and Euclidean norm, first define the *cosine similarity* between two vectors[1] $\underline{z}, \underline{y} \in \mathbb{R}^M$ as

$$s(\underline{z}, \underline{y}) = \frac{\langle \underline{z}, \underline{y} \rangle}{\|\underline{z}\| \, \|\underline{y}\|}. \tag{2.19}$$

An example contrastive loss learning objective on the possibly augmented training dataset is

$$L = -\frac{1}{|\mathcal{X}'|} \sum_{\underline{x} \in \mathcal{X}'} \log \left(\frac{1}{|\mathcal{P}(\underline{x})|} \sum_{\underline{v} \in \mathcal{P}(\underline{x})} \frac{\exp(s(f(\underline{x}), f(\underline{v}))/\tau)}{\sum_{\underline{w} \in \mathcal{N}(\underline{x})} \exp(s(f(\underline{x}), f(\underline{w}))/\tau)} \right)$$

where $\tau > 0$ is a free parameter, see, for example, [13, 121, 138]. Given the contrastive feature embedding, the less parameterized back-end portion of a DNN classifier can be trained using the limited labeled training dataset, using a cross-entropy loss (2.8) (as in transfer learning).

2.13   Other Methods of Extracting Salient Features

Instead of contrastive learning to identify a useful feature embedding, auto-encoding can be used. Auto-encoding involves deep learning with the objective to create an output which *matches* the input, with an internal layer of size M which captures salient features, for example, [78, 332]. That is, the auto-encoding neural network $\hat{c} : \mathbb{R}^N \to \mathbb{R}^N$. Under a sample-wise, input-output MSE training objective,

$$\frac{1}{|\mathcal{X}|} \sum_{\underline{x} \in \mathcal{X}} \|\hat{c}(\underline{x}) - \underline{x}\|^2,$$

auto-encoding does not require the training data to be labeled, in other words, it is unsupervised.

As with contrastive learning, M is an important hyperparameter for auto-encoding, which may be chosen to be much smaller than the input dimension, that is, $M \ll N$.

Non-deep-learning techniques for extracting salient features include principal component analysis (PCA), which is sometimes used to visualize high-dimensional data, see Section 3.5 and Chapter 4. Also, RFE/MFE for support vector machine (SVM) classifiers [4] can be used to identify raw features that are salient for classification, see Section A.4.4 of the Appendix.

2.14   Other Types of Classifiers: Naive Bayes (NB) and Logistic Regression (LR)

While the focus of this book is on the security and robustness of DNNs, there are numerous other classification methods that in some applications are more suitable than

---

[1] $\langle \underline{z}, \underline{y} \rangle = \sum_{i=1}^{M} z_i y_i = \|\underline{z}\| \|\underline{y}\| \cos(a_{\underline{z}, \underline{y}})$ where $a_{\underline{z}, \underline{y}}$ is the angle between the vectors $\underline{z}$ and $\underline{y}$ in $\mathbb{R}^M$.

DNNs. These classifiers may also be subject to attacks. Some widely used alternative classification approaches include SVMs (see the Appendix), decision trees, radial basis function classifiers, nearest-prototype classifiers (recall Section 2.5.2), K-nearest neighbor classifiers (KNN, see Section 4.11), ensemble classifiers, generative classifiers such as those based on mixture models (a mixture model can be estimated for each class, see Chapters 3 and 4), as well as Bayesian network classifiers, including special cases such as (generative) naive Bayes models and hidden Markov models.

Let us consider a two-class setting where $\mathcal{Y} = \{-1, 1\}$. Logistic regression (LR) [192] has $N + 1$ parameters $w_0 \in \mathbb{R}, \underline{w} \in \mathbb{R}^N$. LR is a classifier of the sigmoid form,

$$p(\underline{x}) = \frac{1}{1 + \exp(-w_0 - \underline{w}'\underline{x})} \in (0, 1), \tag{2.20}$$

which is trained so that $\underline{x}$ is deemed to be in class -1 if $p(\underline{x}) < 0.5$; otherwise it is deemed to be in class 1. Note that one can rewrite LR's classification rule as

$$\hat{c}(\underline{x}) = -1 \Leftrightarrow w_0 + \underline{w}'\underline{x} < 0, \tag{2.21}$$

and interpret p as the class posterior,

$$p(\underline{x}) = P(Y = 1 \mid \underline{X} = \underline{x}),$$

where here $\underline{X}$ is the random vector representing the sample data and random variable Y is its class label. So, assuming the training samples are independent, the *conditional data log-likelihood* (log of the probability of the labels $c(\underline{x})$ of the data samples $\underline{x}$ over the whole training dataset) is

$$\mathcal{L}(w_0, \underline{w}) = \log \prod_{\underline{x} \in \mathcal{X}} P(Y = c(\underline{x}) \mid \underline{X} = \underline{x})$$

$$= -\sum_{\underline{x} \in \mathcal{X}} \log(1 + \exp(-c(\underline{x})(w_0 + \underline{w}'\underline{x}))). \tag{2.22}$$

It is left as an exercise to show that $\mathcal{L}$ is a convex function of its $N + 1$ parameters $w_0, \underline{w}$. Though there is no closed-form expression for the $\mathcal{L}$-maximizing parameters, one can exploit the convexity of $\mathcal{L}$, using a simple and quick gradient-based numerical method to learn them.

SVMs are another type of classifier, one which seeks to maximize classification margin, see the Appendix.

The naive Bayes (NB) classifier is generative, while LR and SVM are discriminative. That is, for NB, we learn a joint probability model for the feature vector $\underline{X}$ and the class label random variable, Y. Let random variable X_j be the jth feature of random vector $\underline{X}$. "Naively" assume that the features X_j are conditionally independent given the class label Y. By Bayes' theorem, for any $y \in \mathcal{Y}$ and $\underline{x} \in \mathbb{R}^N$, the posterior probability is:

$$P(Y = y \mid \underline{X} = \underline{x}) = \frac{P(\underline{X} = \underline{x} \mid Y = y)P(Y = y)}{P(\underline{X} = \underline{x})}$$

$$= \frac{P(Y = y) \prod_i P(X_i = x_i \mid Y = y)}{P(\underline{X} = \underline{x})}.$$

The denominator does not depend on the class label and so the following MAP rule used by naive Bayes to make a class decision for a test sample will not depend on it. Assuming discrete distributions, based on the training set $\mathcal{X}$, one can empirically estimate

$$P(X_i = x_i \mid Y = y) \approx \frac{\sum_{\underline{\xi} \in \mathcal{X}} \mathbf{1}\{\xi_i = x_i, c(\underline{\xi}) = y\}}{\sum_{\underline{\xi} \in \mathcal{X}} \mathbf{1}\{c(\underline{\xi}) = y\}}$$

$$P(Y = y) \approx \frac{1}{|\mathcal{X}|} \sum_{\underline{\xi} \in \mathcal{X}} \mathbf{1}\{c(\underline{\xi}) = y\}.$$

These are in fact the maximum likelihood estimates of these parameters. The NB classifier would then classify an (unlabeled) test sample $\underline{z} \in \mathbb{R}^N$ according to the MAP rule:

$$\hat{c}(\underline{z}) = \arg\max_{y \in \mathcal{Y}} P(Y = y) \prod_i P(X_i = z_i \mid Y = y). \qquad (2.23)$$

For continuously distributed data, an NB classifier can instead model the features conditioned on the class using a parametric density function, for example, a Gaussian density,

$$P(X_i = x_i \mid Y = y) = \frac{\exp(-(x_i - \mu_{y,i})^2/(2\sigma_{y,i}^2))}{\sigma_{y,i}\sqrt{2\pi}}, \qquad (2.24)$$

where $\mu_{y,i}$ and $\sigma_{y,i}^2$ are the mean and variance of the ith feature of the class-y subset of the training set, $\mathcal{X}_y = \{\underline{\xi} \in \mathcal{X} \mid c(\underline{\xi}) = y\}$. The parameters can be estimated as:

$$\mu_{y,i} = \frac{1}{|\mathcal{X}_y|} \sum_{\underline{x} \in \mathcal{X}_y} x_i$$

$$\sigma_{y,i}^2 = \frac{1}{|\mathcal{X}_y| - 1} \sum_{\underline{x} \in \mathcal{X}_y} (x_i - \mu_{y,i})^2.$$

Note that the above estimate of the variance (and of the mean) is unbiased. However, the maximum likelihood estimator (MLE) is:

$$\sigma_{y,i}^2 = \frac{1}{|\mathcal{X}_y|} \sum_{\underline{x} \in \mathcal{X}_y} (x_i - \mu_{y,i})^2.$$

This is a biased estimate, but asymptotically unbiased (in the large data limit).

2.15   Discussion: Statistical Confidence

It is common practice to report statistical confidence intervals, for example [251], of performance measures for experiments which involve a degree of randomness. According to the law of large numbers and central limit theorem, for a single performance metric EX (mean of a random variable X), a 95% confidence interval

$$[\hat{\mu} - 2\hat{\sigma}/\sqrt{n}, \ \hat{\mu} + 2\hat{\sigma}/\sqrt{n}]$$

for (unknown) EX satisfies

$$0.95 \approx P(EX \in [-2\hat{\sigma}/\sqrt{n}, \ \hat{\mu} + 2\hat{\sigma}/\sqrt{n}])$$
$$= P(\hat{\mu} - 2\hat{\sigma}/\sqrt{n} \le EX \le \hat{\mu} + 2\hat{\sigma}/\sqrt{n}),$$

where $\hat{\mu}$ is the sample mean and $\hat{\sigma}$ is the square root of the sample variance, based on n i.i.d. samples of X. The number of samples n is set sufficiently large so that the confidence interval is small enough to meet a desired performance "tolerance."

Again, recall that the labeled data is split in a uniformly random fashion between a validation set $\mathcal{H}$ to determine hyperparameters and a training set $\mathcal{X}$ for deep learning of the "main" parameters (those of the DNN's neurons and edges). In addition, there is a similarly distributed test set $\mathcal{I}$ that is used to experimentally evaluate the accuracy of the trained DNN (based both on its main parameters and on hyperparameters), where $\mathcal{I}$ is not involved in choosing any parameters or hyperparameters. Also recall that, in a deep learning setting, the size of these datasets is typically very large and that deep learning is a heuristic process that itself involves several (or even many) hyperparameters. Some hyperparameters are set using a validation set, while others are set to default values.

Thus, for each deep learning experiment, there are a large number of "sources of randomness" to consider. Though we typically report experimental results based on a number of different "cases" or "trials" n, for brevity we typically do not report statistical confidence for the deep learning experiments in this book. While many of the articles we cite also do not report confidence intervals, most do post their code and models online so that third parties can more easily reproduce the reported experimental results [100].

2.16   Chapter Summary

In this chapter we provided a broad overview of deep learning, encompassing a survey of statistical pattern recognition, constituents of feed-forward neural networks that include various neuron activation functions and various types of DNN layers, fundamentals of gradient-based optimization and some of its variants, used within back propagation training of DNNs, different loss functions used for training DNNs, various deep learning tasks/objectives, including auto-encoding and contrastive learning, neural network inversion, which features prominently throughout the rest of this book, and methods for dealing with label-deficient training data. Some questions to test the reader's understanding of the chapter include the following.

- Can (and should) a categorical feature be directly input to a deep neural network?
- Does a neural network take as input both the feature vector and its supervising class label?
- What is meant by the term ground truth? Does a classifier produce ground truth decisions?

- Why is it necessary to evaluate a DNN's accuracy on a test set, rather than on the training set?
- Can a DNN improve on the Bayes error rate?
- What should the vector $\underline{w}$ be in Cover's theorem if there are more than two classes?
- Does it make sense to have a DNN consisting exclusively of layers with linear activation functions?
- Is it necessary to have a softmax layer as the output layer in order to make classification decisions?
- Why is the training set misclassification rate not suitable for gradient descent?
- What is the effect of using dropout during DNN training?
- What are some examples of hyperparameters associated with a DNN architecture?
- What are some examples of hyperparameters associated with DNN training?
- How are contrastive learning and auto-encoding related? (What is the similar goal in both cases?)

2.17　References for Further Reading

There are many good general books on calculus (including multivariate calculus), for example, [126], and linear algebra (including matrix analysis), for example, [103]. Good introductory books on probability include [220, 223, 251]. Introductory references for numerical methods and optimization include [8, 199, 208]. For more details on statistical pattern recognition and neural networks see, for example, [63]. For more details on machine learning, a good reference is [22]. Overviews of deep learning include [62, 81]. An introduction to PyTorch programming (for deep learning) is given in [209, 254].

2.18　Project: Classification of UC Irvine Datasets

Investigate different real datasets from the UC Irvine Machine Learning Repository [276], for example, glass and Hepatitis, as follows.

1. Read the given descriptions of these datasets.
2. Download these datasets from the repository.
3. Train neural networks on the training set provided for the given domain with different numbers of hidden neurons and then evaluate classification accuracy on both the training set and on the test set. The number of parameters to be trained in your neural network should "grow" with the size of your training set.
4. Plot these performance measures as a function of the number of hidden units.
5. Also try other classification methods on these datasets – naive Bayes, logistic regression, and support vector machines. Perform the same evaluations as for the neural network, and compare the performance of the different classification methods.
6. Note any experimental observations that are distinctive for each dataset.

2.19   Project: Membership-Inference Attack

To investigate the membership-inference attack and a defense against this attack described in Chapter 1, consider the Breast Cancer Wisconsin UC Irvine domain [10, 276], and randomly split the training dataset into two equal-sized subsets, X_V, X_S. Similarly split the test dataset I. Use X_V to build a classifier (the victim classifier). Use X_S to build a single shadow classifier of the victim classifier. Then, using X_S and half the test set I_S, build a binary classifier that takes as input a class posterior of the shadow classifier and outputs a decision (Yes/No) of whether the posterior was produced by a training example. Evaluate the accuracy of this binary classifier in predicting whether the posterior output from the victim classifier was elicited by a training sample of the victim classifier, using X_V and the other half of the test set, I_V. Next, implement the defense against this attack which checks a query example against the victim classifier's training set, in other words one may expect that training samples themselves are rarely seen at test time under normal circumstances. Evaluate the true detection rate and false alarm rate of this defense (again on X_V and I_V) when the attacker adds noise to the query patterns, for several different noise variances. Discuss your results.

2.20   Project: Classification for the CIFAR-10 Image Domain

Investigate different DNN training strategies for image-based classification using the CIFAR-10 image domain.

1. Download the CIFAR-10 dataset.
2. Train neural networks (with various numbers of layers and numbers of hidden units per layer) for this domain using several different training approaches. That is, consider networks with multiple feed-forward "stages," with each consisting of a convolutional layer followed by a pooling layer, and a last stage consisting of a fully connected layer yielding logits that are input to a final (softmax) layer, with the class decision based on the MAP rule. Assume individual neurons use ReLU activations. Consider training: (i) without any data augmentation, (ii) with data augmentation, (iii) with pure mini-batch gradient descent, (iv) with momentum-based optimization.
3. Evaluate the training and test set accuracies for the classifiers trained using the different training configurations.
4. Note any interesting observations.

3 Basics of Detection and Mixture Models

In this chapter we introduce mixture models and how to estimate their parameters. Mixture models provide one type of automated *data clustering*, that is, learning of the "groups" present in a given dataset without prior knowledge of the groups present or the number of groups. In this sense, clustering is a form of "unsupervised" learning. Automated clustering techniques may organize a massive image database with millions of images, assigning each image to one of the (estimated) classes; they may organize a text repository with millions of news articles, learning the topics that are present; or they may cluster human genomes to identify distinct human populations, for example, individuals with a common origin or those susceptible to contracting the same disease. In the first two cases, clustering by humans is feasible but extremely onerous, time-consuming, and expensive. In the third example, involving, for example a 30,000-dimensional data vector of human genes, it is difficult if not impossible for a human being to recognize group structure present in high dimensional (non-image) data samples. Mixture models are also used more generally to well-fit complicated, multi-modal data distributions. In this book, these models will be used as *null models* in anomaly detection defenses against several types of attacks – in particular, see Chapters 4 and 13. We also introduce some basic concepts and performance criteria for detection, which will be used for evaluating the performance of anomaly detection defenses throughout this book.

Let us now consider an indexed dataset of "feature vectors":

$$X = \{\underline{x}_i = (x_{i,1}, x_{i,2}, \dots, x_{i,N})' \; : \; i \in \{1, 2, \dots, T\}\}.$$

Suppose the data vectors $\underline{x}_i$ are realizations produced by a stochastic model, that is, define the random vector $\underline{X}$ with an associated stochastic model producing its realizations, $\underline{x}_i$. If all the features are continuously valued, this stochastic model is the joint probability density function (pdf)[1] $f_{\underline{X}}(\underline{x})$, with the T feature vectors typically assumed to be generated independently and identically distributed according to this same pdf (i.e., the data are generated i.i.d.). The joint pdf satisfies $f_{\underline{X}}(\underline{x}) \geq 0 \, \forall \underline{x} \in \mathbb{R}^N$, and

$$\int_{\mathbb{R}^N} f_{\underline{X}}(\underline{x}) d\underline{x} = 1.$$

---

[1] This is also commonly referred to as the "density" or "density function."

Note, though, that $f_{\underline{X}}(\underline{x})$ is *not* constrained to be between 0 and 1 and is *not* the probability of observing $\underline{x}$. For continuously valued observations this probability is zero for any $\underline{x} \in \mathbb{R}^N$. For $B \subset \mathbb{R}^N$,

$$P(\underline{X} \in B) = \int_B f_{\underline{X}}(\underline{x}) d\underline{x}.$$

One widely used model is the multivariate (N-dimensional) Gaussian density,

$$f(\underline{x}) = \frac{1}{\sqrt{(2\pi)^N |\mathbf{C}|}} \exp\left(-\frac{1}{2}(\underline{x} - \underline{\mu})' \mathbf{C}^{-1}(\underline{x} - \underline{\mu})\right) \tag{3.1}$$

where

$$\underline{\mu} = \mathsf{E}\underline{X} \in \mathbb{R}^N$$

is the mean vector and $|\mathbf{C}|$ is the determinant of the $N \times N$ positive-definite covariance matrix,

$$\mathbf{C} = \mathsf{E}[(\underline{X} - \underline{\mu})(\underline{X} - \underline{\mu})'].$$

So, a multivariate Gaussian is determined by just its first-order and second-order statistics (parameters), $\Theta = \{\underline{\mu}, \mathbf{C}\}$.

In this context, for non-singular (positive-definite) covariance matrix $\mathbf{C}$, the *Mahalanobis* distance between $\underline{x} \in \mathbb{R}^N$ and this multivariate Gaussian distribution is defined to be

$$\|\underline{x} - \underline{\mu}\|_{mn} := \sqrt{(\underline{x} - \underline{\mu})' \mathbf{C}^{-1}(\underline{x} - \underline{\mu})}. \tag{3.2}$$

In one dimension ($N = 1$, recall Eq. (2.24)), $\|\underline{x} - \underline{\mu}\|_{mn}$ is just the number of standard deviations ($\sigma = \sqrt{\mathbf{C}}$) between $\underline{x}$ and $\underline{\mu}$, $\frac{1}{\sigma}\|\underline{x} - \underline{\mu}\|_2$.

On the other hand, if all the features are discrete valued, then the distribution of the random vector $\underline{X}$ is described using the joint probability mass function (pmf) $p_{\underline{X}}(\underline{x}) = P(\underline{X} = \underline{x})$. The pmf satisfies $0 \le p_{\underline{X}}(\underline{x}) \le 1$ and

$$\sum_{\underline{x} \in R_{\underline{X}}} p_{\underline{X}}(\underline{x}) = 1,$$

where $R_{\underline{X}} \subset \mathbb{R}^N$ is the countable strict-range of $\underline{X}$, $p_{\underline{X}}(\underline{x}) > 0 \Leftrightarrow \underline{x} \in R_{\underline{X}}$. Using Dirac impulses δ in $\mathbb{R}^N$, one can express a pmf as a pdf,

$$f_{\underline{X}}(\underline{x}) = \sum_{\underline{z} \in R_{\underline{X}}} \delta(\underline{x} - \underline{z}) p_{\underline{X}}(\underline{z}).$$

One joint pmf that is widely used, for example, for modeling the word counts $\{x_i\}$ in a text document, is the multinomial distribution:

$$p_{\underline{X}}(\underline{x}) = \frac{W!}{x_1! x_2! \cdots x_N!} p_1^{x_1} p_2^{x_2} \cdots p_d^{x_N}.$$

Here, W is the number of words in the document, x_i is the number of times the ith unique word in the dictionary occurred in the document, N is the number of unique words in the dictionary, and p_i is the (marginal) probability of occurrence of the *i*th word. Thus, $W = x_1 + \cdots + x_N$, $p_1 + \cdots + p_N = 1$, and $\Theta = \{p_1, p_2, \ldots, p_N\}$. Multinomial mixtures are further discussed in Chapter 13.

If some features are continuous valued while others are discrete, the joint distribution can be expressed as:

$$f_{\underline{X}}(\underline{x}) = f_{\underline{X}_c|\underline{X}_d}(\underline{x}_c|\underline{x}_d)p_{\underline{X}_d}(\underline{x}_d),$$

where here $\underline{x}_c$ is the sub-vector of continuous-valued features and $\underline{x}_d$ is the sub-vector of discrete-valued features.

3.1   Mixture Densities

Unimodal densities like the Gaussian, exponential, and Gamma distributions may not well describe complicated datasets X. Moreover, in some application contexts it may in fact be known that the dataset consists of M different groups, each with a distinct density function model for each group. These different groups could correspond to distinct classes, as in a supervised classification problem. But this is not necessary. Even data all coming from the same class may come from different groups – essentially, in this case, these groups could be considered *components* (sub-classes) of the (parent) class. Each such group for example could correspond to a distinct mode in the joint density function. Thus, in general, there is a need for *multimodal* density functions, which are naturally constructed as *mixture densities*. In the purely continuous-valued case, a mixture density has the form:

$$f_{\underline{X}}(\underline{x}) = \sum_{k=1}^{M} \alpha_k f_{\underline{X}|k}(\underline{x}; \Theta_k). \tag{3.3}$$

Here, $f_{\underline{X}|k}(\cdot; \Theta_k)$ is a valid density function (often referred to as a *component* density) specified by parameters Θ_k, while α_k is the *prior* probability that a feature vector is generated according to the kth component, that is, $\{\alpha_k\}_{k=1}^{M}$ is a pmf. The component densities need not come from the same parametric density function family, for example, they need not all be Gaussian densities. The mixture model's parameters are $\Theta = \{\Theta_k, \alpha_k \mid k = 1, \ldots, M\}$. A mixture density for the case of bivariate Gaussian component densities (i.e., for a two-dimensional feature vector) is shown in Figure 3.1. Note the four modes in the mixture density, each one occurring at the mean of one of the Gaussian component densities.

Now suppose we are given a feature vector $\underline{x}$. We can perform *inference* based on a mixture model to compute the a posteriori probability that $\underline{x}$ was generated by each of the components:

$$p(k|\underline{x}) = \frac{\alpha_k f_{\underline{X}|k}(\underline{x}; \Theta_k)}{\sum_{j=1}^{M} \alpha_j f_{\underline{X}|j}(\underline{x}; \Theta_j)}, \quad k = 1, \ldots, M, \tag{3.4}$$

where

$$p(k|\underline{x}) := P(Y(\underline{X}) = k|\underline{X} = \underline{x}),$$

and here $Y(\underline{x})$ is the mixture component label for $\underline{x}$.

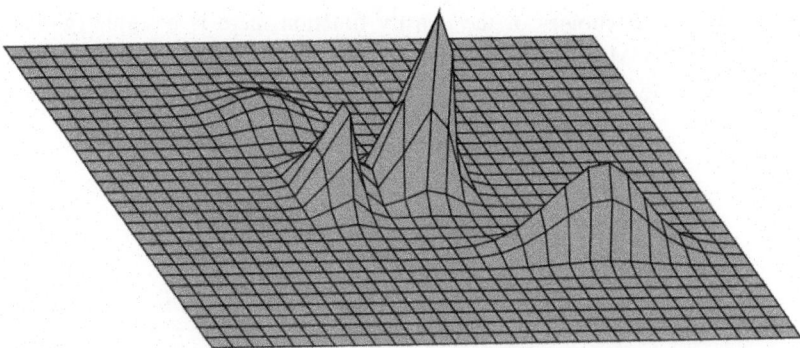

Figure 3.1 An example Gaussian mixture model (GMM) $\sum_{k=1}^{M} \alpha_k f_k(\underline{x}; \Theta_k)$ with $M = 4$ components for an $N = 2$ dimensional random vector. The positive priors $\{\alpha_k\}_{k=1}^{M}$ form a pmf. Each component is a two-dimensional Gaussian density, contributing one mode to the GMM. Plotted using [27].

As one example, consider a mixture of multivariate Gaussian densities, with each component density specified by its parameters $\Theta_k = \{\underline{\mu}_k, \mathbf{C}_k\}$. In this case the a posteriori component probabilities take the form:

$$p(k|\underline{x}) = \frac{\alpha_k |\mathbf{C}_k|^{-1/2} e^{-(\underline{x}-\underline{\mu}_k)'\mathbf{C}_k^{-1}(\underline{x}-\underline{\mu}_k)/2}}{\sum\limits_{j=1}^{M} \alpha_j |\mathbf{C}_j|^{-1/2} e^{-(\underline{x}-\underline{\mu}_j)'\mathbf{C}_j^{-1}(\underline{x}-\underline{\mu}_j)/2}}, \quad k = 1,\ldots,M. \tag{3.5}$$

If a component's covariance matrix is diagonal, then the joint component density factors as a product of marginal Gaussian densities over the individual features (i.e., the features are independent under the given component). This simplifies even further if the covariance matrix is a scaled identity matrix (in this case, the features all have the same variance).

In much of the sequel, to simplify discussion, it will be supposed there is only continuous-valued data.

3.2 Estimating the Parameters: Maximum Likelihood Estimation (MLE) and Expectation-Maximization (EM)

A standard and theoretically supported framework for estimating the parameters of a density function (including the parameters of a mixture density) is to choose the parameters to maximize the joint likelihood (joint density) of the observed data $\mathcal{X}$. Assuming $\mathcal{X}$ consists of independent realizations $\underline{x}_1, \underline{x}_2, \ldots, \underline{x}_T$ of random vector $\underline{X}$, the maximum likelihood (ML) parameters are:

$$\hat{\Theta}_{ML} = \arg\max_{\Theta} \prod_{i=1}^{T} f_{\underline{X}}(\underline{x}_i; \Theta)$$

$$= \arg\max_{\Theta} \sum_{i=1}^{T} \log f_{\underline{X}}(\underline{x}_i; \Theta).$$

For some choices of the density function there is a single (globally optimal) ML solution. Moreover, this solution can be easily found via a "closed form" equation. For example, ML estimation of the parameters of a multivariate Gaussian density is given by

$$\hat{\underline{\mu}} = \frac{1}{T} \sum_{i=1}^{T} \underline{x}_i,$$ (3.6)

followed by

$$\hat{\mathbf{C}} = \frac{1}{T} \sum_{i=1}^{T} (\underline{x}_i - \hat{\underline{\mu}})(\underline{x}_i - \hat{\underline{\mu}})'.$$ (3.7)

That is, $\hat{\mathbf{C}}$ is the average outer product of the centered data samples $\underline{x} \in X$. Note that $\hat{\underline{\mu}}$ is an unbiased estimator of $\underline{\mu}$ ($\mathsf{E}\hat{\underline{\mu}} = \underline{\mu}$) and a consistent estimator of $\underline{\mu}$ ($\lim_{T \to \infty} \hat{\underline{\mu}} = \underline{\mu}$), the latter just an application of the law of large numbers. But though $\hat{\mathbf{C}}$ is a biased estimator of $\mathbf{C}$ ($\mathsf{E}\hat{\mathbf{C}} = \mathbf{C}T/(T-1)$), it is consistent (and so asymptotically unbiased).

On the other hand, for a mixture density function, ML estimation is, in general, a non-convex optimization problem, requiring a non-trivial optimization procedure, and with multiple extrema (including possibly multiple local maxima of varying quality). In this case, the local optimum solution that is obtained depends on the starting point of the optimization (the parameter initialization).

Standard, gradient-based (or second-order Newton-based) optimization methods can be brought to bear on this problem. However, there is an attractive alternative approach that: (i) is guaranteed to converge to an extremum of the likelihood function; (ii) performs a number of iterations, with each iteration guaranteed to increase the likelihood function; (iii) unlike gradient ascent, this algorithm does *not* require the (complicating) choice of a step size hyperparameter; and (iv) for some complicated density functions, it converts an apparently intractable problem into a tractable one [86]. This famous optimization approach is known as the expectation-maximization (EM) algorithm [56]. A brief synopsis of EM is next provided for the particular case of a mixture density.

The EM formulation begins by defining a *new* log-likelihood function that is, in general, more tractable. To start, one writes the log-likelihood of X as:

$$\mathcal{L} = \sum_{i=1}^{T} \log \left(\sum_{j=1}^{M} \alpha_j f_{\underline{X}|j}(\underline{x}_i; \Theta_j) \right).$$ (3.8)

In EM parlance, this is called the *incomplete* data log-likelihood. Note that this has a somewhat complicated form, involving the log of a sum. However, suppose one introduces a special type of new binary data $\{v_{ij}, i = 1, \ldots, T, j = 1, \ldots, M\}$, where

- $v_{ij} = 1$ if sample $\underline{x}_i$ was generated by component j, and
- $v_{ij} = 0$ otherwise.

Supposing that this "indicator" data is known, we can write down the joint log-likelihood of X and $\{v_{ij}\}$. In EM parlance, this is called the *complete data log-likelihood function*,

$$\mathcal{L}_c = \sum_{i=1}^{T} \log \left(\sum_{j=1}^{M} v_{ij} \alpha_j f_{\underline{X}|j}(\underline{x}_i; \Theta_j) \right)$$

$$= \sum_{i=1}^{T} \sum_{j=1}^{M} v_{ij} \log(\alpha_j f_{\underline{X}|j}(\underline{x}_i; \Theta_j)). \tag{3.9}$$

Note that introducing this new data allows the summation to be taken outside of the log, thus simplifying the resulting expression.

Now, unfortunately, the $\{v_{ij}\}$ are not actually known. The closest one can get to these hard $\{0, 1\}$ membership values are the a posteriori mixture component probabilities previously expressed and referred to as the inferences one can make given the parameters of a mixture model; recall Eqs. (3.4) and (3.5). These inferences will figure prominently in the EM algorithm.

Even though the $\{v_{ij}\}$ are not known, one can treat them as random variables $\{V_{ij}\}$ and form the *expected complete data log-likelihood*:

$$\mathsf{E}(\mathcal{L}_c|\mathcal{X}; \Theta) = \sum_{i=1}^{T} \sum_{j=1}^{M} \mathsf{E}(V_{ij}|\mathcal{X}; \Theta) \log(\alpha_j f_{\underline{X}|j}(\underline{x}_i; \Theta_j)),$$

where it is recognized that the only random quantities in $\mathcal{L}_c$ are the $\{V_{ij}\}$. One can further recognize that $\mathsf{E}(V_{ij}|\mathcal{X}; \Theta)$ is just the a posteriori probability according to the mixture density, that is, as in (3.4) and (3.5):

$$\mathsf{E}(V_{ij}|\mathcal{X}; \Theta) = p[j|i] = \frac{\alpha_j f_{\underline{X}|j}(\underline{x}_i; \Theta_j)}{\sum_{l=1}^{M} \alpha_l f_{\underline{X}|l}(\underline{x}_i; \Theta_l)}. \tag{3.10}$$

Here, a further short-hand notation is used for the a posteriori probability:

$$p[j|i] := p(j|\underline{x}_i) := P(Y(\underline{X}) = j|\underline{X} = \underline{x}_i).$$

Thus, the expected complete data log-likelihood is:

$$\mathsf{E}(\mathcal{L}_c|\mathcal{X}; \Theta) = \sum_{i=1}^{T} \sum_{j=1}^{M} p[j|i] \log(\alpha_j f_{\underline{X}|j}(\underline{x}_i; \Theta_j)).$$

The EM algorithm maximizes the *auxiliary function*

$$\mathcal{F} = \sum_{i=1}^{T} \sum_{j=1}^{M} p[j|i] \log(\alpha_j f_{\underline{X}|j}(\underline{x}_i; \Theta_j)) - \sum_{i=1}^{T} \sum_{j=1}^{M} p[j|i] \log p[j|i]$$

over *both* the model parameters Θ and the a posteriori probabilities $\{p[j|i] \mid j = 1, \ldots, M, i = 1, \ldots, T\}$. Note that the second term of the auxiliary function is Shannon's entropy for Y given $\underline{X} = \underline{x}_i$:

$$H = -\sum_{j=1}^{M} p[j|i] \log p[j|i].$$

The auxiliary function is optimized by alternating two optimization steps until convergence: the E-step and the M-step.

In the E-step, we maximize the auxiliary function over the posteriors $\{p[j|i]\}$ given the parameters Θ held fixed. This yields the closed-form expression at iteration $t + 1$ (recall (3.4)):

$$p[j|i]^{(t+1)} = \frac{\alpha_j^{(t)} f_{\underline{X}|j}(\underline{x}_i; \Theta_j^{(t)})}{\sum\limits_{l=1}^{M} \alpha_l^{(t)} f_{\underline{X}|l}(\underline{x}_i; \Theta_l^{(t)})}, \tag{3.11}$$

where here the superscript (t) on the *vector or set* of parameters indicates that the parameters at iteration t, $\Theta^{(t)} = \{\underline{\alpha}^{(t)}, \Theta_l^{(t)} \mid l = 1, 2, \ldots, M\}$, are plugged in to compute the a posteriori probabilities at iteration $t + 1$.

Then, given these E-step quantities fixed, the M-step maximizes the auxiliary function over the parameters Θ (subject to the constraint that the component prior probabilities sum to 1), yielding the parameters at iteration $t + 1$, $\Theta^{(t+1)}$.

As an example, supposing each component is a multivariate Gaussian density, the *closed form* M-step update is:

$$\underline{\mu}_j^{(t+1)} = \frac{\sum\limits_{i=1}^{T} p[j|i]^{(t+1)} \underline{x}_i}{\sum\limits_{i=1}^{T} p[j|i]^{(t+1)}}, \quad j = 1, \ldots, M,$$

$$\alpha_j^{(t+1)} = \frac{1}{T} \sum_{i=1}^{T} p[j|i]^{(t+1)}, \quad j = 1, \ldots, M,$$

followed by

$$\mathbf{C}_j^{(t+1)} = \frac{\sum\limits_{i=1}^{T} p[j|i]^{(t+1)} (\underline{x}_i - \underline{\mu}_j^{(t+1)})(\underline{x}_i - \underline{\mu}_j^{(t+1)})'}{\sum\limits_{i=1}^{T} p[j|i]^{(t+1)}}, \quad j = 1, \ldots, M.$$

As aforementioned, these E- and M-steps are alternated, starting from initial parameter estimates $\Theta^{(0)}$, until a convergence condition is met. Some of the attractive properties of this algorithm are as follows.

1. For some density families, such as for the Gaussian mixture considered above, the M-step is a closed-form update.
2. Each step (E or M above) is non-decreasing in the auxiliary function, $\mathcal{F}$, which is the theoretical basis for convergence of the algorithm.
3. Moreover, each M-step guarantees increase in the actual function of interest – the (incomplete) data log-likelihood function.
4. With closed-form E- and M-steps, the algorithm does not require any setting of a step-size hyperparameter (a necessary complication when performing gradient-based optimization).
5. For mixture densities, the EM algorithm can be seen as a probabilistic generalization of a well-known algorithm used to find meaningful sub-groups (clusters) in a given dataset: the K-means algorithm (also known as the generalized Lloyd algorithm).

Finally, we define a mixture model called the Gaussian *kernel* density, wherein each data point $\underline{x} \in X \subset \mathbb{R}^N$ is the center of an isotropic Gaussian density with common variance σ^2 and uncorrelated features: $\forall \underline{y} \in \mathbb{R}^N$,

$$f(\underline{y}) = \sum_{\underline{x} \in X} \frac{1}{\sigma \sqrt{(2\pi)^N}} \exp\left(-\frac{1}{2\sigma^2} \|\underline{y} - \underline{x}\|^2\right). \tag{3.12}$$

As an exercise, show how the common parameter σ^2 can be estimated to maximize the likelihood of the data X under f.

3.3 *K*-Means Clustering as a Special Case

To show that *K*-means is a special case of EM for Gaussian mixtures, suppose that $\mathbf{C}_j = \sigma^2 I$ and $\alpha_j = \frac{1}{M} \ \forall j$. Also, suppose that in the E-step one forces *hard* $\in \{0, 1\}$ assignments of data points to components (clusters), that is, let

- $v_{ij}^{(t+1)} = 1$ for $j = \arg\max_k p[k|i]^{(t+1)}$ and
- $v_{il}^{(t+1)} = 0 \ \forall l \neq j$.

Hard assignments reduce the E-step to the *nearest-neighbor data assignment rule* (irrespective of the value of σ^2):

$$v_{ij}^{(t+1)} = 1 \quad \text{if} \quad \|\underline{x}_i - \underline{\mu}_j^{(t+1)}\| \leq \|\underline{x}_i - \underline{\mu}_k^{(t+1)}\| \ \ \forall k \neq j.$$

The M-step (optimizing over the mean parameters) reduces to the *centroid rule*,

$$\underline{\mu}_j^{(t+1)} = \frac{\sum_{i=1}^{T} v_{ij}^{(t+1)} \underline{x}_i}{\sum_{i=1}^{T} v_{ij}^{(t+1)}}. \tag{3.13}$$

The resulting algorithm descends in, and yields a local extremum of, the *K*-means (squared error) clustering-distortion objective:

$$\sum_{i=1}^{T} \sum_{j=1}^{K} v_{ij} \|\underline{x}_i - \underline{\mu}_j\|^2.$$

Here "*K*" does not stand for the number of classes (indeed, unsupervised *K*-means does not rely on class labels); rather, it is the number of clusters. The hyperparameter *K* can be automatically selected by, for example, optimizing over the clustering-distortion objective with a model order penalty – such model order selection is the subject of the next section.

3.4 Model Order Selection

EM learns a mixture density function supposing that the number of mixture components (*M* above) is fixed/known. It is in fact ill posed to seek to also maximize the data log-likelihood function $\mathcal{L}$ (3.8) with respect to the number of components in the model. In particular, in an extreme case, if any component is centered on a single data point, and if the variance for that component is decreased to zero, the log-likelihood function will go to infinity.

3.4.1   Background on BIC

Suppose a dataset $X \subset \mathbb{R}^N$ of size $T = |X|$ is to be modeled. Also suppose we have a finite family of model types M where each model is the logarithm of a pdf,

$$\log f(\underline{x}; \underline{\theta}, m), \quad \underline{x} \in \mathbb{R}^N,$$

of type $m \in M$, and has associated parameters $\underline{\theta} \in \Theta_m \subset \mathbb{R}^{d(m)}$, that is, for model m, $\underline{\theta}$ is a vector of $d(m)$ parameters and here Θ_m is the set of such parameters. Here the data log-likelihood is defined as

$$\mathcal{L}(\underline{\theta}; m) = \sum_{\underline{x} \in X} \log f(\underline{x}; \underline{\theta}, m).$$

For each model type m, define the maximum likelihood (ML) model parameters $\underline{\theta}_m^*$:

$$\underline{\theta}_m^* = \arg\max_{\underline{\theta} \in \Theta_m} \mathcal{L}(\theta; m).$$

Assume smooth $\mathcal{L}$ so that it can be differentiated with respect to the model parameters: $\forall m \in M$,

$$\nabla_{\underline{\theta}} \mathcal{L}(\underline{\theta}_m^*; m) - 0$$

$$\mathcal{L}(\underline{\theta}; m) = \mathcal{L}(\underline{\theta}_m^*; m) + \frac{1}{2}(\underline{\theta} - \underline{\theta}_m^*)' \mathbf{H}(\underline{\theta}_m^*; m)(\underline{\theta} - \underline{\theta}_m^*) + o(\|\underline{\theta} - \underline{\theta}_m^*\|^2)$$

where the second equality is just Taylor's theorem with the $d(m) \times d(m)$ Hessian matrix

$$\mathbf{H}(\underline{\theta}_m^*; m) := \frac{\partial^2 \mathcal{L}}{\partial \theta^2}(\underline{\theta}_m^*; m) = \sum_{\underline{x} \in X} \frac{\partial^2 \log f}{\partial \theta^2}(\underline{x}; \underline{\theta}_m^*, m).$$

Assume uniform priors for the parameters ($\underline{\theta} \in \Theta_m$) for all models ($m \in M$) and that θ_m^* is in the interior of the large set Θ_m. So, the mean of the inverse of the likelihood of X taken over the parameters of model m is

$$\frac{1}{p(m)} := \int_{\Theta_m} \exp(-\mathcal{L}(\underline{\theta}; m)) d\underline{\theta}$$

$$\approx \exp(-\mathcal{L}(\underline{\theta}_m^*; m)) \int_{\Theta_m} \exp\left(-\frac{1}{2}(\underline{\theta} - \underline{\theta}_m^*)' \mathbf{H}(\underline{\theta}_m^*; m)(\underline{\theta} - \underline{\theta}_m^*)\right) d\underline{\theta}$$

$$\approx \exp(-\mathcal{L}(\underline{\theta}_m^*; m)) \int_{\mathbb{R}^{d(m)}} \exp\left(-\frac{1}{2}(\underline{\theta} - \underline{\theta}_m^*)' \mathbf{H}(\underline{\theta}_m^*; m)(\underline{\theta} - \underline{\theta}_m^*)\right) d\underline{\theta}$$

$$= \exp(-\mathcal{L}(\underline{\theta}_m^*; m))(2\pi)^{d(m)/2} \sqrt{|\mathbf{H}(\underline{\theta}_m^*; m)|}$$

where the last equality is obtained by integrating the $d(m)$-dimensional (scaled) Gaussian density. By the law of large numbers,

$$\lim_{T \to \infty} \frac{1}{T} \mathbf{H}(\underline{\theta}_m^*; m) = \mathsf{E}_{\underline{X} \sim \mathcal{X}} \frac{\partial^2 \log f}{\partial \theta^2}(\underline{X} : \underline{\theta}_m^*, m) =: h(\underline{\theta}_m^*; m).$$

Note that the determinant $|Th(\underline{\theta}_m^*; m)| = T^{d(m)} |h(\underline{\theta}_m^*; m)|$. So, for large $T = |\mathcal{X}|$,

$$- \log p(m) \approx -\mathcal{L}(\underline{\theta}_m^*; m) + \frac{d(m)}{2} \log(2\pi T) + \frac{1}{2} \log |h(\underline{\theta}_m^*; m)|.$$

Finally, it is shown in [77] that the third term becomes negligible for large T. The (remaining) first two terms on the right-hand side are the maximum data log-likelihood under model m and a term that depends on the model order (number of parameters) $d(m)$ of model m. These two terms form the *Bayesian information criterion* (BIC) cost, which can be minimized to select among different models $m \in \mathcal{M}$ for the dataset $\mathcal{X}$:

$$m^* = \arg \min_{m \in \mathcal{M}} \frac{d(m)}{2} \log(2\pi T) - \mathcal{L}(\underline{\theta}_m^*; m). \tag{3.14}$$

Note that the first term can be interpreted as the number of bits needed to describe the model, and the second (negative data log-likelihood) term as the number of bits to describe the data given knowledge of the model. Thus, the data log-likelihood trades off with the model order (model complexity) in the BIC objective. The BIC cost was shown in [238] to give a consistent estimator of model order.

3.4.2 High-Dimensional Data

While BIC and minimum description length (MDL) [219] are principled *and* practical criteria for selecting model order, they may yield unacceptable results when applied to very high-dimensional data domains (with the number of free parameters in the model growing with the data dimension). For example, for GMMs with full covariances, the number of covariance parameters for a single Gaussian grows quadratically in the feature dimension. In [86], it was shown that BIC chooses the number of mixture components as $M = 1$ for multinomial mixture modeling of the word count (bag of words) representation of some text document datasets even when it is known that the dataset contains documents from *many* different topics. Here, even though the dataset may contain thousands of documents, the document representation has one (word count) feature for each unique word in the dictionary (which may contain 30,000 unique words, even after standard word stemming and stop-listing are applied). The problem here is that there is one free (multinomial probability) parameter for every unique word, for *each* component in the model – for a model with 20 components, this means 600,000 free parameters (assuming a dictionary of size 30,000), even if the number of documents in the dataset is only a few thousand. In this situation, the model complexity term (number of bits to describe the model) *dominates* the BIC function. That is, increasing the number of mixture components M, while increasing the data log-likelihood, does so in a too modest fashion compared with the increase in model complexity. The result is that the BIC function sharply increases as M is increased above 1, with the BIC minimum occurring at $M = 1$ irrespective of the actual number of topics (components) present in the dataset.

To resolve this problem of gross model order underestimation, [86] did not give up on BIC. Rather, the number of free parameters in the model at fixed order M was greatly reduced by allowing tied (shared) parameters across components, with these sharing structures chosen so as to minimize the BIC objective. This "parsimonious" mixture modeling (PMM) approach yields much more reasonable model orders, consistent with the known number of topics present in the dataset; see Figure 3.2 (and Figure 13.1). Subsequent works extended this approach to allow parsimonious modeling of Gaussian mixtures with shared covariance parameters [164], as well as parsimonious topic models [246]. Full covariances can also be *heuristically* introduced to a PMM component (without full accounting under BIC) by simply using the mean outer product of the data samples most likely explained by that component, or all data samples weighted by their probability according to that component.

3.5   Principal Component Analysis (PCA) and Singular Value Decomposition (SVD)

Principal component analysis (PCA) is a linear transform technique for reducing the effective dimensionality of a feature vector $\underline{x} \in \mathbb{R}^N$, while introducing the least amount of distortion/error in the resulting approximation $\hat{\underline{x}}$ of $\underline{x}$. For classification problems, reducing the data dimension can alleviate high computational complexity of classifier decision-making [60]. It may also reduce training data requirements to achieve an accurate classifier, so it is one way to combat the so-called "curse of dimensionality" [63]. For density modeling (which could be the basis of statistical anomaly detection, discussed in the next section), dimensionality reduction associated with PCA can reduce the number of model parameters that need to be estimated. In this way, PCA can be used as a crude alternative approach to PMMs for overcoming the previously mentioned problem of "gross model order underestimation" for mixture models. Finally, closely related techniques, known as *transform coding*, are highly effective for lossy data compression as used, for example, in the standard JPEG image-compression algorithm.

In PCA, a feature vector $\underline{x} \in X = \{\underline{x}_i, i = 1, \ldots, T\}$ is approximated as:

$$\hat{\underline{x}} = \sum_{j=1}^{J} \beta_j \underline{q}_j + \underline{m},$$

where $\{\underline{q}_j\}_{j=1}^{J}$ are a set of *orthonormal vectors* for representing any $\underline{x} \in X$ with $J < N$; the "mean" vector $\underline{m}$ is also common to all $\underline{x} \in X$; and $\beta = (\beta_1, \ldots, \beta_J)' \in \mathbb{R}^J$ are the

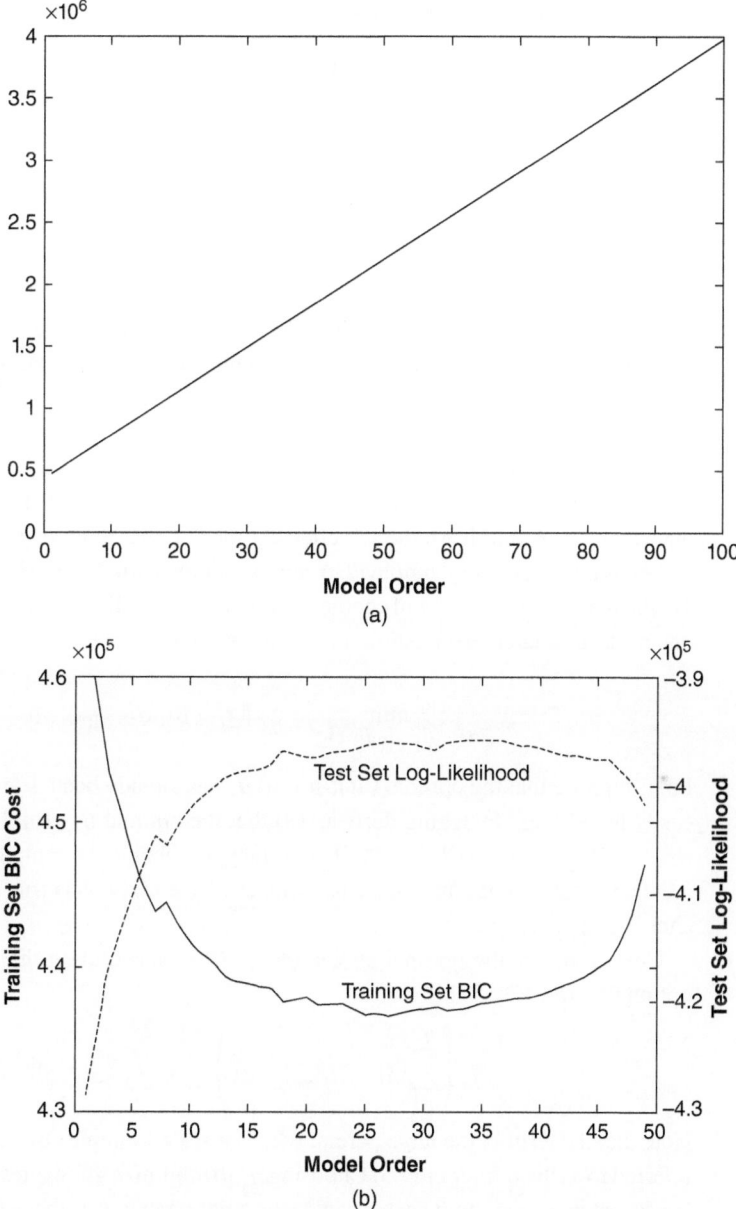

Figure 3.2 Multinomial mixture models applied to the *Reuters* news articles dataset [218], with 2000 articles. (a) BIC curve for a standard multinomial mixture. Note that the minimum BIC cost occurs at $M = 1$, that is, gross model order underestimation is exhibited. (b) BIC curve and the test set incomplete data log-likelihood for a parsimonious multinomial mixture model. Note that the model order where BIC is minimized by the parsimonious model coincides with good test set log-likelihood (which one would expect if the model order is chosen well). Reprinted from [86] with permission.

corresponding "optimal" coefficients for representing $\underline{x}$, that is, these coefficients are chosen to minimize the MSE "distortion"

$$\frac{1}{T} \sum_{i=1}^{T} \|\underline{x}_i - \hat{\underline{x}}_i\|^2.$$

The optimal choice of the mean vector, again in the sense of this MSE distortion, is the empirical mean of X,

$$\underline{m} = \frac{1}{T} \sum_{i=1}^{T} \underline{x}_i.$$

The $\underline{q}_j$ are called "components" (but note that this terminology is distinct from that employed in describing mixture densities – the components in PCA are basis vectors, not density functions). Rather than classifying (or detecting) based on $\hat{\underline{x}}$ explicitly, when PCA is used the input to the classifier (or detector) is the vector of coefficients β, where, in general, one chooses $J \ll N$ to achieve substantial dimension reduction. Likewise, in a density modeling framework (which could be part of a statistical anomaly detector), one would learn the joint density for β, rather than for $\hat{\underline{x}}$.

Let us consider a very simple PCA representation with $J = 1$, where $\hat{\underline{x}}_i = \beta_{1,i}\underline{q}_1 + \underline{m}$. To find the basis vector $\underline{q}_1$ and coefficients (with one coefficient β per data point $\underline{x} \in X$), one poses a squared error estimation problem on the given dataset X,

$$\min_{\beta_{1,1},\beta_{1,2},\dots,\beta_{1,T},\underline{q}_1} \sum_{i=1}^{T} \|\underline{x}_i - \beta_{1,i}\underline{q}_1 - \underline{m}\|^2. \tag{3.15}$$

First, suppose that the optimal (unit-norm) $\underline{q}_1$ has already been determined. Then, it is easily found (e.g., by taking derivatives) that the optimal $\beta_{1,i}$ (in the MSE sense) are $\beta_{1,i} = \underline{q}_1'(\underline{x}_i - \underline{m})$, $i = 1,\dots,T$. That is, they are obtained simply by *projecting* each (centered) data point onto the basis vector $\underline{q}_1$. Note that this is true *irrespective of* the choice of $\underline{q}_1$.

Next, consider the optimal choice of $\underline{q}_1$. After substituting the expression for the optimizing $\beta_{1,i}$, (3.15) becomes

$$-\underline{q}_1'\left(\sum_{i=1}^{T}(\underline{x}_i - \underline{m})(\underline{x}_i - \underline{m})'\right)\underline{q}_1 + \sum_{i=1}^{T}\|\underline{x}_i - \underline{m}\|^2.$$

Note that the term in the large parentheses is a scaled sample covariance matrix, often referred to as the *scatter matrix*. Choosing $\underline{q}_1$ to minimize this expression, subject to the constraint that $\underline{q}_1$ is a unit vector, yields the solution that $\underline{q}_1$ is the *principal eigenvector of the scatter matrix*, that is, the eigenvector with largest eigenvalue. Moreover, it is also clear from this expression that the minimum MSE choice for $\underline{m}$ is the empirical mean.

Similarly, if one considers $\hat{\underline{x}} = \sum_{j=1}^{J} \beta_j \underline{q}_j + \underline{m}$ for $J > 1$, the minimum MSE solution is to choose $\{\underline{q}_j\}_{j=1}^{J}$ as the J principal (orthonormal) eigenvectors of the scatter matrix (i.e., those with the largest eigenvalues), with the optimal coefficients $\underline{\beta}_i = \{\beta_{j,i}\}_{j=1}^{J}$

obtained by projecting $\underline{x}_i$ onto each of the $\underline{q}_j$, as above for $\underline{q}_1$. Thus, PCA can be performed in practice via eigendecomposition on the sample covariance matrix (using any established technique, e.g., [8, 103]), retaining the J components corresponding to the largest eigenvalues.

Theoretical properties of PCA that support its use include the following.

- The PCA representation preserves more variance in $\mathcal{X}$ (essentially, more information) than any other J-component representation.
- The PCA coefficients are completely statistically uncorrelated (i.e., this is a redundancy-free representation).
- Since PCA is based on an orthogonal decomposition, very good lossy compression performance can be achieved by separately (scalar) quantizing each coefficient $\beta_{i,j}$ rather than performing (much more computationally complex) vector quantization [76] on $\underline{\beta}_i = \{\beta_{i,j}\}_{j=1}^{J}$.

The last property greatly simplifies data compression systems that are widely used for digital images – hence, transform coding techniques closely related to PCA are the basis of image compression standards (e.g., JPEG).

For another perspective, consider the $N \times T$ matrix $\mathbf{X}_0$ formed by the *centered* dataset $\mathcal{X}$, that is the ith column of $\mathbf{X}_0$ is $\underline{x}_i - \underline{m}$. Let $Q := \min\{N, T\} \geq \text{rank}(\mathbf{X}_0)$. $\mathbf{X}_0$ has a singular-value decomposition (SVD)

$$\mathbf{X}_0 = \mathbf{A\Sigma B},$$

where $\mathbf{\Sigma} \in \mathbb{R}^{Q \times Q}$ is a diagonal matrix whose diagonal entries are called the singular values of $\mathbf{X}_0$, $\mathbf{A} \in \mathbb{R}^{N \times Q}$ has orthonormal columns, and $\mathbf{B} \in \mathbb{R}^{Q \times T}$ has orthonormal rows. $\mathbf{X}_0$ has $\text{rank}(\mathbf{X}_0)$ positive singular values (the rest are zero) (see, e.g., [103]).

One could reduce the feature dimension by focusing on the $J \leq \text{rank}(\mathbf{X}_0)$ largest (positive) singular values of $\mathbf{X}_0$. Define the $J \times J$ diagonal matrix $\mathbf{\Sigma}_J$ with these J singular values on the diagonal. Obtain $\mathbf{A}_J \in \mathbb{R}^{N \times J}$ by choosing the columns of $\mathbf{A}$ that correspond to these J singular values. Now consider the $J \times T$ matrix given by the Moore–Penrose pseudoinverse [24, 103] of $\mathbf{A}_J$,

$$\mathbf{B}_J = \mathbf{\Sigma}_J^{-1}(\mathbf{A}_J'\mathbf{A}_J)^{-1}\mathbf{A}_J'\mathbf{X}_0.$$

Here, note that we can identify the ith column of $\mathbf{B}_J$, $\underline{\beta}_i$, as a new feature vector with dimension $J < N$ for the ith sample $\underline{x}_i \in \mathcal{X}$,

$$\underline{\beta}_i = \mathbf{\Sigma}_J^{-1}(\mathbf{A}_J'\mathbf{A}_J)^{-1}\mathbf{A}_J'(\underline{x}_i - \underline{m}),$$

where $\underline{\beta}_i$ is the PCA feature vector described earlier.

Note that a solution $\mathbf{B}_J$ to $\mathbf{X}_0 = \mathbf{A}_J\mathbf{\Sigma}_J\mathbf{B}_J$ may not exist because this system of equations is over-specified (the number of variables is equal to $J < N$ which is the number of equations). The pseudoinverse gives, for all $i = 1, \ldots, T$,

$$\underline{\beta}_i = \arg\min_{\underline{b}} \|\underline{x}_i - \underline{m} - \mathbf{A}_J\mathbf{\Sigma}_J\underline{b}\|.$$

A completely different approach to feature reduction (i.e., feature *selection*, rather than feature compaction, which is what is achieved by PCA) is given in Appendix A.4.4. Also, recall the discussion in Section 2.13. One can also employ e.g. kernel-PCA (Appendix A.4.3) or auto-encoders (Section 2.3) when the data is confined to a manifold of a high-dimensional space.

3.6   Some Detection Basics

The maximum likelihood parameter estimation discussed previously is the basis for learning/estimating a generative model for a population that is also referred to as a "class" or a "hypothesis." Given an observed feature vector $\underline{x}$, suppose one wishes to distinguish between two generative hypotheses, H_0 and H_1. H_0 is, by convention, referred to as the "null" hypothesis, while H_1 is the "alternative" hypothesis. Also suppose, optimistically, that one has a training set of feature-vector realizations for *each* of these two hypotheses. Then, one possibility is to train a statistical classifier (such as a support vector machine or a deep neural network), via a supervised learning algorithm (i.e., based on *class-labeled* training data), which can then be used to decide between the hypotheses for any given (unlabeled) $\underline{x}$. Another approach, more in line with the theory of detection, would be to estimate a generative model f_i, separately, for each hypothesis H_i using its training set. One can then use a likelihood ratio test to decide between the two hypotheses, given $\underline{x}$. Here, one evaluates the density (likelihood) $f_i(\underline{x})$ under each hypothesis H_i, computes the ratio $f_0(\underline{x})/f_1(\underline{x})$, and compares this to a threshold $\eta > 0$ to make a decision, that is, to decide H_0 if $f_0(\underline{x})/f_1(\underline{x}) \geq \eta$, otherwise to decide H_1. (See the Neyman–Pearson lemma, e.g., in [228].) The true positive rate (TPR), also called the *power* of the test, is the probability of correctly deciding H_1,

$$P(f_0(\underline{X})/f_1(\underline{X}) < \eta \mid H_1). \tag{3.16}$$

Likewise, the false positive rate (FPR, or false alarm probability) is the probability of deciding H_1 when H_0 is true,

$$P(f_0(\underline{X})/f_1(\underline{X}) < \eta \mid H_0). \tag{3.17}$$

Each threshold value represents a distinct tradeoff between power and FPR. The likelihood ratio test, assuming accurate null and alternative models, has the highest power among all possible tests, given the FPR fixed.

Now, what if there is a training set of examples from H_0, but no examples from H_1? This is a commonly encountered scenario, often called the problem of statistical *anomaly detection*. Here, H_0 represents something that is known or "normal," and one wishes to identify whether a given $\underline{x}$ is unlikely to have been generated under H_0. It is also useful to assess *how unlikely* H_0 itself is.

Statistical anomaly detection applies a threshold to a *detection statistic* which is a function of the observation $\underline{x}$. For example, this statistic could be the density function evaluated at $\underline{x}$, conditioned on H_0, that is, $f_0(\underline{x})$. However, if the density is multimodal, a low density at $\underline{x}$ may not reliably detect anomalies. A more comprehensive detection statistic is commonly referred to as a *p-value*. This is the probability of observing a value "more extreme" than $\underline{x}$ under H_0, which can be obtained via an integral over the density function. For example, the p-value at $\underline{x}$ can be taken to be

$$P(f_{\underline{X}|H_0}(\underline{X}) < f_{\underline{X}|H_0}(\underline{x}) \mid H_0). \tag{3.18}$$

For a (scalar) random variable X, one can define "one-sided" p-values of x respectively as $P(X > x|H_0)$ (right tail) or $P(X < x|H_0)$ (left tail), particularly when $x > E(X|H_0)$ or $x < E(X|H_0)$. Such one-sided p-values represent the FPR when the detection threshold is x itself. For the special case of a Gaussian null density (which is unimodal and symmetric about its mean $\mu = E(X|H_0)$), the right-sided p-value at $x > \mu$ is

$$\int_x^\infty \frac{1}{\sqrt{2\pi}} e^{-\frac{(z-\mu)^2}{2\sigma^2}} \, dz,$$

where σ^2 is the conditional variance of X given H_0. There are several simple ways to numerically approximate this p-value (e.g., [96]).

Note that if $F(x) = P(X \leq x)$, $x \in \mathbb{R}$, in other words if it is the cumulative distribution function (cdf) of random variable X and $1 - F(X)$ is the right-sided p-value of a random sample X, then for arbitrary $x \in [0, 1]$,

$$P(1 - F(X) \geq x) = P(X \leq F^{-1}(1 - x)) = F(F^{-1}(1 - x)) = 1 - x.$$

Thus, the right-sided p-value

$$1 - F(X) \sim \text{uniform}[0, 1]. \tag{3.19}$$

The use of p-values is controversial in statistics, particularly when they are used for validating scientific discoveries. There are numerous reasons for this, including the following (i) one must account for multiple testing in properly assessing the level of significance of a deviation from the null, with controversy in how to properly correct p-values for such multiple testing; and (ii) small p-values, reflecting significant deviation from the null hypothesis, may occur *by chance*. Putting (i) and (ii) together, if one performs enough tests, one is eventually bound to "discover" a significant deviation from the null. As one particularly emphatic example of (ii), it is often of great interest to determine whether two phenomena are dependent, with H_0 the hypothesis that they are independent. [28] gives an example involving "number of people who drowned after falling out of a fishing boat in a given year" and "marriage rate in Kentucky in a given year." These two phenomena are clearly *unrelated* (the first phenomenon does not even limit itself to individuals from Kentucky), and yet they exhibit a statistically significant departure from independence.

However controversial p-values can be in statistics, their use for anomaly detection is on somewhat safer ground, given that the p-value is the FPR. That is, making detections when the p-value in (3.18) is less than ϕ sets the FPR at ϕ when deciding for $\underline{x}$, assuming the null model is accurate. If the null model is inaccurate, then the detection rule could either be too liberal (making too many false detections) or conservative (making too few false detections, and possibly too few true detections).

3.7   Performance Measures for Detection

The key performance measures for a detector have already been mentioned. These are relevant irrespective of whether the problem is supervised detection or unsupervised anomaly detection (where, for the latter, there are no known examples from the alternative hypothesis). Recall that the TPR (power) is the probability of correctly rejecting the null hypothesis, H_0, and the FPR is the probability of *falsely* rejecting the null hypothesis, Eqs. (3.16) and (3.17). Clearly, there is a tradeoff between power and false positives, which can be controlled by the choice of the detection threshold.

In many applications, the FPR must be kept to a very small value, even though this will also limit the attainable TPR. For example, in a cyber security context, each flagged detection may require human analyst confirmation or action (to mitigate the attack). Thus, a "too-high" FPR will overwhelm the analyst. In practice, one can use a held-out set of samples generated according to H_0 to estimate the FPR, with the detection threshold varied until the desired (estimated) FPR is achieved. The power can also be estimated *operationally*, for example, using the human analyst to label detections as true or false, and estimating the TPR based on the normalized count of true positives (this can also be used to operationally estimate the FPR). Moreover, in a controlled (supervised) setting where one has access to known examples from both H_0 and H_1, there are comprehensive measures of detection performance that can be assessed and used, for example, to benchmark-compare different detectors.

A standard such measure is the receiver operating characteristic (ROC) curve, which is a plot of power versus FPR. This plot can be generated by sweeping over a sequence of detection thresholds with increasing FPR, starting with a threshold achieving zero FPR (and possibly zero power as well), and ending with a threshold achieving both FPR and power equal to 1 (i.e., where everything is decided to H_1). The ROC area under the curve (ROC AUC) is a comprehensive measure of detection performance, with a maximum value of 1.0. One can also evaluate the curve only up to a maximum tolerable FPR, for example, $\delta < 1$, and then measure the area under the partial ROC curve (with maximal attainable value of δ).

Finally, accuracy (ACC) is just the probability of a correct decision. When there are only two choices, the accuracy is just the (unconditional) probability of a true positive or true negative:

$$P(f_0(\underline{X})/f_1(\underline{X}) < \eta \mid H_1)P(H_1) + P(f_0(\underline{X})/f_1(\underline{X}) \geq \eta \mid H_0)P(H_0). \qquad (3.20)$$

3.8   Chapter Summary

In this chapter we reviewed *unsupervised* learning techniques (those which do not rely on supervising target information), including expectation-maximization for learning a mixture density function, K-means clustering, which is a special case of EM for Gaussian mixtures, and PCA for determining derived features that, in a well-defined sense, preserve as much information as possible while allowing one to reduce data dimensionality. We also introduced detection criteria (p-values) and performance measures (true positive rate and false positive rate) that will be widely evaluated in experiments throughout the rest of the book.

Some questions to test the reader's understanding of the chapter include the following.

- Does EM maximize the complete data log-likelihood function?
- What does it mean to say that the M-step has a closed-form update?
- Are mixture components classes? Explain.
- What interpretation do you give to the α_j parameter in a mixture model?
- What does the word "parsimonious" mean in the context of parsimonious mixture models?
- What is the problem with the BIC plot of Figure 3.2?
- Can you suggest how to generalize the K-means objective and algorithm so that it also estimates the mass of each cluster?
- Explain the relationship between PCA and auto-encoding from Chapter 2.
- Suggest how PCA can be used within a data compression system.
- What are the potential benefits from (and/or applications of) applying PCA to a given dataset?
- Suggest an application where keeping false positives low is more important than maximizing true positives.
- Suggest an application where maximizing true positives is more important than minimizing false positives.

3.9   References for Further Reading

The material in this chapter is also covered in greater detail in general introductions to machine learning and pattern recognition such as [22, 63, 190]. Unsupervised detection of outliers is discussed in many references, for example, [36, 177, 298, 326]. [296] concerns modeling high-dimensional data. [42] concerns distributionally robust learning.

3.10   Projects: Receiver Operating Characteristic (ROC), Principal Component Analysis (PCA), and Gaussian Mixture Model (GMM)

3.10.1   ROC

Let us now look at a two-class problem. Class 1 has a two-dimensional Gaussian pdf with mean vector $\underline{\mu}_1 = [1, -1]'$ and covariance matrix

$$\mathbf{C}_1 = \begin{bmatrix} 1.01 & 0.2 \\ 0.2 & 1.01 \end{bmatrix}.$$

Class 2 has a two-dimensional Gaussian pdf with mean vector $\mu_2 = [-1, 1]'$ and covariance matrix $C_2 = I$ (the identity matrix). Suppose class 1 is twice as likely as class 2.

You are asked to do the following. (1) Generate 1000 data points according to this model for the two-class data. Note the Cholesky decomposition: $C_1 = AA'$, where upper triangular

$$A = \begin{bmatrix} \sqrt{1.01} & \frac{0.2}{\sqrt{1.01}} \\ 0 & \sqrt{1.01 - \frac{(0.2)^2}{1.01}} \end{bmatrix}. \tag{3.21}$$

Question: How can this decomposition be used in the data generation step? Record the number of points generated from each of the two classes. (2) Suppose class 1 represents "disease presence," with class 2 representing "disease absence." Write a short program to generate the ROC curve for this dataset (true detection rate on the y-axis and FPR on the x-axis). Explain your procedure for "sweeping out" the ROC curve. Produce a plot of your ROC curve and compute its AUC.

3.10.2   PCA

In this problem you will use PCA to "recover" the principal coordinates after a correlating rotation is applied to an (originally) uncorrelated multivariate Gaussian distribution. Do the following.

1. Generate 1000 realizations of a 10-dimensional, zero-mean multivariate Gaussian random feature-vector with $\sigma_1^2 = 2$, $\sigma_2^2 = 1$, $\sigma_i^2 = 0.2$, $i = 3, \ldots, 10$, and with the feature coordinates uncorrelated.
2. Create an orthogonal (rotation) matrix Q (the MATLAB command Q=orth(randn(10,10)) can achieve this). Verify that it is an orthogonal matrix.
3. Rotate the multivariate Gaussian data by multiplying by Q.
4. Compute the sample covariance matrix for the rotated random vector and verify that it is now correlated.
5. Use PCA to recover the principal components (based on eigendecomposition) of the sample covariance matrix.
6. Print out the variances of the ten principal components, in decreasing variance order. Compare with the variances σ_i^2 in (1) used to generate the data.
7. Plot the first two principal component coefficients for the 1000 data points. The vector of these components is often treated as a reduced-dimension feature vector, for example, input to a supervised classifier (in order to reduce the classifier's computational complexity and also its training data requirements).

3.10.3   GMM for Unsupervised Classification

In this problem, you are asked to implement the fixed point maximum-likelihood estimation (MLE, i.e., EM) algorithm for a mixture of Gaussians and apply it to "unsupervised" classification of a real-world dataset.

1. From the dataset directory of [278] get the files 'iris.names' and 'iris.data'. iris.names gives a description of the famous Iris dataset, consisting of example feature vectors measured for each of three types of Iris flowers. This dataset has been widely used, for many years, to illustrate and evaluate classification techniques. The Iris set consists of 150 examples, each consisting of a four-dimensional feature vector and a class label. You will need to preprocess iris.data to remove commas, to change class names to integer labels, and to save the class labels as a separate array.

2. Perform MLE on the 150 four-dimensional features. Assume three mixture components (one per class). For initial means, (randomly) select three feature vectors from the dataset. Assume initial variances are all equal (1.0 in each dimension) and assume initial equal prior probabilities. (You may assume initial off-diagonal covariance matrix entries are zero). Repeat the MLE for several different choices of initial means.

3. Perform unsupervised classification of each training vector, based on the learned model. (How to do this?) Measure and record the fraction of points in error, for each learned model.

4. To verify your MLE routine really works, plot the log-likelihood value versus number of fixed point iterations. Discuss.

5. How does the algorithm "behave" if the means (and other parameters) for each component are all initialized to the same values?

6. Try running with different numbers of components (3, 4, 5, or 6) and compare the BIC cost associated with the solution obtained at each given number of components.

4 Test-Time Evasion Attacks (Adversarial Inputs)

In this chapter we consider attacks that do not alter the machine learning model itself, but rather which seek to "fool" the classifier (plus any supplementary defense) into making erroneous decisions. As introduced in Chapter 1, these attacks are known as test-time evasion attacks (TTEs), adversarial inputs or adversarial samples. In addition to representing a threat to practical deployment of machine learning systems, TTEs also reveal the non-robustness of existing deep learning systems; they show that one can alter the class decision made by the DNN by making small changes to the input, changes which would **not** alter the (robust) decision-making of a human being, for example, performing visual pattern recognition. Thus, TTEs are a foil to claims that deep learning, in its current incarnations, is achieving truly robust pattern recognition, let alone that it is close to achieving the ultimate goal of artificial intelligence. So in addition to being a security threat, TTEs are a spur to the machine learning community to devise more robust pattern recognition systems. Solving this problem may in fact be a "holy grail" problem of AI.

We survey several types of defenses against TTEs in this chapter, including anomaly detection methods as well as robust classifier training methods. In fact, one very promising defense evaluated in this chapter – based on generative adversarial networks – weaves an adversary *controlled by the learner* into a game-theoretic learning framework. Thus, a kind of adversarial learning is effectively being leveraged to *defeat* adversarial learning attacks.

4.1 Previously Proposed Test-Time Evasion (TTE) Attacks

In this section, existing TTE attacks are reviewed in greater detail than in the overview given in Section 1.3. Our focus will be on DNN classifiers (categorical decision-makers). A regressor/predictor DNN, see Chapter 12, whose input is a TTE will produce an output which is a significant distance, assessed by some norm, from the correct output. Also, TTEs against contrastive DNNs, recall Section 2.12.3, are described in [122].

Early work on TTEs considered the spam email domain and relatively simple classifiers such as naive Bayes (recall Section 2.14), using "good word" attacks, wherein words associated with ham were introduced into spam documents in order to fool the classifier [162]. Subsequently, considering a two-class problem, [19] proposed a constrained objective function for the TTE attacker, seeking to choose a perturbed sample so as to minimize the discriminant function output (of the true class) while constraining the amount of perturbation from the original, clean pattern. They demonstrated their approach for SVM classification of images and PDF files and also showed how it could be extended to neural network classifiers. [260] considered DNNs, posed a related attacker optimization objective seeking "imperceptible" image perturbations that induce misclassifications, showed that this approach is highly successful in creating adversarial examples starting from legitimate images, and also showed that these adversarial examples seem to *transfer* well (i.e., they remain adversarial examples for other networks with different architectures and for networks trained on disjoint training sets from the same domain). There are much older optimization approaches closely related to [19] and [260], for example, [107], which was proposed for finding decision boundaries in neural networks, but which was not specifically applied to create adversarial test-time attacks (recall Section 2.10).

[19, 83, 260] are "global" methods, potentially altering all of a pattern's features (e.g., the values of all image pixels), but constraining the overall distortion introduced by the pattern perturbation. A variety of other global methods have also been proposed.

FGSM [83] is a simple form of global TTE attack. For each clean test sample $\underline{v}$ assumed correctly classified to a (source) class s (i.e., $\hat{c}(\underline{v}) = c(\underline{v}) = s$), a single-step perturbation is applied, with the direction related to the gradient of the loss function. That is, the (untargeted) FGSM perturbation is

$$\underline{\delta} = \varepsilon \cdot \text{sgn}(\nabla_{\underline{v}}(-\log \hat{p}(s|\underline{v}))) \tag{4.1}$$

where sgn computes the element-wise sign (± 1) of the components of the negative log class-posterior gradient, and the real hyperparameter $\varepsilon > 0$ controls the perturbation size so that the inferred class $\hat{c}(\underline{v} + \underline{\delta}) \neq s$ while at the same time $\underline{v} + \underline{\delta}$ hopefully (from the attacker's point of view) still resembles a class-s sample without obvious artifacts. The use of sgn greatly simplifies multiplication by ε, which may be more important for the "basic iterative method" (BIM) [133], also called iterative-FGSM (i-FGSM), which is the multi-step version of FGSM: for iteration $k = 0, 1, 2, 3, \ldots$

$$\underline{v}_{k+1} = \underline{v}_k + \varepsilon \cdot \text{sgn}(\nabla_{\underline{v}}(-\log \hat{p}(s|\underline{v}_k))), \tag{4.2}$$

with $\underline{v}_0 = \underline{v}$ and using a naturally smaller step size $\varepsilon > 0$ than for FGSM.

There are many variations of this untargeted attack, including clipping the result of each iteration so that the pixel intensities stay in their valid range (for the image domain), replacing $\hat{p}(s|\underline{v}_k)$ by $\hat{p}(s|\underline{v}_k)/\hat{p}(t|\underline{v}_k)$ or $\max_{i \neq t} \hat{p}(i|\underline{v}_k)/\hat{p}(t|\underline{v}_k)$ to create a class-t targeted version of the FGSM attack ($t \neq s$), and using the class logits $f_\kappa(\underline{v})$ instead of the softmax class posteriors $\hat{p}(\kappa|\underline{v})$ (recall (2.4)) as the former give a smoother cost surface on which to descend. PGD [271] is similar to BIM, but with the perturbation initialized at a random point on a ball around the test sample $\underline{v}$.

JSMA [203], on the other hand, cycles over individual features (pixels), one at a time, at each step modifying the pixel estimated to effect the most progress toward the classifier's decision boundary. This procedure is applied either until a successful decision change is induced or until the modified-pixel budget is reached. That is, JSMA restricts the *number* of modified features (pixels). However, this requires large changes for the modified features in order to induce a change in the classifier's decision (recall Figure 1.2 and see the project of Section 4.10 based on the related ZOO attack).

An improvement over prior TTE attack works is achieved by the CW [32, 33] and EAD [40] attacks. Both optimize regularized objective functions. CW regularization uses either the l_2 or l_∞ distance between the perturbed image and the original image, see (4.3) and see, for example, [110]. EAD regularization instead considers a linear combination of l_1 and l_2 distances.

More specifically, the CW attacker's objective function, to be minimized in crafting perturbations, focuses in a *discriminative* fashion on *two* classes: the target class (t) and the class other than the target class with the largest discriminant function value, which could be the true class of the original, clean sample. Let f_j denote class j's discriminant function, with the classifier using the winner-takes-all rule for input $\underline{x}$,

$$\hat{c}(\underline{x}) = \arg\max_j f_j(\underline{x}).$$

Then, given positive real hyperparameters $q, \lambda, \kappa > 0$, the CW attacker's optimization problem is as follows. Starting from a clean sample $\underline{x}$ that is correctly classified (to some source class $s \neq t$, where t is the target class of the attack), the attacker iteratively solves the following problem:

$$\min_{\underline{z}} \|\underline{z} - \underline{x}\|_q + \lambda \max\{\max_{j \neq t} f_j(\underline{z}) - f_t(\underline{z}), -\kappa\}. \tag{4.3}$$

Recall (2.18). The following comments are noted about this attack.

1. Minimizing (4.3) seeks the perturbed pattern that, while constrained in q-norm distance to $\underline{x}$, maximizes the discriminant function difference between that of the target class and that of the nearest competitor class, that is, it maximizes "confidence" in decision-making to class t. However, misclassifications with very high confidence are not necessarily sought. Thus, the hyperparameter κ controls the maximum allowed confidence in the decision. While the authors show in [33] that increasing κ increases attack *transferability*, they do not suggest how to choose κ in the case where there is a detector in play which is unknown to the attacker – it is unclear what level of decision confidence will be consistent with being detection evasive.
2. The hyperparameter λ controls the tradeoff between inducing a misclassification and the amount of pattern perturbation. If λ is too small, the penalty on the size of perturbations may be too large to allow class-decision alteration. If λ is too large, misclassifications will be induced but the perturbations may be large (and hence human perceptible and/or machine detectable). This hyperparameter is chosen via a binary search procedure, seeking the smallest value inducing misclassifications.
3. Another hyperparameter is the maximum number of iterations. Thus, a (computation constrained) CW attack may not successfully induce a decision to the target class.
4. [32] showed that with just full knowledge of the classifier, the black box CW attack (i.e., with no knowledge of a possible defense) defeats many TTE defense schemes, including some anomaly detection (AD) defenses.

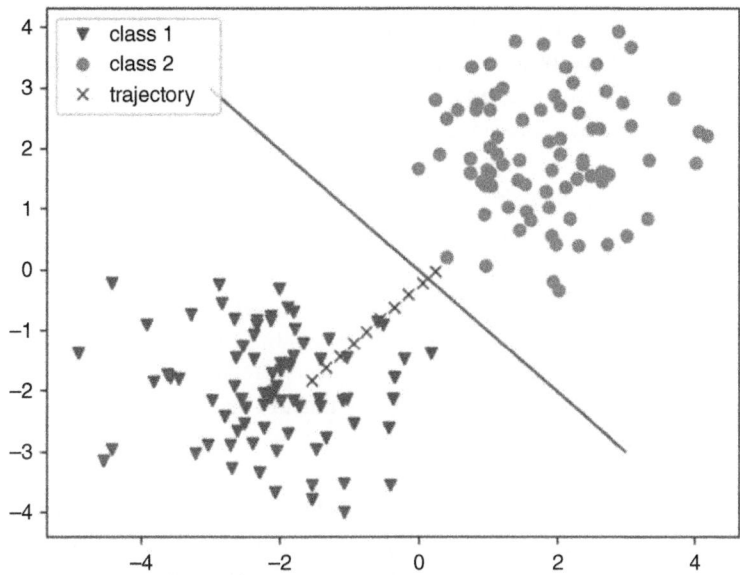

Figure 4.1 Trajectory of a low-confidence CW attack from class 1 to class 2 where the binary classifier involves a single Gaussian density per class in two dimensions.

5. While [32] gives an extensive benchmark experimental study, they do not consistently report FPRs for the evaluated detection methods, for example consider the evaluation of [68] in the "black box" case in [32].
6. [32] also asserts that as a defender "one must also show that an adversary aware of the defense cannot generate attacks that evade detection." We refer to this as the *strong white box* requirement and discuss it further at the end of this chapter.

See Figure 4.1 for a (visualizable) example trajectory of a "low-confidence" CW attack (where the pattern is pushed only *just* across the decision boundary) for a two-class ($K = 2$) problem in the plane ($N = 2$).

Adversarial perturbations $\underline{\delta}$ for the *white box* version of the CW attack applied to a clean, correctly classified input $\underline{x}$ are found by solving the following optimization problem:

$$\min_{\underline{z}} A(\underline{z}) + \gamma \Delta(\underline{z}), \tag{4.4}$$

where A is the loss function of the CW attack (4.3), the hyperparameter $\gamma > 0$, and Δ is positive when a detection is made and is non-decreasing with detection confidence. Note that this approach relies on complete knowledge not only of the classifier but also of the detector, including the threshold value used in making detections. This (additive) cost is minimized when an adversarially perturbed image is *both* misclassified to the target class and undetected.

Universal TTE attacks on DNNs have also been proposed, that is, a *single* perturbation vector that induces classification errors when added to *most* test patterns for a given domain [186]. This work is important because it is suggestive of the fragility of DNN-based classification. However, a *single* perturbation vector required to induce errors on nearly *all* test patterns will, in general, be "larger" than a customized perturbation designed to successfully misclassify a *single* (particular) test pattern. Thus, images perturbed by a universal attack should be more easily detected than those perturbed by the pattern-customized attacks previously discussed.[1]

Although the previous works could in principle be applied to any classification domain working in some (pattern) space, they all focused experimentally on images. There has been related work on other domains, including voice [31, 34, 74], music [118, 119], and text [72, 111, 213, 318]. [31] developed an iterative procedure, with a human attacker in the loop, to generate voice commands that are recognized by a speech recognition system and yet which are not human comprehensible. In [119], the authors showed that changes to the music's tempo degrade the accuracy of a DNN but do not affect a human being's capability to classify the musical genre. This suggests (unsurprisingly) that the DNN is not using the same "reasoning" as a human being in performing music classification. In [118], the authors modify the TTE attack approach in [260] to be suitable for the music domain. This would be straightforward, except that the classification is performed on individual "frames" that are temporally overlapping. Thus, in constructing a TTE attack for a given frame, one should ensure consistency with all frames with which the given frame overlaps. This problem is addressed in [118] using an iterative projection algorithm. A good reference more exhaustively covering the variety of TTE attacks on images that have been proposed, as well as papers that seek (though with no full closure to date) to explain *why* DNNs are susceptible to TTEs, is [3].

Discussion: Proactively Testing a DNN

In some application domains, the range of typical ("natural" or "realistic") inputs to the DNN is significantly smaller than the input space ($\mathbb{R}^N$). To test a DNN for possible operational failure modes or hidden fragilities, a developer may want to try to produce input samples which "look natural" but for which the DNN gives incorrect outputs. To this end, note that the white box TTE attack (4.4) could aim to produce natural inputs (i.e., indistinguishable from the training samples from its source class) if, for example, Δ is chosen as a p-value according to a modeled null distribution of the training dataset (or some DNN-embedded features it activates); see Section 4.8. Retraining the DNN with the training set augmented by such synthetic samples may improve its performance on natural test samples, but this alone may not be an effective defense against TTEs.

4.2   "Robust" and "Certified" Defenses for Test-Time Evasion (TTE) Attacks

Robust classification defenses aim to *correctly* classify TTE examples, while maintaining high test accuracy in the absence of attacks. Previous defenses have tried

---

[1] The following chapters concern backdoor attacks, in which the adversary poisons the training dataset to enable such universal adversarial perturbations (backdoor triggers) against the poisoned DNN at test time.

preprocessing the data, using a robust training objective, or training with adversarial examples. These three approaches are now reviewed.

4.2.1   Feature Obfuscation

This approach alters features so as to hopefully destroy the attack pattern. For example, [288] considers DNNs for digit recognition and malware detection. They randomly *nullify* (zero) input features, both during training and testing/inference. This may "eliminate" perturbed features in a test-time pattern. However, for the malware domain, the features as defined in [288] are *binary* $\in \{0,1\}$. Thus, nullifying (zeroing) does not necessarily alter a feature's original value (if it is already zero). Instead, simply randomly flipping binary features may improve the performance of [288].

In [315] and [151], quantization is used to destroy small perturbations. However, if the perturbation size exceeds a quantization threshold, the perturbation could instead be amplified, possibly making the attack more effective.

[146] performs blurring of test patterns (images) in order to destroy a possible attacker's perturbations. This method was found to be not very effective in [179].

It was also shown in [85] that some attacks are quite fragile and that even the process of image capture (involving, e.g., cropping) may defeat the attack. Assuming the attack is on a physical object, not on an already digital image, image capture may provide some robustness against adversaries.

In [48], rather than blurring, noise is added to the image to potentially destroy adversarial perturbations. In their approach, the class decision of each test sample x is taken as the most common class decision $\hat{c}(x+v)$ by the trained classifier among inputs $x + v$, for different isotropic Gaussian noise realizations v. In this way, $\hat{c}$'s decision is locally "smoothed" to effectively create an ensemble decision function, $\hat{g}$. The noise variance can be chosen to limit misclassifications by $\hat{g}$ on the DNN's ($\hat{c}$'s) training dataset, or on an identically distributed labeled validation set held out of training. A disadvantage of [48] is that, even with this judicious setting of the noise variance, the resulting classifier may be biased, that is, accuracy may be degraded in the absence of attacks. The ODDS method of [221] improves upon [48] by accounting for class confusion using a Z-score.

Note that one common drawback of feature obfuscation is that it may introduce a significant tradeoff between accuracy in correctly classifying attacked examples and accuracy in the *absence* of attacks (i.e., robust classification may introduce classifier bias). Moreover, whereas in principle quantization, being non-differentiable, can defeat gradient-based TTE attacks, such a defense can still be overcome by *transferred* attacks, where the adversary learns a *surrogate* classifier whose gradients can be evaluated [30, 202]. Note that it is sometimes assumed that the attacker has access to its own separate dataset, i.i.d. with the actual training set X, which is used to train a surrogate classifier. A TTE attack is then performed on the surrogate. The premise is that a successful TTE attack on the surrogate will also induce a successful misclassification on the actual classifier. This attack *transferability* is further discussed in Chapter 11.

4.2.2   Certified Training

Several robust training approaches, dubbed *certifiably robust* training, are designed
to ensure decision consistency in a local region, for example, an l_2 ball of radius ϵ
around each training pattern as in [120, 127, 272] ([127] considers ReLU neurons with
bounded outputs). To this end, [272] trains to maximize the classification margin, that is,
a lower bound on the difference between the score for the true class and the largest score
considering all other classes, over all training samples. Alternatively, such robustness
may be achieved by first deriving an upper bound on adversarial loss (the expected loss
incurred for a given distribution of perturbations around a given input pattern) in the
region around the training examples (i.e., the supposed "certified" region), and then
minimizing this upper bound while training the classifier. For example, [216] (focusing
on single-layer classifiers) bounds the adversarial loss in the l_∞ ball by bounding the
gradient for all points in the ball. Compared with approaches that only consider the local
gradient of each training pattern, [216] provides greater secured robustness. But finding
a tight upper bound on adversarial loss is a difficult optimization problem requiring
heavy computation, especially for DNNs with a complicated structure [15, 294]; hence,
certified robustness is hard to achieve in practice. Also, such robust training does not
guarantee a class-consistency region of prescribed size about nominal *test* samples and
often biases the classifier (*reduces* accuracy) in the absence of attacks [216, 272].

In, for example, [46, 120, 272], the authors regularized the DNN training objective to
control the local Lipschitz continuity constant of each layer, so that perturbations added
to input patterns will not significantly affect the signals forward-propagated through
the network. However, the local Lipschitz constant is specific to the type of layer, and
may be difficult to precisely derive for a complex DNN [67]. Recall Section 2.9.

Finally, note that neither [46] nor [272] evaluated whether their classifiers are robust
to TTE attacks that transfer from a surrogate classifier, which is suggested in [30] as a
necessary evaluation step.

4.2.3   Robust Training

Some TTE defenses are based on *robust* training of the classifier, such that a test
pattern from class A that is perturbed by an attacker is still decided to class A by
the classifier. Robust classification is an important goal, especially considering the
presence of "natural" adversaries – additive noise, transformations (image rotation,
translation, scaling, variable lighting, etc.). However, the robust classification works
[55, 146, 204, 288, 322] do not mention achieving robustness to natural adversaries,
but rather solely to TTEs.

An early robust training approach is [55], which modifies the support vector machine
(SVM) training objective to ensure the learned weight vector is not sparse, i.e., that
it makes use of all the features. Thus, if an attacker corrupts some features, other
(unperturbed) features will still contribute to decision-making. However, [55] may fail
if only a few features are strongly class discriminating.

For DNN classifiers, a distillation defense was proposed in [204], first training a
DNN, and then using the class posteriors of each training pattern as "soft" labels,

which are then used to *retrain* the DNN. This scheme essentially amounts to a type of regularization of the DNN. However, this defense was found to be ineffective against the CW attack [33].

4.2.4   Adversarially Robust Training

First proposed in [260], an adversarially trained classifier learns to minimize an *expected* training loss, where the expectation is over a distribution of bounded adversarial perturbations. This is also a customized (adversarial) type of training data augmentation, which can be used to retrain the DNN, to potentially improve its performance. Adversarially perturbed training patterns can be obtained by applying *existing* attacks, for example, FGSM and CW, to clean training patterns using either the victim classifier [134] or a surrogate classifier [266].

Compared with robust "certified" training approaches which use an l_∞ ball to create training dataset perturbations, adversarial training uses an estimate of "worst-case" perturbations, which is less accurate but more computationally efficient. However, these approaches provide limited robustness, as explicated next.

4.2.5   Key Limitations of Robust Classification Defenses

No Guaranteed Test Set Robustness

As mentioned, even though certifiably robust and adversarially robust training may give classification-robustness guarantees in the vicinity of the training patterns, such guarantees do not generalize to the test set. Thus, in practice they may not offer much protection against TTEs. Moreover, these methods may only provide robustness to attacks that were used during the adversarial training. In particular, for the CIFAR-10 domain (low resolution, color images [129]), for which clean test accuracy is $> 90\%$, it was shown in [180] that the adversarially robust classifier training in [271] (based on use of CW attack examples to augment the training set) only achieved 50% accuracy when evaluated on PGD attack examples.

Computational Complexity and Convergence

Let us consider the following iterative process. (i) Given the current trained DNN, use a known TTE attack to create new adversarial samples, which are then added to the training set. (ii) Given the new training set, conventional training is applied to create a newly trained DNN. There are several concerns with such a robust training approach. First, DNN training is already computationally heavy – iterative retraining is even more costly. Second, this iterative algorithm may not converge (e.g., if the stopping condition is that no new, sufficiently evasive, adversarial samples are found). Due to the potentially enormous complexity of decision boundaries, even retraining with a thoroughly thus augmented training set will not guarantee that an attacker with a "clean" test sample $\notin \mathcal{X}$ cannot construct a successful (imperceptible) TTE attack using one of the attack strategies that were used to augment, *let alone* using a new (zero-day) TTE attack, that is, one that was not used to augment the training set. Moreover, adversarial training may not even require an increase in the perturbation size needed to induce successful attacks (and even when it does, imperceptible "high-confidence" TTEs with large perturbation sizes have been demonstrated, recall Figure 1.3 and see Tables 4.3–4.5). Finally, the thus "robustified" DNN may not generalize well for clean test samples (drawn from the same distribution as the training samples in X) since adding TTE samples to the training set may bias the learned decision rule. Thus, even if the robust classifier is good at classifying attacked examples, its accuracy on clean (attack-free) examples may be (unacceptably) poor. This is typical of a classical tradeoff, for example [18, 271].

Semantics of Inference

Another limitation of robust classification to combat TTEs concerns semantics of inferences. Consider digit recognition. Evasion-resistance means a perturbed version of '5' is still classified as a '5'. This *may* make sense if the perturbed digit is still objectively recognizable (e.g., by a human) as a '5'. (Even in this case, the decision may have no legitimate utility, as will be clarified in Section 4.7.1.) However, the perturbed example may not be unambiguously recognizable as a '5'. Recall from Figure 1.2 the perturbed digit examples based on JSMA with significant salt and pepper noise and other artifacts. Some attacked examples from classes '5', '3', and '8' are noticeably ambiguous. This suggests, at a minimum, that there should be a "don't know" category to account for possible TTE attacks.

However, irrespective of assigning the pattern to the correct class (which might in fact be "don't know"), it may be crucial *operationally* to infer that the classifier is being subjected to an evasion attack. Robust classification does not make such an inference. Once an attack is detected, measures to defeat the attack may be taken, for example, blocking the access of the attacker to the classifier through the use of multi-factor (challenge-response) authentication involving a human supervisor. Moreover, actions typically made based on the classifier's decisions may either be preempted or conservatively modified. For example, for an autonomous vehicle, once an attack on its image recognition system is detected, the vehicle may take the following action sequence: (i) slow down, move to the side of the road, and stop; (ii) await further instructions. Similarly, a device that is actuated based on recognized voice commands might require multi-factor authentication, invoke "least privilege" rules, or simply be put into a "sleep" mode once an attack is detected. In a medical diagnostic setting, with an automated classifier used, for example, for pre-screening numerous scans, a radiologist should obviously not try to make a diagnosis based upon an attacked image – if the attack is detected the patient can be re-scanned. In, for example, [55, 204, 288], it is presumed that correctly classifying attacked test patterns is the right objective, without considering attack detection as a separate, important inference objective.

Assumed Full Knowledge of the Classifier

Finally, note that many TTE attacks (whether realistically or not) assume full knowledge of the classifier. Thus, a TTE attack may be successful even when the classifier was "robustly" trained as described above, as the attacker may possess full (or substantial) knowledge of the robust classifier; for example, the proactive distillation defense in [204] was not effective against an attack designed to defeat it [33]. Likewise, [325] is a reactive attack tailored to defeat the classifier from [271]. These are instances of the attack-defense arms race where the *reactive* player with more knowledge (in this case the attacker) has the advantage over the *proactive* player with less knowledge (the defender).

4.3   Anomaly Detection (AD) of Test-Time Evasion (TTE) Attacks

In this section we consider *detection*, rather than robust classification, as a defense against TTEs. The techniques discussed in the sequel for detecting TTE attacks can also be used to detect test samples which are anomalous with respect to the (existing) training dataset, see Section 4.8 on *out-of-distribution detection* (OODD). After careful human labeling, such samples can form the basis of useful retraining or refining of the decision-making system, that is, *active learning* (see Chapter 12), to address

- inadequacies of the current training dataset that are not adversarial in nature,
- "model drift," where the operational/test-set distribution dynamically changes over time and becomes significantly different from the distribution of the (current) training dataset.

In, for example, [32] it is argued that robust classification of attacked images is difficult, while detection is "easier." An argument in support of this is that if one designs a good robust classifier, then one gets a (potentially good) detector essentially "for free" – one may make detections when the robust classifier's decision disagrees with a conventional (non-robust) classifier's decision. Likewise, considering methods which "correct" a test sample (e.g., an image) $\underline{x}$ containing an attack, for example, by blurring it, producing a new sample $\underline{x}'$, one can build a single classifier and make an attack detection when $\hat{c}(\underline{x}) \neq \hat{c}(\underline{x}')$. However, such detection architectures, based on robust classification, are obviously not necessarily optimal. In particular, considering the two-classifier approach, if there is significant classifier error rate, then there are two significant sources for classifier non-consensus: (i) a successful TTE attack on the conventional classifier and its correction by the robust classifier, and (ii) misclassification of a clean (attack-free) pattern by one (or both) of the classifiers. Moreover, irrespective of whether detection is truly "easier," this argument (that detection is essentially a subset of robust classification) is not made by many of the proposed robust classification defenses – it is simply assumed that the only objective of interest is to defeat the attack by correctly classifying in the face of it. Again, attack detection is not even considered in [55, 146, 204, 288, 322].

By contrast, we will point out in Section 4.7.1 that, in some scenarios, when an attack is present, making robust classification inferences in fact has *no* utility. Moreover, it will be argued that the attacker has a natural mechanism for *learning* a robust classifier (and then targeting it) – querying – whereas he/she may have no ability to query so as to learn an AD that may be in play.

Irrespective of the motivation given, there has been substantial recent work on detection of TTEs. Various approaches have been proposed, with an initial benchmark comparison study given in [32] evaluating a number of methods against the CW attack [33], which was demonstrated in [32, 33] to be more difficult to detect than earlier attack methods such as FGSM and JSMA.

4.3.1   Supervised Detection of TTEs

One strategy is to treat the detection problem as supervised, using labeled examples of "known" attacks. The resulting binary classifier (attack versus no attack) can then be experimentally evaluated both on the known attacks and on unknown attacks. Examples of such systems include [87] and the supervised approach taken in [68]. However, [87] failed to detect the (treated as unknown) CW attack on the CIFAR-10 image domain [32]. [68] similarly proved unsuccessful in detecting CW on CIFAR-10 [32]. [146] also treated the problem as supervised, applying a multi-stage classifier, with each stage working on features derived from a deep layer of the trained DNN classifier. A detection is made unless all the stages decide the image is attack-free. [32] demonstrates this detector performs very poorly on CW applied both to the MNIST and CIFAR-10 domains. [173], which feeds a DNN classifier's deep layers as features to a supervised detector, is more successful. The best results reported for this supervised method in detecting CW on CIFAR-10 were 81% true positive rate (TPR) at a false positive rate (FPR) of 28% [32].

We also note SID [262], a supervised method for images, where two networks are trained on the original images and the weighted average wavelet transform (WAWT) of the images respectively. Embedded features of the two networks are fed into a binary classifier to perform detection.

A general problem with supervised detectors is that they may not *generalize* well to detect attacks unseen during their training; see for example, [173]. This is an important limitation, as the defender will not have detailed knowledge/examples of all possible attacks. In the following, *unsupervised* detectors that significantly exceed the performance of supervised detectors will be reviewed.

4.3.2   Unsupervised AD for TTEs Without an Explicit Null Model

Some unsupervised ADs are based on explicit null hypothesis (no attack) statistical models for input patterns, and some are not. One crude approach is simply to reject if the maximum a posteriori class probability (produced by the classifier) is less than a given threshold. Use of such "confidence" was shown to be effective for detection of a classifier's *misclassified* samples in [98], although effective detection of adversarial inputs may require more powerful methods. Another non-parametric approach is based on principal component analysis (PCA) [99] (recall Section 3.5). However, [32] found that, while successful on MNIST, this approach has essentially no power to distinguish attacks from non-attacks on CIFAR-10.

A more sophisticated non-parametric detector is [171]. This method extracts nonlinear components via an auto-encoding neural network; recall Section 2.13. It also uses somewhat unconventional decision-making, *combining* classification and detection – images whose (auto-encoding based) reconstruction error is large are detected as attacks. Images whose reconstruction error is small are sought to be correctly classified. However, it may be desirable to make detections even when the attack is potentially subtle. A primary concern with this detector is that it requires setting a number of hyperparameters (specifying the auto-encoding network architecture, which in fact required different settings for MNIST and CIFAR-10, and softmax "temperature" parameters, recall Eq. (2.5)). Setting hyperparameters in an unsupervised AD setting can be difficult. If labeled examples of an attack are available, one can set hyperparameters to maximize a measure based on a labeled validation set. However, the attack is then no longer "unknown" and the detection method is actually supervised. (An alternative, if only attack-free examples are available, is to set detection hyperparameters to fix the false positive rate (FPR) of the detector.) [171] also incurs some degradation in classification accuracy in the absence of an attack – from 90.6% to 86.8% on CIFAR-10 [171].

4.3.3   Ensemble Defense Strategy

Another defense strategy is to employ an *ensemble* of classifiers. One motivation for an ensemble is that there may be multiple data modalities, with each potentially warranting a dedicated classifier. For example, speech recognition can be performed separately based on audio-only classification and video-only classification (video of the movement of the mouth). Likewise, for automated target recognition, multiple imaging modalities may be used. If the attacker only has knowledge of some of the classifiers in the ensemble, but not all of them, the attacker may fail to defeat an ensemble classification system. Alternatively, even if the attacker has knowledge of all the classifiers in the ensemble, the computational effort of the attacker, to craft an example that defeats an ensemble system, will be greater than that required to defeat a single, standalone classifier. Thus, ensembles do represent a promising approach for achieving resilience against TTE attacks, as well as for making it more difficult and costly to launch successful attacks.

4.3.4   Unsupervised AD Based on an Explicit Null Hypothesis

A generic DNN-based detection plus classification system is shown in Figure 4.2, with classification performed if no attack is detected.

One such detection approach with an explicit null hypothesis is [17]. This approach computes the distance between a DNN internal layer's class-conditional mean feature vector and the test image's feature vector and then evaluates this, under the null hypothesis of no attack, using a Weibull distribution. A few limitations of [17] are that (i) it does not model the *joint* density of a deep layer – such a model would exploit more information than just the (scalar) distance, and (ii) [17] is not truly

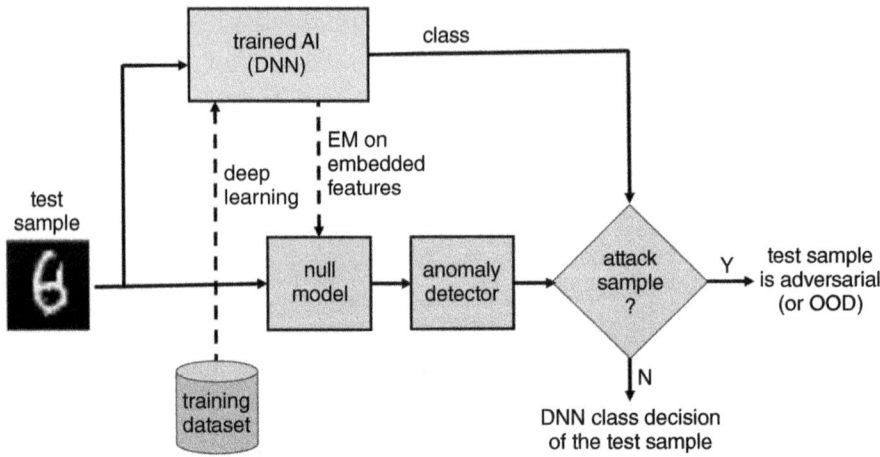

Figure 4.2 Anomaly detection based on detection statistics derived from internal layers (embedded features) of a DNN. Classification of the test sample is performed if no anomaly is detected. Otherwise, the test sample is reported as adversarial (as is the case for the depicted test sample), or more generally as an anomaly with respect to the training dataset, that is, as "out-of-distribution" (OOD). Instead of applying traditional null density based detection (by assuming a particular null density parametric distribution, such as an exponential distribution), GAN based detection can be used, see Section 4.5. Moreover, the null model could be based on other feature representations of the training set, for example, by using PCA (Section 3.5) or an auto-encoder (Section 2.13).

unsupervised – several hyperparameters are set by maximizing a validation measure that requires labeled examples of the attack. The experiments in [179] show that an unsupervised AD outperforms [17] even though [17]'s detector was (optimistically) allowed to use more than 100 labeled examples of the attack as part of its validation set.

One method proposed in [68] used a kernel density estimator (recall (3.12)) to model the penultimate layer of a DNN. However, ultimately, they put forward a *supervised* method, learning to discriminate 'attack' from 'no attack', leveraging their density model to create the discriminator's input features. They ultimately settled on a supervised method because their unsupervised detector did not achieve very good results. In [32], it was found that the unsupervised AD of [68] grossly fails on CW attacks on CIFAR-10 – 80% of the time, attacked images had even *higher* likelihood under the null model in [68] than the original (unattacked) images. The more effective unsupervised anomaly detection of attacks (ADA) [179] method is described next.

Summary of the ADA Method [179]

Let us now consider a successful, targeted TTE attack example $\underline{x}$, one which was obtained by starting from a "clean" (correctly classified) example $\underline{v}$ from some putative source class s (*unknown* to the defender), and then perturbing it until the DNN's decision on this perturbed example (now $\underline{x}$) is no longer s, but is now $d \neq s$ (the "destination" or "target" class). That is,

$$\hat{c}(\underline{x}) = d \neq s = \hat{c}(\underline{v}) = c(\underline{v}).$$

The premise behind [68] is that feeding an *attacked* version $\underline{x}$ of $\underline{v}$, not $\underline{v}$ itself, into the DNN and extracting the vector of activations (embedded features) from some internal layer of the DNN will result in an embedded feature vector $\underline{z}$ that has atypically low likelihood under a learned *null* density model (i.e., the estimated distribution for the random vector $\underline{Z}$ when no attack is present) conditioned on the DNN predicted class $Y = d \in \mathcal{Y}$. Denote these estimated null densities for $\underline{Z}$, conditioned on each class $y \in \mathcal{Y}$, by $f_{\underline{Z}|Y}(\underline{z}|y)$.

If the adversarial perturbation of $\underline{v}$ is not very large (so that the TTE $\underline{x}$ is human imperceptible and/or machine detection evasive), one might *also* expect that $\underline{z}$ will exhibit *too much typicality* (too high a likelihood) under some class other than d, that is, under the *source* category, s. This additional information is exploited by ADA. It does not matter that the source class is unknown to the defender. One can simply determine the best estimate of this class, for example, as:

$$s = \arg\max_{y \in \mathcal{Y} \setminus d} f_{\underline{Z}|Y}(\underline{z}|y). \tag{4.5}$$

(In [179], a hard decision on the source category is not in fact made. Rather, so as not to discard information, the ADA detection statistic is based on an expectation over all classes (other than d) as possible source classes of an attack.) Accordingly, it was hypothesized that attack patterns will be *both* "too atypical" under d and "too typical" under s. This is roughly illustrated by Figure 1.1.

While this may seem to require use of two detection thresholds, a single, theoretically grounded decision statistic that captures both requirements (assessing "atypicality" with respect to d and "typicality" with respect to s) is now given. Specifically, using (4.5) define a two-class posterior pmf evaluated with respect to the (density-based) null model for an embedded feature vector $\underline{z}$ activated by a possible TTE attack input $\underline{x}$ with $\hat{c}(\underline{x}) = d$:

$$P = [P_d, P_s] = \left[\frac{f_{\underline{Z}|Y}(\underline{z}|d)}{f_{\underline{Z}|Y}(\underline{z}|d) + f_{\underline{Z}|Y}(\underline{z}|s)}, \frac{f_{\underline{Z}|Y}(\underline{z}|s)}{f_{\underline{Z}|Y}(\underline{z}|d) + f_{\underline{Z}|Y}(\underline{z}|s)} \right].$$

Similarly define a corresponding pmf based on the normalized two-class DNN posterior:

$$Q = [Q_d, Q_s] = \left[\frac{\hat{p}(d|\underline{x})}{\hat{p}(d|\underline{x}) + \hat{p}(s|\underline{x})}, \frac{\hat{p}(s|\underline{x})}{\hat{p}(d|\underline{x}) + \hat{p}(s|\underline{x})} \right].$$

Both deviations ("too atypical" and "too typical") are captured in the Kullback–Leibler divergence decision statistic:

$$D_{\mathrm{KL}}(P\|Q) = \sum_{k \in \{d,s\}} P_k \log \left(\frac{P_k}{Q_k} \right),$$

that is, a detection is declared when this statistic exceeds a given threshold (which can be set by using a clean dataset to fix the false positive rate).

ADA's hypothesis that an attacked pattern will exhibit both "too high atypicality" (with respect to d) and "too high typicality" (with respect to s) is not based on any strong assumptions about the attacker. It merely assumes the perturbation is constrained to be small to be human imperceptible and/or machine detection evasive. This constraint may necessitate that a TTE attack input x will exhibit unusually low likelihood under class $d = \hat{c}(x)$ and unusually high likelihood under class s given by (4.5). ADA's hypothesis may be best suited to detecting "low-confidence" attacks, rather than "high-confidence" ones (for which the likelihood of the source class may be low).

The baseline ADA method was further improved as follows:

1. modeling the joint density of a deep layer using mixture density-based null hypothesis models (in particular, through log-normal mixture density modeling to match to the *non-negative support* of ReLU layers), recall Chapter 3;
2. exploiting *multiple* DNN layers by taking the *maximum* of the ADA statistic over each of the layers being evaluated (ADA-maxKL);
3. accounting for source class uncertainty by computing an expected ADA statistic based on the estimated probabilities for each of the classes being the source class;
4. exploiting class confusion matrix information (if available), comprehensive *low-order* density modelling [214] and DNN weight information in constructing a best-performing ADA statistic [179], which demonstrated good results against published attacks, including CW.

The resulting method is called L-AWA-ADA-maxKL. [179] directly compared against several benchmark detection methods and also against the results reported in [32].

Note that ADA can also be augmented by a (second) detector using p-values of the estimated class-conditional null densities $f_{Z|Y}$, with the p-value threshold set to limit false positives on the training set, to try to detect high-confidence attacks [21] in particular.

While ADA requires the choice of a parametric null density family, we next discuss a *non-parametric* detection strategy, that is, one that does not require this choice.

4.4   Background on Generative Modeling and Generative Adversarial Networks (GANs)

4.4.1   Scalar Distributions

Suppose a dataset of scalar random samples $X = \{x_1, x_2, \ldots, x_T\}$ has been generated according to a common distribution. An unbiased estimate of the cumulative distribution function (cdf) is simply:

$$F_{\text{data}}(x) = \frac{1}{T} \sum_{i=1}^{T} \mathbf{1}\{x_i \leq x\}, \quad \forall x \in \mathbb{R}.$$

Now consider a cdf F (which was either specified or estimated from data as above) and a random variable U which is uniformly distributed over the real interval $[0, 1]$. It is easy to see that the random variable $F^{-1}(U)$ is distributed as F:

$$P(F^{-1}(U) \le x) = P(U \le F(x)) = F(x), \quad \forall x \in \mathbb{R}.$$

That is, the inverse cdf can be used as a stochastic generator to simulate random variable realizations following a prescribed distribution.

4.4.2 Multivariate Distributions

Suppose a dataset of vector random samples $X = \{\underline{x}_1, \underline{x}_2, \ldots, \underline{x}_T\} \subset \mathbb{R}^N$ has been generated according to a common multivariate distribution, where $N > 1$. Recall from (3.7) and (3.6) that an unbiased empirical estimate of the mean and an unbiased estimate of the covariance matrix of the sampled distribution are respectively given by:

$$\underline{\mu}_{\text{data}} = \frac{1}{T} \sum_{i=1}^{T} \underline{x}_i$$

$$\mathbf{C}_{\text{data}} = \frac{1}{T-1} \sum_{i=1}^{T} (\underline{x}_i - \underline{\mu}_{\text{data}})(\underline{x}_i - \underline{\mu}_{\text{data}})'.$$

If the sampled distribution is a multivariate Gaussian, then the above are the maximum likelihood parameter estimates and the estimated distribution based on X is $N(\underline{\mu}_{\text{data}}, \mathbf{C}_{\text{data}})$; recall (3.1).

Consider an N-dimensional multivariate Gaussian distribution $N(\underline{\mu}, \mathbf{C})$ with non-singular $N \times N$ covariance matrix $\mathbf{C}$ (i.e., its component random variables are a.s. linearly independent).[2] If a Cholesky decomposition on $\mathbf{C}$ is performed (i.e., $\mathbf{C} = \mathbf{A}\mathbf{A}'$ with $\mathbf{A}$ an upper triangular matrix), and N i.i.d. standard normal samples $\underline{Z} = (Z_1, \ldots, Z_N)'$ are generated (i.e., with every random variable $Z_i \sim N(0, 1)$), then it is easy to show that

$$\mathbf{A}\underline{Z} + \underline{\mu} \sim N(\underline{\mu}, \mathbf{C}).$$

Recall (3.21). That is, one can simulate any multivariate Gaussian distribution by generating N i.i.d. standard normal variates, collecting them into a vector, and then applying the above affine transformation. Moreover, given a multivariate Gaussian, an out-of-distribution example $\underline{x}$ can be detected by using p-values (recall (3.18)).

General multivariate distributions can be characterized using Sklar's theorem [64] and related results.

4.4.3 Generative Adversarial Networks (GANs)

GANs [52, 82] are often used to address the problem of modeling data from complicated multivariate distributions of very high dimension $n \gg 1$, and generating samples from the learned model which simulate real data. An attractive aspect of GANs is that it does not make any explicit distribution family assumptions, it is a "non-parametric"

---

[2] Note that if $\mathbf{C}$ is singular, then a sub-vector of a.s. linearly independent random variables can be identified by the Gram–Schmidt process, in other words, this sub-vector has non-singular covariance matrix.

approach to modeling and simulation. A GAN consists of tandem generator G and discriminator D which are trained simultaneously. The generator transforms a uniform random vector $\underline{Z} \in [0, 1]^{n'}$, "$\underline{Z} \sim p_w$," for some large $n' > 1$, into a synthetic sample $\underline{X}_g = G(\underline{Z}) \in \mathbb{R}^n$.

The discriminator takes sample $\underline{x}$ as input and its output $D(\underline{x})$ is the (estimated) probability that $\underline{x}$ comes from the real (training) distribution.

The parameters of the generator and the discriminator are learned via a (somewhat complicated) minimax optimization process over the parameters of D and G:

$$\min_G \max_D \mathbb{E}_{\underline{X} \sim p_{data}}[\log D(\underline{X})] + \mathbb{E}_{\underline{Z} \sim p_w}[\log(1 - D(G(\underline{Z})))] \qquad (4.6)$$

where p_{data} is the uniform empirical distribution of the training dataset X: for any $\underline{v} \in \mathbb{R}^n$,

$$p_{data}(\underline{v}) = \frac{1}{T} \sum_{\underline{x} \in X} \mathbf{1}\{\underline{v} = \underline{x}\} \quad \text{or} \quad p_{data}(\underline{v}) = \frac{1}{T} \sum_{\underline{x} \in X} \delta(\underline{v} - \underline{x}), \qquad (4.7)$$

where the pmf (with indicator functions $\mathbf{1}\{\cdot\}$) is at left and the pdf (with Dirac delta functions $\delta(\cdot)$) is at right.

So if the generator G is fixed, the discriminator is trained to maximize the objective:

$$V(D) := \int_{\mathbb{R}^N} p_{data}(\underline{x}) \log(D(\underline{x})) d\underline{x} + \int_{\mathbb{R}^N} p_g(\underline{x}) \log(1 - D(\underline{x})) d\underline{x},$$

where p_g is the density of $G(\underline{Z})$ when $\underline{Z} \sim p_w$.

From the Euler–Lagrange equations [75], it is easy to see that the discriminator D^* that maximizes the above equation is:

$$D^*(\underline{x}) = \frac{p_{data}(\underline{x})}{p_{data}(\underline{x}) + p_g(\underline{x})}, \quad \underline{x} \in \mathbb{R}^N. \qquad (4.8)$$

While the above suggests a simple, closed-form discriminator (given knowledge of the generator), in practice a discriminator DNN is trained. One reason for this is that the above discriminator cannot generalize to make plausible inferences for samples not in the training set – (4.8) depends on (4.7), which assigns *zero* probability to *any* sample not in the training set, even if this sample is consistent with the training distribution. Thus, (4.8) assigns zero probability to any $\underline{x} \notin X$. Instead, the approach in [82] applies iterative, alternating optimization of the generator and discriminator DNNs, with small optimization steps taken to avoid instability issues (gradient explosion). This optimization process is similar to the classical iterated subgradient method described in Section A.1.5.

GANs training also suffers from generator "mode collapse." Here, a trained generator's output lacks diversity, producing just one output (for different random inputs) in the most extreme case. Mode collapse may be intrinsic to GANs learning, as it appears there is nothing within the minimax objective (4.6) to penalize against it.[3]

If the goal is simply to design a generator, then the discriminator network will be discarded following the optimization procedure. However, GANs discriminators have

---

[3] One could try amplifying the generator's entropy term $-\int p_g(\underline{x}) \log p_g(\underline{x}) d\underline{x}$ in the training objective $U(G)$ given below to possibly avoid mode collapse.

also been used effectively for anomaly (outlier) detection with respect to the training set distribution $\mathcal{X}$. That they form the basis for a powerful TTE detector, one which outperforms the ADA method previously discussed, is demonstrated in the following (again, a GAN gives a non-parametric model of the data while ADA relies on a specific mixture distribution family, e.g., mixture of Gaussians, for the null).

Given the discriminator is fixed based on (4.8) (even though in practice a discriminator DNN is used instead of (4.8)), the generator's training objective becomes:

$$U(G) := \int_{\mathbb{R}^N} p_{\text{data}}(\underline{x}) \log(D^*(\underline{x})) d\underline{x} + \int_{\mathbb{R}^N} p_g(\underline{x}) \log(1 - D^*(\underline{x})) d\underline{x}$$

$$= \int_{\mathbb{R}^N} p_{\text{data}}(\underline{x}) \log\left(\frac{p_{\text{data}}(\underline{x})}{p_{\text{data}}(\underline{x}) + p_g(\underline{x})}\right) d\underline{x} + \int_{\mathbb{R}^N} p_g(\underline{x}) \log\left(\frac{p_g(\underline{x})}{p_{\text{data}}(\underline{x}) + p_g(\underline{x})}\right) d\underline{x}.$$

Since

$$\int_{\mathbb{R}^N} p_{\text{data}}(\underline{x}) \log\left(\frac{1}{2}\right) d\underline{x} + \int_{\mathbb{R}^N} p_g(\underline{x}) \log\left(\frac{1}{2}\right) d\underline{x} = \log\left(\frac{1}{2}\right) + \log\left(\frac{1}{2}\right) = \log\left(\frac{1}{4}\right),$$

$$U(G) = \int_{\mathbb{R}^N} p_{\text{data}}(\underline{x}) \log\left(\frac{2 \times p_{\text{data}}(\underline{x})}{p_{\text{data}}(\underline{x}) + p_g(\underline{x})}\right) d\underline{x} + \int_{\mathbb{R}^N} p_g(\underline{x}) \log\left(\frac{2 \times p_g(\underline{x})}{p_{\text{data}}(\underline{x}) + p_g(\underline{x})}\right) d\underline{x}$$

$$+ \log\left(\frac{1}{4}\right)$$

$$= \text{KL}\left(p_{\text{data}} \| \frac{p_{\text{data}} + p_g}{2}\right) + \text{KL}\left(p_g \| \frac{p_{\text{data}} + p_g}{2}\right) + \log\left(\frac{1}{4}\right),$$

where KL is the Kullback–Leibler divergence. The first two terms added together give twice the Jensen–Shannon divergence (JSD) [66] between the data distribution and the generated distribution:

$$U(G) = 2 \times \text{JSD}(p_g \| p_{\text{data}}) + \log\left(\frac{1}{4}\right). \tag{4.9}$$

The JSD is non-negative and only equal to zero when $p_g = p_{\text{data}}$. So, in order to "defeat" the discriminator, the generator optimization seeks a generator G^* that converts a random vector $\underline{Z} \sim p_w$ to an output distributed according to the training dataset, so the optimal generator is $G^*(\underline{Z}) \sim p_{\text{data}}$. As mentioned above, to train the generator, the discriminator (4.8) is typically *not* used. Instead, a DNN model for the discriminator is used and jointly trained with that of the generator.

4.5 Generative Adversarial Network (GAN) Based Test-Time Evasion (TTE) Attack Detection Methodology

For an out-of-distribution sample $\underline{x} \nsim p_{\text{data}}$, $D(\underline{x}) \in [0, 1]$ will be small, and the probability that any $G(\underline{Z})$ will be close to $\underline{x}$ will be very small (where $\underline{Z} \sim p_w$). Accordingly, GAN based methods have been proposed for anomaly detection, for example, [2, 231, 232, 323]. For example, given a test sample $\underline{x}$, the GAN's discriminator output $D(\underline{x})$ and the GAN's generator reconstruction error ($\rho(\underline{x}) := \min_{\underline{z}} \|G(\underline{z}) - \underline{x}\|$)

have been used as detection statistics. Again, since $D(\underline{x}) \in [0, 1]$ is an estimated probability that the sample comes from the training distribution, a small $D(\underline{x})$ indicates an outlier sample. Also, $\rho(\underline{x})$ tends to be higher for an anomalous test sample $\underline{x}$ compared to that for a sample following the training distribution [232].

The methods in [2, 232] were originally proposed for detecting nodules in CT scans of the lung and macular degeneration in OCT scans of the retina. It is less straightforward to successfully apply GANs to detect adversarial examples. Conventional GANs based detection methods are not very effective for this task because the perturbations of an attack image are often not detectable by the discriminator, and do not significantly influence the reconstruction loss (as will be seen by the experimental results in the sequel).

The following GANs based approach for TTE attack detection is unsupervised (does not require any knowledge of attacks) and can exploit features at any layer of the defended DNN, including the input layer. This approach overcomes limitations of existing GANs methods for attack detection by learning class (decision)-conditional GANs models. The approach illustrated in Figure 4.3, for the example of an image classifier, considers both the cases of a clean (attack-free) sample image and an attacked image. In the former, the discriminator's output is high (indicating that this is a plausible test sample and from the decided class), while the generator's reconstruction error is small. In the latter case, the discriminator's output is low (indicating that the test sample is implausible, i.e., inconsistent with the training distribution), while the generator's reconstruction error is large.

There are multiple class-conditional GANs models, for example, conditional GAN (cGAN) [181], auxiliary classifier GAN (AC-GAN) [200], cGAN with projection discriminator [182], StyleGAN [117], and ReGAN [116]. The following method is a class-conditional GANs based anomaly detector using AC-GAN.

4.5.1   AC-GAN

In AC-GAN, there is a class-conditional generator, which takes a random vector $\underline{Z}$ and a class label y as input and outputs the synthesized sample $\underline{X}_g = G(\underline{Z}|y)$.

Also, for an input $\underline{x}$, the discriminator gives two outputs:

- $D(\underline{x})$, the probability that $\underline{x}$ comes from the training distribution p_{data} (as for the original GANs framework), and
- $\hat{p}_D(y|\underline{x})$, the posterior probability that $\underline{x}$ is from class y, for every $y \in \mathcal{Y}$; that is, part of the discriminator is an auxiliary classifier.

There are two terms in the AC-GAN learning objective – the "source" loss L_{source} and the "class" loss L_{class}:

$$L_{\text{source}} = E_{\underline{X} \sim p_{\text{data}}} \log D(\underline{X}) + E_{\underline{Z} \sim p_w, Y' \sim \text{unif}(\mathcal{Y})} \log(1 - D(G(\underline{Z}|Y')))$$

$$L_{\text{class}} = E_{\underline{X} \sim p_{\text{data}}} \log \hat{p}_D(c(\underline{X})|\underline{X})) + E_{\underline{Z} \sim p_w, Y' \sim \text{unif}(\mathcal{Y})} \log \hat{p}_D(Y'|G(\underline{Z}|Y')),$$

where $c(\underline{x})$ in L_{class} is the true class for data sample $\underline{x}$, and $\text{unif}(\mathcal{Y})$ is the uniform distribution on the set of classes. The discriminator is trained to maximize $L_{\text{source}} + L_{\text{class}}$

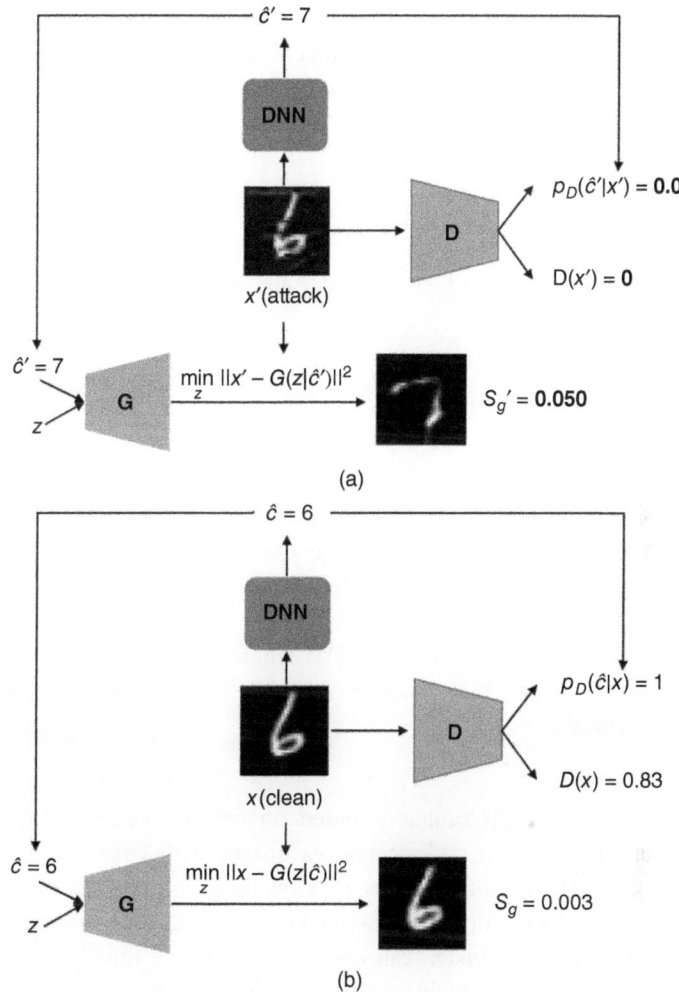

Figure 4.3 Overview of the AC-GAN TTE detection method. (a) The method applied to a TTE attack image $\underline{x}'$. Note that the discriminator's two probabilities are low, indicating that the given image is not plausible. Likewise, the generated image looks like a '7', not a '6' – the associated MSE S_g is large. (b) The method applied to a clean test image. Reprinted from [284] with permission.

while the generator is trained to minimize $L_{\text{source}} - L_{\text{class}}$. (Note that it's unclear why D would want to maximize the second term of L_{class}.)

It has been shown that AC-GAN training may also suffer from gradient explosion and mode collapse [116]. AC-GAN may also tend to only generate images that are easily classified by the discriminator (another indicator that the generator is not doing a very good job). Moreover, when the number of classes increases, the training process becomes more challenging, with an increased chance of mode collapse in the early stage of GANs learning. Experiments show that the performance of anomaly detection (especially generator based anomaly detection) is limited by the quality of the learned

GANs model (see the G-AD row in Table 4.3 and Figure 4.4). However, even with these problems, the following AC-GAN based TTE detector outperforms previous anomaly detection methods, including some other GANs based methods, as we will see in following experiments.

4.5.2   Detection Methods

Under AC-GAN there are three statistics that can be exploited for detection; recall Figure 4.3. Given an input sample $\underline{x}$ and its DNN predicted class $\hat{c} = \hat{c}(\underline{x})$, these test statistics are:

$$S_R = D(\underline{x}) \tag{4.10}$$
$$S_C = \hat{p}_D(\hat{c}|\underline{x}) \tag{4.11}$$
$$S_g = \min_{\underline{z}} \|\underline{x} - G(\underline{z}|\hat{c})\|^2. \tag{4.12}$$

Note that S_R and S_C are the outputs of the discriminator, and S_g is the generator's class-conditional mean-squared reconstruction error.

A detection method can be based on the statistics from either the discriminator, the generator, or from both. Accordingly, three distinct detection methods based on an AC-GAN are now described. A single discriminator test statistic S_d can be obtained by aggregating S_R and S_C based on an independence assumption for these two probabilities, via:

$$S_d = \log D(\underline{x}) + \log \hat{p}_D(\hat{c}|x); \tag{4.13}$$

this is called discriminator based anomaly detection (D-AD). The first (class-independent) term in S_d penalizes images with large perturbation size, while the second term penalizes images with low probability for the class to which the DNN is deciding. A detection is declared when S_d is smaller than a given threshold.

A detection decision can also be made solely relying on the generator, namely generator based anomaly detection (G-AD), with S_g used to detect anomalous images. Again, out-of-distribution (image, class decision) pairs will give larger values of S_g.

All the test statistics can also be combined to make a detection. For example, define the vector $\underline{S} = [S_R, S_C, S_g]$. One can model $\underline{S}$ using a multivariate Gaussian distribution, with anomalies then detected based on a p-value assessed with respect to this distribution. Here this method is called All-AD.

Again, note that all of these methods require setting a threshold to make detections. Generally a threshold can be chosen in an unsupervised fashion based on the largest false positive rate (FPR) that is tolerable.

4.6   Experiments

4.6.1   Datasets

We evaluated the performance of different detection methods on several well-known image classification datasets: MNIST [141], CIFAR-10 [129], and Tiny ImageNet [57].

Table 4.1 Test set accuracy of the ResNet-18 classifier on different datasets.

	MNIST	CIFAR-10	Tiny ImageNet
Test accuracy	99.43%	92.84%	61.35%

MNIST is a hand-written digit grey-scale image dataset used in classification problems. There are 10 classes corresponding to the digits $\{0, 1, 2, \ldots, 9\}$, with 7000 images per class. The MNIST dataset has a standard train-test split with 60,000 images in the training set and 10,000 images in the test set. The size of an image is 28×28.

The CIFAR-10 dataset consists of 60,000 color images in 10 classes, with 6000 images per class. There are 50,000 training images and 10,000 test images. Image sizes are 32×32. See Section 5.5 for additional details regarding CIFAR-10.

Tiny ImageNet is a subset of ImageNet; there are 200 classes in the dataset, with each class consisting of 500 training images and 25 evaluation images. All images are resized to 64×64.

DNN models have achieved high accuracy on these datasets, for example, ResNet-18 (and recall Figure 2.6) achieves 99.5% test accuracy on MNIST and 93.02% test accuracy on CIFAR-10. It has also been shown, though, that a correctly classified image can be easily perturbed (with a relatively small perturbation size) so that it is misclassified to a target class [33]. It was also pointed out in [32] that MNIST has somewhat different security properties than CIFAR-10, with some detection methods effective on MNIST but quite ineffective on CIFAR-10. Most previous works, for example, [68, 142, 179], reported experiments on both MNIST and CIFAR-10. According to [32], due to the lack of diversity of samples in MNIST, the DNN classifier trained on MNIST achieves high certainty (class decision confidence) on the test examples, which makes the perturbation size required for a successful attack larger than that for CIFAR-10.

4.6.2   Model Architectures and Attack Methods

The ResNet-18 [97] model is used as the DNN classifier. The (clean) test set classification accuracy (in the absence of TTE attacks) of the trained DNN on the different datasets is shown in Table 4.1. Note that the significantly lower accuracy on Tiny ImageNet [161] may be attributable to the large number of classes and the small number of training samples per class as compared to either CIFAR-10 or MNIST.

Usually FGSM requires a larger perturbation size than CW to generate an adversarial example. For the targeted CW attack (4.3), the model parameter $\kappa = 14$ (which is a common setting), and the minimum value of the hyperparameter λ to make successful high-confidence and low-confidence attacks was found by grid search. A successful *low-confidence attack* perturbs an image until the target-class posterior of the attacked DNN is just larger than that of any other class. On the other hand, we define that a successful *high-confidence attack* [21] is achieved when the target-class posterior is larger than 90%. Recall Figure 1.3.

Table 4.2 Hyperparameters for AC-GAN training.

	MNIST	CIFAR-10	Tiny ImageNet
Optimizer	Adam ($\alpha = 0.0002$, $\beta_1 = 0.5$, $\beta_2 = 0.999$)		
Learning rate	0.001	0.0002	0.0001
Epochs	60	90	100
Batch size	256	256	64
Weights initialization	$\sim N(\mu, \sigma^2)$, $\mu = 0$, $\sigma = 0.02$		

For the targeted version of the FGSM attack of (4.1), the value $\varepsilon = 0.05$ was chosen for CIFAR-10 and Tiny ImageNet, and $\varepsilon = 0.2$ for MNIST. FGSM is computationally efficient but provides only a crude approach (by varying ε) to achieve high-versus low-confidence attacks. In the following experiments, FGSM is only used to produce low-confidence attacks.

The correctly classified test images were chosen as the clean image set $\mathcal{T}$, and were adversarially perturbed to randomly generated target classes (different from the class labels) using a given attack method; the successfully attacked images from $\mathcal{T}$ are denoted by $\mathcal{T}'$. The union of $\mathcal{T}$ (i.e., the clean images) and $\mathcal{T}'$ (the successful attack images) is used to evaluate anomaly detection performance.

Different AC-GAN structures were used for the MNIST and CIFAR-10 datasets. For MNIST, there are four convolutional layers in the discriminator and four transposed convolutional layers [215] in the generator. For CIFAR-10, both the generator and the discriminator use architectures akin to ResNet-18 [285].

4.6.3   AC-GAN Training

The objective functions defined in Section 4.5.1 were used to train the generator and discriminator. Following the training configuration in [200], mini-batch gradient descent was used to train the generator and the discriminator. In each mini-batch a subset of training images is sampled as real images and a set of fake images is produced by the generator given a randomly generated vector and label; then one discriminator optimization step is performed followed by one generator optimization step. Relatively large batch sizes (256 for MNIST and CIFAR-10 and 64 for Tiny ImageNet) were used to increase the training stability. To mitigate the mode collapse problem, label smoothing [187] was applied to the real/fake labels. The training hyperparameters for different datasets can be found in Table 4.2.

4.6.4   Performance of Anomaly Detection

We now experimentally compare the TTE detection performance of D-AD, G-AD, All-AD, and D-AD-L1, where D-AD-L1 is the D-AD method with the generator modeling embedded features extracted from the DNN's first convolutional layer; for the remaining methods the generator models the DNN's input (raw image features).

Table 4.3 pAUC-0.2 results of different detection methods under different attacks for MNIST and CIFAR-10 datasets.

	MINST			CIFAR-10		
	CW-HC	CW-LC	FGSM	CW-HC	CW-LC	FGSM
f-AnoGAN [231]	0.0981	0.0995	0.0887	0.0576	0.0563	0.0566
KD [68]	0.1892	0.1887	0.1880	0.0533	0.0584	0.1642
MD [142]	0.1861	0.1832	0.1901	0.1042	0.1125	0.1783
ODDS [221]	0.0618	0.0412	0.0537	0.0910	0.0568	0.0436
SID [262]	0.1576	0.1628	0.1726	0.1489	0.1412	0.1388
ADA [179]	0.1715	0.1732	0.1823	0.1593	0.1601	0.1782
G-AD	0.1525	0.1517	0.1612	0.0181	0.0254	0.0203
D-AD	0.1915	**0.1970**	0.1862	**0.1881**	**0.1899**	**0.1819**
All-AD	**0.1923**	0.1964	**0.1905**	0.1798	0.1825	0.1618
D-AD-L1	0.1897	0.1873	0.1824	0.1805	0.1787	0.1768

Also, we compare against several unsupervised anomaly detection methods: kernel density (KD [68], recall (3.12)), Mahalanobis distance (MD [142], recall (3.2)), ADA (recall Section 4.3.4), and F-AnoGAN [231] (a GAN based anomaly detector). Also, ODDS [221] is a noise-based method (recall Section 4.2.1). To make fair comparisons with the supervised SID method [262] (recall Section 4.3.1), the FGSM attack is assumed known for SID when detecting CW attacks, and the CW low-confidence attack is assumed known for SID when detecting FGSM attacks.

The performance measure chosen for all detection methods was the partial area under the ROC curve for FPR below 0.2 (pAUC-0.2). The maximum value of 0.2 for pAUC-0.2 is achieved when the detection rate of adversarial examples is 100% and the false positive rate is 0%. As with pAUC-1, a larger pAUC-0.2 score means better performance. pAUC was assessed because the most practically important detection performance is often in the low false positive regime.

The experimental results for MNIST and CIFAR-10 are shown in Table 4.3.

The f-AnoGAN method, which is a GAN based AD but not class-conditional, has poor performance on both datasets. The blurring-based method [221] is also ineffective on both datasets. Two methods based on the clean distribution of the penultimate layer features – Mahalanobis distance based (MD) [142] and kernel density based (KD) [68] – have good performance on the MNIST dataset, but for CIFAR-10, especially under the CW attack, the performance is poor. The SID method generalizes reasonably well to unknown attacks, but the performance is still not as good as D-AD.

ADA, which assesses multiple hidden layers and uses GMMs to capture the null (clean) distribution for these layers, outperforms all the above-mentioned methods under the two most challenging attack scenarios (CW-HC and CW-LC for CIFAR-10). Note that ADA relies on BIC (recall Section 3.4) to select the number of components in a GMM used to represent a given hidden layer, conditioned on a particular decided class. In order to assist BIC in choosing good model orders, an auto-encoding network was used to reduce the feature dimensionality of a given hidden layer.

Table 4.4 pAUC-0.2 results for the Tiny ImageNet dataset.

	CW-HC	CW-LC	FGSM
f-AnoGAN [231]	0.0571	0.0523	0.0655
KD [68]	0.0542	0.0567	0.1168
MD [142]	0.0918	0.0864	0.1104
ADA [179]	0.1312	0.1348	0.1385
D-AD	**0.1532**	**0.1585**	**0.1496**

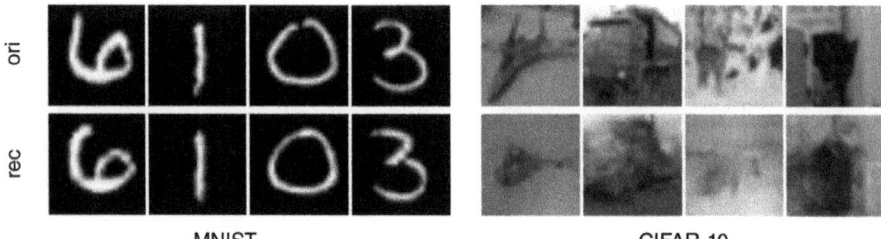

ori

rec

MNIST   CIFAR-10

Figure 4.4 Reconstruction examples of clean images for the MNIST and CIFAR-10 datasets: the first row shows the original clean test images; the second row shows the images reconstructed by the generator. Reprinted from [284] with permission.

From Table 4.3, observe that the methods which combine class-decision conditioned anomaly detection and GANs based anomaly detection outperform both the unconditional GANs based anomaly detection method and the class-conditional ADA method. The best performing versions of AC-GAN based defense either use both the discriminator and generator statistics (All-AD) or just use the discriminator (D-AD) – the generator is modestly helpful for MNIST, but unhelpful for CIFAR-10. Notably, a multiple step (usually around 300 iterations for the MNIST dataset) gradient descent process is needed to obtain S_g (this is *test time* overhead). However, for the discriminator based statistics S_C and S_R, only one forward pass of the discriminator is needed to perform detection. It is experimentally observed that the performance of the pure generator based method is very poor on CIFAR-10. Generator based detection requires accurate reconstruction of a given clean image – for the MNIST dataset, the reconstruction task is relatively easy due to the low diversity of the data in each class. On the other hand, the high data diversity of the CIFAR-10 dataset makes it challenging to reconstruct a given clean test image. Some examples of reconstructed clean images for MNIST and CIFAR-10 are given in Figure 4.4. Observe for the MNIST dataset that the clean images can be reconstructed with high accuracy, but for the CIFAR-10 dataset, the reconstruction error is high even for clean samples.

The experimental results on the Tiny ImageNet dataset are presented in Table 4.4. D-AD and the other methods that have good performance on the MNIST or CIFAR-10 dataset were chosen for evaluation. The D-AD method is seen to outperform all other comparison methods on Tiny ImageNet. The drop in TTE attack detection performance compared to CIFAR-10 and MNIST in Table 4.3 can be explained by the lower accuracy of the ResNet-18 DNN on Tiny ImageNet; recall Table 4.1.

4.6.5   Detecting Based on Embedded Features

Some previously described ADs detect anomalies based on embedded features, that is, from internal layers of the DNN. For example, the null distributions of these features are modeled using a mixture model or Gaussian kernel density estimation, or they use K-nearest neighbors (KNN); recall Chapter 3 and see Section 4.11. As discussed above, the AC-GAN model can also capture the conditional distribution of embedded features. Consider an M-layer DNN h, for example, of the ResNet type. For a test sample x with predicted class $\hat{c} = h_M(x)$, a feature vector from the kth DNN layer $h_k(x)$, with $k < M$, can be extracted and modeled by an AC-GAN. Then the detection statistics of (4.10)–(4.12) can be used just by replacing $x = h_0(x)$ by $h_k(x)$. Table 4.3 also reports the anomaly detection performance of the AC-GAN discriminator based detector using the features from the output of the first convolutional layer (D-AD-L1). Observe that the detection pAUC-0.2 values for this method are comparable to, but not quite as good as, the best performing version (based on use of the raw input features).

The AC-GAN framework also gives a way of visualizing the DNN's internal features. At test time, when an image or internal layer feature vector is fed into the discriminator (depending on which layer the AC-GAN was trained on), the discriminator's penultimate-layer activations can be extracted and visualized using principal component analysis (PCA) (recall Section 3.5). The visualization results are shown in Figure 4.5, considering AC-GAN modeling of different layers of the DNN classifier. Consider in particular images perturbed from class 'cat' to class 'dog' (triangle points, attacked 'cat'). In the input layer, clean 'cat' and attacked 'cat' are well separated from clean 'dog'. In the first convolutional layer, attacked 'cat' images still follow the clean 'cat' distribution (and hence are discriminable from clean 'dog'); for the 11th convolutional layer features, attacked images fall in between clean 'cat' and clean 'dog' (hence, just based on this low-dimensional representation, it is possible that they could be assigned to either class). Finally, for the penultimate layer DNN features (not shown in the figure), some attacked 'cat' images are very close to some clean 'dog' images, which is suggestive that these features cannot be used to reliably discriminate between clean and attacked images.

4.6.6   Correcting the Classifier's Prediction

Beyond detecting attacks, the class-decision conditional detection statistics of the generator and the discriminator can also be used to *correct* the DNN classifier's predictions for samples that are detected as TTE attacks. The discriminator captures the class conditional distribution of the input data, so the class under which the input sample is *least atypical* can be predicted as the correct class. At test time, when an input sample x is detected as an adversarial example, the discriminator's maximum a posteriori class,

$$c_D = \arg\max_i \hat{p}_D(i|x),$$

can be used as the corrected class decision for the test sample x. However, note that the DNN has a class decision $\hat{c}$ for x. Since the image is detected as an adversarial

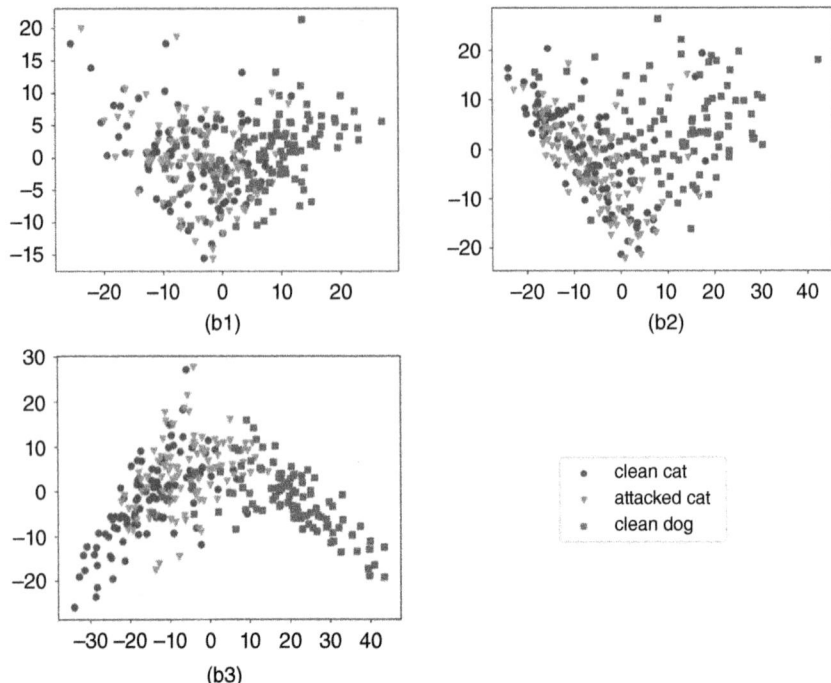

Figure 4.5 Visualization of different ResNet layers for CIFAR-10. The AC-GAN model is trained based on features from the input layer (b1), first (b2) or 11th (b3) convolutional layer; the corresponding discriminator's penultimate layer activations are then visualized using PCA. Reprinted from [284] with permission.

example, the class $\hat{c}$ should be an incorrect class decision; hence it is reasonable to exclude $\hat{c}$ when correcting labels, that is, choosing

$$c_D = \arg\max_{i \neq \hat{c}} \hat{p}_D(i|\underline{x}).$$

The corrected classification accuracy is presented in Table 4.5, with results reported considering both the inclusion of $\hat{c}$ as well as the exclusion of $\hat{c}$ as a possible class prediction.

Similar to the anomaly detection task, class label correction was performed using a GANs based on features from the input layer (D-AD) as well as the output of the first convolutional layer (D-AD-L1). These methods are compared with Defense-GAN (D-GAN) [227], which is a generator based robust classification method using the generator to reconstruct a given test image. The reconstructed image, instead of the original image, is then fed into the DNN classifier.

Observe from Table 4.5 that the performance of D-GAN is better than AC-GAN based methods on MNIST, but the AC-GAN based methods greatly outperform D-GAN on CIFAR-10. As discussed earlier, the performance of the generator based method is limited. For CIFAR-10, if a better generative model is used, then generator based class correction may achieve better performance. To validate this hypothesis,

Table 4.5 Classification accuracy in correcting the DNN decision, for correctly detected adversarial examples. CW-HC means CW high-confidence attack; CW-LC means CW low-confidence attack. D-GAN is the Defense-GAN method.

	Include $\hat{c}$	MINST		CIFAR-10	
		CW-HC	CW-LC	CW-HC	CW-LC
D-GAN [227]	✓	0.9247	0.9273	0.2089	0.2079
		0.9314	0.9291	0.3274	0.3782
D-AD	✓	0.8951	0.8816	0.8266	0.8191
		0.8964	0.8819	0.8423	0.8316
D-AD-L1	✓	0.8295	0.8204	0.7643	0.7420
		0.8421	0.8395	0.7874	0.7535
pix2pix	✓	**0.9504**	**0.9668**	**0.8539**	**0.8566**
		0.9612	**0.9671**	**0.8632**	**0.8788**

an alternative pix2pix image generation model is introduced – the pix2pix method of [108] is modified to essentially act as an auto-encoder to simplify the reconstruction task, inputting the image $\underline{x}$ into the generator to produce a "reconstructed" image $\underline{x}_r = G(\underline{x})$. The modified discriminator, when given the two images $\underline{x}_r$ and $\underline{x}$, outputs the probability $D(\underline{x}_r, \underline{x})$ that $\underline{x}_r$ is real given the reference image $\underline{x}$.[4] The performance of this method for class correction (with the generator's image fed into the DNN to produce the predicted label) is presented in Table 4.5. This method achieves the best class correction performance among all the evaluated methods. Note also from this table that, for all methods, there is modest performance improvement attained by *excluding $\hat{c}$.*

4.6.7   White Box Attack

The AC-GAN based detector was also evaluated under the white box scenario, where the attacker knows everything including the DNN model, the AC-GAN defense model, the detection statistics, and detection rules. In this section, the best performing (from Table 4.3) AC-GAN based defense for the grey box scenario, D-AD, is evaluated under a white box attack. Recall from (4.4) that a white box attack strategy is to minimize a loss function that is a composite of the attack objective (4.3) (classification loss) and a detector loss, that is,

$$\arg \min_{\underline{\delta}} A(\underline{x} + \underline{\delta}) - \alpha(D(\underline{x} + \underline{\delta}) + \hat{p}_D(t|\underline{x} + \underline{\delta})), \qquad (4.14)$$

where the first term is the objective of the standard targeted CW attack (4.3), hyperparameter $\alpha > 0$, the second term is the sum of the discriminator's statistics, $\underline{x}$ is the correctly classified, clean sample based on which the TTE attack is constructed, and the target class of the TTE attack is $t \neq c(\underline{x})$. Minimizing the first term will defeat the classifier while minimizing the second term will defeat the detector.

---

[4] Although the variational auto-encoder (VAE) [124] model is also used for image-to-image translation, without the adversarial training process and without a discriminator model to penalize deviations from a clean image, it can only reconstruct a given image and cannot eliminate adversarial perturbations.

Now suppose the white box attacker wishes to produce a high-confidence (large perturbation) TTE attack, requiring more iterations to minimize (4.14). Note that after a developing adversarial example $\underline{x} + \underline{\delta}$ first becomes classified to the attacker's target class t (after a certain number of iterations), the D term in the white box objective may start to influence subsequent iterations so that the adversarial example appears to be class-t realistic. Recognize that this is *contrary* to the basic goal of a TTE, that is, to fool the classifier and defense while not raising the suspicion of a (possible) human monitor; the TTE should continue to look like a typical sample from the source class $c(\underline{x}) \neq t$. (This problem for the attacker may be amplified when a class-conditional discriminator is used [181], whose input is also the decided upon class of the victim DNN, $\hat{c}(\underline{x}+\underline{\delta}) = t$.) On the other hand, if $D(\cdot)$ is removed from (4.14) after the evolving TTE is classified to class t, then subsequent optimization iterations may result in a TTE that does not evade a detector based on D, that is, it may be detected as an outlier relative to the training set, via D (or, more specifically, as an outlier of the class-t training dataset, according to a class-conditional discriminator). Dealing with such potential problems caused by an anomaly detector D increases the work factor of a high-confidence, white box TTE attacker, and also may require intervention by a human attacker, who may, for example, need to periodically inspect the developing TTE to ensure D is large *and* that the TTE continues to look like it belongs to the source class.

In the following experiment, only overall small adversarial perturbations were considered under (4.14), that is, yielding only low-confidence white box TTE attacks. 1000 test images $\underline{x}$ were randomly sampled from the CIFAR-10 test set such that they are all correctly classified by the DNN classifier. Adversarial examples were then created by solving the optimization problem (4.14) with $\alpha = 5$. Projected gradient descent (PGD) (recall Section 4.1) was used to control the sizes of the (small) adversarial perturbations.

Performance measures evaluated include the attack success rate and system defeat rate. An attack craft success means an image is perturbed such that it will be misclassified by the DNN classifier to the target class. System defeat is achieved when a perturbed image is misclassified to the target class *and* is not detected by the detection method (The detection threshold was chosen to achieve a false alarm rate of 14%.) In Figure 4.6a, these measures are plotted under white box (WB) and grey box (GB) settings (recall that the grey box attacker knows the classifier but not the detector) versus the perturbation size. The grey box system defeat rate is always close to zero, which verifies the effectiveness of AC-GAN based detection under grey box attacks. The figure also shows that a larger perturbation size is needed to defeat the victim DNN classifier and detector than to just defeat the classifier. Also D-AD is computationally much cheaper (lower work factor) than the attacks – an attack requires hundreds of optimization steps, while D-AD only needs one forward network pass to make a detection decision.

It is also observed that, for the same perturbation size, more optimization iterations are required to defeat the system (the classifier and the detector) than only to defeat

Table 4.6 Training and detection time complexity for AC-GAN based defense on different datasets.

	MNIST	CIFAR-10	Tiny ImageNet
GAN training time	4 min 35 s	1 h 25 min 57 s	15 h 13 min 2 s
GDT (per image)	2.96 s	12.9 s	n/a
DDT (per image)	2×10^{-5} s	0.002 s	0.03 s

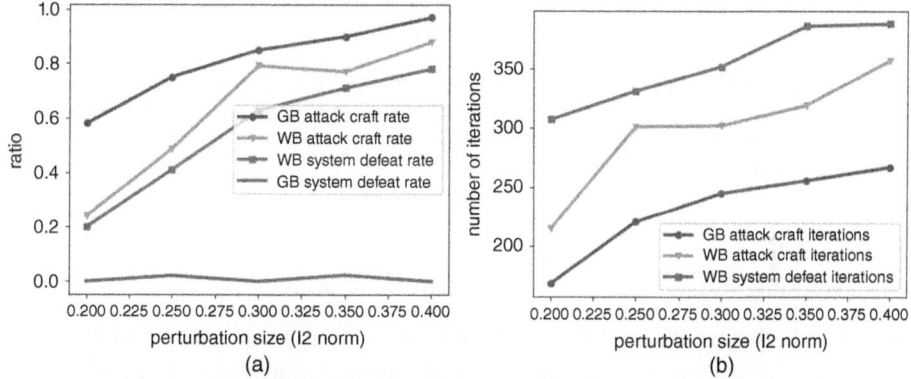

Figure 4.6 (a) Several attack success measures under white box (WB) and grey box (GB) attack scenarios. (b) Average iterations required for successful attacks. The experiments are conducted on the CIFAR-10 dataset. Projected gradient descent (PGD) is used to control the perturbation size. Reprinted from [284] with permission.

the DNN classifier. The average numbers of iterations required to defeat the classifier or to defeat the system are reported in Figure 4.6b.

4.6.8 Measured Computational Complexity

The foregoing experiments were performed on a computer with NVIDIA GeForce RTX 3090 GPU. The GANs model training time, generator based detection time (GDT) and discriminator based detection time (DDT) are presented in Table 4.6. While the GANs training time is high for Tiny ImageNet, this time is comparable to that required for training the DNN.

4.7 Deeper Consideration of Test-Time Evasion (TTE) Attack Scenarios

In this section, we delve more deeply into some issues, both theoretical and practical, involving TTE attacks.

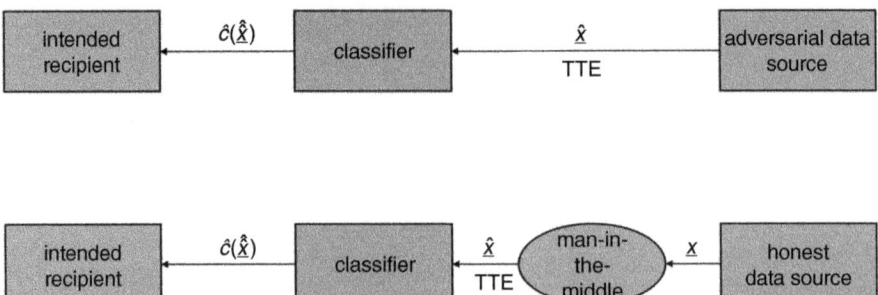

Figure 4.7 The two possible TTE attack mechanisms applied to digital patterns x, with the attacker either an adversarial *source* of patterns directly, or a man-in-the-middle intercepting a pattern on its way to the classifier. In the former mechanism, there is no legitimate utility obtained from the classifier's decision. There may also be a man-in-the-middle attacker between the classifier and the intended recipient.

4.7.1   Analysis of Test-Time Attack Mechanisms

Following the brief discussion in Section 1.3, it is recognized that there are only two *digital* attack mechanisms on a pattern to be classified (see Figure 4.7).

In one mechanism, there is an honest generator of patterns, but the pattern is then intercepted and perturbed by an adversary (a man-in-the-middle attack) before being forwarded to the classifier. However, there is a second mechanism, with the adversary the *originator* of the input pattern (input sample). Here, the adversary may have his/her own cache of labeled patterns from the domain. The adversary selects one (even arbitrarily), perturbs it to induce a desired misclassification, and then sends it to the classifier. In both mechanisms, if the attacker knows the classifier's decision rule, he/she can make a perturbation that is guaranteed to induce a *change* in the classifier's decision to a target class. However, only in the man-in-the-middle scenario, where there is a legitimate pattern, forwarded by an honest party who is interested in the classifier's decision, is there utility in correctly classifying the attacked pattern. For the adversarial source scenario, the classifier's decisions are only being made for the possible benefit of the adversary. Moreover, even for the man-in-the-middle scenario, it is pointless to make correct decisions if they are only going to be intercepted and modified by the adversary on their way to the intended decision recipient. We thus conclude that, *if the pattern has been digitally attacked*, it is only meaningful to correctly classify when there is an honest generator *and* when the intended recipient correctly receives the classifier's decision. While this may be a common scenario, an adversarial source is also a common scenario. However, even under the man-in-the-middle scenario, for the reasons articulated previously, attack detection in high stakes security settings is important, irrespective of making correct decisions. If no attack is detected, one can still make a best effort to correctly classify the pattern. Of course, for a given application one must weigh the importance of detection against that of (unimpeded) classification – patterns falsely detected as attacks may be rejected (they may not be classified). Thus, if, to achieve a desirable TPR, the FPR (equivalently, the classifier's rejection rate) is too high, attack detection may be impractical for the given domain.

4.7.2 Validity of the TTE Requirement that the Attacker Knows the Ground Truth Label

A key assumption made in all TTE attack works [32, 83, 202, 260] is that, in addition to knowing the classifier (or some reasonably accurate proxy), the attacker knows the ground truth label of the input pattern to be attacked. This is required so that an attack perturbation can be crafted that pushes the pattern across the classifier's decision boundary to the decision region for another class, *yielding a misclassification*; recall Figures 1.1 and 4.1. Without knowledge of the true label, an attacker could still perturb a pattern to ensure a *change* in the classifier's decision, but such change might actually alter an *incorrect* decision to a correct one. Thus, in all TTE attack works it is assumed that the true label of the pattern to be attacked is known. But this universal assumption is not generally valid for the man-in-the-middle scenario of Figure 4.7. Here, the attacker is intercepting the input pattern (and perturbing it), before it is fed as input to the classifier. The attacker receives the input test pattern, but not the ground truth label for this pattern. (If it is a pattern generated at test/inference time, no ground truth label may be available/known to *any* entity, let alone to the attacker.) While the attacker may know the classifier or an accurate surrogate for the classifier (and hence the decision the classifier makes on this input pattern), this is not the same thing as knowing ground truth. Thus, while the attacker may perturb the input pattern to induce a decision change, such change may even *correct* the classifier's (incorrect) decision on the original pattern.

4.7.3 Underestimating Susceptibility to AD

Some proposed TTE attacks are highly susceptible to a straightforward AD defense; yet this was not considered when performance evaluating the attack's "success." For example, a simple white region counting defense against the JSMA attack [203] achieves 0.97 ROC AUC on MNIST [179]; see the project of Section 4.10.

4.7.4 Transferability in TTE Attacks: Targeted Versus Non-targeted Cases

[202] considers the case where the TTE attacker does not have knowledge of the classifier but has the ability to query it. Such querying is used to create a labeled training set for learning a surrogate classifier, see Chapter 14. The authors demonstrated that TTE attack patterns crafted to induce misclassifications by the surrogate classifier with high success rate *also* induce misclassifications on the true classifier. Moreover, the authors demonstrated that such *transferability* of the TTE attack does not even require that the true classifier and its surrogate have the same structure; if the true classifier is a DNN, the surrogate could be an SVM or a decision tree. While these

results are quite intriguing, it is also important to note that the results in [202] assume that the TTE attack is *untargeted*, that is successful transferability only requires that a misclassified TTE input pattern for the surrogate is also a misclassified pattern for the true classifier. However, for TTE attacks to be strategic and cause the most damage, the attack may need to be *targeted*, inducing assignment to a particular target class t when the original pattern comes from class $s \neq t$. In the targeted case, a TTE attack only successfully transfers if the perturbed pattern induces the true classifier to misclassify to t. Considering this targeted attack case for CIFAR-100, learning an 8-layer ResNet classifier that is a surrogate of the ResNet-16 true classifier resulted in a targeted transferability success rate for the CW [33] attack of 56% (see Section 4.1). By contrast, the non-targeted transferability success rate was found to be over 80%. This indicates, at any rate, that the targeted case is more challenging, with a significantly lower transferable success rate, than for the non-targeted case.

4.7.5   Black Box or White Box TTE Attacks for Evaluation of a Defense

Very different viewpoints have been put forth on what is required in evaluating a defense (even to meet the standard of publication). Discussing TTE attacks, [32] has asserted (without elaboration) the *strong white box requirement* that "one must also show that an adversary aware of the defense [white box] cannot generate attacks that evade detection." There are several points to make about this. First, it does not mention false positives – there is always a true detection/false detection tradeoff, with the FPR controlled by setting the detection threshold. Clearly, the FPR must be sufficiently low for the deployed system to be practicable (not generating too many false alarms). Thus, one can safely construe the requirement (for a successful defense) from [32] to be that the true detection rate should be nearly perfect, with the FPR acceptably low. One might speciously argue in support of such a requirement by appeal to *worst-case* engineering analysis, that is any successful attack could have worst-case *consequences*, which should be avoided at all cost. However, it is also possible, in this highly asymmetric, fully white box setting, where the attacker knows everything (the classifier *and* the detector, including even the detector's threshold value) and the (proactive) defender knows nothing about the attacker, that meeting the requirements of [32] is theoretically impossible. In fact, [171] is not very sanguine about the prospects for defense against a fully white box attack.

Two fundamental questions need to be asked at this point.

1. In what scenarios is a white box attacker actually realistic?
2. What should be *realistically expected*, performance-wise, for a proactive (AD) defense against a white box attack?

Addressing the first question, note that [32] and other works do not justify or motivate the white box attacker assumption. In some security-sensitive settings where the deployed defense is *not* common knowledge, "omnipotent" white box knowledge of both the DNN *and* the AD defense would have to come from a well-placed "insider" working with the attacker. It is *not* reasonable to expect an AD system alone to defeat an insider attack. There are defenses specifically designed to prevent or to detect insider threats, with the former based on system safeguards (e.g., "need to know" knowledge compartmentalization) and with the latter exploiting information *well beyond* just the attacked data, for example, *monitoring* suspicious behavior of users with sensitive access to the defense system. Thus, a fully white box attack, consistent with an insider threat, should be evaluated against a "holistic" defense that includes both insider threat detection/prevention and AD based attack detection. Moreover, even assuming insider knowledge, true white box knowledge is in fact not always possible, as one can always introduce *randomness* into the defense that even an insider cannot predict. For example, suppose several distinct TTE defenses are mounted, and for each presented test pattern the invoked defense is randomly chosen from the mounted set. In this case, the attacker will not know which defense is being used against the crafted TTE attack pattern. He/she can mount multiple attacked patterns, to increase the possibility of matching an attack to a defense realization, but this will increase the attacker's work factor. Note that this discussion is not intended to imply that a defender can simply rely on the passive tactic of "security through obscurity." But it does indicate that it is difficult for an attacker to truly possess full white box knowledge in practice.

Addressing the second question, a successful attack requires inducing a misclassification *and* evading detection. We have shown experimentally in this chapter that white box attacks require an increased work factor (more computation, more attack iterations) relative to black box (or grey box) attacks. Moreover, as reported in [179], the attacker's computational effort (to induce misclassifications) is quite high even in the absence of an AD defense – the effort to craft CW attacks is hundreds of times heavier than that required to make ADA based detections [179]. To defeat both a classifier and detector, the white box attacker's computational effort is made even greater.

While [32] requires strong detectability of white box attacks, other opinions on proper defense evaluation have been offered. In [79], the authors quote [106] which states,

> if the model gives the adversary an unrealistic degree of information... an omnipotent adversary who knows [everything] can... design optimal attacks... it is necessary to carefully consider what a realistic adversary can know.

One such realistic scenario is where the attacker has full knowledge of the classifier but no knowledge of a possible AD defense (i.e., a black or grey box scenario). This scenario is far less asymmetric (i.e., fairer) than the white box attack scenario, that is, the unsupervised AD defense is unaware of the attacker's strategy and the attacker is unaware of the AD defense's strategy. In particular, for many application settings, the best performing *type* of classifier (e.g., a DNN or SVM) may in fact be common knowledge. Moreover, even if the classifier's parameters are unknown, if the attacker has good labeled data from the domain, he/she can train a surrogate classifier with similar performance as the target classifier. Again, it has been shown that using surrogate classifiers as the basis for TTE attack crafting may yield a high rate of success *transferability* to the target classifier [202]. Moreover, a reverse-engineering

(RE) attack, involving relatively numerous queries to the target classifier, can be used to learn a good surrogate of the target classifier, see Chapter 14.

Thus, it is plausible to start with good knowledge of the classifier in play, and even if one does not start with such knowledge, there is a direct mechanism (*querying*) that allows the attacker to learn the classifier. However, the same cannot necessarily be said for the detector – there may be no natural mechanism for "querying" the detector. (If the attacker might receive the classifier's decision, one should not output a "don't know" decision when attacks are detected, as this would in fact allow detector querying by the attacker.) Moreover, with numerous potential defense approaches and no definitive standard, it seems less realistic for the attacker to possess substantial knowledge of the deployed AD defense. Also, no one has shown there is high transferability of a surrogate *defense*, that is, a *surrogate* AD deployed by the attacker may not closely mirror detections made by the true deployed AD.

We conclude by noting that common, commercial antivirus, intrusion-detection and firewall systems are *supervised* means of defense that may be known to the adversary, are frequently breached, and require periodic updating (together with patching of the operating system and protocols in an attempt to remove associated vulnerabilities, hopefully while not compromising the usability of the defended system). Such an arms race will also occur for unsupervised AD defenses (targeting zero-day attacks), which augment supervised defenses (targeting known attacks).

4.8   Discussion: Out-of-Distribution Detection (OODD)

From the foregoing discussion of TTE defenses, detection of TTEs involves techniques that can also be used to detect not necessarily malicious "out-of-distribution" (OOD) test samples, that is, outliers with respect to the training set. Such detection is obviously important, for example, many such outliers detected may indicate that the current operating environment is different from that under which the training set was collected. In such situations (commonly referred to as domain adaptation or model drift settings), one may need to retrain or refine (fine-tune) the model to better fit the current operating conditions, that is, an active learning (selective reinforcement learning) process, wherein "out-of-distribution" (including TTE) examples detected at test time are ground-truth labelled and incorporated into the training set, with the model then fine-tuned to account for them. This is further discussed next (also see Chapter 12).

4.8.1   Detecting individual OOD test samples

One can attempt to detect individual OOD test samples by simply employing p-values of the null densities of the activations of an internal layer (possibly dimensionally reduced) of the DNN (recall that ADA uses such null densities to detect TTEs) or of a separately trained auto-encoder (e.g., [332], recall Section 2.13). The GAN discriminator, whether class conditional or not, can also be used for OODD of course. (An alternative OODD approach is a one-class neural network, e.g., [37, 201], based on a loss function similar to that of one-class SVMs, see Section A.4.6 of the Appendix).

4.8.2 Detecting Anomalies in a Batch of Test Samples

Consider the scenario where the classifier has been applied to make decisions on a large *batch* of test examples. It is possible that some (a priori unknown) subset of this batch consists of TTE attack examples. Certainly, one could apply a sample-wise detector to make independent detection decisions on individual samples in the batch. However, if the attack perturbations are subtle, a significant number of attack instances may evade such detection. An alternative strategy is to apply a *group* anomaly detection method, that is, a method which essentially identifies a *cluster* of anomalous samples, with these samples clustered together based on (i) their anomalousness relative to a null (no-attack) distribution, and (ii) *similarity* between these samples, especially with respect to their features that are anomalous with respect to the null. That is, even if the anomalies in individual samples are subtle, and may involve very few features, these anomalies become statistically significant when considered *in aggregate*, especially if many of them may involve the same/similar subset of features. A method proposed for such group anomaly detection is [177]. This approach first learns a parsimonious mixture model (PMM, recall Section 3.4.2) as a null distribution, estimated based on a given training dataset. Next, given a test batch of samples, one applies BIC to optimize an *alternative hypothesis* PMM model, one which makes modest (parsimonious) modifications to the null model, only modifying the distribution for the small set of features that are not well explained by the null. This BIC optimization essentially performs both *sample* clustering and *feature* clustering, that is, it iteratively seeks to identify a subset of the test batch (a sample cluster), and a subset of features that require modification of the null distribution model, in order to well explain these features for the samples in the cluster. This method was demonstrated in [177] to give highly promising results both on synthetic examples and on detection of botnet command and control activity in a batch of network traffic flows. This approach may also be able to detect clusters of OOD examples working from an embedded feature space that is some internal layer of a DNN classifier. In particular, a cluster may well capture TTE examples that involve a transition from the same source class (s) to the same target class ($t \neq s$). Such samples may exhibit atypicalities in the same subset of features, and with these atypicalities in the same "direction," so as to induce decision change from s to t.

4.9 Chapter Summary

In this chapter we described in detail test-time evasion attacks (also known as adversarial inputs), we described several well-known TTE attack algorithms, reviewed defenses against TTEs, including both robust classifier training defenses and detection defenses, the latter including ADA and one based on class-conditional generative adversarial networks (GANs), and finally, we delved deeper into important theoretical and practical issues concerning TTEs, including, for example, the underlying attacker scenario (e.g., a man-in-the-middle attack, and white box attacks).

Some questions to test the reader's understanding of the chapter include the following.

- Explain in what sense the CW attack improves on prior TTE attack methods.
- What are the disadvantages of existing robust and certified classifier training methods?
- Describe an application for which robust classification is inadequate by itself as a defense against TTEs, and explain why.
- Explain why the ADA method may not be so effective against high-confidence TTE attacks.
- In what sense is a GANs a "non-parametric" anomaly detection method?
- What is a limitation of the data visualizations shown in Figure 4.4?
- Which will be larger in practice – the transferability rate for a targeted TTE attack, or for an untargeted TTE attack?
- Explain why a man-in-the-middle TTE attacker may not be able to create successful attacks.
- Come up with a practical application involving an adversarial source TTE attack.
- Suggest possible strategies for defeating a white box attack.

4.10   Project: White Region Counting Defense

Note that in this and some of the following projects, the student is expected to read research articles and digest ideas and methods from them, despite varying notation and jargon.

4.10.1   Create and Assess the ZOO Attack on MNIST

Recall that the MNIST dataset [141] has handwritten digit characters, so there are 10 classes $\{0, 1, \ldots, 9\}$ and each image is 28×28 grey-level pixels, that is, each image is a 784-dimensional vector of grey levels $\in \{0, 1, \ldots, 255\}$ where intensity 0 is black and intensity 255 is white.

Notes Regarding the ZOO Algorithm 1 Attack
- See the untargeted attack objective f in Eq. (5) and ZOO Algorithm 1 in [41].
- Start with an MNIST image $\underline{x} = \underline{x}_0$ that is correctly classified to class $t_0 \in \{0, 1, \ldots, 9\}$,

$$f(\underline{x}_0) := [F(\underline{x})]_{t_0} - \max_{j \neq t_0}[F(\underline{x})]_j > 0,$$

where here $F(\underline{x})$ is the softmax output (class posterior vector) of the neural network when the input is $\underline{x}$ (**x** in the notation of [41]).

- In each iteration k of Algorithm 1, select at random pixel index i of image $\underline{x}^{(k)}$ and modify its grey-level $x_i^{(k)}$ to maximize [41]'s objective f. That is,

$$\underline{x}^{(k+1)} = \left(\underline{x}_{-i}^{(k)}, \ \underset{\delta \in \{0,1,\ldots,255\}}{\arg\max} \ f((\underline{x}_{-i}^{(k)}; \delta)) \right),$$

where by definition the jth element of the vector $(\underline{x}_{-i}, a)$ is x_j if $j \neq i$ and is a if $j = i$.

- The stopping condition for Algorithm 1 is $f(\underline{x}^{(k)}) < 0$, that is, the (untargeted adversarial) image $\underline{x}^{(k)}$ is no longer classified to t_0.

Implement and assess the ZOO Algorithm 1 attack on MNIST.

Compare ZOO Algorithm 1 to JSMA [203].

Instead of searching the entire range of values $\{0, 1, \ldots, 255\}$, just search in a small neighborhood above and below the current value $x_{-i}^{(k)}$. Does this change to Algorithm 1 produce different images?

Also implement the ZOO Algorithm 2 attack in [41] which employs a difference quotient (see Eq. (12.4) and [41]'s Eq. (6)) to estimate gradients rather than computing them by back propagation (recall Section 2.10).

MATLAB (With Deep Learning Toolbox) Version

See the MATLAB files available at www.cambridge.org/millersecureAI.

The pseudocode to generate adversarial examples is as follows.

1. Import the MNIST dataset of images with ground truth class labels.
2. Use a pre-trained neural network MATLAB function with F the softmax layer.
3. While any class has fewer than 10 adversarial images classified to it:
   1. select a new, correctly classified MNIST image $\underline{x}$ from a random source class t_0;
   2. perform the ZOO attack described above, starting from $\underline{x}$;
   3. output the created ZOO attack image into a file containing ZOO adversarial examples, and also record its class decision (t) and the source class ($t_0 \neq t$) of the initial clean image $\underline{x}$ used to create it.

Python Version

Follow the directions of the MATLAB project version but instead use the Python files available at www.cambridge.org/millersecureAI.

Alternatively, you can use another prebuilt model for MNIST, for example, VGG-16 available here [265]. Note that with some of these models, you may have to resize the input in your transforms with a command like transforms.Resize if the model was trained on a different dataset.

4.10.2   Contiguous White Region Counting Defense

Visualize ZOO adversarial images to verify salt-and-pepper noise. Next, consider a simple region-counting based AD [179] by first noting that clean (natural) MNIST digits typically consist only of one or two contiguous white regions, where a region is defined as a collection of pixels that are pairwise "connected," with two white pixels pairwise connected if they are in the same first-order (8-pixel) neighborhood, and with white regions defined by extending pixel connectedness through transitive closure over the whole image. Note that a threshold is needed on pixel intensity to determine whether it is "white."

Given such a threshold and an MNIST image, write a program that computes the number of contiguous white regions. When sequentially visiting each pixel of an image, note that a pixel may not be deemed white, may start a new white region, may join one white region, or may join plural white regions and merge them into one. Also note that you can represent the white regions simply using a two-dimensional array of Booleans of the same dimension as an MNIST image. Suppose an image is detected as adversarial if it has more than two contiguous white regions. Applying this detector to a set of clean and of TTE attacked MNIST images, sweep an ROC curve by varying the white-pixel threshold, and compute an associated AUC. Repeat for different numbers of contiguous white regions required to deem a sample a TTE. Also repeat for the case where the ZOO TTEs are iteratively created using a smaller perturbation per iteration, as described above.

For each experiment, choose a single target class and, for each of the remaining classes randomly select 20 clean images. Randomly select another 20 images from each of these classes, and for each of them construct an adversarial example classified to the target class. Run and assess your white region count detector on both sets of 180 images.

4.11   Project: Nearest Neighbor (NN) Classification Defense

In this project, the variable "K" is overloaded: it can mean the number of classes (as elsewhere in this text), the number of clusters (unsupervised K-means, recall Section 3.3), or the number of "nearest neighbors" that are checked to classify a test sample (KNN, also recall Section 2.5.2).

In addition to reading research articles, students working in AI need to learn to forage for code online and write their own. For this project, students can use either the MNIST or CIFAR-10 datasets with a corresponding prebuilt DNN classifier. Using PyTorch, the student can easily access internal layer activations of the DNN.

4.11.1   A K-Means Clustering Based KNN Classifier

Consider the set $\mathcal{A}_i$ of (vector-valued) activations of an internal layer of the DNN by the class-i subset $\mathcal{X}_i$ of the training dataset. Choose the pooling layer after the first convolutional layer. Apply K-means clustering to the vectors in $\mathcal{A}_i$ to obtain κ_i different cluster centers (class-i prototypes). An unlabeled test sample is classified by determining the highest frequency class among the nearest (by some metric) κ^* cluster centers to it (where $\kappa^* < \sum_{i \in y} \kappa_i$), that is, a κ^*NN classification rule.

For an experiment to assess classification accuracy on clean samples, try $\kappa_i = 10$ for all i and $\kappa^* = 3$. Compare the classification accuracy to that of the DNN itself.

Note that a clean validation set held out of training can be used to set the parameters $\{\kappa_i\}$ and κ^*, and to decide which internal layer activations to use, based on maximizing validation-set classification accuracy. One could also perform multi-fold cross validation rather than held-out validation to set these hyperparameters (recall Section 2.8.3).

4.11.2   Assess KNN Defense Against TTEs

Now devise a TTE detection statistic based on K-means clustering of internal-layer activations and evaluate it against the BIM (iterative FGSM) or CW attack.

4.12   Project: Test-Time Evasion (TTE) Attacks and Dropout

Train two DNN classifiers for MNIST. The first has the architecture of the one used in the project of Section 4.10 and is trained without dropout (recall Section 2.7.8). With the same MNIST training dataset, train a second DNN with say 20% more neurons than the first. Dropout is employed during training of the second DNN to achieve a similar accuracy on a clean validation set as the first. Devise and evaluate an experiment to test the hypothesis that TTE attacks are easier to mount on the second (more parameterized) DNN compared to the first.

5 Backdoors and Before/During Training Defenses

Data poisoning (DP) attacks which plant backdoors (Trojans) were introduced in Section 1.4.2. The threat of such attacks is not at all far fetched, considering that cyber attacks occur on a daily basis. The importance of defending against backdoors in DNNs is highlighted by related IARPA TrojAI and DARPA GARD research programs, as well as by machine learning competitions (e.g., that of 2022 NeurIPS). In this chapter, we focus on before/during training backdoor defense, where the defender is also the training authority, with full control of the training process and responsibility for providing an accurate, backdoor-free DNN classifier. Deployment of a backdoor defense during the training phase is supported by the fact that the training authority is usually more resourceful in both computation and storage than a downstream user of the trained classifier. Moreover, in principle, before/during training detection could potentially be somewhat easier than post-training detection since the defender has access to the (possibly poisoned) training set and, thus, to samples that contain the backdoor pattern. On the other hand, before/during training detection is still a highly challenging problem because it is unknown both *whether* there is poisoning and, if so, *which* samples (among the possibly huge number of training samples) are poisoned. The primary defense method developed in this chapter is the first example, in this book, of a *reverse-engineering* defense (RED), wherein the defender aims to estimate a putative backdoor pattern that may have been used by an attacker. The RED paradigm will feature prominently as a defense strategy in much of the remainder of this book.

The before/during training defender needs not only to detect whether the training set is poisoned, but also to cleanse it of poisoning, that is, by accurately identifying and removing the backdoor poisoned training samples. Another possibility, which is also investigated in this chapter, is to cleanse detected poisoned patterns by removing the estimated backdoor pattern from them and replacing a detected poisoned sample's (presumably incorrect) label by a prediction of the sample's true class of origin. In this way, all training samples can still be used for retraining the classifier.

Training set cleansing is an important objective of the defender because it is practically infeasible to reject the entire training set when it is deemed to be poisoned. Also, re-collecting a sufficient training set is costly. Moreover, without identifying the backdoor training samples (and the malicious sources from which they originate), a re-collected training set may *still* be backdoor poisoned. Training set cleansing is also very challenging. First, none of the training set is guaranteed to be clean (i.e., without the backdoor pattern); second, there is no independent/held-out clean dataset as assumed for the post-training scenario, see Chapters 6–9. Hence, there is no reliable baseline reference for the "behavior" of clean samples to assist in identifying backdoor training samples. Third, liberally removing suspicious training samples, which could possibly cause a high fraction of clean training samples to be falsely removed, should be avoided; otherwise, the performance of the resulting trained classifier could be degraded.

In this chapter we cover the following topics.

- A more detailed review of backdoor attacks is given.
- Before/during training defenses [39, 268, 301, 308] are described and experimentally compared using standard image datasets (each with a specific DNN architecture and training setting). The attacks in these experiments involve several backdoor patterns considered in existing works.

5.1 Backdoor Attacks

Following the overview in Section 1.4.2, additional details on backdoor attacks are now given.

5.1.1 Backdoor Patterns and Source and Target Classes

To launch a backdoor attack, the adversary needs to first specify a target class t^*, a set of source class(es) S^*, and a backdoor pattern $\underline{v}^*$ (including a method of its incorporation). Similar to the stealthiness required by TTE attacks, a backdoor pattern, when embedded into clean test samples during operation, should neither be easily noticeable to humans nor easy to automatically detect. In most works, an attack involves a single target class, see for example, [39, 44, 158, 268, 282, 303]. Backdoor attacks involving more than one target class, dubbed an "all-to-all" attack, have been discussed in [89], where the same backdoor pattern, when embedded in a clean test image from class $i \in \mathcal{Y} = \{1, 2, \ldots, K\}$, is supposed to induce a misclassification to class $(i + 1) \mod K$. However, such a backdoor attack can be decomposed into $K = |\mathcal{Y}|$ attacks using the same backdoor pattern, but each involving a unique (source, target) class pair. The backdoor data poisoning detection approach discussed later in this chapter, leveraging elements of a post-training reverse-engineering defense (I-PT-RED) discussed in Chapter 6, will assume a single target class. Although the detection inference approaches of the REDs of Chapters 6 and 7 can only handle a small number of target classes, that of Chapter 8 works for arbitrary numbers of target classes.

From the attacker's perspective, embedding multiple backdoors into the same network may not be advantageous. First, whether multiple backdoors can be embedded such that the attack success rate is high for each backdoor, and such that there is only modest impact on clean (attack-free) test accuracy of the trained classifier (see Section 5.1.3), will depend on the size (capacity) of the network: if the success rate is too low for a backdoor attack, that attack is ineffective; if the clean test accuracy is significantly degraded, the attack is not evasive and it may be easily inferred that the classifier has been compromised.

The number of source classes involved in a backdoor attack could range from 1 to $K - 1$, that is, from a single source class (e.g., [39, 268, 303, 308]) to all classes except for the target class (e.g., [44, 89, 282, 303]).

Effective backdoor patterns in existing works mainly fall into two categories:

- a human imperceptible perturbation applied to a clean sample, dubbed here an *imperceptible* backdoor pattern, for example, a watermark [44, 150, 268, 303, 308];
- a seemingly plausible object patched into a scene, for example, replacing the sample's data in the patch by the attacker's pattern – dubbed here a scene-plausible *perceptible* backdoor pattern, for example, a pair of glasses on a face [44, 89, 93, 282], or a tennis ball in an image with a dog on a lawn.

In this chapter, before/during training defenses will focus on backdoor attacks with an *imperceptible* backdoor pattern. (Before/during training defense against perceptible backdoors is a much easier problem [301], see Chapter 7.) Backdoor patterns can be easily embedded in a clean sample $\underline{x}$, for example, additively by the following function:

$$B(\underline{x}; \underline{v}^*) = [\underline{x} + \underline{v}^*]_\kappa \qquad (5.1)$$

where $[\cdot]_\kappa$ is a domain specific "clipping" operation that constrains the pixel intensity values to their valid range, and where

$$B : I \rtimes I \rightarrow I$$

is the backdoor pattern embedding function and I represents, for example, an image domain. (This clipping operation is an alternative to imposing strict box constraints on the backdoor pattern [260].) For example, for MNIST images, clipping constrains the greyscale pixel intensity values to their valid range $\{0, 1, \ldots, 255\}$. Note that image pixel-channel intensities can be vectorized (and normalized) so that $I \subset \mathbb{R}^N$, consistent with previous notation. However, images are often represented as matrices of (pixel, color channel) intensities in many parts of this book.

The visual stealthiness of an imperceptible backdoor pattern is usually achieved by setting a very small maximum perturbation size $\|\underline{v}^*\|_\infty$ if the pattern is global (e.g., image-wide) [44, 150, 303]; or, in the case of a local pattern, setting a small $\|\underline{v}^*\|_0$, that is, perturbing just a few pixels [268, 303, 308]. Recall that $\| \cdot \|_\infty$ is the l_∞ norm which measures the maximum element in a vector or matrix, while $\| \cdot \|_0$ is the l_0 norm which measures the number of non-zero elements. As an example, Figure 5.1 shows two "truck" images respectively embedded with a global "chessboard" pattern Figure 5.1a and a local "cross" pattern Figure 5.1b, as well as the original, clean "truck" image Figure 5.1c. The backdoor embedding is barely visible to the naked eye, consistent with an "imperceptible" backdoor pattern.

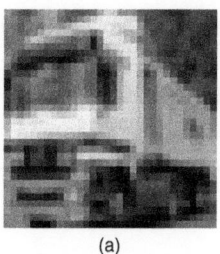 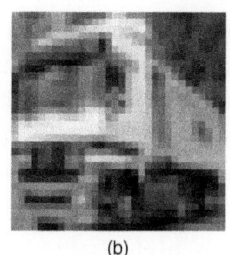 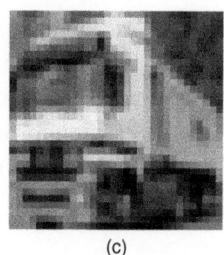

(a)   (b)   (c)

Figure 5.1 Example images embedded with (a) a "chessboard" pattern, (b) a "cross" (embedded near the center), and (c) the original clean (backdoor-free) training image. Reprinted from [301] with permission.

5.1.2   Backdoor Data Poisoning

The (poisoned) training dataset used to learn the victim classifier is the union of the benign (unpoisoned, clean) training set $\mathcal{X}_0$ and a relatively small "backdoor set"

$$\mathcal{B} = \{(B(\underline{x}; \underline{v}^*), t^*) \mid \underline{x} \sim P_{\mathcal{S}^*}\},$$

that is, a set of backdoor training samples from the attack's source classes $\mathcal{S}^* \subset \mathcal{Y}$ embedded with the pattern $\underline{v}^*$ and labeled to target class $t^* \notin \mathcal{S}^*$. Here B is the method of backdoor pattern incorporation, and the original clean samples $\underline{x}$ are collected by the attacker from its source class(es) and are assumed to follow the distribution $P_{\mathcal{S}}^*$ of samples from classes $\mathcal{S}^*$ of the clean training dataset $\mathcal{X}_0$. That is, the training dataset is

$$\mathcal{X} = \mathcal{X}_0 \cup \mathcal{B}.$$

5.1.3   Attacker's Goals

The goals of a backdoor attacker are two-fold. First, the attacker aims to maximize the misclassification rate to the target class t^* when the same backdoor pattern $\underline{v}^*$ used during training is embedded into any test sample following distribution $P_{\mathcal{S}^*}$ of clean training samples from the attack's source class(es). That is, the attacker aims to maximize

$$P_{\underline{X} \sim P_{\mathcal{S}^*}}(\hat{c}(B(\underline{X}; \underline{v}^*)) = t^*), \tag{5.2}$$

where $\hat{c}(\cdot) : \mathcal{I} \to \mathcal{Y}$ is the DNN classifier that maps from the input domain $\mathcal{I}$ to the corresponding set of class labels $\mathcal{Y}$. Second, for clean test samples $\underline{x}$ from any class $y \in \mathcal{Y}$ (i.e., following distribution P_y), the classifier should make correct classifications (i.e., the attack should not degrade classification accuracy when a test pattern does not contain the backdoor pattern). For every class $y \in \mathcal{Y}$ this accuracy is

$$P_{\underline{X} \sim P_y}(\hat{c}(\underline{X}) = y). \tag{5.3}$$

So, the number of poisoned samples $|\mathcal{B}|$ is made small by the attacker to minimize the amount of degradation in clean test set accuracy that is introduced. Thus, both attacker goals can be jointly and automatically achieved by regular training (which the attacker does not influence, unless the attacker also happens to be the training authority) using the poisoned training set, so as to minimize, for example, the cross-entropy training loss objective (recall (2.8)).

5.1.4   More Sophisticated Backdoor Attacks

While the aforementioned backdoor attacks only require that the attacker has the ability to poison the training dataset, there are more powerful attacks which require fewer backdoor training samples and smaller "footprint" (e.g., in l_0 norm) backdoor patterns. However, these attacks require the attacker to possess either a surrogate classifier or the capability to influence the training process of the classifier, which greatly reduces their practical feasibility. In this chapter, as for other existing defenses, only the "classical" backdoor DP attack is considered, wherein the backdoor pattern is chosen by the attacker independent of any knowledge of the classifier structure, the training set, or the classifier's training process, and without leveraging any surrogate classifiers. From experiments, it appears that, with sufficient poisoning, the choice of backdoor pattern is not so important – successful attacks may use local patterns, global patterns, various spatial support shapes, as well as random noise-like patterns. (This is not surprising, given that DNNs have rich representational power.) This also means that the defender has no prior knowledge of the backdoor pattern that may be used by an attacker.

Moreover, while the before/during training defenses considered below focus on imperceptible backdoor patterns that are additively embedded in a sample as in (5.1), other methods of incorporation include local patch replacement (Section 6.9 and Chapter 7), multiplicative embedding (Section 6.4.4), and by a blended method (Eq. (6.1)).

5.2   Before/During Training Defender's Goals

As aforementioned, backdoor defenses can be deployed before/during classifier training, post-training, or during the classifier's operation (test time, in-flight). Here, the focus is on before/during training defense. The defender's objectives, knowledge and capabilities are next summarized. The defender plays the role of the training authority, or helps the training authority to provide users/consumers with a reliable, backdoor-free DNN classifier.

The defender's objectives are the following.

- Detect whether the training set is backdoor poisoned and identify the target class if there is poisoning.
- If there is backdoor poisoning, accurately identify and remove (or cleanse) backdoor training samples.
- Limit the number of clean training samples falsely removed, such that there are sufficient clean samples for adequate training of the classifier.

The defender's knowledge and capabilities are the following.

- The defender has access to the possibly poisoned training set but does not know a priori whether there is data poisoning and, if so, which samples may be poisoned.
- The defender does not possess any independent clean dataset known to be free of backdoor patterns.
- The defender is able to train classifiers.

5.3 Before/During Training Defenses

Some existing before/during training defenses include a "spectral signature" (SS) defense [268], an "activation clustering" (AC) defense [39], "cluster impurity" (CI) defense [308], and TSC-RED [301]. The first three defenses will be reviewed in this section and the reverse-engineering defense TSC-RED will be described in Section 5.4. These defenses will then be compared experimentally in Section 5.5 on the CIFAR-10 dataset [129]. Additional experiments, variations of TSC-RED, and other defenses are discussed in Section 5.6.

Some backdoor defenses deployed before/during training first train a classifier using the possibly poisoned training set. For each class, SS projects the activations of an internal layer of the trained classifier (e.g., the penultimate layer or logit) induced by the training samples – an embedded feature representation of the training samples – onto the principal eigenvector (recall Section 3.5), and then removes outliers. As an early work in this area, SS did not propose any explicit detection inference rule for whether or not the training set was poisoned – SS sanitizes the training set without making explicit inference that the DNN possesses a backdoor. One issue with SS is that the detection threshold is based on knowledge of a hyperparameter that essentially bounds the number of poisoned training patterns. In practice, this number will not be known. While the authors select this guided by validation/test set accuracy, backdoor patterns could also be embedded in the test set (to confound use of this set for setting this hyperparameter). Moreover, a validation set may not even be available in practice. Thus, one cannot, in general, use (good) validation/test set accuracy as a guide for setting this hyperparameter. Second, while the authors do demonstrate both that their approach identifies most of the backdoor patterns and, in removing them, retains high classification accuracy, they do not report how many clean patterns are falsely rejected by their method. For CIFAR-10 there is a sufficient amount of training examples (5000 per class) such that accuracy should be unaffected even if many clean patterns are falsely removed. However, this could be more problematic if fewer training samples are available. Finally, SS [268] assumes that the class that has been poisoned is somehow known to the defender (or that samples can be removed from *all* classes – removing the same number of samples from each – without large impact on the accuracy of the trained classifier). In practice, the training set may not be so large that one has the luxury to eliminate training samples from *all* categories.

AC involves both backdoor detection (based on a Silhouette score) and training set cleansing. For each putative target class, the penultimate layer activations of the associated training samples are projected onto a low-dimensional (e.g., 10-dimensional) space using PCA and clustered using K-means with $K = 2$ (see the respective Sections 3.5 and 3.3). If the activations are well fit by the two-cluster model (evaluated by comparing with a threshold on the Silhouette score), a backdoor attack is detected and this class is deemed the target class of the attack. Then, for the detected target class, the training images associated with the cluster with the smaller mass are identified as the backdoor training images and are removed before retraining.[1] However, in many cases, the backdoor training images are not clearly separable (using, e.g., 2-means) from the clean training images labeled to class t^*, in the projected low-dimensional space of internal layer features [308].

The CI defense first models the penultimate layer activations (without projection to low-dimensional spaces) for each class using a Gaussian mixture model (GMM), with the number of Gaussian components determined by the Bayesian information criterion (BIC), see Section 3.4. Then, for each component, the affiliated training images are blurred by applying an averaging filter and fed into the same trained classifier. If a component contains mainly backdoor training images, the embedded backdoor pattern may be destroyed by blurring; if so, there will be a high fraction of images from this component whose predicted labels are altered by blurring. Although the clustering procedure in CI allows for multiple components, such that the backdoor training images may be mostly captured in one or more clusters, the number of components selected by BIC is very sensitive to the dimension of the activations. When the dimension is too high, BIC usually selects one component, even for the true target class being poisoned, as experimentally shown in Section 5.5.4. (Also recall Section 3.4.2.) Moreover, both CI and AC require setting a detection threshold, which depends on the data domain, whereas the following method requires no such careful threshold choice.

5.4 Training Set Cleansing Reverse-Engineering Defense (TSC-RED)

A before/during training reverse-engineering defense (RED) against imperceptible backdoors is now described. Again, before/during training defense against perceptible backdoors is not discussed in this chapter because these attacks can be easily detected, as shown in [301] (also see Chapter 7).

While the before/during training, not the post-training, scenario is addressed here, the TSC-RED method developed here is inspired by I-PT-RED of Chapter 6 and leverages some of its key ideas. Specifically, post-training detection of imperceptible backdoors is based on the premise that, for a putative backdoor (source, target) class pair (s,t), there exists an unusually small, common "perturbation" that will induce most samples from class s to be misclassified to class t (the backdoor pattern itself would be one such perturbation). We refer to the estimation of such perturbations

---

[1] Since the defense requires training on the possibly poisoned training set, "retraining" refers to training on the cleaned training set. The retrained classifier is the one that will be provided to the consumer.

as "perturbation optimization." Such perturbation optimization (seeking to reverse engineer a putative backdoor pattern) is performed for all possible (source, target) class pairs, with the required perturbation sizes (to induce a π-level misclassification rate from s to t, e.g., $\pi = 0.9$) used as the detection statistics. The fundamental premise behind this detector is experimentally verified in Chapter 6. TSC-RED applies perturbation optimization like I-PT-RED but, unlike I-PT-RED, has access to the possibly poisoned training dataset. That is, a common, small perturbation is sought such that, when *added* to training samples from class s, induces high misclassifications to class t, and when *subtracted* from all training samples labeled to class t, induces an unusually large number of them (the putative backdoor poisoned samples) to be classified to class s. Subtracting out the perturbation is also part of the sample cleansing operation. One main difference between I-PT-RED and TSC-RED is that I-PT-RED relies on a small clean dataset spanning all classes. Another is that TSC-RED has access to the dataset used to train the classifier, while I-PT-RED does not.

5.4.1   Key Ideas

For Detection

Suppose $\hat{c}(\cdot)$ is a DNN classifier trained on the possibly poisoned training dataset to be inspected. If there is successful backdoor data poisoning, that is, $\mathcal{B} \neq \emptyset$ and the probability (5.2) is large enough, for any backdoor class pair (s, t^*) with $s \in S^*$, a large fraction of training samples from class s (since they also follow the distribution P_{S^*}) will be misclassified to class t^* when the backdoor pattern v^* is embedded. The *fundamental premise* of the TSC-RED detector is that, for a true backdoor class pair (s, t), high misclassifications can be induced from s to t using a common, *small* norm perturbation. However, for any non-backdoor class pair (s, t), to achieve a similarly high misclassification rate from s to t, the minimum required perturbation norm will be very large – likely much larger than the norm of the imperceptible backdoor pattern v^* [303]. (As is experimentally supported by several works, when there is no backdoor, the more samples from one class that need to be perturbed to another class using a common perturbation, the larger the required perturbation norm, see Chapter 6.)

This fundamental premise can be understood intuitively as follows. For example, let us consider classification of samples of digits (e.g., the MNIST domain [141]). In particular, take a class pair (s, t) with s the class of digit '3' and t the class of digit '4'. Suppose, first, that the training set is *clean* and the DNN is trained on this clean set. Then, if one desired to add a common perturbation vector to images from class s so that *most* of them are decided as class t by the classifier (which was trained on the clean set), it is expected that one would need to significantly perturb many pixels in the image, or make very large changes to a few pixels, because '3' and '4' are not very similar – either way, the required common perturbation vector will be relatively large (as measured by, e.g., the l_2 norm); recall universal TTE attacks from Section 4.1. On the other hand, suppose that the training set is backdoor poisoned with the class of digit '3' one of the source classes (i.e., $s \in S^*$) and the class of digit '4' the target class (i.e., $t^* = t$). If there are a sufficient number of poisoned samples, one can create a highly successful backdoor attack using a very *small* backdoor pattern vector, for example, modifying a single pixel in the image, or modifying the whole image, but with minute modifications at each pixel location. This should be true even if classes s and t are not very similar (as in this example) – the only way for the DNN to reliably classify images from class '3' (with the backdoor pattern present) as class '4' is by recognizing the backdoor pattern. Thus, the poisoned samples (used in the training objective function) force the classifier to learn to recognize this (*small*) backdoor pattern and to classify to class t when this pattern is recognized in a given sample. Moreover, *small* image modifications may be necessary in order for the backdoor pattern to be imperceptible.

Thus, based on this reasoning, one expects this fundamental premise to hold in practice: for any class pair $(s,t) \in \mathcal{Y} \times \mathcal{Y}$ with $s \neq t$, large perturbations will be needed to induce high misclassifications if (s,t) is not a backdoor class pair (i.e., $s \notin \mathcal{S}^*$ or $t \neq t^*$), while much smaller perturbations will suffice if (s,t) is involved in the backdoor attack (i.e., $s \in \mathcal{S}^*$ and $t^* = t$, with the backdoor pattern itself being one such small perturbation). Again, this premise has been extensively experimentally validated, see Chapter 6. The experimental results in this chapter provide further such validation.

For Training Set Cleansing

It should be clear that additively embedding a pattern $\underline{v}$ and then $-\underline{v}$ to a sample $\underline{x}$ will induce limited changes to it,

$$\|B(B(\underline{x};\underline{v});-\underline{v}) - \underline{x}\|_\infty \leq \|\underline{v}\|_\infty, \tag{5.4}$$

where the infinity norm selects the maximum element in a vector. Moreover, if the clipping function is not activated, the left-hand side of (5.4) will in fact be zero – *no* difference is induced in this case. Hence, if there is an attack, that is, $\mathcal{B} \neq \emptyset$, then for any $\underline{x} \in \mathcal{B}$ where $\underline{x} = B(\tilde{\underline{x}};\underline{v}^*)$ for some $\tilde{\underline{x}} \sim P_{S^*}$ and class label $c(\underline{x}) = t^*$, we have with high probability that

$$\hat{c}(B(\underline{x};-\underline{v}^*)) = \hat{c}(\tilde{\underline{x}}) \in \mathcal{S}^* \tag{5.5}$$

that is, the true class of the originally clean version of a backdoor training sample can be recovered by *removing* the embedded backdoor pattern. However, for *clean* training samples labeled to class t^*, "embedding" the pattern $-\underline{v}^*$, or any arbitrary pattern with a similarly small norm, will likely not change the label predicted by $\hat{c}(\cdot)$. Thus, one can subtract an estimated backdoor pattern $\underline{v}^*$ from $\underline{x}$ and identify $\underline{x}$ as a poisoned training sample if this operation results in a change in the classifier's decision (especially if a high proportion of such misclassifications are to a common class, which is a possible source class of an attack).

5.4.2   Reverse-Engineering Defense

As for other before/during training defenses reviewed in Section 5.3, consider a possibly backdoor poisoned classifier, denoted by $\hat{c}(\cdot)$. TSC-RED (summarized as Algorithm 5.1) consists of three main procedures: pattern estimation, detection inference, and training set cleansing. It is designed for both detection of backdoor attacks and training set cleansing, as well as estimation of the true backdoor pattern $\underline{v}^*$.

Pattern Estimation

Based on the aforementioned fundamental premise, when there is successful backdoor data poisoning, the existence of a small-sized perturbation that induces high misclassification from any $s \in S^*$ to t^* is guaranteed by the existence of $\underline{v}^*$. This motivates a search for such a small-sized perturbation, that is, reverse-engineering the backdoor pattern, for the backdoor class pair(s).

To serve both *detection* and *training set cleansing* purposes, for any class pair $(s,t) \in \mathcal{Y} \times \mathcal{Y}$ with $s \neq t$, under the hypothesis that (s,t) is a backdoor class pair (i.e., $s \in S^*$ and $t = t^*$), one expects the following to hold.

- High misclassifications from s to t are induced by a well-chosen small perturbation.
- The DNN's class decision for a backdoor training sample should change from t when this same perturbation is "removed" from the sample.
- It is not possible for any small perturbation to change the class decision of a significant proportion of the *clean* training samples labeled to t, when the perturbation is "removed" from these samples.

So the goal is to search for a size-limited pattern that induces at least $\pi \in (0,1)$ misclassification fraction from s to t (on the training samples labeled to s) and, at the same time, maximizes the class decision changes for the training samples labeled to t when this pattern is "removed" from them, that is,

$$\text{maximize}_{\underline{v}} \quad \frac{1}{|\mathcal{X}_t|} \sum_{x \in \mathcal{X}_t} \mathbf{1}\{\hat{c}(B(\underline{x}; -\underline{v})) \neq t\}$$

$$\text{subject to} \quad \frac{1}{|\mathcal{X}_s|} \sum_{x \in \mathcal{X}_s} \mathbf{1}\{\hat{c}(B(\underline{x}; \underline{v})) = t\} \geq \pi \tag{5.6}$$

$$\text{and} \quad d(\underline{v}) \leq \Delta_{st}.$$

- $\mathcal{X}_s$ and $\mathcal{X}_t$ represent the subsets of the training dataset labeled to class s and class t, respectively;
- $d(\cdot)$ is any reasonable metric representing the perturbation size (e.g., l_2 norm); and
- Δ_{st} constrains the perturbation size (with reference to metric $d(\cdot)$) to be small.

Since Δ_{st} and the feasible set of $\underline{v}$ for solving (5.6) cannot be easily specified, a gradient-based search algorithm is used, with the perturbation size *implicitly* controlled by the gradient descent termination condition (which will be discussed further, shortly). In principle, consistent with the above goals, it is sought to maximize the Lagrangian objective:

$$\text{maximize}_{\underline{v}} \frac{1}{|\mathcal{X}_t|} \sum_{x \in \mathcal{X}_t} \mathbf{1}\{\hat{c}(B(\underline{x}; -\underline{v})) \neq t\} + \lambda \frac{1}{|\mathcal{X}_s|} \sum_{x \in \mathcal{X}_s} \mathbf{1}\{\hat{c}(B(\underline{x}; \underline{v})) = t\}. \tag{5.7}$$

However, since the indicator $\mathbf{1}\{\cdot\}$ in (5.7) has zero derivative almost everywhere, the following differentiable surrogate objective function can be adopted:

$$J_{st}(\underline{v}) = \frac{1}{|\mathcal{X}_t|} \sum_{\underline{x} \in \mathcal{X}_t} \log(1 - \hat{p}(t|B(t|\underline{x}; -\underline{v}))) + \lambda \frac{1}{|\mathcal{X}_s|} \sum_{\underline{x} \in \mathcal{X}_s} \log \hat{p}(t|B(\underline{x}; \underline{v})). \quad (5.8)$$

Recall Section 2.7.1. Here, the logarithm is taken to make the objective function smoother. The search for $\underline{v}$ is conducted along the gradient of (5.8) with a *relatively small* step size $\delta > 0$, starting from $\underline{v} = \underline{0}$. The step size δ can also be carefully registered in an adaptive way (e.g., using line search) to ensure a smooth increment in the misclassification fraction from s to t (or it can just be periodically reduced, e.g., halved every ten iterations of gradient descent). Note that the choice of δ does not require any prior knowledge about whether (s,t) is a backdoor class pair or not. The searching is stopped immediately once $\underline{v}$ successfully induces at least π fraction of misclassifications from s to t on the training samples labeled to s. This termination condition, paired with a small step-size parameter δ, limits the size of the perturbation. Thus, the resulting perturbation is expected to satisfy both constraints of (5.6), that is, inducing at least π fraction of misclassifications from s to t while being a *small* perturbation. The pattern estimation method is detailed on lines 3–7 of Algorithm 5.1. It is applied to all class pairs independently, with the estimated pattern for any (s,t) pair denoted as $\hat{\underline{v}}_{st}$.

This backdoor pattern estimation (RE) algorithm does require choosing the target misclassification fraction π and the Lagrange multiplier λ. In principle, π should be large, that is, close to 1, and λ should keep the balance between the two terms of (5.7), for example, a default value of $\lambda = 1$. However, as will be experimentally shown, performance of this defense is not very sensitive to these choices.

Also note that the choice of the surrogate objective function for (5.7) is not unique. Although (5.8) is chosen, we may also consider replacing the first term of (5.8), for example, with an objective similar to that associated with the Perceptron algorithm, see (6.7), or with any other mathematically sound, differentiable surrogate for the classifier's (non-differentiable) error rate. Moreover, for each updating of $\underline{v}$ in practice, it is suggested to compute the gradient of (5.8) using two subsets of samples randomly sampled from $\mathcal{X}_s$ and $\mathcal{X}_t$ respectively, especially when the training set is large (so as to reduce the computational complexity). The implementation details of this pattern estimation approach will be described in Section 5.5.

Detection Inference
If backdoor poisoning is detected, the following method also

- infers the target class,
- estimates the backdoor pattern,
- identifies the subset of samples that are deemed to have been poisoned (for purposes of training set cleansing), and
- infers the source class for each sample in this subset.

Algorithm 5.1 For training set cleansing reverse-engineering defense (TSC-RED) backdoor defense.

1: **Inputs**: labeled training set $\mathcal{X} = \{\mathcal{X}_1, \ldots, \mathcal{X}_K\}$, classifier $\hat{c}(\cdot)$
2: **Pattern estimation**:
3: **for** all (s,t) class pairs with $s \neq t$ **do**
4:      $\underline{v} \leftarrow \underline{0}, \rho \leftarrow \frac{1}{|\mathcal{X}_s|} \sum_{\underline{x} \in \mathcal{X}_s} \mathbf{1}\{\hat{c}(\underline{x}) = t\}$
5:      **while** $\rho < \pi$ **do**
6:          $\underline{v} \leftarrow \underline{v} + \delta \nabla J_{st}(\underline{v})$
7:          $\rho \leftarrow \frac{1}{|\mathcal{X}_s|} \sum_{\underline{x} \in \mathcal{X}_s} \mathbf{1}\{\hat{c}(B(\underline{x}; \underline{v})) = t\}$
8:      **end while**
9:      $\underline{\hat{v}}_{st} = \underline{v}, r_{st} = d(\underline{\hat{v}}_{st})^{-1}$
10: **end for**
11: **Detection inference**:
12: **for** all classes i **do**
13:      get null density $g_{-i}(r)$ by MLE using as data all r_{st} with $t \neq i$
14:      evaluate p-value $\text{pv}_{i,\max}$ by Eq. (5.9)
15: **end for**
16: evaluate pv by Eq. (5.10)
17: **if** pv $> \theta$ **then**
18:      there is no attack; defense terminated
19: **else**
20:      backdoor attack detected; $\hat{t} = \arg\min_i \text{pv}_{i,\max}$ is the target class; $\hat{s} = \arg\max_s r_{s\hat{t}}$ is one of the source classes; $\underline{\hat{v}} = \underline{\hat{v}}_{\hat{s}\hat{t}}$ is the estimation of the backdoor pattern $\underline{v}^*$
21: **end if**
22: **Training set cleansing**:
23: **for** all $\underline{x} \in \mathcal{X}_{\hat{t}}$ **do**
24:      **if** $\hat{c}(B(\underline{x}; -\underline{\hat{v}})) \neq \hat{t}$ **then**
25:          remove $\underline{x}$ from the training set (or replace it by the cleansed example $(B(\underline{x}; -\underline{\hat{v}}), \hat{c}(B(\underline{x}; -\underline{\hat{v}}))))$
26:      **end if**
27: **end for**
28: Proceed to retraining if there are samples being removed

Based on the key ideas and the design of the above backdoor pattern estimation algorithm, if there is backdoor poisoning, $d(\underline{\hat{v}}_{st})$ for (s,t) a backdoor class pair should be much smaller than for (s,t) a non-backdoor class pair. Such atypicality can be captured by an unsupervised anomaly detector based on an order statistic hypothesis test as follows [303], see Section 6.3.3.

1. For each class pair (s,t), perform perturbation optimization to obtain the reciprocal statistic $r_{st} = d(\underline{\hat{v}}_{st})^{-1}$. The null hypothesis is that there is no attack – in this case, all

the reciprocal statistics are assumed to come from the same population. Detection of training set poisoning is inferred when there is a reciprocal statistic that is an outlier (unusually large) under the null model. This is assessed in the following.

2. For each putative target class $i \in \mathcal{Y} = \{1, \ldots, K\}$, exclude all the $(K-1)$ reciprocals with $t = i$, and fit a null (e.g., Gamma) density $g_{-i}(r)$ using maximum likelihood estimation (MLE) applied to the *remaining* $K(K-1)-(K-1) = (K-1)^2$ reciprocals.

3. For each putative target class i, evaluate the probability, under the associated null model, that the largest of the $(K-1)$ excluded reciprocals (those with $t = i$) is greater than or equal to the observed maximum reciprocal, $r_{i,\max}$. That is, evaluate the *order statistic p-value*:

$$\mathrm{pv}_{i,\max} = 1 - G_{-i}(r_{i,\max})^{K-1}, \quad i = 1, \ldots, K, \tag{5.9}$$

where G_{-i} is the cumulative distribution function corresponding to the null density g_{-i}.

4. Under the null hypothesis, each of the K order statistic p-values follows a uniform distribution on the interval $[0, 1]$. However, if there is an attack with target class t^*, based on the key detection ideas, $\mathrm{pv}_{t^*,\max}$ should be abnormally small. Hence the probability is evaluated (under the uniform distribution) that the smallest of the K order statistic p-values is no larger than the observed minimum p-value, that is, evaluate an order statistic *on* order statistics:

$$\mathrm{pv} = 1 - (1 - \mathrm{pv}_{\min})^K, \tag{5.10}$$

where $\mathrm{pv}_{\min} = \min_i \mathrm{pv}_{i,\max}$.

5. It is inferred that there is backdoor poisoning with confidence $1 - \theta$ (e.g., $\theta = 0.05$) if $\mathrm{pv} < \theta$; otherwise, declare no attack. If an attack is detected, $\hat{t} = \arg\min_i \mathrm{pv}_{i,\max}$ is inferred to be the target class involved; and $\hat{s} = \arg\max_s r_{s\hat{t}}$ is inferred as one of the source classes involved in the attack. Moreover, $\hat{\underline{v}} = \hat{\underline{v}}_{\hat{s}\hat{t}}$ is our estimate of the backdoor pattern $\underline{v}^*$.

One could alternatively use, for example, a variation of the above method given in [307], MAD-based detection inference of Section 6.2.3, or the method of Section 6.3.3.

Variations of TSC-RED are discussed in Section 5.6, including applying TSC-RED to embedded rather than input features in order to attempt to detect imperceptible backdoor patterns which are not additively incorporated.

5.5   Experiments

In this section, we evaluate the performance of SS, AC, CI and TSC-RED for different DNNs trained on the CIFAR-10 [129] dataset, and using a large variety of imperceptible backdoor attacks. The results demonstrate TSC-RED's superior capability in backdoor detection and training set cleansing (so that the attack is no longer effective).

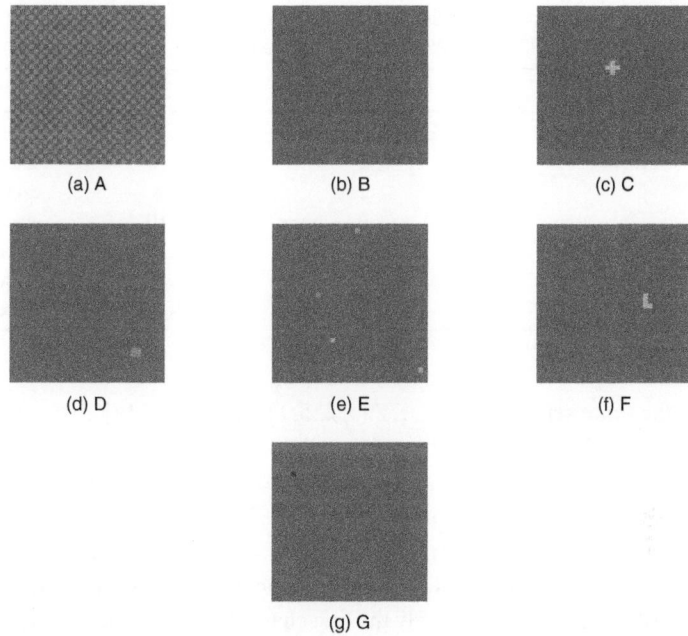

Figure 5.2 Illustration of the backdoor patterns. Some images are offset or scaled for visualization purposes. Reprinted from [301] with permission.

5.5.1 CIFAR-10 Dataset

CIFAR-10 [129] is a dataset of 60k (i.e., 60,000) 32×32 color images from $K = 10$ classes: 'plane', 'car', 'bird', 'cat', 'deer', 'dog', 'frog', 'horse', 'ship', and 'truck'. For convenience, these 10 classes are enumerated as 1 to 10. The training set of a CIFAR-10 classifier contains 50k images (5k per class) and the test set contains the remaining 10k images (1k per class).

5.5.2 Attack Crafting

Backdoor Patterns

Seven *imperceptible* backdoor patterns, shown in Figure 5.2, that have appeared in the backdoor literature are considered, including two "global" patterns (patterns A, B) and five "local patterns" (patterns C–G).

Pattern A is a "chessboard" pattern [303]. For each pair of neighboring pixels, one and only one pixel is perturbed positively. Here, the perturbation size is set to 2/255 for all pixels being perturbed. (Although the TSC-RED defense is designed for the general case where the pixel-channel intensity values are continuous $\in [0, 1]$, real-world attackers are mimicked by imposing an 8-bit finite precision to the pixel values, such that a valid image (with or without a backdoor pattern) should have pixel values in

Table 5.1 Choices of the source class(es) S^* and the target class t^* for the 21 attacks (1SC, 3SC, and 9SC attack for patterns A–G).

Pattern	t^*	S^* of 1SC	S^* of 3SC	S^* of 9SC
A	10	2	2, 5, 8	except 10
B	8	2	2, 3, 10	except 8
C	10	2	5, 7, 8	except 10
D	4	9	8, 9, 10	except 4
E	7	4	2, 4, 6	except 7
F	9	4	4, 5, 6	except 9
G	3	1	1, 4, 8	except 3

the finite set $\{0, 1/255, \ldots, 254/255, 1\}$.) In pattern B [150], a pixel (i, j) is perturbed positively if and only if i and j are both even numbers (where pixel indices start from 0). The perturbation size is 3/255 for all perturbed pixels. Patterns C, D, and F, that is, the "cross," the "square," and the "L," are crafted (with a little modification) based on the backdoor patterns used in [268]. However, the perturbations for pattern C and pattern F are applied to all three channels (i.e., pixel colors) with perturbation size 70/255. For pattern D, only the first channel is modified, with perturbation size 80/255. The locations of the "cross," the "square," and the "L" are randomly selected. In pattern E [303], four pixels are perturbed in one of the three channels. The location of the pixel to be perturbed, the channel to be perturbed, and the sign of the perturbation (either positive or negative) are all randomly selected. The absolute perturbation size is also randomly selected from the set $\{80/255, \ldots, 96/255\}$. Pattern G, a "single-pixel" perturbation, is considered in both [268] and [308], and is generated according to [268]: the position of the pixel and the channel to be perturbed are randomly selected.

Note that pattern generation may involve some randomness (e.g., the choice of the location of the "cross" for pattern C). But once a backdoor pattern is generated for an attack, it is *commonly* embedded in all backdoor training images. In the Appendix of [301], for each backdoor pattern A–G, example images embedded with the backdoor pattern and their originally clean, backdoor-free images are shown – all these backdoor patterns are barely visible to humans.

Attack Configurations

For each backdoor pattern, backdoor attacks are created with one source class, three source classes, or nine source classes (i.e., all classes except for the target class are the source classes in the last case). For convenience, these three attacks are respectively named '1SC', '3SC', and '9SC'. For each backdoor pattern, the three associated attacks use the same target class, which is arbitrarily chosen. The choice of the source classes for each attack is also arbitrary. These choices are summarized in Table 5.1.

For each backdoor pattern, 500, 200, or 60 clean images *per source class* are used to create backdoor training images. Backdoor poisoning in the experiments is conducted by *replacing* these clean images in the training set by the backdoor images created using them. This simulates the practical scenario where the sources for data collection (including a possible attacker) independently contribute training images to the training authority. If all the sources are benign, the training authority obtains the clean CIFAR-10 training set. If any source is an attacker (unbeknownst to the training authority) the subset of training images contributed by this source contains a backdoor pattern.

Note that these experimental settings cover a broader range of cases than some prior works. For example, [268] only considered backdoor attacks with a single source class, that is, the 1SC attack case. [308] only considered attacks with one source class and three source classes. The following experiments cover all these cases, with a large variety of backdoor patterns involved, including those considered by [268] and [308].

5.5.3 Attack Effectiveness on Defenseless DNNs

DNN Architecture: Two slightly different architectures are considered from the standard ResNet model family, which is perhaps the most popular choice of DNN architecture for image classification (recall Figure 2.6). A standard ResNet architecture is featured by *four groups* of residual blocks (see Table 1 of [97]). A ("non-bottleneck") residual block consists of two identical, consecutive convolutional layers (i.e., two sets of identical convolutional filters) in parallel with an identity map (see Figure 2 of [97]). The two architectures considered here are both 18-layer ResNet with two residual blocks in each of the four groups of residual blocks. One is a wide architecture where there are 64, 128, 256, 512 filters in each convolutional layer for the four groups of residual blocks, respectively; while the other is a compact architecture with 16, 32, 64, 128 filters instead. The two architectures are depicted in Figure 2.6.

The wide DNN architecture has a stronger representation power than the compact DNN architecture, but it also contains more parameters and requires more training resources and training time than the compact DNN architecture to achieve high test accuracy. For a dataset containing a large number of classes (e.g., ImageNet [57], CIFAR-100) using a wide DNN structure can achieve a clearly higher test accuracy than using a compact DNN architecture. But for a dataset containing a relatively small number of classes (e.g., CIFAR-10, MNIST [141] or SVHN [194]), using a compact DNN architecture achieves sufficiently high test accuracy with much less training resources/time required. The architecture of the DNN is determined by the trainer, not by the attacker. Both wide and compact architectures are considered for adequate evaluation of the performance of the defenses.

Training Configurations: For both DNN architectures, training is performed for 100 epochs (Section 2.7.5), with batch size 32 and learning rate 0.001. The Adam optimizer is used with decay rates of 0.9 and 0.999, respectively, for the first and second gradient-moment estimates used to compute search direction. Following common practice, training data augmentation is used for training clean image classifiers, including random cropping, random horizontal flipping, and random rotation.

Attack Effectiveness: Table 5.2 shows that all 21 attacks (1SC, 3SC, and 9SC attacks for seven backdoor patterns) are successful against defenseless DNNs, for both the wide and the compact architectures. The attack success rate (ASR) for each attack is the percentage of the CIFAR-10 test images from the source class(es) that are classified

Table 5.2 Attack success rate (ASR) and poisoned classifier accuracy (ACC), as percentages, on the clean test set (jointly represented by ASR/ACC [289]) for each of the 21 attacks (1SC, 3SC, and 9SC attacks for patterns A–G) for defenseless DNNs, for both wide and compact architectures; test ACC of the clean benchmark DNNs is also shown (ASR is not applicable (represented by n.a.) to clean DNNs).

	Pattern	A	B	C	D	E	F	G
Wide DNN	clean	n.a./92.2	n.a./91.8	n.a./91.9	n.a./91.7	n.a./92.3	n.a./91.3	n.a./92.2
	1SC	99.2/92.1	97.3/92.0	98.9/92.2	96.2/92.1	97.0/91.8	86.1/91.7	92.9/91.3
	3SC	99.5/91.6	98.5/92.0	99.3/91.8	99.5/91.8	99.9/92.1	94.2/90.8	97.1/92.2
	9SC	98.8/91.7	97.1/91.9	98.4/91.7	92.6/91.9	99.4/91.7	89.4/92.0	96.2/91.5
Com-pact DNN	clean	n.a./90.4	n.a./90.7	n.a./91.3	n.a./91.2	n.a./90.4	n.a./90.8	n.a./90.5
	1SC	99.1/90.8	99.5/90.5	96.4/90.3	92.4/90.6	96.0/90.7	89.4/90.1	94.3/90.4
	3SC	99.3/90.1	91.0/90.9	98.1/90.2	99.5/90.4	99.6/90.6	90.5/89.8	96.9/90.7
	9SC	99.1/90.3	97.7/90.5	97.3/90.8	86.5/90.6	98.2/90.0	87.6/90.2	97.2/90.1

to the target class when the backdoor pattern is embedded. For each backdoor pattern and each DNN architecture, a DNN was trained on the clean, unpoisoned CIFAR-10 training set to obtain benchmark accuracy (ACC) on the clean test set (with no backdoor patterns). For all attacks, both of the attacker's goals – a high ASR and a negligible degradation in ACC – are achieved.

5.5.4   Defense Performance Evaluation

Implementation Details of TSC-RED

As mentioned in Section 5.4.2, the step size δ for pattern estimation should be relatively small so that the π fraction of group misclassification can be achieved with as small a perturbation size as possible. Here, $\delta = 10^{-4}$ for simplicity. Also, the target misclassification fraction π for pattern estimation should be relatively large in order to distinguish backdoor class pairs from non-backdoor class pairs. In the experimental results given below $\pi = 0.95$, but its choice is not critical to TSC-RED. Similarly, the choice of the Lagrange multiplier is not critical to the TSC-RED based defense, and the default $\lambda = 1$ is used. Robustness analysis for the choices of π and λ are provided in [301]. Moreover, in each iteration of pattern estimation, the gradient of (5.8) is computed on two batches of training images (with batch size 256) randomly sampled from X_t and X_s, respectively. This reduces computational complexity and may help avoid poor local optima. For detection inference, the Gamma form for the null density, the l_2 norm for the perturbation size, and the (typical) confidence-level threshold $\theta = 0.05$ were used. Finally, both the wide and compact DNN architectures of Section 5.5.3 (Figure 2.6) were considered, with the training configuration the same as that used for the defenseless classifiers described in the same section.

In writing $X = X_0 \cup B$ above, we also implicitly assumed that the training dataset augmentation process, as described in Section 2.8.1, was not used (consistent with the experiments reported for this chapter; but augmentation was used in the backdoor experiments reported in subsequent chapters). Alternatively, a more powerful adversary could act *after* this augmentation process, that is, X_0 could represent an *augmented* clean dataset.

Several comments are in order here. First note that the defense, as part of the training authority, could be applied prior to such data augmentation and leverage a DNN trained without data augmentation. Even if the defense is applied after data augmentation, note that such augmentation may (i) significantly increase the size of the training dataset but (ii) will produce additional backdoor pattern examples from the source class(es) to the target class of the attack, each corresponding to the augmentation process acting on a backdoor pattern example contributed by the attacker. Relating to this, it is important to emphasize that the methods described below and in subsequent chapters are robust to the presence of a plurality of different backdoor patterns between the same source and target classes.

Performance Evaluation

The performance of TSC-RED in detecting whether or not there was backdoor data poisoning is evaluated in comparison with AC and CI on the 21 attacks for the two DNN architectures. This performance for SS was not evaluated because it sanitizes the training images for *all* classes, without any explicit inference of whether or not there is poisoning and without identifying which class has been poisoned (see SS Algorithm 1 of [268]).

As described in Section 5.3, AC uses the Silhouette score for detection – an attack is detected if the Silhouette score obtained for any class is larger than a threshold. However, no automatic rule was proposed for selecting the detection threshold [39]. Even for the relatively simple MNIST dataset, there is no threshold on the Silhouette score that leads to perfect detection, as shown in Table 3 of [39]. Moreover, when there is no poisoning, the maximum Silhouette score over all classes depends on the data domain, the DNN architecture, and most importantly, the dimension of the space that the extracted activations are projected onto. In [39], the authors set the projected feature dimension as 10, and claimed that a range of dimension choices work similarly well based on their experiments on relatively easy datasets like MNIST. For the CIFAR-10 domain and the wide ResNet architecture, as shown in Table 5.3, AC achieves almost perfect detection performance *with a properly selected detection threshold* (and impressive training set cleansing performance as shown in Table 5.4) when the projected feature dimension is set to 2. Here, the threshold on the Silhouette score was selected as 0.4055 in a "supervised" fashion – this value is the maximum Silhouette score obtained for the seven benchmark DNNs trained on the clean CIFAR-10 training set. But this knowledge will not be available to the defender, in general, in practice. Choosing this value maximizes AC's accuracy in detecting poisoning while maintaining zero false detections when there is no poisoning – as seen in Table 5.3, AC detects all but one of the attacks.

For the compact DNN architecture, the same projected feature dimension (10) is used as in [39], since other choices yielded very poor detection performance. The detection threshold was set to 0.0881 for the compact architecture (again chosen in a supervised

Table 5.3 Detection performance evaluation of (a) TSC-RED, (b) AC and (c) CI, on the 21 poisoned training sets and the clean training sets for both wide and compact DNN architectures. Symbol ⊗ represents an attack is not detected (or falsely detected for a clean training set). Here, symbol ⊙ represents an attack is detected with the target class correctly inferred (or no attack is detected for a clean training set).

Pattern		A	B	C	D	E	F	G
Wide DNN	clean	⊙	⊙	⊙	⊙	⊗	⊙	⊙
	1SC	⊙	⊙	⊙	⊙	⊙	⊙	⊙
	3SC	⊙	⊙	⊙	⊙	⊙	⊙	⊙
	9SC	⊙	⊙	⊙	⊙	⊙	⊙	⊙
Compact DNN	Clean	⊙	⊙	⊙	⊙	⊙	⊙	⊙
	1SC	⊙	⊙	⊙	⊙	⊙	⊙	⊙
	3SC	⊙	⊙	⊙	⊙	⊙	⊙	⊙
	9SC	⊙	⊙	⊙	⊙	⊙	⊙	⊙

(a) TSC-RED detection

Pattern		A	B	C	D	E	F	G
Wide DNN	Clean	⊙	⊙	⊙	⊙	⊙	⊙	⊙
	1SC	⊙	⊙	⊙	⊙	⊗	⊙	⊙
	3SC	⊙	⊙	⊙	⊙	⊙	⊙	⊙
	9SC	⊙	⊙	⊙	⊙	⊙	⊙	⊙
Compact DNN	Clean	⊙	⊙	⊙	⊙	⊙	⊙	⊙
	1SC	⊗	⊗	⊗	⊙	⊗	⊗	⊗
	3SC	⊗	⊗	⊗	⊙	⊗	⊗	⊙
	9SC	⊗	⊗	⊗	⊗	⊗	⊙	⊗

(b) AC detection

Pattern		A	B	C	D	E	F	G
Wide DNN	Clean	⊙	⊙	⊙	⊙	⊙	⊙	⊙
	1SC	⊗	⊗	⊗	⊗	⊗	⊗	⊗
	3SC	⊗	⊗	⊗	⊗	⊗	⊗	⊗
	9SC	⊗	⊗	⊗	⊗	⊗	⊗	⊗
Compact DNN	Clean	⊙	⊙	⊙	⊙	⊙	⊙	⊙
	1SC	⊙	⊙	⊙	⊗	⊙	⊙	⊗
	3SC	⊙	⊙	⊙	⊙	⊙	⊙	⊙
	9SC	⊙	⊙	⊙	⊙	⊙	⊙	⊙

(c) CI detection

fashion, to ensure no false positive detections while maximizing detection power). As shown in Table 5.4b, for the compact DNN architecture, even with supervised setting of the detection threshold, the detection performance of AC is quite poor. This is due to the fact that the dimension-reduced activations for clean training images and backdoor training images are not separable using K-means with $K = 2$. More details are provided in the Appendix of [301] together with results for the wide DNN architecture with the projected feature dimension set to 10.

CI also requires setting a detection threshold [308]. Here, in the same supervised fashion as for AC, the detection thresholds for the wide and compact DNN architectures are respectively set as 0.62 and 0.65. As shown in Table 5.4c, CI detects all attacks except two for the compact DNN architecture, but fails to detect any of the attacks when the wide DNN architecture is used. This is due to the fact that for the wide DNN architecture, CI estimates only one component by Gaussian mixture modeling with BIC, for all classes, including the true backdoor target class, since the dimension of the penultimate layer activations is too high.

Different from AC and CI, TSC-RED uses a statistical confidence threshold ($\theta = 0.05$); it does not require any careful, supervised hyperparameter tuning. As shown in Table 5.4a, TSC-RED outperforms AC and CI by successfully detecting all attacks regardless of the DNN architecture, with correct inference of the target class for each attack, with only one false detection. (If the target class is incorrectly inferred, backdoor training images will not be removed. Moreover, clean training images will be falsely removed.)

Table 5.4 Training set cleansing true positive rate (TPR) and false positive rate (FPR) of SS, AC, CI, and TSC-RED (represented in TPR/FPR form), for the 21 attacks, for (a) the wide DNN architecture, and (b) the compact DNN architecture. TPR ≥ 90% and FPR ≤ 10% are in bold.

	Pattern	A	B	C	D	E	F	G
1SC	SS	**98.0/5.2**	**100/5.0**	44.2/10.6	**97.4/5.3**	56.0/9.4	76.8/7.3	86.0/6.4
	AC	88.4/0	**98.8/0.0**	87.2/0.5	**95.2/0**	70.4/27.7	**93.6/0**	85.2/0.1
	TSC-RED	**94.8/8.4**	**97.2/0.3**	**95.6/8.6**	**92.8/2.8**	83.0/0.2	98.6/10.8	87.6/0.3
3SC	SS	**99.5/6.1**	**100/6.0**	66.2/10.1	**99.7/6.0**	**92.2/6.9**	84.8/7.8	79.2/8.5
	AC	**97.5/0**	**98.8/0**	**97.0/0**	**97.2/0**	**94.5/0**	**95.5/0.1**	87.7/0.7
	TSC-RED	98.0/12.9	**98.7/1.6**	**99.2/6.2**	**98.2/0**	**90.3/0**	**98.5/2.8**	**92.7/0.1**
9SC	SS	**98.3/5.6**	**100/5.4**	89.1/6.6	**96.1/5.8**	**97.8/5.6**	**90.9/6.4**	**94.8/6.0**
	AC	**97.0/0**	**98.9/0**	**96.5/0**	**91.1/0.1**	**96.7/0**	**95.9/0**	89.6/0
	TSC-RED	**96.1/4.2**	**98.7/7.9**	**99.3/0.4**	**94.1/0**	88.7/0	**99.1/5.1**	**94.3/0**

(a) Wide DNN architecture

	Pattern	A	B	C	D	E	F	G
1SC	SS	23.6/12.6	**96.8/5.3**	39.6/11.0	69.2/8.1	21.2/12.9	49.2/10.1	18.2/13.2
	AC	36.4/47.0	82.6/38.8	72.2/40.5	92.6/25.9	36.4/41.5	95.4/40.9	93.0/37.5
	CI	55.8/7.5	**99.8/0**	93.8/13.1	n.a./n.a.	96.2/55.6	**100/8.4**	n.a./n.a.
	TSC-RED	93.6/20.9	**100/9.5**	91.0/10.6	98.8/12.2	87.8/5.1	98.4/16.7	94.4/14.7
3SC	SS	35.5/13.7	29.5/14.5	14.7/16.2	85/7.8	53.8/11.5	56.5/11.2	55.5/11.3
	AC	56.0/38.2	19.3/52.0	84.5/38.1	80.7/34.5	74.5/38.2	97.0/39.4	**91.5/0.8**
	CI	89.7/1.9	**97.0/0.1**	**98.7/0**	**99.0/0**	97.5/54.6	**97.7/2.2**	**94.2/1.1**
	TSC-RED	94.8/11.3	99.2/12.6	**99.0/4.5**	**95.8/0.1**	**90.2/2.8**	**99.0/2.4**	91.3/12.6
9SC	SS	11.7/14.9	15.4/14.5	19.3/14.1	42.8/11.6	53.0/10.5	70.9/8.5	68.0/ 8.9
	AC	90.9/42.8	58.5/38.0	8.0/52.2	78.9/40.8	65.2/38.7	**93.1/0.2**	60.7/40.1
	CI	**96.5/0**	**95.7/0**	**96.7/0**	**95.9/1.1**	98.3/43.9	**99.1/0.2**	**95.0/0.3**
	TSC-RED	**98.3/9.5**	94.6/10.2	**97.6/1.0**	**92.2/1.0**	**91.5/2.0**	**98.5/4.6**	**91.3/0.4**

(b) Compact DNN architecture

Training Set Cleansing Performance Evaluation

The training set cleansing performance of TSC-RED is compared with SS, AC, and CI on the 21 attacks for the two DNN architectures.

According to Algorithm 1 of [268], SS removes 1.5ϵ training images from *each* class, without considering whether there is an attack, where ϵ is the upper bound on the number of backdoor training images. The experiments of [268] simply set ϵ as the actual number of backdoor training images used by the attacker. However, in practice, whether or not there is an attack present, the target class, and the number of backdoor training images are *all* unknown to the defender. Thus, evaluation of training set cleansing performance for SS is optimistic or "best case" in that SS is provided with this knowledge – whether there is an attack, the target class of the attack, and the number of backdoor poisoned images. (Our implementations of SS and AC (based on the descriptions in [268] and [39]) are posted in the RE-paper folder of [329].) This information was also exploited by SS in the experiments in [268]. In our experiments, 1.5 times the actual number of backdoor training images were removed from the true backdoor target class (with these images selected by the SS algorithm), without touching the other classes.

As shown in Table 5.3b, AC does not detect all 21 attacks (unlike TSC-RED). The detection performance for the compact DNN architecture is particularly poor, as was noted previously. In practice, when there is no detection made, no images will be removed, and so all the backdoor training images will remain if poisoning actually exists. Thus, in evaluating the training set cleansing performance for AC, similar to SS, AC is "assisted" by assuming that it has detected all the attacks, with the target class correctly inferred. In this way, again, the AC results are optimistic or "best case" results. Following the same settings as in [39], for each attack, from the two clusters obtained for the true backdoor target class (using K-means with $K = 2$), the one with the smaller mass is removed (the same criterion as used in [39]).

For CI, training set cleansing is performed simultaneously with attack detection – all training images from a GMM component are removed if its "cluster impurity" measure exceeds the detection threshold [308]. Since for all 21 attacks, CI estimates only one component for the true target class if the wide DNN architecture is used, even if the true target class is known to the defender, CI cannot identify or remove any backdoor training images. Hence, the failing results of CI for the wide DNN architecture are not shown for brevity.

For each attack and each DNN architecture, true positive rate (TPR) and false positive rate (FPR) are used as the metrics for evaluating the training set cleansing performance of each defense. TPR is defined as the percentage of backdoor training images correctly identified and removed. FPR is defined as the percentage of false removals (detected samples that are actually clean) from the *true backdoor target class*.

As shown in Table 5.4, for the wide DNN architecture, both SS and AC achieve very high TPR and low FPR for most of the attacks. The high TPRs of SS are consistent with the results reported in Table 2 of [268]. However, the low FPR of SS is only guaranteed by the (supervised) setting (at 1.5ϵ) of the number of training images to be removed from the true backdoor target class, where ϵ is chosen as the *true* number of backdoor images. In practice, both the true target class and the number of backdoor-poisoned images are unknown to the defender. Moreover, based on its design, which removes samples from all classes, SS will inevitably falsely remove a significant number of clean images from all classes other than the true backdoor target class. While this is not reflected in the results in Table 5.4 since only FPR is evaluated for SS (i.e., considering only the images labeled to the true backdoor class), SS's false removal of samples from other classes may result in significant degradation in the clean test accuracy of the retrained classifier, especially when the training set is not that large.

For the compact DNN architecture, both SS and AC are ineffective against most of the attacks. This is because the activations for the backdoor training images and the clean training images from the true backdoor target class are not separable in the low-dimensional space (see the Appendix of [301] for more details). Also recall that AC has been optimistically "assisted"; otherwise, for all the attacks that are not detected (reported in Table 5.4b), the TPR and FPR would both be zero.

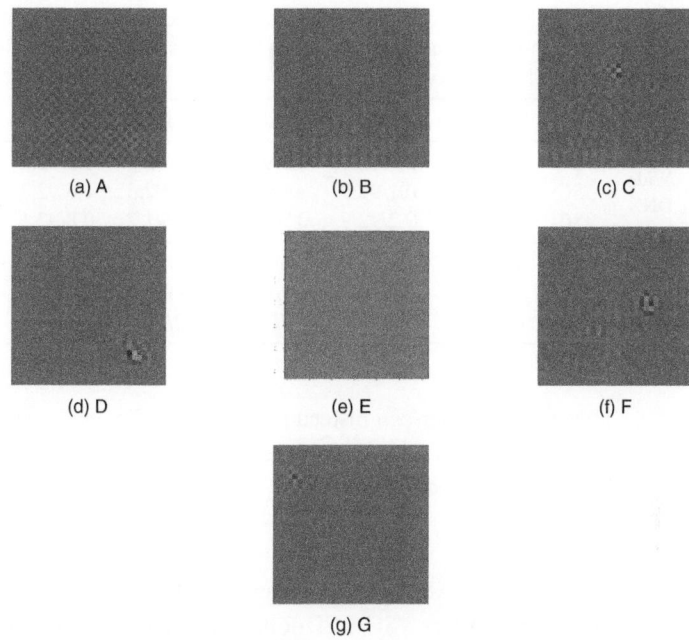

(a) A   (b) B   (c) C

(d) D   (e) E   (f) F

(g) G

Figure 5.3 Pattern estimated by TSC-RED for the seven 1SC attacks for the wide DNN architecture. Some images are offset or scaled for visualization purposes. Reprinted from [301] with permission.

By contrast, though CI fails to detect any attacks for the wide DNN architecture, it works well (for both detection and training set cleansing) for most of the attacks if the defender chooses to use the compact DNN architecture (with a lower dimension for the internal layer features). This is consistent with the results reported in [308].

In practice, an application may have its preferred DNN architecture. In comparison with SS, AC, and CI, TSC-RED is uniformly effective, regardless of which DNN architecture is used for defense. TSC-RED outperforms its competitors (with their optimistic settings) in both **detection** and **training set cleansing**.

Backdoor Pattern Estimation

Figure 5.3 shows the pattern estimated by TSC-RED for the seven 1SC attacks for the wide DNN architecture. These attacks use the backdoor patterns in Figure 5.2. TSC-RED accurately recovers most of these backdoor patterns (with, e.g., 2×10^{-5} squared error per pixel for pattern A). For pattern E, TSC-RED recovers the topmost pixel, which is the actual backdoor pattern learned by the classifier. By embedding this estimated pattern (essentially the single pixel perturbation) into the clean test images from the source class of the 1SC attack, TSC-RED achieves 99.0% ASR on a defenseless DNN with the wide ResNet architecture. Example backdoor training images with the estimated backdoor pattern removed (i.e., cleansed images) are shown in the Appendix of [301]. These images are easily classified to the source class by the classifier trained on the poisoned training set. In practice, rather than removing

Table 5.5 Attack success rate (ASR) and clean test accuracy (ACC), jointly represented by ASR/ACC, of the retrained classifiers for the 21 attacks when TSC-RED is applied, for both wide and compact DNN architectures.

Pattern		A	B	C	D	E	F	G
Wide DNN	1SC	4.9/91.9	2.7/92.1	2.2/91.8	1.1/92.7	3.5/92.6	0.8/91.6	2.2/92.7
	3SC	0.8/92.3	0.1/92.9	0/92.0	0.7/92.3	1.6/92.7	0.3/91.6	1.3/92.6
	9SC	0.6/92.5	0.2/92.9	0.3/92.9	1.4/91.7	0.8/92.1	0.8/91.9	0.4/92.4
Com-pact DNN	1SC	1.9/90.2	0/90.2	2.6/90.4	0.3/90.0	3.1/89.9	0.6/90.5	2.2/89.8
	3SC	1.1/90.1	0.4/90.3	0.1/90.5	0.9/90.5	1.8/90.3	0.5/89.7	2.0/90.1
	9SC	0.9/89.9	0.9/90.0	0.7/90.2	2.2/90.4	0.7/90.1	0.9/90.6	1.4/90.0

these images, the trainer can instead retain these "cleaned" images in the training set (with the class label for a cleaned image chosen as the class decided by the (poisoned) classifier on the cleaned image).

Retraining

Table 5.5 shows the ASR and the clean test ACC of the classifiers retrained on the cleaned training set (for TSC-RED following removal of the suspicious training images). Compelling results for retraining with images cleansed, rather than removed, by TSC-RED are given in the Appendix of [301]. The retrained classifier is the final product that will be provided to users/consumers. The configurations of retraining are determined by the training authority. As an illustration, here the same configurations as for training the defenseless classifiers in Section 5.5.3 are used, for both wide and compact DNN architectures. With the protection of TSC-RED, *the maximum ASR of the 21 attacks is merely 4.9% on CIFAR-10*. Also, no degradation in the clean test ACC of the retrained classifiers is observed, presumably due to the low FPR of TSC-RED in training set cleansing. In comparison, many of the retrained classifiers for SS, AC, and CI still have a high ASR (as shown in the Appendix of [301]).

5.6 Defense Variations and Additional Experiments

In [301], additional experimental results are given to show the robustness of TSC-RED to hyperparameter settings, performance on other datasets, including one with 100 classes (CIFAR-100), and comparisons of different defenses in terms of empirical computational complexity (execution times). Though the number of perturbation optimizations required for TSC-RED scales quadratically with the number of classes, note that before/during training backdoor defenses involve *offline* (i.e., training not test/production time) overhead.

One could consider datasets with more complex images and even more classes, for example, ImageNet [57] has 1000 classes. For such cases, the post-training detector L-RED [305] requires only *one* perturbation optimization for each class. The same ideas can also be exploited to achieve a reduced complexity variant of TSC-RED.

Regarding the attacks themselves, other backdoor embedding mechanisms may be considered wherein the pattern exhibits some variability across the poisoned images, or the backdoor pattern is differently encoded (e.g., multiplicatively or via local patch replacement rather than additively). See the post-training REDs of Chapters 6 and 7. In particular, the TSC-RED approach described above can simply be applied to embedded features in order to attempt to detect backdoors that are not additively incorporated, see Section 6.4.4. Also, when there are few classes, the transferability approach for sample specific perturbations of Chapter 8 can be adapted for TSC.

In [283], an approach to filtering and relabeling the training dataset is proposed using self-supervised representation learning (ignoring the class labels, recall Section 2.12.3) of the possibly poisoned training dataset. (Alternatively, an auto-encoder could be used, recall Section 2.13.) The hypothesis is that the resulting representations will *not* retain the backdoor patterns and backdoor poisoned samples will thus have representations similar to those of samples from their source classes. KNN classification (recall Section 4.11), or classification based on an alternative similarity score, is then applied to this feature representation to detect poisoned training samples – the neighboring samples in the representation space (excepting other poisoned samples) will tend to be labeled to the *source* class of a poisoned sample, while a poisoned sample will be labeled to the target class of the attack. Thus, the poisoned samples will be "outliers" with respect to their class labels. Besides detecting poisoned samples, [283] also applies KNN to relabel them to their (estimated) source class so that they can be safely used for subsequent DNN classifier training. The method is "universal" in the sense that it makes no implicit assumptions about the backdoor pattern or the method of its incorporation. (See Chapter 9 for post-training universal defenses.)

Finally, while this chapter studied before/during training defenses against backdoor data poisoning attacks for the image classification domain, they can be applied to other application domains (e.g., speech [156, 324], documents [212]). In particular, note that even if the features are discrete valued (e.g., for the document domain), the detection method can operate on continuous-valued *embedded* features (internal-layer activations), as described for the post-training scenario in Section 6.4.4. This also gives capability for detecting backdoor attacks that use alternatives to additive embedding of the backdoor pattern (such as multiplicative or patch replacement embedding).

5.7   Chapter Summary

This is the first chapter in the book dealing with defense against backdoor data poisoning attacks, here considering the scenario where the defender has access to the training set (the before/during training scenario). We first described several detection and mitigation methods that are all based on clustering applied to an internal layer of the trained DNN, under the premise that, in this derived (embedded) feature space, backdoor poisoned samples (labeled to a common target class) may form a distinct cluster from "normal" samples, which ground truth originate from this class. Next we developed a more powerful reverse-engineering based defense, wherein putative backdoor patterns are estimated such that, when they are added to samples labeled to a putative source class, they induce high misclassifications to a putative target class *and* such that, when they are subtracted from putative target class samples, they induce a significant number of decision changes back to the putative source class. This defense can be used for backdoor *detection*, for identifying source and target classes of a detected attack, and for identifying the poisoned samples involved in the attack. Retraining following the cleansing of detected poisoned samples was demonstrated to largely mitigate the attack. The experiments demonstrated the effectiveness of the RED defense for a variety of backdoor patterns, for different numbers of source classes involved in attacks, and for both wide and compact DNN architectures.

Some questions to test the reader's understanding of the chapter include the following.

- What are some drawbacks of backdoor detection methods that are based on clustering applied to an internal layer of a DNN?
- Why do we expect that much larger perturbations will be required to induce high misclassifications for non-backdoor (source, target) class pairs, compared to backdoor pairs?
- How, in TSC-RED, is the constraint on finding small-sized perturbations achieved in practice? Are there alternative approaches you can think of?
- What statistical assumption is being made when estimating the null distribution(s) within TSC-RED?
- What is the main limitation of the CI method? Are there ways to mitigate this limitation?

5.8   Project: Principal Component Analysis (PCA) Based Cluster Impurity (CI) Defense

For the CIFAR-10 dataset, investigate an improvement on the CI defense where PCA is applied to reduce the feature dimensionality of the penultimate layer of the DNN, prior to performing mixture modeling on the penultimate layer activations induced by training samples. First, poison the training set with examples embedded with one of the backdoor patterns described in this chapter. Then, train the classifier on the poisoned training set. Then apply the CI defense (with the mixture modeling applied to the PCA dimension-reduced penultimate layer activations). Assess the FPR and TPR associated with the removed samples. Then retrain the classifier (with the detected samples removed) and evaluate its accuracy, as well as the ASR of the attack. Repeat this for different numbers of poisoned samples (i.e., different effective attack strengths).

See the code at www.cambridge.org/millersecureAI.

6 Post-Training Reverse-Engineering Defense (PT-RED) Against Imperceptible Backdoors

In this chapter we focus on the *post-training* (PT) scenario of defense against backdoor data poisoning (Trojans), where the defender has access to the trained DNN but *not* to the possibly backdoor poisoned training set used for its learning. It is also assumed that a clean labeled dataset (no backdoor poisoning present) is available with a relatively small number of examples from each of the classes from the domain [93, 156, 282, 303]. This clean labeled set is insufficient for retraining the DNN from scratch and its small size makes its availability a reasonable assumption in practice. Reliable post-training detection, **without any access to the possibly poisoned dataset**, should appear to be a formidable problem. Indeed, there are enormous degrees of freedom that can be used in defining a backdoor attack, encompassing both the backdoor pattern and the method of incorporating the backdoor (e.g., by adding the pattern to the image or by replacing a patch of pixels by the backdoor pattern). If the training set is available, then at least the defender does possess examples with the backdoor present (even though the backdoor pattern is stealthily encoded and which, if any, samples contain the backdoor pattern is unknown). But *without* access to the training set, the only "signature" of the backdoor is in the learned parameters of the network (and this may affect only a small number of weights/neurons, among possibly millions of weights/neurons in the network). Despite these challenges, a very effective post-training RED is presented. This method reliably infers whether there is an attack and the source and target classes involved in a detected attack. Moreover, the backdoor pattern itself is quite reliably estimated, *even when it is not human perceptible at all*, as will be seen in the sequel. Although this RED employs additively incorporated perturbations, it can be applied to activated embedded features of the DNN, which gives capability to detect backdoors that are not additively incorporated by the adversary.

6.1 The Post-Training (PT) Scenario

The post-training scenario is of practical interest for several reasons. First, deep learning can be extremely computationally intensive; hence learning may be outsourced to a third party who may be compromised [89]. Moreover, there are many pure *consumers* of machine learning systems, for example, an app used on millions of cell phones. The app user will not have access to the training set on which the app's classifier was learned. Still, the user would like to know whether the app's classifier has been

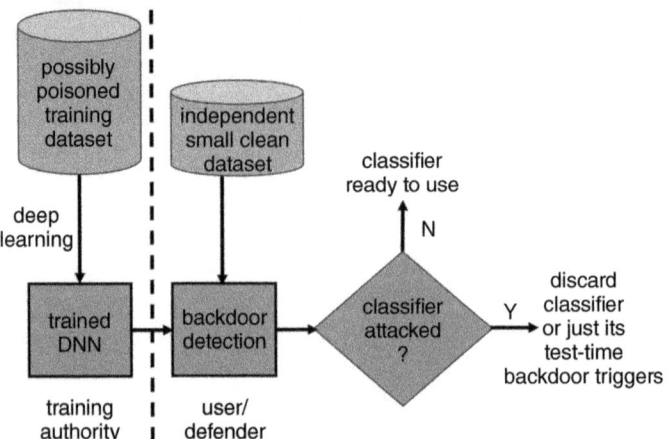

Figure 6.1 Illustration of the post-training scenario. The user/defender receives a classifier trained on a possibly (backdoor) poisoned training set from the training authority. An independent clean dataset is used to detect whether the classifier is backdoor attacked. If a detection is made, the classifier is discarded (or its detected backdoor triggers at test/operation time are either discarded or corrected, see Chapter 10); else, it is certified for use.

backdoor poisoned. Also, consider the scenario of legacy systems (where the training set used to build the classifier may no longer be available) and proprietary systems (e.g., with the government purchasing a classifier from a company, but without any rights to the training set used to build the classifier).

Since the attacker wants the backdoor mapping to be learned *without* affecting the classifier's accuracy on clean (backdoor-free) samples, successful attacks may be inherently evasive. As the user/defender, a fundamental goal is to detect whether the DNN has been backdoor attacked, using only the small, clean, labeled dataset $\mathcal{D}$ available to the defender (again, $\mathcal{D}$ is too small to be used for training an accurate classifier). If deemed attacked, the DNN may be discarded and replaced by a new one from a more trustworthy source. This is illustrated in Figure 6.1 and recall Figure 1.5.

Beyond that, another aim is to infer the source class(es) and the target class of the detected backdoor attack. The defender also aims to estimate the backdoor pattern itself, given that an attack has been detected. The backdoor could be mitigated ("unlearned") if the DNN is refined using a (sufficient number of) clean examples with the estimated backdoor pattern added in (and labeled with the *correct* source class – not the backdoor's target class). If such fine-tuning is not practical and the DNN cannot be discarded, the estimated backdoor pattern may still help to detect and thus reject use of the backdoor operationally, that is, when backdoors are triggered at test time (in-flight), see Chapter 10. Also, beyond detecting backdoor poisoning post-training, the estimated (reverse-engineered) backdoor pattern is fundamental to the goal of "explainable" AI (XAI), that is, the reverse-engineered backdoor pattern is a hidden fragility of the AI that is being revealed.

6.2   Some Post-Training (PT) Defenses

6.2.1   Overview

In this chapter, *unsupervised* anomaly detection (AD) approaches thwarting backdoor attacks post-training (PT) are investigated. While the IARPA TrojAI BAA [269, 270] allowed detector solutions to make use of supervised (known) exemplar DNN classifiers ("with backdoor present" and "without backdoor"), such labeled information is obviously unrealistic in practice and is anyway not needed by AD approaches described in this chapter. If backdoor-free classifiers *were* available, they could simply be used in place of the (possibly poisoned) classifier. Thus, their availability (however unrealistic in practice) would obviate the need for any backdoor detection.

The defenses considered in this chapter detect backdoors post-training and *without access to the poisoned training set*. Without the training set, the only potential hint of a possibly embedded backdoor pattern is *latent* in the learned DNN's parameters (to which the defender has access, in addition to $\mathcal{D}$). Promising work has addressed this problem under two scenarios that collectively cover the evasive backdoor cases of most interest:

- where the backdoor pattern (BP) is evasive by being imperceptible (either by modifying a few pixels or by using a global, image-wide watermark pattern);
- where the BP is *perceptible but scene plausible*, for example, a ball placed in front of a dog, whose presence causes the classifier to misclassify as a cat, or a pair of glasses on a face, which alters the class decision.

This chapter considers the first type of BP. (The second type will be considered in Chapter 7.) We now review some specific post-training defenses.

6.2.2   Fine-Pruning

Under fine-pruning (FP) [156], the defender prunes neurons in the penultimate layer of the DNN in increasing order of their average activations (as measured over a clean, i.e., attack-free, dataset $\mathcal{D}$), doing so up until the point where there is an unacceptable loss in classification accuracy on $\mathcal{D}$. The premise behind FP is that BPs will activate neurons that are not triggered by the clean examples in $\mathcal{D}$ and pruning will likely remove these neurons. However, this premise is not so plausible in general because there is nothing inherent to gradient-based neural net training (on a poisoned training dataset) that would create a propensity for a simple "dichotomization" of neurons, with most *solely* dedicated to "normal" operation and some *solely* dedicated to implementing the backdoor. Indeed, experimentally it is observed that FP gives very limited capability to mitigate backdoor attacks.

6.2.3   Neural Cleanse

For the image domain, define the operation of pixel-wise combining of two images $\underline{x}, \underline{v}$:

$$B_{\text{mask}}(\underline{x}, \underline{v}, \underline{m}) = \underline{x} \odot (1 - \underline{m}) + \underline{v} \odot \underline{m}, \tag{6.1}$$

where $\underline{m}$ is a two-dimensional, image-wide mask which is **relaxed** so that it has real values $\in [0,1]$ at each pixel/channel (so the images are "blended" together under the relaxed $\underline{m}$). Note that $\underline{x} \odot \underline{m}$ zeroes-out all the channel intensities of $\underline{x}$'s pixel i when $m_i = 0$ and does not affect $\underline{x}$'s pixel i when $m_i = 1$. ($\underline{m}$ will be a three-dimensional mask if its values differ for different color channels of the same pixel.) That is, every pixel/channel of the image $B_{\text{mask}}(\underline{x}, \underline{v}, \underline{m})$ is a convex combination according to $\underline{m}$ of the corresponding pixel/channels of $\underline{v}$ and $\underline{x}$.

For each putative target class t, Neural Cleanse (NC) [282] jointly estimates a possible BP $\underline{v}$ and a *relaxed mask* $\underline{m}$ using a relatively small dataset of clean, labelled images from *all* classes except for class t, that is, $\mathcal{D} \backslash \mathcal{D}_t$, by minimizing the following Lagrangian over $\underline{v}$ and $\underline{m}$:

$$\min_{\underline{v}, \underline{m}} -\frac{1}{|\mathcal{D} \backslash \mathcal{D}_t|} \sum_{\underline{x} \in \mathcal{D} \backslash \mathcal{D}_t} \hat{p}(t | B_{\text{mask}}(\underline{x}, \underline{v}, \underline{m})) + \lambda \|\underline{m}\|_1, \tag{6.2}$$

with $\lambda > 0$, until a high misclassification rate to t from all the other classes is achieved. Then anomaly detection is performed on the l_1 norm (size of the support) of the K estimated masks $\|\underline{m}_t^*\|_1$, one for each putative target class t.

An "anomaly index" is derived for each class based on the median absolute deviation (MAD) [95, 222]. If μ is the median of a set of numbers $\mathcal{Z} = \{z_i\}_{i=1}^{|\mathcal{Z}|}$, then the MAD of $\mathcal{Z}$ is the median of absolute (l_1) deviations from μ, $\{|z_i - \mu|\}_{i=1}^{|\mathcal{Z}|}$. Outliers in $\mathcal{Z}$ have less impact on the MAD statistic because of its use of the median (instead of mean) and absolute (instead of squared) deviation. For each putative target class t, one can compute an anomaly index of $\|\underline{m}_t^*\|_1$ with respect to a dataset $\mathcal{M} = \{\|\underline{m}_s^*\|_1\}_{s \in \mathcal{Y}}$ (or $\mathcal{M}_{-t} = \{\|\underline{m}_s^*\|_1\}_{s \in \mathcal{Y} \backslash \{t\}}$) using MAD as the measure of data dispersion. The standard deviation of a given type of null model (estimated using the dataset) can be expressed in terms of MAD, and then a p-value assessed according to the null can be used to detect whether t is a target class of an attack. For the example of a Gaussian null, if $X \sim N(\mu, \sigma^2)$, $\mu \approx$ mean, and $P(|X - \mu| < \text{MAD}) = 1/2$, then $\sigma \approx 1.5 \times \text{MAD}$. In NC, the anomaly detection threshold is $\theta_{\text{MAD}} \times \text{MAD}$ referenced to the median μ with $\theta_{\text{MAD}} \approx 3$ (corresponding to $>95\%$ anomaly detection confidence under this Gaussian null model): that is, x is anomalous if $|x - \mu| > 3 \times \text{MAD}$. In the following experiments, we vary this parameter for NC, initially reporting results for $\theta_{\text{MAD}} = 2$ to boost NC's true positive rate.

NC may have been intended to detect backdoors which are patch incorporated, although this was not explicitly discussed in [282]. That is, in [282], NC's relaxed mask $\underline{m}$ is not encouraged to become a Boolean (all elements $\in \{0,1\}$) mask. If so, the attempt to minimize the l_1 norm of m through (6.2) suggests NC will work better for a BP with smaller total spatial support when the positive hyperparameter λ is made larger. Experimental results in [93, 282] involve attacks which are clearly noticeable "noisy" patches or icons. Note that such BPs $\underline{v}$ could be physically incorporated into clean images, or digitally incorporated, according to (6.1), that is, in a "blended" fashion using a relaxed mask $\underline{m}$.

NC's assumptions limit its performance. First, NC assumes that, if there is an attack, *all* classes except for the target class are source classes. But an attacker may avoid choosing too many source classes when devising the attack; otherwise, too many examples with the BP will be inserted in the training set, making the attack less evasive. Section 6.4 will show that NC fails when there is a single source class involved in the attack. Second, NC generates K statistics for detection inference, such that (assuming a single target class of the attack) there are only $(K - 1)$ "null value realizations" (decision statistics guaranteed to *not* be associated with an attack assuming one target class) against which to assess atypicality of the most extreme statistic. This may lead to an unreliable inference result, particularly when the number of classes K is small. Third, as shown both by the experiments described below and in [93, 303], when there is no attack, NC may still estimate a pattern with an abnormally small spatial support for some classes, resulting in false detections. Fourth, NC was only experimentally evaluated against perceptible attacks (see Chapter 7) – the noisy BP used in their experiments is easily visibly discernible, unlike the imperceptible BPs considered in this chapter.

6.2.4   TABOR

An extension of NC, TABOR [93] focuses on detecting a very special subset of BPs – those located in any one of the four corners of the image. TABOR assumes that the spatial support of the pattern should be very small and non-scattered. It also assumes that the BP should not cover any key features in the image. The (BP, mask) estimation of TABOR uses the same objective function as NC, but with regularization terms penalizing any (pattern, mask) that violates its assumptions.

6.2.5   META

META [316] first generates a substantial number of shadow models "with BA" (backdoor attack) and "without BA" for a given domain. Models "with BA" are created using BAs (chosen by the defender) with a local blended BP, with various blend ratios. Then a few query inputs are fed into each shadow model and the output logits are collected as the representation vector of the model. A meta classifier is then trained on the collected model representations, with a single output node and an associated domain dependent threshold to distinguish models "with BA" and "without BA." However, META easily fails when the architecture of the shadow models used to train the meta classifier is different from the architecture of the model to be inspected (i.e., the DNN under test), even when META's detection threshold is chosen to maximize its detection performance.

6.2.6   TND

For TND [289], there are two patch replacement BP estimation steps for each putative target class t. In the first step, a "universal" BP is estimated to induce images from all classes other than class t to be misclassified to class t. In the second step, for each image from classes other than class t, a sample specific BP is estimated to induce the image to be misclassified to class t. Then, for each image from classes other than t, two penultimate layer feature vectors are obtained respectively by feeding the image with the universal BP and the sample specific BP into the classifier. Then the cosine similarity (recall Section 2.12.3) of the two penultimate layer feature vectors is calculated. The median of the cosine similarities over all these images is obtained as the detection statistic for class t. If the statistic for any class is larger than a prescribed threshold, the class is deemed a backdoor target class.

6.2.7   ABS

ABS [157] is composed of two steps for backdoor detection. In the first step, the "top-10" candidates for compromised neurons in a DNN's internal layer are identified, based on their degree of influence on the output logits. For each of these 10 neurons, the output logit being affected the most and the associated class label of the logit are also recorded. Experiments found that these "top-10" compromised neurons are always from the penultimate layer of the DNN. In the second step, for each of these ten neurons, a patch replacement pattern is reverse engineered by maximizing the activation of the neuron on 30% of the clean images used for detection. Each estimated pattern is then embedded into the remaining 70% of the clean images used for detection. The percentage of these images being misclassified to the recorded class for the candidate neuron, called the "attack success rate of reverse-engineered trojan triggers" (REASR), is measured for each of the top-10 neurons. If the maximum REASR over all top-10 neurons is above a prescribed threshold, the classifier is deemed to be backdoor attacked.

6.3   Imperceptible-Backdoor Post-Training Reverse-Engineering Defense (I-PT-RED)

In this section, an unsupervised AD framework for detecting backdoors in DNN classifiers, herein called I-PT-RED, is described in detail [303, 305, 307].

6.3.1   Key Idea

The premise behind I-PT-RED is that for a classifier that has been backdoor data poisoned using an imperceptible backdoor pattern, with source class s^* and target class t^*, the required perturbation size for a common perturbation to induce misclassification to t^* for most images from class s^* is *much smaller* than for class pairs that have not been backdoor poisoned – in fact, one such common perturbation (it need not be unique) is the backdoor pattern $\underline{v}^*$ itself. Thus, if one can find a small perturbation that induces most patterns from a (putative source) class s to be misclassified to another (putative target) class $t \neq s$, then this is indicative that the DNN is the victim of an (imperceptible) backdoor attack involving the class pair (s,t).

An imperceptible backdoor pattern $\underline{v}$ can be embedded into a clean image $\underline{x}$ as an additive perturbation [150, 226, 268, 308], by

$$B_{\text{add}}(\underline{x}, \underline{v}) = [\underline{x} + \underline{v}]_\kappa, \tag{6.3}$$

where the clipping operation $[\cdot]_\kappa$ constrains the pixel intensity values to their valid range (e.g., $[0, 256)$ for a grey scale intensity); recall (5.1).

In the post-training scenario, for each class pair $(s,t) \in \mathcal{Y} \times \mathcal{Y}$ with $s \neq t$, the optimal additive perturbation $\underline{v}^*_{st}$ that induces at least π-level group misclassification is estimated as the solution to:

$$\begin{aligned} \underset{\underline{v}}{\text{minimize}} \quad & d(\underline{v}) \\ \text{subject to} \quad & \frac{1}{|\mathcal{D}_s|} \sum_{\underline{x} \in \mathcal{D}_s} \mathbb{1}\{\hat{c}(B_{\text{add}}(\underline{x}, \underline{v})) = t\} \geq \pi, \end{aligned} \tag{6.4}$$

where

- $d(\cdot)$ is the metric for measuring the size (e.g., l_1 norm) or the energy (squared l_2 norm) of a perturbation $\underline{v}$,
- $\hat{c}(\cdot)$ is the classifier's decision,
- $\mathcal{D}_s$ is the set of clean (unpoisoned) labeled samples from class s,
- $\mathbb{1}\{\cdot\}$ is an indicator function, and
- $\pi \in (0, 1]$ can be considered the minimum misclassification rate to deem a backdoor attack "successful," for example, $\pi = 0.8$.

Note that the defender's choice of π does not have a strong effect on detection performance because the required perturbation size for a true attack pair (s^*, t^*) is observed to be anomalously small, compared with the size for non-attack class pairs, over a large range of π values, see Section 6.4.5.

The I-PT-RED detection procedure consists of two steps. First, it estimates $\underline{v}^*_{st}$ for each class pair $(s,t) \in \mathcal{Y} \times \mathcal{Y}$ with $s \neq t$. Second, an inference procedure is performed based on the collection of statistics $\{d(\underline{v}^*_{st}), \forall s \neq t\}$. If the classifier is attacked and the backdoor involves, for example, a single (source, target) class pair (s^*, t^*), one would expect $d(\underline{v}^*_{s^*t^*}) \ll d(\underline{v}^*_{st})$ for all $(s,t) \neq (s^*, t^*)$. If the neural network has not been attacked, one would expect there to be no such anomalies. Additional inference details are given in Section 6.3.3.

6.3.2   Perturbation Optimization

Unfortunately, (6.4) does not have a closed-form solution and cannot be solved using gradient-based methods because of the non-differentiable indicator function. So, similar to the previous chapter on before/during training backdoor detection, the perturbation is sought to minimize a *differentiable, surrogate* objective function.

Note that choosing a perturbation to induce group *misclassification* is quite reminiscent of optimization of a parameterized classification model to maximize the *correct* classification rate. Further, note that there is no objective function universally used in practice for learning good classifiers – cross-entropy, discriminative learning that seeks to minimize a soft error count measure [113], classifier margin, as well as other training objectives [63], have all been shown to be "good" surrogate objectives for the (non-differentiable) classification error rate in that minimizing them to determine the classifier leads to good (test set) classification accuracy in practice. Recall Sections 2.7.1 and 5.4.2.

Similarly, there are multiple plausible surrogate objectives for (6.4). In the following experiments, the perturbation (i.e., estimated putative backdoor pattern) is primarily determined by performing gradient descent on the following objective function:

$$J_{st}(\underline{v}) = -\frac{1}{|\mathcal{D}_s|} \sum_{\underline{x} \in \mathcal{D}_s} \hat{p}(t|[\underline{x} + \underline{v}]_\kappa), \tag{6.5}$$

until the constraint in problem (6.4) is satisfied. See Algorithm 6.1.

Algorithm 6.1 Perturbation optimization.

1: Initialization: $\underline{v} \leftarrow \underline{0}$, $\rho \leftarrow \frac{1}{|\mathcal{D}_s|} \sum_{\underline{x} \in \mathcal{D}_s} \mathbf{1}\{\hat{c}(\underline{x}) = t\}$
2: **while** $\rho < \pi$ **do**
3:     $\underline{v} \leftarrow \underline{v} - \delta \cdot \nabla J_{st}(\underline{v})$
4:     $\rho \leftarrow \frac{1}{|\mathcal{D}_s|} \sum_{\underline{x} \in \mathcal{D}_s} \mathbf{1}\{\hat{c}([\underline{x} + \underline{v}]_\kappa) = t\}$
5: **end while**

There are several things to note about Algorithm 6.1. First, ρ is updated in each iteration as the misclassification fraction induced by the current perturbation $\underline{v}$.

Second, note that the algorithm does not *explicitly* impose a constraint on the perturbation size – the perturbation is initially set to zero, with its size tending to grow with iterations. While a smaller sized perturbation inducing π-level misclassification could be achieved by minimizing $J_{st}(\cdot)$ subject to an explicit constraint on the perturbation size (or by minimizing the perturbation size subject to a level of $J_{st}(\cdot)$), this would also lead to an optimization problem that would require the choice of a Lagrange multiplier specifying the value of the constraint – appropriate (likely search-entailed) choice of the Lagrange multiplier would complicate this constrained optimization problem. Experiments in this chapter show that gradient descent on $J_{st}(\cdot)$, with termination once π-level misclassification is achieved, yields small perturbations for backdoor pairs *relative* to those required for non-backdoor pairs. This is sufficient for successful anomaly detection of backdoor pairs.

Third, note that the gradient of $J_{st}(\cdot)$ has non-zero contributions from samples even once they are successfully misclassified. Again, no claim is made that $J_{st}(\cdot)$ is the best surrogate for misclassification count that could be used. Alternative surrogate objectives can also be used within the I-PT-RED framework, see Section 6.3.4.

Fourth, δ is the step size for updating $\underline{v}$. If δ is too small, the execution time can be very long. If δ is too large, the algorithm may terminate in a few steps with a resulting ρ much larger than π and with the resulting perturbation much larger in size/energy than that required to induce π-level group misclassification. In practice, a suitable δ can be chosen via line search or, alternatively, could be periodically reduced, for example, by a factor of 2 every 10 iterations.

Fifth, in the practical implementation of I-PT-RED, an upper bound is set on the size/energy of $\underline{v}$, with the algorithm terminated when the upper bound is reached even if the π target has not been reached – when π is selected too large (e.g., $\pi = 1$), looking for the required perturbation may be hard or even infeasible (even for a ground truth attacked pair (s^*, t^*)).

6.3.3   Detection Inference

As discussed in Section 5.4.2, the statistics for the detection inference are $\{r_{st}\}$, where

$$r_{st} = \frac{1}{d(\underline{v}_{st}^*)},$$

that is, the reciprocal of the "size" of the $K(K-1)$ optimized perturbations (one for each class pair). The reciprocal is taken because otherwise anomalies (corresponding to (s^*, t^*) or (s, t^*) for all $s \in S^*$), if they exist, will be near the origin.

The null hypothesis for detection inference is that the classifier has not been attacked, which requires the $K(K-1)$ detection statistics to follow a null distribution (i.e., a distribution for non-backdoor attack pairs). Alternatively, if the classifier has been attacked, the reciprocal statistics corresponding to the class pairs involved in the attack should be large anomalies, with small p-values under the null. Hence the detection inference for a given classifier consists of the following two steps: (i) estimating a null distribution for non-backdoor class pairs using the computed $\{r_{st} | s \neq t \in \mathcal{Y}\}$; (ii) evaluating whether the largest detection statistic, which is the one most likely associated with a backdoor attack, is very unlikely under the null distribution.

The null parametric density form used in the detection experiments is a Gamma distribution, a right-tailed distribution with positive support. It is noted that other one-tailed distributions (e.g., exponential, inverse Gaussian) can instead be used as the null distribution. Because it is assumed that there is at most one target class, if there is a backdoor attack, there can be at most $K-1$ reciprocal statistics that correspond to backdoor attack class pairs. Thus, the $K(K-1)-(K-1) = (K-1)^2$ *smallest* reciprocals are considered and it is assumed that these are *not* associated with backdoor attacks and thus are suitable for use in learning the null density function. The $(K-1)$ *largest* reciprocals were excluded from being used for such estimation because these could be associated with the backdoor attack and thus could corrupt estimation of the null model, as will be shown in experiments.

However, it is *unknown* which, if any, of the $(K-1)$ largest reciprocals correspond to a backdoor – indeed, there may be no backdoor attack on the DNN. Thus, it is incorrect to assume there are *no* null measurements in the interval $r_{min} < r < r_{max}$, where

r_{min} is the smallest of the $(K-1)$ largest reciprocals and r_{max} is the largest of these statistics – some of these $(K-1)$ statistics could correspond to class pairs not involved in a backdoor attack and follow the true null distribution. To account for this lack of certainty, the $(K-1)^2$ smallest statistics should be used to learn the *conditional* null density, where these statistics are conditioned on being less than r_{min}; that is, conditional on the observed statistics being smaller than the *smallest* of the $(K-1)$ statistics that could correspond to a backdoor attack. Thus, the $(K-1)^2$ smallest statistics are used to learn the conditional null density $g_{R|R<r_{min}}(r)$ by maximum likelihood estimation (MLE). The shape and scale parameters of this conditional density (a density truncated at r_{min}) are then used for the unconditional density g_R. In the following experiments, the superiority of this learned null model will be demonstrated in comparison with the naive null obtained by directly estimating the (unconditioned) null distribution using all the $K(K-1)$ reciprocal statistics; see Section 6.4.6. (An alternative detection inference procedure, with comparable performance to the one described here, was given in Section 5.4.2 and [307].)

Given the learned null, whether any of the $K(K-1)$ reciprocals deviate from the null is next ascertained. In particular, the probability under the null that the largest of these $K(K-1)$ reciprocals is greater than or equal to the observed maximum reciprocal, r_{max}, is evaluated,

$$\text{pv} := P_{null}[\max\{R_1,\ldots,R_{K(K-1)}\} \geq r_{max}]$$
$$= 1 - P_{null}[\max\{R_1,\ldots,R_{K(K-1)}\} \leq r_{max}]$$
$$= 1 - G_R(r_{max})^{K(K-1)} \tag{6.6}$$

where G_R is the null cumulative distribution function corresponding to the density g_R. If this order statistic p-value is less than a threshold θ, the null hypothesis is rejected and the classifier is claimed to be attacked. Since p-values under the null hypothesis are uniformly distributed on $[0,1]$, θ can in principle be set to fix the false detection rate. For example, the "classical" statistical significance threshold $\theta = 0.05$ should induce 5% false detections for classifiers not attacked (assuming an accurate null model). If an attack is detected, the class pair corresponding to r_{max} is inferred to be involved in the backdoor attack. Furthermore, if the attack is detected, the optimized perturbation for the detected pair is the estimate of the backdoor pattern $\underline{v}^*$ used by the attacker. The *complete* detection procedure (which fits into the "backdoor detection" block in Figure 6.1), including this robust null learning and inference strategy, is summarized in Figure 6.2.

Recall that in Section 5.1.1 the possibility of *multiple* backdoor attacks was discussed. An attacker might introduce multiple backdoor attacks involving different target classes in order to make detection more difficult. Specifically, in the above detection inference, the detection statistics not associated with a putative target class are used to learn the null density. But if there are multiple backdoors involving different target classes, some of the detection statistics used to learn the null may be associated with a backdoor attack (which will thus corrupt the null estimation).

To defeat such an attack, one can devise an alternative inference strategy that simply aims to identify whether there are any significant outliers among *all* the detection

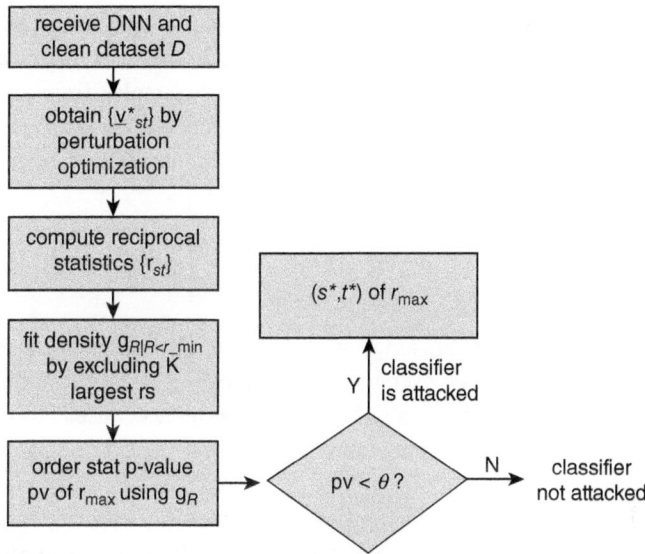

Figure 6.2 Flow chart for the complete I-PT-RED detection procedure.

statistics. For example, one such strategy is as follows. First, order all of the r_{st} statistics from least extreme to most extreme, and then learn a null (using maximum likelihood estimation) based on a subset of least extreme statistics (e.g., based on the statistics that are in the lower 50th percentile of extremity). Now using this null, one can test the next remaining least extreme statistic, for example, based on a p-value. If that statistic is not detected, then add it to the set of least extreme statistics, (re)-learn the null, and then test the next remaining least extreme statistic. The first time that a remaining least extreme statistic is detected, then *all* the remaining statistics are detected. This greedy algorithm gives a way to potentially identify all the outlier statistics (from which one can infer all (source, target) class pairs). Such an approach could also infer that there are multiple backdoor attacks present. In Chapter 8, a PT-RED is developed that in fact does *not* rely on any null density estimation and is intrinsically robust in the presence of multiple backdoor attacks.

6.3.4 Surrogate Objective Function Variants

As noted above, J_{st} of Eq. (6.5) measures a non-zero gradient contribution even from samples already successfully misclassified. This can be remedied by instead minimizing an objective function similar to that associated with the Perceptron algorithm [63]:

$$J_{st-p}(\underline{v}) = -\frac{1}{|\hat{\mathcal{D}}_s(\underline{v},t)|} \sum_{\underline{x} \in \hat{\mathcal{D}}_s(\underline{v},t)} \hat{p}(t|[\underline{x}+\underline{v}]_\kappa), \tag{6.7}$$

where $\hat{\mathcal{D}}_s(\underline{v},t) = \{\underline{x} \in \mathcal{D}_s \mid \hat{c}([\underline{x}+\underline{v}]_\kappa) \neq t\}$.

Another potential concern with $J_{st}(\underline{v})$ in Eq. (6.5) is its use of all of $\mathcal{D}_s$ for perturbation optimization. It is possible that the attacker knows some clean samples from class s that are misclassified and excludes these samples from consideration in crafting the backdoor. Accordingly, to mimic the attacker, the defender might consider group misclassification only on the subset of clean source samples that are *correctly* classified. This leads to the following objective:

$$J_{st-c}(\underline{v}) = -\frac{1}{|\hat{\mathcal{D}}_s|} \sum_{\underline{x} \in \hat{\mathcal{D}}} \hat{p}(t|[\underline{x} + \underline{v}]_\kappa), \tag{6.8}$$

where $\hat{\mathcal{D}}_s = \{\underline{x} \in \mathcal{D}_s \mid \hat{c}(\underline{x}) = s\}$. One can also combine the restrictions in (6.7) and (6.8), summing only over $\underline{x}$ such that both $\hat{c}([\underline{x} + \underline{v}]_\kappa) \neq t$ and $\hat{c}(\underline{x}) = s$.

Likewise, one might also hypothesize the attacker used box constraints [260], rather than clipping, in implementing the backdoor to keep image intensity values in the proper range.

As noted before, one could also consider an optimization problem that explicitly accounts for/constrains the perturbation size. Moreover, one can use a soft error count/discriminative objective function akin to that used in [113].

Based on this discussion, one can see that many surrogate objective function variants are possible. In Section 6.4, experimental results with some of these alternative surrogates are given; in general, the detection performance is not strongly sensitive to this choice. Again, the reason is that all that is needed is that the size of the learned perturbation for a true backdoor pair (s^*, t^*) should be much smaller than for a non backdoor pair. Minimizing any of these surrogate objectives is sufficient to elicit this difference between $r_{s^*t^*}$ and r_{st} for any non-backdoor pair (s, t). While the following experiments primarily focus on minimizing J_{st}, the I-PT-RED detection framework is general and consistent with use of any of the above alternative surrogates, in the search for minimal sized perturbations.

6.3.5   Correcting for Class Confusion

The premise behind I-PT-RED's detection inference is that the perturbation size/energy required to induce π-level group misclassification for (s^*, t^*) is less than for other (unattacked) class pairs. However, if the initial misclassification fraction $\rho_{st}^{(0)}$ (using a zero perturbation vector) is abnormally high for $(s, t) \neq (s^*, t^*)$, then it is expected that the perturbation size/energy needed to reach π-level group misclassification will be smaller than when this initial misclassification fraction is low, that is, $d(\underline{v}_{st}^*)$ may be abnormally small, possibly resulting in (s, t) being falsely detected.

Here, it is sought to correct this effect assuming the class confusion matrix information is available (estimable from the available clean dataset $\mathcal{D}$). For any pair (s, t) such that $\rho_{st}^{(0)} \neq 0$, fit an (Mth order) polynomial using the sequence of (perturbation size, misclassification fraction) pairs obtained while executing Algorithm 6.1 for the pair (s, t). This gives a regression relationship between perturbation size and induced misclassification fraction for the pair (s, t). The "compensation" $d_{st}^{(0)}$ is derived as

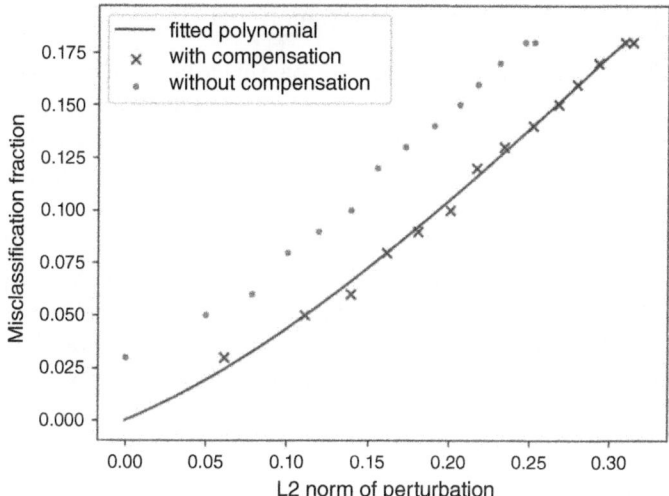

Figure 6.3 An example of correction of perturbation sizes to account for non-zero initial class pair confusion. Reprinted from [303] with permission.

$$d_{st}^{(0)} = \arg\min_{d^{(0)}} \min_{\{a_m\}} \sum_{\tau=0}^{U} \left[\sum_{m=1}^{M} a_m (d(\underline{v}_{st}^{(\tau)}) + d^{(0)})^m - \rho_{st}^{(\tau)} \right]^2, \quad (6.9)$$

where the superscript τ is the index of the iteration when executing Algorithm 6.1. $d_{st}^{(0)}$ is an estimate of the perturbation size needed to induce the initial class confusion $\rho_{st}^{(0)}$. So, to correct for this (non-zero) initial confusion level, add $d_{st}^{(0)}$ to $d(\underline{v}_{st}^*)$ before computing r_{st}. Intuitively, this correction will increase an "abnormally small" $d(\underline{v}_{st}^*)$, making it less likely to be falsely detected. Note that $d(\underline{v}_{st}^{(0)}) = 0$ since $\underline{v}_{st}^{(0)} = \underline{0}$. (In Algorithm 6.1, the iteration index superscripts are omitted for simplicity.) U could be chosen as the index of the first iteration such that either $\rho_{st}^{(U)} \geq \pi$ or such that $d(\underline{v}_{st}^{(U)})$ exceeds an upper bound of the perturbation size. Alternatively, one can base the polynomial fit on a smaller number of (perturbation size, misclassification rate) pairs. For (s,t) with $\rho_{st}^{(0)} = 0$, set $d_{st}^{(0)} = 0$, that is, no correction is required in this case.

Figure 6.3 gives an example of correction to $d(\underline{v}_{st}^*)$ for one class pair using the confusion information. The round dots are the original (perturbation size, misclassification fraction) sample points obtained from Algorithm 6.1. The compensation based on an optimized polynomial with order $M = 3$ (the curve in the figure) is obtained by solving (6.9). The crosses are the sample points after correction. Note that the polynomial is guaranteed to pass through the origin (which is desired, since the purpose of the correction is to ensure that the initial misclassification rate when there is no perturbation is zero). Then the corrected statistics for detection inference are $\{\hat{r}_{st}\}$, where

$$\hat{r}_{st} = [d(\underline{v}_{st}^*) + d_{st}^{(0)}]^{-1}.$$

6.3.6   Exploiting Additional Information

Note that I-PT-RED only exploits some of the information in the estimated perturbation vectors $\{v_{st}\}$. Specifically, it exploits the magnitudes of these perturbation vectors, but not their directions. One can hypothesize that, for a non-backdoor class pair, the perturbation vector v_{st} should be in a direction that is similar to that of the direction between the means of classes s and t (a "natural" direction, in perturbing samples from class s to class t); or more precisely it should be in a direction similar to the perpendicular to the decision boundary between classes s and t. On the other hand, for a backdoor class pair, v_{st} could be in *any* direction. Thus, beyond assessing perturbation size, one could also assess perturbation direction, for example, evaluating the cosine similarity between the direction of the perturbation vector and a chosen "natural" direction between the two classes (recall Sections 2.12.3 and 6.2.6). Exploiting direction, beyond perturbation size, could potentially increase the sensitivity of the detector.

6.3.7   I-PT-RED Applied to Embedded Features

Also note that while it employs an additive-perturbation approach, I-PT-RED can detect perturbations which are *not* additively incorporated by operating on internal layer activations (embedded features) rather than the input (raw features) of $\mathcal{D}_s$, see Section 6.4.4.

6.4   Experiments

In this section, the I-PT-RED framework is sometimes referred to by the acronym AD (anomaly detection) for brevity.

6.4.1   Set-Up of Ensemble Experiments

When doing experiments, one of course has omniscient knowledge of the classifier, the data poisoning, etc. Thus, in doing experiments, we must be careful to compartmentalize this knowledge when implementing the defender and the attacker, so that the defense and attack only exploit information consistent with their stated assumptions.

In the following experiments, we evaluate defenses such as NC, FP and I-PT-RED under different attack settings and two different types of backdoor patterns. Also evaluated is the performance of some variants of I-PT-RED. The experiments involve multiple realizations of classifiers (which is referred to as an *ensemble experiment*, both in this and in subsequent chapters).

The DNN classifier has the ResNet-20 [97] structure (recall Section 5.5.3). Training was performed with cross-entropy loss objective (2.8) on the CIFAR-10 dataset. Recalling Section 5.5.1, the dataset is separated into a training set with 50k images (5k per class) and a test set with 10k images (1k per class). Data augmentation provided by Keras was used for training of the backdoor attacked and the clean classifiers, see [303]. Training was performed for 200 epochs with mini-batch size of 32, using the

Adam optimizer [123]. This training achieves an accuracy of 91% on the clean test set when there are no backdoor attacks. Note that this dataset, DNN structure and training configuration are frequently used in many adversarial learning works.

6.4.2   Devising Backdoor Attacks

The following experiments involve two types of backdoor patterns (BPs), both of which are imperceptible and are in fixed positions in the image support. Backdoor patterns that can be in different positions are considered in Chapter 7. In addition to digitally triggering them at test time, fixed position BPs can also be physically triggered in cases where images are captured in a "registered" fashion with the camera and object in approximately fixed relative positions, for example, in manufacturing quality control or face recognition applications. (Registration can also be part of the preprocessing for both training and test samples so that the object of interest is always of approximately fixed size and in a fixed position, e.g., the MNIST dataset [141] is registered.) For the case of image classification, since pixel values are usually normalized (e.g., from $\{0, 1, \ldots, 255\}$) to the real interval $[0, 1)$ before feeding to a DNN classifier, the valid additive perturbation range per pixel (without clipping) is $[-1, 1]$.

One such type of backdoor pattern that will be used in the following experiments is a sparse pixel-wise perturbation, that is, a backdoor pattern that affects only a small subset of pixels, as considered in [39, 44, 89, 93, 158, 268, 282, 303]. Similar to pattern E of Figure 5.2, the pixel-wise perturbation is created by first randomly selecting a few pixels; for colored images, one of the three channels (i.e., RGB colors) of each selected pixel is randomly selected to be perturbed. The perturbations can be either positive or negative, but the perturbation magnitude is similar, across all the chosen pixels. In the experiments, this was achieved by first fixing a "reference" perturbation magnitude and then, for each of the chosen pixels, multiplying this reference magnitude by a random factor generated by a Gaussian distribution with mean 1 and standard deviation 0.05.

Another type of backdoor pattern is a global (but subtle) perturbation that affects all pixels, akin to a global image watermark as considered in [44, 150, 226]. Similar to pattern A of Figure 5.2, the global pattern is spatially recurrent and looks like a chessboard – one and only one pixel among any two adjacent pixels was perturbed (in all three channels) positively. Again, the perturbation magnitude for each pixel being perturbed is a fixed value multiplied by a random factor generated from the same Gaussian distribution mentioned above. Finally, if the l_2 norm of the perturbation is specified, the perturbation mask can be scaled to achieve it.

Examples of the two types of backdoor patterns for color images are shown in Figure 6.4. In Figure 6.4a, four pixels were randomly selected to be perturbed (in one of the three channels), with the l_2 norm of the perturbation mask equal to 0.6. (There is no strong preference on the norm to be used. The l_2 norm is the default, unless specified otherwise. However, the l_1 norm will also be used in the experiments.) For visualization purposes, a constant offset was added to each pixel of the image (so that all perturbed values are non-negative). In Figure 6.4b, a global perturbation mask with

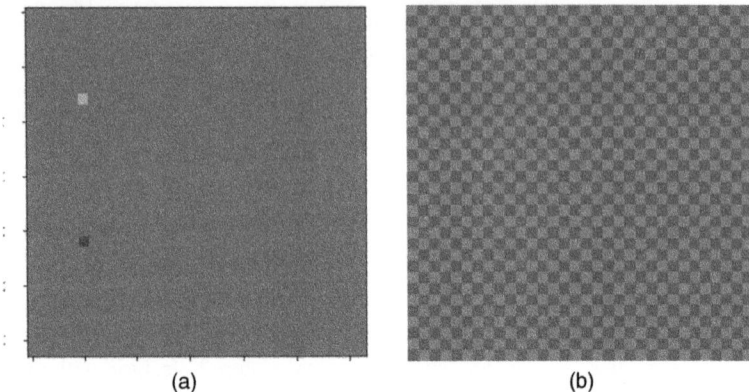

Figure 6.4 A sparse pixel-wise perturbation mask with l_2 norm 0.6 and a 0.5 offset (a), and a global perturbation mask with l_2 norm 10 (b). Some images are offset or scaled for visualization purposes. Reprinted from [303] with permission.

l_2 norm equal to 10 is shown (the large norm is chosen solely to assist visual inspection of the backdoor pattern). To launch a successful backdoor attack with a global backdoor pattern, a perturbation mask with such large l_2 norm is quite unnecessary – the required norm is in fact smaller than for the pixel-sparse attacks.

Consistent with the description in Section 5.1, perturbation (backdoor pattern) sizes were evaluated with respect to the l_2 norm, with the least human perceptible one (as small l_2 norm as possible) picked under the constraints of high attack success rate and low degradation in test accuracy on clean patterns. Such evaluation is given in Figure 6.5. A larger perturbation size could be used but at the risk of being perceivable to humans. For sparse pixel-wise perturbations and global perturbations, l_2 perturbation norms ranging from 0.25 to 1.0 and 0.01 to 0.5 were evaluated, respectively. For each l_2-norm specified backdoor pattern, a single attack realization was created.

One thousand attack images were produced using randomly selected clean training images from the 'automobile' (source) class, adding the backdoor pattern to each image, and then clipping as described by (6.3). (The attacker could alternatively select the images that are easiest to be misclassified to the target class, i.e., those with the smallest difference in DNN posterior probability between the true class and the target class.)

These images (with the backdoor pattern incorporated) were labeled to the 'truck' (target) class and added to the training set of 50k clean images. The poisoned training set was then used to train a DNN classifier. A set of backdoor test patterns was created by adding the same backdoor pattern to the 1k clean test patterns (those not used in training) from the source class. The attack success rate is evaluated as the fraction of backdoor test patterns classified to the target class. Also, the accuracy of the classifier on the original 10k clean test patterns is evaluated.

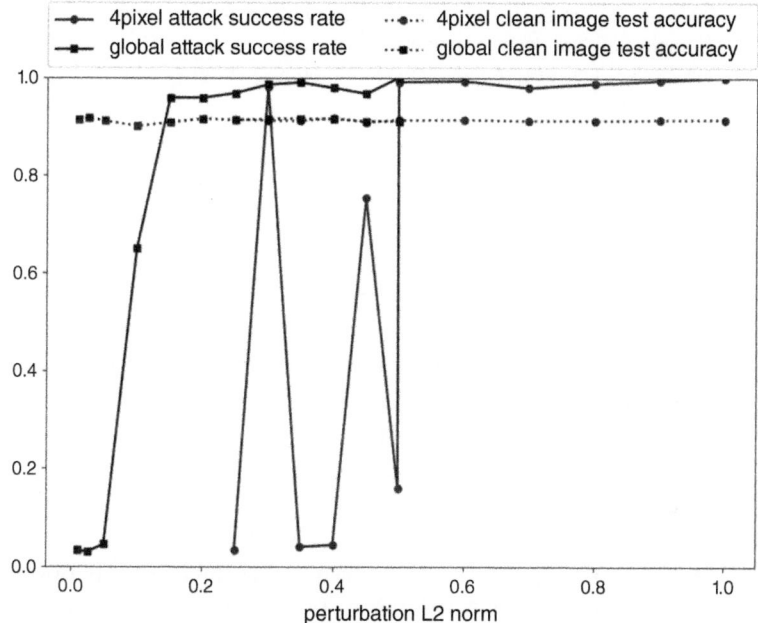

Figure 6.5 Attack success rate (solid) and accuracy on clean test images (dashed) for DNN classifiers under backdoor attacks that use sparse pixel-wise perturbation (round dots) and global perturbation (square dots), for a range of l_2 perturbation norms (attack strengths). The dashed curves overlap in the middle of the figure. Reprinted from [180, 303] with permission.

As depicted in Figure 6.5, for the global perturbation backdoor pattern, the attack success rate tends to grow with the l_2 norm of the perturbation mask. However, for the sparse, pixel-wise backdoor pattern, the attack success rate wildly fluctuates when the perturbation norm is low, only becoming stable with further increases in the perturbation norm. Such fluctuation may be due to one of several causes. For example, by chance, some of the pixels of the BP could be in locations (chosen by the attacker) where significant clipping occurs in the poisoned source class images; thus, the BP is poorly learned by the classifier. Another possibility is that pixels of the BP could be in very noisy regions of the image; again, this could lead to the BP not being well learned by the classifier. Based on the results shown in Figure 6.5, to launch a successful and human imperceptible attack, the attacker should choose the l_2 norm for the global perturbation mask to be 0.2, with an attack success rate of 0.959 and test set accuracy of 0.916 on clean test images. For the sparse, pixel-wise perturbation mask, if the l_2 norm is set to 0.6, an attack success rate of 0.993 and test accuracy of 0.914 on clean test images can be achieved.

In each training iteration, the mini-batch is randomly sampled from the training set. Also, for each training image, the type of data augmentation is randomly chosen. Because of the randomness in the backdoor data poisoning and deep learning process, to evaluate detection performance, ensemble experiments were conducted on four groups of DNN classifiers, 25 classifier realizations per group, as follows.

Table 6.1 Attack success rate and accuracy (+/- one sample standard deviation) on clean test images (over all 25 classifier realizations) for the four groups of DNN classifiers.

	Attack success rate	Test accuracy
BD-P-S	0.978 ± 0.035	0.913 ± 0.003
BD-G-S	0.974 ± 0.014	0.912 ± 0.003
BD-G-M	0.990 ± 0.005	0.912 ± 0.003
Clean	n.a.	0.915 ± 0.003

- **BD-P-S:** Classifiers were trained on the training set poisoned by 1000 backdoor images with 4-pixel perturbations ($\|\underline{v}^*\|_2 = 0.6$). The backdoor images were crafted using clean images from a single source class.
- **BD-G-S:** Classifiers were trained on the training set poisoned by 1000 backdoor images with a global perturbation ($\|\underline{v}^*\|_2 = 0.2$). The backdoor images were crafted using clean images from a single source class.
- **BD-G-M:** Classifiers were trained on the training set poisoned by 900 backdoor images with a global perturbation ($\|\underline{v}^*\|_2 = 0.2$). The backdoor images were crafted using clean images from the nine classes excluding the target class, with 100 images per (source) class.
- **Clean:** Classifiers were trained on the clean training set, without data poisoning.

The four groups of classifiers involve sparse, pixel-wise and global backdoor patterns, single source class and multiple source class attack scenarios, and include a clean classifier group. For each attacked classifier, the clean images used for devising the attack are selected randomly from the 'automobile' (source) class, and the backdoor pattern is generated independently of the selected images. The attack success rate (ASR) and the clean test accuracy (ACC) across the 25 realizations and for the four groups of classifiers are reported in Table 6.1. All backdoor attacks are successful and the degradation in ACC is negligible across all experimental realizations. (The attack success rate for the BD-G-M group is evaluated on backdoor images crafted using all 9000 clean test images from the nine classes other than the target class.) An example of backdoor images with sparse, pixel-wise backdoor pattern (Figure 6.6b), global backdoor pattern (Figure 6.6c) and the original image (Figure 6.6a) are shown in Figure 6.6. The sparse, pixel-wise backdoor pattern (with l_2 norm 0.6) is only human perceived through careful visual scrutiny of the image. The global backdoor pattern (with l_2 norm 0.2), when added to the original image, is imperceptible even under careful human inspection, since the perturbation size per pixel (and per channel) is only about 5.1×10^{-3}.

Collateral Damage: During the experiments, it was noticed that backdoor DP attacks usually induce "collateral damage" to classes other than s^* or t^*. That is, supposing the classifier has been successfully corrupted by a backdoor involving the single pair (s^*, t^*), test images from some classes $\tilde{s} \in \mathcal{Y} \setminus \{s^*, t^*\}$ will be classified to t^* with high probability when the same backdoor pattern is added to them. This

(a)   (b)   (c)

Figure 6.6 Examples of backdoor patterns applied to CIFAR-10 images: (a) the original automobile image; (b) automobile with sparse, pixel-wise perturbation ($\|\underline{v}^*\|_2 = 0.6$); (c) automobile with global perturbation ($\|\underline{v}^*\|_2 = 0.2$). Reprinted from [180, 303] with permission.

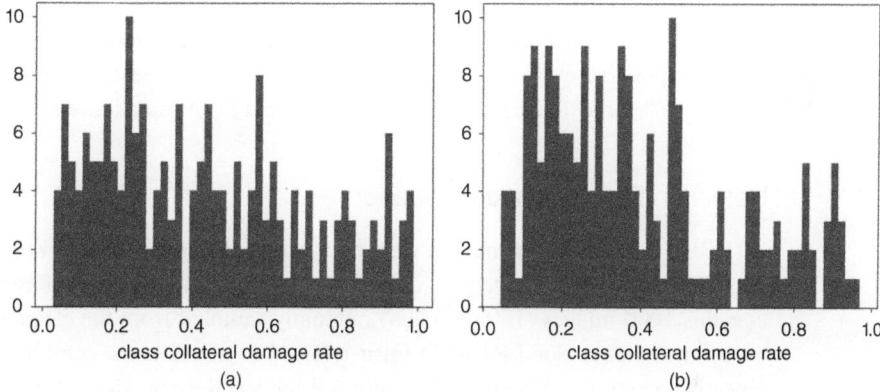

Figure 6.7 Histograms of the collateral damage rate statistics for (a) the BD-P-S group and (b) the BD-G-S group. Reprinted from [303] with permission.

phenomenon was discovered in [303], where the term "collateral damage" was also coined. To demonstrate this effect, for each trained DNN in the BD-P-S and BD-G-S groups, for which only one class is designated to be the source class s^* of the backdoor, eight tests were conducted, one for each of the classes ($\tilde{s}$) other than s^* or t^*. In each test, the backdoor pattern used for attack was added to the 1000 clean test images from $\tilde{s}$, and a class collateral damage rate was obtained as the fraction of images classified to t^*. In Figures 6.7a and 6.7b, histograms of the (8×25) 200 class collateral damage rate statistics for the BD-P-S and BD-G-S groups are respectively shown. Clearly, significant group misclassification to the target class is induced for classes other than the true source class using the true backdoor pattern, for many of the classifiers. This phenomenon may occur because the backdoor attack is not sufficiently "surgical" to induce misclassifications to t^* only from s^*, that is, the network may learn to associate the BP with t^* *irrespective* of the class of origin for the image. Another possibility is that some (unattacked) classes share some distinctive features of source classes of the attack, with the attack thus also successful in inducing misclassification to t^* for images from these (unattacked) classes.

Accordingly, it is not surprising that, for such high "collateral damage" classes, the size/energy of the optimized $\underline{v}^*_{\tilde{s}t^*}$ is close to the size/energy of $\underline{v}^*_{s^*t^*}$. This thus gives further insight into why, in I-PT-RED, the $K-1$ largest statistics in the set $\{\|\underline{v}_{st}\| \mid s \neq t\}$ are excluded from use in estimating the null distribution. This also helps to motivate why the I-PT-RED method only infers a single (source, target) class pair based on the *most extreme* statistic (as illustrated in Figure 6.2). "Collateral damage" classes, paired with the inferred target class, may be prone to false detection, and sometimes it is not so easy to distinguish the "collateral damage" phenomenon for a single source attack from a truly multiple source backdoor attack.

A More Surgical Backdoor Attack: This could be achieved by backdoor poisoning examples not only from class s, but also from all other classes excluding t; however, the poisoned examples from classes $s' \neq s$ should be labeled as s', not as t. This "encourages" the DNN to only learn a backdoor mapping from s to t, not from $s' \neq s$ to t, that is, the source class is (or source classes are) "localized." This idea is similar to that of positive examples in contrastive learning (recall Section 2.12.3). Also, see Section 12.3 for a "localized" backdoor attack on a DNN used for regression.

6.4.3   Detection Performance Evaluation

I-PT-RED and NC performances were first evaluated using the four groups of classifiers. The clean dataset used for detection (for both AD and NC) for each classifier contains 1000 images (100 per class) randomly sampled from the clean test set held out from training. For I-PT-RED (also referred to as AD), the combinations of the objective functions for perturbation optimization and the detection inference strategies to be evaluated are as follows.

- **AD-J-P:** I-PT-RED with the (6.5) objective to obtain candidate backdoor patterns.
- **AD-Jp-P:** I-PT-RED with the (6.7) objective.
- **AD-Jc-P:** I-PT-RED with the objective (6.8).
- **AD-J-C:** I-PT-RED with the (6.5) objective combined with the confusion-corrected detection inference approach described in Section 6.3.5.
- **AD-J-P-L1:** AD-J-P except taking $d(\cdot)$ as the l_1 norm for detection purposes (previous variants use the l_2 norm).

For all the variants above, π, the target misclassification fraction, was set to 0.8. However, detection performance is not sensitive to the choice of π, see Section 6.4.5. For the confusion-corrected detection inference used with the AD-J-C variant, the order of the polynomial was chosen as 3. Again, other choices of polynomial have little impact on detection accuracy, for example, orders $2, 4$, and 5 gave similar results. The only remaining hyperparameter to be selected for all the variants is the detection threshold θ on the p-values (6.6). θ can be set to fix the theoretical false detection rate. Here the "classical" statistical significance threshold $\theta = 0.05$ was used as the default for I-PT-RED, which also matches the choice for NC in terms of the significance level. Performance will also be evaluated for more conservative and liberal choices of θ later in the current section.

Table 6.2 Detection accuracy of several variants of I-PT-RED framework (with detection threshold $\theta = 0.05$) and of the NC approach for the four groups of DNN classifiers, for CIFAR-10.

	BD-P-S	BD-G-S	BD-G-M	Clean
AD-J-P	0.92	0.92	**1.00**	**1.00**
AD-Jp-P	0.92	0.92	**1.00**	**1.00**
AD-Jc-P	0.96	0.92	**1.00**	**1.00**
AD-J-C	0.96	0.92	**1.00**	**1.00**
AD-J-P-L1	**1.00**	0.92	**1.00**	**1.00**
NC-L1-1.5	0.36	0.16	**1.00**	0.84
NC-L2-1.5	0.56	0.64	**1.00**	0.72
NC-L1-1.0	0.40	0.28	**1.00**	0.76
NC-L1-1.5-0.5	0.36	0.16	0.88	0.96

For NC, minimizing (6.2) requires specifying the Lagrange multiplier λ. Both $\lambda = 1.5$ and $\lambda = 1.0$ were tested (The default is $\lambda = 1.5$, see [191].). It is conjectured that if λ is selected too large, perturbation optimization for NC may never reach the π-level group misclassification target. For NC, the same $\pi = 0.8$ target as for I-PT-RED (AD) was used; $\pi = 0.5$ was also evaluated. However, it was found for some classifiers that inducing π-level misclassification to a subset of putative target classes from all source classes (i.e., NC's objective) is not feasible. For these classes, the optimization process is terminated when the size (norm) of the perturbation mask reaches a pre-set upper bound value. When this occurs, the derived detection statistics for these problematic classes skew estimation of the median during NC inference. In the experiments, these abnormal perturbation statistics were discarded in order to make NC inference more robust. Under I-PT-RED, this upper bound on the perturbation size/energy was never reached in the experiments, that is, π-level group misclassification was always achieved by I-PT-RED. Even if the upper bound were to be reached for several class pairs, taking the reciprocal will send these large statistics close to zero and have little effect on the estimation of the tail of the null density.

The variants of NC detection that were evaluated are the following.

- **NC-L1-1.5:** l_1-regularized objective function with $\lambda = 1.5$. The anomaly indices are derived from the l_1 norm of each optimized perturbation.
- **NC-L2-1.5:** l_2-regularized objective function with $\lambda = 1.5$. The anomaly indices are derived from the l_2 norm of each optimized perturbation.
- **NC-L1-1.0:** l_1-regularized objective function with $\lambda = 1.0$.
- **NC-L1-1.5-0.5:** Same as NC-L1-1.5, except that $\pi = 0.5$ instead of $\pi = 0.8$.

In Table 6.2, the accuracy for each variant of the I-PT-RED (AD) and NC detection methods for each group of classifiers is shown. Accuracy for the groups of classifiers under attack, that is, BD-P-S, BD-G-S and BD-G-M, is defined as the fraction of classifiers successfully detected as attacked. For the I-PT-RED variants, a successful detection *also* requires the detected source and target class pair (corresponding to the most extreme detection statistic) to be ground truth involved in the attack. For NC, since it assumes all classes except for the target class are involved in the backdoor attack, there is no inference on the source class(es). In the experiments, NC detection was considered to be successful if the class label corresponding to the most extreme anomaly index, if detected (i.e., above θ_{MAD}), is the true backdoor target class label t^*. Thus, for BD-P-S and BD-G-S, the AD approach meets a stronger true detection requirement than NC. For the group of clean networks, the detection accuracy is defined as the fraction of networks inferred to *not* be attacked.

All I-PT-RED (AD) variants achieved perfect detection for the BD-G-M and Clean group experiments. Detection accuracy for the BD-P-S and BD-G-S groups is also very high (all above 0.90). Note that one can always make more conservative AD inferences and claim a successful detection when *only* the target class is correctly inferred. This is reasonable due to the collateral damage effect shown previously. Allowing such conservative inference, all five AD variants achieve perfect detection for the BD-G-S group. In fact, *all* incorrectly determined source classes by AD variants for the results shown in Table 6.2 have high class collateral damage rates (above 88.4%).

NC detection, as expected, achieves strong performance for the BD-G-M group (except for the NC-L1-1.5-0.5 variant) since it is designed for backdoor attacks that involve all possible $K - 1$ source classes. However, not all the variants of NC are effective at detecting backdoor attacks involving a single source class, as shown in Table 6.2 by the accuracy for BD-P-S and BD-G-S, and this despite collateral damage affecting some non-target classes. Also, the detection power of NC cannot be improved by choosing a smaller θ_{MAD}, since the false detection rate on clean classifiers is then made quite non-negligible. Figure 6.8 shows the histogram of the maximum anomaly indices for BD-G-S and Clean, obtained using NC-L1-1.5; these two groups of anomaly indices are clearly not separable by *any* choice of θ_{MAD}.

Unlike NC, for the I-PT-RED (AD) variants, the order statistic p-values for clean classifiers and for attacked classifiers are easily separable in practice – there is a large range of thresholds θ which yield the same (or very similar) performance. Table 6.3 shows the detection performance for a very liberal detection threshold $\theta = 0.2$ applied to (6.6). One can observe a slight increment in false detection rate for the Clean group. Simultaneously, the true detection rate for the BD-P-S group is slightly increased. If a very conservative detection threshold $\theta = 0.01$ is used, as shown in Table 6.4, only the true detection rate for the BD-P-S group is reduced somewhat. Moreover, Table 6.2 and Table 6.3 show that the false detection rate for the Clean group is much lower than its theoretical value, which is the detection threshold θ. This is because, for the classifiers in the Clean group, the distribution of the reciprocal statistics used for detection is not left skewed like a typical Gamma distribution – few reciprocals sit on the tail of the unconditional null distribution. Hence, the order statistic p-value follows a slightly right-skewed distribution rather than a truly uniform distribution on $[0, 1]$. For example, the mean of the order statistic p-value across the 25 classifier realizations from the Clean group is 0.590 when the AD-J-P variant is applied for detection.

In addition to accurate attack detection inference, I-PT-RED also gives an estimate of the ground truth backdoor pattern. Figure 6.9a is an estimate of one of the 25 4-pixel

Table 6.3 Detection accuracy of all the variants of the I-PT-RED framework with detection threshold $\theta = 0.2$ for the four groups of DNN classifiers.

	BD-P-S	BD-G-S	BD-G-M	Clean
AD-J-P	0.96	0.92	**1.00**	**1.00**
AD-Jp-P	0.96	0.92	**1.00**	0.96
AD-Jc-P	0.96	0.92	**1.00**	0.96
AD-J-C	0.96	0.92	**1.00**	**1.00**
AD-J-P-L1	**1.00**	0.92	**1.00**	0.92

perturbations used to create the BD-P-S group, with a constant offset again added to aid visualization. Compared with the ground truth backdoor pattern of Figure 6.4a, one can see that instead of perturbing all four pixels, perturbing the region near the ground truth backdoor pixel on the top left is most effective to induce group misclassification to the target class. Figure 6.9b is an estimate of one of the 25 global perturbations used to create the BD-G-S group. Since nearly half of the pixels are perturbed negatively, and the perturbation size is too small to be visualized, an offset is first added such that the resulting perturbations are all positive; then the shifted perturbation mask is scaled by 30 times to aid visualization. Clearly, a chessboard pattern similar to the ground truth backdoor pattern is recovered.

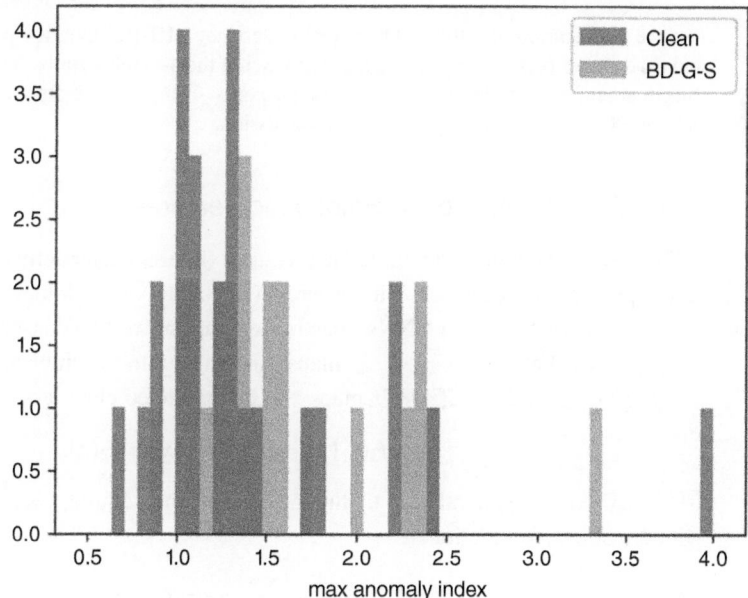

Figure 6.8 Histogram of the maximum anomaly indices for the BD-G-S and Clean groups, obtained using NC-L1-1.5. Reprinted from [303] with permission.

Table 6.4 Detection accuracy of all the variants of the I-PT-RED framework with detection threshold $\theta = 0.01$ for the four groups of DNN classifiers.

	BD-P-S	BD-G-S	BD-G-M	Clean
AD-J-P	0.84	0.92	**1.00**	**1.00**
AD-Jp-P	0.88	0.92	**1.00**	**1.00**
AD-Jc-P	0.88	0.92	**1.00**	**1.00**
AD-J-C	0.96	0.92	**1.00**	**1.00**
AD-J-P-L1	**1.00**	0.92	**1.00**	**1.00**

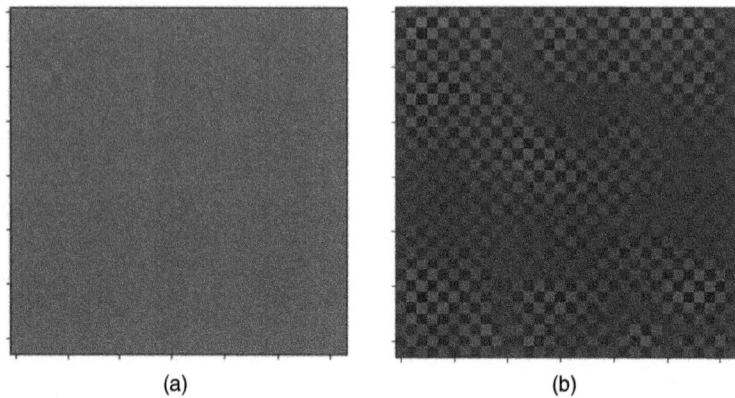

(a)   (b)

Figure 6.9 Examples of estimated backdoor patterns by I-PT-RED: (a) a 4 pixel perturbation and (b) a global perturbation. The upper left pixel of the 4-pixel perturbation is detected. Some images are offset or scaled for visualization purposes. Compare with the ground truth pattern of Figure 6.4. Reprinted from [303] with permission.

6.4.4   I-PT-RED (AD) Applied to Embedded Features

I-PT-RED can be applied to embedded features (internal layer activations) of $\mathcal{D}$ to detect imperceptible backdoors with different (non-additive) backdoor embedding mechanisms. Note that for most DNNs $\hat{c}$ can be decomposed as two consecutive sub-models $f_1 \circ f_2$, such that $f_1 : \mathbb{R}^N \rightarrow \mathcal{Z}$ maps an image $\underline{x}$ to an embedded feature vector $\underline{z} = f_1(\underline{x}) \in \mathcal{Z}$, and $f_2 : \mathcal{Z} \rightarrow \mathcal{Y}$ maps $\underline{z}$ to the predicted class label,

$$\hat{c}(\underline{x}) = f_2(f_1(\underline{x})) = (f_2 \circ f_1)(\underline{x}) = f_2(\underline{z}).$$

I-PT-RED can be generalized, taking AD-J-P as an example, by replacing Eq. (6.5) with the objective function

$$J_{st}^{\mathcal{G}}(\underline{v}) = -\frac{1}{|\mathcal{D}_s|} \sum_{\underline{x} \in \mathcal{D}_s} \hat{p}_{\mathcal{G}}(t | f_1(\underline{x}) + \underline{v}), \qquad (6.10)$$

where $\hat{p}_{\mathcal{G}}(\cdot | \underline{z})$ is the DNN's posterior given the internal layer feature vector $\underline{z}$. That is, for each class pair (s, t), this generalized I-PT-RED searches for the minimal sized (additive) perturbation that induces high misclassification rate from s to t in the *internal*

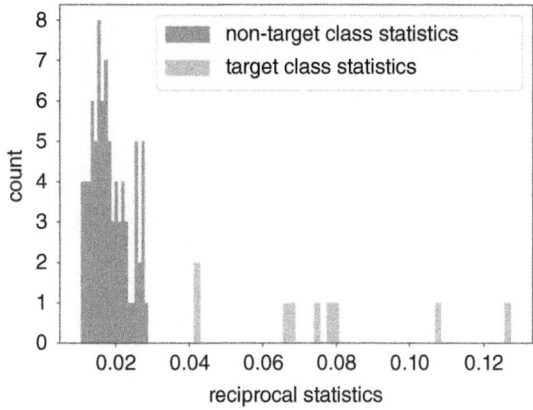

Figure 6.10 Histogram of the reciprocal statistics for AD-J-P with the generalized objective function applied on an attack with the multiplicative chessboard watermark pattern. Reprinted from [303] with permission.

feature space $\mathcal{Z}$ instead of the (input) image space. Note that methods which operate on deep embedded features may also easily generalize to different (non-image) application domains, for example, discrete feature-valued domains such as text documents.

For example, by applying AD-J-P with the generalized objective function Eq. (6.10), with f_1 the first convolutional layer, on the classifiers from the BD-P-S, BD-G-S, and BD-G-M groups, detection rates of 0.88, 1.00, and 1.00 are respectively obtained. Also, no attacks are detected over all 25 classifiers in the Clean group.

Now consider a **multiplicative** perturbation $\underline{u}^*$ that can be applied to a clean image $\underline{x}$ by

$$B_{\text{multi}}(\underline{x}, \underline{u}^*) = [\underline{x} \odot \underline{u}^*]_{\kappa}, \tag{6.11}$$

where $\underline{u}^*$ has the same dimension as the image $\underline{x}$, with u_{ijk} the scaling factor of x_{ijk}. Here we are using a two-dimensional pixel coordinate (i, j) and a color channel coordinate k. We created a backdoor attack with a multiplicative chessboard watermark pattern by setting $u_{ijk} = 1$ if pixel x_{ijk} is not perturbed and setting $u_{ijk} = 1.02$ if pixel x_{ijk} is perturbed. Other configurations of the attack are the same as those of the attacks on the classifiers in the BD-G-S group.

Figure 6.10 shows the histogram of the reciprocal statistics obtained by applying AD-J-P with the generalized objective function Eq. (6.10) on the attack above. Again $f_1(\cdot)$ was chosen as the first convolutional layer. The reciprocals corresponding to the true target class are clearly abnormally large. Generalized AD-J-P successfully detects the attack with order statistic p-value $2.0 \times 10^{-13} \ll \theta = 0.05$, and with correct inference of the (source, target) class pair.

Now consider the **blending-embedding** attack mechanism for local backdoor patterns, that is, Eq. (6.1). Again, the focus is on imperceptible backdoor patterns by setting $\|\underline{m}^*\|_{\infty}$ to be small. An attack on CIFAR-10 was created using the same configurations for creating the BD-P-S group, except that a noisy pattern $\underline{v}^*$ with v_{ijk} uniformly distributed from 0 to 1 is blending-embedded in the clean images with an associated mask

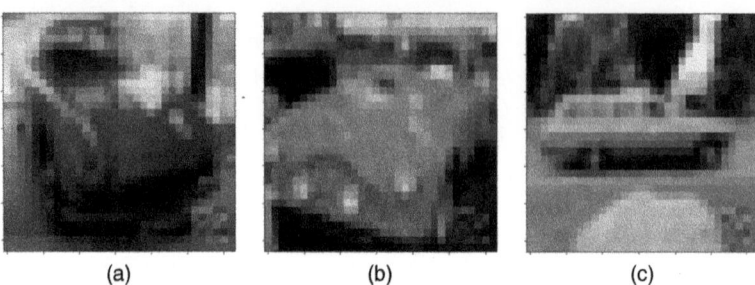

(a)   (b)   (c)

Figure 6.11 Examples of images with backdoor patterns embedded using Eq. (6.1). Reprinted from [303] with permission.

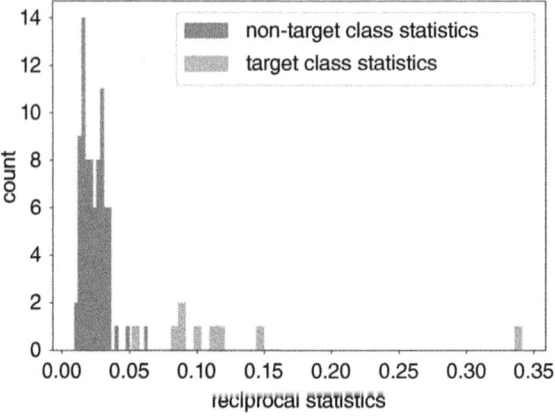

Figure 6.12 Histogram of the reciprocal statistics for AD-J-P with the generalized objective function applied on an attack with a localized pattern embedded using Eq. (6.11). Reprinted from [303] with permission.

$\underline{m}^*$. A localized attack pattern was created such that the non-zero elements of $\underline{m}^*$ are in a 5×5 square at the upper right corner of the image. The non-zero elements of the mask were set to 0.3 for imperceptibility. Examples of images with a backdoor pattern embedded according to Eq. (6.1) are shown in Figure 6.11. The attack success rate and the test accuracy on clean images are 0.966 and 0.912, respectively.

The AD-J-P variant of I-PT-RED was applied with the generalized objective function Eq. (6.10). The histogram of the reciprocal statistics obtained for all class pairs is shown in Figure 6.12. The reciprocal statistic corresponding to the true backdoor class pair is the right-most one – so AD-J-P successfully detects the attack with correct inference of the backdoor class pair (with order statistic p-value numerically equal to zero). Note that this attack cannot be effectively detected by the original I-PT-RED based on (6.5), meaning that I-PT-RED applied to embedded features is necessary here.

6.4.5   Choice of π

Unlike NC, the I-PT-RED approach is not very sensitive to the choice of π. As an example, the detection accuracy of the AD-J-P variant was evaluated on the 25 classifiers

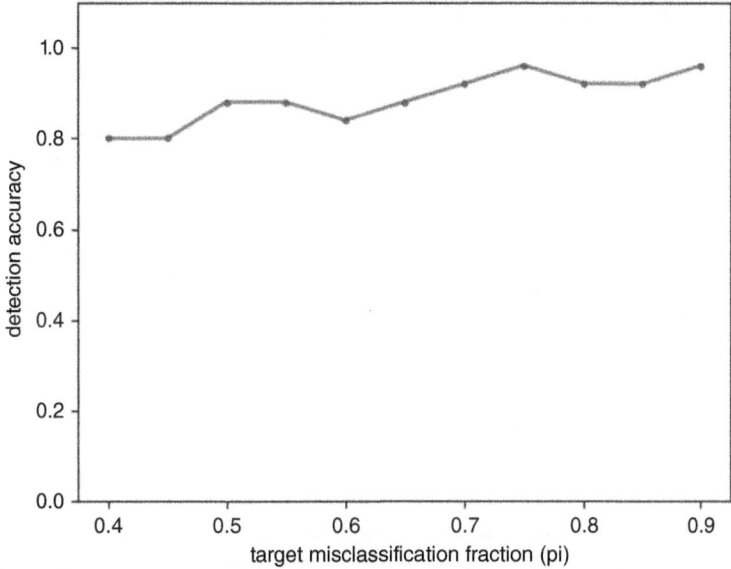

Figure 6.13 Detection accuracy of AD-J-P on the BD-P-S group, with a range of choices of π. Reprinted from [303] with permission.

in the BD-P-S group, with a range of choices of π from 0.4 to 0.9. The default detection threshold $\theta = 0.05$ was used. As shown in Figure 6.13, the detection accuracy does increase, but not dramatically with π. The minimum detection accuracy across the range of choices of π is 0.8, which can be further improved by use of a more liberal detection threshold. This phenomenon can be understood from Figure 6.14, in which the sequences $(\|\underline{v}_{st}^{(\tau)}\|_2, \rho_{st}^{(\tau)})$ are plotted for all (s,t) pairs during the perturbation optimization using Algorithm 6.1 with $\pi = 0.9$, while applying AD-J-P on an example classifier realization in the BD-P-S group. The sequence corresponding to the ground truth backdoor class pair (s^*, t^*) is represented using crosses, and is clearly separated from the sequences for the non-backdoor pairs. In other words, there is a huge range for the choice of π (not exceeding 0.9) to achieve correct detection for this example. For any choice of π in such range, the $(\|\underline{v}_{st}^{(\tau)}\|_2, \rho_{st}^{(\tau)})$ sequence for each (s,t) pair is truncated at the minimum τ such that $\rho_{st}^{(\tau)}$ first exceeds π. The resulting $\|\underline{v}_{st}^{(\tau)}\|_2$ for the backdoor class pair (s^*, t^*), as can be seen from the figure, will be much smaller than those for the non-backdoor pairs, which will lead to a successful detection.

6.4.6   Fitting Null Distribution Using All Statistics

As described in Section 6.3.3, during the detection inference process, a conditional null density is fit using the $(K-1)^2$ smallest statistics. One may also consider a naive approach that fits an unconditional null using all detection statistics. In Table 6.5, the detection accuracy of the AD-J-P variant with detection threshold $\theta = 0.05$ is shown

Table 6.5 Detection accuracy of the AD-J-P variant with detection threshold $\theta = 0.05$ for the four groups of DNN classifiers, where the null density is estimated using all $K(K-1)$ reciprocal statistics.

	BD-P-S	BD-G-S	BD-G-M	Clean
Detection accuracy	0.48	0.44	0.52	**1.00**

for the four groups of DNN classifiers based on this naive null learning. Clearly, there is severe degradation in the accuracy of detecting backdoors.

6.4.7   Size of the Ground Truth Backdoor Pattern

Here, 25 classifier realizations were created using the same setting as for the BD-G-S group, except that the l_2 norm of the backdoor pattern is set to 1.2, much larger than required to launch a successful backdoor attack (and visualizable by carefully scrutinizing the image). When applying AD-J-P for detection, with the detection threshold $\theta = 0.05$, the detection accuracy reaches 1.00. More importantly, the estimated backdoor patterns for the 25 classifier realizations are all scaled chessboard patterns with l_2 norm around 0.101 ± 0.017, while the l_2 norm of the optimized perturbation for all non-backdoor class pairs across the 25 realizations is 1.243 ± 0.321. That is, the estimated backdoor pattern will have the *minimum* norm necessary to achieve the

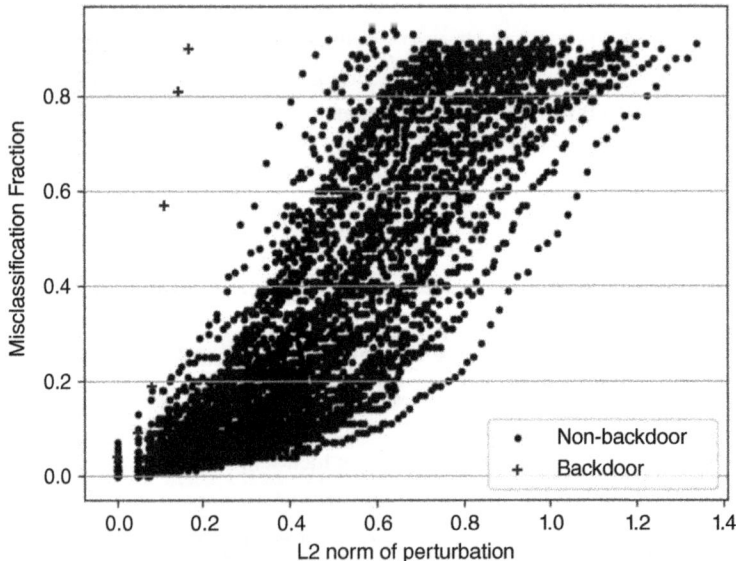

Figure 6.14 Sequences of $(\|\underline{v}_{st}^{(\tau)}\|_2, \rho_{st}^{(\tau)})$ for all (s,t) pairs, including the ground truth backdoor pair (s^*, t^*) represented using crosses (+), during the execution of Algorithm 6.1 with $\pi = 0.9$, while applying AD-J-P on an example classifier realization in the BD-P-S group. All of the backdoor points (+) are at the far left, with clear separation from all the other trajectories for L2 values greater than or equal to 0.1. Reprinted from [303] with permission.

π target level, even if the actual backdoor pattern has much larger norm. The estimated backdoor pattern is nevertheless accurate (it is a chessboard pattern). Also, from this experiment, note that I-PT-RED does not require the size/energy of the ground truth backdoor pattern to be significantly smaller than the size/energy of perturbations required to induce group misclassification for non-backdoor class pairs.

6.4.8 Fine-Pruning Experiments

Fine-pruning (FP) [156] was also evaluated using the classifiers from BD-P-S, BD-G-S, and BD-G-M. Note that FP does not infer whether a classifier has been backdoor attacked. For every classifier, neurons were pruned in the penultimate layer in increasing order of their average activations over the clean dataset. We recorded the attack success rate when the accuracy on the same dataset first drops by 2% and then by 5%. The histograms of attack success rate for the classifiers from the three groups at 2% and 5% clean dataset accuracy degradation are shown in Figure 6.15 – only a small portion of the classifiers are successfully pruned such that the backdoor effect is mitigated. This is likely due to the fact that, for most classifiers, penultimate layer (and, in fact, all) neurons are functionally *shared* by clean and backdoor patterns. Thus, successfully removing the backdoor by pruning will entail inevitable (above 5%) degradation in the usability of the classifier.

6.4.9 Effect of Poisoning Rate

Whether a backdoor attack with an imperceptible backdoor pattern will be successful depends on many factors, among which (perhaps) the most important two are the perturbation size (norm) and the poisoning rate. The following experimental study shows the effect of the poisoning rate on CIFAR-10 when the l_2 norm of the perturbation is fixed. Intuitively, with a higher poisoning rate, that is, with more training images embedded with the backdoor pattern used to poison the training set, the backdoor pattern will likely be more easily learned, which benefits the attacker. However, when the poisoning rate is too high (while not high enough to draw attention from the training authority), will the test accuracy of the trained classifier on clean images be degraded (such that the attack will possibly be noticeable)? This is a reasonable concern of an attacker because as the poisoning rate increases, more images from the source class(es) with the backdoor pattern embedded will be labeled to the target class, which may mislead the classifier to also learn the features of the source class(es), and cause high confusion between these source class(es) and the target class.

Two groups of attacked classifiers are created, with eight classifiers per group. The first group uses the same configuration of BD-P-S, including the same way of generating the 4-pixel backdoor pattern. But the number of backdoor images used to poison the training set for these eight classifiers respectively is set as [250, 500, 750, 1000, 1250, 1500, 1750, 2000] (recall that CIFAR-10 has 5000 clean images per class, including the target class). Note that the same backdoor pattern is used for all eight attacks for this group. For the second group, the same configuration of BD-G-S is used, but in this case the backdoor pattern is the chessboard pattern. Also,

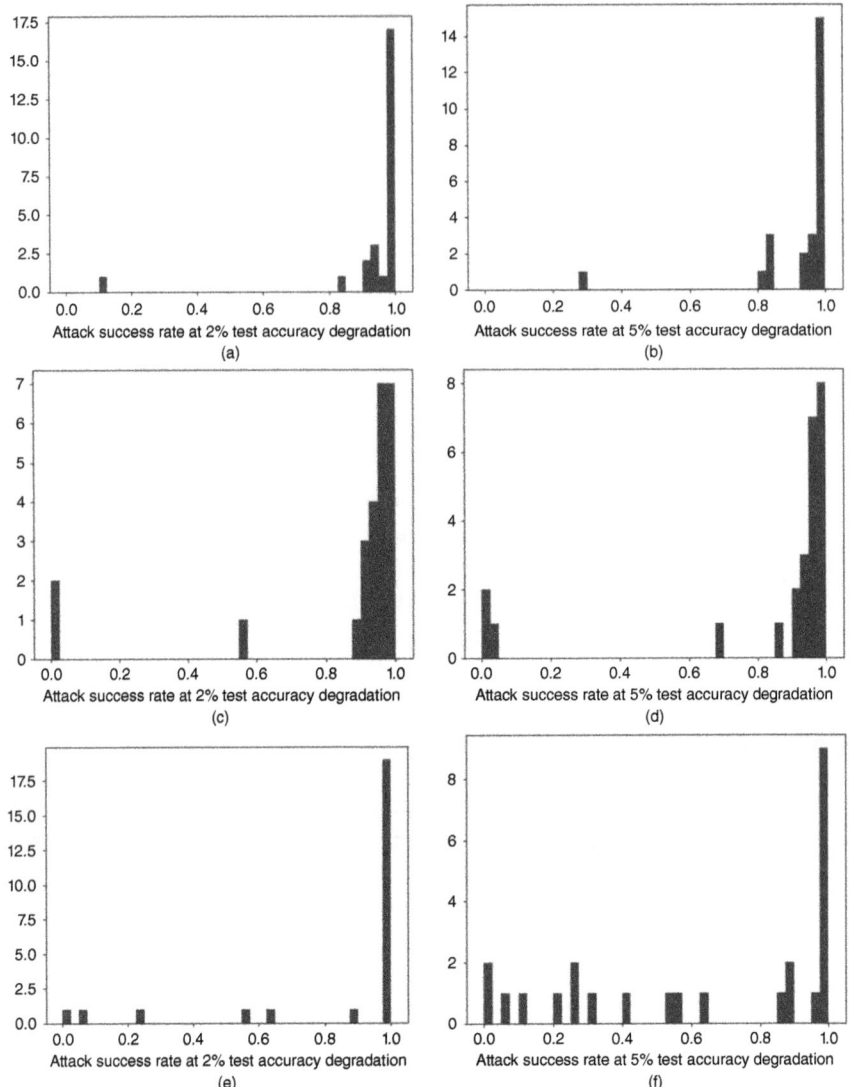

Figure 6.15 Histograms of attack success rate for classifiers from (a, b) BD-P-S, (c, d) BD-G-S, and (e, f) BD-G-M, at 2% (a, c, e) and 5% (b, d, f) absolute classification accuracy degradation, respectively. Reprinted from [303] with permission.

the same numbers of backdoor images to poison the training set are used for the eight classifiers in this group.

The attack success rate and the test accuracy on clean images for these attacked classifiers are shown in Figure 6.16. Note that the attack success rate does increase and remains at a high level as the number of backdoor images (used for poisoning the training set) increases, for both backdoor patterns. However, there is no clear degradation in the test accuracy on clean images for both backdoor patterns, as the number of backdoor training images increases.

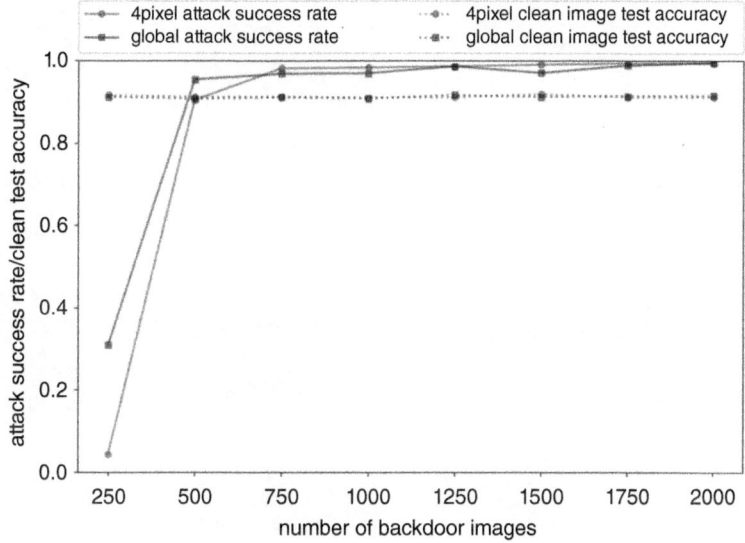

Figure 6.16 Attack success rate (solid) and accuracy on clean test images (dashed) for DNN classifiers under backdoor attacks that use sparse pixel-wise perturbation (dots) and global perturbation (squares) for number of backdoor images used to poison the training set in [250, 500, 750, 1000, 1250, 1500, 1750, 2000]. Reprinted from [303] with permission.

Hence, it is hypothesized that it is the backdoor pattern, rather than the features of the source class(es), that are being learned by the classifier. Grad-CAM is used to test this hypothesis (recall Section 2.11). For each of the eight classifiers attacked using the 4-pixel perturbation, a heat-map is obtained based on Grad-CAM for each backdoor image used to poison the training set of the classifier. The heat-map highlights the spatial region involving the key features. For all eight classifiers, Figure 6.17 shows the average heat-map over all the backdoor images used to poison the training set, respectively, along with the true backdoor pattern used by the attacker. The heat-maps clearly show that it is the backdoor pattern being learned, particularly the perturbation in the bottom right corner.

Moreover, I-PT-RED is applied to all the 16 classifiers being attacked. Using AD-J-P, successful detections are made with correct inferences of the (source, target) class pair for all the attacks, except for the attack using the 4-pixel perturbation and 250 backdoor images – but this attack is anyway unsuccessful, as seen from its low attack success rate in Figure 6.16. Note that for the attack with the chessboard pattern and 250 backdoor training images, where the attack is weak (with an attack success rate near 0.3), I-PT-RED still successfully detects it.

6.4.10 Other Experiments

In [303], additional experiments were conducted involving other design/parameter choices of the defenses: different surrogate objectives for I-PT-RED (AD), sizes of the

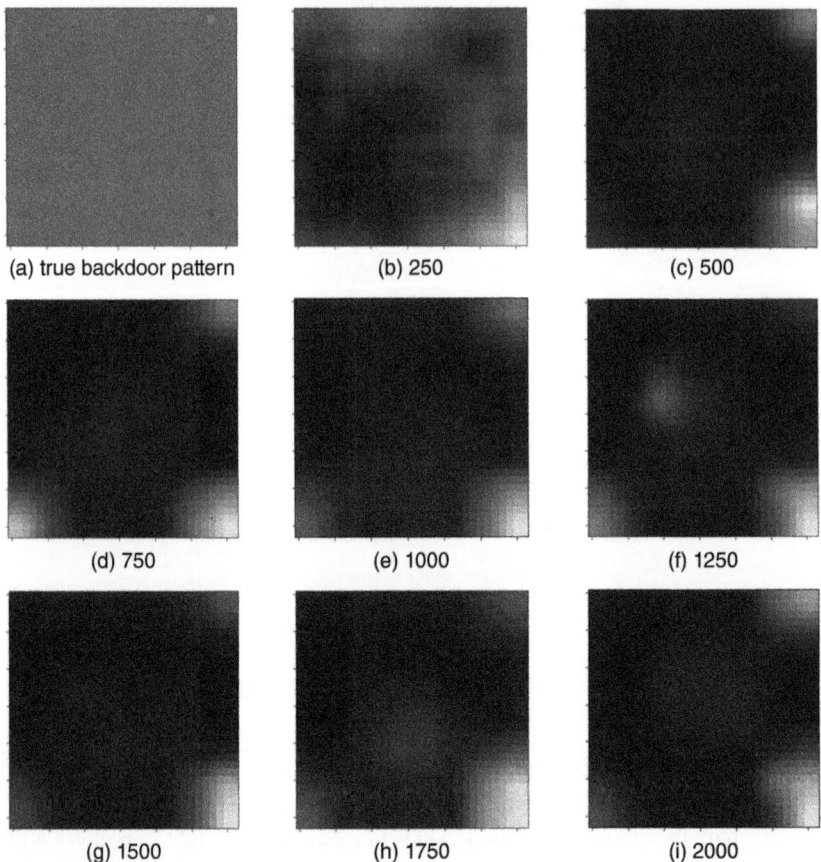

Figure 6.17 Heat-map associated with the target class, averaged over the backdoor images used to poison the training set, for all eight attacked classifiers for the 4-pixel pattern; and the true backdoor pattern used by the attacker. Reprinted from [303] with permission.

clean dataset (see Figure 13 of [303] and see Section 6.5), and polynomial degrees M to account for class confusion. Also, additional experiments were conducted involving varying attack strengths/parameters (e.g., poisoning rate), increased image resolution (i.e., ImageNet [57]), and alternative attack/defense scenarios. In all of these additional experiments, the I-PT-RED framework was robust, showing generally good and superior performance to alternative methods.

6.4.11 Computational Complexity

The experiments were performed on Amazon EC2 g3s.xlarge virtual machines powered by a NVIDIA Tesla M60 GPU. When applying AD-J-P to BD-P-S, the average running time across the 25 classifier realizations is 698 s. In comparison, when applying NC-L1-1.5 to BD-P-S, the average running time across the 25 classifier realizations is

912 s. For both approaches, the perturbation optimization step incurs most of the computational cost.

For the NC defense, each iteration of perturbation optimization requires $2(K-1)M$ back-propagations on the DNN, where here M is the number of clean images per class used for detection, that is, $MK = |\mathcal{D}|$. Since NC solves K perturbation optimization problems, the total computational cost is $2(K-1)MVK$ back-propagations, where V is the number of iterations required to reach π-level misclassification.

For the I-PT-RED (AD) framework, each iteration of perturbation optimization requires $2M$ back-propagations on the DNN since only clean images from a single class are used for detection. The total computational cost is then $2MVK(K-1)$ since $K(K-1)$ perturbation optimization problems are solved. Theoretically, the computational costs of the two defenses are the same. But in practice, the difficulty of inducing group misclassification to a target class from all the other classes can be much higher than inducing misclassification from a single source class to the target class, especially when the backdoor attack is crafted with a single source class. Therefore, the number of iterations in perturbation optimization required for the NC defense is generally larger than that for I-PT-RED.

The time/complexity of post-training detection is well worth the effort, compared with the alternative of deploying a backdoor poisoned classifier. Also note that these computational costs are not borne at test time. Finally, note that Section 6.5 describes a much less complex (more scalable in the number of classes K) variant of I-PT-RED for detecting imperceptible backdoors. This approach also reduces the number of clean samples that are necessary for successful detection.

6.5   Lagrangian Post-Training Reverse-Engineering Defense (L-PT-RED) and Experiments

This section describes a computationally efficient improvement of the backdoor attack detection procedure I-PT-RED, called Lagrangian based PT-RED (L-PT-RED) [305]. L-PT-RED is designed to detect an imperceptible backdoor with *arbitrary* number of source classes, and to infer the target class for any detected attack. L-PT-RED can also be potentially extended with little modification to detect *perceptible* backdoors, see Chapter 7. Compared with I-PT-RED, L-PT-RED requires far fewer clean images for accurate backdoor attack detection (and thus also much lower computational complexity). Even with just two clean images per class, the following experiments show that L-PT-RED detects 56 out of 60 attacks with just 1 out of 10 false detections in experiments on CIFAR-10.

Consider a possible *imperceptible* backdoor attack with arbitrary number of source classes. (i) L-PT-RED detects whether there is a backdoor attack; (ii) if an attack is detected, the target class of the attack is inferred; (iii) the source classes of the attack are inferred; (iv) the backdoor pattern associated with the detected attack is estimated. Like other REDs, L-PT-RED contains a backdoor pattern estimation step followed by an anomaly detection step.

6.5.1   Backdoor Pattern Estimation

BP estimation is performed for each putative target class $t \in \mathcal{Y}$ using all images from $\cup_{s \neq t} \mathcal{D}_s$. So, if there are M clean images per class for detection, then K pattern estimations are performed, one for each putative target class and each using $M(K-1)$ clean images. Recall that I-PT-RED performs $K(K-1)$ pattern estimations, each using M clean images, with M sufficiently large to ensure good detection accuracy. It thus might appear that L-PT-RED and I-PT-RED require the same computational complexity. However, *the minimum M required for L-PT-RED to accurately detect backdoor attacks in practice will be much smaller than for I-PT-RED (especially when K is large)*. Thus, L-PT-RED may have much lower computational complexity (and generally requires a much smaller clean data set) than I-PT-RED.

Instead of assuming that $S^* \cup t^* = \mathcal{Y}$ (i.e., that the set of attack source classes $S^* = \mathcal{Y} \backslash \{t^*\}$), suppose that a backdoor attack may involve an arbitrary $S^* \subset \mathcal{Y} \backslash \{t^*\}$. Correspondingly, consider the following *weighted* pattern estimation problem for each putative $t \in \mathcal{Y}$:

$$\underset{\underline{v}, \underline{w}}{\text{minimize}} \quad \|\underline{v}\|_2$$

$$\text{subject to} \quad Q_t(\underline{v}, \underline{w}) \triangleq \sum_{s \neq t} w_s q_{st}(\underline{v}) \geq \pi,$$

$$\sum_{s \neq t} w_s = 1, \quad \underline{w} \geq \underline{0},$$

(6.12)

where

$$q_{st}(\underline{v}) \triangleq \frac{1}{|\mathcal{D}_s|} \sum_{\underline{x} \in \mathcal{D}_s} \mathbb{1}\{\hat{c}(B(\underline{x}, \underline{v})) = t\}$$

is the misclassification fraction from s to t for putative backdoor pattern $\underline{v}$. It is hypothesized, in solutions to (6.12) for both the weights $\underline{w}$ and $\underline{v}$, when a backdoor attack is present, that the true source classes will be assigned much higher weights than other classes. Note that the above optimization problem extends I-PT-RED to leverage all the classes simultaneously (other than the putative target class) in estimating putative backdoor patterns. At the same time, this formulation is also related to NC, see Eq. (6.2). NC gives the same weight to *all* classes other than t in estimating a putative backdoor pattern involving target class t. If the actual attack involves only a subset of the classes, this may severely impact the accuracy of NC's pattern estimation. By contrast, L-PT-RED simultaneously estimates the backdoor pattern and the involved source classes (via the class weights).

Following DeepFool [185] and I-PT-RED, consider an iterative algorithm to solve (6.12) which alternately updates $\underline{v}$ and $\underline{w}$ until $Q_t(\underline{v}, \underline{w}) \geq \pi$.

Initial $\underline{w}$: *Constant* in all entries (with value $\frac{1}{K-1}$) except that $w_t = 0$, and $\underline{v} = \underline{0}$ (so that initially $Q_t(\underline{v}, \underline{w}) \approx 0$).

Update $\underline{v}$: At iteration $\tau + 1$ ($\tau \geq 0$), given $\underline{v}^{(\tau)}$ and $\underline{w}^{(\tau)}$ from iteration τ, update $\underline{v}$ by

$$\begin{aligned} \underline{v}^{(\tau+1)} &= \underline{v}^{(\tau)} + \Delta \underline{v}^{(\tau+1)}, \text{ where} \\ \Delta \underline{v}^{(\tau+1)} &= \arg\max{}_{\|\underline{z}\|_2 = \delta} \, Q_t(\underline{v}^{(\tau)} + \underline{z}, \underline{w}^{(\tau)}) \end{aligned}$$

(6.13)

with $\delta > 0$ a small step size. Since $Q_t(\underline{v}, \underline{w})$ is not differentiable in $\underline{v}$ due to the indicator function, an approximate solution to (6.13) can be obtained by taking just one gradient ascent step on a differentiable surrogate of Q_t:

$$\Delta\underline{v}^{(\tau+1)} \approx \delta \frac{\nabla_{\underline{v}} J_t(\underline{v}^{(\tau)}, \underline{w}^{(\tau)})}{\|\nabla_{\underline{v}} J_t(\underline{v}^{(\tau)}, \underline{w}^{(\tau)})\|_2}, \quad \text{where}$$

$$J_t(\underline{v}, \underline{w}) \triangleq \sum_{s \neq t} w_s \frac{1}{|\mathcal{D}_s|} \sum_{\underline{x} \in \mathcal{D}_s} \log \hat{p}(t | B(\underline{x}, \underline{v}))$$

(6.14)

and $\hat{p}(i|\underline{x})$ is the classifier's posterior for class $i \in \mathcal{Y}$ for any image $\underline{x} \in \mathbb{R}^N$. Note that the number of samples being used by L-PT-RED to estimate a putative backdoor pattern with target class t is $\sum_{s \neq t} |\mathcal{D}_s|$.

Update $\underline{w}$: The aim is to have the source classes assigned higher weights. In iteration $\tau + 1$, one might naively hard assign $w_i = 1$ to class $i = \arg\max_{s \neq t} q_{st}(\underline{v}^{(\tau+1)})$ because with a small-norm $\underline{v}$, the misclassification fraction from a source class to the true backdoor attack target class tends to be larger than for non-source classes. However, after choosing this class, updating of $\underline{v}$ will be performed on clean images associated with only this class in all subsequent iterations. As uniform weights are initially assigned to all classes except t, in early iterations, updating $\underline{v}$ may cause any class $i \notin \mathcal{S}^*$ to *temporarily* have the largest $q_{it}(\underline{v})$. In this case, under hard assignment, subsequent pattern estimations will be performed for a "non-backdoor" class pair – a poor local optimum with a large $\|\underline{v}\|_2$ will be the result. To avoid this outcome, L-PT-RED uses the following Lagrangian to update $\underline{w}$ in iteration $\tau + 1$ subject to a specified level of "randomness" (entropy of $\underline{w}$):

$$\underline{w}^{(\tau+1)} = \arg\max_{\underline{w}} Q_t(\underline{v}^{(\tau+1)}, \underline{w}) - \lambda^{(\tau+1)} \sum_{s \neq t} w_s \log w_s$$

$$\text{subject to} \sum_{s \neq t} w_s = 1,$$

(6.15)

where the Lagrange multiplier $\lambda^{(\tau+1)} \geq 0$ can be viewed as the current iteration's "temperature" [1]. Note that if $\lambda^{(\tau+1)} = 0$, solving (6.15) is equivalent to hard weight assignment; on the other hand, if $\lambda^{(\tau+1)}$ is made very large, solving (6.15) will yield a maximum entropy solution (uniform weights). In order to avoid poor local optima caused by hard weight assignment, λ should be large when $Q_t(\underline{v}, \underline{w})$ is small in the early iterations. As $Q_t(\underline{v}, \underline{w})$ grows large, λ should be *gradually* decreased, such that higher weights are *gradually* assigned to classes with large $q_{\cdot t}(\underline{v})$; these classes are likely the source classes if t is the true backdoor attack target class. For example, we can schedule λ automatically via:

$$\lambda^{(\tau+1)} = -\log Q_t(\underline{v}^{(\tau+1)}, \underline{w}^{(\tau)}) \in (0, +\infty)$$

(6.16)

for $Q_t(\underline{v}^{(\tau+1)}, \underline{w}^{(\tau)}) > 0$. Note that, in practice, while λ decreases with increasing iterations, it never actually goes to zero because the algorithm is terminated when, for the first time, $Q_t(\underline{v}, \underline{w}) \geq \pi$ for some $\pi < 1$. Given this scheduled $\lambda^{(\tau+1)}$, the closed-form solution to (6.15) is:

$$w_s^{(\tau+1)} = \frac{\exp[q_{st}(\underline{v}^{(\tau+1)})/\lambda^{(\tau+1)}]}{\sum_{i \neq t} \exp[q_{it}(\underline{v}^{(\tau+1)})/\lambda^{(\tau+1)}]}, \quad \forall s \neq t.$$

(6.17)

The derivation of this result and pseudocode for L-PT-RED's pattern estimation algorithm are given in the Appendix of [305].

6.5.2   Detection Inference

Detection for L-PT-RED uses a similar hypothesis testing approach as I-PT-RED. First, a detection statistic is obtained for each putative target class t as $r_t = (\|\underline{v}_t\|_2)^{-1}$, where $\underline{v}_t$ is the *estimated pattern* for class t. To test the null hypothesis that there is no attack, a null distribution G is fit using all statistics except $r_{max} = \max_t r_t$ (i.e., excluding the statistic associated with the class t^* with the smallest estimated pattern norm, the putative target class of a backdoor attack). G is chosen to have the form of a Gamma distribution, but other single-tailed distribution forms should also work [303]. (Unlike the inference approach described in Section 6.3.3, a conditional null with support $[0, r_{max}]$ is *not* first estimated in the L-PT-RED experiments described in the following.) Then the order statistic p-value for r_{max} under G is calculated as $pv = 1 - G(r_{max})^K$. A detection threshold θ is chosen, such that the null hypothesis is rejected with confidence $1 - \theta$ if $pv < \theta$. When an attack is detected, $\hat{t} = \arg\max_t r_t$ is inferred as the target class. One can also estimate the source classes as those with the largest weights w (as obtained after solving target class $\hat{t}$'s optimization problem).

6.5.3   L-PT-RED Experiments

The following experiments evaluate both the effectiveness and *efficiency* of L-PT-RED against other RED defenses for backdoor attacks on the CIFAR-10 domain (with 50k training images and 10k test images, both evenly distributed among 10 classes). Key results for other datasets are also given.

The ResNet-18 DNN architecture is used. For each backdoor attack considered, one classifier is trained on the poisoned training set. Training is performed for 100 epochs with batch size 32 and learning rate 10^{-3}. Data augmentation, including random cropping and random horizontal flipping, are used during training.

The backdoor attacks considered are the global checkerboard and the local 4-pixel pattern of Figure 5.2a and Figure 5.2e, respectively.

In the following, the six groups of classifiers being attacked are respectively called 'G-1', 'G-3', 'G-9', 'L-1', 'L-3', and 'L-9', where 'G' represents 'global' BP, 'L' represents 'local' BP, and the numbers represent the number of attack source classes. Ten classifiers were also trained (using different random weight initialization, for each of the 10 trainings) on the clean CIFAR-10 training set as the control group (named 'C-0'), for false detection rate evaluation.

6.5.4   Attacker: ASR and ACC

From the experimenter's perspective, the effectiveness of the attacks is indicated by attack success rate (ASR) and clean test set accuracy (ACC). ASR of an attack is the fraction of test images from the source class(es) being classified to the target class

Table 6.6 Attack success rate (ASR) and clean test accuracy (ACC) for the six groups of classifiers being attacked.

	G-1	G-3	G-9	L-1	L-3	L-9
ASR	92.1 ± 1.9	94.1 ± 1.1	96.6 ± 0.3	93.1 ± 1.6	91.1 ± 0.8	91.9 ± 0.7
ACC	93.6 ± 0.2	93.5 ± 0.2	93.5 ± 0.2	93.7 ± 0.1	93.6 ± 0.2	93.6 ± 0.2

Table 6.7 Detection accuracy (fraction of successful detection) of the defenses on the seven groups of classifiers.

	G-1	G-3	G-9	L-1	L-3	L-9	C-0
I-PT-RED	5/10	9/10	7/10	2/10	3/10	3/10	7/10
U-RED	2/10	8/10	10/10	2/10	5/10	10/10	10/10
L-PT-RED	10/10	10/10	10/10	10/10	10/10	10/10	10/10
L-PT-RED′	9/10	10/10	10/10	9/10	8/10	10/10	9/10

when the backdoor pattern is embedded. In Table 6.6, for all attacks, the ASRs are uniformly high, with almost no degradation in ACC compared with group C-0 (with ACC 93.8 ± 0.1); the attacks are all highly successful.

Defenses Evaluated: L-PT-RED was evaluated along with two other REDs, I-PT-RED and U-RED which (like NC [282]) assumes $S^* \cup t^* = \mathcal{Y}$. Here U-RED is a special case of L-PT-RED with $\underline{w}$ fixed to uniform weights. For L-PT-RED, I-PT-RED, and U-RED, eight clean images per class were used for detection. A severely "data-limited" case, denoted L-PT-RED′, was also considered, where only two clean images per class are available.

Common Defense Parameters: For all these defenses, $\pi = 0.9$, pattern estimation step size $\delta = 10^{-4}$, and detection (confidence) threshold $\theta = 0.05$ were chosen (in general, these choices are not critical to the performance of REDs against imperceptible backdoor attacks, as seen earlier in this chapter).

For each classifier to be inspected, the clean images used for detection were randomly sampled from the subset of CIFAR-10's test set consisting of correctly classified samples.

Accuracy Evaluation: For all the defenses, a successful detection of an attack requires also a correct inference of the target class. For the clean classifiers in C-0, "no attack detected" is deemed a successful detection.

Table 6.7 shows the fraction of successful detections for all the defenses for the seven groups of classifiers. For U-RED, although perfect detection is achieved for G-9 and L-9 where the $S^* \cup t^* = \mathcal{Y}$ assumption is satisfied, with no false detections on C-0, the detection accuracy on G-1, G-3, L-1, and L-3 (where $|S^*| < |\mathcal{Y}| - 1$) is poor. I-PT-RED shows limited detection capability with $M = 8$ clean images per class for attacks with the "global" pattern (consistent with Figure 13 in [303]), but even worse results (it fails) for most of the attacks with the "local" pattern. In comparison, L-PT-RED achieves perfect detection of all the attacks, *regardless of the number of source classes*, and with no false detections. Notably, with only $M = 2$ clean images per class, L-PT-RED′ detects 56 out of 60 attacks, with only 1 out of 10 false

Table 6.8 Average execution time (in seconds) of the defenses on the seven groups of classifiers.

	G-1	G-3	G-9	L-1	L-3	L-9	C-0
I-PT-RED	480	473	531	478	479	394	541
L-PT-RED	562	615	636	529	482	536	535
L-PT-RED'	136	161	167	129	169	163	157

Table 6.9 Order statistic p-values for both clean and attacked classifiers on MNIST, FMNIST, GTSRB, and CIFAR-100, when applying L-PT-RED (u.f. for underflow).

	MNIST	FMNIST	GTSRB	CIFAR-100
Attacked	u.f.	8.44×10^{-7}	3.41×10^{-9}	u.f.
Clean	0.300	0.331	0.152	0.551

detections, which is a generally better result than that achieved by both I-PT-RED and U-RED.

Efficiency Evaluation: As discussed in Section 6.5.1 and demonstrated experimentally, to achieve high detection accuracy, defenses like I-PT-RED need a "sufficiently large" number of clean images per class (i.e., a large M), while L-PT-RED does not. As shown in Table 6.8, L-PT-RED and I-PT-RED need similar average execution times for each of the seven groups of classifiers. However, L-PT-RED' with $M = 2$ exhibits a much lower time consumption than both L-PT-RED and I-PT-RED with $M = 8$. The execution time for U-RED (not shown) is similar to that for L-PT-RED. All experiments above are performed on an RTX2080-Ti (11GB) GPU.

Experiments on Other Datasets: One attack is created on each of the MNIST, FMNIST [312], GTSRB [250], and CIFAR-100 datasets. For each dataset, one classifier is trained on the backdoor poisoned dataset and one clean classifier is trained (without using the poisoned samples). Details of the attacks and training are given in the Appendix of [305]. L-PT-RED was applied with the same settings as above to inspect these classifiers, except that for classifiers trained on GTSRB and CIFAR-100, **only one** clean image per class is used for detection. Table 6.9 shows the order statistic p-values obtained for each classifier by L-PT-RED. All attacks are detected, with no false detections for any of the clean classifiers using the detection threshold $\theta = 0.05$. For the backdoor attack on CIFAR-100, L-PT-RED requires less than three hours for detection while I-PT-RED requires several days. Additional results are given in the Appendix of [305] including an extension to perceptible backdoor attacks, see Chapter 7.

6.6   Discussion: Robust and Explainable AI

Determining whether a DNN has a backdoor is fundamental not only to security of DNNs but also to their interpretability, that is, to determining whether the DNN is performing as intended for purposes of explainable AI (XAI). Moreover, **even in the absence of an attack**, reverse-engineering based backdoor defenses may identify unexpectedly small perturbations that can cause the DNN to produce incorrect outputs over a region of input space, for example, corresponding to an entire class (for one example, see the discussion of "intrinsic" backdoors in Sections 11.6.1 and 11.7.2). These regions of input space with high output sensitivity may be surprising to data scientists who simply apply deep learning, without close scrutiny of what is being learned. Active learning informed by a RED can be used to attempt to "shore up" such detected deficiencies in the existing DNN model, resulting in a more robust model.

Moreover, to robustly operate a DNN, it is obviously important to detect (and possibly correct) backdoor triggers at test time (see Chapter 10) and "out-of-distribution" test samples (including TTE attacks, recall Chapter 4 and the comment in Section 4.8). Detection of a large number of out-of-distribution samples may also indicate that the testing domain is somehow different from the training domain. This may also necessitate a model retraining or refinement stage, to make the DNN well matched to the current input domain (i.e., applying adaptation/refinement techniques to the DNN to address "model drift").

6.7   Chapter Summary

In this chapter it was demonstrated that *even without access to the (possibly) poisoned training set*, it is feasible to reliably detect backdoor data poisoning in a trained neural network. The I-PT-RED method developed in this chapter has several key components.

- A suitable optimization to estimate a putative backdoor pattern for *each* candidate (source, target) class pair, for example, finding the smallest additive perturbation that induces high misclassifications from the candidate source class to the candidate target class (on a small clean dataset). The sizes of the required perturbations are the resulting detection statistics.
- Robust null modelling of these statistics, that is, estimating the null density *conditioned* on the range of the detection statistics. This density can be, for example, a truncated Gamma distribution, with the *unconditioned* distribution then simply extrapolated from the conditional distribution.
- Order statistic p-value based detection inference. This method infers whether the DNN was poisoned, estimates source and target classes of the attack if a detection was made, and also estimates the backdoor pattern itself.

Moreover, an extension/correction method was developed to account for knowledge of inherent confusion between the classes. Also, I-PT-RED is suitable for detecting backdoors using embedding functions other than additive embedding if the method is applied not to the raw (input) features but rather to internal layer features of the DNN.

We observed an experimental phenomenon that we dubbed "collateral damage," wherein some *non-backdoor* source classes are susceptible to the backdoor trigger. Such collateral damage could be avoided by the attacker if they applied a more targeted attack, for example, by also embedding the backdoor pattern into training examples from classes *not* associated with the attack, but *correctly* labeling these examples.

Neural cleanse (NC) and I-PT-RED are two early foundational methods for reverse-engineering (RED) based backdoor defense. One limitation of NC is that it supposes that all classes other than the target are source classes of the attack. Neural cleanse was shown to fare poorly when this assumption is violated, that is, when the attack involves only one or several source classes.

Some questions to test the reader's understanding of the chapter include the following.

- What is the explanation for why fine-pruning [156] is ineffective at mitigating backdoor attacks?
- It was noted that NC's detection performance would improve if it is not assumed that all non-target classes are source classes when the attack is present. Do you think that NC's performance would also improve if detection were based on the estimated putative pattern in addition to the estimated mask?
- How is the "small perturbation size" constraint imposed by I-PT-RED? Are there alternative ways to achieve this?
- Is I-PT-RED most suitable for detecting digital attacks or physical attacks? Explain.
- Why are ensemble experiments performed in this chapter?
- Explain why for the 4-pixel attack that the attack success rate fluctuates wildly as the attack perturbation size is varied.
- Is it surprising that I-PT-RED is quite accurately estimating the backdoor pattern? (Note that I-PT-RED's objective function is, in general, non-convex.) Explain.
- Explain the relationship between I-PT-RED and TSC-RED from Chapter 5. (Note that I-PT-RED was developed *first*.)
- What are the advantages of L-PT-RED over I-PT-RED? Can L-PT-RED be applied to embedded features?

6.8 Project: Imperceptible Backdoor Post-Training Reverse-Engineering Defense (I-PT-RED) on Images

Python code for this project is available at www.cambridge.org/millersecureAI. Code that can train accurate MNIST and CIFAR-10 classifiers is given in [155]. For those who are only using a CPU, training a DNN may be time consuming. You can use cloud resources which have GPU and TPU hardware accelerators accessible through convenient APIs like CUDA.

6.8.1 Implementing and Assessing a Backdoor Data Poisoning Attack on CIFAR-10

Note that, unlike MNIST images where each pixel has a single greyscale channel, color CIFAR images [129] have three (RGB) channels per pixel.

This project involves the following steps.

1. Load-in the CIFAR-10 dataset.
2. Create a backdoor pattern.
3. Create backdoor training samples and backdoor test samples by embedding the backdoor pattern into clean samples.
4. Insert the backdoor training samples into the training set (i.e., poison it) having, say, 3000 clean (unpoisoned) training samples per class.
5. Load in the model architecture (ResNet-18).
6. Perform training (back-propagation).
7. Evaluate attack performance, that is, accuracy on clean test samples and the attack success rate.
8. Report such performance versus the poisoning rate (0, 250, 500, ..., 1500 total poisoned images, i.e., up to 5% if 30k clean training samples are used across 10 classes). Also vary the size of the perturbation (using either L2 or L1 norms) to see the effect of this on the performance for a fixed poisoning rate.

6.8.2   Implementing and Assessing I-PT-RED

Apply I-PT-RED to the classifiers trained in Section 6.8.1 and evaluate its performance for the following changes to the attack configurations and detection hyperparameters.

1. The attack strength is jointly decided by the perturbation size of an additive perturbation backdoor pattern and the poisoning rate. Evaluate I-PT-RED for a range of backdoor perturbation sizes and number of backdoor training images.

2. Evaluate I-PT-RED with different target misclassification fractions π, observe any changes to the detection accuracy, and interpret your results.

3. Compare the backdoor pattern estimated by I-PT-RED with the ground truth backdoor pattern. Does I-PT-RED successfully estimate the backdoor pattern? How do you evaluate it? Evaluate the collateral damage caused by the estimated backdoor pattern.

4. Apply the following variant of I-PT-RED's anomaly detection to clean classifiers without backdoor attack. Fit a Gamma distribution (or any single-tailed density form) using all the reciprocal statistics and evaluate the p-value of the largest statistic. Repeat for fewer reciprocal statistics and observe the changes of the p-value. What is the main limitation of the above variant based on your observation and which mechanism of the proposed I-PT-RED is designed to address this limitation?

Alternatively or in addition, experiment with the provided I-PT-RED code that perturbs the activations of an internal layer (embedded features) of the DNN rather than the input.

6.9 Project: Consensus Post-Training Reverse-Engineering Defense (C-PT-RED)

The following project considers defenses which can address patch-incorporated back-doors (recall NC in Section 6.2.3 and see Chapter 7). In this project, assume the attacker can use, for example, the 4-pixel pattern (Figure 5.2e) or a more localized pattern (e.g., the square of Figure 5.2d) as the backdoor pattern. The defender can use the inference methods of Section 6.3.3. The proposed defenses, next described, still estimate an additive perturbation as the backdoor pattern. However, they also take account of the following observations.

1. For patch-incorporated backdoors, the (additive) perturbation is much more likely to be distinct for each image in which the patch is incorporated because the perturbation is the patch BP minus the particular clean image's pixel values in the support (mask) of the BP (while for an additively incorporated BP, the perturbation will likely have far less image specific variation, e.g., due to clipping so that the perturbed pixels are feasible).
2. At the same time, the perturbations are expected to not be too different from each other.

6.9.1 An Additive C-PT-RED

This project investigates a particular detector for patch-embedded backdoor attacks based on the above ideas. Suppose that one performs the perturbation optimization in I-PT-RED, but with a separate perturbation estimated for *each* clean labeled sample in the small clean labeled set $\mathcal{D} = \cup_{s \in \mathcal{Y}} \mathcal{D}_s$ (available to the defense). Let $\hat{p}(t|\cdot)$ be the class posterior of the DNN for class t. Let $\lambda > 0$ be a Lagrange multiplier or penalty parameter to "regularize" the sample-wise backdoor perturbation estimates so that they are not too different from each other (i.e., so that their sample variance is not high). For each source target class pair (s,t), find

$$\{\underline{v}^*_{s,t,\underline{x}}\}_{\underline{x} \in \mathcal{D}_s} = \underset{\{\underline{v}_{\underline{x}} \mid \underline{x} \in \mathcal{D}_s\}}{\arg\min} \sum_{\underline{x} \in \mathcal{D}_s} \left(-\hat{p}(t|\underline{x} + \underline{v}_{\underline{x}}) + \lambda \|\underline{v}_{\underline{x}} - \frac{1}{|\mathcal{D}_s|} \sum_{\underline{x}' \in \mathcal{D}_s} \underline{v}_{\underline{x}'}\|^2 \right). \quad (6.18)$$

That is, increase λ until the estimated variance of the sample specific perturbations $\underline{v}$ is relatively small. The motivation for this constraint is the two observations given above. Thus, in the above optimization problem (which involves additive BP reverse-engineering, but performed separately for each sample), the perturbation is allowed to be sample specific, but without too much variation (too much variance) across the clean images from the given class being inspected. As a detection statistic use $r_{s,t}$ given by

$$r_{s,t}^{-1} = \frac{1}{|\mathcal{D}_s|} \sum_{\underline{x} \in \mathcal{D}_s} \|\underline{v}^*_{s,t,\underline{x}}\|.$$

6.9.2   A Patch C-PT-RED

In this project, another approach is applied to detect patch-incorporated backdoor patterns embedded into images. Let $\underline{m}$ be a Boolean pixel image (mask), with each entry in $\{0, 1\}$ (each entry could correspond to a pixel or just to a channel for a pixel).

For each source target class pair (s, t) and each $\underline{x} \in \mathcal{D}_s$, estimate the minimal additive perturbation $\underline{v}_x$ required to cause the class decision to change from s to t (as under I-PT-RED but sample-wise). Now define an approximation of a putative (s, t) patch-replaced backdoor pattern (BP) based just on $\underline{m}, \underline{x}$,

$$\underline{z}(\underline{x}, \underline{m}) = (\underline{x} + \underline{v}_x) \odot \underline{m},$$

that is, the support of the putative BP $\underline{z}(\underline{x}, \underline{m})$ is $\underline{m}$. For each mask $\underline{m}$, also define the mean putative BP

$$\underline{\mu}(\underline{m}) = \frac{1}{|\mathcal{D}_s|} \sum_{\underline{x} \in \mathcal{D}_s} \underline{z}(\underline{x}, \underline{m}).$$

For $\lambda > 0$, now find the detection statistics,

$$r_{s,t}^{-1} := \left\| \arg \min_{\underline{m}} \sum_{\underline{x} \in \mathcal{D}_s} \left(-\hat{p}(t | \underline{z}(\underline{x}, \underline{m}) + \underline{x} \odot (\underline{1} - \underline{m})) + \lambda \| \underline{z}(\underline{x}, \underline{m}) - \underline{\mu}(\underline{m}) \|^2 \right) \right\|. \quad (6.19)$$

The minimization over masks $\underline{m}$ can be found by, for example, simulated annealing [1] or by greedy hill-climbing, that is, by trial-changing chosen pixels from $\underline{m}$. Though performed offline, note that this complex optimization needs to be performed for all class pairs. To simplify it, one can reduce the resolution of the mask, for example, set the resolution of $\underline{m}$ to 3×3 squares of nine pixels. (You should note, in your experiments, the effect of this simplification on the detection performance, for both global and sparse-pixel backdoor patterns.)

Alternatively, in order to perform gradient-based optimization, one can simply relax the Boolean mask $\underline{m}$ so that its elements take values in the real interval $[0, 1]$ (recall Section 6.2.3), and then quantize the optimal values to $\{0, 1\}$ by comparing them to a threshold $\in [0, 1]$ (the threshold being a hyperparameter of the detector). The $r_{s,t}$ statistics can be used as the basis for an order statistic p-value based detector (recall Section 6.3.3).

It will be seen in Chapter 7 that when the BP is learned in a *spatially invariant* fashion, no search for an optimal mask of a putative patch-incorporated BP is needed. Also, another way to leverage sample-wise putative BPs is given in Chapter 8.

6.9.3   The Tasks for the C-PT-RED Projects

- Evaluate on CIFAR-10 the effectiveness of the attacks (ASR and ACC), the detection performance, and the computational costs of these C-PT-REDs, NC, and I-PT-RED.

- Explore sensitivity of performance to the choice of hyperparameters λ or the threshold for the relaxed $\underline{m}$ elements, and to the strength of the attack, that is, the number of pixels involved (or size) of the patch-incorporated backdoor perturbation.
- Compare the performance of I-PT-RED and additive C-PT-RED on additively incorporated imperceptible backdoors.
- Compare the performance of NC and patch C-PT-RED on patch-incorporated, localized, imperceptible backdoors. Be sure to vary the number of source classes involved in the attack.
- If detected, the reverse-engineered backdoor pattern can be taken to be just $|\mathcal{D}_{s*}|^{-1} \sum_{\underline{x} \in \mathcal{D}_{s*}} v_{\underline{x}}$ under additive C-PT-RED or $\mu(\underline{m}^*)$ under patch C-PT-RED, and associated with the detected target class. Visually compare the reverse-engineered BP with the ground truth BP for the various BP estimation approaches.
- Can and, if so, should C-PT-REDs be applied to embedded features rather than input features?
- Suppose an attacker uses a single (source, target) class pair but with more than one backdoor pattern (from the set of BPs, one is selected at random for embedding in a given image). Instead of applying (6.19), cluster the sample specific putative backdoor patterns for C-PT-RED. Also, try to find different backdoor perturbations per clean source class sample by starting the perturbation estimation process at different initial points chosen at random. Discuss attacker and defender work factors in this case. Also, how will NC and I-PT-RED perform in this case?

6.10   Project: Noisy Backdoor Incorporation

Recall that several backdoor data poisoning approaches involve the use of randomness, for example, [93, 197, 275, 282]. Here, consider an imperceptible backdoor pattern type based on an elastic warping operation [80, 109] applied to images, coupled with a "noisy" training scheme [198] (code available in [196]). Assume that the attacker has full control of the training dataset. For each training sample, there is a probability ρ_a for the sample to be embedded with the warping-based backdoor pattern with label flipping (from original/source class to target class); ρ_a should be chosen large enough to ensure a high ASR. With probability ρ_n, the sample is embedded with the warping-based backdoor pattern but with random noise added and *without* label flipping – this is to try to ensure that there are no common features in the pixel domain related to the embedded backdoor pattern that are detectable by reverse-engineering based defenses. And with probability $1 - \rho_a - \rho_n$, a training image is left unchanged. Here, ρ_a and ρ_n should also be chosen small enough so that training involves a sufficient number of clean samples and so that the trained classifier has a sufficiently high accuracy on clean test samples. Details of the training configurations can be found in [198]. Assess the effectiveness of this backdoor poisoning strategy for different choices of ρ_a, ρ_n, and the variance of the noise added without label flipping. Also, assess the effectiveness of this attack against the version of I-PT-RED based on embedded features (recall Section 6.4.4). Another defense against this attack was considered in the Appendix of [286], see Chapter 9.

7 Post-Training Reverse-Engineering Defense (PT-RED) Against Patch-Incorporated Backdoors

In this chapter we focus on post-training detection of backdoor attacks that are embedded by replacing a patch of pixels in the image by a common backdoor pattern. Such attacks are important because they can be implemented not just digitally but also *physically* (where, in the latter case, the backdoor pattern is an object that occludes part of the scene). While the developed methodology can be applied whether the pattern is perceptible or imperceptible, our focus will be on perceptible backdoor patterns that are scene plausible. Scene-plausibility is crucial in order for a perceptible attack to be evasive to cursory human detection. Again, while the focus is on image classification domains, the detection methodology could also be applied, for example, to audio classification – in that context, "scene-plausibility" would mean that the backdoor pattern does not sound artificial or incongruous, among the other sounds in the audio clip. The NC work [282] did not worry about whether the backdoor pattern is scene plausible or *incongruous* with the rest of the image. In the latter case, however, backdoor-trigger images (at test time) might be easily noticed by a human being, thus thwarting the attack. Accordingly, the focus here is on defending against patch attacks that *are* in fact scene plausible. As we will argue in this chapter, in order for the attack to be scene plausible, the backdoor pattern cannot, in general, be embedded into the same location in every (poisoned) image; for example, a backdoor that is a rainbow (one of the attack patterns considered in this chapter) must be embedded into the image in the region where there is sky (and the location of sky may vary from image to image).

Since scene-plausibility requires spatial diversity across the set of poisoned training images, the backdoor mapping learned by the deep neural network will tend to be **spatially invariant**. This property of the learned backdoor mapping will be exploited by a defense described in this chapter: perceptible backdoor PT-RED (P-PT-RED). Moreover, even for patch attacks that *are* placed in a fixed position (either because the attacker ignores scene-plausibility or because it is a pattern that *is* scene plausible in a fixed position across all/most images), a spatially invariant backdoor mapping can still be learned by the DNN if data augmentation (including, e.g., image translations and rotations) is employed. Thus, P-PT-RED is applicable and effective *both* against scene-plausible patch attacks (not in a fixed position), as well as against fixed position patch attacks (where in the latter case data augmentation was used during the training of the DNN).

As verified experimentally, the I-PT-RED method of Chapter 6 will work to detect backdoor poisoning even under data augmentation for the backdoor patterns considered there. P-PT-RED builds on I-PT-RED.

7.1   Perceptible Backdoor Patterns

Consider images of dimension $W \times H$ pixels, with each pixel having C channels whose discretely valued intensities are mapped to the real interval $[0, 1]$. That is, each image is $\in [0, 1]^{W \times H \times C}$ (so when vectorized, an image can be viewed as an element of $[0, 1]^N \subset \mathbb{R}^N$ with $N = WHC$). Recall that a backdoor-modified image $\tilde{x}$ with a (spatially fixed) backdoor pattern $\underline{v}$ can be crafted from a clean image $\underline{x}$ by patching:

$$\tilde{x} = B_{\text{mask}}(\underline{x}, \underline{v}, \underline{m}) = \underline{x} \odot (\underline{1} - \underline{m}) + \underline{v} \odot \underline{m}, \tag{7.1}$$

where $\underline{m}$ is a Boolean image-wide mask of dimension $W \times H$ pixels, with $m_{ij} \in \{0, 1\}$ for any pixel (i, j), so that for any given pixel, the same mask value is used for all channels. Recall that $\odot$ denotes pixel-wise multiplication. The backdoor pattern $\underline{v}$ has the same dimension as $\underline{x}$ but with only a small subset of non-zero pixels (see the tennis ball in Figure 7.1). Often, the (Boolean) mask's spatial support,

$$\{(i, j) \mid m_{ij} = 1\}, \tag{7.2}$$

is contiguous or spans several different contiguous regions. An example is shown in Figure 7.1, where a backdoor image used for attacking a pet breed classifier is created by embedding a tennis ball into an image from class 'Poodle' and labeling to 'Pug'. Patch embedding can be accomplished either digitally or physically, the latter if an actual scene with a dog and ball is captured by a digital camera.

Preferably, from the attacker's point of view, the backdoor pattern should be designed to be *evasive* to possible cursory human inspection of the training set (or of test images). However, perceptible backdoor patterns considered in some existing defense works were not chosen with evasiveness in mind. For example, in [93, 282], a noisy patch or a noticeable icon is *fixed in the same location* in every poisoned image (and backdoor test image) as the backdoor pattern, that is, the mask $\underline{m}$ is a constant for all backdoor images. Regardless of the *incongruousness* of these patterns, which could easily raise human suspicion in practice, there are several issues which should deter such spatially fixed (e.g., to the right bottom corner of the image [282]) perceptible backdoor patterns from being considered by a practical attacker.

- Scene-plausible (i.e., evasive) perceptible backdoor patterns usually cannot be placed *just anywhere* in the image (irrespective of whether the attack is digital or physical). For example, if the backdoor pattern is a pair of glasses on a face, its location will be dependent on the location of the face. So, spatially fixed backdoor patterns cannot, in general, be used in evasive physical attacks.
- If the same perceptible backdoor pattern is embedded at the same location in all backdoor images used to poison the training set, a naive data sanitization applied

Figure 7.1 An example backdoor image used for attacking a pet breed classifier. A clean training image from class 'Poodle' is added with a perceptible backdoor pattern – a tennis ball– following (7.1) and labeled to class 'Pug'. Reprinted from [180, 304] with permission.

"before/during training" could detect the attack by, for example, checking the pixel value distribution and removing suspicious images from the training set; see [304].

• Fixing the spatial location of the backdoor pattern while creating backdoor training images will likely *greatly* harm the robustness of the attack during testing. As will be seen in Section 7.4.4, for a perceptible backdoor pattern fixed to the bottom left corner of the backdoor training images, when there is no data augmentation used during training, even a *single* column/row shift of the backdoor pattern at test time will severely degrade the attack effectiveness. This weakness of spatially fixed perceptible backdoor patterns is fatal. Moreover, for physical attacks, there really is no way to guarantee that the backdoor object is captured at the same location in test images as in the backdoor training images.

So, in this chapter, the focus is on detecting *scene-plausible, perceptible backdoor patterns* that are visually stealthy and which have great potential to be physically implemented in practice. As stated earlier, P-PT-RED is also capable of detecting spatially fixed perceptible backdoors, so long as data augmentation is used during the classifier's training, as shown in Section 7.4.4. This is because the spatial location of the backdoor pattern will likely be changed when data augmentation is applied to training samples, such that the backdoor pattern in the actual augmented training samples is no longer spatially fixed (and, thus, a spatially invariant backdoor mapping will be learned by the DNN).

In the following experiments backdoor patterns were digitally patched into clean images, requiring laborious human effort to choose the object used as the perceptible backdoor pattern and to carefully design the mask to "carve" the *same* backdoor pattern into the best (suitably innocuous) location for each originally clean image (e.g., a bird flying in the sky). In this way, a practical, evasive (scene-plausible) backdoor attacker is simulated. That is, an image with the attacker's backdoor pattern $\underline{v}^*$ is crafted by

$$\tilde{\underline{x}} = B_{\mathrm{mask}}(\underline{x}, \underline{v}^*, \underline{m}(\underline{x}, \underline{v}^*)), \tag{7.3}$$

where $\underline{m}(\underline{x}, \underline{v}^*)$ yields a **customized** mask for each clean image $\underline{x}$, depending on both the image and the backdoor pattern $\underline{v}^*$. Perceptible backdoor patterns embedded in such a way are made scene-plausible through judicious choice of the *image specific location* of the backdoor pattern.

7.2   Choice of Source Class(es) and Target Class

As in previous chapters, it is assumed that if a backdoor attack is present, there is a single backdoor target class and the number of source classes can range from 1 to $K - 1$, that is, all except the target class. As for attacks using an imperceptible backdoor pattern, the source classes could be arbitrarily chosen by the attacker. However, if an innocuous perceptible backdoor pattern is used, the source class(es) and the backdoor pattern should be well matched to achieve stealthiness. For example, a bird flying in the sky could be used as a perceptible backdoor pattern when most of the source class images contain the sky; hence a class for which most of the images capture an underwater scene is not well matched with such a backdoor pattern. Clearly, finding a perceptible backdoor pattern that is seemingly innocuous when embedded in images from *all* classes (except for the target class) is very difficult in many classification domains. So, the number of source class(es) involved in a backdoor attack using a perceptible backdoor pattern depends on both the attacker (who seeks for the attack to be evasive) and the classification domain. Moreover, for both perceptible and imperceptible backdoors, even if the attacker specifies a *single* (source, target) class pair ($|S^*| = 1$), after training on the backdoor poisoned data, the classifier (during operation) could possibly classify images originally from a class $i \neq t$ and $i \notin S^*$ to the target class t^*, if the image contains the same backdoor pattern used by the attacker – recall the discussion of *collateral damage* in Chapter 6. A class pair suffering severe collateral damage is not among the backdoor class pairs specified by the attacker, but it can be viewed as an "effective" backdoor class pair induced by training on the backdoor poisoned training set. Above all, in developing defenses against backdoor attacks, it is very important to note that a robust defense should not require big assumptions concerning the number of source classes involved in an attack. Recall that NC assumes all classes other than the target class are source classes of an attack – if the attack involves only a single source class, NC does not fare well, as seen in both the current chapter and Chapter 6.

7.3   Perceptible Backdoor Post-Training Reverse-Engineering Defense (P-PT-RED)

P-PT-RED, which is designed to detect scene-plausible, perceptible backdoor patterns, is now described. No assumptions about the backdoor pattern, its shape, or its spatial support are made. Moreover, unlike NC and TABOR, no assumptions are made about the number of source classes chosen by the attacker (recall Sections 6.2.3 and 6.2.4). Indeed, P-PT-RED is designed to detect backdoors with any number of source classes, ranging anywhere from 1 to $K - 1$ (without prior knowledge of the number of source classes that may be involved in a putative attack).

Similar to other post-training defenses, P-PT-RED assumes the defender does not have access to the training set used for the DNN's learning, the defender has access to a relatively small clean dataset containing images from all classes, and this clean set is inadequate for retraining a new (accurate) classifier. P-PT-RED is designed both to detect whether or not the classifier has been attacked and to infer the source class(es) and the target class if an attack is detected. While P-PT-RED focuses on detecting innocuous, perceptible backdoor patterns (with variable location in the image), it can also detect spatially fixed backdoors if the classifier was trained using data augmentation, which is often the case, see Section 7.4.4.

7.3.1   Basis of P-PT-RED Detection

The P-PT-RED detector is based on two practical properties of scene-plausible, perceptible backdoor patterns.

Property 1   Spatial invariance of the backdoor mapping: *If the perceptible backdoor pattern is spatially distributed (not at a fixed location) in the backdoor poisoned training images (placed so as to be most innocuous in each image), the learned backdoor mapping will be spatially invariant in inducing targeted misclassifications on test images (with high attack success rate).*

As discussed above, the perceptible backdoor pattern could be spatially located anywhere in a given training image so as to be made scene plausible. Accordingly, the backdoor pattern may be placed in many different locations, across the collection of poisoned training images. The trained DNN will then learn the backdoor pattern, but not its spatial location (as will be demonstrated by experiments in this chapter). This property is actually favored by the attacker, since there is then great freedom in where the attacker can embed the backdoor pattern in clean test images (subject to preserving scene-plausibility). As will be seen in Section 7.4.1, at test time, backdoor images with the backdoor pattern randomly located are still likely to yield misclassifications to the target class prescribed by the attacker (i.e., the attack is spatially robust), which justifies the attacker performing data poisoning so as to satisfy this property.

Property 2   Robustness of perceptible backdoor patterns: *The learned backdoor mapping is robust to variations such as noise, lighting, view, and illumination, thus obviating the need for an attacker to use exactly the same perceptible backdoor pattern in all the training and test images.*

Again, this property is favored by a practical attacker. For a physically implemented backdoor pattern, during testing, though the same object (e.g., the same pair of glasses) is used, it is not guaranteed that the same digital pattern will be captured (due to, e.g., the lighting condition, or to variable image perspective). As will be seen in Section 7.4.3, even when *strong* noise is added to the backdoor pattern while creating backdoor test images (and *not* during training), they will still likely be (mis)classified to the designated target class. More importantly, consistent with potential object occlusion, if only *part* (in terms of spatial support) of the backdoor pattern is added to source class images during testing, this also induces (mis)classification to the target class. This is not surprising because perceptible backdoor patterns, like other patterns, are learned by the DNN by extracting key features, which may occupy a smaller spatial support than the full pattern support.

7.3.2   Detection Overview

The following are two key ideas.

- For a scene-plausible, perceptible backdoor attack, for "effective" backdoor (source, target) class pairs, including those used for devising the attack and those caused by collateral damage, one can find a pattern that induces a high misclassification fraction (from the source class to the target class) on the clean dataset using a **relatively small** spatial support, **arbitrarily located** in the image.
- For non-backdoor class pairs, *much larger* spatial support is required to find a pattern that induces high misclassifications from the source to the target class.

The following analysis shows that the key ideas behind P-PT-RED are well supported by the properties in Section 7.3.1. For convenience, for any class pair $(s, t) \in \mathcal{Y} \times \mathcal{Y}$ with $s \neq t$, and a set $\mathcal{D}_s$ of clean images that are correctly classified to s by the classifier $\hat{c}$ to be inspected, define:

$$\xi_{st}(\underline{v}, \underline{m}) = \frac{1}{|\mathcal{D}_s|} \sum_{\underline{x} \in \mathcal{D}_s} \mathbf{1}\{\hat{c}(B_{\text{mask}}(\underline{x}, \underline{v}, \underline{m})) = t\} \qquad (7.4)$$

as the misclassification fraction from s to t induced by pattern $\underline{v}$ and mask $\underline{m}$.

When there is a scene-plausible, perceptible backdoor attack, the perceptible backdoor pattern will be spatially distributed in the backdoor poisoned training images (as argued above). Then, for any backdoor class pair (s, t^*) with $s \in \mathcal{S}^*$ as well as for class pairs suffering high collateral damage (recall Figure 6.7), based on the spatial invariance of the learned backdoor mapping (Property 1), $\xi_{st^*}(\underline{v}^*, \underline{m}')$ is expected to be large (i.e., close to 1) for any $\underline{m}'$ having the same support as the true mask used by the attacker, but with *arbitrary center* of the support. Here, $\underline{v}^*$ is the same backdoor pattern used by the attacker. Note that in the above statement, although the location of the support of $\underline{m}'$ can be arbitrary, *and could in fact be varied from one image to the next (!)*, for the proposed defense a *common* $\underline{m}'$ is considered for all $\underline{x} \in \mathcal{D}_s$, solely for simplicity.

Following the above and according to the robustness of the learned backdoor mapping (Property 2), there exists a (non-unique) "effective" backdoor pattern $\underline{v}' \neq \underline{v}^*$, such that $\xi_{st^*}(\underline{v}', \underline{m}'')$ is large. Here, the support of the mask $\underline{m}''$ should be matched with the support of $\underline{v}'$. Again, the center of the support (chosen to be the same for $\underline{m}''$

and $\underline{v}'$) can be arbitrarily located in the image according to Property 1. Moreover, the size of the support of $\underline{v}'$,

$$\|\underline{v}'\|_0 = |\{(i,j) \mid v'_{ij} \neq 0\}|$$

(or $\|\underline{m}''\|_0$ equivalently), could be quite small, much smaller than $\|\underline{v}^*\|_0$, so long as sufficiently "representative" features of $\underline{v}^*$ are captured by $\underline{v}'$.

Thus, for any arbitrarily located spatial support with a relatively small support size of, at most, b (i.e., specified by a given Boolean mask $\underline{m} \in \{0,1\}^{W \times H}$ with $\|\underline{m}\|_0 \leq b$), it is expected that the *maximum misclassification fraction*

$$\underset{\underline{v} \in [0,1]^{W \times H \times C}}{\text{maximize}} \quad \xi_{st}(\underline{v}, \underline{m}) \tag{7.5}$$

for (s,t) an effective backdoor class pair (including those suffering severe collateral damage) will be much larger than for (s,t) a non-backdoor class pair. This crucial property, which allows accurate identification of backdoor class pairs in an attack, is borne out experimentally in the sequel.

Motivated by the above, P-PT-RED consists of a pattern estimation step and a detection inference step, as will be described in detail in the following.

7.3.3   Pattern Estimation

P-PT-RED's pattern estimation step, roughly speaking, aims to solve (7.5) for all class pairs. However, to achieve a truly reliable detector, several design choices must be carefully considered, as follows.

Support Size: There is a tradeoff in choosing proper support sizes $\|\underline{m}\|_0 \leq b$ for solving (7.5), in order to achieve accurate backdoor detection. If b is too small, smaller than the minimum required to capture sufficient "representative" features of the true backdoor pattern $\underline{v}^*$, no pattern will be able to induce a high group misclassification for any backdoor class pairs. If b is too large, large enough to capture the "representative" features of any non-backdoor target class, high group misclassification will be achieved for some non-backdoor class pairs. Thus, for each class pair, instead of estimating one pattern for one fixed support size, P-PT-RED considers $\Gamma > 1$ different spatial supports (each specified by a given mask), with increasing sizes, and estimates a pattern for each of them. By "fusing" the pattern estimation results for these Γ supports for each class pair, P-PT-RED can effectively avoid false positives and false negatives.

Support Location: Since, as discussed before, it does not matter where the estimated pattern's spatial support is placed (because a spatially invariant backdoor mapping, consistent with a scene-plausible backdoor, is learned by the classifier), in P-PT-RED's detector the mask position is *fixed* for all the clean images it uses. However, as we emphasized before, accurate detection should be achieved even if the center position of the mask is *varied* from one clean image to the next.

Support Shape: The choice of the support shape is not critical to the detection performance, but it is preferred to use a simple convex support (e.g., a rectangle or a circle) to efficiently capture the "representative" features of the backdoor pattern. Here, square support is chosen as the shape for simplicity. Note that the choice of the support shape used by the detector does not need to be matched to the shape of the mask used by the attacker (which is not known to the defender a priori). In the following experiments, attacks are considered with backdoor patterns having contiguous, non-convex shapes, as well as highly spatially distributed backdoor patterns – these attacks are all detected by P-PT-RED using a simple square spatial support for pattern estimation.

Surrogate Objective Function and Optimizer: Note that the misclassification fraction $\xi_{st}(\underline{v}, \underline{m})$ on $\mathcal{D}_s$ for class pair (s, t) is not differentiable in $\underline{v}$. As in Chapter 6, the following surrogate objective function is thus instead used for a given mask $\underline{m} \in \{0, 1\}^{W \times H}$:

$$\tilde{\xi}_{st}(\underline{v}, \underline{m}) = \frac{1}{|\mathcal{D}_s|} \sum_{\underline{x} \in \mathcal{D}_s} \hat{p}(t | B_{\text{mask}}(\underline{x}, \underline{v}, \underline{m})), \tag{7.6}$$

which can be interpreted as the *average misclassification confidence* or *fraction* from s to t on $\mathcal{D}_s$. By employing the classifier's posterior for class t, the resulting objective is differentiable with respect to $\underline{v}$. Thus, maximizing $\tilde{\xi}_{st}(\underline{v}, \underline{m})$ over $\underline{v} \in [0, 1]^{W \times H \times C}$ can be achieved using a gradient-based optimizer with projection (i.e., clipping). For example, one can use stochastic gradient descent (SGD) with momentum and an adaptive learning rate, where in each step of updating $\underline{v}$, the gradient of (7.6) is computed on a subset of (i.e., a mini-batch from) $\mathcal{D}_s$. Note that the choices of the objective function and the optimizer achieving good detection performance are not unique. As discussed in Chapter 6, one can, for example, alternatively consider a surrogate objective function similar to that associated with the Perceptron algorithm, or take the logarithm of the classifier's posterior in (7.6) for better smoothness.

Note that optimization of the objective (7.6) is closely related to the perturbation optimization that is performed as part of the I-PT-RED procedure. In particular, this optimization is essentially equivalent to performing I-PT-RED's perturbation optimization on a smaller image support (on the support of the mask), and starting from a sub-image on this support that is all zeros (consistent with the fact that patching can be thought of operationally as involving two steps: (i) zeroing-out pixel values, and then (ii) replacing them by the values associated with the backdoor pattern).

The Pattern Estimation Step: Based on the above discussion of design choices, P-PT-RED first creates Γ different masks. Each mask specifies a square spatial support with fixed location, for example, the top left corner of each image. The number Γ and the width of the square spatial support associated with each mask are specified under P-PT-RED as follows. Assuming the image width W is no larger than the image height H (otherwise, rotate the image), choose a minimum *relative* support width $r_{\min} \in [0, 1]$ and a maximum *relative* support width $r_{\max} \in [0, 1]$. Then

$$\mathcal{W} = \mathbb{Z}^+ \cap [r_{\min} W, r_{\max} W] \tag{7.7}$$

is the set of integer support widths to be considered with

$$\Gamma = |\mathcal{W}|.$$

For example, for 32×32 images (i.e., $W = H = 32$), with $r_{\min} = 0.15$ and $r_{\max} = 0.2$, P-PT-RED considers $\Gamma = 2$ masks with support widths $\mathcal{W} = \{5, 6\}$, respectively. As already discussed, the reason for considering a range of support widths for pattern estimation is for more reliable detection. The choices of r_{min} and r_{max} used in the following experiments will be further discussed in Section 7.4.2.

For each of the $K(K-1)$ possible (source, target) class pairs, P-PT-RED performs Γ pattern estimations. That is, for each $(s,t) \in \mathcal{Y} \times \mathcal{Y}$ with $s \neq t$ and $w \in \mathcal{W}$, P-PT-RED solves (using, e.g., the previously suggested optimizer):

$$\max_{\underline{v} \in [0,1]^{W \times H \times C}} \tilde{\xi}_{st}(\underline{v}, \underline{m}_w) =: \rho_{stw}, \tag{7.8}$$

where $\underline{m}_w \in \{0,1\}^{W \times H}$ is a mask with *fixed* $w \times w$ square spatial support. Compared with NC, which *jointly* estimates a pattern and its (relaxed) support mask ($\in [0,1]^{W \times H}$), P-PT-RED's pattern estimation problem (with the mask fixed) is clearly less complicated, as well as possibly less susceptible to finding poor locally optimal solutions.

7.3.4 Detection Inference by MAMF

For each class pair (s,t) and support width $w \in \mathcal{W}$, define an associated **maximum achievable misclassification fraction (MAMF) statistic** (found by solving (7.8) above) as ρ_{stw}. Then for each class pair, P-PT-RED fuses the pattern estimation results for the Γ spatial supports by computing the **average MAMF**

$$\bar{\rho}_{st} = \frac{1}{\Gamma} \sum_{w \in \mathcal{W}} \rho_{stw}$$

over the Γ MAMF statistics. For a relatively small r_{max} (and the Γ associated small spatial supports), if there is an attack, one would expect *at least* one true backdoor pair to have a large average MAMF (whether one or multiple source classes are involved in the attack); otherwise (if there is no attack), the maximum $\bar{\rho}_{st}$ for all (s,t) pairs is expected to be small. Hence, there should be a range of thresholds $\pi \in (0,1]$ (with very high true detection rate and low false positive rate, as confirmed in Section 7.4.2), such that the DNN is correctly inferred to *be attacked* if

$$\rho^* = \max_{(s,t) \in \mathcal{Y} \times \mathcal{Y}, s \neq t} \bar{\rho}_{st} > \pi; \tag{7.9}$$

else, no backdoor is detected. If an attack is detected,

$$(\hat{s}, \hat{t}) = \arg\max_{(s,t) \in \mathcal{Y} \times \mathcal{Y}, s \neq t} \bar{\rho}_{st}$$

is inferred as one (source, target) class pair involved in the attack.

7.3.5 Extensions

MAMF Correction with Class Confusion Information
Pattern estimation for a non-backdoor (source, target) class pair may produce a large MAMF statistic on a small spatial support if the two classes are similar to each other, that is, if they exhibit high class confusion. To avoid false detections caused by

this, following Section 6.3.5, one may build knowledge of confusion matrix information into the detector. For each $(s,t) \in \mathcal{Y} \times \mathcal{Y}$ with $s \neq t$, define baseline class confusion between s and t as:

$$\rho_{st0} = P_{\underline{X} \sim P_s}(\hat{c}(\underline{X}) = t), \tag{7.10}$$

where P_s is the image distribution for class s. The class confusion information may be provided to the defender in advance, or may be empirically estimated using a set of clean images. (Pattern estimation for each class pair is still performed using only a subset $\mathcal{D}$ of clean images that are correctly classified to the source class.) Then the average MAMF $\bar{\rho}_{st}$ for (s,t) is obtained by averaging over Γ "corrected" MAMF statistics defined by:

$$\tilde{\rho}_{stw} = \max\{0, \rho_{stw} - \rho_{st0}\}, \tag{7.11}$$

for each $w \in \mathcal{W}$. When there is no attack, the above correction will prevent class pairs with high class confusion from having overly high MAMF statistics, as will be seen experimentally in the sequel.

Computational Complexity and Extension for Efficiency

Under P-PT-RED, detection computation is mainly incurred by forward and backward propagations during the pattern estimation step. Supposing M clean images per class for detection ($MK = |\mathcal{D}|$), the computational complexity for P-PT-RED is $O(\Gamma M K^2)$, where M should be large enough to avoid any non-backdoor class pair having an overly large MAMF statistic on a small spatial support by chance. The robustness of P-PT-RED regarding the number of clean images per class used for detection is assessed experimentally in [304].

Recall how L-PT-RED of Section 6.5 reduces the complexity of I-PT-RED of Chapter 6 (both sample-wise and computationally). The P-PT-RED perceptible backdoor detector can be extended in a similar way. For each putative target class $t \in \mathcal{Y}$, the following pattern estimation problem can be solved for each $w \in \mathcal{W}$:

$$\begin{aligned}
\underset{\underline{v} \in [0,1]^{W \times H \times C}, \, \underline{\alpha} \in \mathbb{R}^K}{\text{maximize}} \quad & \sum_{s \in \mathcal{Y} \setminus \{t\}} \frac{\alpha_s}{|\mathcal{D}_s|} \sum_{\underline{x} \in \mathcal{D}_s} \hat{p}(t | B_{\text{mask}}(\underline{x}, \underline{v}, \underline{m}_w)) \\
\text{subject to} \quad & \sum_{s \in \mathcal{Y} \setminus \{t\}} \alpha_s = 1, \quad \underline{\alpha} \geq \underline{0},
\end{aligned} \tag{7.12}$$

that is, the weight vector of classes, $\underline{\alpha}$, is in the $(K-1)$-simplex with $\alpha_t = 0$. On the small spatial support specified by $\underline{m}_w$, the optimal "weighted" misclassification fraction (i.e., the objective of (7.12) at convergence) for t the true backdoor target class will likely be larger than for t not the backdoor target class. Also, the weights associated with the effective source classes (including those suffering severe collateral damage) will be large if t is the backdoor target class. Moreover, since pattern estimation is performed on all clean images in $\cup_{s \in \mathcal{Y} \setminus t} \mathcal{D}_s$, accurate detection can possibly be achieved with very few clean images per class, similar to L-PT-RED; thus, the actual computational complexity is expected to be low.

7.4   Experiments

7.4.1   Devising Backdoor Attacks

Our experiments involve nine attacks, five datasets, five DNN structures, and nine backdoor patterns. For each data domain, a clean ("benchmark") DNN was first trained using an unpoisoned training set, with the accuracy on clean test images reported as the "benchmark accuracy." The dataset used, image size, number of classes, training size and test size are shown in Table 7.1. In particular, for Attack G on Oxford-IIIT, the test accuracy using the entire dataset, in absence of backdoor attacks, is very low. A reasonable benchmark test accuracy is achieved on G by using a subset involving only six classes, as reported in the table. For Attack I on PubFig [131], many images cannot be downloaded; hence only 33 (out of 60) classes are considered, each with more than 60 images. The DNN structures involved in the experiments include ResNet-18, ResNet-34 [97], VGG-16 [245], AlexNet [130] and ConvNet [240]. The choices of DNN structure, learning rate, batch size and number of training epochs for each attack instance are also shown in Table 7.1. The Adam optimizer [123] is used for all DNN training in these experiments. For the benchmark training for the datasets involving Attacks F, G and I, training data augmentation is also used, including random cropping, random horizontal flipping and random rotation. For the benchmark training for the dataset involving Attack G, a pretrained AlexNet provided by Pytorch is fine tuned. For the benchmark training for the dataset involving Attack I, transfer learning was adopted by retraining only the last four layers of a pretrained VGG-face model [6].

Under each attack, the DNN is trained using the same training settings as for the benchmark, except that the training set is poisoned by a number of backdoor images. As explained in Chapter 6, the backdoor images are created using clean images from *one* source class, with a backdoor pattern added following Eq. (7.3), and then labeled to a target class.

P-PT-RED was evaluated against backdoor attacks involving one source class for the convenience of crafting scene-plausible backdoor patterns that could possibly be used in practice. As discussed in Section 7.3.4, P-PT-RED's design allows it to detect backdoor attacks with any number of source classes, since only one class pair is needed to have a sufficiently large average MAMF to make a detection. [304] shows the effectiveness of P-PT-RED against backdoor attacks involving $K-1$ source classes, even though the backdoor patterns may not be scene plausible (e.g., a rainbow will be placed in an image without the sky). For the experiments in the current section, the choices of the backdoor pattern, the number of backdoor training images, the source class, and the target class for each attack instance are also shown in Table 7.1.

To create scene-plausible backdoor attacks that can potentially be physically implemented, a large number of candidate backdoor images were first created, each with the backdoor pattern randomly located in the image. Then by manual effort, images were picked in which the backdoor pattern looks scene plausible. For example, for Attack C (source class 'airplane' and backdoor pattern a 'rainbow'), a valid backdoor poisoned training image should have the rainbow in the sky (see Figure 7.2c). Since the focus

Table 7.1 Details of the attacks used in our experiments.

	Attack A	Attack B	Attack C	Attack D	Attack E	Attack F	Attack G	Attack H	Attack I
Dataset	CIFAR-10	CIFAR-10	CIFAR-10	CIFAR-10	CIFAR-10	CIFAR-100	Oxford-IIIT	SVHN	PubFig
Image size	32×32	32×32	32×32	32×32	32×32	32×32	128×128	32×32	256×256
Number of classes	10	10	10	10	10	100	6	10	33
Training size	50000	50000	50000	50000	50000	50000	900	73257	2782
Test size	10000	10000	10000	10000	10000	10000	300	26032	495
DNN structure	ResNet-18	ResNet-18	ResNet-18	ResNet-18	VGG-16	ResNet-34	AlexNet	ConvNet	VGG-16
Learning rate	10^{-3}	10^{-3}	10^{-3}	10^{-3}	10^{-3}	10^{-4}	10^{-5}	10^{-3}	10^{-4}
Batch size	32	32	32	32	32	32	16	32	32
Number of training epochs	200	200	200	200	200	200	120	80	120
Benchmark accuracy (%)	86.7	88.1	86.7	87.6	87.9	71.9	88.7	89.2	76.0
Source class	'cat'	'deer'	'airplane'	'frog'	'truck'	'road'	'Chihuahua'	'3'	'B. Obama'
Target class	'dog'	'horse'	'bird'	'bird'	'automobile'	'bed'	'Abyssinian'	'8'	'C. Ronaldo'
Backdoor pattern	'bug'	'butterfly'	'rainbow'	'bug&butterfly'	'gas tank'	'marmot'	'tennis ball'	'bullet holes'	'sunglasses'
Number of backdoor training images	150	150	150	150	150	100	50	500	40
Attack test accuracy (%)	87.0	86.9	86.8	87.0	89.1	71.7	90.0	90.1	77.0
Attack success rate (%)	99.3	98.0	96.4	98.0	97.9	92.0	84.0	91.4	93.3

here is on automated defense against attacks, the backdoor patterns were not polished (e.g., considering the lighting condition or the angle of the backdoor pattern) to make them completely innocuous to humans. Figure 7.2 shows an example backdoor training image and its original clean image for each attack. The backdoor patterns considered here are representative of multiple types of practical backdoor patterns. The 'bug' for Attack A and the 'butterfly' for attack B represent backdoor patterns at the periphery (not covering the foreground object of interest) of the image and with a modest size. The 'rainbow' for Attack C represents large backdoor patterns with an irregular shape. The backdoor patterns for Attacks D and H represent dispersed patterns. The 'sunglasses' for Attack I represent backdoor patterns overlapping with features of interest. Other approaches for crafting evasive backdoors include [159].

Table 7.1 also reports the accuracy on clean test images and the attack success rate for all attacks. The attack success rate is defined as the fraction of backdoor *test* images classified to the target class prescribed by the attacker. A backdoor test image is created using a clean test image from one of the source class(es), and embedding in it the same backdoor pattern used for creating the backdoor poisoned training images. An automated approach is taken (due to the huge number of test images) to create backdoor test images, randomly placing the backdoor pattern in the image (except for Attack I where the sunglasses were manually placed on the faces). By doing so for a sufficiently large test set, most locations where the attacker could place the backdoor pattern (in creating backdoor test images in practice) are being "covered." In Table 7.1, the attack success rate is high for all attacks, and there is no significant degradation in clean test accuracy compared with the benchmark; hence all attacks are considered successful. *Moreover, such success is achieved with randomly placed backdoor patterns in test images, which experimentally verifies Property 1, that is, the spatial invariance of the learned scene-plausible perceptible backdoor mapping.* More experimental results regarding Property 1 are shown in [304].

7.4.2 Scene-Plausible, Perceptible Backdoor Detection Performance Evaluation

In this section, the performance of P-PT-RED, NC and FP are evaluated using the above mentioned attacks, that is, innocuous perceptible attacks where the backdoor pattern is not in a fixed position, either in the poisoned training images or in the backdoor attacked test images. For each attack, detection is applied to both the DNN being attacked and the clean benchmark DNN.

P-PT-RED

For best discrimination between the two categories of DNNs by P-PT-RED, relatively small spatial supports should be used for pattern estimation so that a DNN being attacked can have a much larger ρ^* than a clean DNN. On the one hand, the spatial support should be smaller than that of the foreground objects associated with (characterizing) the actual classes; otherwise, the actual target class object(s) could possibly be reverse engineered, causing high group misclassification even for a clean DNN.

Figure 7.2 Example backdoor image and the originally clean image for Attacks A–I. Subcaptions describe the object(s) added as the perceptible backdoor pattern for each attack. Reprinted from [304, 310] with permission.

Moreover, if r_{max} (recall Eq. (7.7)) needs to be chosen large to achieve high ρ^* for a DNN that was backdoor poisoned, then the backdoor is likely not innocuous, in other words, it is likely an *overly large* perceptible pattern and likely not scene plausible.

Here, $r_{max} = 0.22$ for all reported experiments. In practice, an r_{max} could be adaptively chosen for each dataset as the *critical* spatial support allowing a proportion of class pairs (e.g., 50%) to achieve a modest MAMF (e.g., 0.4) during the pattern estimation step. On the other hand, the spatial support should be large enough for estimating any pattern related to the backdoor. Here, $r_{min} = 0.08$, such that for a 32×32 image, there is at least 3×3 spatial support for pattern estimation.

The basic version of P-PT-RED without MAMF correction is first considered. The details of the experimental settings are as follows. For Attacks A–E and Attack H, 200 clean images correctly classified *per class* are used for detection. For Attacks F, G and I, 50, 30 and 9 correctly classified clean images per class are used for detection, respectively. For all DNNs, class pairs, and spatial supports, (7.8) is solved using the Adam optimizer with decay rate 0.9 and 0.999 for the first and second moment, respectively, and learning rate 0.5 for 100 epochs. (Fewer epochs are actually needed for decent convergence in all reported experiments.) A mini-batch size of 32 was used for Attacks A–E and H, 10 for Attacks F and G and 3 for Attack I. The spatial support for pattern estimation used by P-PT-RED is a square covering the top left corner of each image. Due to Property 1 other locations yield similar results (as is further investigated and illustrated in [304]).

In Figure 7.3, for both the DNN being attacked and the clean benchmark DNN, for each attack, the ($\Gamma = |\mathcal{W}|$) MAMF statistics are shown for the class pair with the largest average MAMF (i.e., the class pair corresponding to ρ^*). For example, for Attack A (recall the image size is 32×32), the set of (absolute) support widths being considered is $\mathcal{W} = \{3, 4, 5, 6, 7\}$. Instead of performing pattern estimation for each integer support width in the interval $[r_{min}W, r_{max}W]$, images of large size could be efficiently downsampled and pattern estimation performed for fewer support widths. Here, $\Gamma = 9$ and $\Gamma = 7$ support widths are respectively considered for Attacks G and I of Figure 7.3. In each sub-figure of Figure 7.3, a large gap is observed between the clean and attacked curves, clearly distinguishing the DNN being attacked from the clean DNN.

In Figure 7.4, the maximum average MAMF (i.e., ρ^*) is shown for both the clean and attacked DNNs, for all attacks. Note the clear large difference between the two bars for each attack. Thus, any detection threshold π in $(0.6, 0.8)$ could successfully detect whether the DNN has been attacked (for all Attacks A–I). Moreover, for the DNN being attacked, for all attack instances, the class pair corresponding to the maximum average MAMF is precisely the *true backdoor pair*. Hence when a detection is made, the (source, target) class pair (used by the attacker) is also correctly inferred, in all cases.

Next, consider the extension of P-PT-RED where MAMF statistics are corrected using class confusion information (see Section 7.3.5). For each of Attack B, Attack F, and Attack H, an empirical class confusion matrix is estimated using all the test images for the dataset associated with the attack. For each attack, P-PT-RED is used with class confusion correction on both the clean benchmark DNN and the DNN being attacked. Figure 7.5 shows the largest average MAMF ρ^* with correction, compared with ρ^* without correction, for both clean and attacked DNNs, for the three attacks. Although

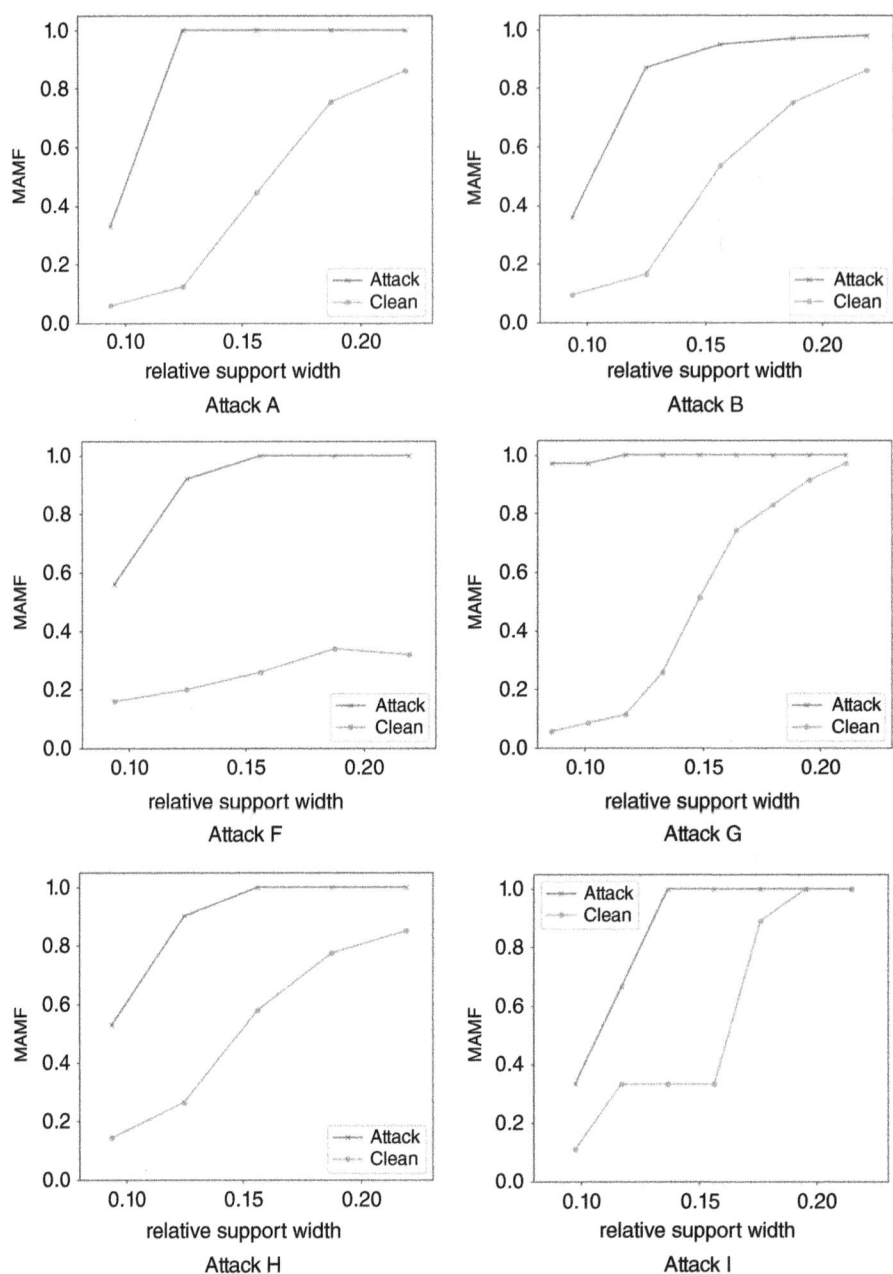

Figure 7.3 Maximum achievable misclassification fraction (MAMF) statistics for the class pair with the largest average MAMF, for both attacked and unattacked (clean) DNNs, for attacks A, B, F–I. The largest average MAMF is plotted as a function of relative support for pattern estimation over $(0.08, 0.22)$. Reprinted from [304] with permission.

class confusion correction does not significantly affect ρ^* for the six classifiers, the decrement in ρ^* for the clean DNN is slightly larger than for the DNN being attacked, for

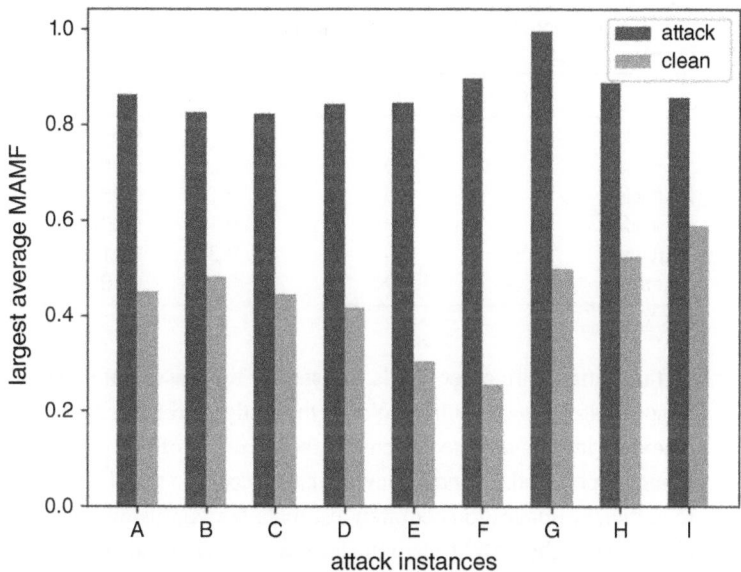

Figure 7.4 Largest average MAMF, ρ^*, over all class pairs for both the attacked DNN and unattacked (clean) DNN, for Attacks A–I. Reprinted from [304, 310] with permission.

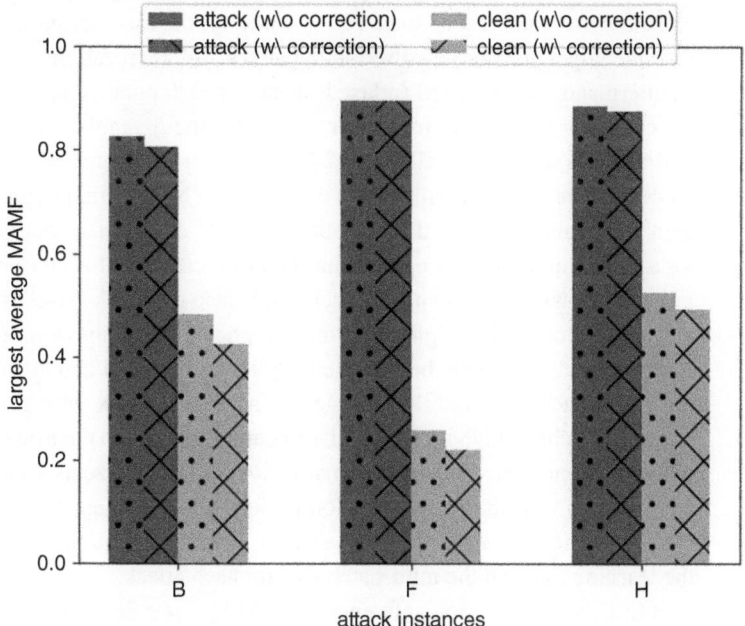

Figure 7.5 Largest average MAMF, ρ^*, with class confusion correction, compared with ρ^* without class confusion correction, for both the attacked DNN and unattacked (clean) DNN, respectively for Attack B, Attack F, and Attack H. Reprinted from [304] with permission.

Table 7.2 Detailed settings of NC, including the number of clean images per class used for detection, the choice of λ, the learning rate and the mini-batch size, for each attack instance.

	Number of images per class	λ	Learning rate	Batch size
Attacks A–D	100	0.1	0.05	90
Attack E	100	0.6	0.05	90
Attack F	10	0.1	0.05	90
Attack G	30	0.5	0.001	60
Attack H	100	0.2	0.01	100
Attack I	9	0.1	0.005	30

all three attacks. In other words, assisted by the class confusion information, the range of successful detection thresholds is modestly increased. Note that in this experiment, abundant images are used to ensure the accuracy of this confusion matrix estimation, though a practical defender may not have access to the class confusion information or to sufficient images to accurately estimate the confusion matrix. Nevertheless, it has already been shown that accurate detection can be achieved by P-PT-RED even without class confusion correction. Thus, in all of the following experiments, class confusion correction is omitted for simplicity.

NC

For the attacks in the current experiment (that use a single source class), NC may not make a correct detection, since NC is based on the assumption that *all classes* other than the target class are involved in the attack. Again, recall that NC jointly estimates a pattern and an associated (relaxed) mask for each putative target class and relies on the choice of the penalty multiplier $\lambda > 0$ (for the l_1-regularization of the mask) and optimization settings (recall Eq. (6.2)). Here, NC is evaluated on the same attacks as P-PT-RED. The Adam optimizer was used to solve NC's optimization problem, with the parameter values suggested by the authors of NC, and with the optimization performed for a sufficient number of epochs (until convergence). If λ is chosen too large, π-level group misclassification cannot be achieved since the mask "size" is over penalized. If λ is made too small, a high group misclassification fraction will be achieved, but the l_1 norm of the mask may be unreasonably large. Hence, λ and the training parameters for each attack are carefully adjusted to achieve a mask with small l_1 norm and a pattern inducing a high group misclassification fraction to the true backdoor class. So, NC's hyperparameter λ is *optimistically tuned* to maximize its accuracy. For all attack cases, $\pi = 0.9$, with the optimization performed for 200 epochs. Table 7.2 shows the number of clean images per class used for pattern estimation by NC, the choice of λ, the learning rate and the mini-batch size for each attack.

Recall NC's detection inference uses MAD, see Section 6.2.3. If the "anomaly index" is larger than 2.0 (i.e., ≈ 3 MAD beyond the median, recall Section 6.2.3), a

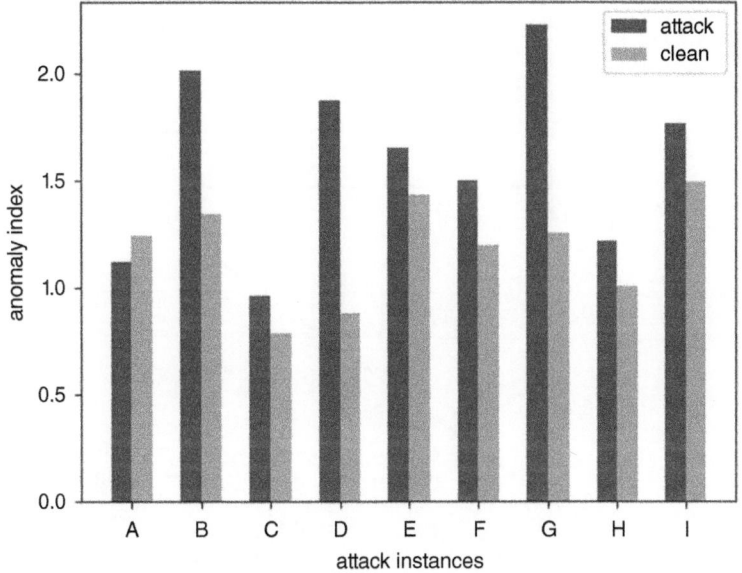

Figure 7.6 Anomaly indices when applying NC to the DNN being attacked and the clean DNN, for Attacks A–I. Reprinted from [304, 310] with permission.

detection is made with 95% confidence. Figure 7.6 shows anomaly indices for both the DNN being attacked and the clean DNN, for each attack. Only for Attack B and Attack G does NC successfully detect the attack – for these attacks, there is a pattern and an associated *relatively small* mask which, when applied to clean test images from all classes other than the target class, induces high group misclassification (even though the backdoor targeted only a single source class – recall the discussion of collateral damage). Note that for Attack A, the anomaly index for the clean DNN is in fact larger than for the backdoor attacked DNN.

For better visualization of the performance comparison between P-PT-RED (without MAMF correction) and NC, the (average) ROC curves for the two approaches against all nine attacks are shown in Figure 7.7. The average area under the curve (AUC) values for P-PT-RED and NC respectively are 1.0 and 0.78.

FP

FP (Section 6.2.2) was also evaluated to show it is ineffective against most of the attacks. The penultimate layer neurons of each classifier being attacked are pruned (until only a few are left), in increasing order of their average activations over all clean test images. For each attack, Figure 7.8 shows the accuracy on clean test images and the attack success rate versus the number of neurons pruned. For most of the attacks (except Attacks E and H), the attack success rate does not drop before the accuracy on clean test images is severely degraded, as the number of pruned neurons grows. Thus, FP is generally unsuccessful against these backdoor attacks.

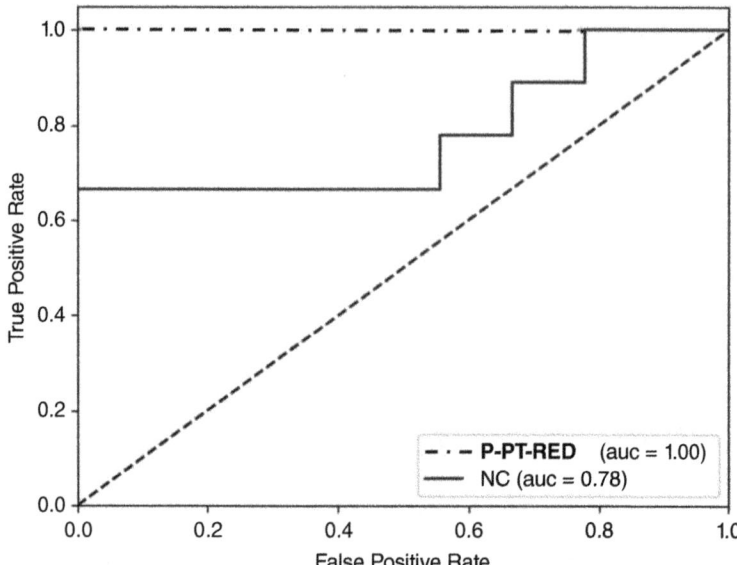

Figure 7.7 Average ROC curves for NC (average AUC is 0.78) and P-PT-RED (average AUC is 1.0) against the nine attacks. Reprinted from [304] with permission.

7.4.3   Verification of Property 2 on Robust Backdoor Triggers

The following experiment assesses Property 2, the robustness property of perceptible backdoor patterns, from two aspects. First, for each attack, the backdoor pattern embedded into *each* clean test image (from the source class) is modified by adding mean-zero Gaussian noise $\sim N(0, \sigma^2)$ to each pixel (and then clipping each normalized pixel intensity value to $[0, 1]$). Second, instead of adding noise, part of the backdoor pattern is cropped outside its center before embedding to the clean test images. Table 7.3 shows the attack success rate for noisy backdoor patterns with $\sigma^2 = 0.1, 0.5, 1$ and cropped backdoor patterns to 64% and 36% of the original size. For the majority of the attacks, using noisy or cropped backdoor patterns at test time still achieves high attack success rate (even though cropping may remove critical features on the periphery of the backdoor pattern).

7.4.4   Backdoor Patterns with Fixed Spatial Location

When all classes except for the target class are source classes of an attack, NC performs well when the backdoor pattern is spatially fixed, see [282] and Table 6.2. Although P-PT-RED is not designed to detect backdoor attacks with a spatially fixed backdoor pattern, the following experiments show that such attacks have poor robustness during testing, if the classifier is trained without data augmentation. It is also shown that P-PT-RED can easily detect attacks with the perceptible backdoor pattern spatially fixed (during its embedding into clean images) if the classifier is trained with simple data

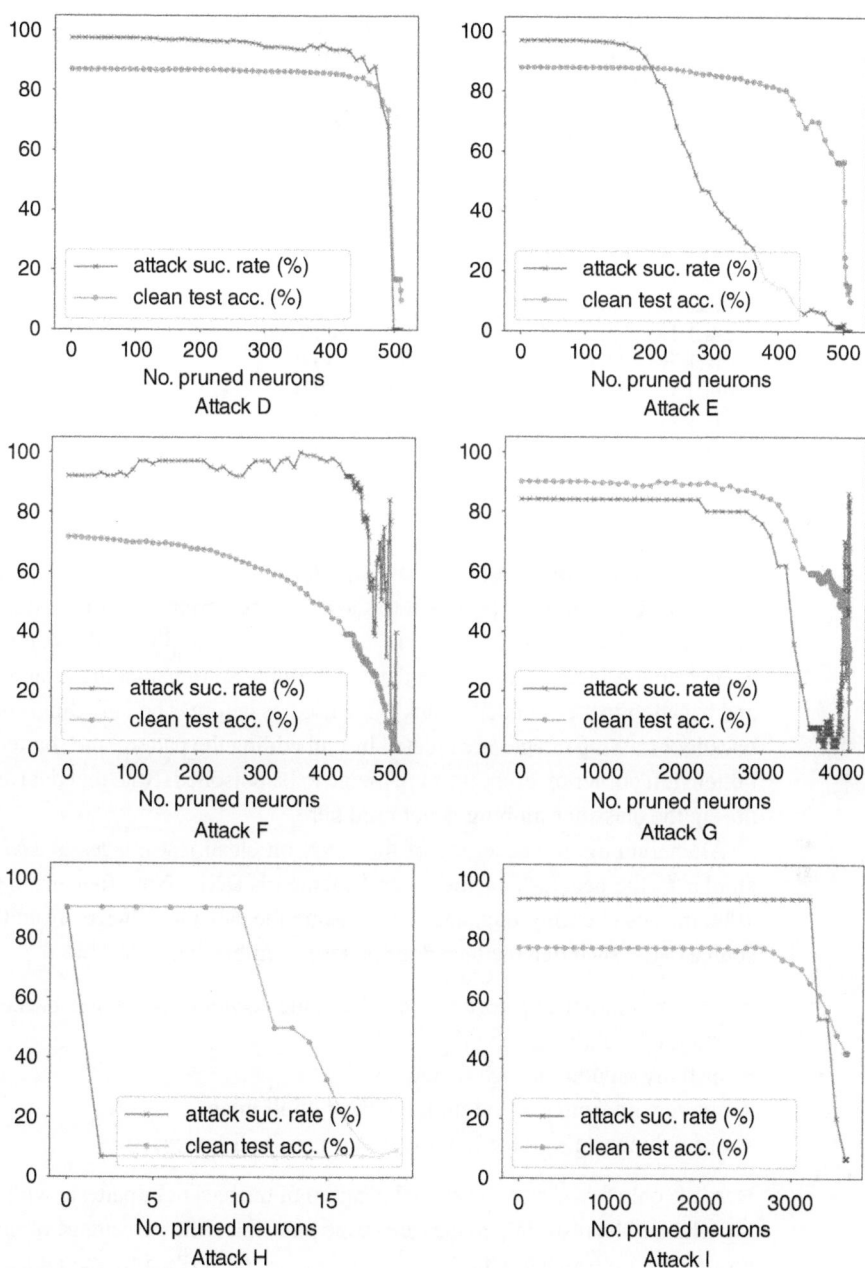

Figure 7.8 Attack success rate and accuracy on clean test images as the number of penultimate layer neurons being pruned by FP is increased, for the DNN being attacked for Attacks D – I (for example). Reprinted from [304] with permission.

augmentation that possibly changes the spatial location of the backdoor pattern in the poisoned images during training.

Table 7.3 Attack success rate (%) on backdoor test
images with (Gaussian) noisy backdoor patterns
with $\sigma^2 = 0.01, 0.25, 1$ and cropped backdoor
patterns to 64% and 36% of the original size.

	σ^2			Crop	
	0.01	0.25	1	64%	36%
Attack A	85.2	53.6	53.7	84.6	73.2
Attack B	97.8	86.7	87.6	67.8	26.3
Attack C	62.4	46.9	23.6	96.0	29.1
Attack D	98.1	99.9	99.0	81.7	60.2
Attack E	78.4	45.6	32.0	91.4	46.0
Attack F	97.0	91.0	83.0	86.0	69.0
Attack G	78.0	38.0	28.0	78.0	62.0
Attack H	91.3	66.7	67.2	41.7	20.7
Attack I	86.7	86.7	80.0	40.0	26.7

Non-robustness of Fixed Position Attacks

First consider a simple experiment to show that the power/robustness of the *attack* will
be degraded if the perceptible backdoor pattern is spatially fixed when poisoning the
clean training images. The same dataset, training settings, (source, target) class pair,
and backdoor pattern under Attack B are used as before. The only difference is that the
backdoor training images are created by embedding the pattern, the 'butterfly', into the
bottom left corner of *every* training image to be poisoned. Note that data augmentation
during the classifier training is not used here.

After training, the accuracy of the DNN on clean test images is 87.2%, which is
similar to the accuracy of the clean benchmark DNN. Now four groups of images,
1000 images in each group, are created using the clean test images from the attacker's
source class, such that the backdoor pattern is embedded as follows:

- into the bottom left corner (i.e., the same location as for the backdoor training
  images) of all images;
- spatially random in each image;
- one row up from the bottom left corner of all images;
- one column right of the bottom left corner of all images.

Here the only focus is on the spatial location of the backdoor pattern, without considering whether the resulting images are scene plausible. The percentage of images in each
group that are (mis)classified to the target class prescribed by the attack respectively
are

$$99.7, \ 4.1, \ 47.8, \ 14.4.$$

Clearly, only if the backdoor pattern during testing is located at the *same* place as
during training, will the backdoor image be reliably (mis)classified to the target class.
Hence, fixing the spatial location of the backdoor pattern when creating backdoor

training images largely degrades the robustness of the attack (and also affects its scene-plausibility).

When Training Data Augmentation is Used

Although P-PT-RED is not designed for attacks with spatially fixed perceptible backdoor patterns, experiments show that P-PT-RED can detect this type of attack when data augmentation is used during the classifier's training (and note that it is the designer, not the attacker, who chooses whether to use data augmentation). Here, the same configurations as in Section 7.4.4 are used to train a classifier on the same poisoned training set, where the 'butterfly' is spatially fixed to the bottom left corner of every poisoned image. However, training-set data augmentation is used, including random cropping, random horizontal flipping, and random rotation (±30°), such that the spatial location of the backdoor pattern in the augmented training images will be modified to some extent. The attack success rate and the clean test accuracy for this DNN are 99.5% and 92.0%, respectively. Note that the images used to measure the attack success rate all have the backdoor pattern fixed to the same spatial location as in the backdoor training images (before being augmented).

P-PT-RED was evaluated for the same configurations as for Attack B in Section 7.4.2, where the fixed square spatial support for pattern estimation covers the top left corner of each image used for detection. Note that the approach to training data augmentation that is used does not include any vertical flipping; hence none of the augmented training images will have the backdoor pattern, the 'butterfly', located in the top left corner, that is, coinciding with the location of the spatial support for this version of P-PT-RED pattern estimation. Figure 7.9 compares the MAMF statistics for the class pair with the largest average MAMF for the above attacked DNN trained with data augmentation with the MAMF statistics for the clean benchmark DNN, for attack B in Section 7.4.2. A similarly large gap can be observed between the two curves; here the largest average MAMF, ρ^*, for the DNN being attacked (with the spatially fixed perceptible backdoor pattern and training data augmentation in use) is as large as 0.87, so the attack can be easily detected. Thus, the location of the spatial support for pattern estimation does not need to coincide with the location of the backdoor pattern in the poisoned training images. Moreover, P-PT-RED is quite effective at detecting backdoors that occur in a fixed location, if data augmentation is used during training.

Additional experimental results are given in [304].

7.5   Chapter Summary

In this chapter we considered backdoor attacks that involve patch replacement, rather than the additive attack embedding function considered in Chapter 6. In order to be evasive, a patch backdoor pattern must either be imperceptible or scene plausible. However, many patch attacks, either introduced or tested against in the literature, are neither imperceptible nor scene plausible. In this chapter we focused on scene-plausible,

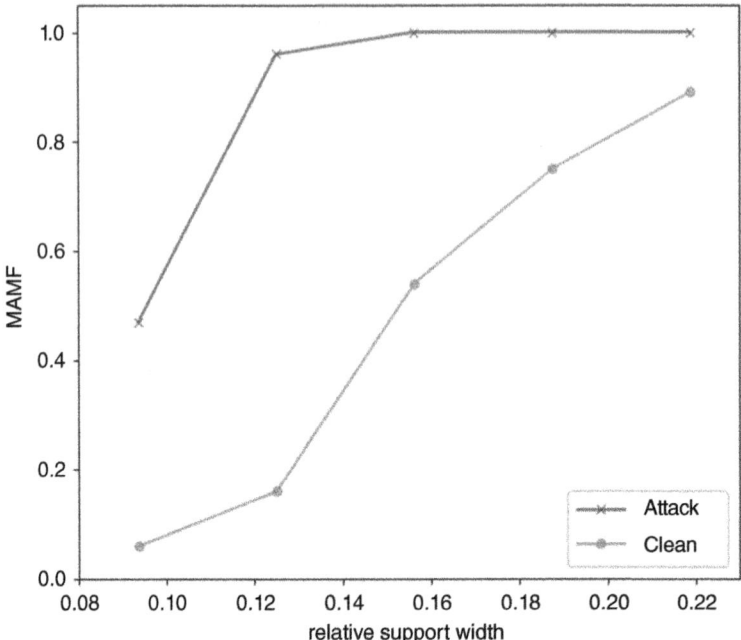

Figure 7.9 MAMF statistics for the class pair with the largest average MAMF, for the attacked DNN trained with data augmentation, and the clean benchmark DNN for Attack B. Reprinted from [304] with permission.

perceptible attacks. Such attacks have several important properties that are exploited by the P-PT-RED defense. (1) In order to be scene plausible the backdoor pattern cannot, in general, be introduced at a fixed location in every poisoned training (or backdoor triggered test) image. Moreover, by introducing the backdoor at different locations, the DNN will learn a robust, spatially invariant backdoor mapping. (On the other hand, if the backdoor *were* introduced in just a single, fixed location, the attack success rate will be severely degraded if, at test time, the backdoor is introduced even at a modestly offset location, compared to its location in the poisoned training images, i.e., the learned backdoor mapping would be quite fragile. Though training data augmentation may improve the attack success in this case, the attack then becomes easily detectable by P-PT-RED.) (2) The learned backdoor mapping is robust to variations such as noise, lighting, image perspective, and, to some extent, occlusion. The P-PT-RED detector exploits both of these properties. P-PT-RED's perturbation optimization is performed on a small clean set, for a sequence of masks of increasing spatial support (with the pixel values in the mask support first zeroed out). The first property above ensures that it does not matter where in the image this spatial support is placed. In fact, the support of the mask can be *varied*, from one clean image to the next, without affecting detection accuracy. The second property ensures that, even if the support of a mask is smaller than the backdoor pattern's spatial support, the backdoor can be detected.

P-PT-RED detection was experimentally shown to be more accurate and robust than both NC (with NC's hyperparameter optimistically tuned) and FP.

Some questions to test the reader's understanding of the chapter include the following.

- Are patch attacks digital attacks or physical attacks? Explain.
- What detection inference approach is suitable for use by P-PT-RED?
- Does P-PT-RED require optimization of the support of a mask (like Neural Cleanse)?
- If it is unknown whether an additive or patch replacement backdoor embedding function was used by a possible attacker, how do you suggest to devise a (robust) detection scheme?
- Can the L-PT-RED framework be applied to the P-PT-RED (scene-plausible patch replacement) scenario?
- What complications arise if one seeks to optimize the mask (as neural cleanse does), in the case of scene-plausible perceptible attacks?
- Explain why varying the mask location, even from one clean image to the next, should not affect P-PT-RED's detection accuracy.
- Should varying the location of the backdoor pattern from one poisoned training image to the next affect NC's detection performance? Explain.

7.6   Project: Exploring What the Deep Neural Network (DNN) is Learning

Perform experiments to assess "how much" patch backdoor patterns need to be shifted around, among the poisoned training samples, in order for the backdoor mapping to be robustly learned. In particular, *randomly* locate the center of a local patch backdoor pattern within each poisoned image. Explore how the test ASR (and the clean test set accuracy), if test patterns randomly place the backdoor pattern *anywhere* in the image, depend on the variance of the random center pixel of the backdoor pattern in the poisoned training images.

7.7   Project: Perceptible Backdoor Post-Training Reverse-Engineering Defense (P-PT-RED) and Variations on Images

7.7.1   P-PT-RED

Modify the I-PT-RED code provided in the project of Section 6.8 to implement P-PT-RED (this should involve only a simple modification), and replicate the evaluation of its performance on clean DNNs and on those which are backdoor poisoned through a patch replacement mechanism, as described above. Also experiment with data augmentation. This project is similar to patch C-PT-RED of Section 6.9.

7.7.2   Source Class Inference

Regardless of the number of source classes involved in devising the attack, P-PT-RED is designed to detect the attack and infer **one** (source, target) class pair. Recalling Section 7.3.5, show that by forming a pattern estimation step that solves (7.12) for each putative target class, the detected source class*es* (those with the largest estimated weights) may be accurately identified.

7.7.3   Detection Efficiency

Section 7.3.5 also discussed the computational efficiency of P-PT-RED. The briefly introduced method (which solves (7.12) for each putative target class and is based on L-PT-RED of Section 6.5) may have lower computational complexity by needing far fewer clean images per class to achieve accurate detection. However, this method still requires performing a lot of forward/back propagation on the DNN. Empirically evaluate the computational efficiency of the L-PT-RED idea applied to P-PT-RED.

7.7.4   Anomaly Detection

Detection under P-PT-RED requires setting a detection threshold. Using (unsupervised) statistical anomaly detection based on p-value estimation, show how a detection threshold can be set using the clean dataset $\mathcal{D}$ to control the false positive rate. This requires proper modeling of the null distribution for MAMF statistics (or other reasonable metrics) associated with the putative non-backdoor class pairs. Is there an alternative way to control the false positive rate?

8 Transfer Post-Training Reverse-Engineering Defense (T-PT-RED) Against Backdoors

In this chapter, we focus on classification problems involving only a few classes $K = |\mathcal{Y}|$, particularly the case of just two classes, and involving cases where there are arbitrary numbers of backdoor attacks (BAs) present in the training set, including multiple backdoor patterns (BPs) with the same source and/or target classes. Examples of two-class problems include biometric (Y/N) authentication for accessing privileged information/premises, determining (Y/N) whether a particular object of interest (e.g., a gun) is found in a given scene, and determining whether a given MRI image is indicative of the presence of cancer. In Chapter 6, null models used to perform detection inference were estimated using $(K - 1)^2$ statistics. When $K = 2$, there is only *one* such statistic available, which is clearly insufficient for estimating a null distribution! Thus, the inference approach of Section 6.3.3 cannot be directly applied in the two-class case. For a similar reason, a MAD based approach, as used by NC (Section 6.2.3), cannot be applied when $K = 2$. Beyond developing a feasible, effective method for the two-class case, the developed approach has the intriguing property that it works very effectively with a *fixed* threshold on its detection statistic (at a value of $\frac{1}{2}$), *irrespective of the classification domain*. This is of great practical importance, as most detection methods require tuning the detection threshold for each new domain. Such tuning is quite laborious, as it requires training *many* "clean" DNN models (e.g., based on different random initializations), with the detection threshold chosen to set the false positive rate of DNN detection. The method next developed does not require such tuning. Moreover, it can detect backdoor poisoning when a plurality of target classes are involved.

8.1 Transferability of Sample-wise Minimal Perturbations

Again, for defense purposes, assume an available clean, correctly classified dataset $\mathcal{D}$, with labeled examples from each class. Consider a classifier $\hat{c} : \mathbb{R}^N \to \mathcal{Y}$ to be inspected, with category space (classes) $\mathcal{Y} = \{1, 2\}$ and *continuous* (training) sample distribution P_i on $\mathbb{R}^N$ for class $i \in \mathcal{Y}$. For any $\underline{x} \in \mathbb{R}^N$ from either class, define

$$\underline{v}^*(\underline{x}) = \arg\min_{\underline{v}} \|\underline{v}\|_2 \quad \text{subject to } \hat{c}(\underline{x} + \underline{v}) \neq \hat{c}(\underline{x}). \tag{8.1}$$

Equation (8.1) is a *sample specific* BP reverse-engineering problem. This problem can be solved using methods from existing REDs like I-PT-RED from Chapter 6. It can also be practically solved by creating an adversarial example for $\underline{x}$ using TTE attack methods from, for example, DeepFool and CW, see Chapter 4. Consider the following definition for the set of *practical* solutions to (8.1).

Definition 7 (ϵ-**solution set**) For any sample $\underline{x}$ from any class, the ϵ-solution set to problem (8.1) is defined by

$$\mathcal{V}_\epsilon(\underline{x}) \triangleq \{\underline{v} \in \mathbb{R}^N \mid \|\underline{v}\|_2 - \|\underline{v}^*(\underline{x})\|_2 \leq \epsilon, \hat{c}(\underline{x} + \underline{v}) \neq \hat{c}(\underline{x})\}, \tag{8.2}$$

where (typically small) $\epsilon > 0$ is the upper "quality gap" of "practical" (approximate) solutions to (8.1).

A practical solution $\in \mathcal{V}_\epsilon(\underline{x})$ to (8.1) for sample $\underline{x}$ may or may not cause a misclassification when embedded in another sample $\underline{y}$ from the same class. Definitions related to such a "transferability" property are now given.

Definition 8 (**Transferable set**) The transferable set for any sample $\underline{x}$ and $\epsilon > 0$ is defined by

$$\mathcal{T}_\epsilon(\underline{x}) \triangleq \{\underline{y} \in \mathbb{R}^N \mid \hat{c}(\underline{y}) = \hat{c}(\underline{x}), \exists \underline{v} \in \mathcal{V}_\epsilon(\underline{x}) \text{ s.t. } \hat{c}(\underline{y} + \underline{v}) \neq \hat{c}(\underline{y})\}. \tag{8.3}$$

Definition 9 (**ET statistic**) For any class $i \in \mathcal{Y} = \{1,2\}$ and $\epsilon > 0$, considering two i.i.d. random samples $\underline{X}, \underline{Y} \sim P_i$, the ET statistic for class i is defined by

$$\text{ET}_{i,\epsilon} \triangleq \mathsf{P}\big(\underline{Y} \in \mathcal{T}_\epsilon(\underline{X})\big).$$

The following theorem shows the connection between ET and a detection threshold (on ET) of $\frac{1}{2}$ regardless of the presence of any BA.

Theorem 10 *For any class $i \in \mathcal{Y}$ and $\epsilon > 0$:*

$$\text{ET}_{i,\epsilon} = \frac{1}{2} + \frac{1}{2}(P_{MT,i} - P_{NT,i}), \tag{8.4}$$

with $P_{MT,i}$ a "mutual-transfer probability" and $P_{NT,i}$ a "non-transfer probability" respectively defined by

$$P_{MT,i} \triangleq \mathsf{P}(\underline{Y} \in \mathcal{T}_\epsilon(\underline{X}), \underline{X} \in \mathcal{T}_\epsilon(\underline{Y}))$$
$$P_{NT,i} \triangleq \mathsf{P}(\underline{Y} \notin \mathcal{T}_\epsilon(\underline{X}), \underline{X} \notin \mathcal{T}_\epsilon(\underline{Y}))$$

where i.i.d. $\underline{X}, \underline{Y} \sim P_i$.

Proof Take i.i.d. $\underline{X}, \underline{Y} \sim P_i$ for some $i \in \mathcal{Y}$. Since $\underline{X}$ and $\underline{Y}$ are i.i.d.,

$$2\text{ET}_{i,\epsilon} = \mathsf{P}(\underline{Y} \in \mathcal{T}_\epsilon(\underline{X})) + \mathsf{P}(\underline{X} \in \mathcal{T}_\epsilon(\underline{Y}))$$
$$= 1 + P_{MT,i} - P_{NT,i}$$

where the second equality follows by inclusion-exclusion and De Morgan's rule. For any events A, B, $\mathsf{P}(A) + \mathsf{P}(B) = \mathsf{P}(A \cup B) + \mathsf{P}(A \cap B) = 1 - \mathsf{P}(\overline{A \cup B}) + \mathsf{P}(A \cap B) = 1 - \mathsf{P}(\overline{A} \cap \overline{B}) + \mathsf{P}(A \cap B)$ where $\overline{A}$ is the complement of event A. □

The intuitive operating hypothesis of T-PT-RED (consistent with the above theorem) is that a successful backdoor attack is present with *source* class i if and only if $P_{MT,i} > P_{NT,i}$, that is, if and only if $ET_{i,\epsilon} > \frac{1}{2}$. Note that this *constant* threshold does not rely on any specific data domain or classifier architecture. Moreover, *it does not even rely on a specific attack embedding function*. In particular, one can simply modify the transferable set definition in (8.3) from an additive attack embedding to any other embedding function choice (multiplicative, patch embedding, *etc.*), see Section 8.2.1. A practical backdoor detector, of course, will rely on good (sample specific) estimates of the backdoor pattern in order to leverage the T-PT-RED hypothesis.

8.2 Transfer Post-Training Reverse-Engineering Defense (T-PT-RED) Detection Procedure

The T-PT-RED procedure, specialized to the two-class case (but easily generalized when there are more than two classes, as discussed in Section 8.2.3), is summarized in Algorithm 8.1. Basically, for each putative target class $t \in \mathcal{Y}$, an estimate of the ET statistic, $\widehat{ET}_i$, is obtained for the remaining class $i \neq t$, and a detection is made if $\widehat{ET}_i > \frac{1}{2}$. Based on practical solutions $\hat{\nu}(x_n^{(i)})$ to (8.1) for each $x_n^{(i)} \in \mathcal{D}_i$, $\widehat{ET}_i$ is obtained by considering the transferability to elements of $\mathcal{D}_i \setminus x_n^{(i)}$.

Given the non-convexity of RED based optimization objectives and, thus, the potential existence of multiple (only) locally optimal solutions with varying quality (and recall the transferable *set* definition of Equation (8.3)), it is insufficient to decide whether or not a sample is in the transferable set of another sample according to merely *one* solution realization to problem (8.1). To address this, for each $x_n^{(i)} \in \mathcal{D}_i$, T-PT-RED solves problem (8.1) *repeatedly* with random initialization. For each practical solution, T-PT-RED embeds it to all elements in $\mathcal{D}_i \setminus x_n^{(i)}$ and finds those that are misclassified – these samples are included into the subset $\widehat{\mathcal{T}_i}(x_n^{(i)})$ (line 9, Algorithm 8.1). Such repetition stops when $\widehat{\mathcal{T}_i}(x_n^{(i)})$ stays unchanged for some τ iterations. This procedure is summarized as the "while" loop in Algorithm 8.1, which is guaranteed to converge in $(M_i - 1)\tau$ iterations. Finally, T-PT-RED obtains the estimated ET by averaging $p_n^{(i)}$, the empirical estimation of the transfer probability, over all samples $x_n^{(i)} \in \mathcal{D}_i$.

T-PT-RED has the following extensibility capabilities.

8.2.1 BP Embedding Mechanism and Reverse-Engineering Problem

First, while the above T-PT-RED procedure is only specified for the two-class case, it is easily generalized to the case where there are more than two classes (again, see Section 8.2.3). Second, for this multi-class case, the transferrable set definition and the associated perturbation optimization method can *either* be *untargeted* (where the perturbation transfers to other samples in the same source class so long as the perturbation induces a misclassification to any other class) or *targeted* (where the perturbation must induce a misclassification to a particular class, t). In this latter

---

Algorithm 8.1 BA detection using ET statistics (T-PT-RED) with $\mathcal{Y} = \{1,2\}$.

1: **Input**: Classifier $\hat{c} : \mathbb{R}^N \to \mathcal{Y}$ for inspection; clean dataset $\mathcal{D}_i = \{\underline{x}_1^{(i)}, \ldots, \underline{x}_{M_i}^{(i)}\}$ for each $i \in \mathcal{Y}$.

2: **Initialization**: attacked $=$ *False*; BA_ targets $= \emptyset$.

3: **for** each putative target class $t \in \mathcal{Y} = \{1,2\}$ **do**

4:      **Step 1**: Obtain empirical estimation $\widehat{ET}_i$ using $\mathcal{D}_i$ for $i \neq t$, i.e., $i = 3 - t$ when $K = 2$

5:      **for** $n = 1 : M_i$ **do**

6:          $\widehat{\mathcal{T}_i}(\underline{x}_n^{(i)}) = \emptyset$; converged $=$ *False*

7:          **while** not converged **do**

8:              Obtain an empirical solution $\hat{\underline{v}}(\underline{x}_n^{(i)})$ to problem (8.1) using random initialization

9:              $\widehat{\mathcal{T}_i}(\underline{x}_n^{(i)}) \leftarrow \widehat{\mathcal{T}_i}(\underline{x}_n^{(i)}) \cup \{\underline{x}_m^{(i)} \mid m \in \{1, \ldots, M_i\} \setminus \{n\}, \hat{c}(\underline{x}_m^{(i)} + \hat{\underline{v}}(\underline{x}_n^{(i)})) \neq \hat{c}(\underline{x}_m^{(i)})\}$

10:             **if** $\widehat{\mathcal{T}_i}(\underline{x}_n^{(i)})$ unchanged for prior τ iterations **then**

11:                 converged $\leftarrow$ *True*

12:                 $p_n^{(i)} = |\widehat{\mathcal{T}_i}(\underline{x}_n^{(i)})|/(M_i - 1)$

13:             **end if**

14:         **end while**

15:     **end for**

16:     $\widehat{ET}_i = \frac{1}{M_i} \sum_{n=1}^{M_i} p_n^{(i)}$

17:     **Step 2**: Determine whether class t is a BA target class

18:     **if** $\widehat{ET}_i > \frac{1}{2}$ **then**

19:         attacked $=$ *True*; BA_ targets $\leftarrow$ BA_ targets $\cup \{t\}$

20:     **end if**

21: **end for**

22: **Output**: attacked; BA_ targets

---

targeted case, one might apply the perturbation optimization and compute an ET statistic for all (s,t) pairs with $s \neq t$. This point will be discussed further, shortly.

Second, as mentioned before, T-PT-RED's detection rule is applicable to *different* backdoor embedding functions:

- additive (Eq. (6.3)),
- multiplicative (Eq. (6.11)),
- patch replacement (Eq. (7.1) with Boolean mask),
- blended replacement (Eq. (6.1) with a relaxed mask), or
- noisy versions of the above (Section 6.10).

All that is necessary is to specialize the search for transferable samples to a particular backdoor embedding mechanism. For example, if one is (also or instead) assessing a possible non-additive backdoor embedding, then just modify the optimization problem (8.1), which is specifically for an additive backdoor, customizing it for the non-additive embedding function of interest. However, note that *at least in principle* this is in fact not even necessary.

In particular, suppose one is searching for the transferable set for sample x, considering the case of a patch replacement backdoor mechanism. One can in fact still apply the *additive* backdoor mechanism in (8.1) to find an (additive) perturbation v. Now recognize that one can infer an estimate of the patch replacement backdoor pattern from v. In particular, in every coordinate j where the perturbation $v_j \neq 0$ the mask value is 1; elsewhere the mask value is 0. (An alternative is to determine the mask by setting the mask to 1 at coordinates j where $|v_j|$ is greater than a threshold.) And for the patch replacement vector, for each coordinate j for which the mask value is 0 the patch value is taken to be x_j; and for each coordinate j for which the mask value is 1, the patch value is taken to be

$$x_j + v_j.$$

The potential practical significance of this observation is that, even if one needs to evaluate multiple candidate backdoor embedding mechanisms, only the additive optimization problem (8.1) may need to be solved, with the resulting backdoor pattern (be it patch replacement or multiplicative) inferrable. This reduces complexity of the detection procedure. Moreover, optimization of an additive perturbation should be "easier" than NC's optimization of a patch replacement pattern, as in the latter one needs to optimize over *both* the backdoor pattern *and* the mask (with potentially more poor local optima than for an additive optimization). This general approach (applying additive perturbation optimization, but then inferring a non-additive mechanism from the additive result) will be experimentally investigated in a project in Section 8.6.

8.2.2 BP Reverse-Engineering Algorithm

T-PT-RED is not limited to any specific algorithm when solving problem (8.1) (line 8 in Algorithm 8.1); other algorithms, for example, those of Chapters 4 and 6 (including operations on embedded features in Section 6.4.4), can be used.

8.2.3 T-PT-RED Variants for Greater than Two Classes and Multiple Attack Scenarios

When there are more than two classes ($K > 2$), where each can possibly be a BA source or target class (and where there may be multiple backdoor attacks present), T-PT-RED can still be used for detection. For each putative *source* class s of one or more BAs, define a single *aggregate target* class $t = \mathcal{Y} \backslash \{s\}$, and then compute an ET estimate for (s, t) using $\mathcal{D}_s$ (based on the above detection procedure). Clearly, for K different ET estimates are computed, one for each putative source class in this "untargeted" defense (untargeted in the sense that for both the ET definition and the pseudocode procedure, it suffices to induce a misclassification, not a misclassification to a particular class). So, all classes other than s are aggregated and a misclassification to any of these classes is considered a valid misclassification for computing the ET statistic for putative source class s. Moreover, it does not matter *which* estimated BP is used for a given clean source sample under T-PT-RED. For identified source classes s of a BA, one can then use a *targeted* variant of the above detection procedure (and with a corresponding targeted misclassification ET definition) to compute an ET estimate for the $K-1$ (s,t') class pairs with $t' \neq s$, in order to identify specific target classes t'.

Alternatively, one can just separately estimate ET (again, using a targeted ET definition and an associated targeted variant of the detection procedure pseudocode) for all $K(K-1)$ putative (source, target) class pairs, which obviously will involve more computation.

The following experiments evaluate T-PT-RED considering some of these extensions, while others are also considered in [302].

8.3   Experiments

The following attack-defense experiments involve six common benchmark image datasets with a variety of image sizes and color scales: CIFAR-10, CIFAR-100 [129], STL-10 [47], Tiny ImageNet [263], FMNIST [312], and MNIST. Additional experiments and analysis are given in [302].

8.3.1   Main Experiment: Two-Class, Multi-attack BA Detection Using ET Statistic

Generating Two-Class Domains: From CIFAR-10, 45 different two-class domains are created (for all unordered class pairs of CIFAR-10). From *each* of the other five datasets, 20 different random two-class domains are created.

Attack Configuration: For each two-class domain generated from CIFAR-10, CIFAR-100, STL-10, and Tiny ImageNet, two *attack instances* are created, one for a BA with an additive perturbation BP, and the other for a BA with a patch replacement BP. For each two-class domain generated from FMNIST and MNIST, one attack instance is created with an additive perturbation BP. (Images from these two datasets commonly have a large area of "black" background. Positively perturbing a few background pixels, which is a common practice to achieve a successful BA [39], is *equivalent* to replacing these pixels with a grey patch.) For convenience, the six ensembles of attack instances with additive perturbation BP and for two-class domains generated from CIFAR-10, CIFAR-100, STL-10, Tiny ImageNet, FMNIST, and MNIST are respectively denoted A_1–A_6. The four ensembles of attack instances with patch replacement BP and for two-class domains generated from CIFAR-10, CIFAR-100, STL-10, and TinyImageNet are respectively denoted A_7–A_{10}. Examples of some BPs (as in prior chapters) and images embedded with them are shown in Figure 8.1.

Consider two-class scenarios where *both classes can possibly be a BA target class*. For each attack instance in ensembles A_1, A_2, A_3, A_7, A_8, and A_{10}, *two* attacks are launched within the same training dataset, each with one of the two classes being the BA target class. For each instance in ensembles A_4, A_5, A_6, and A_9, one attack is

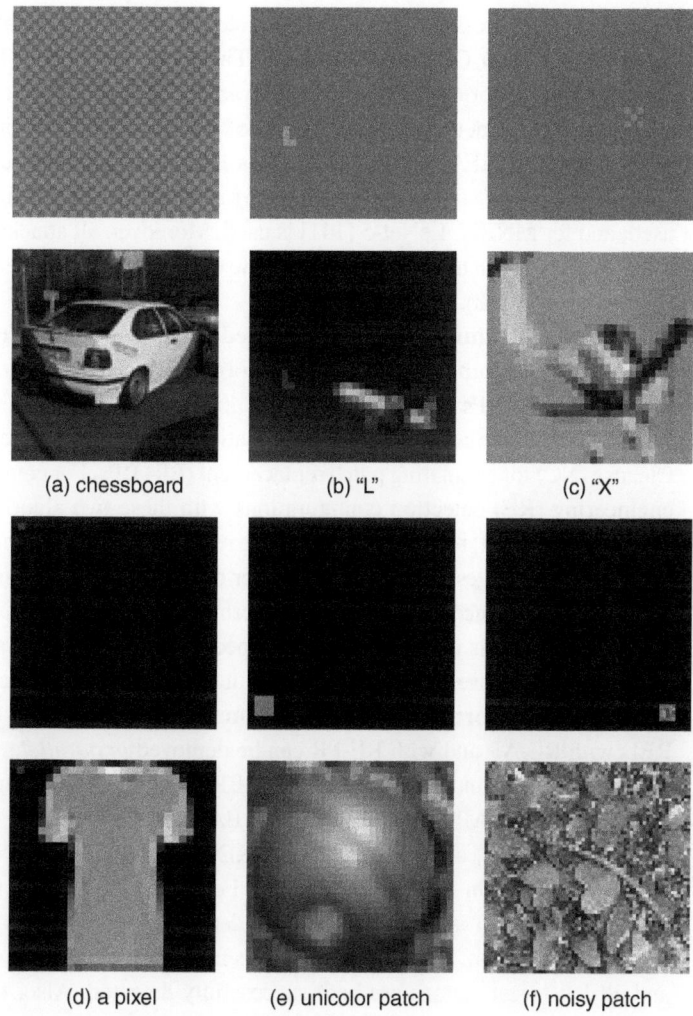

(a) chessboard   (b) "L"   (c) "X"

(d) a pixel   (e) unicolor patch   (f) noisy patch

Figure 8.1 Some of the BPs used in T-PT-RED experiments and images with these BPs embedded. (a)–(d) are additive perturbation BPs and (e)–(f) are patch replacement BPs. Some BP images are offset or scaled for visualization purposes. Spatial locations for BPs in (b)–(f) are randomly selected for each attack.

created, with the second class being the BA target class. For each of these attacks, the BP is randomly selected from the BPs shown in Figure 8.1. To avoid confusion associated with learned backdoor mappings, for all two-attack instances with additive perturbation BPs, the BPs for the two attacks are ensured to have different shapes (e.g., two "X" BPs are not allowed). Similarly, for all two-attack instances where the two attacks both choose to use the unicolor patch BP (Figure 8.1e), it is ensured that the colors for the two BPs are significantly different.

Training Configurations: One classifier is trained for each attack instance using the poisoned training set. For each two-class domain, a clean classifier is also trained in order to evaluate false detections. Denote the six ensembles of clean instances for datasets CIFAR-10, CIFAR-100, STL-10, TinyImageNet, FMNIST, and MNIST as C_1–C_6 respectively. For classifier training, a variety of DNN architectures are considered (with two output neurons, one for each of the two classes). For two-class domains associated with CIFAR-10 and STL-10, a ResNet-18 is used (recall Figure 2.6); for CIFAR-100 and FMNIST, VGG-11 [245] is used; for TinyImageNet, ResNet-34 is used; and for MNIST, LeNet-5 [141] is used. Moreover, all attacks for all the instances are successful, with high attack success rate (ASR) and negligible degradation in clean test accuracy (ACC).

Defense Configurations: As mentioned in Section 8.2, T-PT-RED can be easily generalized to incorporate a variety of algorithms for BP reverse-engineering to detect various types of BPs with different embedding mechanisms. Consider the approach of I-PT-RED for estimating additive perturbation (AP) BPs, and the approach of Neural Cleanse (NC) for estimating patch replacement (PR) BPs. For convenience, the reverse-engineering (RE) detection configurations with these two algorithms are denoted by RE-AP and RE-PR, respectively. Irrespective of the BP reverse-engineering algorithm, only 20 clean images per class are used for detection (similar to most existing REDs). Finally, the "patience" parameter for determination of convergence in Algorithm 8.1 is set to $\tau = 4$; this choice is made irrespective of the possible presence of a BA. A larger τ will increase the execution time but not change the estimated ET significantly.

Detection Performance (Using the Common ET Threshold $\frac{1}{2}$): In practice, T-PT-RED with RE-AP and with RE-PR can be deployed *in parallel* to cover both additive perturbation BPs and patch replacement BPs. Here, just for simplicity, T-PT-RED is applied with RE-AP to classifiers (with BAs using an additive perturbation BP) in ensembles A_1–A_6, and is applied with RE-PR to classifiers (with BAs using patch replacement BP) in ensembles A_7–A_{10}. For each classifier in the clean ensembles C_1–C_6, T-PT-RED is applied with both detector configurations. For each ensemble of attack instances, Table 8.1 reports the fraction of classifiers such that the attack and all BA target classes are both successfully detected. Also, for each ensemble of clean DNNs, the fraction of classifiers that are inferred to be not attacked are reported. While there is a large variety of classification domains, attack configurations, DNN architectures, and defense generalizations mentioned above, *using the common ET threshold $\frac{1}{2}$*, observe that T-PT-RED successfully detects most attacks, with very few false detections.

8.3.2   Compare ET with Other Statistics

T-PT-RED's ET statistic is now compared with some other types of statistics used by existing REDs in terms of their potential to distinguish BA target classes from non-target classes. The types of statistics for comparison include the following:

- the l_2 norm of the estimated additive perturbation used by I-PT-RED (denoted $\mathbf{L_2}$);
- the l_1 norm of the estimated mask used by NC (denoted $\mathbf{L_1}$); and
- the cosine similarity between the BP estimated group-wise and the BP estimated for

Table 8.1 T-PT-RED Detection accuracy for RE-AP and RE-PR inference on attack ensembles A_1-A_{10}, and on clean ensembles C_1-C_6, using *the common threshold $\frac{1}{2}$ on ET statistic.*

	A_1	A_2	A_3	A_4	A_5	A_6	A_7	A_8	A_9	A_{10}	C_1	C_2	C_3	C_4	C_5	C_6
RE-AP	45/45	18/20	16/20	17/20	20/20	20/20	—	—	—	—	45/45	20/20	20/20	20/20	20/20	20/20
RE-PR	—	—	—	—	—	—	45/45	20/20	19/20	19/20	39/45	19/20	20/20	16/20	18/20	19/20

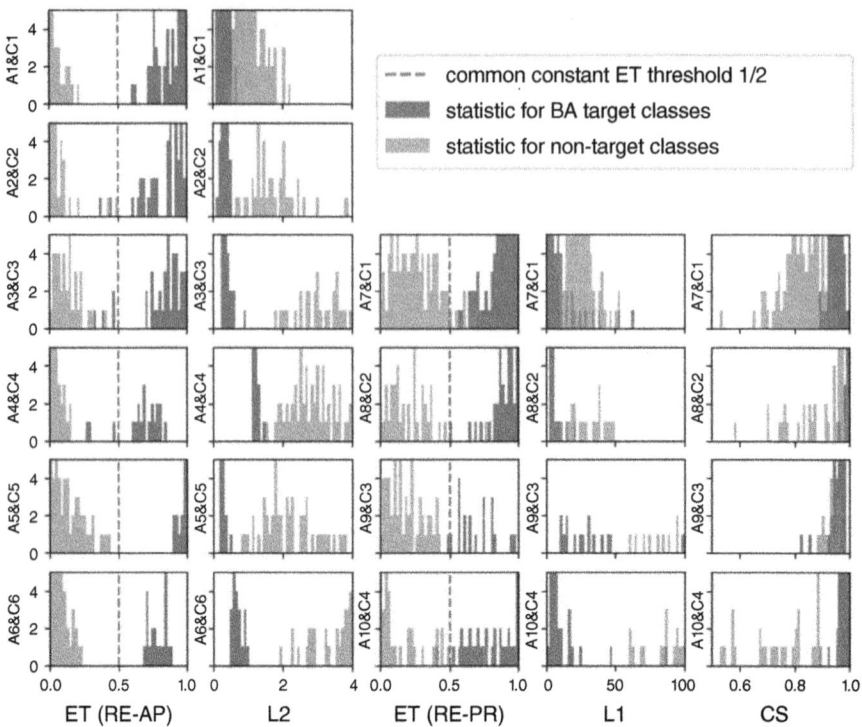

Figure 8.2 Comparison between T-PT-RED's ET statistic (for both RE-AP and RE-PR configurations) and statistic types used by other PT-REDs (L_1, L_2, and CS). Only for ET, there is a common range for all two-class domains for choosing a threshold to distinguish BA target classes (dark) from non-target classes (light); ET's common range contains the constant threshold $\frac{1}{2}$ (dashed line).

each sample with respect to its representation at some internal layer of the classifier (denoted **CS**), see Sections 2.12.3 and 6.2.6.

For each type of statistic mentioned above and for each benchmark dataset, all classifiers are considered (those with and without BA), the classifiers are trained for all two-class domains generated from the given dataset, and a double histogram is plotted for statistics obtained for all BA target classes and all non-target classes across these classifiers, respectively. For example, in the first column of Figure 8.2, for T-PT-RED with RE-AP, a double histogram is plotted for ET statistics obtained for all BA target classes and all non-target classes from all classifiers in each of $A_1\&C_1$, $A_2\&C_2$, $A_3\&C_3$, $A_4\&C_4$, $A_5\&C_5$, and $A_6\&C_6$. Note that all classifiers in, for example, $A_1\&C_1$ are trained for two-class domains generated from CIFAR-10. Here, for simplicity, BA target classes with patch replacement BP (e.g., associated with classifiers in A_7–A_{10}) are not considered for ET (with RE-AP) and L_2 (both designated for additive perturbation BPs). Also, BA target classes with an additive perturbation BP (e.g., associated with classifiers in A_1–A_6) are not considered for T-PT-RED with RE-PR, L_1 and CS (designated for patch replacement BPs).

Based on Figure 8.2, for *all* types of statistics, including T-PT-RED's ET, statistics obtained for BA target classes are generally separable from statistics obtained for non-target classes for classifiers (with and without BA) trained for two-class domains generated from the *same* benchmark dataset (using the same training configurations including DNN architecture). But only for ET (obtained under both RE-AP and RE-PR), there is a *common range* (irrespective of the classification domain, attack configurations, and training configurations) for choosing a detection threshold to effectively distinguish BA target classes from non-target classes for all instances; and such common range clearly includes the *constant threshold* $\frac{1}{2}$ (marked by dashed lines in Figure 8.2). By contrast, for both L_1 and L_2, a proper choice of detection threshold for distinguishing BA target classes from non-target classes is *domain dependent*. For example, in the 4th column of Figure 8.2, the l_1 norm of masks estimated for both BA target classes and non-target classes for domains with larger image size (e.g., 96×96 for domains in $A_9 \& C_3$ generated from STL-10) is generally larger than for domains with smaller image size (e.g., 32×32 for domains in $A_7 \& C_1$ generated from CIFAR-10). The proper threshold on the CS statistic, on the other hand, depends both on the domain and on the DNN architecture.

In summary, all the above mentioned types of statistics are suitable for BA detection *if there is supervision information from the same domain that allows choosing the best proper detection threshold.* However, in most practical scenarios, where such supervision will not be available, only T-PT-RED's ET statistic with the common detection threshold $\frac{1}{2}$ can be used to achieve good detection performance. Finally, Figure 8.3 shows the ROC curves associated with Figure 8.2 for each of ET, L_1, L_2, and CS. Note that T-PT-RED's ET statistic has a clearly larger area under the ROC curve (very close to 1) than the other types of statistics.

8.3.3   More than Two Classes, Multi-attack BA Detection Using ET Statistic

Experiments on datasets with more than two classes are next considered. For each of the CIFAR-10, CIFAR-100, and STL-10 datasets, a different DNN classifier instance is created respectively with one, two, and three attacks (on the *original* domain). That is, nine attacked classifiers are created in total. Here, only BAs with additive BPs are considered, for simplicity. The target class and the BP for each attack are randomly selected and distinct. In each attack, all non-target classes are poisoned as source classes (recall Section 6.2.3). Also, for each domain, a clean classifier (without BA) is trained for evaluating false detections.

A T-PT-RED variant is applied with RE-AP to these classifiers wherein all potential *source* classes are aggregated for each putative *target* class (thus creating a two-class problem). So, this T-PT-RED variant will compute K ET estimates, one for each putative *target* class. (Unlike the "untargeted" T-PT-RED variant of Section 8.2.3, this defense may not work well for BA cases where *not* all non-target classes are attacked source classes, notwithstanding collateral damage – recall the discussion in Chapter 6; this is explored further in the project at the end of this chapter.)

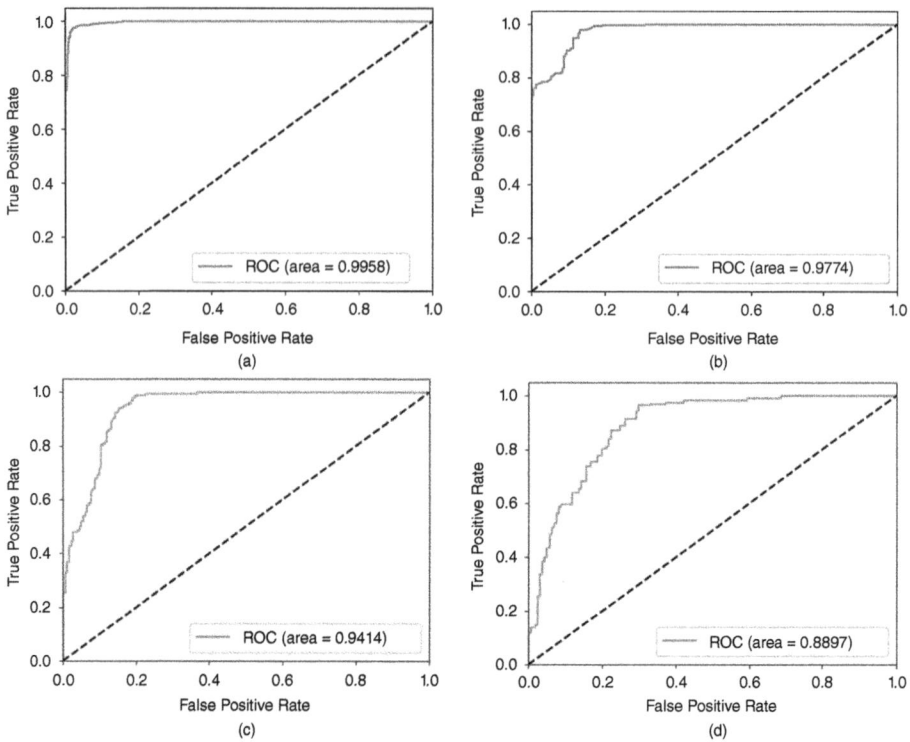

Figure 8.3 ROC curves for T-PT-RED's (a) ET, (c) L_1, (b) L_2, and (d) CS in distinguishing BA target classes from non-target classes for a variety of classification domains and attack configurations.

For CIFAR-10 and STL-10, three clean images per class are used for detection; for CIFAR-100, only one clean image per class is used for detection. Other detection configurations, including the *detection threshold* $\frac{1}{2}$, are the same as in Section 8.3.1. Since a classifier is deemed to be attacked if ET obtained for any class is greater than the threshold 1/2, for each classifier, the maximum ET over all the classes is shown in Table 8.2. Clearly, the maximum ET is greater than 1/2 for all classifiers under attack and less than 1/2 for all clean classifiers. Thus, this T-PT-RED variant (with the same constant threshold on ET) is also applicable to more than two classes and multi-attack scenarios.

8.4   Chapter Summary

In this chapter we developed a post-training backdoor detector, T-PT-RED, considering the cases where the classification problem may involve only a few classes, for example, even the two-class case, or a plurality of target classes. The post-training backdoor inference methods developed in previous chapters are not suitable for this case, as they require estimating a null distribution, with the number of "samples" available for

Table 8.2 Maximum ET statistic over all classes for classifiers respectively with one, two, and three attacks, and a clean classifier, for CIFAR-10, CIFAR-100, and STL-10.

	One attack	Two attacks	Three attacks	Clean
CIFAR-10	0.91	0.92	0.87	0
CIFAR-100	0.95	0.99	0.99	0.27
STL-10	0.65	0.83	0.77	0.0043

estimating this null just $K(K-1)$, where K is the number of classes – so, when K is small there are insufficient samples to estimate a reliable null distribution. To well address problems involving few classes, a novel detection statistic, the expected transferability (ET), was introduced. It was demonstrated experimentally that a universal, constant detection threshold on ET ($\frac{1}{2}$) is effective, independent of the classification domain.

Some questions to test the reader's understanding of the chapter include the following.

- Can T-PT-RED be applied to classification domains where I-PT-RED or P-PT-RED might be applied (such as CIFAR-10)? Which method should be preferable for such domains? Explain.
- I-PT-RED did not require multiple random initializations in performing its perturbation optimization procedure. Why are multiple random initializations required for T-PT-RED?
- Why is averaging performed on line 16 of Algorithm 8.1? What is being assumed, in performing such averaging?
- Explain why it should be possible to perform additive perturbation optimization within T-PT-RED even if the actual backdoor embedding mechanism was patch replacement.
- Does the T-PT-RED procedure of Algorithm 8.1 actually depend on ϵ? If not, explain why.
- Explain when it makes sense to use an "untargeted" definition of transferability rather than a "targeted" definition.
- In some applications, for example, in-flight detection of backdoor triggers at test time, the defender needs to make use of an estimated backdoor pattern (for an assumed backdoor embedding function). Suggest how the backdoor pattern can be estimated within T-PT-RED.

8.5 Project: Targeted Transfer Post-Training Reverse-Engineering Defense (T-PT-RED) for Multiple Classes

Consider a variant of the above pseudocode detection procedure wherein (i) there are more than two classes on the domain and (ii) both the ET definition and the detection procedure use a *targeted* definition of misclassifications (recall Section 8.3.1). Estimate a (targeted) ET statistic for all $K(K-1)$ class pairs, and make a detection if any pair has an ET statistic above the $\frac{1}{2}$ threshold. Apply this approach to single-attack detection on the CIFAR-10 dataset. Report true detection and false positive rates. Also report results when a detection is only deemed successful if both the source and target classes are correctly inferred. Is the threshold of $\frac{1}{2}$ effective for this multi-class, targeted version of T-PT-RED? Compare against the performance of I-PT-RED.

8.6   Project: Transfer Post-Training Reverse-Engineering Defense (T-PT-RED) for Backdoor Patches

Recall the discussion of Section 8.2.1 and suppose sample-wise $(\underline{x})$ additive perturbation optimization is used to find putative adversarial perturbations $(\underline{v})$, as described in this chapter. For a clean sample $\underline{x} \in \mathcal{D}$, zero out the elements of $\underline{v}$ which are less than a threshold z, leaving $\underline{\tilde{v}}$ whose support is essentially a mask $\underline{m}$. That is, for image $\underline{x}$, at every (pixel, channel) coordinate i, $m_i = \mathbf{1}\{|v_i| > z\}$ where $z \geq 0$. A *putative* patch BP for clean sample $\underline{x}$ is thus

$$\underline{\pi} = \underline{m} \circ (\underline{x} + \underline{v}),$$

where $\circ$ is (pixel, channel)-wise multiplication. Here, when transferring $\underline{x}$'s $\underline{\pi}$ to another sample $\underline{y} \in \mathcal{D}$ as in T-PT-RED, $\underline{\pi}$ is incorporated as a patch, that is, the modified $\underline{y}$ sample is

$$\underline{\pi} + (\underline{1} - \underline{m}) \circ \underline{y}.$$

1. Evaluate the performance of this variant of T-PT-RED for patch-incorporated backdoor patterns. In particular, sweep an ROC curve by varying the hyperparameter z for each attack-defense experiment (where the detection threshold is always $\frac{1}{2}$). Note that this may only sweep a partial ROC curve, up to some false positive rate less than 1. Consider either fixed position (imperceptible or perceptible), or perceptible and scene-plausible BPs.
2. Compare this approach with a version of T-PT-RED based on the application of sample-wise NC, which directly estimates the (relaxed) mask and patch for each sample.
3. Also test these defenses against additive, imperceptible BPs. Negative results would indicate that the transferability of *both* patch-replaced and additive putative BPs should be applied, with a detection made if either detector triggers.
4. Do an experiment with $K > 2$ classes and multiple BAs, each with different patch BPs, where some BAs have the same source class(es) and others the same target class. Also, where *not* all non-target classes are source classes of a BA. For this attack scenario, evaluate the "untargeted" T-PT-RED of Section 8.2.3 and compare it against the T-PT-RED of Section 8.3.3 (where the latter aggregates all possible source classes).
5. Explain how a sample-wise additive perturbation can be interpreted as a blended (NC's backdoor embedding representation) or multiplicative one. For blending, take

a special case of (6.1) involving a *Boolean* mask $\underline{m}$, a real parameter $\alpha \in \{k/n \mid k \in \{1, 2, \ldots, n-1\}\}$ with integer $n > 2$, and method of backdoor image $\underline{v}$ incorporated into clean image $\underline{x}$ given by:

$$\alpha \underline{x} \odot (\underline{1} - \underline{m}) + (1 - \alpha) \underline{v} \odot \underline{m}.$$

So, for each additive perturbation of $\underline{x}$, this will create $n - 1$ candidate blended perturbations, and a separate ET statistic can be computed for each α and each putative source class. Conduct an experiment to assess the detection performance of this approach.

9 Universal Post-Training (PT) Backdoor Defenses

In previous chapters, we developed RE based backdoor detectors wherein putative backdoor patterns (BPs) are estimated based on a particular backdoor pattern embedding function assumed to be used by the attacker (e.g., additive or patch-replace backdoor embedding). But there is a vast space of possible embedding functions that could be used by an attacker. Even if applied to embedded features, *RE detectors may fare poorly when the embedding function (or embedding functions in an RE ensemble)* assumed by the defender does not match the embedding function used by the attacker. In this chapter we describe some unsupervised post-training (PT) defenses that do not make any explicit assumptions regarding the backdoor pattern or how it was incorporated into clean samples by the adversary. *In this sense these backdoor defenses aspire to be "universal."* These new detectors exploit an experimentally confirmed property – that for backdoor poisoned DNNs, for the target class of an attack, the maximum achievable margin is unusually large, compared to that for non-target classes. This is likely due to very large magnitude weights triggered by neurons that detect the backdoor pattern, and which conduct (often via unbounded ReLU activations) to the class logits. While these defenses do not *rely* on (nor do they produce) reverse-engineered BPs, there is a tradeoff here – estimated BPs provide valuable explainable AI information and they may be essential for detecting backdoor triggers at test time, see Chapter 10, as well as for cleansing the training dataset (recall Chapter 5).

We start the chapter by describing a universal backdoor detector that *does not* leverage a small set of clean labeled data [286]. (How detection can be potentially improved by exploiting available clean data is discussed in a project.) Then a universal backdoor *mitigation* strategy is described that *does* leverage a small clean dataset, $\mathcal{D}$. In each backdoor attack (BA) scenario that is experimented with in this chapter, various detection and mitigation strategies are compared, where some mitigation strategies are also known as "unlearning" defenses. Note that the "blurring" defense mentioned in Sections 4.2.1 and 5.3 falls in this category, where the hope is that blurring the input destroys the backdoor pattern while not compromising the source (true) class discriminative features. Some unlearning defenses modify or augment the DNN's parameters, while others do not.

9.1 Universal Backdoor Detection (UnivBD) Without Clean Labeled Data

This section describes a universal PT backdoor detector (UnivBD) which is based on a *maximum margin* (MM) detection statistic that is estimated for each class by applying neural network inversion (recall Section 2.10), starting from a set of *randomly* generated input patterns. A fully unsupervised anomaly detector is then applied to the MM statistics as detection inference. Thus, unlike some other PT methods, no hypothesis concerning the backdoor embedding function is required and no clean samples are needed for detection. Moreover, this method detects backdoor attacks (BAs) with an *arbitrary* number of source classes and with lower *computational complexity* than some other PT defenses. Again, it is emphasized that, for the MM based approach, no assumptions are made regarding the backdoor pattern, method of incorporation, or the number of classes involved in the backdoor attack.

9.1.1 Key Ideas of the UnivBD Procedure

Consider a backdoor attack (BA) with target class $t \in \mathcal{Y}$ and denote the DNN classifier's logit function associated with any class $i \in \mathcal{Y}$ as

$$f_i : \mathcal{U} \to \mathbb{R},$$

assuming $\mathcal{U} \subset \mathbb{R}^N$ is the compact set of feasible inputs. (A set $\mathcal{U} \subset \mathbb{R}^N$ is compact if it is closed and bounded, where a set is closed if it contains the limits of all convergent sequences within it.) Consider the following general hypothesis for a backdoor poisoned DNN having target class t:

$$\max_{\underline{x} \in \mathcal{U}} \left[f_t(\underline{x}) - \max_{k \in \mathcal{Y} \setminus t} f_k(\underline{x}) \right] \gg \max_{\underline{x} \in \mathcal{U}} \left[f_i(\underline{x}) - \max_{k' \in \mathcal{Y} \setminus i} f_{k'}(\underline{x}) \right], \quad \forall i \in \mathcal{Y} \setminus t. \quad (9.1)$$

That is, the MM statistic for the true BA target class (defined as the left-hand side of (9.1), recall (2.12)) will tend to be *much larger* than the MM statistics for all other classes (right-hand side of (9.1)).

Why should a BA cause this phenomenon? Note that a BP is typically a *common* pattern[1] embedded in all samples used for poisoning the classifier's training set; and the same BP will be embedded in test samples to induce test-time misclassifications. By contrast, non-BP class-discriminating features typically exhibit high variability – for example, birds of different species, or even the same object captured under different views, range, or lighting conditions. (In extreme cases, class-discriminating features may be highly common across samples from the same class, which creates an "intrinsic backdoor" hardly distinguishable from backdoors planted by an attacker [306], see Chapter 11; a general solution to rule out such "intrinsic backdoors" is still an open problem.) The commonality of a BP is critical for it to override class-discriminating

---
[1] Some recently proposed BAs use BPs that are sample specific, see [144, 197] and recall Section 6.9. However, these BPs embedded in different samples still share common semantic features and are similar to each other in some latent embedding space. Thus, these BAs are still detectable by the UnivBD detector described here, as shown in the Appendix of [286].

features that will favor deciding to the source class and also so that the BP can be easily learned (at a low poisoning rate) by the victim classifier during training (recall Section 1.4.2). However, the repetition of the common BP in the training set also induces an inevitable overfitting which (i) boosts the target class logit (by causing abnormally large activations from neurons positively correlated with this logit), and (ii) suppresses the logits of all other classes (with these phenomena shown empirically in Section 9.3.2). Consequently, an abnormally large margin between the target class logit and the logits of all other classes is engendered by a backdoor, due both to the "boosting" and "suppression" effects.

The following simple calculation supports this hypothesis. Let f_i be the class-i logit (penultimate layer) activation function for a backdoor poisoned DNN with target class t. Suppose an additive backdoor pattern $\underline{v}$ has small magnitude (so that the incorporated backdoor is innocuous or even imperceptible). Consider a clean sample $\underline{x}_s$ from source class $s \neq t$ that was used to create a backdoor poisoned training example. We can use Taylor's theorem at $\underline{x}_s$ to approximate

$$f_i(\underline{x}_s + \underline{v}) \approx f_i(\underline{x}_s) + \langle \underline{w}_i, \underline{v} \rangle, \qquad (9.2)$$

where $\underline{w}_i := \nabla f_i(\underline{x}_s)$ for all classes $i \in \mathcal{Y}$. Assume that after (supervised) deep learning, each training sample $\underline{x} \in \mathcal{X}$ (including the poisoned samples) is classified correctly with margin at least $\tau > 0$, that is:

$$f_{c(\underline{x})}(\underline{x}) - \max_{k \neq c(\underline{x})} f_k(\underline{x}) \geq \tau.$$

Thus, for the poisoned training sample $\underline{x}_s + \underline{v}$ classified to t,

$$f_t(\underline{x}_s + \underline{v}) - f_s(\underline{x}_s + \underline{v}) \geq \tau. \qquad (9.3)$$

Substituting (9.2) gives

$$f_t(\underline{x}_s) + \langle \underline{w}_t, \underline{v} \rangle - (f_s(\underline{x}_s) + \langle \underline{w}_s, \underline{v} \rangle) \geq \tau. \qquad (9.4)$$

By assumption, $\underline{x}_s$ is also classified to s with margin at least τ, that is,

$$f_s(\underline{x}_s) - f_t(\underline{x}_s) \geq \tau. \qquad (9.5)$$

Adding (9.4) and (9.5) gives that the derivative of $f_t - f_s$ at x_s in the direction of small magnitude $\underline{v}$,

$$\langle \underline{w}_t - \underline{w}_s, \underline{v} \rangle \geq 2\tau, \qquad (9.6)$$

(recall (2.7)). For the special case where $f_t - f_s$ is linear, the previous display gives

$$f_t(\underline{v}) - f_s(\underline{v}) \geq 2\tau. \qquad (9.7)$$

This loosely suggests that after deep learning on the backdoor poisoned training dataset, the model has a stronger "affinity" between the target class and the backdoor pattern (9.7) than that between the source class and the class-discriminative features of clean source class samples (9.5).

Note that in the above discussion, it is also being implicitly assumed that *only* the backdoor pattern (or patterns highly correlated with it) will induce such abnormally

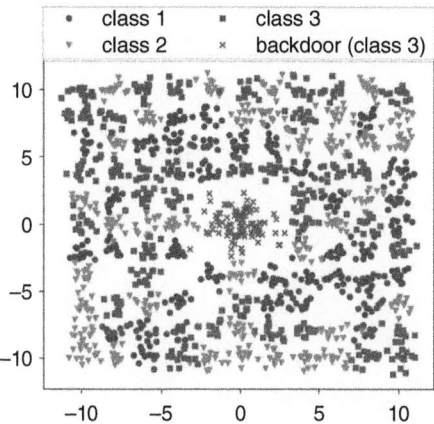

Figure 9.1 Illustration of the distribution of samples from three classes. The backdoor samples with target class 3 (depicted by 'x's) form a component located in the center.

large margins – essentially, the backdoor pattern is in some sense unique in inducing very large margins. If this were not the case, then such *unconstrained* margin maximization might elicit large margins from inputs having nothing to do with the backdoor pattern (and perhaps involving putative target classes that are not in fact backdoor target classes). In such cases, margin maximization would likely produce lots of false positives. While the experiments on real-world image domains in this chapter do not explicitly confirm uniqueness of the backdoor pattern in inducing large margins, they do implicitly support this claim, as good detection accuracy, for different data domains and for various backdoor patterns and embedding functions, will be seen in the sequel.

The above reasoning is visualized in Figures 9.1 and 9.2 using a toy example. Consider two-dimensional inputs from three classes, with the sample distribution for each class specified by a Gaussian mixture model (each with a large number of components to mimic the high variability of class-discriminating features). Five hundred training samples per class were generated, and two BAs were launched (both with target class 3), respectively with 10 (BA-10) and 100 (BA-100) "backdoor samples" inserted for poisoning – the backdoor samples were generated according to a single Gaussian component centered at the origin (*i.e.*, the backdoor pattern is highly reproducible, unlike the non-backdoor class patterns). This is analogous to a patch replacement attack applied to an image (recall Chapter 7), except one that is replacing all (in this case, both) input features, not just a (small) patch of features. For each BA, a multilayer Perceptron was trained with three hidden layers (see [63]), which achieves nearly 91% accuracy on clean test samples for both BAs. The attack success rates of the trained classifiers on test "backdoor samples" are 92% and 99% for BA-10 and BA-100, respectively. In Figure 9.2, for each BA and each class, the margin between the class logit and the largest logit among the other two classes is plotted as a function of the input space (only positive values are kept for better visualization). It is clearly observed that the backdoor target class (class 3, in Figure 9.2c and f) has abnormally large MM for both BAs (which agrees with Eq. (9.1)). Moreover, while there are multiple local maxima for each putative target class, the global maximizer for the true BA target class is much

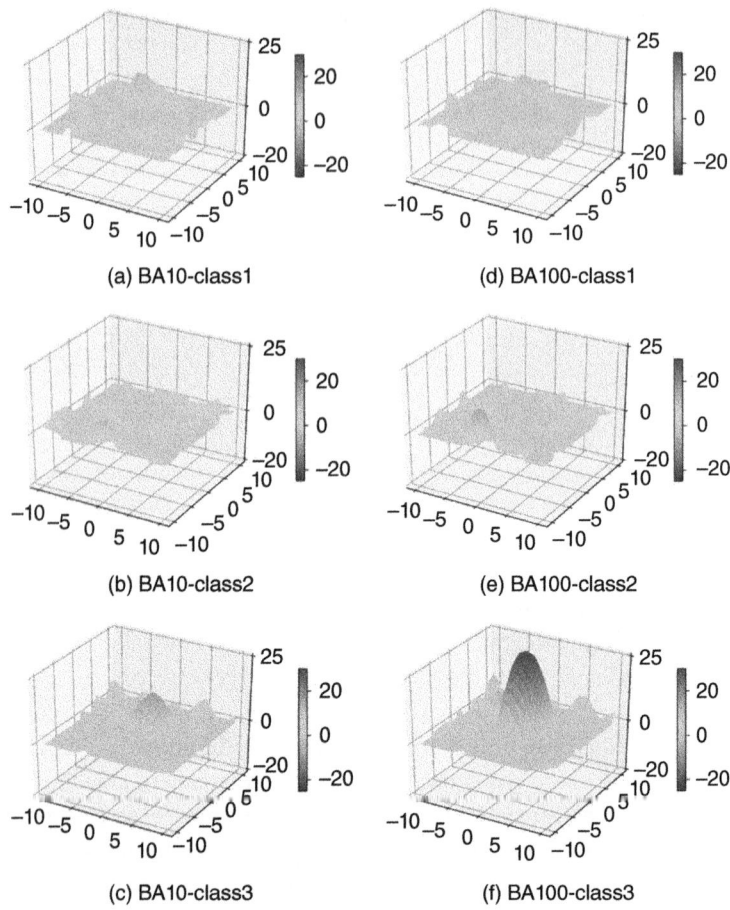

Figure 9.2 Illustration of the key ideas of the universal backdoor detection method. For two-dimensional input and three classes following the sample distribution in Figure 9.1, consider two BAs (BA-10 (a, b, c) and BA-100 (d, e, f)) with different poisoning rate but the same target class, class 3. For both BAs, the maximum margin for class 3 ((c) and (f)) is abnormally large compared with that for the non-target classes ((a, d), class 1; (b, e), class 2).

larger than other local maxima for the true target class, as well as much larger than all maxima for all the other classes. Finally, compared with BA-10, the atypicality of the MM for the BA target class is more obvious for BA-100 (note that the higher poisoning rate may in fact be preferred by the attacker since this yields a higher attack success rate).

9.1.2   UnivBD Detection Procedure

Estimation Step: For each putative target class $i \in \mathcal{Y}$, a MM statistic is estimated by solving:

$$\underset{\underline{x} \in \mathcal{U}}{\text{maximize}} \quad f_i(\underline{x}) - \max_{k \in \mathcal{Y} \setminus i} f_k(\underline{x}) \tag{9.8}$$

using gradient ascent with projection onto $\mathcal{U}$ (e.g., $\mathcal{U} = [0,1]^{H \times W \times C}$ for color images with height H pixels, width W pixels, and C channels) until convergence, which is guaranteed for continuous logit functions and compact $\mathcal{U}$. (If images are vectorized and normalized, then $\mathcal{U} \subset [0,1]^N \subset \mathbb{R}^N$, where $N = HWC$ and 8-bit pixel intensities $\in \{0,1,\ldots,255\}$ are mapped to the real interval $[0,1]$.) As is common practice (and as motivated even by the results for the toy example in Figure 9.2, where there are multiple local maxima when maximizing margin), such optimization is performed for multiple *random* initializations in $\mathcal{U}$ (e.g., for images, pixel values are uniformly randomly initialized in the interval $[0,1]$), with the best solution then selected. Compared with REDs, which may suffer from mismatch between the assumed BP embedding type and the true attack BP type, note that solving the above optimization problem does not require making any hypothesis concerning the BP embedding type. Moreover, the BP estimation of some REDs using clean samples from *all* non-target classes has been found experimentally to fail when the majority of these classes are not source classes [243]. By contrast, this universal backdoor detection method (like I-PT-RED) can detect BAs with an arbitrary number of source classes, since (9.8) above does not require any assumption about the number of involved source classes. Finally, unlike I-PT-RED, (9.8) does not rely on the availability of any clean samples.

Unsupervised Detection Inference Step: Denote the estimated MM statistic for each class $i \in \mathcal{Y}$ as r_i and the largest statistic as $r_{max} = \max_{i \in \mathcal{Y}} r_i$. It is hypothesized that, when there is a BA, r_{max} will be associated with the BA target class and will be an outlier to the distribution of MM statistics for non-target classes. Thus, a null distribution H_0 (a CDF) is estimated using all statistics excluding r_{max}. Given that the MM is strictly positive, single-tailed density forms with non-negative support are chosen for the null distribution, for example, a Gamma distribution in the following experiments. (MM is positive so long as every class has an input region where it is the decided class, and MM was experimentally observed to be positive for all classes.) To evaluate the atypicality of r_{max} under the estimated null, an *order statistic* p-value is computed as:

$$pv = 1 - H_0(r_{max})^{K-1}, \tag{9.9}$$

where $K = |\mathcal{Y}|$ is the total number of classes in the domain; recall Section 6.3.3. It can easily be shown that pv follows a uniform distribution on $[0,1]$ under the null hypothesis of "no attack." (The CDF of the maximum of $K-1$ i.i.d. samples each $\sim H_0$ is $F = H_0^{K-1}$, and recall (3.19).) Thus, a detection with confidence $1 - \theta$ is claimed if $pv < \theta$ (e.g., with $\theta = 0.05$). If a BA is detected, the class associated with r_{max} is inferred as the BA target class.

9.1.3   Detection Experiments

We conducted experiments mainly on four benchmark datasets with different image resolutions, image sizes, and number of classes: CIFAR-10, CIFAR-100, Tiny ImageNet, and GTSRB [250].

In the following, we assess the effectiveness of UnivBD and several other PT detectors in terms of detection accuracy and computational efficiency for a variety of BA configurations (with different BP types and numbers of source classes).

Settings
Consider three commonly used BP types:

- additive (Eq. (6.3)),
- patch replacement (Eq. (7.1) with Boolean mask), or
- blended patch replacement (Eq. (6.1), with a relaxed mask).

For the additive BP, again consider a global chessboard watermark pattern and a local pixel perturbation (recall Section 6.4.2). For the patch replacement BP, consider a noisy patch from [275] and a "unicolor" patch from [282]. The blended BP uses a noisy patch from [307]. For convenience, respectively denote the above five BPs as A_1-A_5. For A_2, the pixel being perturbed is randomly selected and fixed for each attack; for A_3-A_5, both the color and the location of the patch are randomly selected and fixed for each attack. Examples of these five BPs are shown in Figure 9.3. (Additionally, sample-specific BPs, as discussed in Section 6.9, and "warping" based BPs, as discussed in Section 6.10, are considered in the Appendix of [286].)

As is typically done, consider BAs with one target class (randomly selected for each attack). However, BAs are allowed to have one or multiple source classes – for brevity, these two source class settings are respectively denoted as 'S' (for "single") and 'M' (for "multiple"). For each BA with the 'S' setting, the source class is randomly selected. For Tiny ImageNet, ten source classes are randomly selected for each BA with the 'M' setting; while for the other three datasets, all classes other than the target class are selected as the source classes (which is assumed by the detectors in [93, 157, 282]) for the 'M' setting. With the above notations, a BA with "chessboard" BP and multiple source classes is denoted as 'A_1-M'.

An ensemble of backdoor poisoned classifiers is generated by randomly selecting the training samples to be poisoned for each classifier in the ensemble; recall Section 6.4.1. Likewise, an ensemble of clean classifiers is created by randomly selecting a subset of training samples, from the full training pool, for the training of each classifier in the ensemble. For CIFAR-10, ten *ensembles* of BAs are created, one for each combination of A_1-A_5 and 'S'/'M'. For CIFAR-100 and GTSRB, five BA ensembles are created for A_1-A_5, all with the 'M' setting. BAs are not created with a single source class for these two datasets because one cannot generate sufficient backdoor training images to launch a successful BA, given the limited number of images in each class for these two datasets. For Tiny ImageNet, only one BA ensemble is generated with the setting 'A_3-M' since the amount of time needed to train a single classifier on this dataset is extraordinarily high. For each ensemble, ten different BAs are generated independently according to the specified settings using the classical ensemble "data poisoning" protocol from [89].

The DNN architectures used for CIFAR-10, CIFAR-100, Tiny ImageNet, and GT-SRB respectively are ResNet-18 [97], VGG-16 [245], ResNet-34 [97], and MobileNet

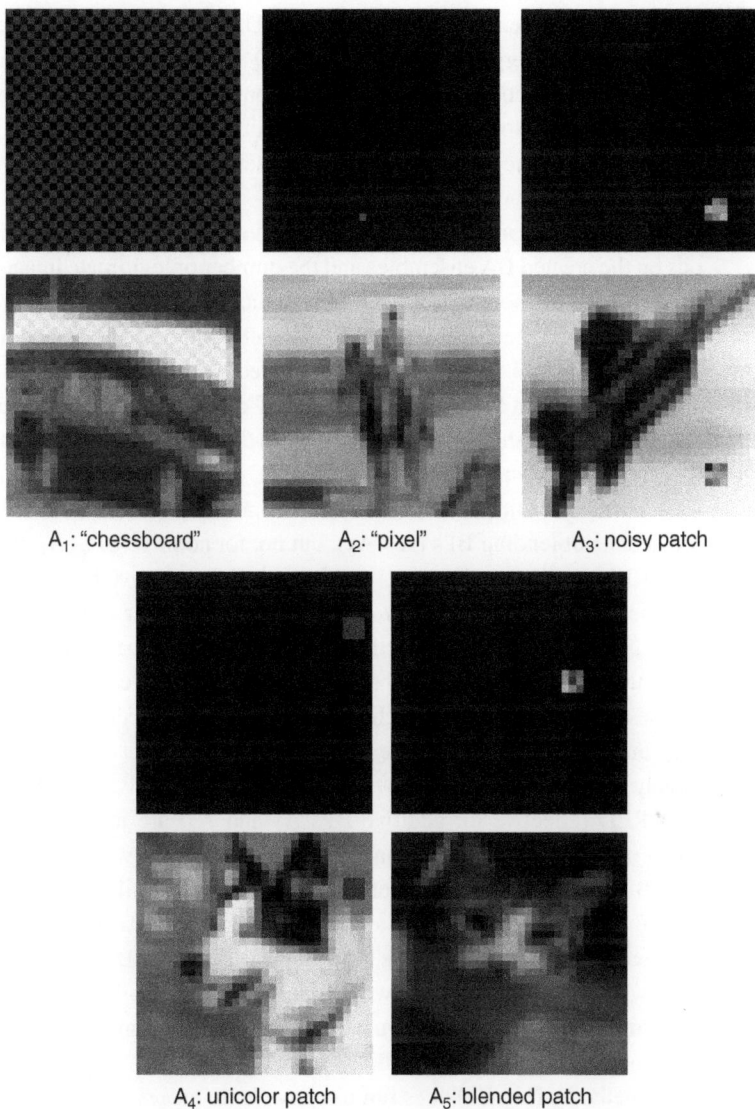

Figure 9.3 Example BPs used in experiments (top) and images with these BPs embedded (bottom). Some BP images are offset or scaled for visualization purposes.

[229]. All the BAs that were created are successful, with high attack success rate (ASR) and negligible degradation in clean test accuracy (ACC).

Detection Performance

Detection Configurations: UnivBD is compared with I-PT-RED (applied to the input, see Section 6.3) and five other PT detection methods: NC, TABOR, ABS, META, and TND (see Section 6.2). The original implementations for these other methods are followed with only modest changes (e.g., choosing the best detection threshold to maximize their performance). For UnivBD, problem (9.8) is solved using gradient ascent with convergence criterion $\epsilon = 10^{-5}$ (i.e., stop when the rate of change of the objective function between any two consecutive iterations is less than ϵ) and 30 random initializations. These choices are not critical to the detection accuracy. For the inference stage, the detection threshold is set to $\theta = 0.05$, that is, with 0.95 detection confidence.

Detection Accuracy: Table 9.1 shows the detection accuracy of the different methods on the created BA ensembles and the number of legitimate images per class $|\mathcal{D}|/K$ used by each method, for each dataset. A successful detection requires both the BA to be detected and the target class to be correctly inferred. Also shown is the proportion of clean classifiers deemed to be not attacked by each detector.

As discussed in Section 6.2, existing PT detectors presume one or more BP types. For example, NC shows strong capability in detecting BAs with patch replacement BPs (A_3 and A_4), for which it is designed; but NC fails to detect BAs with local additive BPs (A_2). Similar results are reported for ABS and META, which are designed for patch replacement/blending BPs (A_3–A_5), but not for additive BPs (A_1 and A_2). In contrast, I-PT-RED (applied to the input) performs well for additive BPs (A_1 and A_2), for which it is designed, but is generally ineffective for the other BP types (A_3–A_5). TABOR and TND do not show competitive performance compared with the other methods, since they adopt additional constraints on the shape or color of the BP. Distinct from all these methods, UnivBD achieves *high detection accuracy* for all BP types (A_1–A_5), and with a *low false detection rate* for all datasets; that is, its performance is largely **invariant to the BP type**. Even if ABS (effective for patch BPs A_3–A_5) and I-PT-RED (effective for additive BPs A_1 and A_2) are jointly deployed (detecting if either one detects), the detection accuracy on classifiers with BAs is just comparable to UnivBD, but with more false detections and a significantly greater computational cost. Moreover, NC, TABOR, ABS, and TND assume that BAs have multiple source classes (i.e., with the 'M' setting); thus they may easily fail for BAs with a single source class (i.e., with the 'S' setting). However, UnivBD is generally effective in detecting BAs with **arbitrary number of source classes**, as shown in Table 9.1, since it does not make any assumptions about the number of source classes. Finally, different from all other methods, UnivBD does **not** use any clean images for detection.

Detection Computational Efficiency: In Table 9.2, the average execution time (in seconds) of UnivBD is shown and compared with all the other detectors on the CIFAR-10 dataset. All experiments are conducted on a NVIDIA RTX-3090 GPU. Clearly, UnivBD is the most efficient among these detectors.

See the project in Section 9.5.

9.2   Universal Mitigation of Backdoor Attack (UnivBM)

When a BA is detected, if the victim classifier cannot be replaced by a new one from another trustworthy training authority, an alternative choice is to *mitigate* the backdoor attack on the poisoned classifier.

Table 9.1 Backdoor detection accuracy (accuracy ≥0.8 is in bold).

	$|\mathcal{D}|/K$	CIFAR-10										
		Clean	A_1-S	A_1-M	A_2-S	A_2-M	A_3-S	A_3-M	A_4-S	A_4-M	A_5-S	A_5-M
NC	10	12/20	4/10	**10/10**	2/10	3/10	**8/10**	**10/10**	**9/10**	7/10	3/10	3/10
TABOR	10	13/20	4/10	**8/10**	7/10	**8/10**	6/10	7/10	0/10	5/10	7/10	**9/10**
ABS	1	**19/20**	2/10	7/10	4/10	6/10	**8/10**	**10/10**	7/10	5/10	7/10	**8/10**
META	10k	15/20	**8/10**	6/10	0/10	0/10	**9/10**	**10/10**	4/10	2/10	**9/10**	7/10
TND	5	11/20	2/10	2/10	3/10	**8/10**	3/10	3/10	1/10	0/10	5/10	6/10
I-PT-RED	100	15/20	**10/10**	**10/10**	**9/10**	**10/10**	1/10	0/10	1/10	1/10	4/10	7/10
I-PT-RED+ABS	100	14/20	**10/10**	**10/10**	**9/10**	**10/10**	**8/10**	**10/10**	7/10	5/10	**8/10**	**10/10**
UnivBD	0	**18/20**	**9/10**	**8/10**	**8/10**	**10/10**	**10/10**	**10/10**	**8/10**	**10/10**	**9/10**	**10/10**

	$|\mathcal{D}|/K$	CIFAR-100				Tiny ImageNet			GTSRB				
		Clean	A_2-M	A_3-M	A_4-M	Clean	A_2-M	A_3-M	Clean	A_1-M	A_2-M	A_4-M	A_5-M
NC	1	4/10	3/10	**10/10**	**9/10**	3/10	3/10	**8/10**	13/20	**9/10**	5/10	2/10	6/10
TABOR	1	4/10	6/10	4/10	4/10	4/10	4/10	7/10	11/20	7/10	6/10	1/10	6/10
ABS	1	**10/10**	2/10	**9/10**	**9/10**	**9/10**	**9/10**	2/10	**17/20**	2/10	**9/10**	4/10	4/10
TND	1	2/10	2/10	2/10	5/10	5/10	5/10	3/10	12/20	3/10	4/10	0/10	6/10
UnivBD	0	**10/10**	**10/10**	**10/10**	**10/10**	**10/10**	**10/10**	**9/10**	**17/20**	7/10	**10/10**	**10/10**	**10/10**

Table 9.2 Average execution times on CIFAR-10.

NC	TABOR	ABS	META	TND	I-PT-RED	UnivBD
308 s	58 s	50 s	32 h	592 s	343 s	27 s

9.2.1   UnivBM Procedure

One mitigation approach (which can be applied if UnivBD makes a backdoor detection) is based on the observation that a BA induces a subset of neurons in each layer to have abnormally large activations (which are accumulated layer by layer, resulting in a large MM for the BA target class); such activations are particularly enabled by the (widely adopted) ReLU neurons, which allow unbounded (positive) activations. This "large activation" phenomenon is also the basis of the BA *detection* approach of ABS, though several hyperparameters are required, for example, to identify the neurons responsible for the large activations.

By contrast, consider the hypothesis that, for *each neuron*, a specific optimized upper bound should be applied in order to suppress any possible large activations caused by a BA, and without significant degradation in the classifier's accuracy on clean samples. Let $\sigma_\ell : \mathbb{R}^{n_{\ell-1}} \to \mathbb{R}^{n_\ell}$ be the activations of layer ℓ (for $\ell \in \Lambda = \{1, 2, \ldots, |\Lambda|\}$) of the victim classifier as a function of the activations of the previous layer. In the following, the number of neurons in each layer ℓ, n_ℓ, and the parameters of each neuron are not indicated for brevity, since none of them will be modified during this mitigation process.

For each input $\underline{x} \in \mathbb{R}^N$, layer ℓ, and neuron $i \in \ell$, define the function

$$\bar{\sigma}_{\ell,i}(\underline{x}) = \max\{\sigma_{\ell,i}(\underline{x}), z_{\ell,i}\}, \tag{9.10}$$

where $\sigma_{\ell,i}$ is the activation function of the DNN's neuron $i \in \ell$, and the scalar limiting activation $z_{\ell,i} > 0$ is used for backdoor mitigation purposes. Let the set of such scalars spanning the whole DNN with layers Λ be

$$\mathbf{Z} = \{\underline{z}_\ell\}_{\ell \in \Lambda} \text{ where the vector } \underline{z}_\ell = \{z_{\ell,i}\}_{i \in \ell}.$$

Also, for each class $k \in \mathcal{Y}$, define the function

$$\bar{g}_k(\underline{x}; \mathbf{Z})$$

as the kth logit of the DNN when the neural activations are $\mathbf{Z}$-bounded as in (9.10).

To find *the minimum activation upper bound for each neuron without affecting the classifier's performance on clean test samples*, one could pose the following problem:

$$\min_{\mathbf{Z}} \quad \sum_{\ell \in \Lambda} \|\underline{z}_\ell\|_2$$

$$\text{subject to} \quad \frac{1}{|\mathcal{D}|} \sum_{\underline{x} \in \mathcal{D}} \mathbf{1}\{c(\underline{x}) = \arg\max_{i \in \mathcal{Y}} \bar{g}_i(\underline{x}; \mathbf{Z})\} \geq \pi, \tag{9.11}$$

where $\mathbf{1}\{\cdot\}$ represents the indicator function, $c(\underline{x})$ is the ground truth class label of input $\underline{x}$, $\mathcal{D}$ is a small set of clean samples that are correctly classified (by the poisoned network) and used for BA mitigation, and π is the minimum accuracy benchmark (e.g., set $\pi = 0.95$). Here, the l_2 norm of the bounding vectors is minimized to penalize activations with overly large absolute values in each layer. However, as noted in Section 6.3.4, the correct classification count (and misclassification count) are not differentiable due to the indicator function, $\mathbf{1}\{\cdot\}$. One could construct a differentiable surrogate of the correct classification count, akin to what was done in Section 6.3.4.

But here a different approach is taken, in order to potentially exploit *more* supervision information than just the ground truth class labels on the clean set $\mathcal{D}$. In particular, suppose that backdoor poisoning, *even if present*, does not alter the real-valued class logits, evaluated on the clean set $\mathcal{D}$. If the classifier correctly classifies all samples in $\mathcal{D}$, then these logits are consistent with the ground truth class labels, that is, $\{\hat{c}(\underline{x}) = c(\underline{x})$ for all $\underline{x} \in \mathcal{D}\}$. However, they are substantially more informative than these class labels, as they provide information about the classifier's confidence in its (correct) decision-making, as well as which classes (with relatively large logits) are the nearest competitor classes to the correctly decided class. Accordingly, rather than seeking to maximize the correct classification rate on $\mathcal{D}$ (while suppressing large activations), we instead seek to agree as closely as possible with the logits f on $\mathcal{D}$. This is achieved by solving the following Lagrangian objective:

$$L(\mathbf{Z}, \lambda; \mathcal{D}) = -\frac{1}{|\mathcal{D}| \times |\mathcal{Y}|} \sum_{\underline{x} \in \mathcal{D}} \sum_{i \in \mathcal{Y}} [\bar{g}_i(\underline{x}; \mathbf{Z}) - f_i(\underline{x})]^2 + \lambda \sum_{\ell \in \Lambda} \|\underline{z}_\ell\|_2. \tag{9.12}$$

This problem is practically solved using gradient descent, where $\mathbf{Z}$ is initialized so that the bounds start off being quite liberal. The Lagrange multiplier λ is updated automatically so as to fulfill the constraint of problem (9.11), for example, see Section A.1.5. Finally, the classifier with the BA mitigated is obtained by applying a softmax to the logits $\{\bar{g}_i(\underline{x}; \mathbf{Z}^*), i \in \mathcal{Y}\}$ using $\mathbf{Z} = \mathbf{Z}^*$ that minimizes (9.12).

9.2.2 FP and NC-M Backdoor Mitigation

Neural cleanse mitigation (NC-M) is the mitigation approach associated with NC, see Section 6.2.3. NC-M embeds the BP reverse-engineered for the target class detected by NC into clean images from all source classes, and then fine-tunes (refines) the classifier deemed to be attacked on these images to "unlearn" the backdoor mapping. (Obviously, similar mitigation methods could be based on other PT-REDs including those discussed in previous chapters.)

On the other hand, fine-pruning (FP, see Section 6.2.2) removes neurons with low activations on clean images (these neurons are hypothesized to be "reserved" for BPs) subject to a prescribed budget of accuracy degradation. Then FP fine-tunes the classifier to recover its accuracy.

9.2.3 Mitigation Experiments

The above three backdoor mitigation approaches are evaluated using the ten BA ensembles created in Section 9.1.3 for CIFAR-10. Experimentally, NC-M is evaluated regardless of whether the BA is successfully detected by NC; NC-M is applied to each BA in each ensemble using the BP estimated by NC for the ground truth target class. Since FP does not perform BA detection, it is directly applied to all BA ensembles on CIFAR-10.

UnivBM is implemented with the accuracy constraint set to $\pi = 0.95$ and $|\mathcal{D}|/K = 20$ clean images per class ($K = |\mathcal{Y}|$) for mitigation. (Again, these settings are not critical to the performance of UnivBM.) For the convolutional neural networks used in the experiments, a common activation upper bound is applied to all neurons associated with the same convolutional filter, since the neuron activations in the feature map produced by a convolutional filter are spatially invariant.

For fairness of comparison, like NC-M, UnivBM is applied to all classifiers in the ten BA ensembles on CIFAR-10 independently of the detection performance.

Table 9.3 shows the average ASR and average ACC of classifiers over each of the ten BA ensembles created on CIFAR-10, for each of NC-M, FP, and UnivBM. Also shown are the number of clean images per class used by each method. Compared with the baseline without backdoor mitigation, NC-M significantly reduces ASR for most BA ensembles, though suffering non-negligible degradation in ACC for some ensembles (e.g., A_3-M). In fact, the performance of NC-M largely relies on the effectiveness of the NC detector in BP reverse-engineering and the hyperparameter choices such as the step size for (un)learning. FP does not perform well in removing the backdoor mapping, possibly because the FP hypothesis – that a subset of neurons are reserved solely for triggering the backdoor mapping – does not hold. However, FP yields the highest ACC among the three mitigation approaches. In comparison, with only 20 images per class (much fewer than the other two methods), UnivBM reduces ASR to much lower levels than the other two methods for BPs A_2–A_5, with only moderate degradation in ACC. In Section 9.3.1, it is shown that even better performance can be achieved by UnivBM for these BPs when a few more clean images are used. Unfortunately, UnivBM fails to mitigate BAs with the global additive BP (A_1).

Ensemble Mitigation: Given that UnivBM *does not* change the architecture or any trained parameters of the classifier, it can be naturally deployed together with other tuning-based mitigation methods. For example, as shown in Table 9.3, if UnivBM is deployed followed by FP, the ASR of the BAs (including those with BP, A_1) will be largely reduced (and close to zero for BPs A_2–A_5), and with little degradation in ACC.

9.3   Some Additional Experiments

9.3.1   Effect of Mitigation Design Choices

For ensembles A_3-M, A_4-S, and A_5-S, Figure 9.4 shows the resulting ASR and execution times over a range of number of clean images used by UnivBM for BA mitigation. For 50 images per class, observe the clear drops in ASR, especially for the A_4-S ensemble, with some (acceptable) increments in execution time. Even with as few as 10 images per class, UnivBM achieves decently low ASRs for all three ensembles.

Table 9.3 Average ASR (%) and average ACC (%) of classifiers in each of the ten BA ensembles created for CIFAR-10, after each of NC-M, FP, and UnivBM is applied for backdoor mitigation.

	$|\mathcal{D}|/K$		A_1-S	A_1-M	A_2-S	A_2-M	A_3-S	A_3-M	A_4-S	A_4-M	A_5-S	A_5-M
Without mitigation		ASR	99.94	99.94	91.09	91.28	99.41	99.92	97.78	98.44	96.36	96.86
		ACC	91.31	91.06	91.80	91.12	91.63	91.59	91.31	91.36	91.35	91.48
NC-M	500	ASR	39.58	38.45	26.94	61.23	21.75	28.30	55.86	93.20	13.37	47.53
		ACC	86.96	87.70	90.78	85.96	84.91	76.66	86.00	85.13	88.42	88.24
Fine-pruning	500	ASR	31.91	52.40	61.12	71.56	86.67	89.50	89.16	86.91	65.38	75.48
		ACC	90.72	90.60	91.19	91.45	91.18	91.59	91.32	90.90	91.59	91.61
UnivBM	20	ASR	99.42	99.46	7.84	8.98	3.05	1.80	12.23	5.02	10.79	9.97
		ACC	90.44	90.65	87.39	88.30	87.22	90.55	89.83	89.77	88.74	90.79
UnivBM with fine-pruning	500	ASR	55.17	53.14	2.44	2.39	1.18	1.70	1.22	1.22	2.30	2.28
		ACC	90.06	90.20	90.19	89.68	89.96	90.15	90.48	90.24	89.59	89.89

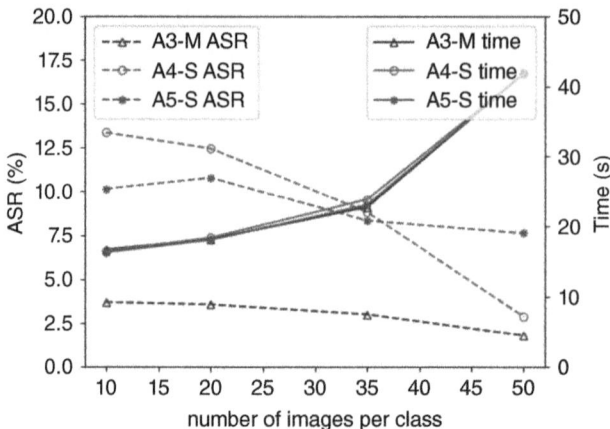

Figure 9.4 ASR and execution time for UnivBM over a range of clean images per class used for mitigation, for BA ensembles A_3-M, A_4-S, and A_5-S.

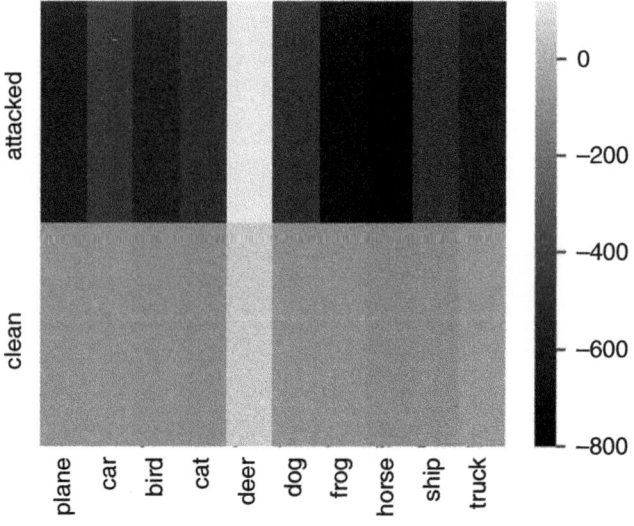

Figure 9.5 Logits of a classifier from A_2-S with target class 'deer' (top) and a clean classifier (bottom), when the logit of the 'deer' class is maximized.

9.3.2   Empirical Analysis of Maximum Margin Statistic

Here, it is shown that the existence of a BA boosts the target class logit, while perhaps even more importantly, suppressing the logits of all other classes. Consider a classifier being attacked with target class 'deer' from the A_2-S ensemble and a clean classifier, both for the CIFAR-10 domain. For both classifiers, UnivBD is applied with its MM objective, but with only the logit term displayed after solving problem (9.8). The logits for all classes for the two classifiers are shown in Figure 9.5. Even though the logits of all classes other than the 'deer' class are not "singled out" for suppression in the

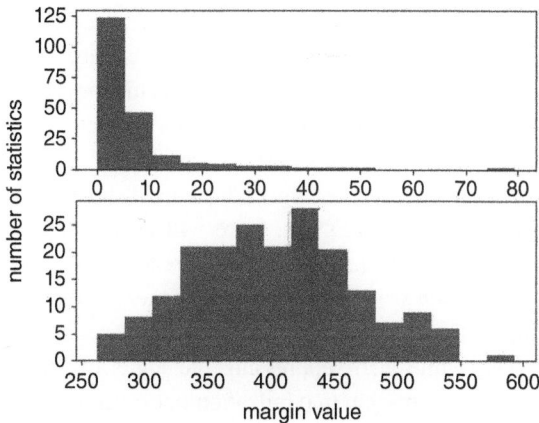

Figure 9.6 Histogram of margin statistics of a clean classifier trained on Tiny ImageNet using different maximization objective functions: maximize logits (top) and maximize margin (bottom).

(margin maximization) objective (9.8), significant decrements in these logits compared with the clean case are observed. Thus, while a BA may evade a detector based on pure *logit* maximization (where the "boosting" effect alone may not generate a sufficiently atypical statistic that is detectable), it will be easily detected by UnivBD based on MM, which produces both "boosting" and "suppression" effects.

However, could one maximize *just* the logit and then obtain a margin statistic for detection? Unfortunately, this alternative will easily lead to false detections, especially when a substantial number of classes have closely "neighboring" classes containing similar semantic features; recall Section 6.3.5. Here, we take a clean classifier trained on Tiny ImageNet for example. By maximizing just the logit (i.e., maximizing the first term of (9.8)) for, for example, the 'plunger' class, a similarly large logit for the 'drumstick' class will be obtained, possibly because the two categories of objects are similar to each other. Thus, the margin statistics obtained for the 'plunger' class will be small. Given a large number of such small margins (seen in the top of Figure 9.6), relatively large margins produced by classes without a "neighboring" class will likely appear as outliers, which will result in false detections. By contrast, UnivBD avoids false detections by directly maximizing the margin instead of the logit, which yields decently large margins for most classes, as shown in the bottom of Figure 9.6.

Additional experimental results are found in the Appendix of [286].

Finally, recall the description of the universal before/during training approach of [283] in Section 5.6.

9.4   Chapter Summary

In Chapters 5–8, we described RE based detectors wherein the detector implicitly assumes a particular backdoor embedding function was used by the attacker, for example, patch replacement, multiplicative, or additive (but recall Sections 6.4.4 and 8.2.1 regarding additive perturbations). If the embedding function implicitly assumed by a detector does not match that of the actual attack, the attack may evade it. Thus, there is motivation to develop a "universal" detector, that is, one that does not attempt to reverse engineer the backdoor pattern.

In this chapter we accordingly conjectured, and then experimentally confirmed, that for backdoor poisoned DNNs, there will exist input patterns that elicit decisions to the attacker's target class with much greater classification margin than for patterns that ground truth originate from the attacker's target class. In fact, we demonstrated experimentally that backdoor patterns simultaneously boost the logit of the attack's target class while also suppressing the logits of other classes (hence boosting the margin). Thus, a margin maximization optimization problem was formulated for each class, with a backdoor detected if there is a class with unusually large margin, compared with the remainder of the maximum margin detection statistics (with this atypicality again assessed by measuring an order statistic p-value). Moreover, unlike the PT-RE detectors from Chapters 6–8, which require availability of a small, clean dataset, the "universal" detector of this chapter, dubbed UnivBD, does not rely on any clean data. The effectiveness of UnivBD and other detectors was assessed on different datasets and various network architectures, and for different backdoor patterns and backdoor embedding functions.

Next, based on the same underlying hypothesis (that backdoors are successful by generating unusually large internal signals), we also described a post-training backdoor *mitigation* scheme dubbed UnivBM that essentially posits that the unboundedness of ReLU activation functions makes it much easier for a backdoor mapping to be learned. If, on the other hand, bounded activation functions replace ReLUs, this may mute/mitigate internal DNN signaling associated with a backdoor. We thus optimize a limiting activation threshold for every neuron in the DNN, choosing the smallest thresholds consistent with the DNN's accuracy on a clean dataset being maximally preserved – but rather than maximizing accuracy explicitly, the class logits on the clean dataset are preserved (which in fact preserves more information than mere class decisions). This method was demonstrated to outperform both the FP and NC-M procedures and to greatly reduce ASR with only moderate degradation in classification accuracy on clean test data.

Some questions to test the reader's understanding of the chapter include the following.

- Explain why it is plausible that a planted backdoor should make the DNN "susceptible" to inputs that elicit much larger margins to the target class of an attack than for non-attack classes. *Hint:* Note that the poisoned training patterns originate from source classes and, assuming the backdoor pattern is subtle, these samples still retain many features representative of their source class of origin.
- Why does (9.6) or (9.7) only *loosely* suggest that there is a stronger affinity between the target class and the backdoor pattern than between the source class and the class-discriminative features of the source class?

- In this chapter we showed that backdoor attacks can be substantially mitigated, post-training, by bounding the activations of neurons. What does this suggest about the choice of ReLU activation functions in DNNs?
- Why, do you believe, does the mitigation procedure fail to mitigate BAs with the global additive (chessboard) pattern?
- Relate the failure of pure logit maximization (as opposed to margin maximization) to the collateral damage phenomenon experimentally observed in Chapter 6.

9.5 Project: Universal Backdoor Detection (UnivBD) Versus Lagrangian Post-Training Reverse-Engineering Defense (L-PT-RED)

Compare detection performance and computational complexity of UnivBD against L-PT-RED (Section 6.5) operating on embedded features (Section 6.4.4), particularly for the additive global chessboard backdoor pattern. Also, create a L-PT-RED mitigation approach (like NC-M from NC) and compare it against UnivBM. Alternatively, use I-PT-RED instead of L-PT-RED.

9.6 Project: Reverse-Engineering Backdoor Patterns (BPs)

For each putative backdoor target class $t \in \mathcal{Y}$, start from an input $\underline{z}_t$ chosen uniformly at random and then perturb it to iteratively maximize the margin for that class (see Eq. (2.12)), yielding $\underline{z}_t + \underline{\delta}_t$. The hope is that $\underline{z}_t + \underline{\delta}_t$ contains the backdoor pattern and not "natural" class-discriminative features of class t when the DNN is backdoor poisoned to target class t. Note that there is no reason to expect that there are natural class-discriminative features in $\underline{z}_t + \underline{\delta}_t$ from any class other than t. Also note that the perturbations $\underline{\delta}$ could be added to activations of an internal layer rather than to the input layer (recall Section 6.4.4). Evaluate this approach as a method for reverse-engineering backdoor patterns.

9.7 Project: Universal Backdoor Detection (UnivBD) Leveraging Clean Labeled Data

Consider a variation of UnivBD which exploits an assumed available small clean (unpoisoned) labeled dataset $\mathcal{D}$ with representatives from each class: $\mathcal{D} = \cup_{i \in \mathcal{Y}} \mathcal{D}_i$. The foregoing UnivBD detection optimization starting from a random initial pattern may not find the global optimum margin statistic. So, one idea is to try starting the UnivBD optimization from clean samples, rather than random samples. Experimentally assess this idea.

Moreover, if one were doing classification using a generative model for each class, one would expect that the greatest discriminant function value for class i would come from the most representative example from class i (e.g., the mean of the distribution of examples from class i). Now, UnivBD maximizes margin in an unconstrained fashion, for example, it in no way constrains the logit values that may be achieved by the optimization. However, it is possible that a more reliable detection statistic will result if UnivBD's MM objective is constrained, based on the information in clean samples. Specifically, suppose one maximizes MM subject to the constraint that the logit value should be, for example, within two standard deviations of the mean logit value for clean samples from the class under consideration. Evaluate this constrained MM maximization approach within the UnivBD detection framework to see whether it gives any benefit compared with "vanilla" MM.

Finally, note that one way to understand UnivBD's maximization over the domain, to find the MM for a given class i, is to see if there is an input vector that has much larger discriminant value (or MM) than representative instances from class $i \in \mathcal{Y}$. This naturally leads to the following inference procedure, to couple with the above constrained MM optimization.

1. For all clean examples from class i, evaluate the margin (and do this for all classes).
2. Learn a null density from the clean example margins, separately for each class.

At test time, assess a p-value of the test sample $\underline{x}$'s classification margin (based on the learned null density for its decided upon class $\hat{c}(\underline{x})$); one can then assess an order statistic p-value (p-value on the p-values) to determine whether the network was backdoor poisoned. Evaluate this strategy on the CIFAR-10 dataset.

9.8 Project: Universal Detector Based on Deep Neural Network (DNN) Weight Outliers

A universal backdoor detection approach that is simple to implement is based on the hypothesis that a backdoor will result in some anomalously large neural network parameters, particularly edge or convolutional kernel weights. This assumption is also consistent with the hypothesis of Section 9.1.1 regarding how backdoors boost the logit of the target class and suppress those of the source class(es). Formulate a detector that (i) examines the ingress weights of each layer, (ii) forms a null distribution based on say the 95th percentile group according to the weight magnitudes, and (iii) evaluates the p-value of the largest magnitude edge weight. Formulate and assess a backdoor detection statistic considering all $|\Lambda|$ of these p-values (one for each layer). Alternatively, use the MAD to detect weight outliers.

9.9 Project: Mitigation Using Surrogates for Correct Decision Rate

Consider the backdoor mitigation approach of Section 9.2, but replacing the least squares objective to the logits by one of the surrogates for correct classification rate from Chapter 6. Compare the use of these two objectives for backdoor mitigation.

9.10   Project: Testing the Hypothesis that a Backdoor Preserves Clean Logits

Evaluate the hypothesis which motivated the backdoor mitigation objective (9.12), that is that a backdoor compromised classifier does not significantly alter the classifier's logits, evaluated on a clean dataset $\mathcal{D}$. Toward this end, design two classifiers on CIFAR-10, one containing a backdoor and the other backdoor-free, for different backdoor patterns. On a clean dataset, compute the logits for both classifiers. Then apply a softmax function to these logits, yielding a class posterior. Compute the average Kullback–Leibler pmf dissimilarity measure between the two class posteriors on $\mathcal{D}$ (recall Section 4.3.4). Is this measure small? Does the result support the hypothesis that a backdoor does not significantly alter the logits on clean examples?

9.11   Project: Modified UnivBM Objective to Reduce Margin

Again recall the hypothesis that the backdoor attack relies on overfitting. Modify the objective (9.12) of UnivBM to replace the second (activation-bounding) term with a penalty term involving the estimated maximum margin. Evaluate this variation of UnivBM.

9.12   Project: Defense Against Error-Generic Data Poisoning

Conduct an experiment to test the efficacy of UnivBM against "error-generic" poisoning, e.g., by label flipping, see Chapter 13.

10 Test-Time Detection of Backdoor Triggers

Previous chapters considered detection and remediation of backdoors before/during training and post-training. Here, our objective is to detect the exploitation of a backdoor trigger operationally, that is at test time. We use the phrase "in-flight" to refer to such detections. Such detection may prevent potentially catastrophic decisions, as well as potentially catching culprits in the act of exploiting a learned backdoor mapping. The described detector relies on either a before/during training RED or a post-training RED to infer that the DNN was poisoned and *also* relies on the estimated backdoor pattern produced by such a RED. In this sense, this chapter leverages the results from Chapters 5–8. An alternative "universal" approach based on classification margin, inspired by UnivBD of Chapter 9, is the subject of a project.

10.1 Some Test-Time Backdoor Detection Methods

Though the following methods were formulated for the image domain, they can also be applied to other data domains.

Neural cleanse (NC) [282] detects test images embedded with backdoor triggers by their activations on neurons that are "most relevant to" the backdoor pattern (recall Section 6.2.3). If the input image has activations higher than a given threshold for those neurons, it is deemed a backdoor trigger sample. Performance of this detector highly depends on the choice of these "relevant" neurons and on the detection threshold. For inferring the class of origin for a detected backdoor trigger image, NC exploits the reverse-engineered backdoor trigger obtained by applying the NC post-training detector (again recall Section 6.2.3). Post-detection, NC proposes to patch the poisoned DNN by fine-tuning it on 10% of the original training set (all identified by NC as backdoor free), 20% of which are embedded with the reverse-engineered backdoor pattern and correctly labelled.

B3D [61] is a black box detector which captures backdoor triggers based on the difference in model outputs for a test image with $(\underline{x} + \underline{v})$ and without $(\underline{x})$ the reverse-engineered backdoor pattern $(\underline{v})$ embedded. The two model outputs $(\hat{c}(\underline{x}), \hat{c}(\underline{x} + \underline{v}))$, are hypothesized to be very different if the test image is clean. The idea is that in this case one input, the clean input $\underline{x}$, will not possess the backdoor trigger, while the other, $\underline{x} + \underline{v}$, does. This should result in a change in the classifier's decision, relative to that of the clean input, that is, $\hat{c}(\underline{x}) \neq \hat{c}(\underline{x} + \underline{v})$. However, for a test image that *already* has the backdoor pattern embedded (i.e., $\underline{x}$ contains a backdoor trigger), embedding the reverse-engineered backdoor pattern "on top of this" is not expected to alter the class decision. Note that, for both backdoor trigger images classified to the target class and clean target class images, embedding a backdoor trigger may have little impact on the model outputs and, if so, they cannot be effectively distinguished by B3D.

Strong intentional perturbation (STRIP) [73] linearly blends a test image $\underline{x}$ with a few clean images $\in \mathcal{D}$ and detects backdoor triggers based on the entropy of the DNN's class posterior $\hat{p}(\cdot|\underline{b})$ for the blended image $\underline{b}$. A small entropy may indicate a backdoor trigger input $\underline{x}$. The hypothesis here is that, for clean test images $\underline{x}$, blending may distort the class-discriminating features, resulting in less confident decision-making. On the other hand, for backdoor triggered test images, the presence of the backdoor trigger should allow for confident decision-making even in the presence of blending. STRIP performance is sensitive to the size of the DNN model, as will be shown in Section 10.3.

All of these methods require careful choice of hyperparameters, including the detection threshold, whereas no such careful choice is needed for the following method.

10.2   In-Flight Reverse-Engineering Defense (IF-RED)

An in-flight (IF) detector of backdoor triggers (at test time), dubbed IF-RED, is now described. IF-RED leverages a PT-RED.

Defender's Goals: Given any *single* test image predicted to the target class t of a BA detected by a post-training (or before/during training) defense, IF-RED aims to (i) detect whether the test image contains the backdoor pattern (i.e., the backdoor trigger), and, if so, (ii) infer the true class of origin (source class) of the test image.

Defender's Knowledge: The defender has access to (i) the DNN detected as backdoor attacked, together with the target class t assumed correctly inferred by a PT-RED; (ii) the backdoor pattern (and its type) estimated by the PT-RED, and (iii) a (small) set of clean, labeled images from all classes. IF-RED does not make any assumptions about the location of the attacker's backdoor pattern. Thus, IF-RED can be coupled with any PT-RED and addresses a variety of backdoor patterns. Finally, IF-RED assumes no knowledge of the source classes involved in the attack (even though the PT-RED might identify the source classes), nor does it require enough clean data or computational resources to train a clean DNN *from scratch*.

10.2.1   Notation

Again denote the DNN (for which a post-training defense has detected an attack) by $\hat{c} : \mathbb{R}^N \rightarrow \mathcal{Y}$. Let f_ℓ be the outputs/activations of an internal layer ℓ of the DNN. Let t be the detected target class. Then, the actual source classes S_A involved in the attack, unknown to IF-RED, are a subset of all classes excluding the target class, that is, $S_A \subset \mathcal{Y} \setminus \{t\}$. Let $\mathcal{D} = \bigcup_{i \in \mathcal{Y}} \mathcal{D}_i$ be the small clean dataset possessed by the defender, where $\mathcal{D}_i$ contains images labeled to class i and correctly classified. Backdoor patterns of different types may be crafted and embedded in images in very different ways. Here let Δ be the true (ground truth) backdoor pattern and define the embedding function associated with Δ as

$$B(\cdot, \Delta) : \mathbb{R}^N \to \mathbb{R}^N,$$

such that a clean image $\underline{x} \in \mathbb{R}^N$ embedded with Δ can be written as $\underline{\tilde{x}} = B(\underline{x}, \Delta)$. Finally, denote the backdoor pattern estimated by the post-training defense as $\widehat{\Delta}$.

10.2.2   In-Flight Backdoor Defense

The estimated backdoor pattern $\widehat{\Delta}$ (with embedding function $\widehat{B}$) obtained by an effective post-training defense will likely elicit misclassification to the backdoor target class t, just as the true backdoor pattern Δ (used by the attacker and unknown to the defender), when they are embedded in source class images (as will be shown experimentally). But these two patterns may have very different intensity values in the image space, as visualized in [282]. Therefore, it is unreliable to determine whether a test image classified to class t is embedded with Δ by directly looking for the estimated $\widehat{\Delta}$ in the image. Even if a test image embedded with Δ is successfully detected, directly removing an estimated $\widehat{\Delta}$ (e.g., subtracting the estimated additive perturbation pattern, recall Chapter 5) from the image is not likely to remove the true backdoor pattern Δ completely; the image may still be classified to the target class t.

However, in deep layers close to the DNN output (e.g., the penultimate/logit layer), the true backdoor pattern Δ and its empirical estimate $\widehat{\Delta}$ will likely activate the *same* set of neurons when embedded in images from the same source class. These neurons are trained (on the poisoned training set) to activate for the backdoor mapping, and are hypothesized to be not wholly the same as the neurons activating for *typical* target class images. Thus, if a test image classified to the target class t is actually an image from some source class embedded with the backdoor pattern Δ, its deep layer activations are expected to be (i) similar to the activations for most images from the same source class embedded with the estimated pattern $\widehat{\Delta}$, and (ii) different from the activations for typical images from class t.

Based on the above intuition, IF-RED's detection steps are as follows. First, for each non-target class $i \in \mathcal{Y} \setminus \{t\}$, the estimated backdoor pattern $\widehat{\Delta}$ is embedded in the clean images used for detection, yielding

$$\tilde{\mathcal{D}}_i = \{\widehat{B}(\underline{x}, \widehat{\Delta}) | \underline{x} \in \mathcal{D}_i\}.$$

Then, all images in $\bigcup_{i \in \mathcal{Y} \setminus \{t\}} \tilde{\mathcal{D}}_i$ and the clean target class images $\mathcal{D}_t$ are respectively fed into the attacked DNN to get their deep layer ℓ (internal, embedded) features

$$\mathcal{Z}_i = \{f_\ell(\underline{\tilde{x}}) | \underline{\tilde{x}} \in \tilde{\mathcal{D}}_i\}, \quad \forall i \in \mathcal{Y} \setminus \{t\} \quad \text{and}$$
$$\mathcal{Z}_t = \{f_\ell(\underline{x}) | \underline{x} \in \mathcal{D}_t\}.$$

All the embedded features are then standardized to have mean 0 and standard deviation 1. For each class $i \in \mathcal{Y}$, a density model P_i (e.g., Gaussian mixture model) with parameters

$$\underline{\theta}_i = \arg\max_{\theta} \prod_{\underline{z} \in \mathcal{Z}_i} P_i(\underline{z}|\theta)$$

is then learned. *e.g.*, via the EM algorithm (see Chapter 3).

Then, *at test time*, for any test image $\underline{w}$ with class decision $\hat{c}(\underline{w}) = t$, its likelihood

$$\mathcal{L}_i = P_i(f_\ell(\underline{w})|\underline{\theta}_i)$$

is evaluated under the density model for each $i \in \mathcal{Y}$.

- If $\arg\max_{i \in \mathcal{Y}} \mathcal{L}_i \neq t$, $\underline{w}$ is deemed to contain the backdoor pattern and the prediction of the DNN is then rejected and, instead, the predicted class is chosen as $s = \arg\max_{i \in \mathcal{Y}} \mathcal{L}_i$.
- Otherwise, $\underline{w}$ is deemed clean and its class prediction $\hat{c}(\underline{w}) = t$ is accepted.

Note that, by learning density models for classes $i \neq t$ using the clean images from class i with the estimated BP embedded, one is learning the density for class i *in the presence of* the backdoor trigger – this is matched to the scenario where a test image from class $i \neq t$ is classified to class t due to presence of the backdoor trigger.

IF-RED has the following advantages over existing methods. Unlike NC, B3D and STRIP which are sensitive to the choice of hyperparameters, for example, a detection threshold, *no* hyperparameters are needed by IF-RED. Besides, IF-RED needs relatively few clean images (100 images per class in the experiments) for detection, compared with other methods, and is computationally cheap, as it does not involve tuning a complicated DNN. Note that the most time-consuming part of IF-RED, learning class-conditional density models, is also done offline.

10.3   Experiments

10.3.1   Experiment Set-Up

Dataset: We first report experimental results for the CIFAR-10 [129] dataset. We report experimental results on other datasets including MNIST [141], PubFig [131], and FMNIST [312] in Section 10.3.3.

Data Allocation: The test set of CIFAR-10 is randomly split into $\mathcal{D}$ and $\mathcal{I}$, where $\mathcal{D}$ consists of 100 images per class, and $\mathcal{I}$ is used for performance evaluation. $\mathcal{D}$ is used both for the PT detector (which estimates the backdoor pattern that is used by the IF-RED detector) and by the IF-RED (test-time) detector.

Attack Settings: Typical backdoor attacks described in previous chapters are considered. Class 9 is arbitrarily chosen as the target class for all attacks. The following three backdoor patterns are considered:

- CB, a global, additive chessboard perturbation, see Figure 6.4;
- SP, a single pixel set to 255; and
- WB, a 3 × 3-pixel white box embedded in the bottom right corner of an image as in [90].

For each type of backdoor pattern, two attacks are respectively created by (i) embedding the backdoor pattern in 1000 training images randomly selected from class 0 (single class attack), and (ii) embedding the backdoor pattern in 100 training images randomly selected from each class, except for the target class (multi-class attack).

Training Settings: For each attack, a DNN is trained with the ResNet-18 architecture (recall Figure 2.6) on the backdoor poisoned CIFAR-10 training set. Training is performed for 150 epochs with learning rate 0.1 (reduced by 0.5 per 50 epochs) and batch size 32.

Defense Settings: For each attack, a post-training detector, leveraging $\mathcal{D}$, is first applied to the DNN being attacked to infer the target class t and to reverse engineer the backdoor pattern $\widehat{\Delta}$. In particular, I-PT-RED (Chapter 6) is applied to attacks with additive backdoor pattern CB, and the NC detector [282] is applied to attacks with backdoor patterns SP or WB as they are embedded as small patches in the image. Thus, in these experiments, $\widehat{B} = B$. For IF-RED, the penultimate layer features are chosen for (maximum likelihood) estimation of a full covariance Gaussian mixture model (GMM) density for each class. BIC was used to decide the model order; recall Chapter 3.

10.3.2   Main Experimental Results on CIFAR-10

First, it is shown that the created attacks are sufficiently effective for their use in evaluating detection performance. Such effectiveness is evaluated by

- ACC, the clean test accuracy (ACC) defined as the DNN's accuracy on $\mathcal{I}$; and
- GT/ASR, the attack success rate (ASR) defined as the fraction of images from the source classes in $\mathcal{I}$ that are misclassified to the target class when the ground truth (GT) backdoor pattern (Δ) is embedded.

We also evaluate RE/ASR: the ASR for each attack using the backdoor pattern reverse-engineered (RE) by the post-training defense ($\widehat{\Delta}$) instead of the GT pattern. As shown in Table 10.1, all attacks have high ASR and almost no degradation in ACC compared with the baseline ACC of a DNN trained with no backdoor. The RE patterns induce similarly high misclassification rates to the target class as the GT patterns, when embedded in clean source class images from $\mathcal{I}$.

The effectiveness of IF-RED is evaluated in comparison with NC, B3D, and STRIP. The metrics for performance evaluation include true positive rate (TPR, i.e., the fraction of backdoor triggered test images correctly detected), false positive rate (FPR, i.e., the fraction of clean test images falsely detected), and source class inference accuracy (SIA, i.e., the fraction of backdoor trigger images with correct inference of the source class). As shown in Table 10.2, for all attacks, IF-RED performs very well – almost all the backdoor trigger images are correctly identified, and no clean target class images are falsely reported. Following [61, 73, 282], in-flight detectors for NC, B3D, and STRIP were built. As these papers do not disclose the thresholds used for detection, they were tested with various thresholds, with the best TPR at an FPR of around 5% reported. (A 5% FPR is not achievable by B3D for some attacks, even as the detection

Table 10.1 ASR and ACC for attacks using GT patterns; and ASR for the RE patterns obtained by post-training defenses applied to these attacks.

Attack pattern	Single class attack		Multi-class attack	
	ACC	ASR	ACC	ASR
No attack	0.9387	—	0.9387	—
CB-GT	0.9360	0.9955	0.9381	0.9954
CB-RE	—	1.0000	—	0.9876
SP-GT	0.9354	0.9488	0.9337	0.9565
SP-RE	—	0.9900	—	0.9953
WB-GT	0.9324	0.9411	0.9340	0.9497
WB-RE	—	0.9970	—	0.9354

Table 10.2 TPR, FPR and SIA for IF-RED, NC, B3D, and STRIP, against all the created attacks.

Attack pattern	Single class attack			Multi-class attack		
	TPR	FPR	SIA	TPR	FPR	SIA
			IF-RED			
CB	0.9922	0.0	0.8392	0.9997	0.0	0.6946
SP	0.9813	0.0	0.7728	0.9454	0.0	0.632
WB	0.9847	0.0	0.8607	0.9992	0.0	0.8945
			NC			
CB	0.9855	0.0488	0.9444	0.9962	0.0533	0.8765
SP	0.8088	0.0544	0.8833	0.9043	0.0511	0.8963
WB	0.0	0.0522	0.8667	0.8644	0.0522	0.8086
			B3D			
CB	0.0788	0.0511	—	0.9872	0.9955	—
SP	0.5333	0.1066	—	0.1814	0.0522	—
WB	0.0011	0.0500	—	0.0535	0.0511	—
			STRIP			
CB	0.0822	0.0533	—	0.0218	0.0555	—
SP	0.1333	0.0588	—	0.1555	0.0588	—
WB	0.0088	0.0588	—	0.0011	0.0633	—

threshold is varied over a wide range.) For STRIP, the weight of the incoming input is set to 0.5 in image blending. NC does not correctly detect any backdoor trigger images in a single class attack using the pattern WB. B3D does not perform well under all the attacks, as embedding the estimated backdoor pattern has little impact on the model outputs for both backdoor trigger images and clean target class images. STRIP does not perform well either (for ResNet-18 and CIFAR-10). STRIP is more effective for the DNN architectures, datasets, and attack configurations used in [73].

Since the NC paper does not mention the learning rate used for fine-tuning the DNN, in the experiments the poisoned DNN was fine tuned using various learning rates. From

Table 10.3 SIA of NC fluctuates with the learning rate (LeRa) used for DNN fine-tuning.

LeRa	10	1	10^{-1}	10^{-2}	10^{-3}	10^{-4}
SIA	0.1114	0.4291	0.6033	0.8086	0.7103	0.6348

Table 10.3, the severe fluctuation in SIAs for models poisoned by the multi-class attack using pattern WB, across different learning rates, shows the sensitivity of NC to the learning rate. Thus, NC was applied with all the learning rates, with the *best* SIA reported in Table 10.2. IF-RED performs relatively well in inferring source classes for the detected backdoor trigger images, though it is not as good as the *best results* of NC. However, note that IF-RED requires neither a clean dataset as large as the one used by NC for its fine-tuning, nor careful choices of hyperparameters.

IF-RED is also implemented on the last four convolutional layers of ResNet-18, the internal layers just before the penultimate layer. The dimensionality of the internal layer activations is reduced to that of the penultimate layer activations by simple average pooling. As shown in Table 10.4, the nearly perfect TPRs and FPRs demonstrate that the choice of the deep layer has little impact on IF-RED's detection performance. However, the choice of the deep layer affects source class inference accuracy for backdoor trigger images. IF-RED achieves the best SIA when applied to the penultimate layer.

10.3.3   Experimental Results on Other Datasets

IF-RED was also evaluated on datasets including PubFig, MNIST and FMNIST. For PubFig, 20 classes were randomly chosen, each with 80 training samples and 20 test samples. Class 19 was arbitrarily selected as the target class, with the backdoor pattern embedded in two training samples from each class except for the target class. The backdoor patterns considered for PubFig are Trojan square (SQ) and Trojan watermark (WM) [158], and the poisoned training set was used for training a DNN with the VGG-16 architecture [245]. The detector used five clean images per class (exclusive of the test samples used for evaluating detector performance). For each of MNIST and FMNIST, two attacks with backdoor patterns CB and WB, respectively, were used, and with the same attack settings as for the multi-class attacks described in Section 10.3.1. For each attack, a DNN with LeNet-5 [140] architecture was trained on the poisoned training set. Detector performance was evaluated on the (remaining) 15 test samples from each class – both clean and backdoor triggered versions of these samples. As shown in Table 10.5, IF-RED achieves overall good performance on these datasets.

10.4   Chapter Summary

Previous chapters considered defense against backdoors before/during training (Chapter 5) and post-training (Chapters 6–9). Here we considered detection of test-time

Table 10.4 TPR, FPR and SIA for IF-RED against all the created attacks on different DNN internal layers.

Attack pattern	Single class attack			Multi-class attack		
	TPR	*FPR*	*SIA*	*TPR*	*FPR*	*SIA*
Penultimate layer						
CB	0.9922	0.0	0.8392	0.9997	0.0	0.6946
SP	0.9813	0.0	0.7728	0.9454	0.0	0.632
WB	0.9847	0.0	0.8607	0.9992	0.0	0.8945
1st convolutional layer before penultimate layer						
CB	0.9977	0.0	0.7897	0.9996	0.0	0.6488
SP	0.9894	0.0	0.7562	0.9807	0.0	0.5271
WB	0.9941	0.0057	0.8598	0.9997	0.0034	0.8638
2nd convolutional layer before penultimate layer						
CB	0.9977	0.0011	0.7035	0.9998	0.0	0.6106
SP	0.9976	0.0011	0.5962	0.9948	0.0011	0.4923
WB	0.9976	0.0126	0.8544	0.9998	0.0267	0.8085
3rd convolutional layer before penultimate layer						
CB	0.9888	0.0023	0.6117	0.9997	0.0	0.5336
SP	0.9941	0.0081	0.6266	0.9922	0.0046	0.3738
WB	0.9976	0.0207	0.7857	0.9997	0.0500	0.7049
4th convolutional layer before penultimate layer						
CB	0.9888	0.0	0.5349	0.9997	0.0	0.4926
SP	0.9988	0.0302	0.6248	0.9976	0.0058	0.3705
WB	0.9952	0.0288	0.7581	0.9997	0.0848	0.6351

Table 10.5 TPR, FPR and SIA for IF-RED on datasets PubFig, MNIST and FMNIST.

	PubFig		MNIST		FMNIST	
	SQ	*WM*	*CB*	*WB*	*CB*	*WB*
TPR	0.9856	1.0	1.0	1.0	1.0	0.9951
FPR	0.1428	0.1428	0.0033	0.0022	0.0023	0.0127
SIA	0.7194	0.5507	0.9413	0.9764	0.6948	0.8039

samples that contain the backdoor pattern, that is, "in-flight" detection of backdoor triggering. Such detection can defeat the exploitation by an attacker of the planted backdoor mapping. Moreover, such detection may allow one to catch attackers in the act of backdoor triggering. IF-RED's detector assumes that a before/during training or post-training RE detector has already been applied to produce a backdoor detection decision (Y/N) and, if a backdoor is detected, an estimate of the backdoor pattern and identification of the target class. This information is coupled with a small clean dataset in order to learn a (e.g., GMM) density model for deep internal layer features of the DNN conditioned on the input (classified to the target class) being a clean example from the target class of the attack, and conditioned on the input being a backdoor embedded sample from each of the remaining classes from the domain. Thus, a hypothesis testing detection approach is applied, with a test sample that is classified to the target class of the attack deemed a backdoor trigger if its likelihood under the (clean) target class distribution is smaller than its likelihood under the (backdoor triggered) density model for one of the other classes. The class with the greatest likelihood can also be chosen to "correct" the classifier's decision, on detected backdoor trigger test instances. This method was demonstrated to outperform both alternative methods for test-time trigger detection, as well as for source inference accuracy (correcting the classifier's decision on backdoor triggered samples).

Some questions to test the reader's understanding of the chapter include the following.

- Is IF-RED a standalone detector, or must it be used in concert with other backdoor defenses?
- What are some disadvantages of IF-RED?
- Why does IF-RED *not* involve density models for non-target classes conditioned on the input being a *clean* sample originating from this (non-target) class?
- Why should IF-RED achieve its best source inference accuracy when applied to penultimate layer activations (as opposed to deep internal signals closer to the input)?
- Why does IF-RED not depend on hyperparameters?
- Can you suggest a modification of IF-RED that *does* use a detection threshold hyperparameter? Why, in practice, might this be needed?

10.5   Project: Trigger Detection via Test-Time Evasion (TTE) Attack Detection Strategy

An alternative backdoor trigger detector can be devised simply by applying the same anomaly detection techniques used to detect TTEs to detect backdoor triggers. Following this strategy, apply the basic ADA detector (Chapter 4) to detect backdoor triggers.

1. Choose a deep layer of the DNN (internal, embedded features) upon which the anomaly detection will be performed.
2. Perform null density modeling of this internal layer, conditioned on the DNN's correctly decided class, using a clean dataset of samples correctly decided to this class (perform this null modeling separately for each class).
3. At test time, evaluate a test sample decided to class i by the DNN using the null density conditioned on class i, and make a detection if the ADA test statistic is greater than the detection threshold.

Evaluate this detector with respect to TPR and FPR using the CIFAR-10 dataset (and compare with the reported results in this chapter).

10.6   Project: In-Flight Reverse-Engineering Defense (IF-RED) Using Imperceptible Backdoor Post-Training Reverse-Engineering Defense (I-PT-RED) Applied to Embedded Features

Apply I-PT-RED based on an internal layer feature representation (Section 6.4.4) to estimate BPs that are not additively incorporated. Use an internal layer closer to the input than that used by IF-RED, where the penultimate/logit layer is typically used for the latter. This can be coupled with the IF-RED detection procedure in one of two ways.

- Recall that IF-RED embeds the estimated BP into clean images, in the *image* space. Thus, to apply IF-RED as explicitly defined in this chapter, given a BP estimated in an internal space, one must first reverse engineer an estimated BP in image space via DNN inversion starting from the estimated BP in the internal layer space.
- Alternatively, one can simply add the estimated BP in the embedded feature space to the representation (activations) of clean images in this (internal layer) space.

Apply and compare both of these approaches for IF-RED based detection of backdoor triggers and source class inference.

For both of the above approaches, prior to density modeling the internal layer to be used by IF-RED, also apply PCA to reduce the dimensionality of the internal layer feature vector; recall Section 3.5. Evaluate whether PCA helps to reduce the number of clean samples needed for accurate density modeling (i.e., consistent with achieving good TPRs and FPRs for test-time trigger detection).

10.7   Project: Margin as an In-Flight Detection Statistic

Recall the MM based UnivBD method from Chapter 9 (see Eq. (9.1) and Section 9.7) used for post-training detection of whether a DNN was backdoor poisoned. Here consider margin as a detection statistic for whether or not a test image contains a backdoor trigger. Toward this end, for each class i, first learn a null density for the margins of clean samples $\mathcal{D}_i$ correctly decided to this class by the DNN. Then, for a given test sample decided to class t, evaluate its classification margin and assess an associated p-value, based on the null density for class t, to decide whether the sample contains a backdoor trigger. Note that this method, unlike IF-RED, does not rely on an estimated BP. If a backdoor trigger is detected, how can you apply this method to also estimate the source class? Compare this approach (for both trigger detection and source class inference) with the results of IF-RED from this chapter. Alternatively, null model the entire posterior distribution rather than just the classification margin.

11 Backdoors for 3D Point Cloud (PC) Classifiers

In previous chapters we exclusively considered attacks against image classifiers. Backdoor attacks have been considered in non-image data domains, for example, [9, 53, 158, 236, 328], and for non-classification applications, see Chapter 12. In this chapter, we consider classification of point cloud (PC) data (e.g., LiDAR), which has important applications, for example, in object recognition for autonomous driving and in industrial robotics. PC data is quite different from image data – a PC data object essentially captures the periphery/*shape* of an object. Thus, PC based DNN classifiers, in particular PointNet [38], are also quite different in architecture from image based classifiers. Moreover, concepts such as "imperceptibility" and "scene-plausibility" still exist for PC data, but are characterized differently for PC data compared to images. Accordingly, both attacks and defenses must be customized for the PC domain. Both backdoor attacks against PC classifiers, as well as defenses against such attacks, are devised and experimentally assessed in this chapter.

A point cloud is a collection of points that are typically obtained by sensing signal reflections off the surface of an object, with this collection essentially capturing the object's shape. Tools for 3D PC classification have been developing rapidly due to the increasing popularity of 3D applications in industry such as autonomous driving, industrial robotics, and augmented/virtual reality [43, 92]. Recently, DNN models (like PointNet), have demonstrated very good performance in 3D PC classification; hence they are widely used as the backbone of many 3D PC processing modules. For each PC input sample, a DNN may, for example, output up to a certain maximum number of detected objects, each with a class label and bounding box. However, these models are vulnerable to attacks, which typically aim to induce misclassifications during the classifier's operation [314]. In safety-sensitive domains, such as autonomous driving, such misclassifications, for example, incorrectly recognizing a pedestrian as a car (Figure 11.1), may have catastrophic consequences.

Test-time evasion (TTE) attacks have been devised against 3D PC classifiers. These attacks may involve adding points [274, 300], perturbing points [154, 293, 300], and/or deleting points [330]. Also, related spoofing attacks have been described [258]. As discussed in Chapters 1 and 4, TTEs are sample specific, innocuous modifications which are obtained by optimizing an objective function that (typically) assumes full knowledge (the architecture and parameters) of the victim classifier to be "fooled." However, in many practical cases, the victim classifier is not accessible to the attacker. Moreover, the *transferability* of existing PC TTEs is poor, that is, adversarial test

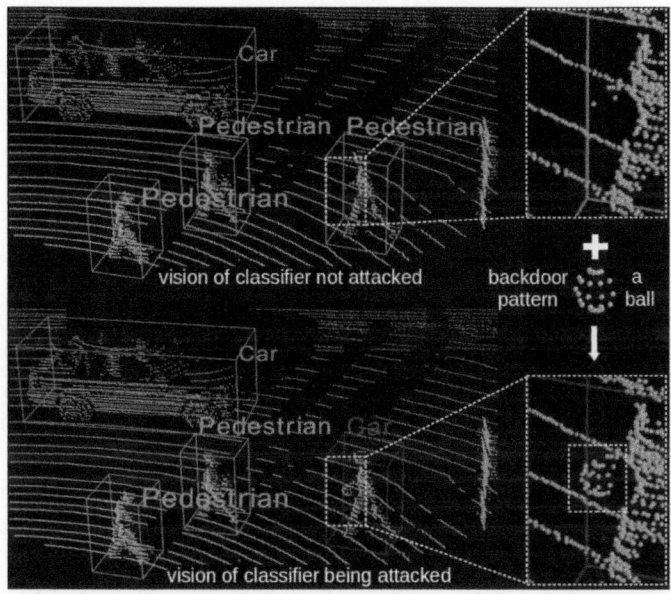

Figure 11.1 Illustration of a backdoor attack (BA) during the operation of a 3D PC classifier as part of an autonomous driving system. Top: If the classifier is not attacked it functions normally. Bottom: The attacker embeds a backdoor pattern to a PC associated with a pedestrian (e.g., by having the pedestrian carry a ball). The backdoor attacked classifier incorrectly recognizes the pedestrian as a car. Reprinted from [309] with permission.

samples created using a surrogate classifier *independently* trained by the attacker do not reliably fool the victim classifier [154, 300]. Thus, the threat of PC TTE attacks in practice may not be so high.

Devising a BA against 3D PC classifiers is challenging in several respects.

- **Challenge 1**: Existing backdoor patterns for image BAs considered in prior chapters do not apply to point clouds.
- **Challenge 2**: Designing a backdoor pattern learnable by 3D PC classifiers is difficult since they extract different features than image classifiers, especially different features than those of convolutional neural networks widely used for image classification such as ResNet and LeNet (recall Figure 2.6).
- **Challenge 3**: The backdoor pattern should be robust to test-time preprocessing of 3D PCs such as random sampling, should be evasive in the presence of anomaly detection (AD), and should be scene plausible (recall Chapter 7).

The PC BA considered here inserts a small cluster of points as the backdoor pattern (Challenge 1), dubbed "backdoor points," which can be implemented either digitally (to mimic, e.g., spurious points caused by vehicle exhaust), or physically using an object (e.g., a ball) captured along with the scene by the 3D sensor. The spatial location of the backdoor cluster is optimized by making use of a surrogate classifier that is *independently* trained by the attacker using their own (separate) dataset (for Challenge

2). Such optimization is necessary to ensure that the victim classifier will learn the backdoor pattern during its training. The local geometry of the actual backdoor points embedded in each PC sample is also optimized, such that these points have similar local density as the original points in the PC (for Challenge 3).

In this chapter we cover the following topics.

- A BA against 3D PC classifiers is described. Typical for BAs and unlike TTE attacks, it *does not* require any knowledge of the victim classifier design or of the clean data possessed by the trainer.
- The BA involves inserting "backdoor points" customized for 3D PCs, along with approaches for optimizing their spatial location and local geometry.
- The effectiveness of this BA is shown for four different types of backdoor point local geometries, three different architectures for the victim classifier, and for two data domains.
- It is shown through experiments that effectiveness of this BA mostly depends on the spatial location of the backdoor points, while careful design of their local geometry helps the BA evade state-of-the-art PC ADs.
- Finally, a general anomaly detection framework is described for defending against PC BAs, and its effectiveness is experimentally demonstrated.

Additional experiments can be found in [306, 309].
A different PC BA is proposed in [145].

11.1   3D Point Cloud (PC) Classification

A three-dimensional (3D) point cloud is a set of points in 3D space ($\mathbb{R}^3$) commonly captured by 3D sensors including radio detection and ranging (RADAR) [237], light detection and ranging (LiDAR) [321], and ultrasonic sensors [128]. Techniques for 3D PC classification have rapidly developed due to the increasing popularity of 3D sensors in many applications like autonomous driving [43]. Early approaches include 3D convolutional neural networks, for example, VoxNet [166], which represents 3D PCs using a series of voxels for classification. Multi-view based methods combine features associated with different views of an object into a global descriptor [256, 257]. PointNet directly takes a 3D PC as input and achieves permutation invariance of points by using a symmetric function, max pooling. Due to the simplicity and strong representation capability of PointNet, it is used as the backbone of many 3D learning modules [43], and is also the basis for many subsequent methods, for example, [211, 292, 317, 327]. PointNet (and its variants) is the DNN architecture we focus on in this chapter.

11.2   Backdoor Attacks against 3D Point Cloud (PC) Classifiers

Let

$$\mathbf{X} = \{\underline{x}_i \in \mathbb{R}^3 \mid i = 1, \ldots, |\mathbf{X}|\}$$

denote a PC[1] with points $\underline{x}_i$ and with associated class label $c(\mathbf{X}) \in \mathcal{Y}$, where here the (possibly poisoned) training set is

$$\mathcal{X} = \{\mathbf{X}_j \mid j = 1,\ldots,T\}.$$

It is also assumed that the number of points in each PC is bounded by, say, $m < \infty$, so that $\max_{\mathbf{X} \in \mathcal{X}} |\mathbf{X}| \le m < \infty$. With null-point padding and vectorizing, one can consider the input space of a PC classifier $\hat{c}$ to be fixed dimensional, $\mathbb{R}^N$, with $N = 3m$, that is, $\hat{c} : \mathbb{R}^N \to \mathcal{Y}$.

The class decision made for a PC should be invariant to translations and rotations of its point set. Thus, the training should be augmented to include translated and rotated PCs. Moreover, the class decision for each PC $\mathbf{X}$ should also be invariant under permutations of its points. This suggests that the training set should also be augmented to consider all possible permutations of its points. Fortunately, this is unnecessary since the DNN architecture considered here, based on PointNet, encodes a permutation invariant representation of its input, $\mathbf{X}$.

As in previous chapters, the loss function (whose minimization over classifier parameters is the training objective), the architecture of the classifier, $\hat{c}$, and other training settings are all specified by the trainer, without consideration of the possible presence of a BA, that is, without considering whether $\mathcal{X}$ is backdoor poisoned.

In this chapter, it is assumed that the classifier $\hat{c}$ identifies a **single** object in every PC sample $\mathbf{X}_j$ and assigns it to one of a set of ($|\mathcal{Y}|$) classes.

Recall that the backdoor attacker has two criteria for success.

1. Having the classifier learn the *backdoor mapping*. That is, for any test PC from an attacker prescribed source class $s \in \mathcal{Y}$, the trained classifier should classify to the attacker's target class $t \in \mathcal{Y}$ $(t \ne s)$ whenever the test PC is embedded with the attacker's backdoor pattern $\mathbf{V}$. The attacker aims to maximize:

$$P_{\mathbf{X} \sim P_s}(\hat{c}(B(\mathbf{X}; \mathbf{V})) = t), \tag{11.1}$$

where P_s is the distribution of (training set) PCs from class s, and $B(\cdot; \mathbf{V})$ is the embedding function associated with the backdoor pattern $\mathbf{V}$ (whose design requires a surrogate classifier independently trained by the attacker on a small dataset, see Section 11.3).

2. *Not* degrading the accuracy of the trained classifier on clean test PCs. That is, the attacker aims not to compromise the trainer's objective, which is to maximize:

$$P_{\mathbf{X} \sim P_y}(\hat{c}(\mathbf{X}) = y), \quad \forall y \in \mathcal{Y} \tag{11.2}$$

Recall the motivation for criterion 2 is so that (clean) validation set accuracy degradation *cannot* be reliably used to detect BAs.

To achieve these two goals, similar to image BAs, the attacker uses a set $\mathcal{B}$ of samples from class s, but with the backdoor embedded and labeled to class t, to poison the

---

[1] General PCs may involve higher-dimensional point representations with additional features beyond 3D coordinates for each point [327].

training set. Then, (11.1) and (11.2) are jointly and automatically maximized during training, where the loss function involves a differentiable surrogate of the indicator function in the estimates of (11.1) and (11.2) based on the training dataset $X = X_0 \cup \mathcal{B}$.

Now consider a specific PC BA whose outline is shown in Figure 11.2. The scenario for this point cloud BA is as follows.

1. The attacker has no access to the training process, that is, no knowledge of the victim classifier's architecture, the loss function, and other training configurations.
2. The attacker has *no access* to X_0, the clean training data collected by the trainer from other (benign) sources.
3. The attacker is able to collect data independently. This collected data, denoted $\mathcal{A}$ is assumed to be i.i.d. with X_0. $\mathcal{A}$ will be used by the attacker in two ways. First, $\mathcal{A}$ will be used to train the attacker's surrogate classifier. Second, PCs from $\mathcal{A}$ will be embedded with the backdoor pattern, resulting in the set $\mathcal{B}$ used to poison the victim's training set.
4. The attacker has the capability to contribute its data $\mathcal{B}$ to the training set of the victim classifier, yielding the poisoned training set.

The first two assumptions are consistent with the role of a backdoor attacker, who is merely one of the data donors. (Thus, BAs may be more practical than existing PC TTE attacks, which rely on knowledge of the victim classifier.) The third and fourth assumptions are the basis of image BAs and traditional DP attacks – the classifier can be more adequately trained by collecting data from as many sources as possible, (unfortunately) among which there may be an attacker. These assumptions are strictly adhered to in the attack/defense experiments that follow.

11.3   A Small Cluster of Backdoor Points

The key to the following PC BA is the design of the backdoor pattern and the associated embedding function. Due to the irregularity of 3D PCs, and inspired by PC TTE attacks [300, 330], candidate backdoor embedding mechanisms include adding points, dropping points, and perturbing points. Backdoor patterns that are created by adding/inserting a small cluster of points are considered here for two reasons. First, in practice, a set of inserted points can potentially be implemented physically by placing an object, for example, a ball, in the scene captured by a 3D sensor; or, these points can be digitally inserted into a PC to *mimic* an object or a cluster of spurious points (which could be physically caused by vehicle exhaust in the context of autonomous driving). Second, an ideal backdoor pattern is a *common* pattern; but point dropping and point perturbations are a function of the original points – it is thus difficult to create a common backdoor pattern using these mechanisms, unlike point addition.

The *backdoor embedding function* is defined as:

$$B(\mathbf{X}; \mathbf{V}) = \mathbf{X} \cup \mathbf{V}, \tag{11.3}$$

where the backdoor pattern (BP) $\mathbf{V}$, dubbed "backdoor points," is defined as

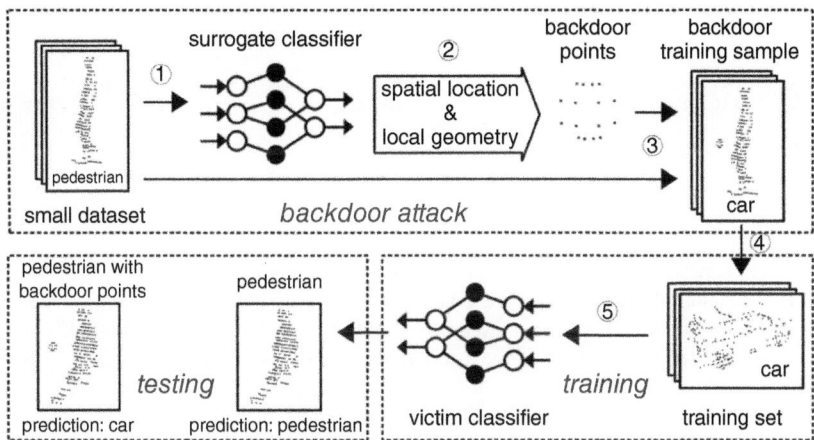

Figure 11.2 Outline of the considered BA. The attacker collects a small dataset to train a surrogate classifier ①. The backdoor points are generated using the surrogate classifier with optimized spatial location (Section 11.3.2) and local geometry (Section 11.3.1) ②. The backdoor points are embedded in clean PCs from a source class, for example, 'pedestrian' ③, to generate backdoor training samples labeled to a target class, for example, 'car'. These samples are used to poison the training set possessed by the trainer ④, on which the victim classifier is trained ⑤. During testing, the victim classifier is likely to classify source class PCs embedded with the backdoor points to the target class (Eq. (11.1)), while correctly classifying backdoor-free test PCs (Eq. (11.2)). Reprinted from [309] with permission.

$$V = \{\underline{u}_i + \gamma \mid \underline{u}_i, \gamma \in \mathbb{R}^3, i = 1, \ldots, |V|\} = \gamma + U, \tag{11.4}$$

with V jointly determined by its **local geometry**:

$$U = \{\underline{u}_i \in \mathbb{R}^3 \mid i = 1, \ldots, |U| = |V|\}.$$

U is chosen to be "centered" at the origin $\underline{0} \in \mathbb{R}^3$, that is, $\sum_{\underline{u} \in U} \underline{u} = \underline{0}$, and V's spatial location (center position) is γ. Here, $X \in \mathcal{A}$ is a clean PC sample classified to the source class of the BA, while $X \cup V \in \mathcal{B}$ is desired by the attacker to be classified to its target class. How to specify the local geometry and center position of the backdoor points is discussed in the following.

Note also that, in addition to a translation, U may be rotated about an arbitrary axis before being translated by γ to produce the PC BP V.

Finally, note that some points in the PC BP V may be removed to meet the DNN classifier's upper bound (m) on the total number of points in the input PC $X \cup V$.

11.3.1   Local Geometry of Backdoor Points

Ideally, the embedded backdoor points should have the same local geometry for all backdoor training/test PCs. However, this is not feasible for BAs physically implemented using even the same object – the actual points associated with the object captured by a 3D sensor are likely different from PC to PC. Fortunately, the local

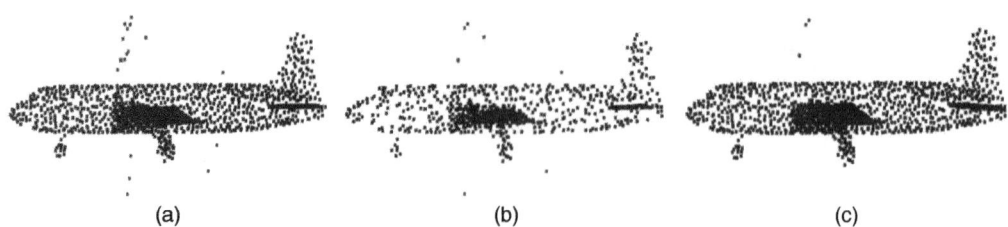

Figure 11.3 Preprocessing and anomaly detection of test PCs. (a) A PC with randomly inserted points above and below the plane, prior to processing. (b) PC undergoes random sampling (with half the points removed). (c) PC is processed by the point AD in [331], which removes outlier points – most of the inserted points are removed. Reprinted from [309] with permission.

geometry of backdoor points is less critical than its spatial location for the victim classifier to learn the backdoor mapping (Eq. (11.1)), as will be empirically shown by experiments in Section 11.4.4. Here, backdoor points embedded in each PC are allowed to have slightly *different* (optimized) local geometries.

Our design of the local geometry of the backdoor points focuses, with practical consideration, on the *robustness* of the pattern to possible PC preprocessing, for example, point sub-sampling, and PC anomaly detectors (ADs) deployed during testing. As shown in Figure 11.3, point sub-sampling keeps a subset of points for classification; thus, some of the inserted backdoor points will inevitably be removed. A PC AD, for example, [331], removes outlier points, that is those with an abnormal local density. Accordingly, the backdoor pattern should: (i) contain a sufficient number of points, and (ii) have a similar local point density as the PC into which they are embedded. For BAs implemented physically using an object, criterion (i) can be achieved if the object is sufficiently large. Criterion (ii) is automatically achieved due to the usually stable scanning frequency of 3D sensors.

For digitally implemented BAs, the local geometry of the backdoor points $\mathbf{U}$ can be specified by the attacker by defining a suitable stochastic point generator. For example, in one of the following experiments, to mimic a physically implemented BA using a ball, backdoor points are placed on a sphere according to the random generator:

$$g(r, \Theta, \Phi) = [r \sin \Theta \cos \Phi, r \sin \Theta \sin \Phi, r \cos \Theta]', \qquad (11.5)$$

where Θ and Φ are random angles uniformly distributed respectively in $[0, \pi]$ and $[0, 2\pi]$ and the sphere's radius r is a parameter to be specified. Here, if $\mathbb{R}^3$ is described by a pair of horizontal (x, y) axes and a vertical (z) axis, all perpendicular, then the azimuthal angle Φ is the angle (measured counter-clockwise) from the positive x-axis, while the polar angle Θ is the angle from the positive z-axis.

Regardless of the generator's form, to achieve attacker criterion (i) a sufficient number of points should be generated. For criterion (ii), one can optimize (over the parameters of the generator) the distribution of the local density of all points in $\mathbf{U}$ by an approach based on median absolute deviation (MAD) (recall Section 6.2.3). Following [331], the local density of a point is measured using its kNN distance (recall Section 4.11). Then, the median kNN distance of a PC $\mathbf{X} \in \mathcal{A}$ for backdoor point embedding is:

$$D_{\text{knn}}(\mathbf{X}) = \underset{i \in \{1,\ldots,|\mathbf{X}|\}}{\text{median}} \frac{1}{k} \sum_{\underline{x}_j \in \mathcal{S}_{\mathbf{X}}(\underline{x}_i, k)} \|\underline{x}_i - \underline{x}_j\|_2, \tag{11.6}$$

where $\mathcal{S}_{\mathbf{X}}(\underline{x}_i, k)$ contains the k nearest neighbors of $\underline{x}_i$. For the example of generating random points $\underline{U}$ on a sphere with radius r to embed in a particular PC $\mathbf{X}$, the optimal radius r is found by solving:

$$\min_{r>0} \quad \mathsf{E}_{\Theta,\Phi} \underset{i \in \{1,\cdots,|\mathbf{U}|\}}{\text{median}} \left| D_{\text{knn}}(\mathbf{X}) - \frac{1}{k} \sum_{\underline{U}_j \in \mathcal{S}_{\mathbf{U}}(\underline{U}_i, k)} \|\underline{U}_i - \underline{U}_j\|_2 \right| \tag{11.7}$$

$$\text{such that} \quad \underline{U}_i = g(r, \Theta_i, \Phi_i), \quad \forall i \in \{1, \cdots, |\mathbf{U}|\},$$

where $\{\Theta_i\}_{i=1}^{|\mathbf{U}|}$ and $\{\Phi_i\}_{i=1}^{|\mathbf{U}|}$ are independent sets of i.i.d. random variables, so that the $\underline{U}_i$ are i.i.d. Equation (11.7) is solved in practice via a grid search, that is, evaluating the objective in (11.7) for $r = n\varepsilon$, for small real $\varepsilon > 0$ and positive integers $n \geq 1$ over a sufficiently large range, in particular so that the largest value $n_{\text{max}}\varepsilon$ is not a minimizer over the range. Also, for each such r, the expectation can be approximated to within a certain degree of statistical confidence (recall Section 2.15). Note that for other geometries, for example, a cube, a different generator function would be chosen, possibly with different parameters to be optimized.

11.3.2   Spatial Location of Backdoor Points

Given the local geometry $\mathbf{U}$ fixed, the spatial location $\underline{\gamma}$ should be specified following two criteria.

C1   The backdoor mapping (Eq. (11.1)) should be well learned by the victim classifier.

C2   The backdoor points should be spatially *close* to the PC into which they are embedded so that the inserted backdoor object can be captured along with the object associated with the PC (i.e., in the same bounding box) by a 3D sensor.

(Note that the classifier may, in general, classify multiple objects in a scene, residing in different bounding boxes, but we only consider single-object classification here.)

Empirically, a BA with randomly located backdoor points is not guaranteed to be successful, as will be shown in Section 11.4.5. Thus, the attacker *optimizes* the spatial location $\underline{\gamma}$ using a surrogate classifier $\tilde{c}$ independently trained on a small (attack-free) dataset, $\mathcal{A}$. The landscape of the surrogate classifier's posterior probability for the target class will likely be similar to that of the victim classifier $\hat{c}$ due to the fact that $\mathcal{X}_0$ and $\mathcal{A}$ are assumed to come from the same distribution. In other words, for both classifiers, the target class posterior probability will likely be large for a *typical* (backdoor-free) target class PC, and be small for a *typical* source class PC. However, there is no guarantee that the two classifiers will have the same (or even a very similar) decision boundary between the source class and the target class. This intuition is jointly illustrated in Figure 11.4a and Figure 11.4b.

To reiterate, the purpose of backdoor poisoning is to have the victim classifier learn to classify backdoor poisoned samples to the target class (i.e., **C1**). For these PCs, the

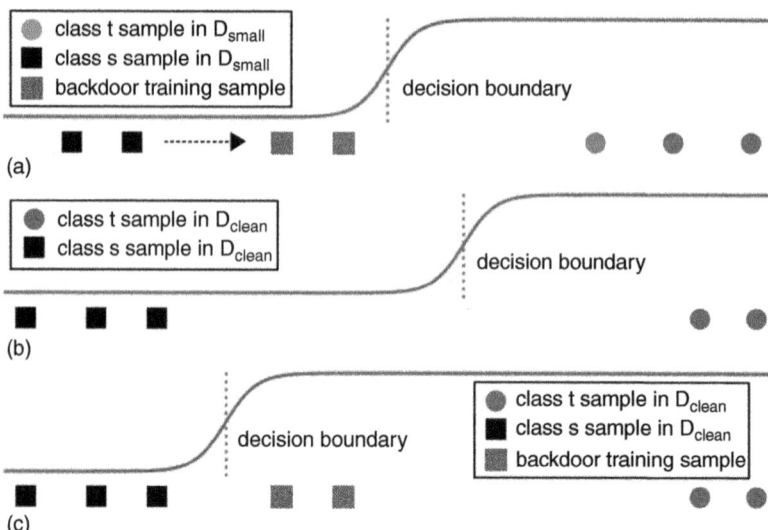

Figure 11.4 An intuitive illustration of the class t posterior probability for (a) the attacker's surrogate classifier ($\tilde{c}$) trained on $\mathcal{A}$. Clean samples from class s are "pushed toward" class t by backdoor points being embedded, which are labeled to class t. (b) The victim classifier ($\hat{c}$) without backdoor poisoning (trained on X_0). (c) The victim classifier trained on the backdoor poisoned training set X; the backdoor training samples influence the learned decision boundary. Reprinted from [309] with permission.

target class posterior probability (produced by the victim classifier) should be large following the victim classifier's training on the poisoned training set. Thus, the spatial location $\underline{\gamma}$ is optimized by the attacker such that the embedded backdoor points are "pushed toward" typical target class PCs (see the parameter ε in (11.8) below). A simple illustration of the *expected* landscape of the target class posterior probability function (and the learned decision boundary) for the (poisoned) victim classifier is shown in Figure 11.4c. For this classifier, a typical source class test PC, but with backdoor points embedded that are similar to those used to poison the classifier, should have a large target class posterior probability.

Denote the *surrogate classifier's* posterior probability function for target class t as $\tilde{p}(t|X)$. For a non-target class PC, $\tilde{p}(t|\cdot)$ should increase when the PC is pushed toward the target class t. Thus, considering also **C2**, the attacker aims to find a **single point** $\underline{\gamma}$ with minimum average distance to a set of source class PCs such that, if $\underline{\gamma}$ is added to the source class PCs, it induces these source class PCs to have at least a certain average level of posterior probability in class t, that is,

$$\min_{\underline{\gamma} \in \mathbb{R}^3} \quad \frac{1}{|\mathcal{A}_s|} \sum_{X \in \mathcal{A}_s} d(\underline{\gamma}, X)$$

$$\text{such that} \quad \frac{1}{|\mathcal{A}_s|} \sum_{X \in \mathcal{A}_s} \tilde{p}(t|B(X; \{\underline{\gamma}\})) \geq \varepsilon + \varepsilon_0. \tag{11.8}$$

Here, $\mathcal{A}_s \subset \mathcal{A}$ is the subset of samples from class s possessed by the attacker, and $d(\underline{\gamma}, \mathbf{X})$ measures the distance from point $\underline{\gamma}$ to PC $\mathbf{X}$. The following experiments use

$$d(\underline{\gamma}, \mathbf{X}) = \min_{\underline{x} \in \mathbf{X}} \|\underline{\gamma} - \underline{x}\|_2 \qquad (11.9)$$

for its simplicity and differentiability with respect to $\underline{\gamma}$. The *initial* (before inserting the additional point) "soft" class confusion from class s to class t,

$$\varepsilon_0 = \frac{1}{|\mathcal{A}_s|} \sum_{\mathbf{X} \in \mathcal{A}_s} \tilde{p}(t|\mathbf{X}),$$

may be close to zero due to possible over fitting on $\mathcal{A}$ during the surrogate classifier's training. Finally, ε is a small positive number controlling how much the source class PCs are "pushed toward" class t by inserting the point $\underline{\gamma}$. Unlike for the image domain, where a small, common perturbation can induce a group of images from one class to be misclassified to another class [186], the feasible set of (11.8) for even a moderately large ε may contain only spatial locations $\underline{\gamma}$ far away from the original PCs in $\mathcal{A}_s$, which violates **C2**. Thus, in practice, ε is chosen to ensure that there is at least one solution with sufficiently small objective value for (11.8); for example, $\varepsilon = 0.02$ is used in the following experiments.

Equation (11.8) is solved using Algorithm 11.1, where

$$J(\underline{\gamma}, \lambda) = \frac{1}{|\mathcal{A}_s|} \sum_{\mathbf{X} \in \mathcal{A}_s} \left[\lambda d(\underline{\gamma}, \mathbf{X}) - \log \tilde{p}(t|B(\mathbf{X}; \{\underline{\gamma}\})) \right] \qquad (11.10)$$

is the Lagrangian corresponding to (11.8). Here, λ is updated automatically (using a scaling factor $\alpha > 1$). $N(\underline{0}, \mathbf{I})$ is a standard normal distribution used to initialize $\underline{\gamma}$; PCs are usually aligned (registered) to the origin for classification [38]. To avoid poor local optima, one can perform Algorithm 11.1 multiple times, with different initialization, and pick the best solution to (11.8).

Note that an alternative approach (which is not explored here) is to insert a *full* cluster of points, that is, $\mathbf{U}$, in (11.8) (i.e., replacing $\{\underline{\gamma}\}$ by $\underline{\gamma} + \mathbf{U}$).

11.4   Attack Experiments

In this section we provide results of attack experiments. Additional experimental results are found in [306, 309].

11.4.1   Datasets

Just as it was used to evaluate existing PC TTE attacks [94, 154, 300], the aligned benchmark dataset ModelNet40 [299] is used here for backdoor attacks. ModelNet40 contains 12, 311 CAD models (2048 points for each PC) from 40 common object categories. Following the original train-test split of ModelNet40, 2468 PCs are used for testing. From the remaining 9843 PCs, 1000 PCs are randomly chosen as the

---

Algorithm 11.1 Optimized spatial location for backdoor points.

1: **Inputs**: source class s, target class t, data subset $\mathcal{A}_s$, surrogate classifier $\tilde{c}$, ε and ε_0, step size δ, maximum iteration count $\tau_{\max}$, scaling factor $\alpha > 1$
2: **Initialization**: $\underline{\gamma}^{(0)} \sim N(\underline{0}, \mathbf{I})$, $\lambda^{(0)}$ set to a small positive number (e.g., 10^{-5}), $\underline{\gamma}^* = \infty$, $\rho^{(0)} = 0$
3: **for** $\tau = 0 : \tau_{\max} - 1$ **do**
4:     $\underline{\gamma}^{(\tau+1)} = \underline{\gamma}^{(\tau)} - \delta \nabla_{\underline{\gamma}} J(\underline{\gamma}^{(\tau)}, \lambda^{(\tau)})$
5:     $\rho^{(\tau+1)} = \frac{1}{|\mathcal{A}_s|} \sum_{\mathbf{X} \in \mathcal{A}_s} \tilde{p}(t | B(\mathbf{X}; \{\underline{\gamma}^{(\tau+1)}\}))$
6:     **if** $\rho^{(\tau+1)} \geq \varepsilon + \varepsilon_0$ **then**
7:         $\lambda^{(\tau+1)} = \lambda^{(\tau)} \cdot \alpha$
8:         **if** $\sum_{\mathbf{X} \in \mathcal{A}_s} \left[d(\underline{\gamma}^{(\tau+1)}, \mathbf{X}) - d(\underline{\gamma}^*, \mathbf{X}) \right] < 0$ **then**
9:             $\underline{\gamma}^* = \underline{\gamma}^{(\tau+1)}$
10:         **end if**
11:     **else**
12:         $\lambda^{(\tau+1)} = \lambda^{(\tau)} / \alpha$
13:     **end if**
14: **end for**
15: **Outputs**: $\underline{\gamma}^*$

"small" dataset ($\mathcal{A}$) possessed by the attacker. The remaining 8843 PCs are possessed by the trainer ($\mathcal{X}_0$) and are not accessible to the attacker.

Additionally, a practical street-view light detection and ranging (LiDAR) dataset KITTI [172] is used. From each scene, PCs are extracted corresponding to labeled objects inside their bounding boxes provided with the dataset. Due to high class imbalance of the original KITTI dataset, two (super) classes are constructed: a 'vehicle' class consisting of 'car', 'van', and 'truck' from the original dataset; and a 'human' class consisting of 'pedestrian' and 'cyclist' from the original dataset. PCs with no less than 256 points are considered and 256 points for each PC are randomly kept. Also, only a subset of PCs is kept for the 'vehicle' class such that the two super-classes have an equal number of samples. Consequently, 2662 PCs are evenly distributed between the two super-classes: 200 are possessed by the attacker, 1800 are possessed by the trainer, and 662 are used for testing.

11.4.2   Attack Implementation

Thirty-six attacks were implemented involving nine (source, target) class pairs in total for the two datasets – for each class pair, four attacks were created with different types of local geometry for the embedded backdoor points.

Specify Source and Target Classes: For ModelNet40, seven (source, target) class pairs were arbitrarily chosen, namely: (chair, toilet), (vase, curtain), (laptop, chair), (night stand, table), (sofa, monitor), (cone, lamp), (airplane, wardrobe). For KITTI, only two ordered class pairs were considered: (human, vehicle) and (vehicle, human). For brevity, these nine class pairs are respectively called Q1, Q2, ..., Q9.

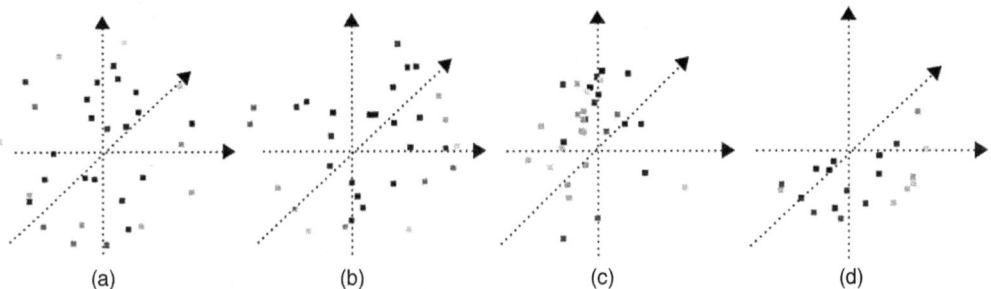

Figure 11.5 Illustration of the four types of local geometry. (a) GS is a non-optimized geometry, while (b) RS, (c) RP, and (d) HS are optimized geometries with stochastic generators. The lighter grey points are on the back side of the sphere from the reader's point-of-view. Reprinted from [309] with permission.

Train a Surrogate Classifier: For each dataset, a PointNet was trained with the same architecture as in [38], on the PCs possessed by the attacker. Training was performed for 250 epochs with batch size 32 and learning rate 10^{-3} (with 0.5 decay per 20 epochs).

Specify the Spatial Location of Backdoor Points: For each of the four attacks associated with each (source, target) class pair, one *common* spatial location is specified for backdoor point embedding using Algorithm 11.1. The parameters for the attacker's optimization are set to $\varepsilon = 0.02$, $\delta = 0.01$, $\tau_{max} = 3000$, $\alpha = 1.5$. In particular, although $\varepsilon = 0.02$ is numerically small, even this value for ε results in a moderate distance between the optimized spatial location (solution to (11.10)) and the PCs used for backdoor embedding, as shown in the Appendix of [309]. A larger ε may cause the embedded backdoor points to be too far from the PC to be captured in the same bounding box by a 3D sensor. The choices of the other three parameters are not critical to the performance of the proposed BA.

Specifying the Local Geometry of Backdoor Points: For each class pair, the following four attacks are created, based on different types of local geometry. The parameter value $k = 4$ in Eq. (11.6) and (11.7) is used for local geometry optimization. Examples of these local geometries are shown in Figure 11.5.

GS: 32 points uniformly spaced on a sphere, generated by Eq. (11.5) with deterministic angles $\theta \in \{\frac{1}{8}\pi, \frac{3}{8}\pi, \frac{5}{8}\pi, \frac{7}{8}\pi\}$ and $\phi \in \{\frac{1}{8}\pi, \frac{3}{8}\pi, \cdots, \frac{15}{8}\pi\}$. The radius is manually set to $r = 0.04$ for scene plausibility, that is, *without* performing the optimization in (11.7).

RS: 32 points randomly distributed on a sphere generated by Eq. (11.5), with random angles Θ and Φ uniformly sampled respectively from $[0, \pi]$ and $[0, 2\pi]$. Radius r is obtained by solving (11.7).

RP: 32 points randomly distributed in a ball generated in the same way as RS, except that r is now a random variable uniformly distributed in $[0, r_{max}]$, where r_{max} is optimized, instead of r, in (11.7).

HS: Points randomly distributed on a half-sphere with random orientation (to mimic a surface of a ball facing a 3D scanner), generated from RS by keeping points having positive inner product with a random vector.

Create Backdoor Training Samples: For each attack, with the specified spatial location and local geometry, backdoor training samples are generated using a subset of clean PCs, possessed by the attacker, from the source class, following Eq. (11.3) and (11.4). Example backdoor training samples are shown in the Appendix of [309]. For ModelNet40 and KITTI, 15 and 30 backdoor training samples are generated for poisoning the training set, respectively.

11.4.3   Training

The victim classifier is learned using the poisoned training dataset X. Based on the assumptions in Section 11.2, the entire training process is not accessible to the attacker. Like PC TTE attacks [293, 300], three DNN architectures for the victim classifier are considered: PointNet [38], PointNet++ [211], and DGCNN [292]. The same DNN architectures and training protocols are used for these models as described in their original papers. Notably, for ModelNet40, each PC is *preprocessed* by randomly sampling 1024 points before feeding to the classifier *(both during training and test)*. Similarly, 128 points are randomly chosen to remain for each PC for KITTI. As a benchmark, without poisoning, the test accuracies of the trained PointNet, PointNet++, and DGCNN are 88.5%, 91.5%, and 91.4% for ModelNet40, and 99.5%, 99.7%, and 99.7% for KITTI.

11.4.4   BA Performance Evaluation

As in previous chapters, the performance of the BA is evaluated using the test set and the following two metrics for each created attack.

- Attack success rate (ASR): for each test PC from the source class, backdoor points are embedded with the same type of local geometry and spatial location as used to create the backdoor training samples. Recall that the ASR is defined as the percentage of such test backdoor triggers that are successfully misclassified to the target class.
- Clean test accuracy (ACC): the accuracy of the victim classifier on the clean test PCs from all classes.

Based on the attacker's goals in Section 11.2, a successful BA should have a high ASR and negligible degradation in ACC compared with the clean benchmarks in Section 11.4.3. Thus, *all 36 attacks are successful* (with all ASR $\geq$ 87%) regardless of the victim classifier's architecture, as shown in Table 11.1 (ASR and ACC for each attack are shown in the Appendix of [309]). Apart from this, it is observed that for each class pair, *with the same optimized spatial location, the choice of the local geometry*

Table 11.1 Average and minimum ASR and ACC (in %), respectively, over the nine attacks (for class pairs Q1, Q2, ..., Q9), for the four local geometries (GS, RS, RP, and HS), the two datasets (ModelNet40 and KITTI), and the three victim classifier architectures (PointNet, PointNet++, and DGCNN). All attacks are successful with ASR ≥ 87%.

		ModelNet40				KITTI			
		ASR (avg)	ASR (min)	ACC (avg)	ACC (min)	ASR (avg)	ASR (min)	ACC (avg)	ACC (min)
Point-Net [38]	GS	94.0	91.9	88.7	88.2	92.8	89.1	99.3	99.2
	RS	96.0	93.0	88.7	88.2	93.4	87.3	99.4	99.4
	RP	94.9	90.0	88.6	87.8	94.0	90.9	99.4	99.1
	HS	96.0	93.0	88.6	88.2	91.2	91.2	99.5	99.5
Point-Net++ [211]	GS	94.6	89.5	91.4	91.0	95.9	92.7	99.5	99.5
	RS	96.9	92.0	91.0	90.2	93.1	87.6	99.4	99.4
	RP	96.9	95.0	91.0	90.2	93.5	89.7	99.7	99.5
	HS	93.7	88.0	91.4	91.1	88.6	87.6	99.5	99.5
DG-CNN [292]	GS	93.2	90.0	92.9	90.8	96.7	95.5	99.5	99.5
	RS	93.9	87.0	91.1	90.7	95.0	91.5	99.8	99.7
	RP	96.1	90.0	91.0	90.6	96.4	93.1	99.6	99.4
	HS	93.7	87.0	91.0	90.8	92.8	90.6	99.5	99.4

does not significantly affect the learning of the backdoor mapping. Especially noteworthy, for attacks with geometry RP, the backdoor points inserted to each PC have high randomness; but the ASRs for these attacks are still uniformly high. For physically implemented BAs, this property allows more freedom in choosing the geometry of the inserted object to achieve scene plausibility. Also, since high ASRs are achieved when each test PC is sub-sampled to 1024 points – nearly half of the points are removed – *the BA is robust to test-time sub-sampling.* Moreover, Figure 11.6 shows ASR curves for the three attacks with local geometry RP for class pairs Q1, Q2, and Q3, over a range of number of backdoor training samples used for poisoning the victim classifier's training set. The BA is effective when only a few backdoor training samples are inserted in the training set containing 8843 clean PCs; thus it is also very stealthy.

Additionally, the BA is compared to PC TTE attacks implemented by point addition, under the same scenario described in Section 11.2. Following [300], for each of the nine class pairs, adversarial PCs are created by inserting 32 points to test PCs from the source class. The locations for the inserted points are optimized such that the adversarial PCs are classified to the target class by the surrogate classifier. As shown in Table 11.2, these adversarial PCs cannot reliably "fool" the victim classifier trained on clean PCs possessed by the trainer. That is, PC TTEs transfer poorly. Thus, they are less threatening than the BA in cases where the victim classifier is not accessible to the attacker.

Table 11.2 Success rate of targeted PC TTE attacks (for class pairs Q1–Q9) transferred from the surrogate classifier, for victim classifier architectures PointNet, PointNet++, and DGCNN. Note that PC TTE attacks transfer poorly.

	Q1	Q2	Q3	Q4	Q5	Q6	Q7	Q8	Q9
PointNet	11.4	32.0	10.5	25.0	44.7	45.5	39.4	18.2	28.5
PointNet++	0	45.0	0	16.7	1.1	18.2	0	1.3	0
DGCNN	12.4	40.5	38.9	20.8	7.2	27.3	11.6	0	0.3

11.4.5   Backdoor Points with Random Spatial Location

Now the *necessity of spatial location optimization* for the BA is shown. For class pair Q1 and local geometry GS, 50 attacks are created as described in Section 11.4.2, but *without* spatial location optimization. In particular, for each attack, a random spatial location $\gamma \sim N(0, I)$ is picked and is scaled such that the average distance from the scaled γ to the source class PCs (the objective (11.10) in the following) is the same as for the optimized spatial location obtained for the attack associated with Q1 and GS. As shown in Figure 11.7, all 50 attacks (with maximum ASR 91.0%) have smaller ASRs than the attack with the optimized spatial location (which has an ASR of 94.0%, as shown in the Appendix of [309]). Moreover, some of the 50 attacks are not reliable, with quite low ASRs.

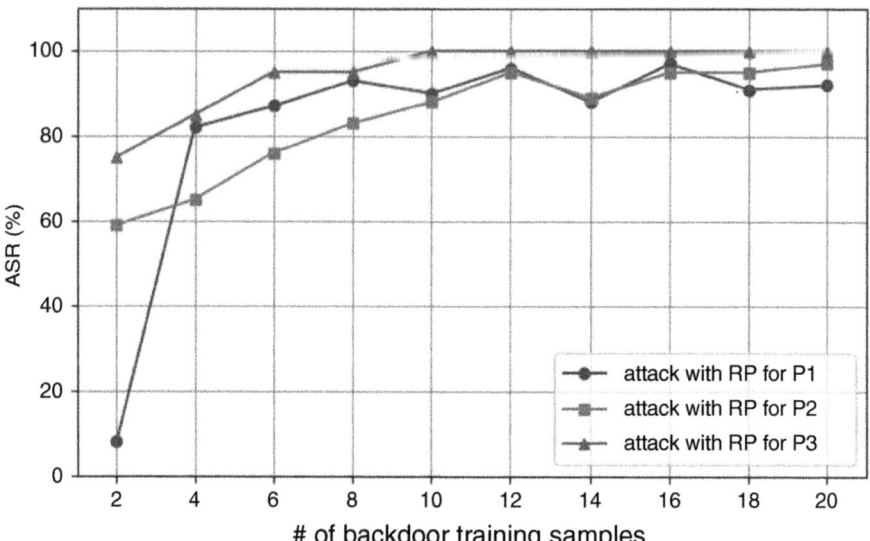

Figure 11.6 ASR versus number of backdoor training samples for attacks with local geometry RP associated with class pairs Q1, Q2, and Q3 (for example). With merely eight backdoor training samples, all three attacks achieve ASR > 80%. Reprinted from [309] with permission.

Table 11.3 Attack success rate (ASR) (in %) for the 36 backdoor attacks for victim classifier architecture PointNet, when the PC AD in [331] is deployed during testing. ASRs (in %) without AD deployed are shown in parenthesis for reference.

	GS	RS	RP	HS
Q1	49.0 (94.0)	90.0 (93.0)	88.0 (94.0)	81.0 (93.0)
Q2	9.0 (93.0)	97.0 (98.0)	96.0 (96.0)	87.0 (97.0)
Q3	51.0 (95.0)	100 (100)	100 (100)	90.0 (100)
Q4	8.1 (91.9)	94.0 (95.0)	95.3 (96.5)	81.4 (95.3)
Q5	2.0 (95.0)	90.0 (95.0)	87.0 (90.0)	84.0 (93.0)
Q6	35.0 (95.0)	90.0 (95.0)	90.0 (90.0)	95.0 (100)
Q7	63.0 (94.0)	94.0 (96.0)	98.0 (98.0)	88.0 (94.0)
Q8	97.0 (96.4)	99.7 (99.4)	98.8 (97.0)	92.4 (91.2)
Q9	87.9 (89.1)	85.2 (87.3)	90.9 (90.9)	90.6 (91.2)

11.5 Point Cloud (PC) Anomaly Detectors (ADs) against Backdoor Attacks (BAs)

An AD defense against PC TTE attacks is considered in [331]. This method aims to remove points inserted/perturbed by a TTE attacker. It measures the kNN distance (with $k = 2$) for each point in a test PC and removes points with abnormally high or low kNN distance (falling outside of a ± 1.1 standard deviation interval around the average as measured for each test sample). Table 11.3 shows ASRs for the 36 backdoor attacks on a PointNet victim classifier, when the above PC AD is deployed during testing. Results associated with PointNet++ and DGCNN are found in the Appendix of

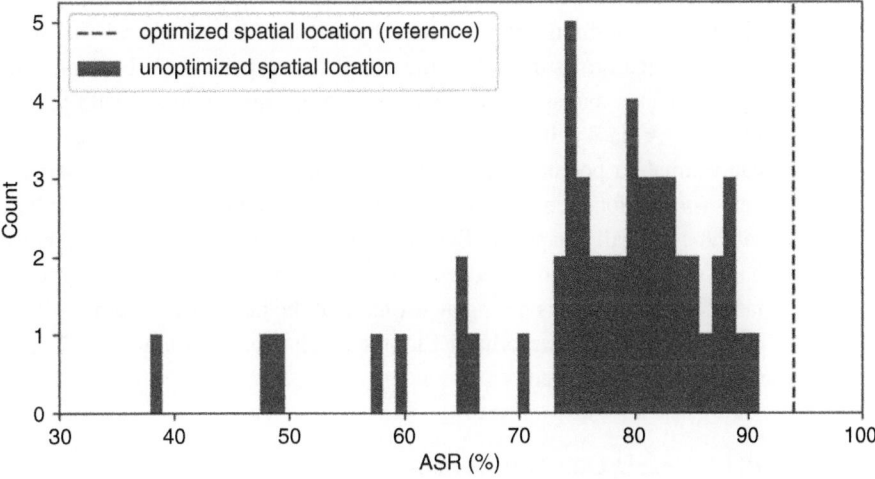

Figure 11.7 Histogram of ASR for 50 attacks created without spatial location optimization; all of them are clearly outperformed by the BA with optimized spatial location. Reprinted from [309] with permission.

[309]. For the non-optimized geometry GS, most attacks are no longer reliable because the backdoor points embedded in many test PCs are entirely removed. For the three optimized geometries (RS, RP, and HS), the PC AD only causes limited degradation in ASR compared with the no detector case. There is still an 81.0% minimum ASR for the 27 attacks for these three local geometries. Hence, **local geometry optimization helps the BA evade state-of-the-art PC ADs.**

11.6 Point Cloud Post-Training Reverse-Engineering Defense (PC-PT-RED)

Existing REDs targeting additive or local patch image backdoor patterns are not suitable for detecting the PC BA described above (with a different backdoor embedding mechanism). Thus, a PT-RED (without access to the training dataset X) designed to detect whether a trained PC classifier was backdoor attacked, PC-PT-RED, is now described. PC-PT-RED performs BP reverse engineering for each putative *source class* and simultaneously estimates a target class. PC-PT-RED addresses the generally strong robustness of PC classifiers [38, 300], for which BP estimation is a hard problem when there are a large number of putative target classes. Moreover, for some putative source classes, there may exist a spatial location *close to* most source class PCs, such that a single point inserted there will cause most of these PCs to be misclassified to a *common* target class, *irrespective of the existence of a BA*. Such an **intrinsic backdoor** can easily cause false detections when there is actually no attack. PC-PT-RED uses a combinatoric detection statistic to address this challenging problem, as will be demonstrated on the benchmark ModelNet40 dataset.

Recall the PT-RED scenario wherein a small, clean dataset ($\mathcal{D}$) independent of the (unavailable) training set is collected by the defender. Also recall that when there is an attack, the pattern estimated for the true BA class pair should be related to the BP used by the attacker and should exhibit some atypicality compared with patterns estimated for non-BA class pairs. Given a sufficiently large number of classes $K = |\mathcal{Y}|$, a RED can estimate a potential backdoor pattern between all possible (source, target) class pairs (or just for each possible target class) and apply null hypothesis based detection inference; recall Chapter 6. Such an approach not only detects whether the classifier has been backdoor poisoned, but also determines the associated source class(es) and target class, as well as giving an estimate of the backdoor pattern itself. Alternatively, a sample-wise transferability RED (recall Chapter 8) or a non-RED approach (recall Chapter 9) can be used.

11.6.1 PC-PT-RED Defense Details

The following intuition behind PC-PT-RED not only guides its design but is also verified experimentally through its (in the sequel) demonstrated success against the PC backdoor attack described above.

I1: For *most* non-BA class pairs, a *common* set of inserted points that induces high group misclassification from source class to target class will be spatially *far* from the points of source class PCs; but for a BA class pair (s^*, t^*), the existence of the *backdoor mapping* guarantees the existence of a *common* spatial location close to the *source* class PCs (likely near γ^*), where a set of inserted points can induce most source class PCs to be misclassified to the target class.

I2: A few non-BA class pairs may be associated with an "intrinsic backdoor." For these class pairs, as for a true BA class pair, there exists a spatial location close to most PCs from the source class, such that a common set of points inserted there will induce most of these PCs to be misclassified to the target class. However, such a spatial location, different from γ^* (specified by the attacker) for the true backdoor, will *also* likely be close to the points of most *target class* PCs.

I3: Unlike backdoor mappings caused by an attack with a *single common* spatial location γ^*, an intrinsic backdoor is likely due to the source and target classes being "semantically" similar, such that there may exist *several* intrinsic backdoor points for a given non-BA class pair, with each one close to source class PCs (see Figure 1 of [306]). In this case (for a source class with an intrinsic backdoor), the *closest* spatial location for a set of inserted points to induce a misclassification to the target class (for a particular point cloud) may be different for different PCs from the same source class.

PC-PT-RED's detection method consists of a BP estimation step followed by a detection inference step.

Step 1: BP Estimation

To find BA class pairs, if there are any, based on I1, we first find, for each class pair, the *common* spatial location *closest* to the source class PCs such that a set of points inserted there induces most of these PCs to be misclassified to the target class, that is, this step reverse engineers putative BPs. Based on the first part of this chapter, which developed an effective PC BA, the backdoor mapping mostly relies on the spatial location γ^* but not on the local geometry $\mathbf{U}^*$ of the inserted points. Thus, one can focus on reverse-engineering the spatial location of the BP with arbitrary local geometry; for simplicity, one can insert a *single* point at this spatial location. That is, we aim to solve the following problem for each class pair $(s, t) \in \mathcal{Y} \times \mathcal{Y}$ with $s \neq t$:

$$\min_{\underline{\gamma} \in \mathbb{R}^3} \quad \sum_{\mathbf{X} \in \mathcal{D}_s} d(\underline{\gamma}, \mathbf{X})$$

$$\text{such that} \quad \frac{1}{|\mathcal{D}_s|} \sum_{\mathbf{X} \in \mathcal{D}_s} \mathbf{1}\{\hat{c}(\mathbf{X} \cup \{\underline{\gamma}\}) = t\} \geq \pi, \tag{11.11}$$

where $\mathcal{D}_s$ is the subset of clean samples from class s possessed by the defender; $\pi \in [0, 1]$ is a group misclassification fraction, which is typically set large (e.g., $\pi = 0.9$ was chosen for I-PT-RED experiments); and $d(\cdot, \cdot)$ is the distance measure defined previously in (11.9).

However, problem (11.11) is difficult to solve in practice. First, the indicator function in the constraint is not differentiable. Second, unlike image BPs (e.g., an additive or patch perturbation) typically constrained by some range of valid pixel values, the search space for a point's spatial location is unbounded in general. Also, due to the generally strong adversarial robustness of recent PC classifiers [38, 300], for many class pairs there may not even exist a spatial location reasonably close to the source class PCs, such that an inserted point can induce high (e.g., at least π) group misclassification to the target class. For these class pairs, finding *any* solution to satisfy the constraint of (11.11) may be infeasible in practice. To address the two challenges above, BP estimation is performed for each putative *source class* by minimizing a *differentiable surrogate* objective *and* by altering the misclassification count constraint in the above. In particular, for each putative source class $s \in \mathcal{Y}$, PC-PT-RED searches for the closest spatial location to PCs from class s such that a point inserted there causes at least π fraction of these PCs to be misclassified to *any class other than* s (untargeted misclassifications). That is, with respect to γ, we minimize the loss function:

$$l(\gamma; \mathcal{D}_s, \lambda) = \sum_{\mathbf{X} \in \mathcal{D}_s} \left[f(s|\mathbf{X} \cup \{\gamma\}) - \max_{k \neq s} f(k|\mathbf{X} \cup \{\gamma\}) \right] + \lambda \sum_{\mathbf{X} \in \mathcal{D}_s} d(\gamma, \mathbf{X}) \quad (11.12)$$

using Algorithm 11.2. The first sum in Eq. (11.12) is similar to the *untargeted* CW loss function (recall Section 1.3 and (4.3)), where $f(k|\mathbf{X})$ is the DNN's penultimate (logit) layer activation for PC input $\mathbf{X}$. Using such untargeted loss, the source class PCs "vote" for a target class by:

$$\hat{t}(s) = \arg\max_{k \neq s} \sum_{\mathbf{X} \in \mathcal{D}_s} \mathbf{1}\{\hat{c}(\mathbf{X} \cup \{\hat{\gamma}(s)\}) = k\} \quad (11.13)$$

where $\hat{\gamma}(s)$ is the spatial location estimated for class s. Note that, like L-PT-RED, PC-PT-RED performs only $O(K)$ BP estimations (instead of $O(K^2)$) and so is more efficient than I-PT-RED when the number of classes K is large. The second sum in Eq. (11.12) is a regularizer which constrains the distance of γ to the points of the source class PCs. The coefficient λ is automatically adjusted according to lines 6–10 of Algorithm 11.2.

In addition to the *group* BP estimation above, based on intuition I3, for each putative source class $s \in \mathcal{Y}$, PC-PT-RED also estimates a *sample-wise* spatial location for each clean sample $\mathbf{X} \in \mathcal{D}_s$, given the estimated target class $\hat{t}(s)$. That is, the following loss is minimized using the same Algorithm 11.2:

$$\tilde{l}(\gamma; \mathbf{X}, \lambda) = f(s|\mathbf{X} \cup \{\gamma\}) - f(\hat{t}(s)|\mathbf{X} \cup \{\gamma\}) + \lambda d(\gamma, \mathbf{X}), \quad (11.14)$$

that is, with $\mathcal{D}_s$ replaced by a single PC $\mathbf{X}$, and with the loss used in line 4 now the sample-wise loss given in Eq. (11.14). We denote the estimated sample-wise (SW) spatial location for $\mathbf{X} \in \mathcal{D}_s$ as $\hat{\gamma}_{sw}(s, \mathbf{X})$.

Step 2: Detection Inference
PC-PT-RED's detection is based on three basic statistics (obtained from BP estimation for each putative source class), corresponding to the three intuitions in this section. For each $s \in \mathcal{Y}$ we compute the following.

Algorithm 11.2 Spatial location estimation for class $s \in \mathcal{Y}$.

1: **Inputs:** data subset $\mathcal{D}_s$, classifier $\hat{c}(\cdot)$, fraction π, step size δ, maximum iteration count $\tau_{\max}$, scaling factor $\alpha > 1$
2: **Initialization:** $\underline{\gamma}^{(0)} \sim N(\underline{0}, \mathbf{I})$, $\lambda^{(0)}$ set to a small positive number (e.g., 10^{-5}), $\underline{\hat{\gamma}}(s) = \infty$, $\rho^{(0)} = 0$
3: **for** $\tau = 0 : \tau_{\max} - 1$ **do**
4:     $\underline{\gamma}^{(\tau+1)} = \underline{\gamma}^{(\tau)} - \delta \nabla_{\underline{\gamma}} l(\underline{\gamma}^{(\tau)}; \mathcal{D}_s, \lambda^{(\tau)})$
5:     $\rho^{(\tau+1)} = \frac{1}{|\mathcal{D}_s|} \sum_{\mathbf{X} \in \mathcal{D}_s} \mathbb{1}[\hat{c}(\mathbf{X} \cup \{\underline{\gamma}^{(\tau+1)}\}) \neq s]$
6:     **if** $\rho^{(\tau+1)} \geq \pi$ **then**
7:         $\lambda^{(\tau+1)} = \alpha \cdot \lambda^{(\tau)}$
8:         **if** $\sum_{\mathbf{X} \in \mathcal{D}_s} [d(\underline{\gamma}^{(\tau+1)}, \mathbf{X}) - d(\underline{\hat{\gamma}}(s), \mathbf{X})] < 0$ **then**
9:             $\underline{\hat{\gamma}}(s) = \underline{\gamma}^{(\tau+1)}$
10:        **end if**
11:    **else**
12:        $\lambda^{(\tau+1)} = \lambda^{(\tau)}/\alpha$
13:    **end if**
14: **end for**
15: **Output:** $\underline{\hat{\gamma}}(s)$

---

1. The average distance from the (group-wise) estimated spatial location to points of source class PCs:

$$r_S(s) = \frac{1}{|\mathcal{D}_s|} \sum_{\mathbf{X} \in \mathcal{D}_s} d(\underline{\hat{\gamma}}(s), \mathbf{X}).$$

2. The average distance from the (group-wise) estimated spatial location to points of PCs from the estimated target class $\hat{t}(s)$:

$$r_T(s) = \frac{1}{|\mathcal{D}_{\hat{t}(s)}|} \sum_{\mathbf{X} \in \mathcal{D}_{\hat{t}(s)}} d(\underline{\hat{\gamma}}(s), \mathbf{X}).$$

3. A normalized similarity score:

$$w(s) = \frac{z(s) - \min_{k \in \mathcal{Y}} z(k)}{\max_{k \in \mathcal{Y}} z(k) - \min_{k \in \mathcal{Y}} z(k)},$$

where

$$z(k) = \frac{1}{|\mathcal{D}_k|} \sum_{\mathbf{X} \in \mathcal{D}_k} \frac{\underline{\hat{\gamma}}(k) \cdot \underline{\hat{\gamma}}_{sw}(k, \mathbf{X})}{||\underline{\hat{\gamma}}(k)|| \, ||\underline{\hat{\gamma}}_{sw}(k, \mathbf{X})||}$$

is the average cosine similarity between the estimated sample-wise spatial location for each $\mathbf{X} \in \mathcal{D}_k$ and the group-wise estimated spatial location for (putative source) class $k \in \mathcal{Y}$. (Recall that PCs are usually aligned to the origin for classification.) The normalization limits the similarity score to the interval $[0, 1]$ for generalization to different domains.

According to intuition I1, $r_S(s)$ will likely be large if $(s, \hat{t}(s))$ is a non-BA class pair; otherwise, $r_S(s)$ will likely be small. If for some class s, $(s, \hat{t}(s))$ is associated with an intrinsic backdoor mapping, such that $r_S(s)$ is abnormally small, based on I2 and I3, $r_T(s)$ or $w(s)$ (or both) will likely be abnormally small. Thus, for each putative source class $s \in \mathcal{Y}$, PC-PT-RED computes the combined detection statistic:

$$r(s) = w(s)\frac{r_T(s)}{r_S(s)}, \tag{11.15}$$

which should be abnormally large only if $(s, \hat{t}(s))$ is a BA pair.

Thus, PC-PT-RED's inference step performs *unsupervised* anomaly detection. It checks, among the r-statistics for all $s \in \mathcal{Y}$, if there exists an abnormally large one. As with other PT-REDs, one can fit a null distribution using all statistics excluding the *largest one* and evaluate its *atypicality* under the null using the maximum *order statistic* p-value, which is generally insensitive to the number of statistics used for detection. However, just as for image domains, a PC BA may cause *collateral damage*: a backdoor mapping with the same BP may be learned for some class pair (s, t^*) with $s \in \mathcal{Y} \setminus \{s^*, t^*\}$, even if the attacker only intended to encode a backdoor mapping involving the pair (s^*, t^*). In such a case, there may be *multiple* abnormally large statistics associated with *the same target class* t^* but different source classes; thus, the null distribution estimated with only the largest statistic excluded may be biased. To resolve this problem, PC-PT-RED excludes statistics for all $s \in \mathcal{Y}$ such that $\hat{t}(s) = \hat{t}(s_{max})$ when estimating the null, where $s_{max} = \arg\max_{k \in \mathcal{Y}} r(k)$. Given that PC-PT-RED's detection statistic $r(\cdot)$ lives in $[0, \infty)$, similar to [303], a single-tailed parametric density form is chosen (a Gamma distribution in the experiments that follow in this chapter, just as for I-PT-RED [303]) as a null distribution, with CDF $G(\cdot)$, such that any abnormally large statistics (likely corresponding to BA class pairs) will likely appear in the tail (e.g., Figure 11.8). Then the *maximum order statistic p-value* is:

$$pv = 1 - G(r(s_{max}))^{K-J}, \tag{11.16}$$

where J is the number of statistics being excluded when estimating the null distribution. A detection threshold φ is chosen (e.g., $\varphi = 0.05$ is commonly used), such that a BA is detected with confidence $1 - \varphi$ if $pv < \varphi$. When a BA is detected, $\hat{t}(s_{max})$ is inferred as the target class.

11.7   Attack/Defense Experiments

11.7.1   Experiment Settings

Dataset: Recall that the benchmark ModelNet40 dataset contains $12,311$ aligned CAD models from 40 object categories [299]. 9843 and 2468 PCs are in the training set and test set, respectively.

Attack Configurations: Consider the seven attacks for ModelNet40, where the BP for each attack is a set of points inserted at an optimized spatial location and with a random local geometry (i.e., the RS geometry). The source and target class pair for these seven attacks are Qn for $n \in \{1, 2, \ldots, 7\}$ as defined in Section 11.4.2. For each attack, 15 source class PCs embedded with the BP and labeled to the target class are used for poisoning the training set.

Classifier, Training, and Attack Effectiveness: Consider the PointNet classifiers [38] trained for all seven attacks, and the PointNet++ classifier [211] and the DGCNN

Table 11.4 Order statistic p-value (pv), in the form (attack pv, clean pv), for nine pairs of classifiers being attacked and for the associated clean classifier, for the statistic r (Eq. (11.15)) used by PC-PT-RED, and for three alternative statistics ($1/r_S$, r_T/r_S, and w/r_S), as part of an ablation study. Attacks are associated with class pairs $Q1,\ldots,Q7$; classifier architectures include PointNet (PN), PointNet++ (PN++), and DGCNN. "u.f." represents "underflow" for numerically computed positive numbers less than 10^{-323}, that is, numerically zero. Also, here e^k is short for $\times 10^k$.

	Q1-PN	Q2-PN	Q3-PN	Q4-PN	Q5-PN
$1/r_S$	$(6.2e^{-3}, 0.36)$	$(3.8^{-3}, 0.16)$	$(4.3e^{-15}, 0.33)$	$(2.2e^{-7}, 2.6e^{-2})$	$(0.24, 0.11)$
r_T/r_S	$(4.5e^{-2}, 9.2e^{-6})$	$(\text{u.f.}, 0.32)$	$(6.1e^{-6}, 9.8e^{-2})$	$(2.8e^{-3}, 0.58)$	$(0.12, 0.19)$
w/r_S	$(1,7e^{-7}, 0.19)$	$(3.5e^{-3}, 0.26)$	$(\text{u.f.}, 0.27)$	$(5.6e^{-9}, 9.2e^{-3})$	$(1.4e^{-2}, 6.1e^{-2})$
$r = w \cdot r_T/r_S$	$(3.3e^{-3}, 0.38)$	$(\text{u.f.}, 0.19)$	$(\text{u.f.}, 0.20)$	$(\text{u.f.}, 0.22)$	$(5.4e^{-2}, 0.27)$

	Q6-PN	Q7-PN	Q1-PN++	Q1-DGCNN
$1/r_S$	$(0.24, 1.6e^{-2})$	$(4.3e^{-3}, 9.7e^{-2})$	$(\text{u.f.}, 8.2e^{-6})$	$(4.4e^{-5}, 4.3e^{-2})$
r_T/r_S	$(0.21, 0.60)$	$(6.7e^{-5}, 9.0e^{-3})$	$(\text{u.f.}, 0.99)$	$(0.10, 0.59)$
w/r_S	$(1.4e^{-2}, 2.6e^{-2})$	$(5.5e^{-9}, 7.0e^{-3})$	$(\text{u.f.}, 0.94)$	$(0.22, 2.9e^{-2})$
$r = w \cdot r_T/r_S$	$(7.6e^{-4}, 0.33)$	$(\text{u.f.}, 9.3e^{-2})$	$(5.5e^{-13}, 0.99)$	$(1.9e^{-3}, 0.18)$

classifier [292] trained for the attack associated with class pair $Q1$, with the training configurations detailed in [306]. All the attacked classifiers exhibit high attack success rate and almost no degradation in clean test accuracy (reported in [306]). To evaluate false detections, for each attacked classifier, a corresponding classifier with no BA was also trained using the same training configurations.

11.7.2 Detection Performance Evaluation Results

Detector Configurations: Following the assumptions in Section 11.6.1, for each class, 10 clean PCs were randomly selected from the ModelNet40 dataset, to form the clean set used for detection; these PCs are not used for training. For BP estimation (both group-wise and sample-wise) using Algorithm 11.2, the following settings were used: $\pi = 0.9$, $\delta = 0.1$, $\tau_{max} = 3k$, and $\alpha = 1.5$. These choices are not critical to the performance of the detector. Moreover, in practice, these values can be chosen so as to minimize the loss function at convergence. The best solution is picked from 10 random initializations, which is a common practice to address highly non-convex problems.

Detection Performance: For each attacked classifier and its associated clean classifier, Table 11.4 (last row) reports the order statistic p-values obtained using PC-PT-RED's statistic $r = w \cdot r_T/r_S$ (Eq. (11.15)). In general, the p-values are large for most clean classifiers and are small when there is a BA, as expected.[2] Applying the commonly used $\varphi = 0.05$ detection threshold to these p-values, *PC-PT-RED only missed*

---

[2] Note also that different clean p-values are reported for the same (PN) architecture in Table 11.4. This is due to different random initializations being used for the different attack experiments (involving the same (PN) DNN architecture).

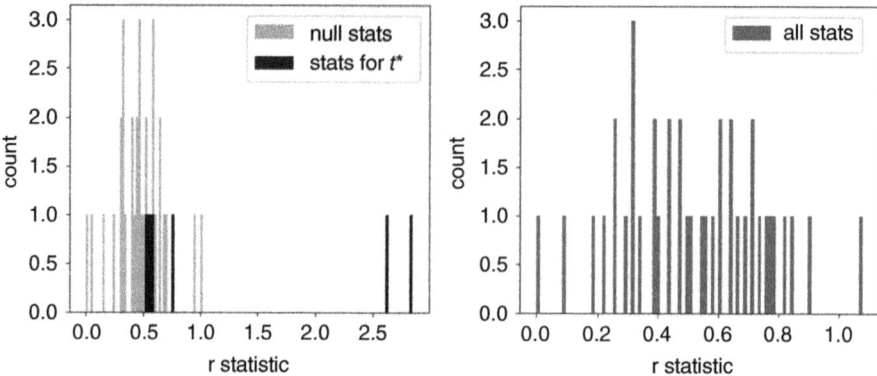

Figure 11.8 Histogram of r statistics for the classifier with BA (a) and its associated clean classifier without BA (b). For the attack case, statistics for two source classes "voting" to the BA target class t^* are abnormally large. Reprinted from [306] with permission.

one attack ($Q5$-PN, and barely, since the p-value is 0.054) *with zero false detections.* For each detected attack, the BA target class is also correctly inferred.

Ablation Study: As the *first* defense designed for PC BAs, there is no competitor with which to compare PC-PT-RED. So, detection performance is also shown using three different simplified statistics instead of the combined one used by PC-PT-RED, that is, (11.15). In Table 11.4, for these simplified statistics, the p-values for some clean classifiers (e.g., $Q4$-PN, $Q6$-PN) are small due to the existence of intrinsic backdoors, which easily cause false detections – in fact, in some cases, for these simplified statistics, the clean classifier p-value is smaller than the attacked classifier's p-value. Even for some attacked classifiers (e.g., $Q5$-PN, $Q6$-PN), using these simplified statistics, the null estimation will be affected by intrinsic backdoors, such that the resulting p-value will not be small enough to trigger a detection. These results highlight the importance of including all three components (each motivated by the intuition in Section 11.6.1) in PC-PT-RED's detection statistic.

Detection Visualization: Figure 11.8 shows the distribution of PC-PT-RED's statistic for both the attacked classifier and the clean classifier for $Q4$-PN, for example. When there is a BA, two statistics associated with the true BA target class clearly appear in the "tail" of the null distribution, triggering a detection with correct inference of the BA target class.

11.8   Chapter Summary

In this chapter, we focused on backdoor attacks and defenses on DNNs for the point cloud domain. Unlike images, point cloud data captures the periphery/shape of 3D (or higher-dimensional) objects, with important applications both for object recognition in autonomous driving systems and for industrial robotics applications. DNNs applied to point cloud data have unique architectures, for example, PointNet's architecture, compared to typical CNN based image classifiers. Moreover, the unique nature of point cloud data requires different attack mechanisms, including *evasion* mechanisms, compared to that for image data. We noted that, unlike for images, TTE attacks against point cloud classifiers do not transfer well from one classifier to another. This motivated consideration of backdoor attacks. We first developed a backdoor attack on PC classifiers that involves inserting points into a point cloud data object that (i) do not significantly alter the local point density, and (ii) increase the a posteriori probability (for the attacker's surrogate classifier) of the target class of the attack. It was shown in the resulting experiments that the devised attack is highly successful, achieving a high ASR and with very little degradation in clean test set accuracy. It was further shown that the attacker's optimization of the spatial location of inserted points is necessary – if inserted points are randomly chosen the attack is not *consistently* successful (some attack instances have quite low ASRs).

Next, we devised a defense to defeat this PC backdoor attack. This defense first involves a reverse-engineering step – for the PC domain this step amounts to finding, for each candidate source class, a single point insertion that is as close as possible to the source class PCs, while inducing a large fraction of source class PCs to be misclassified. Next, a detection statistic was formulated, for each putative source class of an attack, based on three components: (i) the average distance from the inserted point to the source class PCs (this distance should be small for a backdoor attack involving this source class, otherwise a PC anomaly detector is likely to remove the inserted backdoor points as outliers); (ii) the average distance from the inserted point to the target class PCs (this distance should be large for a malicious backdoor attack involving this target class, on the other hand this distance may be small for an *intrinsic* backdoor); and (iii) large agreement (a large average cosine similarity) between putative backdoor points estimated *group-wise* and those estimated sample-wise. This score helps to distinguish between malicious backdoors and intrinsic backdoors (for which there will tend to be less agreement between backdoor points estimated group-wise and those estimated sample-wise). The resulting detection method was demonstrated to detect nearly all instances of the proposed PC backdoor attack.

Some questions to test the reader's understanding of this chapter include the following.

- Is the PC attack in this chapter a digital attack or a physical attack? Explain.
- Instead of inserting points, another possible attack vector involves *deleting* points from PCs. What is the disadvantage of such an approach compared to point insertion?
- Why is it important that a PC classifier's operation be permutation invariant?
- Explain why, for the attacker's optimization problem, it is sufficient that the inserted point need only achieve an average posterior to the target class of the attack of $\varepsilon = 0.02$, that is, why is it *not* required that the inserted point should induce the source class PCs to have the MAP class be the target class of the attack?
- For DNN based PC classification, is it necessary that every PC object to be classified possess the same number of points?

- Does ASR depend much on the local geometry of inserted points?
- Why were intrinsic backdoors not discussed in previous chapters involving image classification examples?
- Why are *untargeted* misclassifications used in the BP estimation step of the proposed defense?
- How does PC-PT-RED avoid introducing bias when estimating null distributions for each source class, s?

11.9   Project: During-Training Defense or Robustification of Point Cloud (PC) Classifiers

Recall that one idea for robustifying a DNN is to retrain it with additional samples that embed a (detected) backdoor pattern, but supervised with the correct label. Evaluate this simple (data augmentation) backdoor defense specifically for PC classifiers.

In one variant of this defense, the poisoned training samples themselves are detected and their labels are corrected (so no additional training samples are added). See the Appendix of [301], that is, TSC-RED of Chapter 5.

Repeat the data augmentation experiment in an attempt to make the PC classifier more robust to detected intrinsic (non-adversarial) backdoors. Does this result in improved generalization accuracy of the PC classifier? A useful starting point is the code available in the PCBA folder [329].

12 Robust Deep Regression and Active Learning

Previous chapters exclusively considered attacks against classifiers. In this chapter, we look at deep regression (and prediction) models. Deep regression [137], active learning for regression [65, 115, 273, 297], and deep active learning [217] have received significant interest over the past few years. Regression has important applications in science, engineering, and economics. The following list gives some examples.

- Signal processing to remove noise, remove interference, perform signal enhancement, or perform signal prediction are all regression problem instances.
- Reinforcement learning problems [183, 184], for example, in control, are well cast as regression problems.
- In scientific ML [167, 195], DNNs are now being used to solve complicated partial differential equations (DEs) from physics, again cast as a regression problem. Regularizing constraints from physics are introduced into deep learning, allowing predictions for complex systems using both DEs and training data. The data complements gaps in physical knowledge, while the DEs significantly reduce training dataset size requirements and allow extrapolation where there is no labeled data. Such DNN inference based equation solving is much faster than traditional numerical solvers.
- Investment banks rely on Monte Carlo estimates to accurately price complicated financial instruments. But such estimates are quite costly in time and computation. Once trained, a DNN regressor also requires much less computation for inference in this setting, and thus is an attractive alternative to Monte Carlo techniques to support high-speed trading.

More specifically, in regression based signal processing, a signal $\underline{x}$ may have noise or distortion which is to be removed, to produce a clean version of $\underline{x}$. Let us now consider a training dataset X consisting of pairs $(\underline{x}, \underline{c}(\underline{x}))$, where $\underline{c}(\underline{x})$ is the supervision (labeling) information, that is, the clean reference for the noisy input $\underline{x}$. Here, the regression problem is to train a DNN $\underline{\hat{c}}(\underline{x})$ so that, for example, the mean-squared error (MSE, recall Eq. (2.10)) between $\underline{\hat{c}}$ and $\underline{c}$ on X (a commonly used training objective for regression) is minimized:

$$\frac{1}{|X|} \sum_{\underline{x} \in X} \|\underline{\hat{c}}(\underline{x}) - \underline{c}(\underline{x})\|^2. \tag{12.1}$$

Note that here the *vectors* $\underline{\hat{c}}(\underline{x})$ and $\underline{c}(\underline{x})$ obviously have the same dimension.

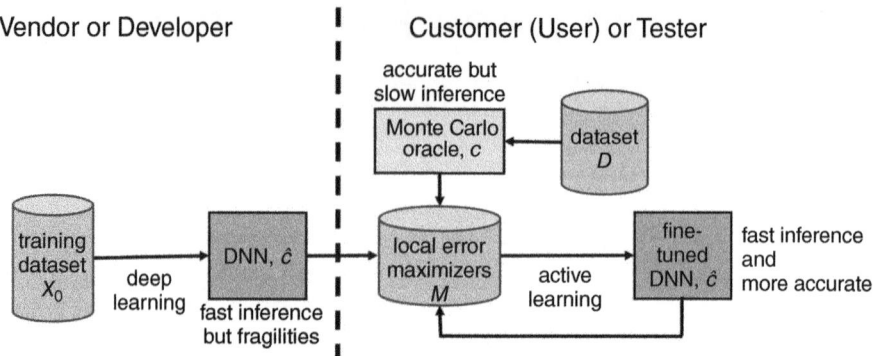

Figure 12.1 A vendor or developer creates a deep regression model $\hat{c}$ using training dataset X_0 with associated ground truth labels. $\hat{c}$ is thereafter used, tested or improved upon by another party, who may or may not have access to X_0, but does have access to one or more supervising "oracles" c which can label new training data for purposes of testing and retraining $\hat{c}$. In the RDR-AL approach developed in the sequel, the new samples will be local error maximizers ($\in M$) of the existing trained model.

Let us now look at Figure 12.1. Here, a vendor (or developer) employs deep learning to produce a regression model $\hat{c}$ which is then passed to a user (or tester). The user evaluates the model and may adjust it in light of any detected problems. To this end, the user may or may not have access to the training dataset X_0 used to learn $\hat{c}$, but does have access to one or more oracles c that can provide supervising labels for new training instances. As aforementioned, in some cases the DNN $\hat{c}$ is able to perform inference much faster than c; see the example of Eq. (12.6) in the sequel, where c is based on Monte Carlo estimates of the expected present value of a financial option [35, 169].

In the following, we will develop an *active learning* approach [241] to be employed by the user/tester, that is, a method by which the learner *chooses* which samples to label, to incorporate within the training set used to learn a model. Our approach will be to apply gradient-based optimization (again, essentially an application of neural network inversion) to find feasible input samples for which c and $\hat{c}$ significantly disagree; this will be the basis of our active learning algorithm. If one selects samples to label from a *pool* of unlabeled samples, this is referred to as pool based active learning [241]. On the other hand, if one chooses new samples to label from *anywhere* within the feasible input space, this is referred to as query-synthesis based active learning [25]. The method we will develop is a query-synthesis active learning approach.

We will then consider the problem where there is a small, localized region of the input space within which the regression error is unusually large. Such regions may exist for multiple reasons, including inadequacy of the available training data or a poor choice of the model architecture. But another possible (adversarial) cause is that the training set has been corrupted by a data poisoning attack. We will assess the effectiveness of our active learning approach for discovering (and also mitigating) such regions.

12.1   Background on Active Learning

A number of active learning schemes have been proposed in the research literature, for building both classification and regression models, with a survey of such techniques given in [241]. As aforementioned, two common approaches are pool based active learning and query-synthesis driven active learning. Most active learning works have focused on the proposal of new criteria for sample selection. In particular, note that the sample selection criterion is a *surrogate* for the actual benefit that will be obtained from labeling samples and then retraining the model in light of these newly labeled samples, that is, the reduction in the number of misclassified samples (in the case of a classifier) or the reduction in the mean-squared regression error (in the case of a regression model). Prior to labeling these samples and retraining based on them, one cannot precisely know the actual benefit that will be gained from such labeling. Thus, sample selection criteria are designed to select samples that are *expected* to provide the most benefit.

Unlike active learning, in online learning one is not (actively) *selecting* which new samples to label. Also unlike active learning, in reinforcement learning there may not be clear ground truth for these samples. See Section 12.5.2.

For classification, a variety of such selection criteria/policies for active learning have been proposed, selecting, for example: the sample nearest to the existing classifier's decision boundary [241]; the sample with high expected utility [105]; the sample with maximum class decision entropy [214]; the sample least likely to belong to a common category (with many existing labeled samples) – such a criterion was demonstrated in [214] to be very efficient for discovering samples from heretofore *unknown* categories; samples in low-density regions of the feature space; the sample for which there is the least consensus among a committee/ensemble of models [242]; or random selection.

Likewise, for regression, a variety of sample selection criteria/policies have also been proposed, selecting, for example: samples in regions with low labeled sample density as measured by, for example, the average K-nearest neighbor (KNN) distance to labeled samples (recall Section 4.11); samples in regions with high unlabeled sample density; samples in the vicinity of training samples with the largest errors; samples to maximize the expected model change [26]; samples with large interpolation errors (with the interpolation function based on the existing labeled samples); samples for which the model *variance* is the highest where, for example, the variance is computed based on an ensemble/committee of models [25, 242, 273] ([273] proposed to construct a committee by random neuron dropout applied to an existing (trained) deep neural network); or samples based on Bayesian criteria which provide some balance between breadth and depth of search [65] (however, this approach was only investigated for linear models, applied to the problem of learning a price-demand function). There are also approaches matched to a particular generative statistical model, for example, a mixture of Gaussians [49]. In the following, we develop a new active learning approach that is particularly suited to discerning where the current model "fails," that is, identifying regions of feature space where the model is (potentially) grossly inaccurate.

12.2   Robust Deep Regression by Active Learning (RDR-AL)

We now describe in detail an active learning approach for robust deep regression (RDR-AL). Let us consider the scenario of Figure 12.1. For each initial seed $\underline{x}_0$, a gradient ascent sequence (with index $n = 0, 1, 2, \ldots$, recall Section 2.6) seeks a local error maximizer (LEM) with respect to the error objective:

$$\mathcal{E}(\underline{x}) = \frac{1}{2}|\hat{c}(\underline{x}) - c(\underline{x})|^2, \tag{12.2}$$

that is

$$\underline{x}^{(n+1)} = \underline{x}^{(n)} + \varepsilon \nabla \mathcal{E}(\underline{x}^{(n)})$$
$$= \underline{x}^{(n)} + \varepsilon(\hat{c}(\underline{x}^{(n)}) - c(\underline{x}^{(n)}))(\nabla \hat{c}(\underline{x}^{(n)}) - \nabla c(\underline{x}^n)). \tag{12.3}$$

Here, the step size ε may be fixed or non-increasing with n. A difference quotient approximation can be used for ∇c when, for example, c is a Monte Carlo estimator:

$$\widehat{\nabla c}(\underline{x}) = [\widehat{\partial_1 c}(\underline{x}), \ldots, \widehat{\partial_N c}(\underline{x})]', \quad \text{with} \tag{12.4}$$
$$\widehat{\partial_i c}(\underline{x}) \approx \frac{c(\underline{x} + \delta \underline{e}_i) - c(\underline{x} - \delta \underline{e}_i)}{2\delta}$$

and for small $\delta > 0$ in this first-order difference quotient, where $\underline{e}_i$ is the standard unit vector with 1 in the ith row ($e_{i,i} = 1$) and 0s elsewhere ($e_{i,j} = 0 \ \forall j \neq i$). $\nabla \hat{c}$ is computed by back-propagation; recall Section 2.10. Gradient ascent can be terminated when the one-step change in $\mathcal{E}$ is less than a certain threshold, $|\Delta \mathcal{E}|/\mathcal{E} < \sigma$.

At each stage of (iterative) active learning, LEMs are found starting from each sample in a batch of seeds, a process that is easily parallelized. The LEMs are then clustered to remove redundant (nearly identical) ones. For example, we can take two local maximizers $\underline{x}$ and $\underline{\xi}$ discovered by gradient ascent on $\mathcal{E}$ to be the same if

$$\|\underline{x} - \underline{\xi}\|^2 < a \cdot \max\{\|\Delta \underline{x}\|^2, \|\Delta \underline{\xi}\|^2\},$$

where $\Delta \underline{x}$ and $\Delta \underline{\xi}$ are the last gradient steps taken and where a larger parameter $a > 0$ results in more aggressive clustering. See Figure 12.2 for an illustration. Then the regression model $\hat{c}$ is retrained or refined (fine-tuned) using these newly labeled samples.

In subsequent active learning stages, the initial points can be chosen considering the unique LEMs found at previous stages, selecting in particular the ones exhibiting the greatest errors, in the manner of classical gradient-based "hill-climbing" methods (a version of which is called Cuckoo search [319]).

To increase search depth in a given LEM region, in subsequent active learning stages one should use a smaller step size ε and smaller parameter δ for the difference quotient approximating ∇c. To reduce the amount of oracle labeling compared to that needed when using a very small step size, subsequent AL stages could use step sizes ε that are initially calibrated based on a line search. That is, regarding (12.3), choose ε over a discrete set, for example, $\{\eta, \eta/2, \eta/4, \eta/8, \ldots, \eta/2^k\}$, so as to maximize $\mathcal{E}(\underline{x}^{(n+1)})$.

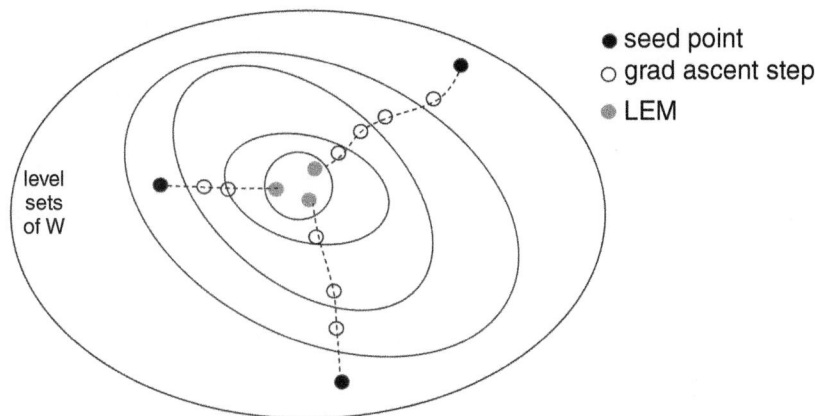

Figure 12.2 An illustrative example of clustering three LEMs.

The parameters $\eta, k > 0$ may be informed by those used for gradient ascent operating near $\underline{x}^{(0)}$ in previous active learning stages.

Also, to reduce the number of required oracle labelings, let us consider a LEM region U ("hill" of $\mathcal{E}$) that contains several previously oracle labeled samples. In subsequent AL stages operating in U, one can use a closed-form $\nabla \kappa$ instead of an approximate ∇c where κ is an interpolator of c based on the previously oracle labeled samples within U, for example, recall Eq. (2.1). Here we obviously may be trading off accuracy for the expense of oracle labeling.

Finally, note that we have implicitly assumed that the model $\hat{c}$ is sufficiently large to "accommodate" additional training samples under active learning. On the other hand, overfitting can be prevented, for example, through the use of random dropout during the training of $\hat{c}$ on $\mathcal{X}_0$; recall Section 2.7.8.

12.2.1   Depth and Breadth of Search for LEMs

In addition to exploring existing/known LEM regions, it may be important to further explore the feasible input space for new ones. The following AL approach uses two parameters, $\beta \in [0, 1]$ and $D \in \mathbb{Z}^+$, to trade off breadth and depth of search when a supervising oracle c is available.

1. Suppose L' unique LEMs and $D' \geq 0$ randomly selected labeled samples are carried forward from the previous AL stage to the current one.
2. Choose βD samples as seeds for finding new LEMs in the current stage – these may include some or all of the L' and D' from the previous stage (e.g., selected as those with the largest errors) and, as needed, newly selected random samples (which are then labeled). Perform LEM discovery starting from these seeds. Let L be the number of unique LEMs discovered in this step.

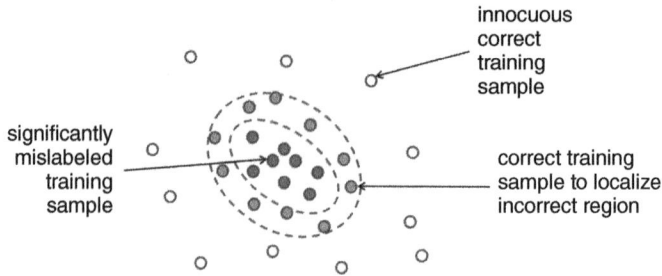

Figure 12.3 Illustrative example of a localized error region.

3. Choose $(1 - \beta)D$ samples independently and uniformly at random from feasible input space and label them.
4. The $(1 - \beta)D$ random samples and the L unique LEMs (discovered starting from the βD seeds) are used to retrain or refine the DNN.
5. The next stage's $D' = (1 - \beta)D$ and $L' = L$.

Note that β acts roughly like the inverse temperature in an annealing based search, for example, [1]; that is, *smaller β* is associated with *more search breadth*.

This iterative retraining or refining AL process has many variations. For example, selection of the $(1-\beta)D$ could be according to a deterministic sampling policy sweeping across the input space. Also, the parameter β may be periodically adjusted. For example, if after five retraining stages no new LEMs are found, then β may be increased (resulting in more depth of search in subsequent stages and, thus, a lower effective temperature).

Recall that oracle labelings c may be very costly computationally (if, e.g., they are based on Monte Carlo techniques, or on solving complicated partial differential equations). Thus, to assess the value of such an "annealing" method, one needs to fairly compare it against a baseline method, for example, one which just selects a number (n') of uniformly random samples equal to the *total* number of oracle labelings used by the annealing method, including all of those needed for LEM discovery. Such a comparison is given in the sequel.

12.3   A Localized Region of Regression Error

A particularly challenging scenario for an active learning system is to detect a highly "localized" region of significant error, as illustrated in Figure 12.3. In this figure, the error is due to training samples that were erroneously labeled. Such mislabelings (i) could "naturally" occur due to a hidden bias in the labeling process, (ii) could be caused by a data poisoning attack, or (iii) could be intentionally introduced by the learner (as a "challenge response" to the system), in order to assess the thoroughness and effectiveness of the active learning process. When the errors in such a region are "coherent," for example, $\hat{c}(\underline{x}) \approx 1.5c(\underline{x})$ for all the mislabeled training samples $\underline{x}$

(i.e., 50% over the ground truth c), then this may be a localized *backdoor* attack introduced into $\hat{c}$ via data poisoning of X_0 by an adversary. For the example of a financial derivative, the adversary could wait until market conditions approach the backdoor region, at which point she/he can manipulate the implied volatility V (one of the DNN's inputs) by placing fake bids (as discussed in, e.g., [29]) to perturb the input into the backdoor region. Alternatively, the adversary could simply wait until the market conditions reach the backdoor region, that is, a "triggerless" backdoor attack.

Obviously, smaller localized regions of error are harder to find, so one may need more search breadth (smaller β) in order to have a high likelihood of detecting them. If a localized region of error is by volume a fraction ρ of the feasible input space, the probability of selecting a seed in this region after n' random samples is obviously

$$\phi = 1 - (1 - \rho)^{n'}.$$

That is, to *achieve* a probability ϕ of finding this region, one would need to choose

$$n' = \frac{\log(1 - \phi)}{\log(1 - \rho)}. \tag{12.5}$$

One could instead deterministically sample the feasible input space by selecting on the order of ρ^{-1} equidistant points (i.e., forming a regular lattice spanning feasible input space). But note that the error region need not be a regular polytope or even convex. So such deterministic sampling would not guarantee detection of the error region.

12.4   Experimental Results for Valuation of a Financial Option

Let us now look at an example from finance: a down-and-out put option [70, 225]. The input, $x = (B, S, M, V, R)'$, is five-dimensional: barrier over spot-price-upon-inception of the security (e.g., a stock) involved in the option (B), strike over spot-price-upon-inception (S), time to maturity (M), implied volatility (V), and interest rate (R). The barrier, strike, and time to maturity are contract terms, while the interest rate, volatility and spot-price-upon-inception of the contract are derived from the market. (Upon inception of the contract, both R and V may be predicted by their own dedicated neural networks whose inputs could be a large number of market signals.) For a down-and-out put option, $B < \min\{S, 1\}$ and, upon maturity at time M (supposing the inception time of the option is time 0), the option has positive value equal to the present (time of inception) value of the strike price minus the spot-price-at-maturity, spot(M), *only if* (i) spot(M) is less than the strike price, and (ii) spot(t) never reaches the barrier over the lifetime $[0, M]$ of the option. So, $\hat{c}$ and c estimate

$$(1 + R)^{-M} E[(\text{strike} - \text{spot}(M))\mathbf{1}\{\text{spot}(t) > \text{barrier } \forall t \in [0, M]\}]. \tag{12.6}$$

For purposes of AL, c is computed by Monte Carlo means [35, 169], which involves much more computational cost than the DNN inference that yields $\hat{c}$.

12.4.1   Initial DNN Training

In an idealized experiment, X_0 is formed by random sampling of a "realistic" input domain – each input signal was accordingly normalized so that

$$X_0 \subset \{\underline{x} = (B, S, M, V, R) \in [0, 1]^5 \mid B < S\}.$$

But the output of the DNN is unnormalized and so has units of dollars. The initial training set size $|X_0| = 200{,}000$ (200k). A test set of 10k samples is used to evaluate accuracy. Under PyTorch, we used a feed-forward DNN with five fully connected internal layers respectively having 128, 256, 512, 256, and 128 ReLU neurons. The Adam optimizer ([123] and recall Section 2.7.7) was used on the MSE training objective (12.1) without dropout or SGD. The initial learning rate 0.001 was divided by 10 every 100 epochs. Training of the DNN halted when the normalized change in training MSE was less than 0.001 over 10 epochs or after 300 total epochs.

Γ_{attack} mislabeled and Γ_{clean} "localizing" clean samples were added to the training set to plant a localized backdoor; see Figure 12.3. Mislabeled samples were given a label that is 50% larger than that prescribed by the oracle c. The mislabeled samples $\underline{x} = (B, S, M, V, R)'$ were randomly chosen with (normalized) features in the ranges:

$$0.9 < B < S < 1; \quad M, R \in [0.45, 0.55]; \quad V \in [0.15, 0.25]. \tag{12.7}$$

(For example, the *un*normalized range for interest rate R is $[0.04, 0.06]$.) Thus, with reference to (12.5),

$$\rho = 10^{-5}.$$

The localizing clean samples were also randomly chosen such that $0.9 < B < S < 1$ but with $M, R \in [0.40, 0.45] \cup [0.55, 0.60]$ and $V \in [0.10, 0.15] \cup [0.25, 0.30]$, that is, so that they surround the mislabeled samples.

The results after (initial) training of the DNN $\hat{c}$ are shown in Table 12.1, including training and test MSE and test mean absolute (l_1) error (MAE). In the rightmost columns, attack and clean respectively indicate whether the reported statistics are computed based on test samples falling inside or outside of the backdoor region.

The first row shows the performance when there is no backdoor attack, that is, the "baseline" test set MSE and MAE are, respectively, 0.307 and 0.1103.

Recall that a *successful* backdoor attack satisfies two properties.

- The performance of the poisoned DNN, in this case measured by MSE and MAE on the correctly labeled (clean) test set, should not change significantly, compared to the performance of an unpoisoned DNN.
- The attack success rate, for example, in this case the percentage of backdoor region test samples whose DNN predicted value $\hat{c} \in (1.4c, 1.6c)$, is as high as possible, after poisoning with as few poisoned training samples as possible.

From Table 12.1, adding 2000 or 4000 (mislabeled) attack samples into the training set without using localizing correctly labeled (clean) samples ($\Gamma_{clean} = 0$) are indeed pretty effective attacks, with respective attack success rates of 0.9702 and 0.9822.

Table 12.1 Performance of DNN regression under different "strengths" of localized backdoor data poisoning. The MAE unit of measure is dollars.

Γ_{attack}	Γ_{clean}	Training MSE	Training MAE	Clean test MSE	Clean test MAE	$\hat{c}/c<1$ (clean)	$\hat{c}/c<1$ (attack)	$1.4<\hat{c}/c<1.6$ (attack)
0	0	0.0234	0.1061	0.0307	0.1103	0.4711	0.4743	0.0042
2000	0	0.0286	0.1133	0.0399	0.1186	0.5005	0.0001	0.9702
4000	0	0.0334	0.1189	0.0396	0.1221	0.4787	0	0.9822
2000	2000	0.0344	0.1193	0.0369	0.1244	0.5017	0.0003	0.876
2000	4000	0.0265	0.1096	0.0379	0.1151	0.5059	0.0008	0.9535
2000	8000	0.0241	0.1047	0.0315	0.1134	0.4921	0.0001	0.9654
4000	2000	0.0263	0.1094	0.0395	0.1131	0.5098	0	0.976
4000	4000	0.0239	0.1044	0.0371	0.1131	0.4976	0	0.983
4000	8000	0.0236	0.1017	0.0366	0.1087	0.4849	0.0004	0.9723
4000	12000	0.0225	0.1001	0.0291	0.1101	0.4982	0	0.9805

However, the clean test set MSE and MAE are somewhat inflated, compared with those of the unpoisoned DNN. The test MSE increased by about 30%, compared with baseline performance. Next, we tried adding clean labeled samples surrounding the mislabeled samples. As we can see, this helps reduce clean test set MSE and MAE, while maintaining a high attack success rate. $\Gamma_{attack} = 2000$ mislabeled samples localized with $\Gamma_{clean} = 8000$ correctly labeled samples achieves the best performance: clean test set MSE is 0.0315, only a 2.6% increase relative to 0.0307. Clean test set MAE is 0.1134, only a 2.8% increase relative to 0.1103. The attack success rate is 0.9654, with the total poisoned set only 5% of the total training set. For $\Gamma_{attack} = 4000$, localizing with $\Gamma_{clean} = 12,000$ clean samples performs best: clean test set MSE and MAE are even lower than for the baseline (unpoisoned) DNN, and the attack success rate is 0.9805. The total poisoned set is 8% of the total training set.

12.4.2 Mitigating Backdoor Poisoning by AL

Let us now focus on the case of 2000 mislabeled samples and 8000 localizing correctly labeled (clean) samples from Table 12.1. Here the AL objectives are both to reduce the overall test MSE and MAE and to discover and "tamp down" any localized backdoor regions in feasible input space.

Referring to Section 12.2: $D = 1000$ samples are selected independently and uniformly at random from feasible input space such that none are in the (misclassified) backdoor region. A fraction βD of them are used to discover LEMs of $\mathcal{E}$. The parameters used for LEM discovery are $\delta = \sigma = 10^{-3}$, $a = 5$, and the initial step-size ε is found by line search with parameters $\eta = 10^{-3}$, $k = 7$. The DNN is refined, using the same settings as when it was originally trained (see the previous subsection), to minimize MSE on the dataset consisting of the unique LEMs and the remaining $(1 - \beta)D$ randomly selected samples.

Table 12.2 After one stage of DNN refinement by active learning with $D = 1000$ (with none of these selected samples in the misclassified (backdoor) region) and with βD seeds for LEM discovery (i.e., with $\leq \beta D$ unique LEMs discovered). The mean total oracle labelings across 10 trials is given by n, where in each trial the number of oracle labelings is βD plus all those needed to discover the LEMs. ϕ is also empirically estimated from 10 trials, where a trial detects the backdoor region if an LEM is found there. Given ϕ and the relative volume of the backdoor region $\rho = 10^{-5}$, n' is given by (12.5). Both test MSE and test MAE were obtained from 10k test samples randomly chosen within feasible input space. Both backdoor MSE and backdoor MAE were obtained from 10k test samples randomly chosen in the backdoor region. The performance of the poisoned DNN before any AL mitigation is performed is indicated in the bottom row.

β	n	ϕ	n' (12.5)	Test MSE	Test MAE	Backdoor MSE	Backdoor MAE
0	1000	0.0	1000	0.0331	0.1130	19.69	3.973
0.25	2681	0.2	22314	0.0333	0.1134	19.31	3.926
0.5	4303	0.6	91628	0.0311	0.1131	18.84	3.869
0.75	6322	0.5	69314	0.0313	0.1137	19.01	3.903
1	8345	0.1	10535	0.0311	0.1141	19.65	3.962
Before				0.0315	0.1134	20.12	4.012

The results after refining are shown in Table 12.2. The improvements are best for $\beta = 0.5$. Though the improvements in the backdoor region are modest, note that the number of samples used in this single stage of AL is less than 5% of those used to train the DNN ($|\mathcal{X}_0| = 200k$). Moreover, it is important to emphasize that the AL approach did, with significant frequency (over 10 trials), find LEMs in the backdoor region, that is, in many cases it succeeded in *discovering* the backdoor. This is by itself very important – once such regions are discovered, the training authority can be notified, with more serious measures potentially taken (such as discarding all training samples in the vicinity of the backdoor region, re-collecting (and labeling) a substantial amount of clean data in this region, and then retraining).

Note that we can adaptively select the β parameter for each AL stage, for example, by selecting the jth value β_j with probability p_j where the pmf p (over a discrete set of values for β) is simply adapted after every AL stage according to, say, the change in test (or a validation set's) MAE. Let ΔMAE_i be the test MAE after stage i minus that after stage $i - 1$. For example, if β_j is used in stage i, then after stage i, $p_j \leftarrow p_j \exp(-\gamma\Delta\text{MAE}_i)$, and then $p_l \leftarrow (1 + bp_l)/\sum_{l'}(1 + bp_{l'})$ for all l, where parameters $\gamma, b > 0$. Note that if b is chosen very small, then p is approximately uniform.

12.5   Discussion Topics: Query by Committee, Reinforcement Learning (RL), Test-Time Evasion (TTE), Classification

In this section, we briefly discuss other related topics of interest.

12.5.1   Query by Committee AL

Note that if there is a group (pool, committee) of $n > 1$ "reference" models $c_1(\underline{x}), \ldots, c_n(\underline{x})$ available to the user, with the average inference $\mu(\underline{x}) = n^{-1} \sum_{i=1}^{n} c_i(\underline{x})$, then active learning could be based on finding feasible inputs $\underline{x}$ for which $\hat{c}(\underline{x})$ significantly deviates from $\mu(\underline{x})$ and for which there is also significant variance in the group inference, that is, where

$$(\hat{c}(\underline{x}) - \mu(\underline{x}))^2 + \lambda \frac{1}{n} \sum_{i=1}^{n} (c_i(\underline{x}) - \mu(\underline{x}))^2$$

is large, with parameter $\lambda > 0$. This is an example of "query by committee" active learning [25].

12.5.2   Online Learning and Reinforcement Learning

In practice, one can *operationally* (at test time), but *passively*, observe the system being modeled to obtain samples with ground truth labels (observed outcomes). That is, unlike for AL, the learner may not be able to control *which* samples are operationally observed. Then some or all of these samples can be periodically selected for purposes of retraining or refining the DNN model $\hat{c}$ as part of an online learning process. The focus may naturally be on observations for which the current model $\hat{c}$ did not well predict the observed outcome.

For the financial application considered in this chapter, operationally observed recent instances of the contract terms and market conditions upon inception (inputs) and the value of a financial option upon maturity (output label) could be the basis for refining the DNN $\hat{c}$ (and the oracle c). But the DNN is predicting the *expected* present value of the option, so care needs to be taken not to bias the regressor through such online learning based on only a few such samples in a given input region.

Also note that deep reinforcement learning (DRL) typically refers to more complex *offline* refinement of DNN embodied policies acting on sequential data [183, 184]. Adversarial inputs to such DNNs are discussed in [152, 207]. Backdoor attacks on DRL are discussed in [125, 287].

12.5.3   TTEs on Deep Regression

Given the DNN $\hat{c}$, a TTE for regression is just a point in the neighborhood of a LEM of $\mathcal{E}$. Such a TTE may be most effective (most covert) when the LEM is highly localized (recall Figure 12.3). Recall that a TTE adversary does not poison the training dataset but instead searches for a suitable LEM using the DNN or some reasonably accurate proxy; the search may be conducted as described above for RDR-AL. One can apply OODD to TTEs in deep regression just as for classifiers, for example, based on a GAN (discriminator output) or mixture model (p-value) learned from the training dataset (although a LEM used by a TTE attacker may not in fact be an OOD sample). Recall the detection methods discussed in Chapter 4, including Section 4.8.

12.5.4   Classification

Note that regression is often part of a discrete decision-making process. For example, a customer may purchase an option if they perceive that its value (by their calculation) minus its price (by the vendor's calculation) is greater than a certain threshold. In this case, the attacks and defenses (tailored for classification) described in previous chapters are relevant. Adversarial active learning for SVM classifiers (see the Appendix) is discussed in [175, 176].

12.6   Chapter Summary

This chapter introduces problems of regression and prediction involving, for example, a MSE loss training objective. An example framework for active learning (AL) was described which identifies local error maximizers (LEMs), by gradient-based optimization, for purposes of retraining or refining a deep regression model. This "query by synthesis" AL can trade off breadth and depth of search of the feasible input space. A kind of worst-case scenario with a small localized region with significant error was considered; this scenario could be the result of deliberate data poisoning to plant a backdoor. Through a numerical example involving prediction of the value of a financial option, using a computationally costly (Monte Carlo based) oracle to provide supervising labels, it was shown how a localized backdoor could be planted in the neural network and how AL can detect it and reduce the test error. The chapter also included discussion of sundry topics, including query by committee AL and TTE attacks on deep regression.

Some questions to test the reader's understanding of the chapter include the following.

- Explain why Figure 12.2 may *not* illustrate steepest ascent.
- Suppose a population of samples in feasible input space have been pre-selected for labeling. Devise methods for selecting *which* of these to label based on known samples that have already been labeled.
- How would the AL approach described in this chapter be extended to deep regression where the output is vector valued?
- Can the AL approach from this chapter also be applied to statistical classifiers? How would it need to be modified to be most suitable for classification?
- Do the experiments in this chapter support the use of RDR-AL for detecting localized backdoors in regression models, compared with a uniform random sampling strategy? Explain.

12.7   Project: Clean Label Backdoor Attack

Implement a "clean label" backdoor data poisoning attack (recall Section 1.4.2) on deep regression for the UC Irvine Boston Housing dataset [153, 277], which involves "poisoning" the training set by adding many additional training samples in a local region, but without any mislabeling. Assess how successful such an attack is in degrading the learned regression model's accuracy (outside of the region where the attack is concentrated). Note that, to implement this attack, which involves the addition of samples that were not in the original training set, one may need to interpolate the supervising target values for the poisoned samples (since there is no known supervision for them).

13 Error Generic Data Poisoning Defense

In this chapter, we address so-called "error generic" data poisoning (DP) attacks (hereafter called DP attacks) [21] on classifiers. Unlike backdoor attacks, DP attacks aim to degrade *overall* accuracy. (Previous chapters were concerned with "error specific" DP attacks involving specific backdoor patterns and source and/or target classes.) To effectively mislead classifier training using relatively few poisoned samples, an attacker introduces feature collision [102] to the training samples, in particular by altering the class labels of clean samples. (Another possibility is to generate *synthetic* data, not typical of a given class, but labeling the synthetic data samples to this class.) The information extracted from the clean and poisoned samples labeled to the same class (as well as from clean samples that originate from the same class as the mislabeled poisoned samples) is largely inconsistent, which prevents the learning of an accurate class decision boundary.

DP attacks have been successfully demonstrated against support vector machines (SVMs, see the Appendix), logistic regression (LR) models (Section 2.14), autoregressive models ([7] and Section 2.7.6), collaborative filtering systems [143], differentially private learners [163], and neural networks [188]. Akin to the before/during training backdoor defenses considered in Chapter 5, we assume that the defender *does* have access to the training set. However, the poisoned samples (if there is data poisoning) are an *unknown* subset embedded among the clean training samples. That is, the defender does not know whether an attack is present, and if so, *which* samples are poisoned and *which* class(es) are corrupted. This *embedded data poisoning* attack scenario, while a formidable problem for the defender, is of great practical interest, as it is the most common scenario that will be encountered in practice. Studies on defending against such embedded data poisoning attacks are either tailored to a specific type of classifier (e.g., SVM [136], LR [69]), are only suitable for a specific type of DP attack, or make assumptions about the available data (e.g., availability of a clean/attack-free validation set for use by the defender [193]). The BIC based defense (BIC-MM-TSC) described below does not make any such assumptions about the attack, does not require a clean validation set, and can be deployed to protect various types of classifiers.

Poisoned samples are generally *atypical* of the distribution of the class to which they are labeled. Thus, mixture modeling (recall Chapter 3, see [63, 168]) can be applied to accurately explain the potentially multi-modal data and to capture poisoned samples within a subset of the mixture components used to model a class's data distribution. Consider the following observations. If the poisoned samples are typical of another class (different from the class to which they are labeled), *re-distributing* them to this other class is expected to increase the overall data likelihood. Furthermore, removing a poisoned component will reduce the model complexity of a mixture. Thus, both the data likelihood and model complexity terms which together constitute the Bayesian information criterion (BIC) cost function (recall Section 3.4) should improve when data poisoning is mitigated (by sample re-assignments and/or component removals). This motivates making poisoned sample inferences consistent with minimizing BIC.

So, it is suggested to first apply mixture modeling separately to each class, with the number of components chosen to minimize the BIC criterion. Then components are assessed for possible poisoning, with a detected component either removed or revised (whichever results in a lower BIC cost for the "meta" mixture across all classes). After poisoned samples have been detected and removed, the classifier can be trained on the resulting (sanitized) dataset.

Note also that if the poisoned samples are synthetically generated, are *not* typical of *any* of the classes, and are all labeled to a *common* class, detecting (and mitigating) data poisoning will be very difficult (and possibly even ill posed) – for such a scenario, detection may only be reliably achieved if clean validation data (from all classes) is available.

13.1 Threat Model

This chapter considers K-class ($K \geq 2$) classification tasks, where the classifier, $\hat{c} : \mathbb{R}^N \rightarrow \mathcal{Y} = \{1, 2, \ldots, K\}$, is trained on $\mathcal{X}$ and then tested on $\mathcal{I}$. $\mathcal{X}$ and $\mathcal{I}$ are assumed i.i.d. from the same (unknown) distribution. Each feature x_l, $l = 1, \ldots, N$, may be either discrete or continuous valued – discrete-valued feature spaces will be considered in the experiments in this chapter, but experiments on real-valued image datasets are also given in [148].

Assume the attacker

1. has sufficient knowledge of the classification domain to generate or acquire samples that are legitimate instances of the different classes,
2. has access to insert poisoned samples into the training set ($\mathcal{X} = \mathcal{X}_0 \cup \mathcal{B}$),
3. may simultaneously poison any subset of the classes, possibly with different attack strengths (i.e., different amounts of poisoned samples) for individual classes, and
4. is unaware of any deployed defense (i.e., this is not a white box attack scenario).

Recall that the goal of the DP attacker is to degrade the classifier's (test set) generalization accuracy, that is,

$$\text{ACC} = \frac{1}{|\mathcal{I}|} \sum_{\underline{x} \in \mathcal{I}} \mathbf{1}\{\hat{c}(\underline{x}) = c(\underline{x})\},$$

as much as possible.

Assume the defender

1. can only use the training set $\mathcal{X}$ manipulated by the attacker – not any additional samples known to be clean (attack-free) – which is consistent with the embedded DP scenario, and

2. does not know whether an attack is present, and if so, does not know the subset of attacking samples ($\mathcal{B}$), nor which class(es) are corrupted.

The defender *aims* to

1. identify and remove as many poisoned samples as possible and as few clean samples as possible, before classifier training/retraining, and in so doing
2. achieve classification accuracy as close as possible to that of a classifier trained on a clean (unpoisoned) dataset.

13.2   Data Poisoning Defenses

An obvious strategy for defending against DP attacks is to conduct "data sanitization" on the training dataset, that is, identifying and cleansing attack samples as training set outliers. Recall that there are two types of outlier identification – supervised and unsupervised. Some supervised detection methods are in fact a form of supervised learning – the defender trains a binary discriminator based on labeled examples of anomalies and normalities, for example, [320]. The resulting discriminator can then be applied to identify and sanitize anomalies (possibly poisoned examples) in the classifier's training dataset. However, such a learned discriminator may only reliably identify anomalies in a dataset that are similar to those seen during the discriminator's training – that is, the discriminator may only be good at identifying *known* anomalies, not *unknown* anomalies. Another issue with this approach is that anomalies (attack instances) may be rarer and more difficult to collect than "normalities." Thus, the performance of the discriminator may suffer from highly skewed class imbalance ("anomalous" versus "normal") in the supervised examples used to train it.

Other supervised detection methods are more akin to *unsupervised* anomaly detection methods, except that they possess hyperparameters whose setting, to achieve good detection performance, requires either a clean validation set (which is contrary to the embedded DP scenario considered here) or, again, a labeled set of "normalities" and "anomalies," for example, [59, 102, 206, 216, 247, 253] (recall Section 4.2.4).

On the other hand, truly unsupervised detection methods do not require labeled examples of what is normal and what is anomalous, and are analogous to unsupervised clustering methods. They model data distributions and flag potential outliers. The false positive rate (FPR) and false negative rate (FNR) may be relatively high for an unsupervised detector. Thus, [36] proposed to leverage human intelligence to correctly identify outliers from among a set of outlier candidates automatically detected by a machine learning method. However, such an approach is only suitable for domains where humans are skilled at analyzing data – images, speech, text, low-dimensional data domains, and/or high-dimensional ones that can be visualized with fidelity in a low-dimensional space. Moreover, such an approach may be very costly and time consuming, as there may be a large set of outlier candidates for the human to inspect.

Due to the large space of possible attacks, in practice there will always be *unknown* attacks, ones which have not been encountered before (and thus, with no labeled examples available for training of a supervised detector). For various types of attacks (test-time evasion attacks, as well as data poisoning attacks), it has been observed that the performance of supervised detectors may fare poorly on unknown attacks [180]. Given a defender that first performs outlier removal followed by margin based loss minimization, [253] generates an approximate upper bound on the efficacy of any DP attack. They also established a dual method which generates an attack that nearly achieves this upper bound. However, their attack requires full knowledge of the clean training dataset (prior to its poisoning) and cannot handle non-convex loss functions, which limits its application in practice. [216] proposes a method for producing certificates of robustness for two-layer neural networks. Such certificates are differentiable and can be jointly optimized with the network parameters, providing an adaptive regularizer that encourages robustness against attacks. However, they neither characterize nor discuss the inherent tradeoff between robustness and model bias (i.e., the degradation in the classifier's accuracy on *clean* data that results from making the classifier robust to attacks).

[206] proposed a label sanitization strategy tailored to label flipping attacks. The poisoned samples are expected to be outliers relative to untainted samples with the same labels. Thus, they relabel a sample based on the plurality label of its K nearest neighbors (KNN) to enforce label homogeneity (recall Section 4.11). However, this defense will fail when the number of poisoned samples is sufficiently large such that some of the neighbors of an attack sample are also attack samples. This defense also relies on the availability of a clean validation set to tune the hyperparameter K. This choice highly impacts the detector's performance, as will be seen (see Section 13.4).

[59, 102] proposed to defend DP attacks by analyzing training sample gradients (measured with respect to the loss function used for classifier training). They posited a unified view of the effects of DP on learned classifier parameters: (i) the l_2 norm of the gradient from a poisoned sample is larger than that of a clean sample, on average; (ii) there is an orientation difference between poisoned and clean sample gradients. [59] detects such effects by singular value decomposition (SVD, recall Section 3.5) applied to the matrix of gradients, taken with respect to the model parameters, with each row of this matrix corresponding to one sample's contribution to the training loss function. They derive an outlier score for each training sample, which is the squared magnitude of the projection of the gradient onto the top right singular vector. For classification tasks, [59] separately constructs the matrix of gradients for the training samples from each class, and computes outlier scores for each class, to improve performance. At each detection step, the top ε/m fraction of samples with highest scores over all classes are removed, where m is the total number of detection steps and ε is the total fraction of samples to be ultimately removed (after m steps); the classifier is then retrained on the remaining samples. The performance of this detector is sensitive to the choice of the hyperparameters m and ε, as well as to the chosen training loss function. Note that there is no a priori knowledge of a good choice for ε. Also, their method is only applicable to linear classifiers, for example, an SVM (see the Appendix). Moreover, they only reported the improvement in the test set error rate – the false positive rate was not mentioned, even though this is an important criterion for assessing a defense against

DP attacks. [59] is computationally expensive as it requires performing an SVD for each class, at each detection step, and then retraining the classifier after each detection step.

[102] mitigates the effects of DP by gradient shaping (GS), that is, constraining the magnitude and orientation of poisoned gradients to make them close to clean gradients. For example, one can adopt a differentially private mechanism based optimizer (e.g., differentially private stochastic gradient descent (DP-SGD)) in training. A DP-SGD optimizer clips gradients according to the hyperparameter $l_2\_norm\_clip$ and then adds noise to the gradients, whose size is controlled by the hyperparameter $noise\_multiplier$. [102] is computationally cheap – it does not require extra computation pre-training/post-training. However, their method only reduces the effect of poisoning, rather than eliminating the poisoned samples. Efficacy of their defense is dramatically degraded as an increasing number of attack samples are injected, as will be seen from our experimental results.

[147] applied a BIC based defense against DP attacks for binary classification tasks (BIC-C-D). The fundamental difference between BIC-C-D and the BIC-MM-TSC method described in the sequel pertains to *untainted data availability*. BIC-C-D assumes that the attacker only poisons one of the two classes, with this class known to the defender. Thus, the defender can always take the clean class as reference in helping to identify poisoned samples in the corrupted class. (This should be especially helpful for label-flipping attacks, where the poisoned samples, labeled to one class, will be typical of the other (clean) class.) However, in practice, the attacker is able to poison more than one class, and the defender does not know which class(es) are poisoned. Under this most realistic attack scenario, [147] may fail even if only one class is poisoned, as the defender might sanitize the clean class based on the poisoned one (see Section 13.4).

[59, 102, 206] are supervised detection methods, with their performances highly impacted by the choices of hyperparameters. By contrast, the BIC-MM-TSC method described below is unsupervised. At each optimization step, it separately assesses the hypothesis that each individual mixture component, in each class, is poisoned. Only the component whose trial sanitization yields the lowest BIC cost is actually sanitized. This process is repeated until the total BIC cost, defined over all classes, converges.

13.3 Bayesian Information Criterion Based Mixture Model Training Set Cleansing (BIC-MM-TSC)

This section describes a cleansing strategy on the training dataset, that is, identifying and removing poisoned samples as training dataset outliers prior to classifier training. To accurately describe the possibly poisoned dataset, mixture modeling is applied to each class. Mixture modeling is a sound statistical approach for well fitting potentially multi-modal data (recall Chapter 3) and also gives the potential for concentrating the poisoned samples into just a few components, which assists in accurately identifying and removing them. Note that, in practice, poisoned components may own both poisoned and untainted samples, with the poisoning ratio for each component unknown.

An attacker can confound the learning of class discriminating features by choosing, for poisoning, samples typical of one class, but then labeling them to other class(es) (i.e., a label flipping attack). *Accordingly, such samples are expected to be better explained by the mixture model for a class other than the class to which they are labeled.* Thus, poisoned samples in the training dataset are identified as those with greater likelihood under a class different from the one to which they are labeled. Such samples are effectively *re-assigned* to the class (and mixture component) under which they have the greatest likelihood.

Bayesian Information Criterion (BIC): Now, suppose the vast majority of a mixture component's samples are re-assigned in this way to another class. In this case, there may be insufficient remaining samples to reliably (or even in a well-posed fashion) estimate the component's parameters. (For example, for a multivariate Gaussian component, with a full covariance matrix of size $d \times d$, one needs at least d samples to estimate a (full rank) covariance matrix.) In such a case, rather than retaining this component, it may be better to *remove* it, with its remaining samples assigned to the class and component under which it has the greatest log-likelihood fit.

A principled, theoretically supported criterion for model order selection, suitable for use in deciding between revising and (wholesale) removing a mixture component from a class's model, is the Bayesian information criterion (BIC), which expresses an inherent tradeoff between data likelihood fit and model complexity. Recalling Section 3.4, the BIC objective function for a given dataset $\mathcal{X}$ is defined as:

$$\text{BIC} = |\theta|\kappa - L(\mathcal{X}; \theta) \tag{13.1}$$

where θ is the set of free parameters specifying a density function model for the data, $|\theta|$ is the number of free parameters in this set, κ is the cost (penalty) for describing an individual model parameter, and $L(\mathcal{X}; \theta)$ is the log-likelihood of the dataset $\mathcal{X}$, based on the density function model. Within an approximate Bayesian setting, the BIC cost for describing an individual model parameter is derived, and found to be $\kappa = \frac{1}{2} \log |\mathcal{X}|$. This model penalty will be used in the following. The form of the BIC objective seen above is equivalent to the minimum description length (MDL) [219], and is amenable to interpretation as a two-part codelength: (i) the first term,

$$\Omega := |\theta|\kappa = \frac{1}{2}|\theta| \log |\mathcal{X}|,$$

is the number of bits needed to describe the parameters of the density model for the data; (ii) the second, negative data log-likelihood term, $-L$, is the number of bits to describe the dataset, given the model.

Mixture Model for the Data: The training data labeled to each class can be modeled by a (class specific) mixture of density functions (or probability mass functions in the case of discrete data). That is, for an individual sample $\underline{x}$, labeled to class $n \in \mathcal{Y} = \{1, 2, \ldots, K\}$ (i.e., $\underline{x} \in \mathcal{X}_n$, $c(\underline{x}) = n$), its density (likelihood) is:

$$p_n[\underline{x}; \theta_n] = \sum_{j=1}^{M_n} \alpha_{n,j} p_{n,j}[\underline{x}; \theta_{n,j}],$$

where $\alpha_{n,j}$ is the probability mass (prior probability) of mixture component j for class n (i.e., $\sum_{j=1}^{M_n} \alpha_{n,j} = 1, \alpha_{n,j} \geq 0\, \forall n, j$), $p_{n,j}[\cdot; \theta_{n,j}]$ is the jth mixture component density under class n, $\theta_{n,j}$ is the set of parameters specifying that component density, and M_n is the number of mixture components for class n. Note that

$$\theta_n = \bigcup_{j=1}^{M_n} (\theta_{n,j} \cup \{\alpha_{n,j}\}) \quad \text{and} \quad \theta = \bigcup_{n=1}^{K} \theta_n.$$

In the above, a data sample from class n is associated probabilistically with all components from the class's mixture density. Alternatively, consider the *complete data* BIC objective function, based on the complete data log-likelihood function, wherein each data sample is hard (fully) assigned to the mixture component under which it has the greatest log-likelihood. That is, the complete data log-likelihood for the data from class n is:

$$L_n = \sum_{j=1}^{M_n} L_{n,j} \quad \text{where}$$

$$L_{n,j} = \sum_{\underline{x} \in X_{n,j}} \log p_{n,j}[\underline{x}; \theta_{n,j}],$$

and $\underline{x} \in X_{n,j}$ if and only if $\underline{x}$ is labeled to class n and $p_{n,j}[\underline{x}; \theta_{n,j}] > p_{n,j'}[\underline{x}; \theta_{n,j'}]$ $\forall j' \neq j$. Thus, the complete data log-likelihood is

$$L = \sum_{n=1}^{K} L_n.$$

(Here component priors are assumed uniform and hence they are absent from the complete data log-likelihood. In practice, these terms do not affect detection performance significantly.)

Likewise, the complete data BIC objective is:

$$\text{BIC}_{\text{cmplt}} = |\theta|\kappa - L = |\theta|\kappa - \sum_{n=1}^{K} \sum_{j=1}^{M_n} L_{n,j}. \tag{13.2}$$

In short, the principle behind a complete data BIC based defense is that *a component is identified as poisoned if removing or revising it and re-assigning its samples to other classes reduces the BIC cost; moreover, samples which are redistributed to other class(es) are deemed poisoned.* Thus, this anomaly detection method is *unsupervised* and consistent with solving a BIC minimization problem. (Apart from poisoned samples, the BIC based method might also remove any outliers, if it is BIC efficacious to do so.) In the sequel, an algorithm is developed for mitigating data poisoning via (locally optimal) minimization of the above complete data BIC objective.

13.3.1   BIC Based Defense

The model parameters θ_n of the mixture for class n are first estimated via the expectation-maximization (EM) algorithm (recall Section 3.2), applied to the subset X_n of the training dataset X labeled as class $n \in \mathcal{Y}$. The chosen model order M_n is the one that yields the least BIC cost (13.1) over the set $\{1, 2, \ldots, M^{\max}\}$, with $M^{\max}$ an upper bound on the number of components in a mixture (recall Section 3.4). ($M^{\max}$ is in fact not truly a hyperparameter, as one can observe the changes of BIC to adjust the range of model orders. For example, if $M^{\max}$ yields the least BIC, one can increase $M^{\max}$ and repeat model selection until $M_n < M^{\max}$.) Finally, let the set of component indices across all classes be

$$S = \{(n, j) \mid n = 1, \ldots, K, \ j = 1, \ldots, M_n\}.$$

As aforementioned, a mixture model for each class is first estimated and then poisoned components and samples are identified by minimizing the complete data BIC cost (13.2). This BIC minimization involves sample re-distribution, component removal/revision, and parameter updates. To reflect these model changes, several types of "indicator" variables are introduced.

- The class t_i and component under this class j_i that best explain sample $\underline{x}_i$ are

$$(t_i, j_i) = \underset{t \in \{1, \ldots, K\}, \ j \in \{1, \ldots, M_t\}}{\arg \max} \ p_{t,j}[\underline{x}_i; \theta_{t,j}],$$

- $r_{n,j} = \begin{cases} 1 & \text{component } j \text{ in class } n \text{ is poisoned} \\ 0 & \text{else} \end{cases}$

- $q_{n,j} = \begin{cases} 1 & \text{component } j \text{ in class } n \text{ needs to be revised} \\ 0 & \text{component } j \text{ in class } n \text{ needs to be removed.} \end{cases}$

Note that $q_{n,j}$ is configured only when $r_{n,j} = 1$.

To account for possible data poisoning, the complete data BIC cost to be minimized is

$$\text{BIC}_{\text{cmplt}}(\theta) = \sum_{n=1}^{K} \sum_{j=1}^{M_n} \left((1 - r_{n,j}(1 - q_{n,j})) \kappa |\theta_{n,j}| + 1 + \mathbf{1}\{r_{n,j} = 1\} \right)$$

$$- \sum_{n=1}^{K} \sum_{j=1}^{M_n} \left((1 - r_{n,j}) L_{n,j}(\theta_{n,j}) + r_{n,j} \sum_{\underline{x}_i \in X_{n,j}} \log p_{t_i,j_i}[\underline{x}_i; \theta_{t_i,j_i}] \right).$$

$$(13.3)$$

In (13.3), the model parameters are $\theta = \cup_{n=1}^{K} \cup_{j=1}^{M_n} (\theta_{n,j} \cup r_{n,j} \cup q_{n,j})$, where the binary "structural" parameters $r_{n,j}$ and $q_{n,j}$ each require one bit to specify (hence the '1' and $\mathbf{1}\{r_{n,j} = 1\}$ contributions to the model complexity term). By contrast, t_i and j_i are hidden data assignments (as part of the complete data log-likelihood, and complete data BIC), not model parameters.

To minimize (13.3) in a locally optimal fashion, the BIC based approach will involve cycling over the mixture components, one at a time, effecting changes to the mixture models that reduce the BIC objective. The new BIC cost, in light of changes to component j from class n, can be expressed as the "old" BIC cost plus the (negative) change resulting from sample re-assignments or the component's removal, denoted $\Delta \text{BIC}_{n,j}$.

Each feasible joint configuration of the variables for component j in class n corresponds to one of three cases.

1. $r_{n,j} = 0$: The component is formed by clean samples, and there is no need to re-distribute its samples or modify the component. That is, the change in model complexity is $\Delta\Omega_{n,j,1} = 0$ and the change in log-likelihood is $\Delta L_{n,j,1} = 0$. The change in BIC in this case is thus

$$\Delta\text{BIC}_{n,j} = \Delta\Omega_{n,j,1} - \Delta L_{n,j,1} = 0.$$

2. $r_{n,j} = 1, q_{n,j} = 0$: Component j is poisoned and is chosen to be removed from the mixture, thus changing the model complexity term by

$$\Delta\Omega_{n,j,2} = -|\theta_{n,j}|\frac{1}{2}\log|\mathcal{X}|,$$

where $|\theta_{n,j}|$ is the number of parameters in component j from class n. The component's samples are re-distributed consistent with maximizing the log-likelihood: each sample $\underline{x}_i \in \mathcal{X}_{n,j}$ is re-assigned to component j_i of class t_i, where

$$(t_i, j_i) = \operatorname*{arg\,max}_{(t',j') \in \mathcal{S}\setminus\{(n,j)\}} p_{t',j'}[\underline{x}_i; \theta_{t',j'}].$$

Let

$$Q = \{(t_i, j_i) \mid \underline{x}_i \in \mathcal{X}_{n,j}\}$$

be the set of components which receive the re-assigned samples. For each component $(t', j') \in Q$, its parameters are re-estimated by maximum likelihood estimation (MLE):

$$\theta_{t',j'}^{\text{new}} = \operatorname*{arg\,max}_{\theta} \sum_{\underline{x} \in \widehat{\mathcal{X}}_{t',j'}} \log p_{t',j'}[\underline{x}; \theta],$$

where

$$\widehat{\mathcal{X}}_{t',j'} = \mathcal{X}_{t',j'} \cup \{\underline{x}_i \in \mathcal{X}_{n,j} \mid t_i = t', j_i = j'\}.$$

This optimization has a closed form, globally optimal solution for the component density model forms considered in this chapter. The total data log-likelihood changes by

$$\Delta L_{n,j,2} = \sum_{(t',j') \in Q} \sum_{\underline{x} \in \widehat{\mathcal{X}}_{t',j'}} \log p_{t',j'}[\underline{x}; \theta_{t',j'}^{\text{new}}]$$

$$- \sum_{(t',j') \in Q} \sum_{\underline{x} \in \widehat{\mathcal{X}}_{t',j'}} \log p_{t',j'}[\underline{x}; \theta_{t',j'}] - \sum_{\underline{x} \in \mathcal{X}_{n,j}} \log p_{n,j}[\underline{x}; \theta_{n,j}].$$

The change in BIC in this case is

$$\Delta\text{BIC}_{n,j} = \Delta\Omega_{n,j,2} - \Delta L_{n,j,2}.$$

3. $r_{n,j} = 1, q_{n,j} = 1$: Similar to case 2 but instead of removing it, the parameters of component j are re-estimated using its surviving samples (i.e., samples with $t_i = n$). Revising a component does not change the model complexity cost, since the

code length is untouched (i.e., $\Delta\Omega_{n,j,3} = 0$). Again, for each sample $\underline{x}_i \in X_{n,j}$, let $(t_i, j_i) = \arg\max_{(t',j') \in S \setminus \{(n,j)\}} p_{t',j'}[\underline{x}_i; \theta_{t',j'}]$. Also, again, let $Q = \{(t_i, j_i) \mid \underline{x}_i \in X_{n,j}\}$, that is, it is the set of components which receive the re-assigned samples. The parameters $\theta_{n,j}$ are re-estimated by MLE on the surviving samples:

$$\theta_{n,j}^{\text{new}} = \arg\max_{\theta} \sum_{\underline{x} \in \widehat{X}_{n,j}} \log p_{n,j}[\underline{x}; \theta],$$

where

$$\widehat{X}_{n,j} = \{\underline{x}_i \in X_{n,j} \mid t_i = n\}.$$

That is, samples that are best represented by class $t' \neq n$ (i.e., $t_i = t' \neq n$) are re-distributed to their fittest components in class t', but the remaining samples (i.e., those with $t_i = n$) are explained by the updated component j. Let

$$Q' = \{(t', j') \in Q \mid t' \neq n\} \cup \{(n, j)\}$$

be the set of components to be updated. The total data log-likelihood changes by

$$\Delta L_{n,j,3} = \sum_{(t',j') \in Q'} \sum_{\underline{x} \in \widehat{X}_{t',j'}} \log p_{t',j'}[\underline{x}; \theta_{t',j'}^{\text{new}}] - \sum_{(t',j') \in Q'} \sum_{\underline{x} \in X_{t',j'}} \log p_{t',j'}[\underline{x}; \theta_{t',j'}],$$

where $\widehat{X}_{t',j'}$ and $\theta_{t',j'}^{\text{new}}$ $\forall (t', j') \in Q'$ are defined in the same way as in case 2. The BIC change in this case is

$$\Delta \text{BIC}_{n,j} = -\Delta L_{n,j,3}.$$

To minimize the complete data BIC objective, for each component in class $n \in \{1, \ldots, K\}$, the configuration of the parameters that reduces BIC the most should be chosen. However, the optimal configuration for any component j depends on the configurations for other components. It is thus intractable to define an algorithm guaranteed to find a globally optimal configuration over all components (e.g., by exhaustively evaluating over the huge combinatorial space of component configurations). Instead, at each optimization step, each component's configuration (for all components, over all classes) is separately *trial* updated, and then only permanently updated for the component that yields the greatest reduction in BIC. This is repeated until there are no further changes. This optimization approach is non-increasing in the BIC objective and results in a locally optimal solution.

The null hypothesis of BIC based detection inference is that the training dataset is not poisoned (and is generated according to the existing mixture model). If there is data poisoning, the training dataset is hypothesized to be generated by an alternative model (with some components removed and/or modified). Thus, the following hypothesis testing is performed: after BIC minimization, if $r_{n,j} = 0$ holds for all components in all classes, then no components and samples are inferred to be poisoned and the null hypothesis is accepted. Otherwise, the null hypothesis is rejected, and the training dataset is deemed poisoned. The samples that were re-assigned to other classes, via the BIC minimization, are deemed poisoned and are removed from the training dataset.

13.3.2   Implementation

Consistent with the above description, an iterative, locally optimal approach is applied to minimize the total BIC cost and optimize its parameters, as shown in Algorithm 13.1. As discussed above, at each algorithm step, only the component whose removal/revision decreases the total BIC cost the most is sanitized. That is, the reduction in the total BIC cost $\Delta\mathrm{BIC}_{n,j}$ caused by trial removal/revision of each component j in each class n is first evaluated. Then, the component j^* in class n^* which decreases the total BIC cost the most is sanitized, that is,

$$(n^*, j^*) = \underset{n\in\{1,...,K\},\ j\in\{1,...,M_n\}}{\arg\min} \Delta\mathrm{BIC}_{n,j},$$

where

$$\Delta\mathrm{BIC}_{n,j} = \min_{m=1,2,3} \{\Delta\Omega_{n,j,m} - \Delta L_{n,j,m}\}.$$

The above procedure is repeated until the total BIC cost converges, that is, until no trial component updates further reduce the BIC cost. Finally, all samples with $t_i \neq y_i$ (i.e., the detected poisoned samples) are removed from the training dataset, resulting in the sanitized dataset

$$\hat{X} = \{\underline{x}_i \in X \mid t_i = y_i\}$$

that can be used for classifier training.

Note that (i) the same component may be re-optimized multiple times during the course of this algorithm, but (ii) removal of a component is permanent, that is, once removed, a component will not be reinstated.

13.4   Experiments on Binary, Discrete Feature Classification Tasks

In this section, we give experimental results for a discrete feature dataset with $K = 2$ classes.

13.4.1   Experiment Set-Up

Dataset and Mixture Model: For binary ($K = 2$) classification, the TREC 2005 spam corpus (TREC05) [50] is used. TREC05 contains 39,999 real ham and 52,790 spam emails which are labeled based on the sender/receiver relationship. For training, 9000 ham emails and 9000 spam emails are randomly selected. (There are 8651 ham emails and 8835 spam emails remaining in the training dataset after preprocessing, where some emails are removed since there are no tokens left after, e.g., stop word removal and low-frequency word filtering.) For testing, 3000 ham emails and 3000 spam emails are randomly selected. The remaining samples are used for poisoning. The dictionary, following case normalization, stop word removal, stemming and low-frequency word filtering, has about 30,000 unique words.

Parsimonious mixture modeling (PMM, recall Section 3.4.2) is applied on both the ham and spam datasets. PMMs allow parameter sharing across multiple

---

Algorithm 13.1 BIC based mixture model training dataset cleansing (BIC-MM-TSC) defense against DP attacks.

- **Input:** $\mathcal{X} = \{(\underline{x}_i, y_i)\}_{i=1}^{N}, \{\{\theta_{n,j}\}_{j=1}^{M_n}\}_{n=1}^{K}$
- **Initialize:**
  - $\forall n, j: r_{n,j} = 0, q_{n,j} = 0, \Delta\text{BIC}_{n,j} = 0$
  - $\forall i: t_i = y_i$
  - Determine $\mathcal{X}_{n,j}$, the set of samples $\underline{x}$ labeled to class n and such that $p_{n,j}[\underline{x}; \theta_{n,j}] > \max_{j' \neq j} p_{n,j'}[\underline{x}; \theta_{n,j'}], \forall n, j$
- While $\sum_{n,j} \Delta\text{BIC}_{n,j} < 0$ do
  - For $n = 1, \ldots, K$ and for each component j in class n do
    - o compute BIC reduction from j for the three cases:
      $\{\Delta\Omega_{n,j,m} - \Delta L_{n,j,m}\}, m = 1, 2, 3$
    - o configure $\{t_i : \underline{x}_i \in \mathcal{X}_{n,j}\}, r_{n,j}, q_{n,j}$ to minimize
      $\{\Delta\Omega_{n,j,m} - \Delta L_{n,j,m}\}_{m=1}^{3}$
    - o $\Delta\text{BIC}_{n,j} = \min_{m=1,2,3}\{\Delta\Omega_{n,j,m} - \Delta L_{n,j,m}\}$
  - $(n^*, j^*) = \arg\min_{n \in \{1,\ldots,K\}, \, j \in \{1,\ldots,M_n\}} \Delta\text{BIC}_{n,j}$
  - If $r_{n^*,j^*} = 1$ then
    - o For $\underline{x}_i \in \mathcal{X}_{n^*,j^*}$, if $t_i \neq n^*$ then
      - ◇ re-distribute $\underline{x}_i$ to component
        $m = \arg\max_{m'} p_{t_i,m'}[\underline{x}_i; \theta_{t_i,m'}]$ in class t_i
        and update component m's parameters via MLE
    - o If $q_{n^*,j^*} = 0$ then
      - ◇ remove component j^* from $\{\theta_{n^*,j}\}_{j=1}^{M_{n^*}}$
      - ◇ re-distribute each $\underline{x}_i \in \mathcal{X}_{n^*,j^*}$ to component
        $(n'', m'') = \arg\max_{n',m'} p_{n',m'}[\underline{x}_i; \theta_{n',m'}]$
        and update component (n'', m'')'s parameters via MLE
      - else
      - ◇ update component j^*'s parameters on $\mathcal{X}_{n^*,j^*}$
    - o Update $\mathcal{X}_{n,j} \, \forall n, j$ based on the sample re-assignments
- **Output:** $\widehat{\mathcal{X}} = \{\underline{x}_i \in \mathcal{X} \mid t_i = y_i\}$

---

components, which greatly reduces the number of model parameters compared with standard (unstructured) mixtures, and which allows BIC to choose good model orders in high feature dimensions, rather than grossly underestimating the model order (number of mixture components). As another illustration of this, Figure 13.1 shows that, for class "soc.religion.christian" of the clean 20-Newsgroups dataset, PMM chooses a reasonable model order (14) that minimizes the training dataset BIC cost. Note that this also results in good generalization (i.e., test set log-likelihood). PMMs' superiority over standard unstructured mixture models for high-dimensional datasets such as text is also indicated by Figure 3.2.

Initially for the experiments, $M^{\max} = 25$ was chosen for all classes. Again, if the chosen model order $M_n = M_n^{\max}$, then $M_n^{\max}$ is increased and the model is retrained.

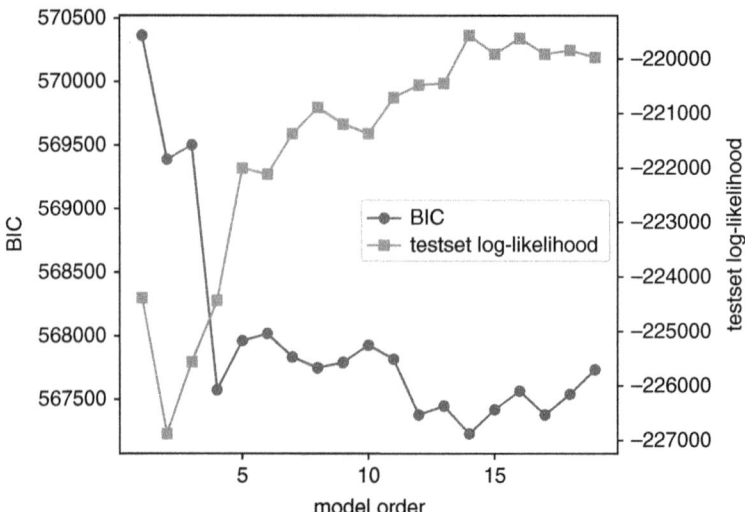

Figure 13.1 Training set BIC cost and test set log-likelihood as a function of the model order of the PMM on class "soc.religion.christian" of clean 20-Newsgroups dataset.

For both datasets, the training and test samples are represented using a bag-of-words. Each PMM component is thus a multinomial joint probability mass function modeling the word-counts in a document.

DP Attack and Target Classifiers: To simulate a reasonable and potent embedded data poisoning attack, real samples are used as attacking samples. That is, samples from class n are injected into the training set, with each intentionally mislabeled to (in the two-class case) the other class, $w \neq n$. The attack strength, that is, the number of attacking samples, may not be the same for each class. The poisoned samples are randomly selected (from the sample pool left over from the training and test datasets).

Twelve poisoning attacks were launched on TREC05. For half of the attacks, only one class is poisoned (e.g., spam), with attack strength from 1000 to 6000 samples. For the other attacks, the ham and spam training datasets are simultaneously poisoned with various attack strengths (see Table 13.1).

The chosen classifiers are

- linear SVM (see the Appendix),
- logistic regression (LR, see Section 2.14), and
- bi-directional one-layer long short-term memory (LSTM) [101] recurrent neural networks with 128 hidden units, since they are effective in the classification of text data (recall the brief discussion in Section 2.5.1).

Evaluation Criteria: The performance of BIC-MM-TSC was measured by: ACC, test set classification accuracy after data sanitization and classifier training; TPR, the fraction of poisoned samples that are detected; and FPR, the fraction of non-poisoned samples falsely detected. Other methods evaluated on this dataset are: the alternative BIC based defense that assumes one of the two classes is clean (BIC-C-D) [145],

Table 13.1 Test set classification accuracy of victim classifiers as a function of attack strength on poisoned and sanitized TREC05 datasets. (Poisoned ham and poisoned spam samples in increments of 1k=1000.)

Number of poisoned ham,spam	0,0	0,1k	0,2k	0,3k	0,4k	0,5k	0,6k	1k,1k	1k,2k	2k,1k	2k,2k	2k,4k	4k,2k
SVM													
Poisoned	0.95	0.89	0.85	0.82	0.79	0.77	0.75	0.83	0.79	0.78	0.75	0.71	0.71
BIC-MM-TSC	**0.97**	**0.96**	**0.95**	**0.94**	**0.94**	**0.94**	**0.93**	**0.95**	**0.93**	**0.94**	**0.91**	**0.90**	**0.87**
KNN-D	0.90	0.90	0.88	0.87	0.84	0.80	0.78	0.90	0.89	0.89	0.88	0.84	0.84
GS-D	0.96	0.94	0.92	0.90	0.81	0.70	0.63	0.91	0.88	0.87	0.86	0.82	0.77
BIC-C-D	0.96	0.94	0.91	0.85	0.69	0.60	0.57	0.92	0.91	0.91	0.83	0.64	0.72
LR													
Poisoned	0.96	0.92	0.88	0.84	0.82	0.78	0.75	0.88	0.85	0.85	0.82	0.76	0.74
BIC-MM-TSC	**0.97**	**0.97**	**0.96**	**0.95**	**0.95**	**0.94**	**0.94**	**0.95**	**0.94**	**0.95**	**0.93**	**0.91**	**0.88**
KNN-D	0.91	0.91	0.90	0.88	0.85	0.81	0.78	0.92	0.90	0.90	0.90	0.86	0.87
GS-D	0.96	0.94	0.92	0.86	0.82	0.71	0.67	0.93	0.91	0.90	0.88	0.81	0.78
BIC-C-D	0.96	0.96	0.92	0.86	0.69	0.62	0.58	0.94	0.92	0.92	0.84	0.64	0.72
LSTM													
Poisoned	0.96	0.93	0.91	0.89	0.87	0.82	0.80	0.88	0.87	0.87	0.85	0.78	0.80
BIC-MM-TSC	**0.97**	**0.97**	**0.96**	**0.96**	**0.95**	**0.95**	**0.94**	**0.96**	**0.95**	**0.96**	**0.94**	**0.92**	**0.90**
KNN-D	0.93	0.93	0.92	0.89	0.87	0.85	0.80	0.93	0.91	0.90	0.91	0.89	0.88
GS-D	0.83	0.82	0.81	0.78	0.73	0.72	0.68	0.84	0.82	0.82	0.82	0.77	0.79
BIC-C-D	0.96	0.96	0.92	0.87	0.69	0.61	0.59	0.94	0.92	0.93	0.84	0.65	0.74

a KNN based defense (KNN-D) [206], and a GS based defense (GS-D) [102]. The SVD based defense [59] was not applied on TREC05 since it is too computationally expensive to perform SVD on the matrix of gradients whose size is approximately 20000×60000.

Hyperparameter Setting: For the KNN based defense, the number of neighbors is set to $K = 10$, which is suggested by [206]. For the GS based defense, a DP-SGD optimizer with *clip-norm* of 2.0 and *noise-multiplier* of 0.1 is applied for training; these values were used in [102].

13.4.2 Experimental Results

The results are listed in Table 13.1 and 13.2. Table 13.1 shows the performance of victim classifiers as a function of attack strength on poisoned and sanitized TREC05 datasets. The target classifiers were first trained on the clean dataset (attack (0,0) in Table 13.1), yielding clean test accuracies (baselines) for SVM, LR, and LSTM of 0.9522, 0.9616, and 0.9632, respectively. The test accuracies of the classifiers poisoned by the 12 DP attacks (described in Section 13.4.1) are shown as poisoned SVM/LR/LSTM in Table 13.1. As the total attack strength (the sum of the attacking ham and spam samples) is strengthened to 6000, the classification accuracies of SVM/LR drop below 0.75 and

Table 13.2 TPRs and FPRs of three defenses on the TREC05 dataset under all attack cases.

Number of poisoned ham,spam	0,0	0,1k	0,2k	0,3k	0,4k	0,5k	0,6k	1k,1k	1k,2k	2k,1k	2k,2k	2k,4k	4k,2k
True positive rates (TPR)													
BIC-MM-TSC	-	**0.89**	**0.90**	**0.90**	**0.87**	**0.90**	**0.89**	0.86	**0.87**	0.89	0.84	0.81	0.81
KNN-D	-	0.84	0.82	0.79	0.73	0.65	0.58	**0.90**	0.85	**0.91**	**0.88**	**0.84**	**0.83**
BIC-C-D	-	0.88	0.83	0.73	0.36	0.20	0.11	0.86	0.84	0.83	0.75	0.21	0.44
False positive rates (FPR)													
BIC-MM-TSC	**0.018**	**0.02**	**0.08**	**0.09**	**0.06**	**0.09**	**0.07**	**0.05**	**0.06**	**0.06**	**0.07**	**0.08**	**0.11**
KNN-D	0.07	0.08	0.09	0.11	0.14	0.18	0.21	0.09	0.11	0.10	0.11	0.13	0.15
BIC-C-D	0.05	0.07	0.08	0.09	0.32	0.36	0.39	0.06	0.07	0.06	0.21	0.30	0.27

LSTM drops to 0.8. Thus, embedding real ham into the spam set and real spam into the ham set is indeed a significant poisoning attack on SVM/LR/LSTMs.

Then, the four defenses are applied to the corrupted training sets, with the classifiers then trained/retrained on the sanitized datasets. The corresponding test accuracies are shown for BIC-MM-TSC, KNN-D, GS-D, and BIC-C-D in Table 13.1. Since BIC-C-D [145] unrealistically assumes the defender knows which class is clean (whereas in reality (i) this is unknown and (ii) both classes may in fact be poisoned), BIC-C-D is alternately applied on ham and spam until the total BIC cost over the two classes converges. The order of sanitization was fixed; it was always initiated from class ham. As expected, the test accuracies of the classifier with BIC-C-D drop rapidly when the total attack strength exceeds 4000. The test accuracies of classifiers using KNN/GS based defenses also decline gradually as the attack strength increases, while BIC-MM-TSC performs well and stably. In all cases, BIC-MM-TSC surpasses the other three defenses in classification accuracy (marked in bold). When the attack is strengthened to 5000 ham emails in the spam training dataset, the KNN based defense exhibits little improvement in test accuracy over that of the poisoned classifier. The classifiers equipped with the GS based defense perform even worse than the poisoned classifiers in many cases in Table 13.1. However, BIC-MM-TSC significantly improves test accuracies even under strong attacks, restoring the test accuracies close to the clean baselines. For LSTM with the GS based defense, its accuracy is even worse than the poisoned LSTM in all cases. The performance of the GS based defense is affected by the choice of its hyperparameters, clip norm and noise multiplier. The hyperparameter settings from [102] were directly used; these are tuned for LR, not LSTM. See [11, 170] for tuning the hyperparameters of a DP-SGD optimizer. Note that for the embedded data poisoning scenario considered in this chapter, there is no clean validation set available for (principled) tuning of hyperparameters.

Table 13.2 shows the TPRs and FPRs of the BIC/KNN based defenses (since the GS based defense does not identify the poisoned samples). Compared with KNN-D and BIC-C-D, the BIC-MM-TSC defense has relatively low FPRs for all cases.

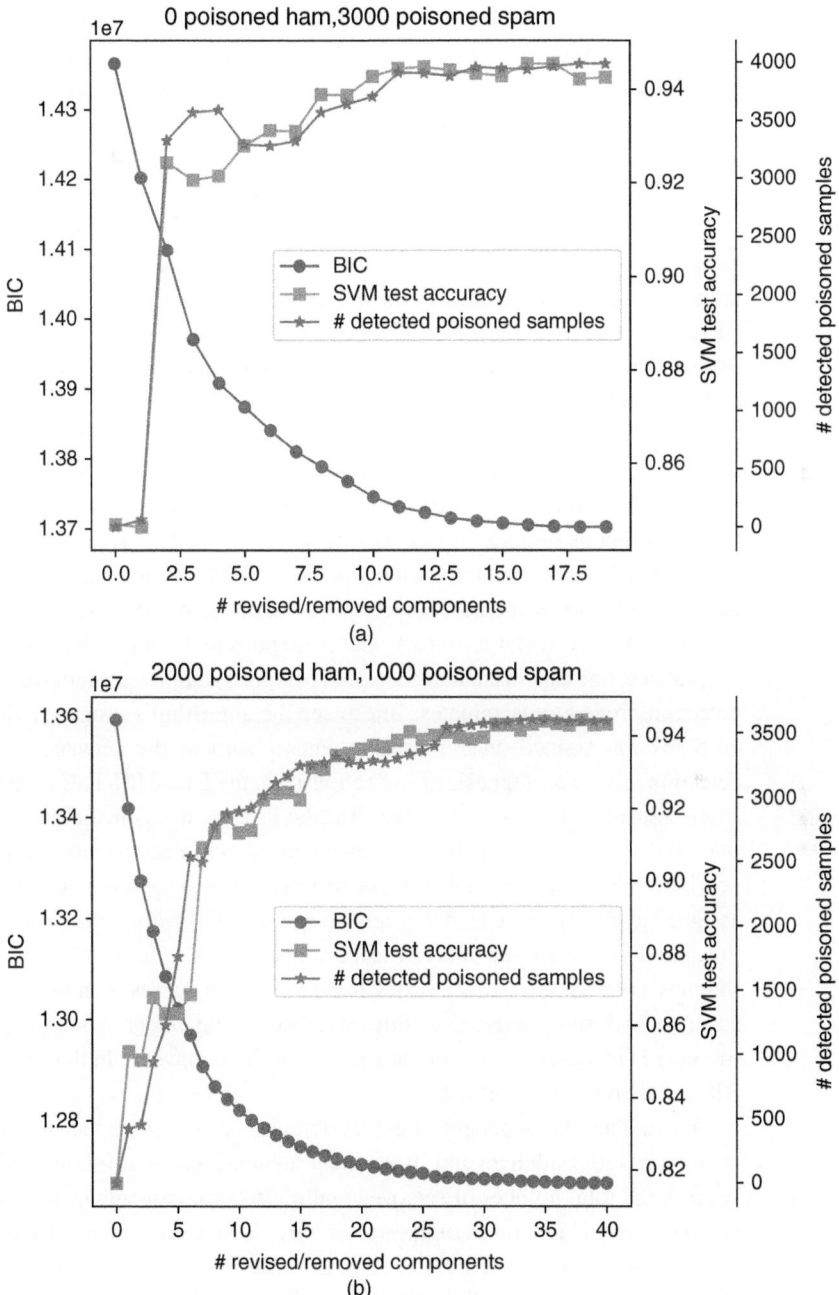

Figure 13.2 BIC cost, SVM test accuracy, and the number of detected poisoned samples for BIC-MM-TSC as a function of the number of component change steps for attacks against TREC05 using (a) 0 poisoned ham samples, 3000 poisoned spam samples, and (b) 2000 poisoned ham samples, 1000 poisoned spam samples.

Besides, the BIC-MM-TSC defense has higher TPRs than the KNN based defense when only the spam set is poisoned and has comparable TPRs when both of the classes are poisoned. When the attack strength exceeds 4000, BIC-C-D fails to detect most poisoned samples and falsely removes a large number of clean samples. In short, compared with the other three defenses, the BIC-MM-TSC defense does not require any additional (clean) validation set or elaborate hyperparameter tuning. Moreover, its performance is superior to that of the other defenses.

When there is no attack, BIC-MM-TSC still sanitizes several components in both classes and falsely detects 789 clean training samples as poisoned samples. The average log-likelihoods of these removed samples under ham and spam respectively are -879.77 and -852.88 (i.e., the likelihoods are similar). Also, for an SVM trained on a clean dataset, with these samples removed, the classification accuracy on the set of removed samples is only 0.5855. That is, these falsely detected samples are close to the decision boundary and are well explained by both classes. Given the similar likelihoods, it is BIC efficacious to remove/revise the components formed by these samples; thus BIC-MM-TSC inevitably produces some (outlier) false positives. Besides, removing these ambiguous samples in fact slightly *increases* the test accuracy.

Figure 13.2 shows how the total BIC cost, SVM test accuracy, and the number of detected poisoned samples change with the number of components removed/revised by BIC-MM-TSC under the attack with 3000 poisoned samples injected into TREC05. (In practice, one expects that the detected poisoned samples are removed only when the detection procedure terminates. But to see the algorithm's progress, via Figure 13.2, an SVM was trained on the training dataset without the detected samples at each detection step.) As emphasized in Section 13.3, the BIC-MM-TSC method guarantees strict descent in the BIC objective. But the test accuracy or the number of detected poisoned samples cannot be guaranteed to be non-decreasing. Samples that were previously deemed poisoned might be restored clean at subsequent detection steps (reassigned to the class to which they are labeled) and vice versa, which explains the slight fluctuation in the curves of SVM test accuracy and the number of detected poisoned samples. Overall, though, the strong trend of the two curves is an increase in detection accuracy and true positive detections with increasing detection steps. Specifically, the two curves increase sharply in the early stages and converge in the final stages, as the BIC cost is further decreased.

The number of components, number of revised components and number of removed components for both ham and spam under all attack cases are shown in Table 13.3. In general, the total number of removed and revised components increases as the attack is strengthened. For most of the cases, BIC-MM-TSC prefers revising a poisoned component rather than removing it. A possible reason is that, given a large number of features (30,000 for TREC05), it is difficult to cluster the clean samples and the poisoned samples into separate groups [252]. Most of the poisoned components are formed by both clean and poisoned samples, and it is apparently most BIC efficacious to revise them.

Table 13.3 The number of components (Cmps), and the number of revised (Rev) components and removed (Rem) components by BIC-MM-TSC, for each class, under all attack cases, on the TREC05 dataset.

Number of poisoned ham,spam	0,0	0,1k	0,2k	0,3k	0,4k	0,5k	0,6k	1k,1k	1k,2k	2k,1k	2k,2k	2k,4k	4k,2k
Cmps	(21,18)	(29,16)	(22,18)	(25,17)	(19,20)	(24,20)	(24,31)	(49,27)	(25,15)	(37,29)	(48,28)	(40,29)	(36,28)
Rev Cmps	(1,5)	(0,6)	(6,11)	(5,10)	(1,16)	(2,9)	(7,11)	(19,18)	(11,7)	(17,12)	(9,7)	(14,11)	(14,13)
Rem Cmps	(0,1)	(5,3)	(2,6)	(1,2)	(2,4)	(3,4)	(4,11)	(7,4)	(4,2)	(4,6)	(12,5)	(10,5)	(8,11)

13.5   Discussion: Experiments with $K > 2$ Classes

In [148], experimental results are given for several different datasets with $K > 2$ classes, including some of the image datasets considered in previous chapters. These results include the SVD-D defense, but not BIC-C-D, and the experimental comparisons include assessment of computational complexity of the defenses. As one example involving the ResNet-18 classifier for the MNIST dataset, the (offline) computation time associated with BIC-MM-TSC is comparable to the training time of the (undefended) ResNet-18, while, as expected, KNN-D requires negligible computation, and the GS-D and SVD-D defenses require much more computation than BIC-MM-TSC.

13.6   Chapter Summary

This chapter distinguishes itself from previous chapters from three different standpoints. First, it considers "error generic" data poisoning attacks, where the attacker simply aims to degrade the trained classifier's accuracy, rather than getting the classifier to learn a backdoor mapping. Second, this chapter considers text classification domains. Third, this chapter investigates SVMs and logistic regression models, as well as recurrent DNN (LSTM based) classifiers. The chapter first reviewed prior work on defenses against data poisoning attacks, including KNN based, SVD based, and gradient-shaping based defenses. Next, a novel defense framework was developed based on the Bayesian information criterion (BIC) statistical model selection criterion. This approach first separately learns a mixture model representation for the data labeled to each class (with the mixture distribution chosen consistent with minimization of the BIC criterion). Next, further improvements in the BIC objective defined over all classes are sought, considering two types of "moves" which are associated with potential data poisoning: (i) identifying samples that are better explained (in the BIC sense) by classes (and associated mixture components) *other than* the class to which they are labeled; (ii) identifying mixture components whose *removal* reduces BIC – such components are hypothesized to be highly contaminated by poisoned samples. This BIC minimization thus performs data cleansing (poisoned sample removal) prior to classifier learning, and is suitable for coupling with any classifier model.

This defense was compared with the aforementioned KNN, SVD, and gradient-shaping defenses, for label flipping attacks with various attack strengths applied to the TREC05 document classification task. Toward this end, for the BIC based defense, parsimonious mixture modeling (PMM) was used to model the data from each of the classes (as PMMs are highly suitable for accurate model order selection, and for informative-feature identification in high-dimensional feature spaces, as discussed previously in Chapter 3). The experiments demonstrated that: (i) classification accuracy is significantly degraded as the attack strength (number of poisoned samples) is increased in the absence of a defense, with accuracy dropping from about 97% to less than 75% for SVMs and logistic regression models and to less than 80% for LSTMs, for the highest strength poisoning attacks; (ii) the BIC defense outperforms the other defenses for *every* attack – for the highest strength attack, the BIC defense "rehabilitated" classification accuracy to 87%, 88%, and 90% respectively for the SVM, LR and LSTM classifiers. While results were only shown for document classification in this chapter, [148] reports results for other data domains, including image classification.

Some questions to test the reader's understanding of the chapter include the following.

- Label flipping applied to existing training samples is one type of data poisoning attack; can you suggest another way of producing poisoned training samples?
- The BIC based defense from this chapter was applied before the classifier is trained. Can you suggest another way of applying the BIC based defense which may be more suitable for some other application domains?
- Did the BIC based defense require a choice of hyperparameters? Explain.
- Why is the BIC objective referred to as "the complete data BIC objective"?
- Does the BIC approach remove samples even when no data poisoning is present? If so, explain why this may in fact be useful.
- Suggest how the BIC approach could be most sensibly applied, for example, for image classification domains.
- What is the key takeaway from Figure 13.1?
- What is the key takeaway from Figure 13.2?

13.7   Project: _K_-Nearest Neighbor (_K_NN) Defense

Python code for this project can be found at www.cambridge.org/millersecureAI. Also, recall the comment made in Section 6.8 regarding using GPUs for deep learning.

13.7.1   Error Generic DP Attack

This project involves the following steps.

1. Load training and test datasets of MNIST.
2. Keep training and test samples of five classes: [0, 1, 2, 3, 4] For each class, split the training dataset as 2000 images used for training and 800 images used for poisoning. Poisoned samples are stored in another dataset named attackset.
3. Poison the training dataset. There are five inputs: N0, N1, N2, N3, N4. If Nn is 1, then evenly distribute poisoning samples of class n into the training datasets of the remaining four classes. For example, if N0 = 1, add 200 poisoning samples of class 0 into class 1, and label them as class 1. Do the same to poison classes 2, 3, 4 by class 0. If Nn = 0, then class n's samples are not used for poisoning.
4. Train a ResNet-18 DNN on the poisoned training dataset. The training framework (epoch, net, Train_loader) is given. The learning rate, the number of training epochs, the loss function and the optimizer are given.
5. Test the trained ResNet-18 on the clean (attack-free) test dataset. The test framework (net, Test_loader) is given.

6. Do the experiment six times. In experiment j, use j classes for poisoning. The number of classes used for poisoning is the attack strength. For example, in experiment 0, N0 = 0, N1 = 0, N2 = 0, N3 = 0, N4 = 0, that is, there is no poisoning (this is the control experiment). In experiment 3, N0 = 1, N1 = 1, N2 = 1, N3 = 0, N4 = 0, that is, three classes are used for poisoning, and all five classes are poisoned. Plot the test accuracy versus the attack strength. The stronger the attack, the lower the test accuracy that is expected.

13.7.2   Error Generic DP Defense

Now consider the goal of detecting poisoned MNIST training images. The method now investigated relabels an image as the plurality label of its K nearest neighbors [206] ([206] only considers a KNN based anomaly detector for binary classification tasks, but it is straightforward to extend it for cases with more than two classes).

1. Poison the training dataset of MNIST as above and keep the ground truth indicators of malicious samples: 0 = clean, 1 = malicious. (Note: that the ground truth indicators are used in performance evaluation in step 4, but they are **not** allowed to be used for anomaly detection.)
2. Train an SVM classifier on the poisoned training dataset or load the ResNet-18 trained in the project of the previous subsection.
3. Implement the KNN based defense with K a hyperparameter (number of nearest neighbors). By default, $K = 10$. For each training sample carry out the following steps.
    (i) Find its K nearest neighbors. (Check sklearn.neighbors library for functions finding the K nearest neighbors of a data sample.)
    (ii) Find the plurality label of the K nearest neighbors. (Check scipy.stats library for functions finding the plurality.)
    (iii) If the plurality label is different from its original label, it is deemed a malicious sample. Otherwise, it is deemed clean.
4. Evaluate the performance of the KNN based detector by TPR, FPR and test set accuracy (ACC) of the classifier trained on the sanitized dataset (with the detected malicious samples removed).
5. Vary the value of K and observe how it affects the performance of the detector.

13.8   Project: White Box Data Poisoning Attack

Devise and evaluate a white box attack against BIC-MM-TSC, that is, one where the adversary is aware of the defense. Evaluate the attack, comparing attacker and defender work factors in particular.

14 Reverse-Engineering Attacks (REAs) on Classifiers

In this chapter we focus on *reverse-engineering attacks* (REAs) on classifiers and defenses against them. REAs [202, 267] involve querying (probing) a classifier to discover its decision-making rule. One application of REAs is to *enable* TTEs (Chapter 4) by providing an attacker with knowledge of the classifier to be targeted. (Related "membership-inference" threats targeting the training set itself were discussed in Section 1.6.) Another application amounts to "stealing" a proprietary classifier, for example, learning the rubrics an insurance company uses to decide whether to approve a home loan. As another example, an adversary may seek to discover how an automated target recognition system makes decisions. Such knowledge, once acquired through a probing attack, might help the adversary to devise strategies (e.g., camouflage) to fool the system, giving them a warfare advantage. Since the attacker may have little prior knowledge about the distribution of classes for the given domain, he/she may need to be quite exploratory with queries. Thus, some attacker queries may "stand out" as extreme outliers relative to the data distribution. Detection of such outliers is the defense strategy employed in this chapter.

[267] demonstrates that, with a *relatively* modest number of queries (perhaps about ten thousand), using the classifier's answers on query examples as supervising ground truth labels, one can learn a surrogate classifier on a given domain that closely mimics an unknown classifier. One weakness of [267] is that it considers neither very large (feature space) domains nor very large networks (DNNs); for orders of magnitude more queries may be needed to reverse-engineer a DNN on a large-scale domain. However, a much more critical weakness stems from one of the greatest purported advantages in [267] – the authors emphasize their REA does not require the attacker to possess *any* actual samples from the domain. (For certain sensitive domains, or ones where obtaining real examples is expensive, the attacker may not have access to legitimate examples.) Their queries are *randomly* drawn, for example, uniformly, over the given feature space. What was not recognized in [267] is that this random querying makes the attack easily detectable – randomly selected query patterns will typically look nothing like legitimate examples from any of the classes. They are very likely to be extreme outliers, of all the classes. Each such query is thus *individually* highly suspicious; thus, even ten, let alone ten thousand such queries will be easily anomaly detected as jointly improbable under a null distribution (estimable from the training set defined over all the classes from the domain). Even if the attacker employed bots, each of which makes a small number of queries, each bot's random queries should be easily detected as

anomalous, likely associated with an REA. On the other hand, [202] proposed an REA that does require some initial known data from the domain. It uses these examples to create more legitimate, "stealthier" queries, over a series of query stages, with the resulting labeled data used to train a surrogate classifier that is then used to launch a TTE.

This chapter concerns detection of REAs. One approach is based on the observation that, even for the stealthier approach in [202], query images are expected to *not* be typical of the underlying classes in the given domain. Thus, these samples should be detectable as outliers, much in the way that TTE attacks are themselves susceptible to anomaly detection approaches. Accordingly, the detection method considered here is an extension of ADA from Chapter 4, which is capable of detecting the stealthy REA of [202], and so may prevent TTEs potentially even before they are launched.

14.1   Reverse-Engineering Attacks (REAs) Given Domain Samples

The REA procedure in [202] aspires to discover class boundaries as follows. First, the adversary collects a small set of representative labeled samples $\mathcal{A}^{(0)}$ from the input domain and uses this to train an initial surrogate classifier, $\tilde{c}^{(0)}$. Then, there is data collection and classifier retraining or refining, beginning with the parameters of the current model, over a sequence of stages. In each stage, the adversary augments the current training set by querying the victim classifier using the stage's newly generated samples. For the "untargeted" attacker querying objective in [291], which is based on [202], the adversary's training dataset at stage $k + 1$ is augmented by the samples

$$\mathcal{A}^{(k+1)} = \{\underline{x} - \lambda \cdot \text{sgn}[\nabla \tilde{p}^{(k)}(\tilde{c}^{(k)}(\underline{x})|\underline{x})] \mid \underline{x} \in \mathcal{A}^{(k)}\} \tag{14.1}$$

where $\tilde{p}^{(k)}$ is the surrogate model's class posterior at stage k, and with small real parameter $\lambda > 0$. Note that the labels for these samples are obtained by querying the victim classifier using these samples. The surrogate classifier is then retrained (or fine tuned) using the labeled samples in $\mathcal{A}^{(k+1)}$, yielding the new (stage $(k + 1)$) surrogate classifier $\tilde{c}^{(k+1)}$. Each successive stage crafts samples closer to the victim classifier's true boundary, which is helpful for RE learning but which also makes these samples less class representative and thus more detectable. Once a sufficiently accurate surrogate classifier is learned, the adversary can launch a TTE. Recall, for example, (4.2) from Section 4.1.

14.2   Overview of Defense Against Reverse-Engineering Attacks (REAs)

One interesting idea for defending against REAs, developed for SVMs (see the Appendix), is to make the *classifier* evasive (a moving target) [5]. That is, the authors proposed a *randomized* classifier, adding multivariate Gaussian noise to the classifier's weight vector, with the covariance matrix chosen to ensure both high classifier accuracy and as much "spread" in weight vector realizations as possible. This is nicely formulated as a convex optimization problem. One limitation of [5] is that this approach may not naturally extend to DNNs. A more serious concern is that the authors did not show that randomization prevents an RE attacker from learning a good classifier for the domain – they only showed that RE learned weight vectors deviate significantly from the mean SVM weight vector. Moreover, the authors evaluated the success rate of TTE attacks following the RE classifier learning phase. While TTE success rates were reduced by classifier randomization compared with those for a fixed classifier, the TTE success rate was still quite high, for example, dropping from 80% to only 65% on some datasets. The problem here is that because the randomization retains high classification accuracy, RE querying, even of *random* classifier realizations, acquires generally accurate labels for its queries.

An alternative approach for RE defense, proposed in [291], is to *detect* RE querying, in much the same way as one detects TTE attacks. That is, because the attacker does not know that much about the classifier (and may have limited legitimate examples from the domain), he/she will have to be "exploratory" with queries. However, one can then hypothesize that query patterns, just like TTE attack examples, may be atypical of legitimate examples from the domain. In fact, [291] directly leverages the ADA detector, designed to detect TTE attacks, to detect RE querying. In [291], it is shown that this approach achieves high ROC AUC (0.97 or higher) in detecting the RE querying proposed in [202] for MNIST, and at a "stage" of querying *before* the attacker has learned an accurate surrogate classifier, suitable for mounting a high success rate TTE attack.

14.3   Anomaly Detection of Attacks (ADA) Based Defense Against Reverse-Engineering Attacks (REA-ADA)

Recall ADA from Section 4.3. Since, in REAs, the attacker submits batches of query samples to the classifier, ADA (the L-AWA-ADA version [179] is considered here) is modified to jointly exploit batches of samples in seeking to detect attacks (in this case RE query attacks, not TTE attacks); recall Section 4.8.2. Several schemes for *aggregating* L-AWA-ADA detection statistics, produced for individual samples in a batch, are investigated: (i) arithmetically averaging the L-AWA statistic over all samples in a batch; (ii) *maximizing* the L-AWA statistic over all samples in a batch; (iii) dividing a batch into mini-batches, for example, a batch of 50 samples could be divided into mini-batches of size 5. For each mini-batch, apply either scheme (i) or scheme (ii). Then, make a detection if *any* of the mini-batches yields a detection statistic greater than the threshold. This last scheme will be seen to perform the best.

14.4   Experiments

We conducted experiments on the MNIST dataset. Recall MNIST has 60,000 greyscale images of handwritten digits '0' through '9'. There are 50,000 training images and 10,000 test images. The Lenet-5 architecture was used for the defended classifier and

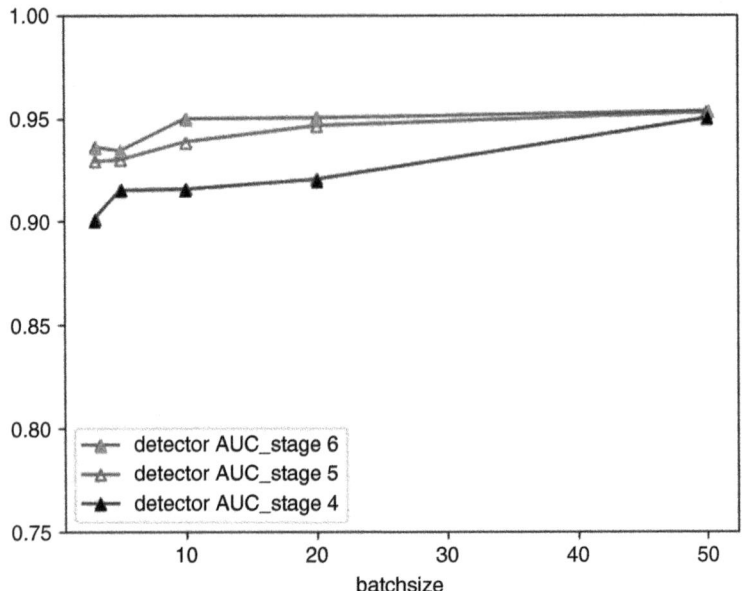

Figure 14.1 REA detection ROC AUC at different stages versus batch size for the arithmetic averaging scheme. Reprinted from [291] with permission.

for the RE attacker's surrogate. 150 MNIST samples (15 from each class) were used for $\mathcal{A}_0$. Five stages of retraining (six training stages) of the surrogate DNN were applied. The number of queries generated by the five stages respectively were 150, 300, 600, 1200 and 2400, with parameter $\lambda = 0.1$. Two maxpooling layers and the penultimate layer were used in generating the ADA detection statistics. Mini-batches of size 5 for the detector were used in experiments.

Figure 14.1 shows that good detection accuracy is achieved using the arithmetic averaging scheme, with the ROC AUC increasing with batch size and with the attack stage, as expected. However, the ROC AUC appears to saturate at about 0.95; one would hope that approximately perfect detection accuracy could be approached with increasing batch size, especially in the latter stages. This better behavior is exhibited by the mini-batch scheme with union detection rule in Figure 14.2. Thus, this latter aggregation scheme is the most promising one.

Figure 14.3 shows the surrogate classifier's accuracy versus the attack stage and also the TTE attack success rate (based on a TTE attack on the surrogate classifier, with this attack then transferred to the actual classifier) if the RE attacker stops after a particular attack stage. Stages 4, 5, and 6 were the focus in the REA experiments because the TTE attack success rate is higher at these stages. For example, from Figure 14.2, a detection ROC AUC of close to 0.95 can be attained after the fourth stage of querying (whereas, if the querying is stopped after three stages, the success rate of the resulting TTE attack will only be ~60%). Thus, this detector does give substantial potential to detect REAs, as well as forcing the attacker to limit the number of querying stages in

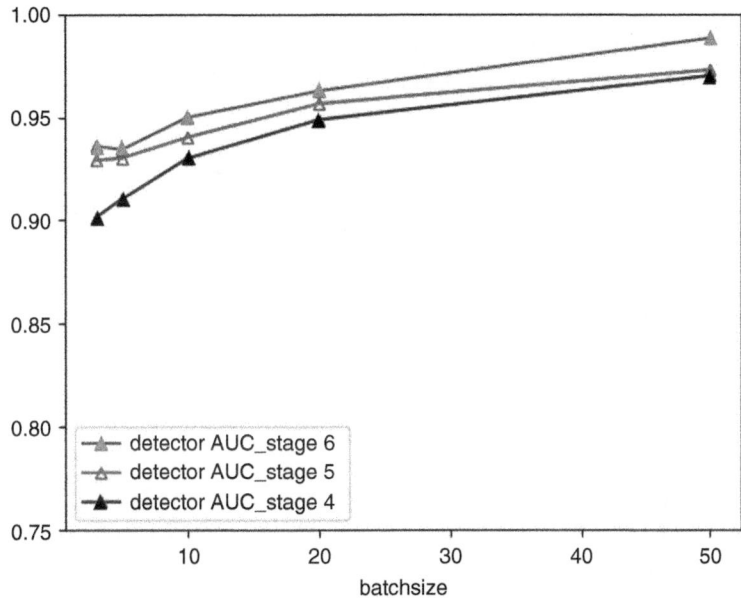

Figure 14.2 REA detection ROC AUC at different stages versus batch size for the mini-batch union aggregation scheme. Reprinted from [291] with permission.

order to evade detection (which limits the transferrable success rate of a TTE attack mounted based on the surrogate classifier learned from the queries).

14.5   Chapter Summary

In this chapter we considered reverse-engineering attacks on classifiers. Here, the classifier may start out as an unknown "black box" to the attacker. This may be due to the classifier being proprietary or because it is being used for sensitive decision-making, for example, associated with critical infrastructure or for military use. The attacker can reverse engineer the victim classifier's decision rule by querying the victim classifier, treating the classifier's decisions as ground truth, and then learning a surrogate classifier based on the labeled queries. It was noted that use of purely *random* queries, while not relying on any knowledge of the data distribution, is a quite weak attack, as random queries are likely to be extreme outliers of the data distribution. Thus, even a small number of such queries, *far* fewer than are needed to accurately learn the classifier's decision rule, may trigger an anomaly detector (and an action such as blocking the entity from further query access to the classifier). The more judicious attack from [202] involves a series of stages where, in each stage, a surrogate classifier is learned given all of the queries made until now, and then a new round of queries is made. The queries made in each stage are not random, but rather are chosen in the vicinity of the current surrogate classifier's decision boundary; in other words, these queries are chosen so as to further explore and refine knowledge of the true decision

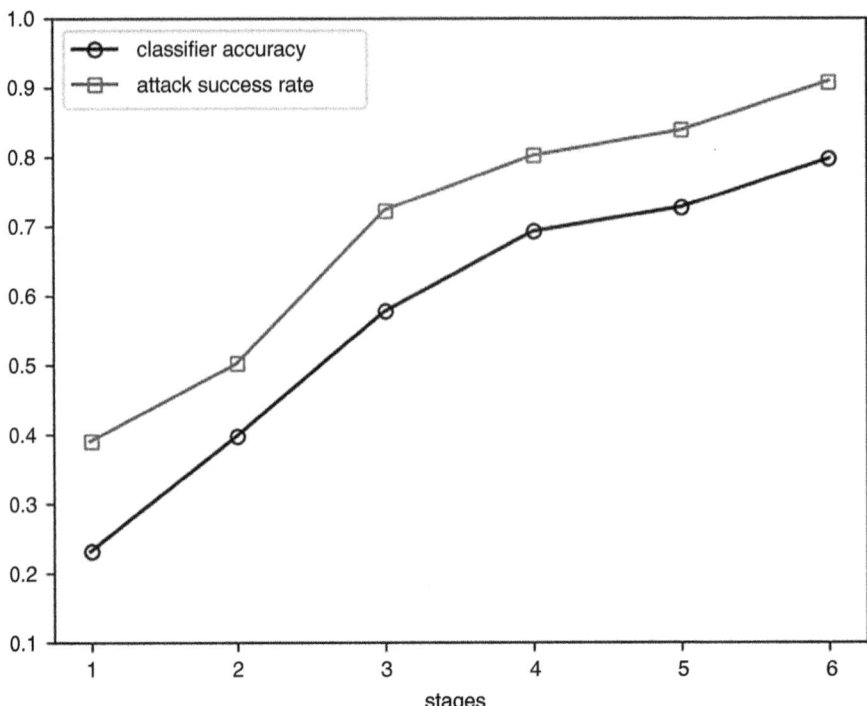

Figure 14.3 Attack success rate and surrogate classifier accuracy versus number of RE stages. Reprinted from [291] with permission.

boundary/decision rule. It was noted that, while the ADA defense from Chapter 4 was designed to detect TTE attacks, it may also have utility more generally for detecting training set outliers (recall Section 4.8), for example, queries associated with an RE attack. Several different schemes were proposed for pooling the detection statistic over all samples in a batch of queries. Dividing a batch into mini-batches, with a union detection rule applied to the detection decisions made for each mini-batch, was found to be the most effective detection scheme. For experiments on MNIST it was found that good detection accuracy (ROC AUCs of at least 0.9) was attained against the attack from [202], and at a stage before the attacker has learned a very accurate surrogate of the actual classifier's rule.

Some questions to test the reader's understanding of the chapter include the following.

- Are the samples added at each stage by (14.1) always feasible? Produce some variations of (14.1) based on Section 2.10 and the TTE attacks discussed in Chapter 4.
- Could the GANs TTE detector from Chapter 4 be applied to detect reverse-engineering attacks? Do you expect this approach to be effective? Explain.
- Explain the connection between reverse-engineering attacks on classifiers and active learning of a classifier.

- Suppose that the attacker does not generate delineated stage-wise queries, but rather makes queries sequentially, one at a time. Can the batch detection schemes described in this chapter still be applied? Explain.
- Identify some application domains where an attacker is likely to have virtually unlimited access to query a classifier numerous times (as needed to successfully reverse engineer the decision rule).

14.6   Project: Defense Against Random Querying

Implement an anomaly detection defense against the REA from [267], which uses random queries (you can consider a simple dataset for this purpose, such as the UC Irvine *Iris* [278]). Evaluate the ROC AUC of attack detection as a function of the number of queries that are performed. Is the attack highly detectable even when the number of queries is small?

Appendix Support Vector Machines (SVMs)

In this Appendix we give detailed development of support vector machine (SVM) classifiers. Though DNNs are state-of-the-art in many domains, SVMs are still widely used. Moreover, hybrid systems, with deep learning based front-end feature extraction and back-end SVM decision-making, are also commonly used.

A.1   Relevant Background on Constrained Optimization and Duality

We now give some background on optimization, for which there are many references providing further details, for example, [208].

Consider a *primal* optimization problem with a set of m inequality constraints. Find

$$\arg\min_{\underline{x} \in D} f_0(x), \tag{A.1}$$

where the constrained domain of optimization (assumed to be non-empty) is

$$D \equiv \{\underline{x} \in \mathbb{R}^n \mid f_i(\underline{x}) \le 0, \forall i \in \{1, 2, \ldots, m\}\}. \tag{A.2}$$

To study the primal problem, define the corresponding *Lagrangian* function on $\mathbb{R}^n \times [0, \infty)^m$:

$$L(\underline{x}, \underline{v}) \equiv f_0(\underline{x}) + \sum_{i=1}^{m} v_i f_i(\underline{x}), \tag{A.3}$$

where, by implication, the vector of *Lagrange multipliers* (dual variables) is $\underline{v} \in [0, \infty)^m$, that is, $\underline{v} \ge \underline{0}$ (non-negative).

A.1.1   Primal Constrained Optimization with Lagrange Multipliers

Theorem:

$$\min_{\underline{x} \in \mathbb{R}^n} \max_{\underline{v} \ge \underline{0}} L(\underline{x}, \underline{v}) = \min_{\underline{x} \in D} f_0(\underline{x}) \equiv p^*.$$

Proof: Simply,

$$\max_{\underline{v} \ge \underline{0}} L(\underline{x}, \underline{v}) = \begin{cases} \infty & \text{if } \underline{x} \notin D, \\ f_0(\underline{x}) & \text{if } \underline{x} \in D. \end{cases} \qquad \square$$

Note that if $\underline{x} \notin D$, then $\exists\, i > 0$ such that $f_i(\underline{x}) > 0$, which implies the associated optimal $v_i^* = \infty$. So, one can maximize the Lagrangian in an *unconstrained* fashion to find the solution to the constrained primal problem.

A.1.2   Complementary Slackness of Primal Solution

Define the maximizing values of the Lagrange multipliers,

$$\underline{v}^*(\underline{x}) \equiv \arg \max_{\underline{v} \geq \underline{0}} L(\underline{x}, \underline{v})$$

and note that the *complementary slackness* conditions

$$v_i^*(\underline{x}) f_i(\underline{x}) = 0$$

hold for all $\underline{x} \in D$ and $i \in \{1, 2, \ldots, m\}$. That is, if there is slackness in the ith constraint, that is, $f_i(\underline{x}) < 0$, then there is no slackness in the constraint of the corresponding Lagrange multiplier, that is, $v_i^*(\underline{x}) = 0$. Conversely, if $f_i(\underline{x}) = 0$, then the value of the Lagrange multiplier $v_i^*(\underline{x})$ has no bearing on the Lagrangian.

A.1.3   The Dual Problem

Now define the *dual* function of the primal problem:

$$g(\underline{v}) = \min_{\underline{x} \in \mathbb{R}^n} L(\underline{x}, \underline{v}),$$

that is, unconstrained optimization with respect to *primal* variables first. Note that $g(\underline{v})$ may be infinite for some values of $\underline{v}$ and that g is always concave.

Theorem: For all $\underline{x} \in D$ and $\underline{v} \geq \underline{0}$,

$$g(\underline{v}) \leq f_0(\underline{x}).$$

Proof: For $\underline{v} \geq \underline{0}$ and $\underline{x} \in D$,

$$g(\underline{v}) \leq L(\underline{x}, \underline{v}) \leq \max_{\underline{v} \geq \underline{0}} L(\underline{x}, \underline{v}) = f_0(\underline{x}),$$

where the last equality is the bound on L assuming $\underline{x} \in D$.   □

So, by the previous theorem, if one solves the *dual problem*, that is, finds

$$d^* \equiv \max_{\underline{v} \geq \underline{0}} g(\underline{v}),$$

then one will have obtained a (hopefully good) lower bound to the primal problem,

$$\max_{\underline{v} \geq \underline{0}} g(\underline{v}) = \max_{\underline{v} \geq \underline{0}} \min_{\underline{x} \in \mathbb{R}^n} L(\underline{x}, \underline{v}) = d^* \leq p^* = \min_{\underline{x} \in \mathbb{R}^n} \max_{\underline{v} \geq \underline{0}} L(\underline{x}, \underline{v}) = \min_{\underline{x} \in D} f_0(\underline{x}).$$

Under certain conditions in this finite-dimensional setting, in particular when the primal problem is convex and a *strictly feasible* solution exists, the *duality gap*,

$$p^* - d^* = 0.$$

A.1.4   The Dual Problem for a Linear Program

If $f_0(\underline{x}) = \sum_{j=1}^{n} \phi_j x_j$ and all $f_i(\underline{x}) = \xi_i + \sum_{j=1}^{n} \gamma_{i,j} x_j$ are linear functions, then the above primal problem is called a linear program (LP). As an exercise, to obtain an *equivalent* dual LP, first show the Lagrangian of the primal problem can be written as

$$L(\underline{x},\underline{v}) = \sum_{i=1}^{m} \xi_i v_i + \sum_{j=1}^{n} x_j \left(\phi_j + \sum_{i=1}^{m} v_i \gamma_{i,j} \right).$$

LPs can be solved by the simplex algorithm (along feasible region boundaries) or by interior point methods.

A.1.5   Iterated Subgradient Method

Using duality to find p^* and $\underline{x}^* = \arg\min_{\underline{x}\in D} f_0(\underline{x})$, consider a *slow* ascent method that is used to maximize g,

$$\underline{v}_n = \underline{v}_{n-1} + \alpha_1 \nabla_{\underline{v}} L(\underline{x}^*(\underline{v}_{n-1}),\underline{v}_{n-1}),$$

and between iterations n of the ascent method, a *fast* descent method is used to evaluate $g(\underline{v}_n)$ by minimizing $L(\underline{x},\underline{v}_n)$,

$$\underline{x}_k = \underline{x}_{k-1} - \alpha_2 \nabla_{\underline{x}} L(\underline{x}_{k-1},\underline{v}_n) \rightarrow \underline{x}^*(\underline{v}_n)$$

using multiple iterations k. The process described by such an ascent/descent method is called an iterative subgradient method. The step sizes $\alpha > 0$ can be chosen dynamically, for example, steepest ascent/descent (recall Section 2.6). Instead of slow ascent, the descent step can be projected on the feasible domain D.

A.1.6   The KKT Conditions

Consider again a *primal* optimization problem (A.1) with a set of m inequality constraints f_i given by (A.2). So the Lagrangian L on $(\underline{x},\underline{v}) \in \mathbb{R}^n \times [0,\infty)^m$ is (A.3) and the objective is to find $\min_{\underline{x}} \max_{\underline{v}\geq 0} L(\underline{x},\underline{v})$. If f_0 is convex and, $\forall i \in \{1,\ldots,m\}$, f_i is linear, then the following Karush–Kuhn–Tucker (KKT) conditions suffice for optimality:

$$\forall j, \ \partial L/\partial x_j = 0 \text{ and}$$
$$\forall i, \ v_i f_i = 0 \text{ (complementary slackness)}.$$

A.2   Linear Separability of a Two-Class Dataset

Recall that in Section 2.3 it was discussed how to construct a mapping so that a two-class dataset becomes linearly separable. Here cases are considered with an already high feature dimension, N, such that the dataset is already linearly separable.

Suppose the training dataset $X = \{\underline{x}_i\}_{i=1}^T$ forms a matrix,

$$\mathbf{X} = [\underline{x}_1 \ \underline{x}_2 \ \cdots \ \underline{x}_T] \in \mathbb{R}^{N \times T}.$$

Assume

$$N \geq T \quad \text{and} \quad \text{rank}(\mathbf{X}) = T, \tag{A.4}$$

(recall Section 3.5). Thus by assumption, the range (span of the columns) of $\mathbf{X}'$ is $\mathbb{R}^T$ and $\mathbf{X}'\mathbf{X} \in \mathbb{R}^{T \times T}$ is non-singular [103]. So, for any $\underline{\beta} \in \mathbb{R}^T$, there exist solutions $\underline{w} \in \mathbb{R}^N$ to the (underspecified) equations

$$\mathbf{X}'\underline{w} = \underline{\beta}. \tag{A.5}$$

In particular, using the Moore–Penrose pseudoinverse of $\mathbf{X}$, the minimum l_2 norm solution is

$$\underline{w} = \mathbf{X}(\mathbf{X}'\mathbf{X})^{-1}\underline{\beta}. \tag{A.6}$$

Now suppose there are two classes $\{1, 2\}$ of data samples (i.e., $K = 2$). Fix $b \in \mathbb{R}$ and consider any $\mathbb{R}^T$ vector $\underline{\beta} = (\beta^{(1)}, \beta^{(2)}, \dots, \beta^{(T)})'$ with $\beta^{(i)} < b$ if $c(\underline{x}_i) = 1$ else $\beta^{(i)} > b$. By (A.5), the two classes of training data,

$$X_1 = \{\underline{x} \in X : c(\underline{x}) = 1\} \quad \text{and} \quad X_2 = \{\underline{x} \in X : c(\underline{x}) = 2\}$$

are separated by the hyperplane $\underline{x}'\underline{w} = b$ where $\underline{w}$ is given, for example, by (A.6).

Now consider the assumption in (A.4). If $\text{rank}(\mathbf{X}) < T$, then one could, for example, apply the Gram–Schmidt process to $\mathbf{X}$'s columns to remove linearly dependent samples $\underline{x}$ (columns of $\mathbf{X}$), toward making $\mathbf{X}$ full rank.

Also, it may be advantageous in terms of generalization performance to reduce N, for example, [4]. In the following figures depicting illustrative examples, typically $N = 2$ and $T \gg 2$, that is, (A.4) does not hold.

Allowing for $T > N$ (i.e., $\mathbf{X}'\underline{w} = \underline{\beta}$ is *over*specified), the Ho–Kashyap classification framework [63] considers the MSE $\|\mathbf{X}'\underline{w} - \underline{\beta}\|^2$ and optimizes over $\underline{w}$ and $\underline{\beta}$. If this method achieves a zero error solution, a linear separator has been found. Otherwise, a linear separator does not exist. Data separability has also been studied through the more general concept of VC dimension and its extensions [279].

A.3   Background: Distance to a Hyperplane

For a fixed N-dimensional vector $\underline{w} \in \mathbb{R}^N$, $\underline{w} \neq 0$, and scalar $b \in \mathbb{R}$, define the hyperplane in $\mathbb{R}^N$,

$$\mathcal{F} = \left\{ \underline{x} \in \mathbb{R}^N \mid 0 = f(\underline{x}) = b + \langle \underline{x}, \underline{w} \rangle = b + \sum_{i=1}^N x_i w_i \right\}.$$

For $N = 2$, note that the line $x_2 = b + mx_1$ can be written as $0 = b + \langle \underline{x}, \underline{w} \rangle$ where $\underline{w} = (m, -1)' \perp (1, m)'$. If $\underline{x}, \underline{z} \in \mathcal{F}$ and $\underline{x} \neq \underline{z}$, then the vector $\underline{x} - \underline{z}$ must be parallel to

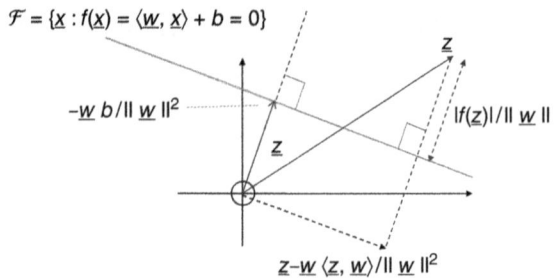

$\mathcal{F} = \{\underline{x} : f(\underline{x}) = \langle \underline{w}, \underline{x} \rangle + b = 0\}$

$-\underline{w}\, b/\|\underline{w}\|^2$

$|f(\underline{z})|/\|\underline{w}\|$

$\underline{z} - \underline{w}\,\langle \underline{z}, \underline{w} \rangle / \|\underline{w}\|^2$

Figure A.1 Distance to a hyperplane, with two axes shown meeting at the origin.

the hyperplane since $0 = f(\underline{x}) - f(\underline{z}) = \langle \underline{w}, \underline{x} - \underline{z} \rangle$ with $\underline{w} \perp \mathcal{F}$. Equivalently, one can define the hyperplane $\mathcal{F}$ given *any particular* vector $\underline{x}^*$ such that $f(\underline{x}^*) = 0$:

$$\mathcal{F} = \{\underline{x}^* + \underline{v} \mid \underline{v} \perp \underline{w}\}.$$

One such $\underline{x}^* = -b\,\underline{w}/\|\underline{w}\|^2 \perp \mathcal{F}$. See Figure A.1.

Recall one can project $\underline{z}$ onto $\underline{w}$ to write

$$\underline{z} = \alpha \frac{\underline{w}}{\|\underline{w}\|} + \left(\underline{z} - \alpha \frac{\underline{w}}{\|\underline{w}\|} \right),$$

where the component of $\underline{z}$ in the direction $\underline{w}$ is

$$\alpha = \frac{\langle \underline{z}, \underline{w} \rangle}{\|\underline{w}\|}$$

and $\underline{w}/\|\underline{w}\|$ is a vector of unit (Euclidean) norm.

The distance from $\underline{z}$ to $\mathcal{F}$ is $|d_{\underline{z}}|$ for a scalar $d_{\underline{z}} \in \mathbb{R}$ such that $\underline{z} - d_{\underline{z}}\underline{w}/\|\underline{w}\| \in \mathcal{F}$, that is,

$$0 = f(\underline{z} - d_{\underline{z}}\underline{w}/\|\underline{w}\|) = f(\underline{z}) - d_{\underline{z}}\|\underline{w}\|.$$

Thus, $d_{\underline{z}} = f(\underline{z})/\|\underline{w}\|$ and

$$|d_{\underline{z}}| = \frac{|f(\underline{z})|}{\|\underline{w}\|}.$$

If $d_{\underline{z}} > 0$ then $\underline{z}$ is on the side of the hyperplane $\mathcal{F}$ in $\mathbb{R}^N$ where $f > 0$ since

$$0 = f(\underline{z} - d_{\underline{z}}\underline{w}) = f(\underline{z}) - d_{\underline{z}}\|\underline{w}\|.$$

Else if $d_{\underline{z}} < 0$ then $\underline{z}$ is on the side of the hyperplane $\mathcal{F}$ where $f < 0$.

A.4   Support Vector Machine Development

A.4.1   Linear SVMs

In the following, let the ground truth class label of $\underline{x} \in X$ be

$$y_{\underline{x}} := c(\underline{x}).$$

Support vector machines (SVMs), for example, [165], are classifiers f of real, vector-valued, two-class samples, designed based on a (labeled) training set $\mathcal{X} \subset \mathbb{R}^N$ and $K = |\mathcal{Y}| = 2$, where the classes are enumerated

$$\{-1, 1\} = \mathcal{Y}.$$

An SVM $f : \mathbb{R}^N \to \mathbb{R}$ that is a separator possesses the following property on the training set: $\forall \underline{x} \in \mathcal{X}$,

- if $\underline{x}$'s class label $y_{\underline{x}} = 1$ then $f(\underline{x}) > 0$,
- else (when $y_{\underline{x}} = -1$) $f(\underline{x}) < 0$,
- that is, the sign of $f(\underline{x})$ indicates the true class $y_{\underline{x}}$.

So the classifier is actually

$$\hat{c} = \text{sgn} \circ f : \mathbb{R}^N \to \mathcal{Y} = \{-1, 1\}.$$

Linear SVMs and Separable Data

If the data is *linearly separable*, then there is a classifier

$$f(\underline{x}) = \langle \underline{w}, \underline{x} \rangle + b$$

such that

$$y_{\underline{x}} f(\underline{x}) > 0 \quad \text{for all } \underline{x} \in \mathcal{X},$$

where the scalar $b \in \mathbb{R}$ and the vector $\underline{w} \in \mathbb{R}^N$. The classification margin of a class separating classifier f is

$$\min_{\underline{x} \in \mathcal{X}} \frac{|f(\underline{x})|}{\|\underline{w}\|} = \min_{\underline{x} \in \mathcal{X}} \frac{y_{\underline{x}} f(\underline{x})}{\|\underline{w}\|}.$$

Consistent with achieving good generalization performance, choose $\underline{w}, b$ to solve the following optimization problem:

$$\min_{\underline{w}, b} \|\underline{w}\|^2 \quad \text{such that}$$
$$y_{\underline{x}} f(\underline{x}) = y_{\underline{x}}(\langle \underline{w}, \underline{x} \rangle + b) \geq 1 \quad \forall \underline{x} \in \mathcal{X}, \tag{A.7}$$

where minimizing $\|\underline{w}\|^2$ (easier to differentiate than $\|\underline{w}\|$) subject to the constraints is equivalent to maximizing classification *margin*, that is, maximizing the shortest distance to the decision boundary (hyperplane $\mathcal{F} = \{x : f(x) = 0\}$) among all the points in both classes.

Note that the linear optimization constraints are ≥ 1 instead of ≥ 0 so as to "normalize" the resulting weight vector $\underline{w}$ with respect to the **closest points (support vectors)** to the hyperplane $\mathcal{F}$,

$$\mathcal{X}^* \subset \mathcal{X}.$$

Define the Lagrangian with Lagrange multipliers $\underline{\lambda}$:

$$L((\underline{w}, b), \underline{\lambda}) = \frac{1}{2}\|\underline{w}\|^2 - \sum_{\underline{x} \in \mathcal{X}} \lambda_{\underline{x}}(y_{\underline{x}}(\langle \underline{w}, \underline{x} \rangle + b) - 1).$$

Taking the dual approach:

$$\nabla_w L = 0 \Rightarrow \underline{w}^* = \sum_{\underline{x} \in X} \lambda_{\underline{x}} y_{\underline{x}} \underline{x}$$

$$\frac{\partial L}{\partial b} = 0 \Rightarrow \sum_{\underline{x} \in X} \lambda_{\underline{x}} y_{\underline{x}} = 0.$$

Thus by substitution one gets

$$L((\underline{w}^*, b^*), \underline{\lambda}) = \frac{1}{2} \left\| \sum_{\underline{x} \in X} \lambda_{\underline{x}} y_{\underline{x}} \underline{x} \right\|^2 - \sum_{\underline{x} \in X} \lambda_{\underline{x}} y_{\underline{x}} \left(\sum_{\underline{z} \in X} \lambda_{\underline{z}} y_{\underline{z}} \underline{z}, \ \underline{x} \right)$$

$$- \sum_{\underline{x} \in X} \lambda_{\underline{x}} y_{\underline{x}} b^* + \sum_{\underline{x} \in X} \lambda_{\underline{x}}$$

$$= -\frac{1}{2} \sum_{\underline{x} \in X} \sum_{\underline{z} \in X} \lambda_{\underline{x}} \lambda_{\underline{z}} y_{\underline{x}} y_{\underline{z}} \langle \underline{x}, \underline{z} \rangle + \sum_{\underline{x} \in X} \lambda_{\underline{x}}.$$

Now, one needs to maximize $L((\underline{w}^*, b^*), \underline{\lambda})$ over $\underline{\lambda}$, subject to

$$\sum_{\underline{x} \in X} \lambda_{\underline{x}} y_{\underline{x}} = 0, \quad \text{and } \lambda_{\underline{x}} \geq 0, \forall \underline{x} \in X,$$

which is a quadratic program.

Recall complementary slackness,

$$\forall \underline{x} \in X, \quad \lambda_{\underline{x}} (y_{\underline{x}} (\langle \underline{w}^*, \underline{x} \rangle + b^*) - 1) = 0.$$

Thus,

$$\lambda_{\underline{x}} = 0 \Leftrightarrow \underline{x} \notin X^*$$

$$\underline{w}^* = \sum_{\underline{x} \in X^*} \lambda_{\underline{x}} y_{\underline{x}} \underline{x}$$

$$b^* = y_{\underline{x}} - \langle \underline{w}^*, \underline{x} \rangle = y_{\underline{x}} - \sum_{\underline{z} \in X^*} \lambda_{\underline{z}} y_{\underline{z}} \langle \underline{z}, \underline{x} \rangle, \quad \underline{x} \in X^*.$$

For robustness to errors, one can average b^* over the support vectors:

$$b^* = \frac{1}{|X^*|} \sum_{\underline{x} \in X^*} \left(y_{\underline{x}} - \sum_{\underline{z} \in X^*} \lambda_{\underline{z}} y_{\underline{z}} \langle \underline{z}, \underline{x} \rangle \right).$$

Inference by Linear SVM

Suppose the class of test sample $\underline{z}$ is to be inferred. Again, this is achieved by evaluating the sign of the SVM at the given test sample $\underline{z}$,

$$\hat{c}(\underline{z}) = \text{sgn}(f(\underline{z})) = \text{sgn}\left(\langle \underline{w}^*, \underline{z} \rangle + b^* \right) = \text{sgn}\left(\sum_{\underline{x} \in X^*} \lambda_{\underline{x}} y_{\underline{x}} \langle \underline{x}, \underline{z} \rangle + b^* \right).$$

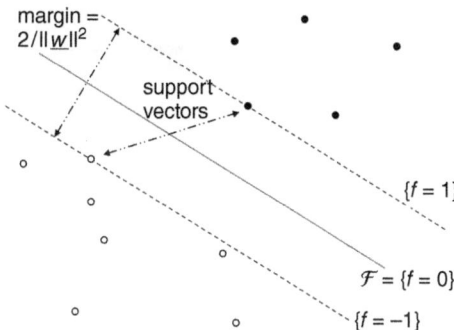

margin =
2/‖$\underline{w}$‖^2

support
vectors

{f = 1}

$\mathcal{F}$ = {f = 0}

{f = −1}

Figure A.2 Illustrative example of linear SVM with linearly separable data.

Note that this depends only on inner products of $\underline{z}$ with support vectors, $\langle \underline{z}, \underline{x} \rangle$ for $\underline{x} \in \mathcal{X}^*$, and of support vectors with each other (b^*). This recognition allows one to also learn non-linear (kernel based) SVMs, by replacing the inner products in the original feature space by inner products in an (in general) infinite-dimensional space, one consistent with a specified kernel function (which efficiently computes inner products in this new feature space, even if infinite dimensional). This will be developed in the sequel, see the *kernel trick*.

In summary, the SVM is the decision boundary that maximizes classification margin over both classes for improved generalization performance; see Figure A.2.

A.4.2   Linear SVM with Slackness for Non-separable Data

When the labeled training data $\mathcal{X}$ is not linearly separable, instead of (A.7), find:

$$\min_{\underline{w}, b} \frac{1}{2} \left\| \underline{w} \right\|^2 + \sigma \sum_{\underline{x} \in \mathcal{X}} \gamma_{\underline{x}} \quad \text{where}$$

$$\gamma_{\underline{x}} = \max\{0, \ 1 - y_{\underline{x}} f(\underline{x})\} = (1 - y_{\underline{x}}(\langle \underline{w}, \underline{x} \rangle + b))^+ \quad \forall \underline{x} \in \mathcal{X}.$$

(A.8)

Here, the slackness term $\gamma_{\underline{x}} \geq 0$ measures the degree to which $\underline{x} \in \mathcal{X}$ violates the margin. The scale term $\sigma \geq 0$ is a hyperparameter which can be chosen by grid search to minimize the classification error rate on a held-out evaluation subset of the training set $\mathcal{X}$ (or the error rate estimated based on cross validation, if a held-out set is unavailable).

See Figure A.3 for an illustrative example.

A.4.3   Kernel SVMs with Nonlinear Decision Boundaries

Again, suppose that the training data $\mathcal{X}$ is not linearly separable, but suppose there is a feature mapping function $\Phi : \mathbb{R}^N \rightarrow \mathbb{R}^{N'}$ for $N' > N$ (the original number of features) such that $\{(\Phi(\underline{x}), y_{\underline{x}})\}_{\underline{x} \in \mathcal{X}}$ *is linearly separable*. Recall Cover's theorem in Section 2.3. Repeating the above procedure gives the SVM in $\mathbb{R}^{N'}$:

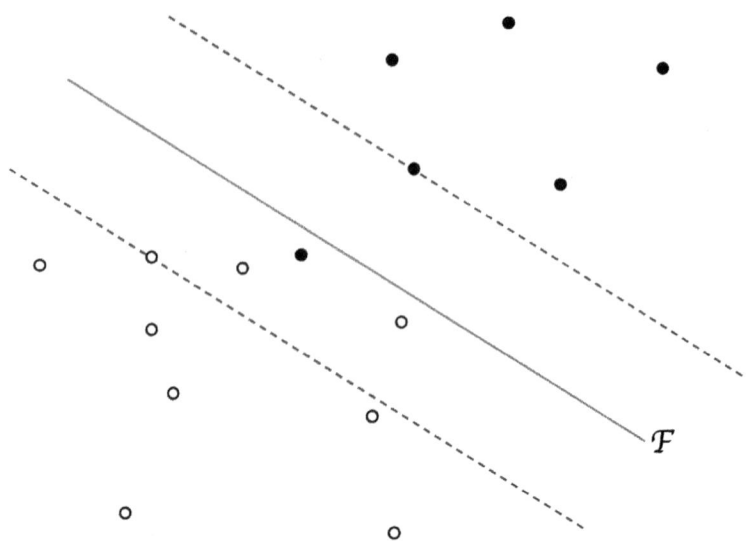

Figure A.3 Linear SVMs with not linearly separable data: two white margin violators, one black sample misclassified.

$$f^*(\underline{x}) = \langle \underline{w}^*, \Phi(\underline{x}) \rangle + b^* \;=\; \sum_{\underline{z} \in \mathcal{X}^*} \lambda_{\underline{z}} y_{\underline{z}} \kappa(\underline{z}, \underline{x}) + b^*,$$

where for any $\underline{\zeta} \in \mathcal{X}^*$,

$$b^* = y_{\underline{\zeta}} - \sum_{\underline{z} \in \mathcal{X}^*} \lambda_{\underline{z}} y_{\underline{z}} \kappa(\underline{z}, \underline{\zeta})$$

and the *kernel* κ is given by

$$\kappa(\underline{z}, \underline{\zeta}) = \langle \Phi(\underline{z}), \Phi(\underline{\zeta}) \rangle.$$

Note that the SVM classifier f^* depends on the feature map Φ only implicitly through κ and $\mathcal{X}^*$. Computation of the SVM typically *begins* by selecting the kernel κ (which determines N'), hoping that the data can be separable with the choice made, and attempting to discover the Lagrange multipliers $\lambda_{\underline{x}}$ (and hence the support vectors $\mathcal{X}^*$) without explicitly determining Φ, that is, using the "kernel trick." The corresponding "weight vector norm squared" (classification margin) in the nonlinear classifier case is

$$\sum_{\underline{z}, \underline{\zeta} \in \mathcal{X}} \lambda_{\underline{z}} \lambda_{\underline{\zeta}} y_{\underline{z}} y_{\underline{\zeta}} \kappa(\underline{z}, \underline{\zeta}),$$

clearly generalizing $\|\underline{w}^*\|^2$ for a linear SVM.

For example, suppose $\Phi(\underline{x})$ contains all polynomial components that can be created with the elements of $\underline{x}$ of degree ≤ 2. Specifically, if $x = (x_1, x_2, x_3)'$ (i.e., $N = 3$) and

$$\Phi(\underline{x}) = (1, x_1\sqrt{2}, x_2\sqrt{2}, x_3\sqrt{2}, x_1^2, x_2^2, x_3^2, x_1 x_2\sqrt{2}, x_2 x_3\sqrt{2}, x_3 x_1\sqrt{2})'$$

then

$$\kappa(\underline{x}, \underline{z}) = \langle \Phi(\underline{x}), \Phi(\underline{z}) \rangle = (1 + \langle \underline{x}, \underline{z} \rangle)^2$$

with $N' = 10$.

As another example, for Gaussian radial basis functions, which are commonly used,

$$\kappa(\underline{z}, \underline{x}) = \exp\left(-\frac{\|\underline{z} - \underline{x}\|^2}{2s^2}\right),$$

for which $N' = \infty$! Note that one does not need to know Φ to train the SVM or to make inferences and that the variance term s^2 is a hyperparameter.

Allowing for slackness with scale $\sigma \geq 0$, the optimization objective is:

$$\frac{\|\underline{w}\|^2}{2} + \sigma \sum_{\underline{x} \in \mathcal{X}} \gamma_{\underline{x}} \quad \text{where}$$

$$\gamma_{\underline{x}} = (1 - y_{\underline{x}}(\langle \underline{w}, \Phi(\underline{x}) \rangle + b))^+ \ \forall \underline{x} \in \mathcal{X}.$$

A.4.4   Feature Selection Using SVMs

Use of many features may confound or may not contribute much to reliable class decision-making. (Recall Section 3.5 regarding feature selection.) One can promote sparsity in the weights (recall Section 2.7.1) by adding a penalty term to the Lagrangian:

$$\|w\|_q^q = \sum_i |w_i|^q \quad \text{for } 0 < q \ll 1,$$

that is, penalize non-zero weights ($q \ll 1$) while preserving differentiability ($q > 0$).

Recursive methods have been proposed to reduce features used for classification (making the SVM weight vector sparser). One approach is to eliminate features associated with smallest magnitude weight-vector components (RFE). Margin based feature elimination (MFE) [4] removes the feature which results in the largest preserved margin.

A.4.5   SVMs for More Than Two Classes

Assume $K = |\mathcal{Y}| \geq 2$ classes and recall Section 2.4. Suppose one finds $\binom{K}{2} = K(K-1)/2$ SVMs $\hat{c}_{y,y'}$, one for each different pair of classes $y' \neq y \in \mathcal{Y}$. For example, one can then create a multi-class SVM by labeling test samples $\underline{x}$ as follows,

$$y_{\underline{x}} = \arg\max_y \sum_{y' \in \mathcal{Y}, \ y' \neq y} \mathbf{1}\{\hat{c}_{y,y'}(\underline{x}) = y\},$$

that is, the class decision for $\underline{x}$ is obtained by plurality "voting" by the SVMs. See Figure A.4 for an illustrative example with pairwise SVMs for three linearly separable classes. Note, though, that, in general, this pairwise multi-class SVM may have indeterminate regions, that is, regions in feature space where more than one class has the same (maximum) number of votes. In such regions, a tie-breaker rule is needed in order to make class decisions.

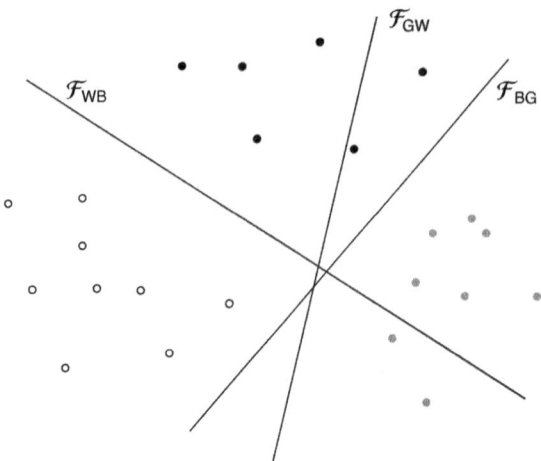

Figure A.4 If two SVMs vote "grey" (G) while $\mathcal{F}_{WB}$ votes either "black" (B) or "white" (W), then the "grey" class is decided.

Alternatively, one could find just K SVMs, each discriminating between a different class y and the rest of the classes treated as a single super-class

$$\bar{y} := \mathcal{Y}\backslash y = \{y' \in \mathcal{Y} \mid y' \neq y\}$$

(i.e., lump together the rest of the classes giving "one versus rest"). Note, though, that the one versus rest SVM is not guaranteed to find a separator when the training set is in fact (multi-class) linearly separable. Moreover, it also may have indeterminate regions.

A.4.6 One-Class SVMs

The idea of one-class SVMs is to try to train the SVM to return 1 for a region containing the training samples; otherwise return -1.

In the approach of Tax and Duin, the problem is:

$$\min_{R,\underline{v}} R^2 + \sigma \sum_{\underline{x} \in \mathcal{X}} \gamma_{\underline{x}} \text{ where}$$

$$\gamma_{\underline{x}} = (\|\Phi(\underline{x}) - \underline{v}\|^2 - R^2)^+ \quad \forall \underline{x} \in \mathcal{X}.$$

Here the decision boundary is a hypersphere of radius $|R|$ and center $\underline{v} \in \mathbb{R}^{N'}$. That is, the SVM is $\hat{c}(\underline{x}) = \text{sgn}(R^2 - \|\Phi(\underline{x}) - \underline{v}\|^2)$. Misclassified training samples $\underline{x}$ are such that $\gamma_{\underline{x}} > 0$, that is, $\Phi(\underline{x})$ is outside of the sphere and $\hat{c}(\underline{x}) = -1$. Other one-class loss objectives include [235].

Note that the mapping $\Phi : \mathbb{R}^N \to \mathbb{R}^{N'}$ could be the output activations of a DNN, where the objective of the previous display is also minimized over Φ's parameters.

References

[1] E. Aarts and J. Korst. *Simulated Annealing and Boltzmann Machines*. Wiley, 1989.

[2] S. Akcay, A. Atapour-Abarghouei, and T. P. Breckon. GANomaly: semisupervised anomaly detection via adversarial training. In *Asian Conference on Computer Vision*, pages 622–637. Springer, 2018.

[3] N. Akhtar and A. Mian. Threat of adversarial attacks on deep learning in computer vision: a survey. *IEEE Access*, 6:14410–14430, 2018.

[4] Y. Aksu, D. J. Miller, G. Kesidis, and Q. X. Yang. Margin-maximizing feature elimination methods for linear and nonlinear kernel SVMs. *IEEE Transactions on Neural Networks and Learning Systems*, 21(5):701–717, 2010.

[5] I. Alabdulmohsin, X. Gao, and X. Zhang. Adding robustness to support vector machines against adversarial reverse engineering. In *ACM International Conference on Information and Knowledge Management, CIKM*, 2014.

[6] S. Albanie. Pretrained VGG Face Model. https://www.robots.ox.ac.uk/~albanie/pytorch -models.html.

[7] S. Alfeld, X. Zhu, and P. Barford. Data poisoning attacks against autoregressive models. In *AAAI Conference on Artificial Intelligence*, 2016.

[8] U. M. Ascher and C. Greif. *A First Course in Numerical Methods*. SIAM Computational Science & Engineering, Philadelphia, PA, 2011.

[9] A. Azizi, I. Tahmid, A. Waheed, N. Mangaokar, J. Pu, M. Javed, C. K. Reddy, and B. Viswanath. T-Miner: a generative approach to defend against Trojan attacks on DNN-based text classification. In *USENIX Security Symposium*, 2021.

[10] K. Bache and M. Lichman. UCI machine learning repository. http://archive.ics.uci.edu/ ml, 2013.

[11] E. Bagdasaryan, O. Poursaeed, and V. Shmatikov. Differential privacy has disparate impact on model accuracy. In Hanna M. Wallach, Hugo Larochelle, Alina Beygelzimer, Florence d'Alché-Buc, Emily B. Fox, and Roman Garnett, editors, *Conference on Neural Information Processing Systems, NeurIPS*, 2019.

[12] J. Bai, B. Wu, Y. Zhang, Y. Li, Z. Li, and S.-T. Xia. Targeted attack against deep neural networks via flipping limited weight bits. arXiv:2102.10496, 2021.

[13] R. Balestriero and Y. LeCun. Contrastive and non-contrastive self-supervised learning recover global and local spectral embedding methods. arXiv:2205.11508v3, 2022.

[14] M. Barreno, B. Nelson, R. Sears, A. D. Joseph, and J. D. Tygar. Can machine learning be secure? In *ACM Symposium on Information, Computer and Communications Security*, 2006.

[15] P. Bartlett, D. Foster, and M. Telgarsky. Spectrally-normalized margin bounds for neural networks. In *International Conference on Neural Information Processing Systems, NIPS,* 2017.

[16] BATCHNORM2D. https://pytorch.org/docs/stable/generated/torch.nn.BatchNorm2d.html.

[17] A. Bendale and T. E. Boult. Towards open set deep networks. In *IEEE Conference on Computer Vision and Pattern Recognition, CVPR,* 2015.

[18] D. Bertsimas and M. Sim. The price of robustness. *Operations Research,* 52(1):35–53, 2004.

[19] B. Biggio, I. Corona, D. Majorca, B. Nelson, N. Srndic, P. Laskov, G. Giacinto, and F. Roli. Evasion attacks against machine learning at test time. In *European Conference on Machine Learning and Principles and Practice of Knowledge Discovery in Databases, ECML PKDD,* 2013.

[20] B. Biggio, B. Nelson, and P. Laskov. Support vector machines under adversarial label noise. In *Asian Conference on Machine Learning,* 2011.

[21] B. Biggio and F. Roli. Wild patterns: ten years after the rise of adversarial machine learning. *Pattern Recognition,* 84:317–331, 2018.

[22] C. M. Bishop. *Pattern Recognition and Machine Learning.* Springer, 2006.

[23] M. Bishop. *Computer Security: Art and Science,* 2nd edn. Addison-Wesley, 2018.

[24] W. L. Brogan. *Modern Control Theory.* Prentice-Hall, Englewood Cliffs, NJ, 1991.

[25] R. Burbidge, J. J. Rowland, and R. D. King. Active learning for regression based on query by committee. In *International Conference on Intelligent Data Engineering and Automated Learning, IDEAL,* 2007.

[26] W. Cai, Y. Zhang, and J. Zhou. Maximizing expected model change for active learning in regression. In *IEEE International Conference on Data Mining,* 2013.

[27] CalcPlot3D. https://github.com/adambielski/siamese-triplet.

[28] C. Calude and G. Longo. The deluge of spurious correlations in big data. *Foundations of Science,* 22:595–612, 2017.

[29] Y. Cao, Y. Li, S. Coleman, A. Belatreche, and T. M. McGinnity. Detecting price manipulation in the financial market. In *IEEE Conference on Computational Intelligence for Financial Engineering & Economics,* March 2014.

[30] N. Carlini, A. Athalye, N. Papernot, W. Brendel, J. Rauber, D. Tsipras, I. Goodfellow, A. Madry, and A. Kurakin. On evaluating adversarial robustness. https://github.com/evaluating-adversarial-robustness/adv-eval-paper, February 18, 2019.

[31] N. Carlini, P. Mishra, T. Vaidya, Y. Zhang, M. Sherr, C. Shields, D. Wagner, and W. Zhou. Hidden voice commands. In *USENIX Security Symposium,* 2016.

[32] N. Carlini and D. Wagner. Adversarial examples are not easily detected: bypassing ten detection methods. In *ACM Workshop on Artificial Intelligence and Security, AISec,* 2017.

[33] N. Carlini and D. Wagner. Towards evaluating the robustness of neural networks. In *IEEE Symposium on Security and Privacy, S&P,* 2017.

[34] N. Carlini and D. Wagner. Audio adversarial examples: targeted attacks on speech-to-text. In *IEEE Security and Privacy, S&P, Workshops,* May 2018.

[35] M. Cesa and L. Clancy. Deep XVAs and the promise of super-fast pricing. https://www.risk.net/derivatives/7848521/deep-xvas-and-the-promise-of-super-fast-pricing icing, June 29, 2021.

[36] C. Chai, L. Cao, G. Li, J. Li, Y. Luo, and S. Madden. Human-in-the-loop outlier detection. In *ACM SIGMOD International Conference on Management of Data,* June 2020.

[37] R. Chalapathy, A. K. Menon, and S. Chawla. Anomaly detection using one-class neural networks. arXiv:1802.06360, 2018.

[38] R. Q. Charles, H. Su, M. Kaichun, and L. J. Guibas. PointNet: deep learning on point sets for 3D classification and segmentation. In *IEEE Conference on Computer Vision and Pattern Recognition, CVPR*, 2017.

[39] B. Chen, W. Carvalho, N. Baracaldo, H. Ludwig, B. Edwards, T. Lee, I. Molloy, and B. Srivastava. Detecting backdoor attacks on deep neural networks by activation clustering. arXiv:1811.03728, November 8, 2018.

[40] P.-Y. Chen, Y. Sharma, H. Zhang, J. Yi, and C.-J. Hsieh. EAD: elastic-net attacks to deep neural networks via adversarial examples. In *AAAI Conference on Artificial Intelligence*, 2018.

[41] P.-Y. Chen, H. Zhang, Y. Sharma, J. Yi, and C.-J. Hsieh. ZOO: zeroth order optimization based black-box attacks to deep neural networks without training substitute models. In *ACM Workshop on Artificial Intelligence and Security*, 2017.

[42] R. Chen and I. Ch. Paschalidis. Distributionally robust learning. arXiv:2108.08993, 2020.

[43] S. Chen, B. Liu, C. Feng, C. Vallespi-Gonzalez, and C. Wellington. 3d point cloud processing and learning for autonomous driving: impacting map creation, localization, and perception. *IEEE Signal Processing Magazine*, 38(1):68–86, 2021.

[44] X. Chen, C. Liu, B. Li, K. Lu, and D. Song. Targeted backdoor attacks on deep learning systems using data poisoning. arXiv:1712.05526v1, 2017.

[45] M. Chui, J. Manyika, M. Miremadi, N. Henke, R. Chung, P. Nel, and S. Malhotra. Notes from the AI frontier: applications and value of deep learning. https://www.mckinsey.com/featured-insights/artificial-intelligence/notes-from-the-ai-frontier-applications-and-value-of-deep-learning#part3, April 2018.

[46] M. Cisse, P. Bojanowski, E. Grave, Y. Dauphin, and N. Usunierr. Parseval networks: improving robustness to adversarial examples. In *International Conference on Machine Learning, ICML*, 2017.

[47] A. Coates, H. Lee, and A. Y. Ng. An analysis of single layer networks in unsupervised feature learning. In *International Conference on Artificial Intelligence and Statistics, AISTATS*, 2011.

[48] J. Cohen, E. Rosenfeld, and Z. Kolter. Certified adversarial robustness via randomized smoothing. In *International Conference on Machine Learning, ICML*, 2019.

[49] D. Cohn, Z. Ghahramani, and M. I. Jordan. Active learning with statistical models. *Journal of Artificial Intelligence Research*, 4(1):129–145, 1996.

[50] G. V. Cormack and T. R. Lynam. Trec 2005 spam public corpora. https://plg.uwaterloo.ca/~gvcormac/trecspamtrack05, 2005.

[51] T. M. Cover. Geometrical and statistical properties of systems of linear inequalities with applications in pattern recognition. *IEEE Transactions on Electronic Computers*, 14:326–334, 1965.

[52] A. Creswell, T. White, V. Dumoulin, K. Arulkumaran, B. Sengupta, and A. A. Bharath. Generative adversarial networks: an overview. arXiv:1710.07035, October 19, 2017.

[53] J. Dai and C. Chen. A backdoor attack against lstm-based text classification systems. arXiv:1905.12457, 2019.

[54] D. T. Davis and J.-N. Hwang. Solving inverse problems by Bayesian neural network iterative inversion with ground truth incorporation. *IEEE Transactions on Signal Processing*, 45(11):2749–2757, 1997.

[55] A. Demontis, M. Melis, B. Biggio, D. Maiorca, D. Arp, K. Rieck, I. Corona, G. Giacinto, and F. Roli. Yes, machine learning can be more secure! A case study on android malware detection. *IEEE Transactions on Dependable and Secure Computing*, 16(4):711–724, 2017.

[56] A. P. Dempster, N. M. Laird, and D. B. Rubin. Maximum likelihood from incomplete data via the EM algorithm. *Journal of the Royal Statistical Society, Series B (Methodological)*, 39(1):1–38, 1977.

[57] J. Deng, W. Dong, R. Socher, L.-J. Li, K. Li, and L. Fei-Fei. ImageNet: a large-scale hierarchical image database. In *IEEE Conference on Computer Vision and Pattern Recognition, CVPR*, 2009.

[58] J. Devlin, M.- W. Chang, K. Lee, and K. Toutanova. BERT: pre-training of deep bidirectional transformers for language understanding. arXiv:1810.04805, May 24, 2019.

[59] I. Diakonikolas, G. Kamath, D. Kane, J. Li, J. Steinhardt, and A. Stewart. Sever: a robust meta-algorithm for stochastic optimization. In *International Conference on Machine Learning, ICML*, 2019.

[60] K. I. Diamantaras and S. Y. Kung. *Principal Component Neural Networks: Theory and Applications*. Wiley, New York, 1996.

[61] Y. Dong, X. Yang, Z. Deng, T. Pang, Z. Xiao, H. Su, and J. Zhu. Black-box detection of backdoor attacks with limited information and data. In *IEEE International Conference on Computer Vision, ICCV*, 2021.

[62] I. Drori. *The Science of Deep Learning*. Cambridge University Press, 2023.

[63] R. O. Duda, P. E. Hart, and D. G. Stork. *Pattern Classification*, 2nd edn. Wiley, 2001.

[64] F. Durante, J. Fernández-Sánchez, and C. Sempi. How to prove Sklar's theorem. In *Aggregation Functions in Theory and in Practise – Advances in Intelligent Systems and Computing*, volume 228. Springer, 2013.

[65] D. Elreedy, A. F. Atiya, and S. I. Shaheen. A novel active learning regression framework for balancing the exploration-exploitation trade-off. *Entropy*, 21:651, 2019.

[66] D. M. Endres and J. E. Schindelin. A new metric for probability distributions. *IEEE Transactions on Information Theory*, 49(7):1858–1860, 2003.

[67] M. Fazlyab, A. Robey, H. Hassani, M. Morari, and G. J. Pappas. Efficient and accurate estimation of Lipschitz constants for deep neural networks. arXiv:1906.04893, 2019.

[68] R. Feinman, R. Curtin, S. Shintre, and A. Gardner. Detecting adversarial samples from artifacts. arXiv:1703.00410v2, 2017.

[69] J. Feng, H. Xu, S. Mannor, and S. Yan. Robust logistic regression and classification. In *International Conference on Neural Information Processing Systems, NIPS*, 2014.

[70] R. Ferguson and A. Green. Deeply learning derivatives. arXiv:1809.02233, October 14, 2018.

[71] M. Fredrikson, S. Jha, and T. Ristenpart. Model inversion attacks that exploit confidence information and basic countermeasures. In *ACM Conference on Computer and Communications Security, ACM CCS*, 2015.

[72] J. Gao, J. Lanchantin, M. L. Soffa, and Y. Qi. Black-box generation of adversarial text sequences to evade deep learning classifiers. In *IEEE Security and Privacy, S&P, Workshops*, 2018.

[73] Y. Gao, C. Xu, D. Wang, S. Chen, D. C. Ranasinghe, and S. Nepal. STRIP: a defence against Trojan attacks on deep neural networks. arXiv:1902.06531, 2019.

[74] C. Geer. Anomaly Detection of Test-Time Evasion Attacks in the Audio Domain. Master's thesis, CSE Department, Pennsylvania State University, May 2022, https://etda.libraries .psu.edu/catalog/20200crg5567.

[75] I. M. Gelfand and S. V. Fomin. *Calculus of Variations*. Prentice-Hall, Englewood Cliffs, NJ, 1963.

[76] A. Gersho and R. M. Gray. *Vector Quantization and Signal Compression*. Springer, 1992.

[77] J. K. Ghosh, M. Delampady, and T. Samanta, editors. *An Introduction to Bayesian Analysis: Theory and Methods*. Springer Science+Business Media, 2006.

[78] P. Ghosh, A. Losalka, and M. J. Black. Resisting adversarial attacks using gaussian mixture variational autoencoders. In *AAAI Conference on Artificial Intelligence*, 2019.

[79] J. Gilmer, R. P. Adams, I. Goodfellow, D. Anderson, and G. E. Dahl. Motivating the rules of the game for adversarial example research. arXiv:1807.06732, 2018.

[80] C. A. Glasbey and K. V. Mardia. A review of image-warping methods. *Journal of Applied Statistics*, 25(2):155–171, 1998.

[81] I. Goodfellow, Y. Bengio, and A. Courville. *Deep Learning*. MIT Press, 2016.

[82] I. Goodfellow, J. Pouget-Abadie, M. Mirza, B. Xu, D. Warde-Farley, S. Ozair, A. Courville, and Y. Bengio. Generative adversarial networks. In *International Conference on Neural Information Processing Systems, NIPS*, 2014.

[83] I. Goodfellow, J. Shlens, and C. Szegedy. Explaining and harnessing adversarial examples. In *International Conference on Learning Representations, ICLR*, 2015.

[84] H. Gouk, E. Frankeib, and B. Pfahringer. Regularisation of neural networks by enforcing Lipschitz continuity. arXiv:1804.04368, September 2018.

[85] A. Graese, A. Rosza, and T.E. Boult. Assessing threat of adversarial examples on deep neural networks. In *International Conference on Machine Learning, ICML*, 2016.

[86] M. W. Graham and D. J. Miller. Unsupervised learning of parsimonious mixtures on large spaces with integrated feature and component selection. *IEEE Transactions on Signal Processing*, 54(4):1289–1303, 2006.

[87] K. Grosse, P. Manoharan, N. Papernot, M. Backes, and P. McDaniel. On the (statistical) detection of adversarial examples. arXiv:1702.06280, 2017.

[88] S. Gruppetta. Image processing with the Python pillow library. https://realpython.com/ image-processing-with-the-python-pillow-library/, March 23, 2022.

[89] T. Gu, K. Liu, B. Dolan-Gavitt, and S. Garg. Badnets: evaluating backdooring attacks on deep neural networks. *IEEE Access*, 7:47230–47244, 2019.

[90] T. Gu, K. Liu, B. Dolan-Gavitt, and S. Garg. BadNets: evaluating backdooring attacks on deep neural networks. *IEEE Access*, 7:47230–47244, 2019.

[91] D. Gunning. Explainable artificial intelligence research at DARPA. https://sites .nationalacademies.org/cs/groups/pgasite/documents/webpage/pga_184754.pdf.

[92] J. Guo, P. V. K. Borges, C. Park, and A. Gawel. Local descriptor for robust place recognition using LiDAR intensity. *IEEE Robotics and Automation Letters*, 4(2):1470–1477, 2019.

[93] W. Guo, L. Wang, X. Xing, M. Du, and D. Song. TABOR: a highly accurate approach to inspecting and restoring Trojan backdoors in AI systems. arXiv:1908.01763, 2019.

[94] A. Hamdi, S. Rojas, A. Thabet, and B. Ghanem. Advpc: transferable adversarial perturbations on 3d point clouds. In *European Conference on Computer Vision, ECCV*, pages 241–257, 2020.

[95] F. R. Hampel. The influence curve and its role in robust estimation. *Journal of the American Statistical Association*, 69(346):383–393, 1974.

[96] A.G. Hawkes. Approximating the normal tail. *The Statistician*, 31(3):231–236, 1982.

[97] K. He, X. Zhang, S. Ren, and J. Sun. Deep residual learning for image recognition. In *IEEE Conference on Computer Vision and Pattern Recognition, CVPR*, 2016.

[98] D. Hendrycks and K. Gimpel. A baseline for detecting misclassified and out-of-distribution examples in neural networks. In *International Conference on Learning Representations, ICLR*, 2017.

[99] D. Hendrycks and K. Gimpel. Early methods for detecting adversarial images. In *International Conference on Learning Representations, ICLR, Workshop Track*, 2017.

[100] S. Higginbotham. Hey, data scientists: show your machine-learning work. *IEEE Spectrum*, November 20, 2019.

[101] S. Hochreiter and J. Schmidhuber. Long short-term memory. *Neural Computation*, 9(8):1735–1780, 1997.

[102] S. Hong, V. Chandrasekaran, Y. Kaya, T. Dumitras, and N. Papernot. On the effectiveness of mitigating data poisoning attacks with gradient shaping. arXiv:2002.11497, 2020.

[103] R. A. Horn and C. R. Johnson. *Matrix Analysis*, 2nd edn. Cambridge University Press, 2013.

[104] D. A. Hoskins, J.-N. Hwang, and J. Vagners. Iterative inversion of neural networks and its application to adaptive control. *IEEE Transactions on Neural Networks*, 3(2):292–301, 1992.

[105] T. M. Hospedales, S. Gong, and T. Xiang. Finding rare classes: active learning with generative and discriminative models. *IEEE Transactions on Knowledge and Data Engineering*, 25(2):374–386, 2011.

[106] L. Huang, A. D. Joseph, B. Nelson, B. I. P. Rubinstein, and J. D. Tygar. Adversarial machine learning. In *ACM Workshop on Artificial Intelligence and Security, AISec*, 2011.

[107] D.A. Hoskins and J.-N. Hwang and J. Vagners. Iterative inversion of neural networks and its application to adaptive control. IEEE Trans. Neural Networks 3, Mar. 1992.

[108] P. Isola, J.-Y. Zhu, T. Zhou, and A. A. Efros. Image-to-image translation with conditional adversarial networks. In *IEEE Conference on Computer Vision and Pattern Recognition, CVPR*, 2017.

[109] M. Jaderberg, K. Simonyan, A. Zisserman, and K. Kavukcuoglu. Spatial transformer networks. In *International Conference on Neural Information Processing Systems, NIPS*, 2015.

[110] S. Jain. An overview of regularization techniques in deep learning. https://www.analyticsvidhya.com/blog/2018/04/fundamentals-deep-learning-regularization-techniques/, April 19, 2018.

[111] D. Jin, Z. Jin, J. T. Zhou, and P. Szolovits. Is BERT really robust? A strong baseline for natural language attack on text classification and entailment. In *AAAI Conference on Artificial Intelligence*, 2020.

[112] A. D. Joseph, B. Nelson, B. I. P. Rubinstein, and J. D. Tygar. *Adversarial Machine Learning*. Cambridge University Press, 2019.

[113] B.-H. Juang and S. Katigiri. Discriminative learning for minimum error classification (pattern recognition). *IEEE Transactions on Signal Processing*, 40(12):3043–3054, 1992.

[114] D. Jurafsky and J. H. Martin. Speech and Language Processing (3rd edn. draft). https://web.stanford.edu/~jurafsky/slp3/, December 29, 2021.

[115] C. Kading, E. Rodner, A. Freytag, O. Mothes, B. Barz, and J. Denzler. Active learning for regression tasks with expected model output changes. In *British Machine Vision Conference*, 2018.

[116] M. Kang, W. Shim, M. Cho, and J. Park. Rebooting acgan: auxiliary classifier gans with stable training. In *Conference on Neural Information Processing Systems, NeurIPS*, 2021.

[117] T. Karras, S. Laine, M. Aittala, J. Hellsten, J. Lehtinen, and T. Aila. Analyzing and improving the image quality of stylegan. In *IEEE/CVF Conference on Computer Vision and Pattern Recognition, CVPR*, pages 8110–8119, 2020.

[118] C. Kereliuk, B. Sturm, and J. Larsen. Deep learning and music adversaries. *IEEE Transactions on Multimedia*, 17(11):2059–2071, 2015.

[119] C. Kereliuk, B. Sturm, and J. Larsen. Deep learning, audio adversaries, and music content analysis. In *IEEE Workshop on Applications of Signal Processing to Audio and Acoustics*, 2015.

[120] G. Kesidis, D. J. Miller, and Z. Xiang. Notes on Lipschitz margin, Lipschitz margin training, and Lipschitz margin p-values for deep neural network classifiers. arXiv:1910.08032, October 15, 2019.

[121] P. Khosla, P. Teterwak, C. Wang, A. Sarna, Y. Tian, P. Isola, A. Maschinot, C. Liu, and D. Krishnan. Supervised contrastive learning. In *Conference on Neural Information Processing Systems, NeurIPS*, 2020.

[122] M. Kim, J. Tack, and S. J. Hwang. Adversarial self-supervised contrastive learning. In *Conference on Neural Information Processing Systems, NeurIPS*, 2020.

[123] D. Kingma and J. Ba. Adam: a method for stochastic optimization. arXiv:1412.6980, 2014.

[124] D. P. Kingma and M. Welling. Auto-encoding variational Bayes. arXiv:1312.6114, 2013.

[125] P. Kiourti, K. Wardega, S. Jha, and W. Li. TrojDRL: Trojan attacks on deep reinforcement learning agents. arXiv:1903.06638, 2019.

[126] M. Kline. *Calculus: An Intuitive and Physical Approach*, 2nd edn. Dover, 1998.

[127] J. Kolter and E. Wong. Provable defenses against adversarial examples via the convex outer adversarial polytope. In *International Conference on Machine Learning, ICML*, 2018.

[128] G. Korres and M. Eid. Haptogram: ultrasonic point-cloud tactile stimulation. *IEEE Access*, 4:7758–7769, 2016.

[129] A. Krizhevsky. The CIFAR-10 dataset. https://www.cs.toronto.edu/~kriz/cifar.html, 2010.

[130] A. Krizhevsky, I. Sutskever, and G. E. Hinton. ImageNet classification with deep convolutional neural networks. In *International Conference on Neural Information Processing Systems, NIPS*, pages 1097–1105, 2012.

[131] N. Kumar, A. C. Berg, P. N. Belhumeur, and S. K. Nayar. Attribute and simile classifiers for face verification. In *IEEE International Conference on Computer Vision, ICCV*, 2009.

[132] R. S. S. Kumar, M. Nystrom, J. Lambert, A. Marshall, M. Goertzel, A. Comissoneru, M. Swann, and S. Xia. Adversarial machine learning – industry perspectives. arXiv:2002.05646, March 19, 2021.

[133] A. Kurakin, I. Goodfellow, and S. Bengio. Adversarial examples in the physical world. In *International Conference on Learning Representations, ICLR, Workshop Track*, 2017.

[134] A. Kurakin, I. Goodfellow, and S. Bengio. Adversarial machine learning at scale. In *International Conference on Learning Representations, ICLR*, 2017.

[135] J. F. Kurose and K. W. Ross. *Computer Networking*, 8th edn. Pearson, 2022.

[136] R. Laishram and V. V. Phoha. Curie: a method for protecting SVM classifier from poisoning attack. arXiv:1606.01584, 2016.

[137] S. Lathuiliere, P. Mesejo, X. Alameda-Pineda, and R. Horaud. A comprehensive analysis of deep regression. *IEEE Transactions on Pattern Analysis and Machine Intelligence*, 42(9):2065–2081, 2019.

[138] P. H. Le-Khac, G. Healy, and A. F. Smeaton. Contrastive representation learning: a framework and review. arXiv:2010.05113, October 27, 2020.

[139] Y. LeCun. LeNet-5, convolutional neural networks. http://yann.lecun.com/exdb/lenet/, 1998.

[140] Y. LeCun, L. Bottou, Y. Bengio, and P. Haffner. Gradient-based learning applied to document recognition. *Proceedings of the IEEE*, 86(11):2278–2324, 1998.

[141] Y. LeCun, C. Cortes, and C. J. C. Burges. The MNIST database of handwritten digits. http://yann.lecun.com/exdb/mnist/, 1998.

[142] K. Lee, K. Lee, H. Lee, and J. Shin. A simple unified framework for detecting out-of-distribution samples and adversarial attacks. In *Conference on Neural Information Processing Systems, NeurIPS*, 2018.

[143] B. Li, Y. Wang, A. Singh, and Y. Vorobeychik. Data poisoning attacks on factorization based collaborative filtering. In *International Conference on Neural Information Processing Systems, NIPS*, 2016.

[144] S. Li, Z. Zhao, J. Yu, M. Xue, D. Kaafar, and H. Zhu. Invisible backdoor attacks against deep neural networks. arXiv:1909.02742, 2019.

[145] X. Li, D. J. Miller, Z. Xiang, and G. Kesidis. A scalable mixture-model based defense against data-poisoning attacks on classifiers. In *Dynamic Data Driven Applications Systems Conference, DDDAS*, 2020.

[146] X. Li and F. Li. Adversarial examples detection in deep networks with convolutional filter statistics. In *IEEE International Conference on Computer Vision, ICCV*, 2017.

[147] Xinke Li, Z. Chen, Y. Zhao, Z. Tong, Y. Zhao, A. Lim, and J. T. Zhou. PointBA: towards backdoor attacks in 3D point cloud. In *IEEE International Conference on Computer Vision, ICCV*, 2021.

[148] X. Li, D. J. Miller, Z. Xiang, and G. Kesidis. A BIC based mixture model defense against data poisoning attacks on classifiers. arXiv:2105.13530v2, May 12, 2022.

[149] X. Li, Z. Xiang, D. J. Miller, and G. Kesidis. Detecting backdoor triggers in deep neural networks. In *IEEE International Conference on Acoustics, Speech, and Signal Processing, ICASSP*, 2022.

[150] C. Liao, H. Zhong, A. Squicciarini, S. Zhu, and D. J. Miller. Backdoor embedding in convolutional neural network models via invisible perturbation. In *ACM Conference on Data and Application Security and Privacy, CODASPY*, 2019.

[151] J. Lin, C. Gan, and S. Han. Defensive quantization: when efficiency meets robustness. In *International Conference on Learning Representations, ICLR*, 2019.

[152] Y.-C. Lin, Z.-W. Hong, Y.-H. Liao, M.-L. Shih, M.-Y. Liu, and M. Sun. Tactics of adversarial attack on deep reinforcement learning agents. arXiv:1703.06748, 2017.

[153] Linear Regression on Boston Housing Datase. https://github.com/adityatiwari13/Boston_Dataset.

[154] D. Liu, R. Yu, and H. Su. Extending adversarial attacks and defenses to deep 3d point cloud classifiers. In *IEEE International Conference on Image Processing, ICIP*, pages 2279–2283, 2019.

[155] K. Liu. Train CIFAR10 with PyTorch. https://github.com/kuangliu/pytorch-cifar.

[156] K. Liu, B. Doan-Gavitt, and S. Garg. Fine-pruning: defending against backdoor attacks on deep neural networks. In *Research in Attacks, Intrusions, and Defenses, RAID*, 2018.

[157] Y. Liu, W. Lee, G. Tao, S. Ma, Y. Aafer, and X. Zhang. ABS: scanning neural networks for back-doors by artificial brain stimulation. In *ACM Conference on Computer and Communications Security, ACM CCS*, 2019.

[158] Y. Liu, S. Ma, Y. Aafer, W.-C. Lee, and J. Zhai. Trojaning attack on neural networks. In *Network and Distributed System Security Symposium, NDSS*, 2018.

[159] Y. Liu, X. Ma, J. Bailey, and F. Lu. Reflection backdoor: a natural backdoor attack on deep neural networks. In *European Conference on Computer Vision, ECCV*, 2020.

[160] Z. Liu, Y. Lin, Y. Cao, H. Hu, Y. Wei, Z. Zhang, S. Lin, and B. Guo. Swin transformer: hierarchical vision transformer using shifted windows. arXiv:2103.14030, August 17, 2021.

[161] Z. Liu, Siyuan Li, Di Wu, Zihan Liu, Zhiyuan Chen, Lirong Wu, and Stan Z. Li. Unveiling the power of mixup for stronger classifiers. arXiv:2103.13027, 2021.

[162] D. Lowd and C. Meek. Good word attacks on statistical spam filters. In *International Conference on Email and Anti-Spam, CSEAS*, 2005.

[163] Y. Ma, X. Zhu, and J. Hsu. Data poisoning against differentially-private learners: attacks and defenses. In Sarit Kraus, editor, *International Joint Conference on Artificial Intelligence, IJCAI*, 2019.

[164] S. Markley and D. J. Miller. Joint parsimonious modeling and model order selection for multivariate Gaussian mixtures. *IEEE Journal of Selected Topics in Signal Processing*, 4(3):548–559, 2010.

[165] S. Marsland. *Machine Learning: An Algorithmic Perspective*, 2nd edn. Chapman & Hall/CRC, 2015.

[166] D. Maturana and S. Scherer. VoxNet: a 3D convolutional neural network for real-time object recognition. In *IEEE/RSJ International Conference on Intelligent Robots and Systems, IROS*, 2015.

[167] L. D. McClenny and U. M. Braga-Neto. Self-adaptive physics-informed neural networks using a soft attention mechanism. arXiv:2009.04544, 2020.

[168] G. McLachlan and D. Peel. *Finite Mixture Models*. John Wiley & Sons, 2004.

[169] D. L. McLeish. *Monte Carlo Simulation & Finance*. Wiley, 2005.

[170] H. B. McMahan, D. Ramage, K. Talwar, and L. Zhang. Learning differentially private recurrent language models. In *International Conference on Learning Representations, ICLR*, 2018.

[171] D. Meng and H. Chen. Magnet: a two-pronged defense against adversarial examples. In *ACM Conference on Computer and Communications Security, ACM CCS*, 2017.

[172] M. Menze and A. Geiger. Object scene flow for autonomous vehicles. In *IEEE Conference on Computer Vision and Pattern Recognition, CVPR*, 2015.

[173] J. Metzen, T. Genewein, V. Fischer, and B. Bischoff. On detecting adversarial perturbations. In *International Conference on Learning Representations, ICLR*, 2017.

[174] T. Mikolov, I. Sutskever, K. Chen, G. S. Corrado, and J. Dean. Distributed representations of words and phrases and their compositionality. In *International Conference on Neural Information Processing Systems, NIPS*, 2013.

[175] B. Miller, A. Kantchelian, S. Afroz, R. Bachwani, E. Dauber, L. Huang, M. C. Tschantz, A. D. Joseph, and J. D. Tygar. Adversarial active learning. In *ACM Workshop on Artificial Intelligence and Security, AISec*, 2014.

[176] D. J. Miller, X. Hu, Z. Qiu, and G. Kesidis. Adversarial learning: a critical review and active learning study. In *IEEE International Workshop on Machine Learning for Signal Processing, MLSP*, 2017.

[177] D. J. Miller, Z. Qiu, and G. Kesidis. Parsimonious cluster-based anomaly detection (PCAD). In *IEEE International Workshop on Machine Learning for Signal Processing, MLSP*, 2018; US Patent 10,846,308.

[178] D. J. Miller and H. S. Uyar. A mixture of experts classifier with learning based on both labeled and unlabeled data. In *International Conference on Neural Information Processing Systems, NIPS*, 1997.

[179] D. J. Miller, Y. Wang, and G. Kesidis. When not to classify: anomaly detection of attacks (ADA) on DNN classifiers at test time. *Neural Computation*, 31(8):1624–1670, 2019.

[180] D. J. Miller, Z. Xiang, and G. Kesidis. Adversarial learning in statistical classification: a comprehensive review of defenses against attacks. *Proceedings of the IEEE*, 108:402–433, 2020.

[181] M. Mirza and S. Osindero. Conditional generative adversarial nets. arXiv:1411.1784, 2014.

[182] T. Miyato and M. Koyama. cGANs with projection discriminator. arXiv:1802.05637, 2018.

[183] V. Mnih, A. P. Badia, M. Mirza, A. Graves, T. Harley, T. P. Lillicrap, D. Silver, and K. Kavukcuoglu. Asynchronous methods for deep reinforcement learning. arXiv:1602.01783, June 2016.

[184] V. Mnih, K. Kavukcuoglu, D. Silver, A. A. Rusu, J. Veness, M. G. Bellemare, A. Graves, M. Riedmiller, A. K. Fidjeland, G. Ostrovski, S. Petersen, C. Beattie, A. Sadik, I. Antonoglou, H. King, D. Kumaran, D. Wierstra, S. Legg, and D. Hassabis. Human-level control through deep reinforcement learning. *Nature*, 518:529–533, 2015.

[185] S.-M. Moosavi-Dezfooli, A. Fawzi, and P. Frossard. DeepFool: a simple and accurate method to fool deep neural networks. In *IEEE Conference on Computer Vision and Pattern Recognition, CVPR*, 2016.

[186] S.-M. Moosavi-Dezfooli, A. Fawzi, and P. Frossard. Universal adversarial perturbations. In *IEEE Conference on Computer Vision and Pattern Recognition, CVPR*, 2017.

[187] R. Müller, S. Kornblith, and G. E. Hinton. When does label smoothing help? In *International Conference on Neural Information Processing Systems, NeurIPS*, 2019.

[188] L. Muñoz-González, B. Biggio, A. Demontis, A. Paudice, V. Wongrassamee, E. C. Lupu, and F. Roli. Towards poisoning of deep learning algorithms with back-gradient optimization. In *ACM Workshop on Artificial Intelligence and Security, AISec*, 2017.

[189] J. Murdock. Google's AI health screening tool claimed 90 percent accuracy, but failed to deliver in real world tests. *Newsweek*, April 28, 2020.

[190] K. P. Murphy. *Machine Learning – A Probabilistic Perspective*. MIT Press, Cambridge, MA, 2012.

[191] Neural Cleanse code. https://github.com/bolunwang/backdoor.

[192] J. A. Nelder and R. W. M. Wedderburn. Generalized linear models. *Journal of the Royal Statistical Society, Series A (General)*, 135(3):370–384, 1972.

[193] B. Nelson, M. Barreno, F. J. Chi, A. D. Joseph, B. I. P. Rubinstein, U. Saini, C. Sutton, J. D. Tygar, and K. Xia. Misleading learners: Co-opting your spam filter. In *Machine Learning in Cyber Trust: Security, Privacy, and Reliability*, 2009.

[194] Y. Netzer, T. Wang, A. Coates, A. Bissacco, B. Wu, and A. Y. Ng. Reading digits in natural images with unsupervised feature learning. In *NIPS Workshop on Deep Learning and Unsupervised Feature Learning*, 2011.

[195] A. New, B. Eng, A. C. Timm, and A. S. Gearhart. Tunable complexity benchmarks for evaluating physics-informed neural networks on coupled ordinary differential equations. arXiv:2210.07880, 2022.

[196] A. Nguyen and A. Tran. Warping based backdoor attack. https://github.com/VinAIResearch/Warping-based_Backdoor_Attack-release.

[197] A. Nguyen and A. Tran. Input-aware dynamic backdoor attack. In *Conference on Neural Information Processing Systems, NeurIPS*, 2020.

[198] A. Nguyen, J. Yosinski, and J. Clune. Deep neural networks are easily fooled: high confidence predictions for unrecognizable images. In *IEEE Conference on Computer Vision and Pattern Recognition, CVPR*, pages 427–436, 2015.

[199] J. Nocedal and S. J. Wright. *Numerical Optimization*, 2nd edn. Springer Series in Operations Research, New York, 2006.

[200] A. Odena, C. Olah, and J. Shlens. Conditional image synthesis with auxiliary classifier GANS. In *International Conference on Machine Learning, ICML*, pages 2642–2651, PMLR, 2017.

[201] one-class-learning. https://github.com/topics/one-class-learning.

[202] N. Papernot, P. McDaniel, I. Goodfellow, S. Jha, Z. B. Celik, and A. Swami. Practical black-box attacks against machine learning. In *Asia Conference on Computer and Communications Security, Asia CCS*, 2017.

[203] N. Papernot, P. McDaniel, S. Jha, M. Fredrikson, Z. B. Celik, and A. Swami. The limitations of deep learning in adversarial settings. In *IEEE Symposium on Security and Privacy, S&P*, 2016.

[204] N. Papernot, P. McDaniel, X. Wu, S. Jha, and A. Swami. Distillation as a defense to adversarial perturbations against deep neural networks. In *IEEE Symposium on Security and Privacy, S&P*, 2016.

[205] N. J. Parmar, A. Vaswani, J. Uszkoreit, L. Kaiser, N. Shazeer, A. Ku, and D. Tran. Image transformer. In *International Conference on Machine Learning, ICML*, 2018.

[206] A. Paudice, L. Muñoz-González, and E. C. Lupu. Label sanitization against label flipping poisoning attacks. In *European Conference on Machine Learning and Principles and Practice of Knowledge Discovery in Databases, ECML PKDD 2018 Workshops*, 2018.

[207] L. Pinto, J. Davidson, R. Sukthankar, and A. Gupta. Robust adversarial reinforcement learning. arXiv:1703.02702, 2017.

[208] E. Polak. Notes on Fundamentals of Optimization for Engineers. https://www2.eecs.berkeley.edu/Pubs/TechRpts/1989/ERL-89-40.pdf, Spring 1990.

[209] PyTorch Tutorials. https://pytorch.org/tutorials.

[210] PyTorch. ResNet-18 for ImageNet. https://download.pytorch.org/models/resnet18-5c106cde.pth.

[211] C. R. Qi, L. Yi, H. Su, and L. J. Guibas. PointNet++: deep hierarchical feature learning on point sets in a metric space. In *International Conference on Neural Information Processing Systems, NIPS*, 2017.

[212] F. Qi, Y. Chen, M. Li, Y. Y. Yao, Z. Liu, and M. Sun. ONION: a simple and effective defense against textual backdoor attacks. In *Conference on Empirical Methods in Natural Language Processing, EMNLP*, 2021.

[213] F. Qi, Y. Chen, X. Zhang, M. Li, Z. Liu, and M. Sun. Mind the style of text! Adversarial and backdoor attacks based on text style transfer. In *Conference on Empirical Methods in Natural Language Processing, EMNLP*, 2021.

[214] Z. Qiu, D. J. Miller, and G. Kesidis. A maximum entropy framework for semisupervised and active learning with unknown or label-scarce categories. *IEEE Transactions on Neural Networks and Learning Systems*, 28(4):917–933, 2016.

[215] A. Radford, L. Metz, and S. Chintala. Unsupervised representation learning with deep convolutional generative adversarial networks. arXiv:1511.06434, 2015.

[216] A. Raghunathan, J. Steinhardt, and P. Liang. Certified defenses against adversarial examples. In *International Conference on Learning Representations, ICLR*, 2018.

[217] P. Ren, Y. Xiao, X. Chang, P.-Y. Huang, Z. Li, X. Chen, and X. Wang. A survey of deep active learning. arXiv:2009.00236, September 16, 2020.

[218] Reuters dataset. https://archive.ics.uci.edu/ml/machine-learning-databases/reuters21578-mld/reuters21578.html.

[219] J. Rissanen. Modeling by shortest data description. *Automatica*, 14(5):465–471, 1978.

[220] S. M. Ross. *Introduction to Probability Models*. Academic Press, San Diego, CA, 1989.

[221] K. Roth, Y. Kilcher, and T. Hofmann. The odds are odd: a statistical test for detecting adversarial examples. In *International Conference on Machine Learning, ICML*, pages 5498–5507, PMLR, 2019.

[222] P. J. Rousseeuw and C. Croux. Alternatives to the median absolute deviation. *Journal of the American Statistical Association*, 88(424):1273–1283, 1993.

[223] Y. A. Rozanov. *A Concise Course in Probability*. Dover, 1977.

[224] S. Ruder. An overview of gradient descent optimization algorithms. https://ruder.io/optimizing-gradient-descent/, January 19, 2018.

[225] J. Ruf and W. Wang. Neural networks for option pricing and hedging: a literature review. arXiv:1911.05620, May 12, 2020.

[226] A. Saha, A. Subramanya, and H. Pirsiavash. Hidden trigger backdoor attacks. In *AAAI Conference on Artificial Intelligence*, 2020.

[227] P. Samangouei, M. Kabkab, and R. Chellappa. Defense-GAN: protecting classifiers against adversarial attacks using generative models. arXiv:1805.06605, 2018.

[228] F. J. Samaniego. *Stochastic Modeling and Mathematical Statistics: A Text for Statisticians and Quantitative Scientists*. Chapman & Hall/CRC Texts in Statistical Science, 2014.

[229] M. Sandler, A. G. Howard, M. Zhu, A. Zhmoginov, and L.-C. Chen. Inverted residuals and linear bottlenecks: mobile networks for classification, detection and segmentation. In *IEEE Conference on Computer Vision and Pattern Recognition, CVPR*, 2018.

[230] S. Sattarzadeh, M. Sudhakar, K. N. Plataniotis, J. Jang, Y. Jeong, and H. Kim. Integrated Grad-CAM: sensitivity-aware visual explanation of deep convolutional networks via integrated gradient-based scoring. arXiv:2102.07805, 2021.

[231] T. Schlegl, P. Seeböck, S. M. Waldstein, G. Langs, and U. Schmidt-Erfurth. f-AnoGAN: fast unsupervised anomaly detection with generative adversarial networks. *Medical Image Analysis*, 54:30–44, 2019.

[232] T. Schlegl, P. Seeböck, S. M. Waldstein, U. Schmidt-Erfurth, and Georg Langs. Unsupervised anomaly detection with generative adversarial networks to guide marker discovery. In *International Conference on Information Processing in Medical Imaging*, pages 146–157. Springer, 2017.

[233] J. Schmidhuber. Annotated history of modern AI and deep learning. arXiv:2212.11279, 2022.

[234] J. Schmidhuber. Critique of paper by "Deep Learning Conspiracy" (Nature 521 p 436). http://people.idsia.ch/~juergen/deep-learning-conspiracy.html, June 2015.

[235] B Schölkopf, J. C. Platt, and J. Shawe-Taylor. Estimating the support of a high-dimensional distribution. *Neural Computation*, 13(7):1443–1471, 2001.

[236] J. R. Schuessler. Adversarial Attacks and Defense in Long Short-term Memory Recurrent Neural Networks. Master's thesis, Electrical Engineering Department, Pennsylvania State University, December 2021; https://etda.libraries.psu.edu/catalog/21965jrs510.

[237] O. Schumann, M. Hahn, J. Dickmann, and C. Wöhler. Semantic segmentation on radar point clouds. In *21st International Conference on Information Fusion (FUSION)*, pages 2179–2186, 2018.

[238] G. Schwarz. Estimating the dimension of a model. *The Annals of Statistics*, 6(2):461–464, 1978.

[239] R. R. Selvaraju, M. Cogswell, A. Das, R. Vedantam, D. Parikh, and D. Batra. Grad-CAM: visual explanations from deep networks via gradient-based localization. In *IEEE International Conference on Computer Vision, ICCV*, pages 618–626, 2017.

[240] P. Sermanet, S. Chintala, and Y. LeCun. Convolutional neural networks applied to house numbers digit classification. In *21st International Conference on Pattern Recognition, ICPR*, 2012.

[241] B. Settles. Active learning literature survey. University of Wisconsin, Madison, 2010.

[242] H. Seung, M. Opper, and H. Sompolinksy. Query by committee. In *5th Workshop on Computational Learning Theory, COLT*, 1992.

[243] G. Shen, Y. Liu, G. Tao, S. An, Q. Xu, S. Cheng, S. Ma, and X. Zhang. Backdoor scanning for deep neural networks through K-arm optimization. arXiv:2102.05123, February 9, 2021.

[244] R. Shokri, M. Stronati, C. Sogn, and V. Shmatikov. Membership inference attacks against machine learning models. In *IEEE Symposium on Security and Privacy, S&P*, 2017.

[245] K. Simonyan and A. Zisserman. Very deep convolutional networks for large-scale image recognition. In *International Conference on Learning Representations, ICLR*, 2015.

[246] H. Soleimani and D. J. Miller. Parsimonious topic models with salient word discovery. *IEEE Transactions on Knowledge and Data Engineering*, 27:824–837, 2014.

[247] S. Song, F. Gao, R. Huang, and Y. Wang. On saving outliers for better clustering over noisy data. In *ACM SIGMOD International Conference on Management of Data, Virtual Event*, pages 1692–1704. ACM, 2021.

[248] N. Srivastava, G. Hinton, A. Krizhevsky, I. Sutskever, and R. Salakhutdinov. Dropout: a simple way to prevent neural networks from overfitting. *Journal of Machine Learning Research*, 15(56):1929–1958, 2014.

[249] W. Stallings and L. Brown. *Computer Security: Principles and Practice*, 4th edn. Pearson, 2017.

[250] J. Stallkamp, J. Salmen, M. Schlipsing, and C. Igel. Man vs. computer: benchmarking machine learning algorithms for traffic sign recognition. *Neural Networks*, 32:323–332, 2012.

[251] H. Stark and J. W. Woods. *Probability, Random Processes and Estimation Theory for Engineers*. Prentice Hall, Upper Saddle River, NJ, 1986.

[252] M. Steinbach, L. Ertöz, and V. Kumar. The challenges of clustering high dimensional data. In *New Directions in Statistical Physics*, pages 273–309. Springer, 2004.

[253] J. Steinhardt, P. W. Koh, and P. Liang. Certified defenses for data poisoning. In *International Conference on Neural Information Processing Systems, NIPS*, 2017.

[254] E. Stevens, L. Antiga, and T. Viehmann. *Deep Learning with PyTorch*. Manning, 2020.

[255] E. Strickland. How IBM Watson overpromised and underdelivered on AI health care. *IEEE Spectrum*, April 2, 2019.

[256] H. Su, S. Maji, E. Kalogerakis, and E. G. Learned-Miller. Multiview convolutional neural networks for 3d shape recognition. In *IEEE International Conference on Computer Vision, ICCV*, 2015.

[257] J.-C. Su, M. Gadelha, R. Wang, and S. Maji. A deeper look at 3d shape classifiers. In Laura Leal-Taixé and Stefan Roth, editors, *European Conference on Computer Vision, ECCV 2018 Workshops*, 2019.

[258] J. Sun, Y. Cao, Q. A. Chen, and Z. M. Mao. Towards Robust LiDAR based perception in autonomous driving: general black-box adversarial sensor attack and countermeasures. In *USENIX Security Symposium*, 2020.

[259] I. Sutskever, J. Martens, G. Dahl, and G. Hinton. On the importance of initialization and momentum in deep learning. In *International Conference on Machine Learning, ICML*, 2013.

[260] C. Szegedy, W. Zaremba, I. Sutskever, J. Bruna, D. Erhan, I. Goodfellow, and R. Fergus. Intriguing properties of neural networks. In *International Conference on Learning Representations, ICLR*, 2014.

[261] M. Thomas. 14 deep learning applications you need to know. https://builtin.com/artificial-intelligence/deep-learning-applications, December 4, 2018; updated April 9, 2020.

[262] J. Tian, J. Zhou, Y. Li, and J. Duan. Detecting adversarial examples from sensitivity inconsistency of spatial-transform domain. In *AAAI Conference on Artificial Intelligence*, 2021.

[263] Tiny ImageNet. https://www.kaggle.com/competitions/tiny-imagenet/.

[264] R. Toews. Deep learning has limits. But its commercial impact has just begun. https://www.forbes.com/sites/robtoews/2020/02/09/deep-learning-has-limits-but-its-commercial-impact-has-just-begun/#4bcff4e76e1a, February 9, 2020.

[265] Torchvision. Models and pre-trained weights. https://pytorch.org/vision/stable/models.html.

[266] F. Tramer, A. Kurakin, N. Papernot, I. Goodfellow, D. Boneh, and P. McDaniel. Ensemble adversarial training: attacks and defenses. In *International Conference on Learning Representations, ICLR*, 2018.

[267] F. Tramer, F. Zhang, A. Juels, M. Reiter, and T. Ristenpart. Stealing machine learning models via prediction APIs. In *USENIX Security Symposium*, 2016.

[268] B. Tran, J. Li, and A. Madry. Spectral signatures in backdoor attacks. In *International Conference on Neural Information Processing Systems, NIPS*, 2018.

[269] TrojAI: Leaderboard. https://pages.nist.gov/trojai/.

[270] TrojAI: Trojans in artificial intelligence. https://www.iarpa.gov/index.php/research-programs/trojai/trojai-baa, 2019.

[271] D. Tsipras, S. Santurkar, L. Engstrom, A. Turner, and A. Madry. Robustness may be at odds with accuracy. In *International Conference on Learning Representations, ICLR*, 2019.

[272] Y. Tsuzuku, I. Sato, and M. Sugiyama. Lipschitz-margin training: scalable certification of perturbation invariance for deep neural networks. In *International Conference on Neural Information Processing Systems, NIPS*, 2018.

[273] E. Tsymbalov, M. Panov, and A. Shapeev. Dropout-based active learning for regression. arXiv:1806.09856v2, July 5, 2018.

[274] J. Tu, M. Ren, S. Manivasagam, M. Liang, B. Yang, R. Du, F. Cheng, and R. Urtasun. Physically realizable adversarial examples for lidar object detection. In *IEEE/CVF Conference on Computer Vision and Pattern Recognition, CVPR*, June 2020.

[275] A. Turner, D. Tsipras, and A. Madry. Clean-label backdoor attacks. http://people.csail.mit.edu/tsipras/pdfs/TTM18.pdf, 2018.

[276] UCI Machine Learning Repository. https://archive.ics.uci.edu/ml/index.php.

[277] UCI Machine Learning Repository – Housing. https://archive.ics.uci.edu/ml/machine-learning-databases/housing/.

[278] UCI Machine Learning Repository – Iris Dataset. https://archive.ics.uci.edu/ml/datasets/iris.

[279] V. N. Vapnik and A. Y. Chervonenkis. On the uniform convergence of relative frequencies of events to their probabilities. *Theory of Probability & Its Applications*, 16(2):264–280, 1971 (English translation).

[280] A. Vaswani, N. Shazeer, N. Parmar, J. Uszkoreit, L. Jones, A. N. Gomez, L. Kaiser, and I. Polosukhin. Attention is all you need. In *International Conference on Neural Information Processing Systems, NIPS*, 2017.

[281] Y. Vorobeychik and M. Kantarcioglu. *Adversarial Machine Learning*. Morgan & Claypool, 2018.

[282] B. Wang, Y. Yao, S. Shan, H. Li, B. Viswanath, H. Zheng, and B. Y. Zhao. Neural cleanse: identifying and mitigating backdoor attacks in neural networks. In *IEEE Symposium on Security and Privacy, S&P*, 2019.

[283] H. Wang, S. Karami, O. Dia, H. Ritter, E. Emamjomeh-Zadeh, K. Chen, Z. Xiang, D. J. Miller, and G. Kesidis. Training set cleansing of backdoor poisoning by self-supervised representation learning. arXiv:2210.10272, October 2022.

[284] H. Wang, D. J. Miller, and G. Kesidis. Anomaly detection of test-time evasion attacks using class-conditional generative adversarial networks. *Computers and Security*, 124, Article 102953, 2023.

[285] H. Wang, Z. Xiang, D. J. Miller, and G. Kesidis. AC-GAN-ADA for detecting adversarial examples. https://github.com/wanghangpsu/acgan-ada, 2022.

[286] H. Wang, Z. Xiang, D. J. Miller, and G. Kesidis. Universal post-training backdoor detection. arXiv:2205.06900, May 2022.

[287] L. Wang, Z. Javed, X. Wu, W. Guo, X. Xing, and D. Song. BACKDOORL: backdoor attack against competitive reinforcement learning. arXiv:2105.00579, 2021.

[288] Q. Wang, W. Guo, K. Zhang, A. Ororbia, X. Xing, L. Giles, and X. Liu. Adversary resistant deep neural networks with an application to malware detection. In *ACM SIGKDD, International Conference on Knowledge Discovery and Data Mining*, 2017.

[289] R. Wang, G. Zhang, S. Liu, P.-Y. Chen, J. Xiong, and M. Wang. Practical detection of Trojan neural networks: data-limited and data-free cases. In *European Conference on Computer Vision, ECCV*, 2020.

[290] S. Wang, Y. Chen, A. Abdou, and S. Jana. MixTrain: Scalable training of verifiably robust neural networks. arXiv:1811.02625, November 2018.

[291] Y. Wang, D. J. Miller, and G. Kesidis. When not to classify: detection of reverse engineering attacks on DNN image classifiers. In *IEEE International Conference on Acoustics, Speech, and Signal Processing, ICASSP*, 2019.

[292] Y. Wang, Y. Sun, Z. Liu, S. E. Sarma, M. M. Bronstein, and Justin M. Solomon. Dynamic graph CNN for learning on point clouds. *ACM Transactions on Graphics*, 38(5), Article 146, 2019.

[293] Y. Wen, J. Lin, K. Chen, C. L. P. Chen, and K. Jia. Geometry-aware generation of adversarial point clouds. *IEEE Transactions on Pattern Analysis and Machine Intelligence*, 44:2984–2999, 2022.

[294] T.-W. Weng, H. Zhang, H. Chen, Z. Song, C.-J. Hsieh, D. Boning, I. S. Dhillon, and L. Daniel. Towards fast computation of certified robustness for ReLU networks. In *International Conference on Machine Learning, ICML*, 2018.

[295] P. J. Werbos. Generalization of backpropagation with application to a recurrent gas market model. *Neural Networks*, 1(4):339–356, 1988.

[296] J. Wright and Y. Ma. *High-Dimensional Data Analysis with Low-Dimensional Models: Principles, Computation, and Applications*. Cambridge University Press, 2022.

[297] D. Wu, C.-T. Lin, and J. Huang. Active learning for regression using greedy sampling. arXiv:1808.04245v1, August 8, 2018.

[298] W. Wu, L. He, W. Lin, Y. Su, Y. Cui, C. Maple, and S. A. Jarvis. Developing an unsupervised real-time anomaly detection scheme for time series with multi-seasonality. *IEEE Transactions on Knowledge and Data Engineering*, 34(9): 4147–4160, 2022.

[299] Z. Wu, S. Song, A. Khosla, F. Yu, L. Zhang, X. Tang, and J. Xiao. 3d shapenets: a deep representation for volumetric shapes. In *IEEE Conference on Computer Vision and Pattern Recognition, CVPR*, June 2015.

[300] C. Xiang, C. R. Qi, and B. Li. Generating 3d adversarial point clouds. In *IEEE/CVF Conference on Computer Vision and Pattern Recognition, CVPR*, June 2019.

[301] Z. Xiang, D. J. Miller, and G. Kesidis. Reverse engineering imperceptible backdoor attacks on deep neural networks for detection and training set cleansing. *Computers and Security*, 106, Article 102280, 2021.

[302] Z. Xiang, D. J. Miller, and G. Kesidis. Post-training detection of backdoor attacks for two-class and multi-attack scenarios. In *International Conference on Learning Representations, ICLR*, 2022.

[303] Z. Xiang, D. J. Miller, and G. Kesidis. Detection of Backdoors in Trained Classifiers Without Access to the Training Set. In *IEEE Transactions on Neural Networks and Learning Systems, TNNLS*, December 2020. (online)

[304] Z. Xiang, D. J. Miller, and G. Kesidis. Detecting scene-plausible perceptible backdoors in trained DNNs without access to the training set. *Neural Computation*, 33(5):1329–1371, 2021.

[305] Z. Xiang, D. J. Miller, and G. Kesidis. L-RED: efficient post-training detection of imperceptible backdoor attacks without access to the training set. In *IEEE International Conference on Acoustics, Speech, and Signal Processing, ICASSP*, 2021.

[306] Z. Xiang, D. J. Miller, S. Chen, X. Li, and G. Kesidis. Detecting backdoor attacks against point cloud classifiers. In *IEEE International Conference on Acoustics, Speech, and Signal Processing, ICASSP*, 2022.

[307] Z. Xiang, D. J. Miller, and G. Kesidis. Revealing backdoors, post-training, in DNN classifiers via novel inference on optimized perturbations inducing group misclassification. In *IEEE International Conference on Acoustics, Speech, and Signal Processing, ICASSP*, 2020.

[308] Z. Xiang, D. J. Miller, and G. Kesidis. A benchmark study of backdoor data poisoning defenses for deep neural network classifiers and a novel defense. In *IEEE International Workshop on Machine Learning for Signal Processing, MLSP*, 2019.

[309] Z. Xiang, D. J. Miller, S. Chen, X. Li, and G. Kesidis. A backdoor attack against 3D point cloud classifiers. In *IEEE International Conference on Computer Vision, ICCV*, 2021.

[310] Z. Xiang, D. J. Miller, H. Wang, and G. Kesidis. Revealing perceptible backdoors in DNNs, without the training set, via the maximum achievable misclassification fraction

statistic. In *IEEE International Workshop on Machine Learning for Signal Processing, MLSP*, 2020.

[311] H. Xiao, B. Biggio, B. Nelson, H. Xiao, C. Eckert, and F. Roli. Support vector machines under adversarial label contamination. *Neurocomputing*, 160(C):53–62, 2015.

[312] H. Xiao, K. Rasul, and R. Vollgraf. Fashion-MNIST: a novel image dataset for benchmarking machine learning algorithms. arXiv:1708.07747, 2017.

[313] C. Xie, J. Wang, Z. Zhang, Y. Zhou, L. Xie, and A. Yuille. Adversarial examples for semantic segmentation and object detection. In *IEEE International Conference on Computer Vision, ICCV*, 2017.

[314] H. Xu, Y. Ma, H.-C. Liu, D. Deb, H. Liu, J.-L. Tang, and A. K. Jain. Adversarial attacks and defenses in images, graphs and text: a review. *International Journal of Automation and Computing*, 17:151–178, 2020.

[315] W. Xu, D. Evans, and Y. Qi. Feature squeezing: detecting adversarial examples in deep neural networks. In *Network and Distributed System Security Symposium, NDSS*, 2018.

[316] X. Xu, Q. Wang, H. Li, N. Borisov, C. A. Gunter, and B. Li. Detecting AI Trojans using meta neural analysis. arXiv:1910.03137, 2019.

[317] J. Yang, Q. Zhang, B. Ni, L. Li, J. Liu, M. Zhou, and Q. Tian. Modeling point clouds with self-attention and gumbel subset sampling. In *IEEE/CVF Conference on Computer Vision and Pattern Recognition, CVPR*, pages 3318–3327, 2019.

[318] P. Yang, C.-J. Hsieh, J. Chen, J.-L. Wang, and M. I. Jordan. Greedy attack and gumbel attack: generating adversarial examples for discrete data. arXiv:1805.12316, 2018.

[319] X.-S. Yang and S. Deb. Cuckoo search via Levy fights. In *World Congress on Nature & Biologically Inspired Computing*, 2009.

[320] Y. Yi, W. Zhou, Y. Shi, and J. Dai. Speedup two-class supervised outlier detection. *IEEE Access*, 6:63923–63933, 2018.

[321] X. Yue, B. Wu, S. A. Seshia, K. Keutzer, and A. L. Sangiovanni- Vincentelli. A lidar point cloud generator: from a virtual world to autonomous driving. In *2018 ACM International Conference on Multimedia Retrieval, ICMR*, pages 458–464, 2018.

[322] V. Zantedeschi, M. Nicolae, and A. Rawat. Efficient defenses against adversarial attacks. In *ACM Workshop on Artificial Intelligence and Security, AISec*, 2017.

[323] H. Zenati, C. S. Foo, B. Lecouat, G. Manek, and V. Ramaseshan Chandrasekhar. Efficient GAN-based anomaly detection. arXiv:1802.06222, 2018.

[324] T. Zhai, Y. Li, Z. Zhang, B. Wu, Y. Jiang, and S.-T. Xia. Backdoor attack against speaker verification, *IEEE International Conference on Acoustics, Speech, and Signal Processing, ICASSP*, 2021.

[325] H. Zhang, H. Chen, Z. Song, D. Boning, I. Dhillon, and C.-J. Hsieh. The limitations of adversarial training and the blind-spot attack. arXiv:1901.04684, 2019.

[326] Yuxin Zhang, Yiqiang Chen, Jindong Wang, and Zhiwen Pan. Unsupervised deep anomaly detection for multi-sensor time-series signals. *IEEE Transactions on Knowledge and Data Engineering*, 35(2):2118–2132, 2021.

[327] H. Zhao, L. Jiang, C. Fu, and J. Jia. Pointweb: Enhancing local neighborhood features for point cloud processing. In *IEEE/CVF Conference on Computer Vision and Pattern Recognition, CVPR*, 2019.

[328] Shihao Zhao, Xingjun Ma, Xiang Zheng, James Bailey, Jingjing Chen, and Yu-Gang Jiang. Clean-label backdoor attacks on video recognition models. In *IEEE/CVF Conference on Computer Vision and Pattern Recognition, CVPR*, 2020.

[329] zhenxianglance on GitHub. https://github.com/zhenxianglance.

[330] Tianhang Zheng, Changyou Chen, Junsong Yuan, Bo Li, and Kui Ren. Pointcloud saliency maps. In *IEEE/CVF International Conference on Computer Vision, ICCV*, 2019.

[331] Hang Zhou, Kejiang Chen, Weiming Zhang, Han Fang, Wenbo Zhou, and Nenghai Yu. Dup-net: denoiser and upsampler network for 3d adversarial point clouds defense. In *IEEE International Conference on Computer Vision, ICCV*, pages 1961– 1970, 2019.

[332] Bo Zong, Qi Song, Martin Renqiang Min, Wei Cheng, Cristian Lumezanu, Daeki Cho, and Haifeng Chen. Deep autoencoding Gaussian mixture model for unsupervised anomaly detection. In *International Conference on Learning Representations, ICLR*, 2018.

Index